Study Guide

for

Berk

Development Through the Lifespan

Fifth Edition

prepared by

Laura E. Berk
Illinois State University

Claire G. Christensen
University of Illinois at Chicago

Jessica Carloni

Leah Shriro

Allyn & Bacon

Boston Columbus Indianapolis New York San Francisco Upper Saddle River
Amsterdam Cape Town Dubai London Madrid Milan Munich Paris Montreal Toronto
Delhi Mexico City Sao Paulo Sydney Hong Kong Seoul Singapore Taipei Tokyo

10 9 8 7 6 5 4 3 2 1   13 12 11 10 09

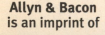

Allyn & Bacon is an imprint of

PEARSON

www.pearsonhighered.com

ISBN-10: 0-205-73763-3
ISBN-13: 978-0-205-73763-5

CONTENTS

PREFACE

As you embark on the fascinating journey of studying human development, it is our hope that this workbook will help you master the material in your text, *Development Through the Lifespan,* Fifth Edition, by Laura E. Berk. Our intention in preparing the workbook is to provide you with active practice in learning the content in your textbook and thought-provoking questions that help you clarify your own thinking. Each chapter in the workbook is organized into the following seven sections:

BRIEF CHAPTER SUMMARY

We begin with a brief summary of the material, mentioning major topics covered and general principles emphasized in text discussion. Each text chapter includes two additional summaries: an informal one at the beginning of the chapter, and a structured summary at the end of the chapter. Thus, the summary in the workbook will be your third review of the information covered in each chapter. It is intended to remind you of major points in the text before you embark on the remaining activities in the workbook.

LEARNING OBJECTIVES

We have organized the main points in each chapter into a series of objectives that indicate what you should be able to do once you have mastered the material. We suggest that you look over these objectives before you read each chapter. You may find it useful to take notes on information pertaining to the objectives as you read. When you finish a chapter, try to answer the objectives in a few sentences or a short paragraph. Then check your answers against the text and revise your responses accordingly. Once you have completed this exercise, you will have generated your own review of chapter content. Because it is written in your own words, it should serve as an especially useful chapter overview that can be referred to when you prepare for examinations.

STUDY QUESTIONS

The main body of each chapter consists of study questions, organized according to major headings in the textbook that assist you in identifying main points and grasping concepts and principles. Text pages on which answers can be found are indicated next to each entry. The study question section can be used in a number of different ways. You may find it helpful to answer each question as you read the chapter. Alternatively, try reading one or more sections and then testing yourself by answering the relevant study questions. Finally, use the study question section as a device to review for examinations. If you work through it methodically, your retention of chapter material will be greatly enhanced.

ASK YOURSELF

In each chapter of the textbook, critical thinking questions appear at the end of each major section. Four types of questions are included: Review questions, which assist with recall and comprehension of information in the text; Apply questions, which encourage application of your knowledge to controversial issues and problems; Connect questions, which help you to integrate what you have learned across age periods and aspects of development; and Reflect questions, which help make the study of lifespan development personally meaningful by encouraging you to relate theory and research to your own life. In each chapter of the Study Guide, you will be asked to log in to the text's MyDevelopmentLab to access the Ask Yourself questions. Answering the questions will help you analyze important theoretical concepts and research findings. On the companion website, each question is page-referenced to chapter material that will help you formulate a response. Model answers are also provided.

SUGGESTED READINGS

A list of three to four suggested readings complements each text chapter. The readings have been carefully selected for their interest value and readability; the majority are recently published. A brief description of the content of each suggested reading is provided.

CROSSWORD PUZZLES

To help you master the central vocabulary of the field, we have provided crossword puzzles that test your knowledge of important terms and concepts. Answers can be found at the back of the workbook. If you cannot think of the term that matches a clue in the puzzles, your knowledge of information related to the term may be insecure. Reread the material in the text chapter related to each item that you miss. Also, try a more demanding approach to term mastery: After you have completed each puzzle, cover the clues and write your own definitions of each term.

PRACTICE TESTS

Once you have thoroughly studied each chapter, find out how well you know the material by taking the two multiple choice practice tests. Then check your answers using the key at the back of the workbook. Each item is page-referenced to chapter content so you can look up answers to questions that you missed. If you answered more than a few items incorrectly, spend extra time rereading the chapter, writing responses to chapter objectives, and reviewing the study questions in this workbook.

Now that you understand how the workbook is organized, you are ready to begin using it to master *Development Through the Lifespan.*

We wish you a rewarding and enjoyable course of study.

Laura E. Berk
Claire G. Christensen

STUDENT REGISTRATION & LOGIN

MyDevelopmentLab & MyDevelopmentLab CourseCompass

MyDevelopmentLab is a state of the art, interactive and instructive online solution for child and lifespan development. MyDevelopmentLab combines multimedia, tutorials, video, simulations, animations, tests and quizzes to make teaching and learning fun. Below you will find instructions to register and access MyDevelopmentLab and MyDevelopmentLab CourseCompass. If you are not sure which access you will need, check with your instructor.

STUDENT REGISTRATION & LOGIN: MyDevelopmentLab
Refer to the following page for registration information for MyDevelopmentLab CourseCompass.

Before You Begin
To complete your registration and access MyDevelopmentLab you will need:

- ☑ Your school zip code
- ☑ A MyDevelopmentLab student access code (packaged with your text or available for purchase at www.mydevelopmentlab.com)
- ☑ A valid email address
- ☑ Course ID (available from your instructor)

Registration

1. Enter **www.mydevelopmentlab.com** in your Web browser.
2. Under "Register or Buy Access," click **Students.**
3. Click the **MyDevelopmentLab** link.
4. If you have an access code, click **I already have an access code**.
   Click **It came with my textbook** or **I bought it separately from my textbook.**
   If you need to purchase access, click **I need to buy access.**
   Select **I want to buy MyDevelopmentLab WITH an E-book of my textbook** or **I want to buy MyDevelopmentLab WITHOUT E-book of my textbook.**
5. Select *Development Through the Lifespan,* Fifth Edition, (the title of your text).
6. After reading through the License Agreement and Privacy Policy, click "I Accept."
7. Do you have a Pearson Education account?
   a. If **Yes**—fill in your username and password.
   b. If **No**—Create a username and password per the guidelines provided.
   c. If **Not Sure**—Enter your email address and click **Search**.
8. Check or enter required information in the appropriate fields.

If successful, you will receive a **Confirmation Screen** with your information (this screen is also emailed to you).

Login and Accessing the Ask Yourself Questions

1. Enter **www.mydevelopmentlab.com** in your Web browser.
2. Under "Log In," click **MyDevelopmentLab**.
3. Select *Development Through the Lifespan,* Fifth Edition (the title of your text).
4. Enter the **Login Name** and **Password** you created and click **"Login."**
5. From the Table of Contents page, select the **Chapter** you wish to view.
6. Under **Chapter Topics**, select the **Topic** you wish to view. This **opens the E-Book** for that topic.
7. Next to the **Ask Yourself** box, select the **Explore** Icon.
8. Complete questions and choose **Submit Answers for grading** or Clear answers to start over.

STUDENT REGISTRATION & LOGIN: MyDevelopmentLab CourseCompass

Before You Begin

To register for MyDevelopmentLab CourseCompass you will need:

- ☑ Course ID (available from your instructor)
- ☑ Your school zip code
- ☑ A MyDevelopmentLab CourseCompass student access code (packaged with your text)
- ☑ A valid email address

Registration

1. Enter **www.mydevelopmentlab.com** in your Web browser.
2. Under "Register or Buy Access," click **Students.**
3. Click the **MyDevelopmentLab CourseCompass** link.
4. Confirm that you have everything you need to register, then click **Next**.
5. Enter your **Course ID**, then click **Find Course**.
6. If you have a code, select the **Access Code** button. If you need to purchase access, click **Buy Now**.
7. After reading through the License Agreement and Privacy Policy, click "I Accept."
8. Do you have a Pearson Education account?
    a. If **Yes**—fill in your username and password.
    b. If **No**—Create a username and password per the guidelines provided.
    c. If **Not Sure**—Enter your email address and click **Search**.
9. Check or enter required information in the appropriate fields.

If successful, you will receive a **Confirmation Screen** with your information (this screen is also emailed to you).

Login and Accessing the Ask Yourself Questions

1. Enter **www.mydevelopmentlab.com** in your Web browser.
2. Under "Log In," click **MyDevelopmentLab CourseCompass**.
3. Enter the **Login Name** and **Password** you created and click **"Login."**
4. You will see your **Course** listed under **Courses.**
5. Click on this Course and select the **Chapter Contents** from the left navigation menu.
6. From the Table of Contents page, select your **chapter**.
7. Under **Chapter Topics,** select the Topic you wish to view. This opens the **E-Book** for that topic.
8. Next to the Ask Yourself box, select the **Explore** Icon.
9. Complete questions and choose **Submit Answers for grading** or Clear answers to start over.

CHAPTER 1
HISTORY, THEORY, AND RESEARCH STRATEGIES

BRIEF CHAPTER SUMMARY

Human development is an interdisciplinary field of study devoted to understanding human constancy and change throughout the lifespan. Although great diversity exists among investigators who study human development, all have a single goal in common: the desire to describe and identify those factors that influence consistencies and transformations in people from conception to death.

Theories of human development take a stance on three basic issues: (1) Is development a continuous or discontinuous process? (2) Is there one course of development or many possible courses? (3) Is development determined primarily by nature or nurture, and is it stable or open to change? Modern theories include elements from both sides of these debates. The lifespan perspective recognizes that great complexity exists in human change and the factors that underlie it. This perspective assumes (1) that development is lifelong; (2) that it is multidimensional and multidirectional; (3) that it is plastic, or flexible, at all ages; and (4) that it is influenced by multiple, interacting forces.

The scientific study of human development dates to the late nineteenth and early twentieth centuries. After Charles Darwin constructed his theory of evolution in the nineteenth century, the scientific study of development evolved quickly. Sigmund Freud's psychosexual theory and Erik Erikson's psychosocial theory viewed development as discontinuous (occurring in stages), but Erikson added three adult stages to Freud's five stages of childhood.

The behaviorist perspective—rejecting the psychoanalytic concern with the unseen workings of the mind—focused on directly observable events: stimuli and responses. Albert Bandura's social learning theory, which expanded on the principles of conditioning, emphasizes modeling as a powerful source of development and is still influential today. Swiss cognitive theorist Jean Piaget, disagreeing with the behaviorists, developed a cognitive-developmental theory, based on the idea that children actively construct knowledge. Recent theoretical perspectives include information processing, which examines the human mind as a symbol-manipulating system; ethology and evolutionary developmental psychology, which are concerned with the adaptive value of behavior; Lev Vygotsky's sociocultural theory, which looks at the role of culture; and Urie Bronfenbrenner's ecological systems theory, which examines development in the context of a complex system of relationships.

Research in human development, like all scientific research, begins with a hypothesis, or prediction about behavior drawn from a theory. Research methods commonly used to study development include systematic observation, self-reports, clinical, or case studies, of single individuals, and ethnographies of cultures or social groups.

Investigators of human development generally choose either a correlational research design, which looks at relationships but cannot determine causality, or an experimental design, which uses dependent and independent variables to determine cause and effect. Experiments may be carried out in the laboratory or in the field. To study how individuals change over time, investigators use longitudinal, cross-sectional, and sequential designs. Each method and design has both strengths and limitations. Finally, conducting research with human subjects poses special ethical dilemmas, particularly for children or elderly people who are ill or cognitively impaired.

LEARNING OBJECTIVES

After reading this chapter, you should be able to:

1.1 Explain the importance of the terms interdisciplinary and applied as they help to define the field of developmental science. (p. 5)

1.2 Explain the role of theories in understanding human development, and describe three basic issues on which major theories take a stand. (pp. 5–7)

1.3 Describe factors that sparked the emergence of the lifespan perspective, and explain the four assumptions that make up this point of view. (pp. 7–13)

1.4 Describe the major early influences on the scientific study of development. (pp. 14–15)

1.5 Describe theoretical perspectives that influenced human development research in the mid-twentieth century, and cite the contributions and limitations of each. (pp. 15–20)

1.6 Describe recent theoretical perspectives on human development, noting the contributions of major theorists. (pp. 21–26)

1.7 Identify the stand that each contemporary theory takes on the three basic issues presented earlier in this chapter. (pp. 26, 27)

1.8 Describe the research methods commonly used to study human development, citing the strengths and limitations of each. (pp. 26–31)

1.9 Contrast correlational and experimental research designs, and cite the strengths and limitations of each. (pp. 31–34)

1.10 Describe three research designs for studying development, and cite the strengths and limitations of each. (pp. 34–38)

1.11 Discuss ethical issues related to lifespan research. (pp. 39–40)

STUDY QUESTIONS

A Scientific, Applied, and Interdisciplinary Field

1. *Developmental science* is a(n) ________________ field, comprised of research from diverse disciplines, including psychology, neuroscience, and education. (p. 5)

Basic Issues

1. List the three elements of a good *theory*. (p. 5)

   A. ______________________________ B. ______________________________

   C. ______________________________

2. Theories are important to the study of developmental science because they help us ________________ our observations and give us a sound basis for ___________________. (p. 5)

3. True or False: Theories differ from opinion and belief in that they are subject to scientific verification. (p. 5)

4. Match each theoretical view with the appropriate description. (pp. 6–7)

   _______ Views early traits as constant across the lifespan.
   _______ Views development as a process of gradually building on preexisting skills.
   _______ Regards the environment as the most important influence on development.
   _______ Regards human change as possible if new experiences support change.
   _______ Views development as a progression through a series of qualitatively distinct stages.
   _______ Views heredity as the most important influence on development.

   A. *Continuous development*
   B. *Discontinuous development*
   C. Nature
   D. Nurture
   E. Stability
   F. Plasticity

5. The existence of diverse developmental *contexts* (supports / refutes) stage theorists' assumption that most people follow the same sequence of development. (p. 6)

The Lifespan Perspective: A Balanced Point of View

1. True or False: Most modern theories of development take an extreme position on controversial issues such as the nature–nurture debate. (p. 7)

2. Explain how gains in average life expectancy have altered our view of human development. (p. 8)

____

____

____

3. The _______________ *perspective* is a broad dynamic systems approach to human development. List the four assumptions that comprise this approach. (p. 8)

   A. ____

   B. ____

   C. ____

   D. ____

Development Is Lifelong

1. List the eight periods of human development. (p. 8)

   A. ____

   B. ____

   C. ____

   D. ____

   E. ____

   F. ____

   G. ____

   H. ____

2. Cite the three broad domains of development in which change takes place across the lifespan. (pp. 8–9)

   A. _______________________ B. _______________________

   C. _______________________

Development Is Multidimensional and Multidirectional

1. Explain what is meant by "development is multidimensional." (p. 9)

____

____

2. Cite two ways in which lifespan development is multidirectional. (p. 9)

   A. ____

   B. ____

Development Is Plastic

1. True or False: Lifespan researchers emphasize that development is plastic at all ages. Briefly explain your response. (p. 10)

____

____

Biology and Environment: Resilience

1. What is *resilience*? (p. 10)

____

____

2. Briefly elaborate on the four broad factors that appear to offer protection from the damaging effects of stressful life events. (pp. 10–11)

   Personal characteristics: ____

   ____

   Warm parental relationship: ____

   ____

   Outside social support: ____

   ____

   Community resources and opportunities: ____

   ____

3. Research on resilience highlights the influence of (heredity / environment / heredity–environment interactions). (p. 11)

Development Is Influenced by Multiple, Interacting Forces

1. According to the lifespan perspective, biological, historical, social, and cultural forces work (together / independently) to fashion highly (predictable / diverse) pathways of change. (pp. 10–11)
2. ______________________ *influences* are strongly related to age. Therefore, it is (possible / impossible) to predict when they will occur and how long they will last. (p. 11)
3. ______________________ *-graded influences* explain why people born around the same time tend to be alike in ways that set them apart from people born at other times. Provide two examples of such influences. (p. 13)

   A. ____

   B. ____

4. What are *nonnormative influences*? (p. 13)

   ____

   ____

   ____

5. True or False: In contemporary adult development, nonnormative influences have become less powerful, while age-graded influences have become more so. (p. 13)
6. True or False: The lifespan perspective emphasizes multiple potential pathways and outcomes of development. (p. 13)

A Lifespan Vista: The Baby Boomers Reshape the Life Course

1. (Age-graded / History-graded / Nonnormative) influences led to an explosion in birth rates in the United States between 1946 and 1964. (p. 12)
2. True or False: The boomers' expressive and socially conscious collective identity was likely influenced by nature, as opposed to nurture. (p. 12)

3. How are the baby boomers changing commonly held stereotypes about aging? (p. 12)

____

____

____

Scientific Beginnings

Darwin: Forefather of Scientific Child Study

1. Explain the two principles emphasized in Darwin's theory of evolution. (p. 14)

   Natural selection: ____

   ____

   Survival of the fittest: ____

   ____

2. Based on Darwin's observations, early scientists concluded that child growth ____________________ human evolution. These conclusions were eventually (confirmed / rejected), and the scientists' investigations of this theory formed the beginnings of scientific child study. (p. 14)

The Normative Period

1. ____________________ is generally regarded as the founder of the child study movement. (p. 14)
2. The ____________________ *approach* to child development uses age-related averages to represent typical development. (p. 14)

The Mental Testing Movement

1. Who constructed the first successful intelligence test? (p. 15)

   ____

2. A translated version of this test was developed for use with English-speaking children. What is the name of this instrument? (p. 15)

   ____

Mid-Twentieth-Century Theories

The Psychoanalytic Perspective

1. True or False: The *psychoanalytic perspective* emphasizes understanding the unique life history of each person. (p. 15)
2. Summarize the basic tenets of the psychoanalytic perspective. (p. 15)

   ____

   ____

   ____

3. Freud's ____________________ *theory* emphasized that how parents manage their child's sexual and aggressive drives in the first few years of life is crucial for healthy personality development. (p. 15)

4. According to Freud, the (id / ego / superego), or conscience, encourages individuals to act in accordance with society's values and norms. The (id / ego / superego) is the source of basic biological needs and desires. The (id / ego / superego) ensures that these impulses are acted upon in acceptable ways. (p. 15)

5. Match each of the following stages of psychosexual development with the appropriate description. (p. 16)

_______ During this stage, sexual instincts die down.	A. Genital
_______ The infant's needs are met through sucking activities.	B. Anal
_______ The Oedipal and Electra conflicts arise.	C. Oral
_______ This stage is marked by mature sexuality.	D. Latency
_______ Toilet training becomes a major issue between parent and child.	E. Phallic

6. Discuss three criticisms of Freud's theory. (p. 15)

A. ____

____

B. ____

____

C. ____

____

7. In what way did Erikson build upon and improve Freud's theory? (pp. 15–16)

____

____

____

8. Match each of Erikson's stages with the appropriate description. (p. 17)

_______ Successful resolution of this stage depends on nurturing others and engaging in productive work.	A. Industry vs. inferiority
_______ The primary task of this stage is the development of a sense of self and of one's place in society.	B. Autonomy vs. shame and doubt
_______ Successful resolution of this stage depends on a warm, loving relationship with the caregiver.	C. Intimacy vs. isolation
_______ In this stage, children experiment with adult roles through make-believe play.	D. Identity vs. role confusion
_______ Children successfully resolve this stage if parents grant them reasonable opportunities for free choice.	E. Basic trust vs. mistrust
_______ Resolution of this stage involves reflecting favorably on one's life story.	F. Generativity vs. stagnation
_______ The development of close relationships with others is key to successfully resolving this stage.	G. Initiative vs. guilt
_______ Children who develop the capacity for cooperation and productive work will successfully resolve this stage.	H. Integrity vs. despair

9. Cite two contributions of psychoanalytic theory. (pp. 16–17)

A. ____

B. ____

10. Why is psychoanalytic theory no longer in the mainstream of human development research? (p. 17)

____

____

Behaviorism and Social Learning Theory

1. True or False: *Behaviorism* focuses on the inner workings of the mind. (p. 17)
2. Watson's study of little Albert, an 11-month-old baby who was taught to fear a white rat by associating it with a loud noise, supported Pavlov's concept of ______________________________. (pp. 17–18)
3. Skinner, who proposed ____________________ conditioning theory, believed that behavior could be increased by following it with ____________________, such as food or praise, and decreased by following it with ____________________, such as disapproval or withdrawal of privileges. (p. 18)
4. Albert Bandura's ______________ *learning theory* posits that children acquire both favorable and unfavorable behaviors through the process of ____________________, also known as imitation or observational learning. (p. 18)
5. Bandura's theory has been revised to include the importance of cognition, and is now referred to as a(n) ____________________ approach rather than a social learning approach. Briefly explain this view of development. (p. 18)

____

____

____

6. What two procedures are combined in *behavior modification* to eliminate undesirable behaviors and increase socially acceptable ones? (p. 18)

A. ____

B. ____

7. Discuss two limitations of behaviorism and social learning theory. (p. 19)

A. ____

____

B. ____

____

Piaget's Cognitive-Developmental Theory

1. Summarize the basic principles of Piaget's *cognitive-developmental theory.* (p. 19)

____

____

____

2. According to Piaget's notion of ____________________, structures of the mind develop to more accurately represent the external world. (p. 19)
3. Match each of Piaget's stages with the appropriate description. (p. 20)

_______ During this stage, thought becomes more complex, and children develop the capacity for abstract reasoning.
_______ This stage is characterized by the use of eyes, ears, and hands to explore the environment.
_______ Children in this stage begin using symbols and make-believe play to represent reality.
_______ This stage is marked by the development of logical, organized reasoning skills.

A. Sensorimotor
B. Preoperational
C. Concrete
D. Formal Operational

4. What was Piaget's chief method for studying child and adolescent thought? (p. 19)

____

5. Describe two major contributions of Piaget's theory. (p. 19)

A. ____

____

B. ____

____

6. Research indicates that Piaget (underestimated / overestimated) the competencies of infants and preschoolers. Critics also suggest that Piaget's theory does not account for (social and cultural / individual) influences on development. In addition, many disagree with Piaget's assertion that major cognitive development ends in (middle childhood / adolescence / late adulthood). (p. 20)

Recent Theoretical Perspectives

Information Processing

1. Briefly describe the *information-processing* view of human development. (p. 21)

____

____

____

2. Information-processing theorists use ____________________ to map the precise steps that individuals use to solve problems and complete tasks. (p. 21)

3. Indicate whether the following statements can be attributed to Piaget's cognitive-developmental theory (P), the information-processing approach (I), or both Piaget's theory and the information-processing approach (B). (p. 21)
____ Cognitive development is continuous.
____ Cognitive development occurs in stages.
____ People actively make sense of their own thinking.

4. Cite one strength and two limitations of the information-processing approach. (p. 22)

Strength: ____

Limitation: ____

Limitation: ____

5. *Developmental cognitive neuroscience* explores the relationship between ____________________ and the development of cognitive processing and behavior patterns. (p. 22)

6. How is developmental cognitive neuroscience transforming our understanding of development? (p. 22)

____

____

Ethology and Evolutionary Developmental Psychology

1. *Ethology* is the study of ____. (p. 22)

2. Name the two European zoologists who laid the modern foundations of ethology. (p. 22)

A. ____

B. ____

3. Certain baby birds ________________ on their mothers, following them to ensure protection and feedings. (p. 22)
4. The term (*critical* / *sensitive*) *period* is more applicable to human development because its boundaries are less well-defined. (p. 22)
5. Explain how John Bowlby applied the principles of ethology to the infant–caregiver relationship. (p. 23)

____

____

____

____

6. Briefly explain what is studied in the field of *evolutionary developmental psychology*. (p. 23)

____

____

____

Vygotsky's Sociocultural Theory

1. Cite one benefit of cross-cultural and multicultural research. (p. 23)

____

____

2. According to Vygotsky, ______________________________ is necessary for children to acquire ways of thinking and behaving that make up a community's culture. (p. 23)
3. Indicate whether each statement can be attributed to Vygotsky's *sociocultural theory* (V), Piaget's cognitive-developmental theory (P), or both theories (B). (p. 24)
   ____ Children are active, constructive beings.
   ____ Cognitive development is a socially mediated process.
   ____ Cognition develops through independent exploration.
4. True or False: Because cultures select tasks for their members, individuals in every culture develop unique strengths not present in others. (p. 24)
5. Vygotsky's emphasis on culture and social experience led him to neglect ______________________ contributions to development. (p. 24)

Ecological Systems Theory

1. Briefly explain Bronfenbrenner's *ecological systems theory*. (p. 24)

____

____

____

2. Match each level of ecological systems theory with the appropriate description or example. (pp. 24–25)

_______	Relationship between the child's home and school	A. Exosystem
_______	The influence of cultural values	B. Microsystem
_______	The parent's workplace	C. Mesosystem
_______	The child's interaction with parents	D. Macrosystem

3. Provide examples of factors in each system that can enhance development. (pp. 24–25)

   Microsystem: ______________________________

   Mesosystem: ______________________________

   Exosystem: ______________________________

   Macrosystem: ______________________________

4. Describe Bronfenbrenner's notion of bidirectional relationships within the microsystem. (p. 24)

   ____

   ____

   ____

5. Bronfenbrenner's ____________________ refers to temporal changes that affect development, such as the timing of the birth of a sibling. (p. 26)

6. True or False: In ecological systems theory, development is molded by the interaction of environmental circumstances and inner dispositions. (p. 26)

Comparing and Evaluating Theories

1. The psychoanalytic perspective and ethology both focus on (changes in thinking / emotional and social development), while Piaget's cognitive-developmental theory, information processing, and Vygotsky's sociocultural theory stress (changes in thinking / emotional and social development). (p. 26)

2. List theories that view development as continuous, discontinuous, or both. (p. 27)

   Continuous: ______________________________

   Discontinuous: ______________________________

   Both continuous and discontinuous: ______________________________

3. Indicate whether each of the following theories emphasizes one course of development (O) or many possible courses of development (M). (p. 27)

   ____ Psychoanalytic perspective
   ____ Piaget's cognitive-developmental theory
   ____ Ethology and evolutionary developmental psychology
   ____ Ecological systems theory
   ____ Behaviorism and social learning theory
   ____ Information processing
   ____ Vygotsky's sociocultural theory
   ____ Lifespan perspective

Studying Development

1. Research usually begins with a ____________________, or a prediction about behavior drawn from a theory. (p. 26)

2. Distinguish between research methods and research designs. (p. 26)

   Research methods: ______________________________

   ____

   Research designs: ______________________________

   ____

Common Research Methods

1. (*Naturalistic* / *Structured*) *observation* reflects participants' everyday lives, but offers the researcher little control over conditions. (*Naturalistic* / *Structured*) *observation*, conducted in a laboratory, permits greater researcher control but may not reflect real-world behaviors. (pp. 27–29)

2. Explain how *clinical interviews* differ from *structured interviews*, and note the benefits of each technique. (p. 29)

   Clinical: ____

   ____

   ____

   Benefits: ____

   ____

   Structured: ____

   ____

   ____

   Benefits: ____

   ____

3. It can be difficult to compare individuals' responses to (clinical / structured) interviews, while (clinical / structured) interviews often do not yield as great a depth of information. (pp. 29–30)

4. True or False: Researchers can eliminate problems with inaccurate self-reports by conducting structured interviews rather than clinical interviews. (p. 29)

5. Cite the primary aim of the *clinical,* or *case study, method.* (p. 30)

   ____

6. The clinical method has been used to investigate what contributes to the accomplishments of ____________________, extremely gifted children who attain the competence of an adult in a particular field before age 10. (p. 30)

7. Discuss the drawbacks of using the clinical method. (p. 30)

   ____

   ____

   ____

8. ____________________ is a research method aimed at understanding a culture or distinct social group. This goal is achieved through ____________________, a technique in which the researcher lives with the cultural community and participates in all aspects of daily life. (p. 30)

9. Cite two limitations of the ethnographic method. (p. 31)

   A. ____

   ____

   B. ____

   ____

Cultural Influences: Immigrant Youths: Amazing Adaptation

1. True or False: The scholastic performance of students who are first-generation (foreign-born) and second-generation (American-born with immigrant parents) immigrants is often as good as or better than students of native-born parents. (p. 32)

2. Compared with their agemates, adolescents from immigrant families are (more / less) likely to commit delinquent and violent acts, use drugs and alcohol, and engage in early sex. (p. 32)

3. Discuss two ways in which family and community exert an influence on the academic achievement of adolescents from immigrant families. (p. 32)

   A. ____

   B. ____

General Research Designs

1. Describe the basic features of the *correlational design.* (p. 31)

____

____

____

2. True or False: The correlational design allows researchers to infer cause and effect. Explain your answer. (p. 31)

____

____

____

3. Investigators examine relationships among variables using a(n) ____________________, a number that describes how two measures, or variables, are associated with one another. (p. 33)

4. A *correlation coefficient* can range from ____________ to ____________. The magnitude of the number shows the (strength / direction) of the relationship between the two variables, whereas the sign indicates the (strength / direction) of the relationship. (p. 33)

5. A positive correlation coefficient means that as one variable increases, the other (increases / decreases); a negative correlation coefficient indicates that as one variable increases, the other (increases / decreases). (p. 33)

6. A researcher determines that the correlation between warm, consistent parenting and child delinquency is –.80. Explain what this indicates about the relationship between these two variables. (p. 33)

____

____

7. If the same researcher had found a correlation of +.45, what would this have indicated about the relationship between warm, consistent parenting and child delinquency? (p. 33)

____

____

8. What is the primary distinction between a correlational design and an *experimental design*? (p. 33)

____

____

9. The researcher anticipates that the (*independent / dependent) variable* will cause changes in the (*independent / dependent) variable.* (p. 33)

10. In an experimental design, it is possible to infer a cause-and-effect relationship between the variables because the researcher ____________________ the independent variable. (p. 33)

11. True or False: *Random assignment* of participants to treatment conditions allows investigators to control for characteristics that could reduce the accuracy of their findings. (p. 34)

12. In ____________________ experiments, researchers randomly assign people to treatment conditions in natural settings. (p. 34)

13. True or False: Natural experiments differ from correlational research in that groups of participants are carefully chosen to ensure that their characteristics are as much alike as possible. (p. 34)

Designs for Studying Development

1. In a ____________________ *design*, a group of participants is studied repeatedly at different ages, and changes are noted as the participants mature. List two strengths of this design. (p. 34)

   A. ______________________________

   B. ______________________________

2. Practice effects and *cohort effects* are (strengths of / limitations to) longitudinal research. (p. 35)
3. True or False: The term "cohort effect" applies to individuals born in different time periods who do not share similar historical and cultural conditions. (p. 35)
4. Describe the *cross-sectional design*. (p. 36)

   ____

   ____

5. In cross-sectional designs, researchers (do / do not) need to worry about participant dropout and practice effects. (p. 36)
6. Describe two problems associated with conducting cross-sectional research. (p. 36)

   A. ______________________________

   ____

   B. ______________________________

   ____

7. In ____________________ *designs*, researchers merge longitudinal and cross-sectional research strategies. List two advantages of this design. (pp. 36–37)

   A. ______________________________

   ____

   B. ______________________________

   ____

Social Issues: Can Musical Experiences Enhance Intelligence?

1. True of False: The "Mozart effect" has a long-lasting influence on intelligence. (p. 38)
2. To produce lasting gains in mental test scores, interventions must have the following two features: (p. 38)

   A. ______________________________

   B. ______________________________

3. Explain how enrichment activities, such as music or chess lessons, can aid a child's developing intelligence. (p. 38)

   ____

   ____

   ____

Ethics in Lifespan Research

1. List participants' research rights. (p. 39)

   A. ______________________________

   B. ______________________________

   C. ______________________________

   D. ______________________________

   E. ______________________________

2. In addition to parental consent, researchers should obtain the informed consent of children ______ years and older prior to participation in research. (p. 40)

3. True or False: Like children, most older adults require more elaborate informed consent procedures. (p. 40)

4. In __________________, the investigator provides to participants in a study a full account and justification of research in which deception was used. (p. 40)

ASK YOURSELF . . .

For *Ask Yourself* questions for this chapter, along with feedback on the accuracy of your answers, please log on to MyDevelopmentLab (for registration and access, please visit mydevelopmentlab.com or follow the instructions on page ix).

(1) Select the Multimedia Library.

(2) Choose the explore option.

(3) Find your chapter from the drop down box.

(4) Click find now.

(5) Complete questions and choose "Submit answers for grading" or "Clear answers" to start over.

SUGGESTED READINGS

Bekman, S., & Aksu-Kok, A. (Eds.). (2009). *Perspectives on human development, family, and culture.* New York: Cambridge University Press. A collection of chapters highlighting the relationship between culture and human development. Topics include the importance of cross-cultural research, culture and family, cross-cultural conceptions of gender, and cultural considerations when developing intervention programs.

Schoon, I. (2006). *Risk and resilience: Adaptations in changing times.* New York: Cambridge University Press. Using findings from Britain's National Child Development and British Cohort Studies, this book examines factors that promote and undermine resilience in childhood and during the transition to adulthood.

Smith, J. W., & Clurman, A. (2007). *Generation ageless: How baby boomers are changing the way we live today... and they're just getting started.* New York: HarperCollins. Based on more than 30 years of research, this book examines the life experiences of the baby boomers, including how this group has changed our perceptions of middle age. According to the authors, the baby boomers remain one of the largest and most influential generations in American history.

CROSSWORD PUZZLE 1.1

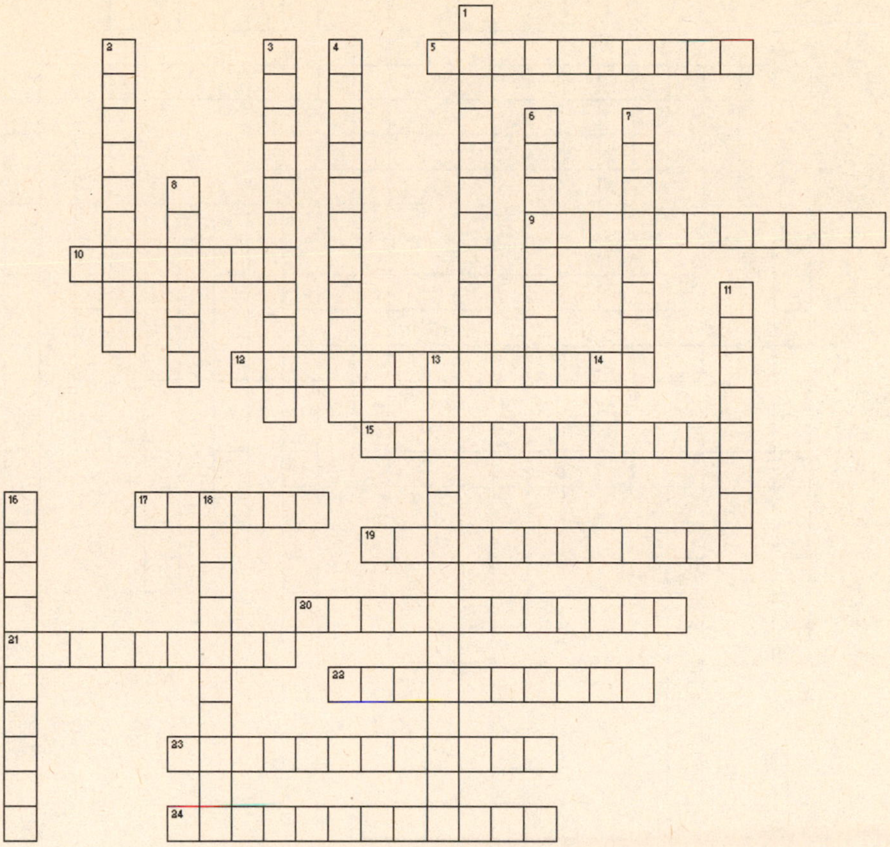

Across

5. In ecological systems theory, connections between the child's immediate settings
9. Participant observation of a culture
10. _____-graded influences explain why agemates tend to share distinguishing characteristics.
12. ______ science: study of constancy and change throughout the lifespan
15. Freud's _____ theory emphasizes management of early sexual and aggressive drives.
17. _____ learning theory emphasizes the role of modeling in the development of behavior.
19. _____ developmental psychology studies the adaptive value of a species' mental competencies.
20. In ecological systems theory, temporal changes in children's environments
21. Piaget's _____-developmental theory: children actively construct knowledge through exploration
22. _____ systems theory: children develop within complex relationships, affected by the environment
23. _____ influences affect one or a few people and do not follow a predictable timetable.
24. Erikson's _____ theory focuses on resolution of psychological conflicts over the lifespan.

Down

1. Emphasizes the study of directly observable events
2. _____ approach: age-related averages are computed to represent typical development
3. In ecological systems theory, activities and interaction patterns in the child's immediate surroundings
4. In ecological systems theory, cultural characteristics that influence inner levels of the environment
6. _____ perspective: development is lifelong, multidimensional, plastic, and context-dependent
7. _____ interview method: uses a flexible, conversational style
8. _____-nurture controversy: is development influenced more by genes or by the environment?
11. Study of the adaptive value of behavior and its evolutionary history
13. Freud's _____ perspective: children develop in stages, negotiating biological drives and social expectations
14. _____-graded influences are fairly predictable in their timing and duration.
16. _____ interview: the researcher asks all participants the same questions in the same way
18. View of development as gradually adding to innate skills

CROSSWORD PUZZLE 1.2

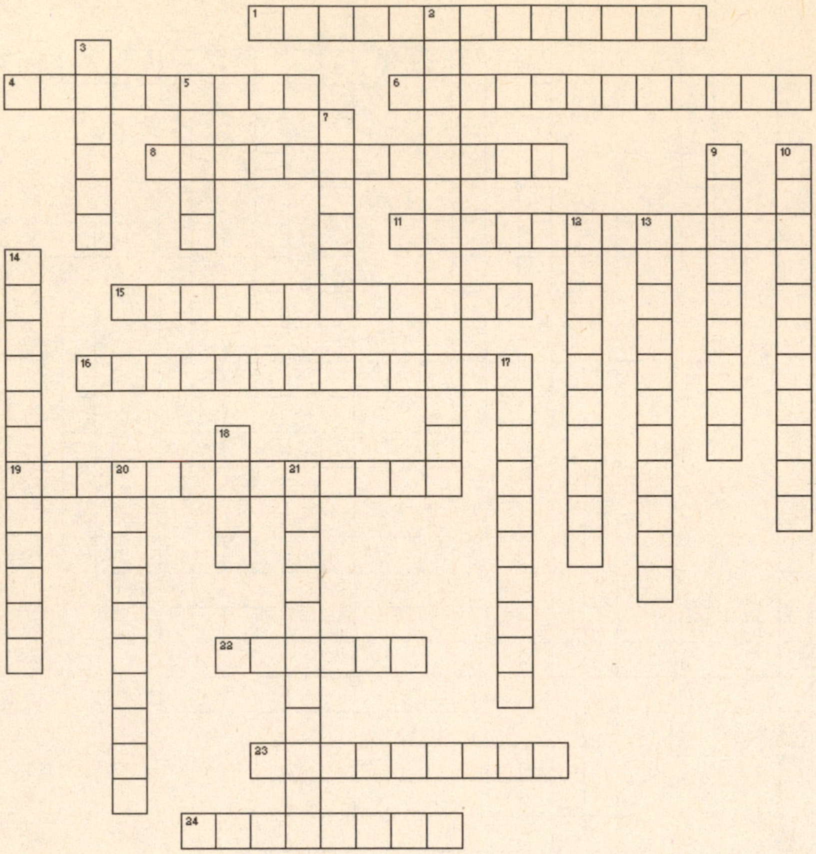

Across

1. Vygotsky's _____ theory: interpersonal interaction facilitates development
4. In ecological systems theory, social settings that do not contain children but still affect them
6. _____ design: one group of participants is studied repeatedly at different ages
8. _____ observation occurs outside the laboratory environment.
11. Developmental cognitive _____: interdisciplinary study of links between changes in the brain and development
15. _____ design: random assignment to multiple treatment conditions permits causal inferences
16. _____ development: new understandings and responses emerge at specific times
19. _____ design: the researcher gathers information without altering the participants' experience
22. An orderly, integrated set of statements that describes, explains, and predicts behavior
23. Variable expected to be influenced by the experimental manipulations
24. Combinations of genetic and environmental circumstances that affect development

Down

2. _____-_____design: groups of people differing in age are studied at the same point in time (2 words, hyph.)
3. _____ effects: cultural-historical change affects the accuracy of findings
5. A specific period of development marked by qualitative changes in thoughts, feelings, and behavior
7. _____assignment: even-handed procedure for assigning participants to treatment conditions
9. _____ period: optimal time for certain capacities to emerge
10. Correlation _____: describes how two variables are related
12. _____ observation: researchers evoke the behavior of interest in a laboratory setting
13. _____ processing approach: the mind is a symbol-manipulating system through which information flows
14. Behavior _____ combines modeling and conditioning to alter behaviors.
17. _____ designs combine longitudinal and cross-sectional studies conducted at different times.
18. Clinical, or _____ study, method
20. The ability to adapt effectively despite threats to development
21. Variable manipulated by the researcher

PRACTICE TEST #1

1. Theories of development __________ (p. 5)
   a. depend upon scientific verification for their continued existence.
   b. are rarely influenced by cultural values or beliefs of their times.
   c. describe and explain, but cannot predict, behavior.
   d. provide frameworks for understanding people, but have little practical value.

2. The study of human development provides no ultimate truth because __________ (p. 6)
   a. most research focuses on animal behavior.
   b. researchers are rarely able to replicate findings.
   c. its theories cannot be scientifically verified.
   d. investigators do not always agree on the meaning of what they see.

3. In stage theories, development is like __________ (p. 6)
   a. a gradual slope.
   b. climbing a staircase.
   c. the unfolding of a flower.
   d. the metamorphosis of a butterfly.

4. Stage theorists assume that people ____________, yet contemporary theorists are increasingly aware of __________. (p. 6)
   a. follow the same course of development; the distinct contexts in which individuals live
   b. live in distinct, complex contexts; universal experiences
   c. are shaped by their environments; the importance of heredity in human development
   d. develop slowly and gradually; the periods of rapid transformation that people undergo

5. A theorist who emphasizes plasticity is likely to believe that __________ (p. 7)
   a. heredity is the major influence on individual growth.
   b. development moves in a single direction.
   c. individual change can occur, especially when it is supported by new experiences.
   d. negative events in the early years are formative and difficult to overcome.

6. Lifespan researchers believe that development is multidirectional. What does this mean? (p. 9)
   a. In each developmental period, performance is continually improved.
   b. In each developmental period, growth and decline occur.
   c. Gains occur in early life, and losses occur in later life.
   d. Within one developmental period, an individual can make gains in a wide range of skills.

7. For a child growing up in disadvantaged circumstances, personal characteristics, such as an easygoing temperament, __________ (p. 10)
   a. rarely offset negative outcomes.
   b. are less important than good health.
   c. can offset the impact of a stressful home life.
   d. only offset the impact of a stressful home life if the child has social support.

8. Today, the baby boomers are __________ (p. 12)
   a. financially better off than any previous midlife cohort.
   b. financially worse off than any previous midlife cohort.
   c. less likely to engage in volunteer work than any previous midlife cohort.
   d. perceived as a drain on national resources.

9. Which of the following events is a nonnormative influence on human development? (p. 13)
   a. At age 16, Malcolm got his driver's license.
   b. At age 13 months, Bree took her first steps.
   c. At age 14, Gabriela is more comfortable with computer technology than her grandfather is.
   d. At age 15, Jill gave birth to her son, Corey.

10. Hall and Gesell launched the _________ approach to the field of child development. (p. 14)
    a. psychoanalytic
    b. behaviorist
    c. normative
    d. mental testing

11. Freud believed that the __________ develops through interactions with parents, who insist that children conform to the values of society. (p. 15)
    a. id
    b. ego
    c. superego
    d. external world

12. A special strength of the psychoanalytic perspective is its emphasis on __________ (p. 17)
    a. the individual's unique life history as worthy of study and understanding.
    b. nature rather than nurture.
    c. the child as a tabula rasa, or "blank slate."
    d. a genetically determined, naturally unfolding course of growth.

13. Piaget's preoperational stage is marked by the development of __________ (p. 19)
    a. language and make-believe play.
    b. sensorimotor skills.
    c. logical reasoning and organization of information.
    d. abstract, systematic thinking.

14. Which statement about Piaget's theory is true? (p. 19)
    a. Contemporary researchers unanimously accept Piaget's stages.
    b. Piaget overestimated the competencies of infants and preschoolers.
    c. Piaget believed that major cognitive changes occur throughout the lifespan.
    d. Piaget's theory influenced educational ideas of discovery learning over direct instruction.

15. Which of the following models is likely to be used by an information-processing researcher? (p. 21)
    a. chronosystem
    b. bioecological model
    c. flowchart
    d. stagewise model

16. Unlike Piaget's theory, Vygotsky's theory emphasizes the __________ (p. 23)
    a. child's independent development.
    b. concept of adaptation.
    c. importance of social interaction.
    d. evolutionary roots of development.

17. Ecological systems theory views the individual as __________ (p. 24)
    a. the product of a static environment.
    b. the follower of a fairly predictable, uniform life course.
    c. a tabula rasa.
    d. both a product and producer of his or her environment.

18. In every science, research is usually based on a(n) __________ (p. 26)
    a. theory.
    b. hypothesis.
    c. urban legend.
    d. longitudinal approach.

19. A major strength of the clinical interview is that it __________ (p. 29)
    a. provides more accurate information than other interview techniques.
    b. provides a large amount of information in a brief period of time.
    c. makes comparing individuals' responses very easy.
    d. combines naturalistic observation with self-report.
20. The clinical research method is best suited to studying the development of __________ (p. 30)
    a. a large group of kindergartners.
    b. a family with strong hereditary traits.
    c. extremely gifted children.
    d. diverse animal species in their natural habitats.
21. The major limitation of correlational studies is that they __________ (p. 31)
    a. are often harmful to participants.
    b. are vulnerable to participant dropout.
    c. do not permit inferences about cause and effect.
    d. take longer to conduct than experimental studies.
22. Compared with their agemates, adolescents from immigrant families are more likely to __________ (p. 32)
    a. suffer from poor self-esteem.
    b. use drugs or alcohol.
    c. feel disconnected from their families.
    d. value education.
23. Which of the following questions would be best answered using an experimental design? (pp. 33–34)
    a. Are men more satisfied with marriage than women?
    b. Do children experience increased behavior problems following the birth of a sibling?
    c. Does adult modeling of kindness affect toddlers' social behavior?
    d. Does growing up during an economic depression affect spending habits in adulthood?
24. One way to protect the accuracy of findings in experimental studies is to use __________ (p. 34)
    a. cohort effects.
    b. random assignment.
    c. behavior modification techniques.
    d. a correlational coefficient.
25. Dr. Hopkins is interested in the changing nature of sibling relationships over the lifespan. He designs a study in which a group of participants are interviewed every five years for several decades starting at age 10. This is an example of a __________ (p. 34)
    a. field experiment.
    b. natural experiment.
    c. longitudinal design.
    d. cross-sectional design.
26. Cohort effects __________ (pp. 35–36)
    a. are a threat to findings in both cross-sectional and sequential research designs.
    b. can occur in an entire generation or in a group of individuals within a generation.
    c. occur when a participant becomes "test-wise."
    d. are revealed by longitudinal research designs.
27. The cross-sectional research design __________ (p. 36)
    a. is less efficient than the longitudinal or sequential design.
    b. permits the study of individual developmental trends.
    c. is often plagued by the problem of participant dropout.
    d. is susceptible to distorted findings due to cohort effects.

28. In a study examining the relationship between musical experiences and intelligence, researchers found that __________ (p. 38)
    a. children exposed to classical music scored 10 to 15 points higher in IQ than children in a control group.
    b. children enrolled in music lessons improved in social maturity, but showed no increase in intelligence.
    c. sustained music lessons led to intellectual benefits unmatched by any other enrichment activity.
    d. sustained music lessons led to small increases in intelligence.

29. The ultimate responsibility for the ethical integrity of research lies with the __________ (p. 39)
    a. parent or guardian.
    b. institution.
    c. participant.
    d. investigator.

30. Which of the following statements about the use of deception in studies with children is true? (p. 40)
    a. Children are rarely affected by participation in a deceptive research situation.
    b. Children may experience serious emotional consequences after learning they have been deceived.
    c. Deception is never justified in research with children under the age of 10.
    d. Deception is permitted in any study involving children as long as debriefing occurs when the session is over.

PRACTICE TEST #2

1. Our knowledge of human development is interdisciplinary. What does this mean? (p. 5)
   a. Our knowledge of human development is based exclusively on research conducted by people in the field of human development.
   b. Human development is not recognized as a distinct field of study.
   c. Individuals from diverse fields have contributed to our knowledge of human development.
   d. Human development is part of a larger discipline known as developmental psychology.

2. A researcher who believes that a child's ability to use language is similar to that of adults, only differing in amount and complexity of her knowledge of words, has a __________ view of development. (p. 6)
   a. stagelike
   b. contextual
   c. continuous
   d. discontinuous

3. Stage theorists view development as __________ (p. 6)
   a. the gradual augmentation of skills.
   b. unique, circumstantial growth.
   c. slow, ongoing transformation.
   d. a process of qualitative changes.

4. Theorists who emphasize stability typically view __________ as the most important developmental influence. (p. 7)
   a. social forces
   b. culture
   c. heredity
   d. reinforcement

5. Lifespan researchers maintain that __________ (p. 10)
   a. age-graded influences are more powerful than nonnormative influences.
   b. development is plastic at all ages.
   c. plasticity is limited to early childhood.
   d. development occurs in a process of stages, much like a staircase.

6. The most consistent asset of resilient children is __________ (p. 11)
   a. athletic skill.
   b. high intelligence.
   c. extracurricular involvement.
   d. a strong bond to a competent, caring adult.

7. According to the lifespan perspective, starting school at around age 6 is an example of a(n) __________ (p. 11)
   a. family-graded influence.
   b. social-graded influence.
   c. history-graded influence.
   d. age-graded influence.

8. As young adults, baby boomers were __________ than previous generations. (p. 12)
   a. more economically disadvantaged
   b. more family- and marriage-centered
   c. less socially aware
   d. more concerned with individual recognition

9. In the normative approach to child study, researchers __________ (p. 14)
   a. jot down day-to-day descriptions and impressions of a youngster's behavior beginning in early infancy.
   b. take measures of behavior on large numbers of children and then compute age-related averages to represent typical development.
   c. investigate children's cognitive development through the use of clinical interviews in which children describe their thinking.
   d. use flowcharts to map the precise steps that individuals take to solve problems and complete tasks.

10. In the early 1900s, Alfred Binet's intelligence test sparked interest in __________ (p. 15)
    a. individual differences in development.
    b. child-rearing advice.
    c. development as a maturational process.
    d. the subconscious mind.

11. Unlike Freud, Erikson __________ (p. 16)
    a. believed that normal development must be understood in relation to each culture's life situation.
    b. was concerned with the individual's inner thoughts and feelings.
    c. believed that people move through a series of stages in which they confront conflicts.
    d. stressed the influence of the early parent–child relationship.

12. Which of the following is a limitation of the psychoanalytic perspective? (p. 17)
    a. It underestimates the importance of early childhood experiences.
    b. Psychoanalysts are overly focused on recording observable stimuli.
    c. It fails to acknowledge the uniqueness of individual lives.
    d. Many psychoanalytic ideas are so vague they cannot be tested empirically.

13. A limitation of behaviorism and social learning theory is that they __________ (p. 19)
    a. have little value in treating developmental problems.
    b. offer too narrow a view of environmental influences.
    c. overestimate individuals' contributions to their own development.
    d. rely too heavily on the clinical approach.

14. In Piaget's concrete operational stage, __________ (p. 20)
    a. infants "think" by acting on the world with their eyes, ears, hands, and mouths.
    b. children develop language and make-believe play.
    c. children's reasoning becomes logical.
    d. adolescents develop the capacity for abstract, systematic thinking.

15. Unlike Piaget's theory, the information-processing approach __________ (p. 21)
    a. underestimates the competencies of infants and toddlers.
    b. emphasizes the development of imagination and creativity.
    c. divides development into stages.
    d. views development as continuous.

16. Observations of imprinting in baby birds led to the concept of __________ (p. 22)
    a. the critical period.
    b. equilibrium.
    c. behavior modification.
    d. modeling.

17. Critics of Vygotsky's sociocultural theory point out that Vygotsky ________ (p. 24)
    a. ignored the role of language in children's development.
    b. overemphasized children's capacity to shape their own development.
    c. neglected the biological side of development.
    d. viewed children as passive participants in their own development.

18. To understand human development at the level of the microsystem, one must keep in mind that all relationships are __________ (p. 24)
    a. universal.
    b. unidirectional.
    c. predetermined.
    d. bidirectional.

19. Pablo's mother works for a company that provides generous sick leave and a flexible work schedule. In Bronfenbrenner's model, this is an example of a(n) __________ support. (p. 25)
    a. microsystem
    b. mesosystem
    c. exosystem
    d. macrosystem

20. A major limitation of naturalistic observation is that __________ (p. 28)
    a. it fails to reflect everyday, real-world behavior.
    b. participants often provide inaccurate information.
    c. not all participants have the same opportunity to display a particular behavior in everyday life.
    d. only one observation can be conducted at a time.

21. Structured interviews __________ (p. 29)
    a. provide more depth of information than clinical interviews.
    b. require interviewers to ask each set of questions in the same way.
    c. are less efficient than clinical interviews.
    d. eliminate the problem of participants' inaccurate self-reporting.

22. A strength of the ethnographic research method is that __________ (p. 30)
    a. it provides a more complete description than can be derived from a single visit, interview, or questionnaire.
    b. it is unlikely to be biased by researchers' theoretical preferences.
    c. its findings can be universally applied.
    d. it provides a large amount of information in a relatively short time.

23. To uncover the cultural meanings of children's and adults' behavior in a community of Haitian immigrants, Dr. Garcia spends several months living in the community, conducting interviews, and recording her observations. This is an example of the __________ research method. (p. 30)
    a. clinical
    b. naturalistic
    c. systematic
    d. ethnographic

24. Which of the following statements about immigrant youths is true? (p. 32)
    a. Recently arrived immigrant high school students have lower achievement than those who came at younger ages.
    b. Adolescents from immigrant families often reject their parents' values.
    c. Youths from low-SES immigrant families experience significant academic problems, regardless of when they arrive in the U.S.
    d. Recently arrived immigrant high school students do as well in school as those who came at younger ages.

25. A correlation coefficient of –.52 indicates a ______ relationship between two variables. (p. 33)
    a. weak
    b. moderate
    c. strong
    d. nonexistent

26. An experimental design permits inferences about cause and effect because __________ (p. 33)
    a. the researcher controls changes in the independent variable.
    b. the researcher controls changes in the dependent variable.
    c. the researcher systematically assigns participants to specific treatment conditions based on their known characteristics.
    d. these studies are conducted in natural settings rather than laboratory settings.

27. A researcher concludes that today's school-age children are more intelligent than children in the 1950s. This example illustrates ________ (pp. 35–36)
    a. biased sampling.
    b. a randomization error.
    c. cohort effects.
    d. selective attrition.

28. To examine the stability of certain personality traits throughout the lifespan, a researcher designs a study in which 18-year-olds of three different cohorts, each a decade apart, are interviewed every 10 years for 40 years. This is an example of a(n) __________ design. (pp. 36–37)
    a. sequential
    b. longitudinal
    c. cross-sectional
    d. experimental

29. Follow-up research on the Mozart effect indicates that brief exposure to classical music __________ (p. 39)
    a. results in higher achievement test scores, but has no effect on arousal and mood.
    b. results in a 10 to 15 point gain in IQ.
    c. leads to gains in IQ and achievement for boys but not girls.
    d. improves arousal and mood, resulting in better concentration for a short time.

30. Which of the following statements about informed consent is true? (p. 40)
    a. The right to informed consent applies to all research participants except young children and the elderly.
    b. In most cases, researchers need only obtain the child's assent; parental consent is not required.
    c. For children 7 years and older, their own informed consent should be obtained in addition to parental consent.
    d. Unless the research is potentially harmful to the participant, researchers are not required to obtain informed consent.

CHAPTER 2
BIOLOGICAL AND ENVIRONMENTAL FOUNDATIONS

BRIEF CHAPTER SUMMARY

This chapter examines the foundations of development: heredity and environment. The discussion begins at the moment of conception, an event that establishes the new individual's hereditary makeup. At conception, chromosomes containing genetic information from each parent combine to determine characteristics that make us human and also contribute to individual differences in appearance and behavior. Several different patterns of inheritance are possible, ensuring that each individual will be unique. Serious developmental problems often result from the inheritance of harmful recessive genes and by chromosomal abnormalities. Fortunately, genetic counseling and prenatal diagnostic methods make early detection of genetic problems possible. Many families turn to adoption, and most adoptees ultimately fare well, despite some challenges.

Just as complex as heredity are the environments in which human development takes place. The family has an especially powerful impact on development, operating as a network of interdependent relationships in which members exert direct, indirect, and third-party influences on one another. Family functioning and individual well-being are influenced considerably by child-rearing practices as well as by socioeconomic status. Poverty and homelessness can pose serious threats to development, while children in affluent families may suffer from overscheduling and lack of emotional closeness. The availability of education of women in particular promotes a better quality of life for both parents and children.

Beyond the immediate family, the quality of community life in neighborhoods, schools, towns, and cities also affects children's and adults' development. Cultural values—for example, the degree to which a society emphasizes collectivism versus individualism—combine with laws and government programs to shape experiences in all of these contexts. Public policies are needed to support the economic and social well-being of both children and the elderly. Compared to many other Western countries, the United States lags behind in adequate programs for low-income families and elderly people who live alone.

Heredity and environment are involved in every aspect of development. Some researchers believe it is useful and possible to determine how much heredity and environment contribute to individual differences. Others are more interested in discovering how these two major determinants of development work together in a complex, dynamic interplay, and then using that information to improve environments and further the development of individuals.

LEARNING OBJECTIVES

After reading this chapter, you should be able to:

2.1 Explain the role and function of genes and how they are transmitted from one generation to the next. (p. 46)

2.2 Describe the genetic events that determine the sex of the new organism. (pp. 46–47)

2.3 Identify two types of twins, and explain how each is created. (pp. 47–48)

2.4 Describe various patterns of genetic inheritance. (pp. 48–52)

2.5 Describe major chromosomal abnormalities, and explain how they occur. (pp. 52–53)

2.6 Explain how reproductive procedures can assist prospective parents in having healthy children. (pp. 53–57)

2.7 Summarize the research on adoption. (pp. 57–59)

2.8 Describe the social systems perspective on family functioning, along with aspects of the environment that support family well-being and development. (pp. 59–60)

2.9 Discuss the impact of socioeconomic status and poverty on family functioning. (pp. 60–63)

2.10 Summarize the roles of neighborhoods, towns, and cities in the lives of children and adults. (pp. 63–65)

2.11 Explain how cultural values and practices, public policies, and political and economic conditions affect human development. (pp. 65–70)

2.12 Explain the various ways heredity and environment can influence complex traits. (p. 70)

2.13 Describe and evaluate methods researchers use to determine "how much" heredity and environment influence complex human characteristics. (pp. 70–72)

2.14 Describe concepts that indicate "how" heredity and environment work together to influence complex human characteristics. (pp. 72–74)

STUDY QUESTIONS

1. (*Genotypes* / *Phenotypes*) are directly observable characteristics, determined in part by the individual's (*genotype* / *phenotype*), the blend of genetic information that influences all of our unique characteristics. (p. 45)

Genetic Foundations

The Genetic Code

1. Explain the relationship among *chromosomes*, *DNA*, and *genes*. (p. 46)

   ____

   ____

2. The process of ______________ allows a fertilized ovum to develop into a human being whose cells contain the same number of chromosomes and identical genetic information. (p. 46)
3. Genes send instructions for making proteins to the ____________, the area surrounding the cell nucleus. (p. 46)
4. True or False: Proteins are the biological foundation on which our characteristics are built. (p. 46)
5. Humans have far more (genes / proteins) than simpler organisms, which contributes to our complexity. (p. 46)

The Sex Cells

1. Cells that have 23 chromosomes and combine to form a new individual are called ________________. (p. 46)
2. Sex cells are formed through (*mitosis* / *meiosis*), which ensures genetic variation. When sex cells unite, the resulting individual grows through (*mitosis* / *meiosis*). (pp. 46–47)
3. A ________________ results when a sperm and ovum unite at conception. (p. 47)
4. True or False: When one cell undergoes meiosis, it creates four sperm or four ova. (p. 47)

Boy or Girl?

1. The 22 matching pairs of chromosomes are called (*autosomes* / *sex chromosomes*). The 23rd pair is made up of (*autosomes* / *sex chromosomes*). (p. 47)

Multiple Offspring

1. The following characteristics describe either *identical twins* or *fraternal twins*. Indicate your answer using "I" for identical or "F" for fraternal. (pp. 47–48)
   _____ Occur in the same frequency throughout the world
   _____ The most common type of multiple birth
   _____ Genetically no more alike than ordinary siblings
   _____ Created when a *zygote* duplicates and separates into two clusters of cells
   _____ Associated with older maternal age, fertility drugs, and in vitro fertilization
   _____ Associated with temperature changes, variation in oxygen levels, and late fertilization
2. True or False: Children of single births are often healthier and develop more rapidly than twins in the early years. (p. 48)

Patterns of Genetic Inheritance

1. If the *alleles* from both parents are (alike / different), the child is (*heterozygous* / *homozygous*) and will display the inherited trait. If the *alleles* are (alike / different), then the child is (*heterozygous* / *homozygous*), and relationships between the *alleles* determine which trait will appear. (p. 48)

2. True or False: When alleles display *dominant–recessive inheritance*, the individual's phenotype reflects a combination of both alleles. (p. 48)

3. True or False: Inheriting unfavorable genes always leads to an untreatable condition. Explain, citing PKU as an example. (p. 50)

   ____

   ____

   ____

4. Why are serious diseases only rarely due to dominant alleles? Explain why Huntington disease, a dominant disorder, has endured in the population. (p. 50)

   A. ____

   ____

   B. ____

   ____

5. In ________________________, both alleles influence the individual's characteristics. Under what conditions is the sickle cell trait expressed by heterozygous individuals? (p. 50)

   ____

6. True or False: Males are more likely than females to be affected by *X-linked inheritance*. (p. 56)

7. Describe *genomic imprinting*. (p. 51)

   ____

   ____

8. How are harmful genes created? (p. 51)

   ____

   ____

9. (Germline / Somatic) *mutation* occurs in cells that give rise to *gametes*, which pass affected DNA to offspring. In (germline / somatic) *mutation*, normal body cells mutate and spread defective DNA when they replicate. (pp. 51–52)

10. Characteristics such as height, weight, intelligence, and personality reflect ________________, in which many genes determine the characteristic in question. (p. 52)

Chromosomal Abnormalities

1. ________________________, the most common chromosomal abnormality, often results from a defect in the twenty-first chromosome. (p. 52)

2. Cite factors that promote favorable development among children with Down syndrome. (p. 53)

   ____

   ____

3. In contrast to autosomal disorders, sex chromosomal disorders often go undetected until ____________________. (p. 53)

4. Evaluate whether these statements about individuals with sex chromosome disorders are true or false. (p. 53)
   (T / F) Males with XYY syndrome are not necessarily more aggressive and antisocial than XY males.
   (T / F) Most children with sex chromosome disorders suffer from mental retardation.
   (T / F) Altering the usual number of X chromosomes affects the development of certain brain structures.

Reproductive Choices

Genetic Counseling

1. ______________________ helps couples evaluate the chance that their offspring will inherit a genetic disorder and choose a course of action. Who is most likely to seek this course of action? (pp. 53–54)

   ____

   ____

2. When affected relatives are identified in a ______________, it is possible to estimate the likelihood that parents will have an abnormal child. (pp. 54–55)

Social Issues: The Pros and Cons of Reproductive Technologies

1. Explain the following reproductive technologies. (p. 54)

   Donor Insemination: ____

   ____

   ____

   In Vitro Fertilization: ____

   ____

   ____

2. (Donor insemination / In vitro fertilization) can be used to treat both male and female infertility problems. (p. 54)
3. List three concerns surrounding the use of donor insemination and in vitro fertilization. (p. 54)

   A. ____

   B. ____

   C. ____

4. Cite three risks involved with surrogate motherhood. (pp. 54–55)

   A. ____

   B. ____

   C. ____

5. True or False: Strong national laws in the United States govern screening of gamete donors, recording and release of donor identities, and in vitro fertilization of post-menopausal women. (p. 55)

Prenatal Diagnosis and Fetal Medicine

1. Which two *prenatal diagnostic methods* are frequently used with women of advanced maternal age? (p. 56)

   A. ____

   B. ____

2. True or False: Prenatal diagnosis and fetal medicine techniques frequently result in complications, most commonly premature labor and miscarriage. (p. 56)

3. Advances in genetic ______________ offer hope for correcting heredity defects. (p. 56)

4. ___________________ allows scientists to correct genetic abnormalities by delivering functional genes to affected cells. Scientists can also use __________________ to modify gene-specified proteins. (pp. 56–57)

Adoption

1. List three possible reasons why adopted children have more learning and emotional difficulties than other children. (p. 58)

   A. ____

   B. ____

   C. ____

2. The decision to search for birth parents usually occurs during (adolescence / early adulthood). Why is the search more likely during this period of development? (p. 58)

   ____

   ____

3. True or False: Most adoptees appear well-adjusted as adults. (p. 58)

Environmental Contexts for Development

The Family

1. When a mother asks her son to clean his room, she is exerting a(n) (direct / indirect) influence on her son. Relationships with third parties, such as the mother's feelings toward her husband, may exert a(n) (direct / indirect) influence on this mother–son interaction. (pp. 59–60)

2. Explain how important events and historical time period contribute to the dynamic, ever-changing nature of the family. (p. 60)

   ____

   ____

Socioeconomic Status and Family Functioning

1. What three interrelated variables define *socioeconomic status (SES)*? (p. 60)

   A. ____

   B. ____

   C. ____

2. People who work in skilled and semiskilled manual occupations tend to marry and have children (earlier / later) and have (fewer / more) children than people in professional and technical occupations. (p. 61)

3. Lower-SES parents tend to desire __________________ characteristics in their children, while higher-SES parents hope their children will develop ___________________ traits. (p. 61)

4. Explain how life conditions, such as parental stress and education, contribute to SES differences in family interaction. (p. 61)

____

____

____

A Lifespan Vista: Worldwide Education of Girls: Transforming Current and Future Generations

1. List two ways that education of girls has a powerful impact on the welfare of families, societies, and future generations. (p. 62)

   A. ____

   B. ____

2. Years of schooling strongly predict women's preventive health behavior. How does education influence family health? (p. 62)

____

____

____

3. True or False: The empowerment that education provides women is associated with more equitable husband–wife relationships and a reduction in harsh disciplining of children. (p. 62)

Affluence

1. True or False: Affluent parents often engage in high levels of family interaction and parenting that promote favorable development. (p. 61)
2. Explain why affluent youth may be troubled or poorly adjusted. (p. 61)

____

____

3. What simple routine is associated with a reduction in adjustment difficulties for both affluent and low-SES youths? (p. 61)

____

Poverty

1. What two groups are hit hardest by poverty? (p. 63)

   A. ______________________ B. ______________________

2. True or False: The poverty rate is higher among children than any other age group. (p. 63)
3. List five outcomes that children of poverty are more likely to experience than other children. (p. 63)

   A. ____

   B. ____

   C. ____

   D. ____

   E. ____

4. A rise in homelessness is mostly due to which two factors? (p. 63)

   A. ______________________________

   B. ______________________________

Beyond the Family: Neighborhoods, Towns, and Cities

1. Explain why neighborhood resources have a greater impact on economically disadvantaged than well-to-do children and adolescents. (p. 64)

   ____

   ____

   ____

2. List two ways that high resident stability and social cohesion in low-SES neighborhoods can affect adults' well-being. (p. 64)

   A. ______________________________

   B. ______________________________

3. Why do neighborhoods become increasingly important during late adulthood? (p. 64)

   ____

   ____

4. Summarize the benefits and drawbacks of living in a small town. (pp. 64–65)

   Benefits: ______________________________

   ____

   Drawbacks: ______________________________

   ____

The Cultural Context

1. Which central North American beliefs and values contribute to the public's slow endorsement of government support and benefits for all families? (p. 65)

   ____

   ____

2. Some citizens belong to ______________ that do not share some of our nation's dominant values. (p. 66)

3. In (*collectivist* / *individualistic*) *societies*, people define themselves as part of a group and stress group goals. In (*collectivist* / *individualistic*) *societies*, people think of themselves as separate entities and are largely concerned with their own needs. (p. 66)

4. Collectivist societies value an ______________ self, while individualistic societies value an ______________ self. List three values of each. (p. 67)

A. ______________	A. ______________
B. ______________	B. ______________
C. ______________	C. ______________

5. The United States (lags behind / leads) other industrialized nations in creating ______________ to safeguard children and the elderly. (p. 67)

6. Why has it been difficult to help children through *public policy* in the United States? (pp. 67–68)

____

____

7. True or False: The U.S. government adequately funds a national network for planning, coordinating, and delivering assistance to the aged. (p. 68)

8. Identify three reasons why many senior citizens remain in dire economic conditions. (p. 68)

   A. ____

   B. ____

   C. ____

9. The number of aging poor has (decreased / increased) since 1960. Senior citizens are (more / less) independent than ever before. (p. 69)

10. The ____________________ releases an Annual Report, which analyzes programs for children and families and details initiatives to improve those programs. (p. 69)

11. The ____________________ has a large membership who advocate for increased government benefits to the aged. (p. 69)

Cultural Influences: The African-American Extended Family

1. Cite characteristics of the African-American extended family that help reduce the stress of poverty and single parenthood. (p. 66)

____

____

____

2. How does the extended family help transmit African-American culture? (p. 66)

____

____

____

Understanding the Relationship Between Heredity and Environment

1. True or False: All contemporary researchers agree that both heredity and environment are involved in every aspect of development. (p. 70)

The Question, "How Much?"

1. ____________________, which compare the characteristics of family members, allow us to calculate ____________________, which describe the role of genetic factors in individual differences. (p. 70)

2. Most current research supports a (weak / moderate / powerful) role for heredity. (p. 70)

3. Both the heritability of intelligence in adulthood and the resemblance between adopted children's mental test scores and their biological parents' scores (support / refute) the role of heredity. (pp. 70–71)

4. True or False: Unlike intelligence, heritability of personality does not increase over the lifespan. (p. 71)

5. List three limitations of *heritability estimates*. (p. 71)

   A. ______________________________

   B. ______________________________

   C. ______________________________

The Question, "How?"

1. If a trait displays *(range of reaction / canalization*), its expression varies widely across individuals and environment. Traits that exhibit *(range of reaction / canalization*) develop similarly across a wide range of individuals and environments. (p. 72)
2. Describe two important points highlighted by reaction range. (p. 72)

   A. ______________________________

   B. ______________________________
3. Identify one trait that is strongly canalized and another that is less strongly canalized. (p. 72)

   A. ______________________________

   B. ______________________________
4. Match the following types of *genetic–environmental correlation* with their appropriate descriptors. (pp. 72–73)

   ________ Children increasingly seek out environments that fit their genetic tendencies (called *niche-picking*).

   ________ A child's style of responding influences others' responses, which then strengthen the child's original style.

   ________ Parents provide an environment consistent with their own heredity.

   A. Passive correlation
   B. Evocative correlation
   C. Active correlation
5. True or False: Partially as a result of niche-picking, identical twins become more similar and fraternal twins and adopted siblings become less similar in intelligence with age. (p. 73)
6. ______________ means development resulting from ongoing, bidirectional exchanges between heredity and all levels of the environment. (p. 74)
7. Cite a major reason why researchers are interested in the nature–nurture issue. (p. 75)

   ____

   ____

ASK YOURSELF . . .

For *Ask Yourself* questions for this chapter, along with feedback on the accuracy of your answers, please log on to MyDevelopmentLab (for registration and access, please visit mydevelopmentlab.com or follow the instructions on page ix).

(1) Select the Multimedia Library.

(2) Choose the explore option.

(3) Find your chapter from the drop down box.

(4) Click find now.

(5) Complete questions and choose "Submit answers for grading" or "Clear answers" to start over.

SUGGESTED READINGS

Lindsey, D. (2007). *Future of children: Wealth, poverty, and opportunity in America.* New York: Oxford University Press. Presents an overview of child and family poverty in the United States, including the role of public policy in child development.

Mundy, L. (2007). *Everything conceivable: How assisted reproduction is changing men, women, and the world.* New York: Knopf. A compelling look at reproductive technologies, this book examines current research, as well as controversies, surrounding assisted reproduction. The author also includes personal narratives, myths, and the social consequences of assisted reproduction.

Rutter, M. (2006). *Genes and behavior: Nature–nurture interplay explained.* Malden, MA: Blackwell. Written by a leading expert in human development, this book examines the complex relationship between genes and behavior. Topics include the nature–nurture controversy, the heritability of diseases and mental disorders, patterns of genetic inheritance, and environmental contributions to risk and resilience.

CROSSWORD PUZZLE 2.1

Across

2. _____ inheritance: a recessive gene is carried on the X chromosome (hyph.)
3. Genomic _____: one allele in a pair is activated, regardless of its makeup
4. A sudden, permanent change in a segment of DNA
5. Having two identical alleles at the same place on a pair of chromosomes
6. Directly observable characteristics
9. Development resulting from bidirectional heredity–environment exchanges
11. 22 matching chromosome pairs in each cell
14. Rodlike structures in the cell nucleus that store and transmit genetic information
15. ______ inheritance: many genes determine a characteristic
17. ______-______ inheritance: only one allele of a heterozygous pair influences the phenotype (2 words, hyph.)
18. Having two different alleles at the same place on a pair of chromosomes

Down

1. Blend of genetic information that influences all our unique characteristics
3. Both alleles are expressed, resulting in a combined trait. (2 words)
7. Process of cell duplication
8. Double-stranded molecules that make up chromosomes (abbr.)
10. ______ chromosomes: the 23rd pair; XX in females, XY in males
12. Human sperm and ova
13. Each form of a gene is called a(n) ______.
16. A segment of DNA along the length of the chromosome

CROSSWORD PUZZLE 2.2

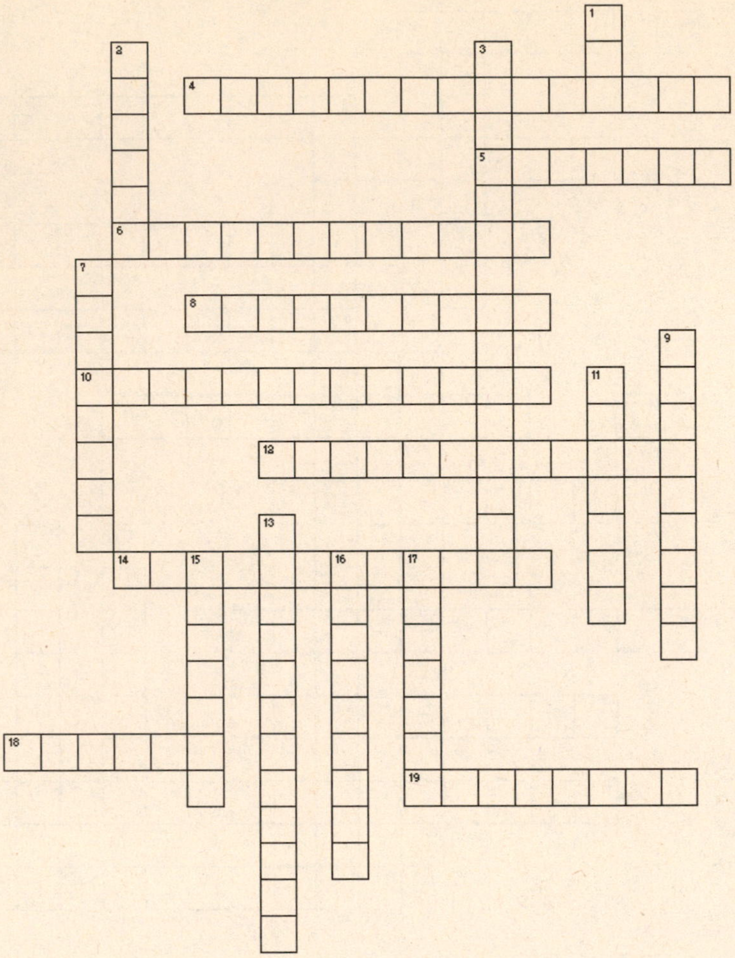

Across

4. In ______ societies people view themselves as separate entities and focus on personal needs.
5. ______ counseling assesses a couple's likelihood of passing on a hereditary disorder.
6. Heredity tends to restrict the development of some characteristics.
8. Group whose beliefs and customs differ from the larger culture
10. Genetic- ______ correlation: heredity influences the experiences to which we are exposed
12. In ______ societies people define themselves as part of a group and stress group goals.
14. Actively choosing environments that compliment one's heredity (2 words, hyph.)
18. Results from the union of the sperm and ova at conception
19. ______ diagnostic methods detect developmental problems before birth.

Down

1. Measure of a family's social position and economic well-being (abbr.)
2. ______ policies: laws and government programs to improve current conditions
3. Each person's unique, genetically determined response to varied environments (3 words)
7. ______ -family household: parent and child live with adult relative(s)
9. ______ twins develop from two ova; also known as dizygotic twins
11. Process of cell division
13. ______ estimate: measures the influence of genetic factors on individual trait differences
15. A heterozygous individual who can pass a recessive trait to offspring
16. ____ twins start as one zygote; also known as monozygotic twins
17. ____ studies compare family members to determine the influence of heredity.

PRACTICE TEST #1

1. A molecule of DNA resembles __________ (p. 46)
   a. a globe or sphere.
   b. a twisted ladder.
   c. either an X or a Y.
   d. a staircase.

2. The control center of the cell, or __________, contains rodlike structures called __________. (p. 46)
   a. nucleus; chromosomes
   b. nucleus; genes
   c. gene; gametes
   d. genotype; DNA

3. One reason that humans are able to develop into such complex beings is because __________ (p. 46)
   a. humans have many times more genes than other species.
   b. 98 percent of their genetic makeup is unique to the human species.
   c. human genes make fewer proteins than the genes of other species.
   d. human genes make far more proteins than the genes of other species.

4. Gametes __________ (pp. 46–47)
   a. are formed through the process of meiosis.
   b. duplicate themselves through the process of mitosis.
   c. contain twice as many chromosomes as regular body cells.
   d. contain the same number of chromosomes as regular body cells.

5. Which of the following statements about sex chromosomes is true? (p. 47)
   a. Twenty-two of the 23 pairs of chromosomes are sex chromosomes.
   b. The sex of a new organism is determined by whether an X-bearing or Y-bearing sperm fertilizes the ovum.
   c. The Y chromosome is quite large, whereas the X is short and carries little genetic material.
   d. The gametes that form in males all carry a Y chromosome.

6. Fraternal twinning __________ (p. 47)
   a. is less likely with each additional birth.
   b. occurs in more than 15 percent of all births.
   c. rises with maternal age, and then rapidly drops.
   d. occurs more often among women whose mothers and sisters gave birth to fraternal twins.

7. If parents each pass on a different allele to their child, the child is __________ (p. 48)
   a. dominant.
   b. recessive.
   c. heterozygous.
   d. homozygous.

8. Which of the following is an example of a recessive characteristic? (p. 48)
   a. dark hair
   b. blonde hair
   c. dimples
   d. normal vision

9. The case of phenylketonuria (PKU) demonstrates that __________ (p. 49)
   a. serious inherited disorders are more often due to dominant than to recessive genes.
   b. most inherited disorders are untreatable unless they are identified and treated in early childhood.
   c. even if we know the genetic makeup of the parents, it is difficult to predict the likelihood that children in a family will display a disorder.
   d. changes in the environment can alter the extent to which an inherited disorder influences a person's well-being.

10. The sickle cell trait, a heterozygous condition present in many black Africans, is an example of __________ because the recessive sickle cell allele asserts itself in certain conditions. (p. 50)
    a. X-linked inheritance
    b. incomplete dominance
    c. genomic imprinting
    d. dominant–recessive inheritance

11. The most common chromosomal disorder, occurring in one out of every 1,000 live births, is __________ (p. 52)
    a. Down syndrome.
    b. Klinefelter syndrome.
    c. Turner syndrome.
    d. XYY syndrome.

12. Beth and Richard want to have a child but are concerned about a genetic disorder that runs in Richard's family. Which of the following can help them understand their risk of passing on the disorder to their offspring? (pp. 53–54)
    a. genetic engineering
    b. amniocentesis
    c. genetic counseling
    d. gene therapy

13. __________ is a particularly controversial method of conception, in part because it may promote exploitation of financially needy women. (pp. 54–55)
    a. Donor insemination
    b. In vitro fertilization
    c. Cloning
    d. Surrogate motherhood

14. Three-year-old Jonah cries often, throws tantrums, and has unpredictable eating and sleeping habits. His mother often becomes upset with Jonah, responding to his behavior with anger and harshness, which causes Jonah to act out even more. Which of the following is being described in the example? (p. 59)
    a. third parties
    b. bidirectional influences
    c. dynamic influences
    d. extraneous variables

15. Donor nations and international organizations are increasingly coming to the conclusion that __________ is the most effective means of combating the most profound, global threats to human development. (p. 62)
    a. good nutrition
    b. family planning
    c. the education of girls
    d. reducing crime

16. In the United States, the poverty rate is higher among __________ than any other age group. (p. 63)
    a. children
    b. young adults
    c. middle-aged adults
    d. the elderly

17. In several studies, children of low-SES families who moved into low-poverty neighborhoods __________ (p. 63)
    a. showed signs of increased stress.
    b. showed no improvement in physical or mental health.
    c. showed improved health and school achievement.
    d. were unlikely to establish new friendships.

18. Which of the following is true of residents of small towns? (p. 64)
    a. The elderly living in small towns tend to feel less safe than the elderly in urban areas.
    b. Youths of small towns are less likely to be taught social skills and responsibility than youths of urban areas.
    c. Civic participation is greater in small towns than in large urban areas.
    d. Children growing up in small towns spend less time with adults than children in urban areas.

19. The African-American extended family tradition __________ (p. 66)
    a. has virtually disappeared in recent generations.
    b. protects children's development.
    c. decreases the likelihood of effective parenting.
    d. is a source of stress and confusion for many children.

20. Collectivist societies value __________ (p. 67)
    a. an interdependent self.
    b. personal needs over group needs.
    c. individual choice in relationships.
    d. privacy.

21. Why have attempts to help children and youths been difficult to realize in the United States? (p. 68)
    a. There is little research to support the effectiveness of programs for families with young children.
    b. Most government programs focus on the elderly instead of children and youths.
    c. Cultural values of self-reliance and privacy have made government hesitant to become involved in family matters.
    d. Cultural values of group needs over personal needs have made government hesitant to become involved in family matters.

22. The Children's Defense Fund and the AARP are examples of __________ (p. 69)
    a. organizations devoted to citizens' well-being.
    b. organizations that have disbanded due to lack of funding and participation.
    c. for-profit institutions with a stake in the betterment of citizens' living conditions.
    d. government programs that research living conditions and make policy recommendations.

23. Contemporary researchers agree that __________ (p. 70)
    a. heredity is the primary influence on development.
    b. environment is the primary influence on development.
    c. genetic and environmental influences are inseparable.
    d. both heredity and environment are involved in every aspect of development.

24. Currently, most kinship findings __________ (p. 70)
    a. are unanimously accepted by researchers.
    b. support a moderate role for heredity in intelligence.
    c. suggest that genetic factors have little or no influence on personality.
    d. attempt to answer the question of how nature and nurture work together.

25. Because it would take unusual, extreme conditions for a baby to never learn to walk, walking is considered a highly __________ behavior. (p. 72)
    a. reactive
    b. variable
    c. canalized
    d. environmental

26. Luke's mother, a classical musician, exposed Luke to music constantly as a baby and enrolled him in violin lessons at the age of 3. The combination of inherited musical ability and environment shaped Luke into a skilled musician. Luke's situation is an example of a(n) __________ correlation. (p. 72)
    a. passive
    b. active
    c. evocative
    d. epigenetic

27. Because all normal human babies roll over, sit up, crawl, and walk, one can conclude that infant motor behavior is a strongly __________ trait. (p. 72)
    a. canalized
    b. imprinted
    c. instinctive
    d. encouraged

28. Research suggests that the less genetically alike siblings are, the more their parents treat them differently. This is an example of a(n) _________ correlation. (pp. 72–73)
    a. passive
    b. active
    c. evocative
    d. canalized

29. Ross, an artistically gifted teenager, chooses to spend his free time drawing, painting, and visiting art museums. This is an example of _________ (p. 73)
    a. passive correlation.
    b. canalization.
    c. heritability.
    d. niche-picking.

30. Two-year-old Ray's parents provide him with a stimulating environment. As a result, his brain grows and new connections between his nerve cells transform gene expression. Ray is therefore interested in continued exploration of his environment, which further enhances his brain growth and gene expression. This series of complex exchanges between nature and nurture is known as __________ (pp. 74–75)
    a. niche-picking.
    b. the epigenetic framework.
    c. genetic–environmental correlation.
    d. reaction range.

PRACTICE TEST #2

1. Which of the following is an example of a phenotype? (p. 45)
   a. Cassie and her mother are both avid swimmers.
   b. Like both of his parents, Vinny is above average in height.
   c. Unlike the rest of his family, Chris enjoys spicy food.
   d. Zoe and her father speak both English and French fluently.

2. Chromosomes are made up of __________ (p. 46)
   a. cells.
   b. mutations.
   c. DNA.
   d. alleles.

3. As a result of __________, each body cell contains the same number of chromosomes and identical genetic information. (p. 46)
   a. phenotypes
   b. genotypes
   c. mitosis
   d. meiosis

4. When gametes form in males, the X and Y chromosomes __________ (p. 47)
   a. separate into different sperm cells.
   b. combine with each other to form one chromosome.
   c. are destroyed by the chemical reaction.
   d. multiply to two sets of Xs and Ys.

5. Which of the following maternal factors is linked to greater likelihood of fraternal twinning? (p. 47)
   a. The mother has had no previous pregnancies.
   b. The mother is between 20 and 29 years of age.
   c. The mother has a poor diet.
   d. The mother is a fraternal twin.

6. Allie inherited a homozygous pair of alleles for straight hair, a recessive characteristic. Her sister, Lauren, inherited a heterozygous pair of alleles—one for curly hair and one for straight hair. Which of the following statements is true? (p. 48)
   a. Both of the sisters' parents definitely have curly hair.
   b. One of the sisters' parents definitely has straight hair.
   c. Allie has straight hair and Lauren has curly hair.
   d. Allie's children could only have straight hair, whereas Lauren's children could have straight or curly hair.

7. Homozygous individuals __________ (p. 48)
   a. have one dominant and one recessive allele.
   b. have two identical alleles.
   c. are carriers of a recessive allele.
   d. result from mutation.

8. The sickle cell trait, a heterozygous condition present in many black Africans, is an example of __________ (p. 50)
   a. incomplete dominance.
   b. concordance.
   c. dominant–recessive inheritance.
   d. monogenic inheritance.

9. Which of the following explains why males are more likely than females to be affected by X-linked disorders? (p. 50)
   a. Males are more often homozygous for harmful recessive genes.
   b. Males are more likely than females to be born to women over the age of 35.
   c. Males' sex chromosomes do not match.
   d. Males tend to have fewer autosomes.

10. People with asthma tend to have mothers, rather than fathers, with asthma. Which of the following patterns of inheritance explains this? (p. 51)
    a. X-linked inheritance
    b. mutation
    c. genomic imprinting
    d. dominant–recessive inheritance

11. _________ shows us that the genetic makeup of each cell can change over time. (p. 52)
    a. Germline mutation
    b. Somatic mutation
    c. Incomplete dominance
    d. Polygenic inheritance

12. Other than Down syndrome, disorders of the autosomes usually _________ (p. 53)
    a. disrupt development so severely that miscarriage occurs.
    b. do not occur in humans.
    c. have few, if any, lasting effects on development.
    d. are not recognized until adolescence.

13. Which of the following statements about reproductive technologies is true? (p. 54)
    a. Donor insemination and in vitro fertilization are rarely performed in North America.
    b. Most U.S. states have strict legal guidelines for reproductive procedures.
    c. Children conceived through donor insemination and in vitro fertilization are as well-adjusted as naturally conceived children.
    d. In vitro fertilization is no riskier to the infant than natural conception.

14. Which of the following prenatal diagnostic methods is routine and safe for the developing organism? (p. 56)
    a. amniocentesis
    b. fetoscopy
    c. chorionic villus sampling
    d. maternal blood analysis

15. Which of the following statements about adoption is true? (p. 58)
    a. Adopted children and adolescents fare as well as or better than children growing up with their biological parents.
    b. The older children are at the time of adoption, the better adjusted they tend to be.
    c. Adopted children and adolescents have more learning and emotional difficulties than other children.
    d. Adopted children are more similar in intelligence and personality to their adoptive parents than to their biological parents.

16. Seven-year-old Miriam's parents have a tense relationship, and she regularly witnesses them expressing anger toward one another. As a result, Miriam is often anxious. This is an example of a _________ influence on development. (p. 60)
    a. direct
    b. bidirectional
    c. third party
    d. macrosystemic

17. Socioeconomic status (SES) is based on income, job prestige, and _________ (p. 60)
    a. geographical location.
    b. years of education.
    c. number of family members.
    d. intelligence.

18. Which of the following is associated with a reduction in adjustment difficulties for both low- and high-SES youths? (p. 61)
    a. after-school employment
    b. high expectations for achievement
    c. coercive discipline
    d. eating dinner with parents

19. The greatest barrier to the education of girls in many developing nations is __________ (p. 62)
    a. fees for public schooling.
    b. distance to public schools.
    c. cultural beliefs about gender roles.
    d. poor health.

20. In the United States, homelessness rates have __________ (p. 63)
    a. increased in the past few decades, despite an increase in government spending on government-supported, low-cost housing and community treatment programs.
    b. increased in the past few decades, partly due to a decline in the availability of government-supported, low-cost housing.
    c. decreased in the past few decades, mostly due to an increase in government-supported, low-cost housing and community treatment programs.
    d. decreased in the past few decades, but families with children continue to make up the majority of homeless people.

21. Neighborhood resources __________ (p. 64)
    a. become less important to people's well-being as they grow older.
    b. have a greater impact on lower-SES youth than higher-SES youth.
    c. have no apparent long-term effects on children's well-being.
    d. are unnecessary for the elderly, as most older adults live in planned housing.

22. The African-American tradition of __________ can help protect family members from the harmful effects of poverty. (p. 66)
    a. extended family households
    b. nuclear family households
    c. self-reliance
    d. privacy

23. When widespread social problems arise, nations attempt to solve them through ____________ (p. 67)
    a. collectivism.
    b. individualism.
    c. subcultures.
    d. public policies.

24. Which of the following statements about senior citizens in the United States is true? (p. 68)
    a. Medicare covers essentially all health care costs for U.S. senior citizens.
    b. As a whole, U.S. senior citizens are in a greater financial crisis than they were in the past.
    c. Senior citizens in the United States are less well off than those in many other Western nations.
    d. Social Security benefits are usually an adequate sole source of income for U.S. retired citizens.

25. Heritability estimates measure the extent to which __________ (p. 70)
    a. individual differences in complex traits are due to genetic factors.
    b. the environment can modify genetic influences.
    c. nature and nurture work together to influence development.
    d. economic and cultural influences affect development.

26. Heritability estimates are obtained from __________ (p. 70)
    a. reaction ranges.
    b. genetic–environmental correlation studies.
    c. kinship studies.
    d. the epigenetic framework.

27. Reaction ranges show that __________ (p. 72)
    a. people respond to different environments in similar ways.
    b. their unique genetic makeups cause people to respond differently to the same environment.
    c. environments play a minimal role in shaping human characteristics.
    d. our genes influence our environments.

28. Charlene is an easygoing, friendly baby. Because of her good nature, her caregivers tend to be attentive to her needs and positive in their interactions with her. This is an example of __________ (pp. 72–73)
    a. niche-picking.
    b. a passive correlation.
    c. an evocative correlation.
    d. canalization.

29. The well-coordinated, muscular teenager who spends a lot of time participating in after-school sports is an example of a(n)__________ correlation. (p. 73)
    a. active
    b. passive
    c. evocative
    d. disciplined

30. The concept of epigenesis reminds us that __________ (p. 75)
    a. people can be changed in almost any way.
    b. timing of intervention is unimportant.
    c. heredity tends to dictate development.
    d. development is a series of complex exchanges between nature and nurture.

CHAPTER 3
PRENATAL DEVELOPMENT, BIRTH, AND THE NEWBORN BABY

BRIEF CHAPTER SUMMARY

With conception, the story of prenatal development begins to unfold. The vast changes that take place during the 38 weeks of pregnancy are usually divided into three phases: (1) the period of the zygote, (2) the period of the embryo, and (3) the period of the fetus.

Although the prenatal environment is far more constant than the world outside the womb, many factors can affect the developing embryo and fetus. Various environmental agents, or teratogens, and other maternal factors can damage the developing organism, making the prenatal period a vulnerable time. For this reason, early and regular prenatal health care is vitally important to ensure the health of mother and baby.

Childbirth takes place in three stages: (1) dilation and effacement of the cervix, (2) delivery of the baby, and (3) delivery of the placenta. Production of stress hormones during labor helps infants withstand oxygen deprivation, clear the lungs for breathing, and arouse them into alertness at birth. Doctors and nurses use the Apgar Scale to assess the infant's physical condition quickly after birth.

Childbirth practices are molded by the society of which the mother and baby are a part. Alternatives to traditional hospital childbirth include natural, or prepared, childbirth and delivery in a freestanding birth center or at home. When pregnancy and birth complications are likely, medical interventions help save the lives of many babies, but when used routinely, they may inaccurately identify infants as being in danger when they are not. Preterm and low-birth-weight infants are at risk for many problems. Interventions for preterm and low-birth-weight babies, such as special infant stimulation, can help these infants develop favorably.

Infants begin life with remarkable skills relating to their physical and social worlds. Reflexes are the newborn baby's most obvious organized patterns of behavior. Throughout the day and night, newborns move in and out of five different states of arousal. Rapid-eye-movement (REM) sleep seems to be especially critical, providing young infants with stimulation essential for central nervous system development. Crying is the first way babies communicate, letting parents know that they need food, comfort, and stimulation. The senses of touch, taste, smell, and sound are well-developed at birth, while vision is the least mature of the newborn's senses.

After childbirth, all family members need to meet the challenges of living in the new family unit that has been created, but when parents support each other's needs, the stress remains manageable.

LEARNING OBJECTIVES

After reading this chapter, you should be able to:

3.1 List the three phases of prenatal development, and describe the major milestones of each. (pp. 80–85)

3.2 Define the term teratogen, and summarize the factors that affect the impact of teratogens on prenatal development. (pp. 85–86)

3.3 List agents known or suspected of being teratogens, and discuss evidence supporting the harmful impact of each. (pp. 86–93)

3.4 Discuss other maternal factors that can affect the developing embryo or fetus. (pp. 93–95)

3.5 Explain the importance of early and regular health care during the prenatal period. (pp. 95–96)

3.6 Describe the three stages of childbirth. (pp. 96–97)

3.7 Discuss the baby's adaptation to labor and delivery, and describe the appearance of the newborn baby. (pp. 97–98)

3.8 Describe natural childbirth and home delivery, noting the benefits and concerns associated with each. (pp. 99–100)

3.9 List common medical interventions during childbirth, circumstances that justify their use, and any dangers associated with each. (pp. 100–101)

3.10 Describe the risks associated with preterm and small-for-date births, along with factors that help infants who survive a traumatic birth recover. (pp. 101–106)

3.11 Describe the newborn baby's reflexes and states of arousal, including sleep characteristics and ways to soothe a crying baby. (pp. 106–111)

3.12 Describe the newborn baby's sensory capacities. (pp. 111–113)

3.13 Explain the usefulness of neonatal behavioral assessment. (pp. 113–114)

3.14 Describe typical changes in the family after the birth of a new baby. (pp. 114–115)

STUDY QUESTIONS

Prenatal Development

Conception

1. About once every 28 days, an ovum is released from one of a woman's two ________________. The ovum is drawn into one of the two ________________, which are long, thin structures that lead to the uterus. (p. 80)
2. True or False: After release, a sperm can survive much longer than an ovum. (p. 80)

Period of the Zygote

1. The period of the zygote is the (shortest / longest) period of prenatal development. (p. 81)
2. Match each of the following terms with its description. (pp. 81–82)

_____	Will provide protective covering and nourishment to the new organism	A. Blastocyst
_____	A hollow, fluid-filled ball that is formed four days after fertilization	B. Embryonic disk
_____	Will become the new organism	C. Trophoblast

3. List two functions of the amniotic fluid. (p. 82)

   A. ____

   B. ____

4. Many zygotes do not survive. What is the adaptive function of their failure to implant? (p. 82)

   ____

5. The ________________ permits food and oxygen to reach the developing organism and waste products to be carried away. (p. 82)
6. True or False: The mother and *embryo* exchange nutrients and waste through direct blood exchange. (p. 82)

Period of the Embryo

1. True or False: The most rapid prenatal changes take place during the period of the embryo. (p. 82)
2. Indicate which layer of the embryonic disc—mesoderm (M), ectoderm (C), or endoderm (N)—forms each organ or structure. (pp. 82–83)

_______	Nervous system	_______	Skeleton
_______	Glands	_______	Skin
_______	Muscles	_______	Lungs
_______	Digestive system	_______	Circulatory system
_______	Other internal organs	_______	Urinary tract

3. In the second month, prenatal growth (slows / continues rapidly). The embryo develops the ability to sense its world through (smell / touch / taste). (p. 83)

Period of the Fetus

1. The period of the *fetus* is a phase of ______________ and ______________. (p. 83)
2. Prenatal development is divided into ______________, or three equal periods of time. (p. 83)
3. The white, cheese-like substance that completely covers the fetus to protect the skin from chapping in the amniotic fluid is called ______________. (p. 84)
4. ______________ is the white, downy hair that covers the entire body of the fetus. (p. 84)
5. True or False: By the end of the second *trimester*, most of the brain's neurons are in place. (p. 84)
6. The age at which the baby can first survive if born early is called the *age of* ______________. When does this typically occur? ______________________________ (p. 84)
7. A (modest / strong) link has been found between fetal activity and infant temperament. Fetuses who were (more / less) active during the third trimester are better able to handle frustration and are less fearful as 2-year-olds. (pp. 84–85)
8. List two ways in which infants' responsiveness to stimulation changes in the third trimester. (p. 85)

   A. ____

   ____

   B. ____

   ____

Prenatal Environmental Influences

Teratogens

1. A *teratogen* is any environmental agent that causes damage during (the prenatal period / infancy). Describe four factors that affect the impact of teratogens. (p. 85)

   Dose: ____

   ____

   Heredity: ____

   ____

   Other Negative Influences: ____

   ____

   Age: ____

   ____

2. A ______________ period is a limited time span in which a part of the body or a behavior is biologically prepared to develop rapidly and is especially vulnerable to its surroundings. (p. 85)
3. Teratogens are most likely to cause serious defects during the period of the (zygote / embryo / fetus). (p. 85)

4. Match each medication with its description and potential effects on a developing fetus. (pp. 86–87)

Medication	Description	Potential Effects on Developing Fetus
___ ___ Thalidomide	A. Vitamin A derivative used to treat severe acne	1. Cancer of the vagina and reproductive difficulties
___ ___ Diethylstilbestrol (DES)	B. Prescribed between 1945 and 1970 to prevent miscarriages	2. Gross bodily deformities and below-average intelligence scores
___ ___ Accutane or isotretinoin	C. Sedative widely available in the 1960s	3. Eye, ear, brain, heart, and immune system abnormalities

5. True or False: Any drug with a molecule small enough to penetrate the placental barrier can enter the embryonic or fetal bloodstream. (p. 87)

6. True or False: Heavy caffeine intake during pregnancy is associated with low birth weight, miscarriage, and newborn withdrawal symptoms. (p. 87)

7. Describe the difficulties faced by babies who are born to users of heroin, cocaine, or methadone. (p. 87)

____

____

____

____

8. Explain why it is difficult to isolate the precise damage caused by prenatal exposure to cocaine. (p. 87)

____

____

____

9. Several studies have linked prenatal ________________ exposure to smaller head size; to sleep, attention, and memory difficulties in childhood; and to poorer problem solving in adolescence. Lasting effects (are / are not) well-established. (pp. 87–88)

10. Summarize physical and behavioral effects of maternal smoking during the prenatal period. (p. 88)

Physical: ____

____

____

Behavioral: ____

____

____

11. True or False: If the mother stops smoking at any time during the pregnancy, even during the last trimester, she reduces the chances that her baby will be negatively impacted. (p. 88)

12. Explain the mechanisms through which smoking harms the fetus. (p. 89)

____

____

____

13. True or False: Passive smoking has not been linked with any adverse effects on the infant. (p. 89)

14. Match each *fetal alcohol spectrum disorder* diagnosis with its distinguishing characteristics. Some diagnoses may correspond with more than one characteristic, and characteristics may be used more than once. (pp. 89–90)

_______	*Fetal alcohol syndrome*	A. Facial abnormalities
_______	*Partial fetal alcohol syndrome*	B. Impaired cognitive functioning
_______	*Alcohol-related neurodevelopmental disorder*	C. Slow physical growth

15. Of the fetal alcohol spectrum disorders, (FAS / p-FAS / ARND) is associated with the most pervasive prenatal alcohol exposure. (p. 90)

16. True or False: Mental impairments in babies with FAS typically lessen by adolescence or early adulthood. (p. 90)

17. Explain two ways in which alcohol harms the fetus. (p. 90)

A. ____

____

B. ____

____

18. (Most / Half of / One quarter of) U.S. mothers report drinking at some time during their pregnancies. (p. 90)

19. True or False: Even mild drinking, less than one drink per day, is associated with reduced head size and body growth in children. (p. 90)

20. True or False: Low doses of radiation exposure, such as through medical X-rays, are believed to be safe for the developing fetus and have not been linked to any negative outcomes. (p. 91)

21. Match each of the following environmental pollutants with its effects on development. (p. 91)

_____	This teratogen, commonly found in paint chippings from old buildings and other industrial materials, is related to prematurity, low birth weight, brain damage, and physical defects.	A. Mercury
_____	This toxic compound, resulting from incineration, is linked to brain, immune system, and thyroid damage in babies and an increased incidence of breast and uterine cancer in women.	B. Lead
_____	Women who ate fish contaminated with this substance gave birth to babies with slightly reduced birth weights, smaller heads, persisting attention and memory difficulties, and lower intelligence test scores in childhood.	C. PCBs
_____	In the 1950s, children prenatally exposed to this teratogen in a Japanese community displayed mental retardation, abnormal speech, and uncoordinated movements. Prenatal exposure disrupts production and migration of neurons, causing widespread brain damage.	D. Dioxins

22. _________________________, or 3-day measles, is a virus associated with eye cataracts; deafness; heart, genital, urinary, and intestinal abnormalities; and mental retardation. (p. 91)

23. True or False: Prenatal exposure to rubella increases the risk for serious mental illness in adulthood. (p. 92)

24. When women carrying the AIDS virus become pregnant, they pass the deadly virus to the developing organism approximately ___________ to ___________ percent of the time. (p. 92)

25. Most prenatal AIDS babies pass away in (infancy / childhood / adolescence). (p. 92)

26. Pregnant women may become infected with _____________, a parasitic disease, by eating raw or undercooked meat or from contact with the feces of infected cats. If it strikes during the first trimester, this disease can cause _________ and ________ damage. (pp. 92–93)

A Lifespan Vista: The Prenatal Environment and Health in Later Life

1. True or False: Fairly subtle prenatal environmental factors, such as the flow of nutrients and hormones across the placenta, have no effect on an individual's health in adulthood. (p. 88)

2. True or False: A consistent link between low birth weight and heart disease, stroke, and diabetes in middle adulthood has emerged for both sexes and in diverse countries. (p. 88)
3. What adult health condition has been linked to high birth weight in females? (p. 89)

____

4. Describe preventative measures low-birth-weight and high-birth-weight individuals can take to protect their health during adulthood. (p. 89)

____

____

Other Maternal Factors

1. In healthy, physically fit women, regular, moderate exercise during pregnancy is associated with (increased / decreased) birth weight. Meanwhile, frequent, vigorous exercise, especially late in pregnancy, results in (increased / decreased) birth weight. (p. 93)
2. Indicate which of the following behavioral and health problems may result from prenatal malnutrition. (p. 93)

_______ Damage to the central nervous system
_______ Decreased brain weight
_______ Increased susceptibility to respiratory illnesses
_______ Low intelligence and learning problems
_______ Increased brain weight
_______ Distorted organ structure
_______ Irritability and unresponsiveness
_______ Facial abnormalities

3. Describe two benefits of maternal folic acid intake before and during pregnancy. (p. 93)

A. ____

B. ____

4. True or False: The U.S. Special Supplemental Food Program for Women, Infants, and Children (WIC) provides food packages to about 90 percent of qualified low-income pregnant women. (p. 93)
5. Describe two mechanisms through which maternal stress affects the developing organism, and note outcomes associated with severe emotional stress during pregnancy. (p. 94)

Mechanism A: ____

Mechanism B: ____

Outcomes: ____

____

6. True or False: Stress-related prenatal complications are greatly reduced when mothers have access to social support. (p. 94)
7. *Rh factor incompatibility* results when the mother is Rh-(positive / negative) and the baby inherits an Rh-(positive / negative) blood type from the father. What are some potential outcomes of this condition? (p. 94)

____

____

8. True or False: The physical immaturity of teenage mothers leads to pregnancy complications. (pp. 94–95)

The Importance of Prenatal Health Care

1. If untreated, ______________ can cause convulsions in the mother and fetal death. What is usually recommended to lower blood pressure to a safe level? (p. 95)

____

2. Which groups of women are most likely to wait until after the first trimester to seek prenatal care or receive no care at all? (p. 95)

____

3. Discuss some of the barriers to obtaining prenatal health care for expectant mothers who delay or never seek such care. (p. 95)

____

____

____

____

Childbirth

The Stages of Childbirth

1. Match each stage of labor with its description. (pp. 96–97)

_____ Dilation and effacement of the cervix

_____ Delivery of the baby

_____ Delivery of the placenta

A. Labor comes to an end and the placenta separates from the wall of the uterus.

B. Longest stage of labor; contractions become more frequent and powerful as the cervix widens and thins.

C. The mother experiences strong uterine contractions and a natural urge to push.

The Baby's Adaptation to Labor and Delivery

1. Cite three ways in which infant production of stress hormones during childbirth is adaptive. (p. 97)

A. ____

B. ____

C. ____

The Newborn Baby's Appearance

1. True or False: Newborn girls tend to be slightly longer and heavier than boys. (p. 98)
2. At birth, the head is very (small / large) in relation to the trunk and legs. (p. 98)

Assessing the Newborn's Physical Condition: The Apgar Scale

1. List the five characteristics assessed by the *Apgar Scale*. (p. 98)

A. ____

B. ____

C. ____

D. ____

E. ____

2. On the Apgar Scale, a score of _________ or better indicates that the infant is in good physical condition; a score between _________ and _________ indicates that the baby requires assistance in establishing breathing and other vital signs; a score of _________ or below indicates the infant is in serious danger and requires emergency medical attention. (p. 98)

Approaches to Childbirth

Natural, or Prepared, Childbirth

1. What is the goal of the *natural childbirth* approach? (p. 99)

____

____

____

2. List and describe three activities in a typical natural childbirth program. (p. 99)

   A. ______________________________

   ____

   B. ______________________________

   ____

   C. ______________________________

   ____

3. True or False: Research has yet to reveal a strong link between social support and birth complications, length of labor, and mother–infant interactions. (pp. 99–100)

Home Delivery

1. Home births are typically handled by certified ______________, who have degrees in nursing and additional training in childbirth management. (p. 100)
2. True or False: For healthy women assisted by a trained professional, it is as safe to give birth at home as in a hospital. (p. 100)

Medical Interventions

1. ______________ refers to oxygen deprivation during labor and delivery. (p. 100)
2. True or False: Infants in the *breech position* are turned in such a way that the head would be delivered first. (p. 100)

Fetal Monitoring

1. Explain the purpose of *fetal monitoring*. (p. 100)

____

____

2. True or False: Most U.S. hospitals require fetal monitoring, which is used in over 80 percent of American births. (p. 100)
3. Cite reasons why fetal monitoring is a controversial procedure. (p. 100)

____

____

____

Labor and Delivery Medication

1. True or False: According to recent statistics, labor and delivery medication is used in 10 to 20 percent of U.S. births. (p. 101)

2. Summarize potential problems associated with the use of labor and delivery medication. (p. 101)

____

____

____

Cesarean Delivery

1. Briefly describe a *cesarean delivery*. Under what circumstances is this type of delivery warranted? (p. 101)

   A. ____

   ____

   B. ____

   ____

2. True or False: New evidence supports the adage, "Once a cesarean, always a cesarean." (p. 101)
3. The worldwide rise in cesarean deliveries can largely be attributed to (repeated cesareans / medical control over childbirth). (p. 101)
4. Cite two drawbacks of cesarean delivery. (p. 101)

   A. ____

   ____

   B. ____

   ____

Preterm and Low-Birth-Weight Infants

1. Babies are considered premature if they are born _______ weeks or more before the end of a full 38-week pregnancy or if they weigh less than _______ pounds. (p. 101)
2. True or False: Birth weight is the best available predictor of infant survival and healthy development. (p. 101)
3. Frequent illness, inattention, sensory impairments, poor motor coordination, language delays, learning difficulties, and emotional and behavioral problems are associated with (low / high) birth weight. These problems (do / do not) persist into adulthood. (p. 102)

Preterm versus Small-for-Date Infants

1. Match each group of low-birth-weight infants with its appropriate description. Multiple descriptions may apply. (p. 102)

   __________ *Preterm infants*

   __________ *Small-for-date infants*

   A. All are born several weeks or more before their due date.
   B. Weight may be appropriate for length of pregnancy.
   C. All are below expected weight for length of pregnancy.
   D. May be full-term or born before due date.

2. Of the two types of low-birth-weight infants, (preterm / small-for-date) infants usually have more serious problems. What difficulties do these babies face? (p. 102)

____

____

____

Consequences for Caregiving

1. Describe the characteristics of preterm infants, and explain how those characteristics may affect caregiving. (p. 102)

   Characteristics: ____

   ____

   Caregiving: ____

   ____

Interventions for Preterm Infants

1. Discuss several forms of special infant stimulation that can help preterm infants develop favorably. (p. 103)

   ____

   ____

   ____

   ____

   ____

2. Describe "kangaroo care," and list its benefits. (p. 103)

   Description: ____

   ____

   Benefits: ____

   ____

3. True or False: Research confirms that preterm babies and economically disadvantaged babies require intensive intervention to achieve lasting changes in their development. (p. 105)
4. True or False: Supportive home and school environments, coupled with societal advantages, can "fix" the serious biological risks associated with being born severely underweight. (p. 105)

Social Issues: A Cross-National Perspective on Health Care and Other Policies for Parents and Newborn Babies

1. *Infant* ____________ refers to the number of deaths in the first year of life per 1,000 live births. (p. 104)
2. True or False: In the United States, African-American and Native-American infants are twice as likely as white infants to die in the first year of life. (p. 104)
3. Neonatal mortality, the rate of death in the first month of life, accounts for (most / half / less than half) of the U.S. infant death rate. (p. 104)
4. Which cause of neonatal mortality is mostly preventable? (p. 104)

   ____

5. List two societal factors largely responsible for the relatively high infant mortality rate in the United States. (p. 104)

   A. ____

   B. ____

6. What factors promote infant health in all of the countries that outrank the United States in infant survival? (p. 104)

____

____

____

7. True or False: Paid, job-protected employment leave is a vital societal intervention for new parents. Describe research findings on the length of childbirth leave for new parents. (pp. 104–105)

____

____

____

Birth Complications, Parenting, and Resilience

1. Describe how the quality of the home environment affects the development of infants who experienced birth complications. (p. 106)

____

____

2. The influence of early biological risks often (increases / decreases) as the child's personal characteristics and social experiences increasingly contribute to their functioning. (p. 106)

The Newborn Baby's Capacities

Newborn Reflexes

1. A *reflex* is a(n) (learned / inborn) response to a particular form of stimulation. (p. 106)
2. Match each reflex with the appropriate response or function descriptor. (p. 107)

_____	Spontaneous grasp of adult's finger	A. Eye blink
_____	When the sole of the foot is stroked, the toes fan out and curl as the foot twists in	B. Tonic neck
_____	Helps infant find the nipple	C. Palmar grasp
_____	Prepares infant for voluntary walking	D. Babinski
_____	Permits feeding	E. Rooting
_____	Infant lies in a "fencing position"; may prepare infant for voluntary reaching	F. Sucking
_____	Protects infant from strong stimulation	G. Stepping
_____	In our evolutionary past, may have helped infant cling to mother	H. Moro

3. Cite three functions of newborn reflexes. (pp. 106–107)

   A. _______________

   B. _______________

   C. _______________

4. When do most newborn reflexes disappear? (p. 108)

____

5. Pediatricians test newborn reflexes carefully because they can reveal the health of the baby's ___________ system. (p. 108)

Newborn States

1. Match each *state of arousal* with its characteristics. (p. 108)

_____	Regular sleep	A. Inactive body, open and attentive eyes, even breathing
_____	Irregular sleep	B. Bursts of uncoordinated body activity, irregular breathing
_____	Drowsiness	C. Eyes open and close, glazed when open; even breathing
_____	Quiet alertness	D. Minimal body activity, no eye movements, even breathing
_____	Waking activity and crying	E. Gentle limb and rapid eye movements, irregular breathing

2. True or False: A newborn's sleep–wake cycles are affected more by fullness–hunger than by darkness–light. (p. 108)

3. Describe how individual differences in infants' daily rhythms affect parents' attitudes toward and interaction with the baby. (p. 108)

4. During (*REM / NREM*) sleep, brain-wave activity resembles that of the waking state; eyes dart beneath the lids; heart rate, blood pressure, and breathing are uneven; and slight body movements occur. During (*REM / NREM*) sleep, the body is almost motionless, and heart rate, breathing, and brain-wave activity are slow and even. (p. 108)

5. Why do infants spend more time in REM sleep than children, adolescents, and adults? (p. 108)

6. Describe sleep behavior of infants who are brain damaged or who have experienced serious birth trauma, and briefly explain possible consequences of this sleep behavior. (p. 108)

   Sleep behavior: ______

   Consequences: ______

7. What is the most effective way to soothe a crying baby when feeding and diaper changing do not work? (p. 109)

8. How do the cries of brain-damaged babies and those who have experienced prenatal and birth complications differ from those of healthy infants, and how does this difference affect parental responding? (pp. 109, 111)

   Differences: ______

   Parental responding: ______

Biology and Environment: The Mysterious Tragedy of Sudden Infant Death Syndrome

1. What is *sudden infant death syndrome (SIDS)*? (p. 110)

2. True or False: In industrialized countries, SIDS is the leading cause of infant mortality between 1 and 12 months of age. (p. 110)

3. True or False: Researchers have recently determined the precise cause of SIDS. (p. 110)

4. Indicate which of the following physical problems are common among SIDS victims. (p. 110)

_____ Prematurity
_____ High birth weight
_____ Misshapen skull
_____ Limp muscle tone
_____ Disturbances in sleep cycles
_____ Low birth weight
_____ Poor Apgar scores
_____ Mild respiratory infections
_____ Abnormal heart rate and respiration
_____ Persistent rash

5. Explain how impaired brain functioning might contribute to SIDS. (p. 110)

____

____

____

6. Cite four environmental factors associated with SIDS. (p. 110)

A. ____

B. ____

C. ____

D. ____

7. Discuss several preventative measures that reduce the incidence of SIDS. (p. 110)

____

____

____

Sensory Capacities

1. True or False: Infants are born with a poorly developed sense of touch, and consequently, they are not sensitive to pain. (p. 112)

2. During the prenatal period, which four areas of the body are first to become sensitive to touch? (p. 112)

A. ______________________________ B. ______________________________

C. ______________________________ D. ______________________________

3. Discuss the effects of allowing a newborn to endure severe pain. (p. 112)

____

____

____

4. Newborns' ______________________ reveal that they can distinguish several basic tastes. Their taste aversions (can / cannot) be altered readily. (p. 112)

5. True or False: Certain odor preferences are present at birth. (p. 112)

6. What is the adaptive function of newborns' attraction to the odor of their mother and to that of breast milk? (pp. 112–113)

____

____

7. Newborns prefer (pure tones / complex sounds). (p. 113)

8. True or False: Newborns can discriminate almost all of the speech sounds of any human language. (p. 113)

9. Cite the characteristics of human speech preferred by infants. (p. 113)

____

____

10. Vision is the (most / least) mature of the newborn baby's senses. (p. 113)

11. Describe the newborn baby's *visual acuity*. (p. 113)

____

____

12. True or False: Infants have well-developed color vision at birth, and they are immediately capable of discriminating colors. (p. 113)

Neonatal Behavioral Assessment

1. The ______________________________ *Assessment Scale* evaluates the newborn's reflexes, muscle tone, state changes, responsiveness to stimuli, and other reactions. (p. 113)

2. Since the NBAS is given to infants all around the world, researchers have been able to learn a great deal about individual and cultural differences in newborn behavior and the ways in which various child-rearing practices affect infant behavior. Briefly discuss these findings. (pp. 113–114)

____

____

____

____

3. The best estimate of the baby's ability to recover from the stress of birth can be gleaned from (a single NBAS score / changes in NBAS scores over time). (p. 114)

4. How are NBAS interventions beneficial for the early parent–infant relationship? (p. 114)

____

____

Adjusting to the New Family Unit

1. Describe birth-related hormonal changes in both the mother and father that prepare expectant parents for their new role. (p. 114)

____

____

____

2. Discuss several changes in the family system following the birth of a new baby. (p. 115)

____

____

____

____

ASK YOURSELF . . .

For *Ask Yourself* questions for this chapter, along with feedback on the accuracy of your answers, please log on to MyDevelopmentLab (for registration and access, please visit mydevelopmentlab.com or follow the instructions on page ix).

(1) Select the Multimedia Library.

(2) Choose the explore option.

(3) Find your chapter from the drop down box.

(4) Click find now.

(5) Complete questions and choose "Submit answers for grading" or "Clear answers" to start over.

SUGGESTED READINGS

Hopkins, B., & Johnson, S. P. (Eds.). (2007). *Prenatal development of postnatal functions.* Westport, CT: Praeger. Examines the link between prenatal and postnatal development, including brain development, the effects of maternal stress, the importance of nutrition, and learning experiences before and after birth.

Miller, M. W. (2006). *Brain development: Normal processes and the effects of alcohol and nicotine*. New York: Oxford University Press. Examines the effects of alcohol and nicotine on the developing nervous system. The author explores the immediate and long-term consequences of prenatal exposure to alcohol and nicotine, including research on brain plasticity and resilience.

Simonds, W., Rothman, B. K., & Norman, B. M. (2006). *Laboring on: Birth in transition*. New York: Taylor & Francis. The book examines a variety of issues concerning pregnancy and labor, including approaches to childbirth, medical interventions, debate over midwifery, and women's health care reform.

CROSSWORD PUZZLE 3.1

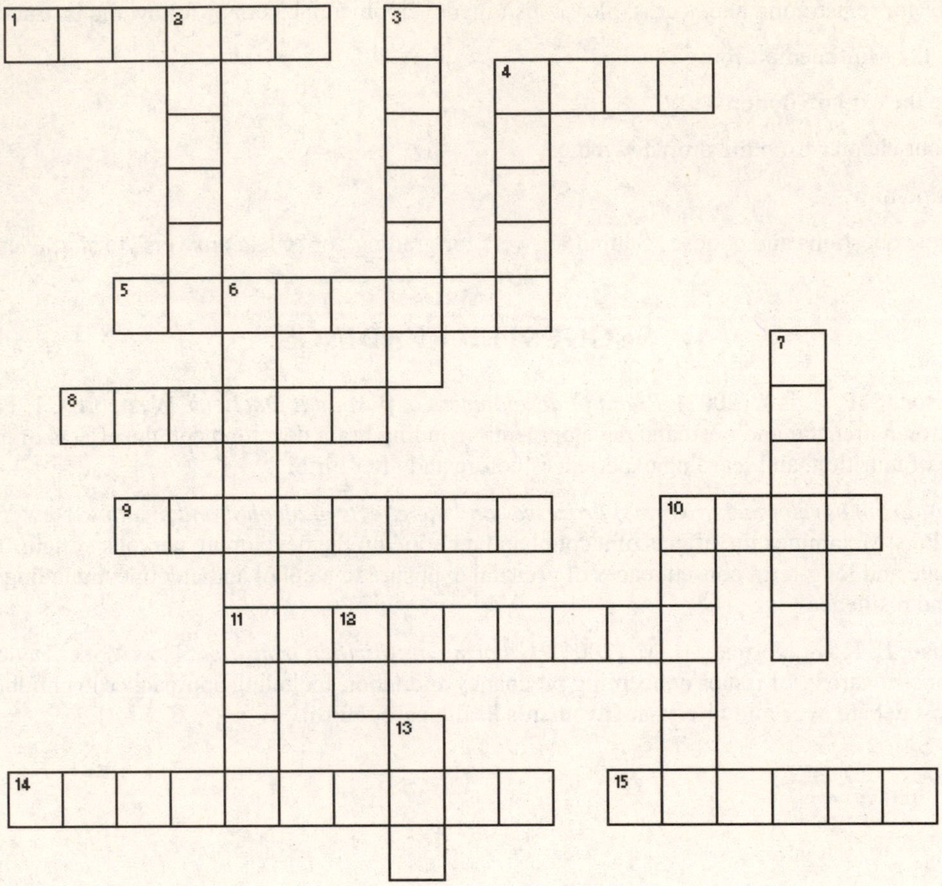

Across

1. Position of the baby in the uterus such that the buttocks or feet would be delivered first
4. A range of physical, mental, and behavioral outcomes caused by prenatal alcohol exposure (abbr.)
5. Fetal _____: electronic instruments that track the baby's heart rate during labor
8. White, downy hair that covers the fetus
9. Permits exchange of nutrients and waste; keeps the mother's bloodstream separate from her baby's
10. FASD diagnosis; impaired mental functioning, despite typical physical growth and facial features (abbr.)
11. Any environmental agent that causes damage during the prenatal period
14. Three equal prenatal time periods, each of which lasts three months
15. Inadequate oxygen supply

Down

2. Prenatal organism from 2 to 8 weeks after conception
3. Outer membrane; forms a protective covering around the prenatal organism
4. Prenatal organism from the beginning of the third month to the end of pregnancy
6. Primitive spinal cord, the top of which swells to form the brain (2 words)
7. White, cheese-like substance; covers the fetus and prevents chapped skin
10. Inner membrane; encloses the prenatal organism in fluid
12. ______ factor incompatibility can cause the mother's antibodies to destroy the fetus' red blood cells.
13. "Irregular" sleep state; brain wave activity is similar to that of the waking state (abbr.)

CROSSWORD PUZZLE 3.2

Across

5. Results when women consume large amounts of alcohol during most or all of their pregnancy (abbr.)
6. States of ______: different degrees of sleep and wakefulness
8. Attachment of the blastocyst to the uterine lining 7 to 9 days after fertilization
9. Infant ______ rate: the number of deaths in the first year of life per 1,000 live births
11. ______ infants' birth weight is below normal for the length of the pregnancy. (3 words, hyph.)
13. FASD diagnosis; facial abnormalities and impaired functioning, despite typical physical growth (abbr.)
14. ______ delivery: the doctor makes an incision in the mother's abdomen and lifts the baby out
16. "Regular" sleep state: heart rate, breathing, and brain waves are slow and regular (abbr.)

Down

1. At the age of ______ the fetus can survive if born early.
2. Scale used to assess the newborn's physical condition immediately after birth
3. Assesses the infant's behavioral status during the newborn period (abbr.)
4. Inborn, automatic response to a particular stimulus
7. Connects the prenatal organism to the placenta; delivers nutrients and removes waste (2 words)
10. Childbirth approach designed to reduce pain and medical intervention
11. Unexpected, unexplained death of an infant (abbr.)
12. Infants born several weeks or more before their due date
15. Visual ______: fineness of visual discrimination

PRACTICE TEST #1

1. The vast changes that take place during the 38 weeks of pregnancy are usually divided into three phases: ________ (p. 81)
   a. the period of the zygote, the period of the embryo, and the period of the newborn.
   b. the period of conception, the period of the embryo, and the period of the fetus.
   c. the period of the zygote, the period of the embryo, and the period of the fetus.
   d. the period of preconception, the period of conception, and the period of the fetus.

2. During the third and fourth weeks of pregnancy, the developing organism _________ (p. 81)
   a. burrows into the uterine lining.
   b. begins to develop muscles, a heart, and a digestive tract.
   c. can move.
   d. is about 3 inches long.

3. The period of the embryo lasts about ________ (p. 82)
   a. two days.
   b. two weeks.
   c. six weeks.
   d. ten weeks.

4. During the period of the embryo, the ectoderm folds over to form the ____________, which will become the spinal cord and brain. (p. 83)
   a. mesoderm
   b. endoderm
   c. embryo
   d. neural tube

5. At the end of the second trimester, ________ (p. 84)
   a. most of the brain's billions of neurons are in place.
   b. the organs, muscles, and nervous system start to become organized and connected.
   c. the fetus can survive if born early.
   d. the fetus will blink its eyes in reaction to nearby sounds.

6. During the fetal period, teratogenic damage is ________ (p. 85)
   a. usually severe.
   b. usually minor.
   c. limited to the limbs and circulatory system.
   d. reversible.

7. Currently, the most widely used potent teratogen is ________ (p. 86)
   a. thalidomide.
   b. diethylstilbestrol.
   c. Accutane.
   d. aspirin.

8. Research indicates that prenatally growth-stunted babies ________ (p. 88)
   a. often remain underweight throughout childhood.
   b. are at no greater risk of long-term health complications than average-weight babies.
   c. may be protected from developing diabetes in adulthood.
   d. have a greater chance of dying of heart disease and stroke in adulthood.

9. Which of the following statements about smoking during pregnancy is true? (p. 88)
   a. Even if a pregnant woman stops smoking during the last trimester, the damage to the baby is permanent.
   b. If a pregnant woman stops smoking during the last trimester, she reduces the likelihood that her infant will suffer negative consequences.
   c. Passive, or second-hand, smoking has no long-term effects on the developing fetus.
   d. About 45 percent of U.S. women smoke during their pregnancies.

10. A child born with fetal alcohol spectrum disorder ________ (p. 90)
    a. will be permanently affected.
    b. will completely recover if provided with an enriched diet.
    c. is unlikely to survive infancy.
    d. is likely to have normal cognitive functioning but will be physically larger than non-FAS children.

11. High levels of prenatal mercury exposure disrupt __________, causing widespread brain damage. (p. 91)
    a. oxygen flow to the uterus
    b. production and migration of neurons
    c. hormones
    d. DNA

12. Which of the following statements about AIDS in infancy is true? (p. 92)
    a. AIDS progresses rapidly in infants, causing weight loss, diarrhea, respiratory illnesses, and brain damage before death.
    b. HIV-infected mothers pass the virus to their babies 100 percent of the time.
    c. No drug is currently available for safely reducing prenatal AIDS transmission.
    d. Most HIV-positive babies lead fairly long and normal lives.

13. When women experience severe emotional stress during pregnancy, ________ (p. 94)
    a. they must take antidepressant medication to protect the fetus from the effects of stress.
    b. their babies are at risk for a wide variety of complications.
    c. the fetus releases antibodies that buffer against the effects of stress.
    d. stress hormones cross the placenta, causing a drop in fetal heart rate.

14. Rh factor incompatibility ________ (p. 94)
    a. occurs when mother and baby both have the Rh-negative blood type.
    b. primarily affects firstborn children.
    c. is usually fatal to infants, and there is currently no safe vaccine.
    d. can be prevented with a vaccine to stop the buildup of antibodies.

15. Infants born to teenage mothers have a higher risk of problems because __________ (p. 95)
    a. most pregnant teenagers come from low-income backgrounds and lack quality health care.
    b. teenagers' bodies are too immature for pregnancy.
    c. most doctors will not provide prenatal care to teenagers.
    d. they are more likely to be born with chromosomal defects.

16. Which of the following takes place during Stage 2 of childbirth? (p. 97)
    a. dilation and effacement of the cervix
    b. the mother feels the first contractions
    c. delivery of the baby
    d. delivery of the placenta

17. The infant's production of stress hormones during childbirth is adaptive because it ________ (p. 97)
    a. causes the baby's lungs to build up with fluid.
    b. causes sleepiness in the baby, making for an easier delivery.
    c. reduces the force of contractions.
    d. helps the baby withstand oxygen deprivation.

18. Which of the following statements about home birth is true? (p. 100)
    a. Most home births in North America are attended by doctors.
    b. Home births are always safe as long as fetal monitors are used.
    c. When home-birth attendants are not properly trained, the infant death rate is high.
    d. Currently, about 10 percent of North American mothers choose home birth.

19. Critics of routine fetal monitoring believe that it results in ________ (p.100)
    a. poor Apgar scores.
    b. newborn sleepiness and/or irritability.
    c. fetal heartbeat irregularities.
    d. unnecessary cesarean deliveries.

20. What is the best available predictor of infant survival and healthy development? (p. 101)
    a. reflexive responses
    b. heart rate
    c. birth weight
    d. color

21. Hayden was born several weeks before his due date, but his weight was appropriate based on time spent in the uterus. Keegan was full-term but was below expected weight considering length of pregnancy. Which of the following statements about Hayden and Keegan is true? (p. 102)
    a. Keegan will probably have more serious problems than Hayden.
    b. Hayden will probably have more serious problems than Keegan.
    c. Hayden probably experienced inadequate nutrition before birth.
    d. Neither Hayden nor Keegan are at-risk for long-term problems.

22. The United States has ________ (p. 104)
    a. one of the highest infant mortality rates in the world.
    b. older, less reliable health care technology than other industrialized nations.
    c. one of the lowest infant mortality rates in the world.
    d. slipped in international rankings of infant mortality in the past few decades.

23. When 2-month-old Sage feels her father's finger in her palm, she wraps her tiny fingers around it and holds on tightly. Which reflex is Sage using? (p. 107)
    a. palmar grasp
    b. rooting
    c. Babinski
    d. moro

24. Which of the following statements about newborn sleep is true? (p. 108)
    a. Newborns spend 4 to5 hours per day in each of the 5 states of arousal.
    b. REM sleep accounts for 80 percent of a newborn baby's sleep time.
    c. Newborns' sleep–wake cycles are mainly driven by darkness–light.
    d. Newborns' sleep–wake cycles are mainly driven by fullness–hunger.

25. REM sleep ________ (p. 108)
    a. accounts for a lower percentage of sleep time in infants than in children and adults.
    b. seems to fulfill young infants' need for stimulation since they spend so little time in an alert state.
    c. is a "regular" sleep state in which the body is almost motionless, and heart rate, breathing, and brain wave activity are slow and regular.
    d. is less frequent in fetuses and preterm infants than in full-term infants.

26. Crying ________ (p. 109)
    a. typically increases during the early weeks, peaks at six weeks, then declines.
    b. increases steadily during the first six months, particularly when parents respond to cries immediately.
    c. decreases gradually during the early weeks in cultures that promote close physical contact between the infant and caregiver.
    d. decreases steadily during the first six weeks, even in colicky babies.

27. What can parents and caregivers do to reduce Sudden Infant Death Syndrome? (p. 110)
    a. Remove the infant's pacifier before sleep.
    b. Wrap the infant very warmly before sleep.
    c. Provide the infant with a pacifier before sleep.
    d. Provide the infant with soft bedding.

28. Research on the sense of smell indicates that ________ (pp. 112–113)
    a. infants do not have a well-developed sense of smell until several months after birth.
    b. newborns can recognize the smell of their own mother's breast.
    c. odor preferences are gradually developed through environmental exposure to a variety of scents.
    d. newborns cannot discriminate between the odor of breast milk and formula.

29. __________ is the least developed of the newborn baby's senses. (p. 113)
    a. Hearing
    b. Smell
    c. Taste
    d. Vision

30. NBAS scores reveal that Asian and Native American babies are __________ than Caucasian infants. (p. 113)
    a. less irritable
    b. more irritable
    c. less responsive
    d. more responsive

PRACTICE TEST #2

1. Most conceptions result from intercourse __________ (pp. 80–81)
   a. during the 3-day period after ovulation.
   b. on the day of ovulation or the 2 days preceding it.
   c. about a week before ovulation.
   d. about a week before menstruation.

2. The period of the zygote lasts about two weeks, from ________ (p. 81)
   a. fertilization until the blastocyst is formed.
   b. fertilization until implantation.
   c. fertilization until the zygote's first cell duplication is complete.
   d. formation of the blastocyst until formation of the trophoblast.

3. The placenta ________ (p. 82)
   a. permits food and oxygen to reach the organism and waste products to be carried away.
   b. first appears as a tiny stalk and eventually grows to a length of one to three feet.
   c. helps keep the temperature of the prenatal world constant.
   d. surrounds the amnion.

4. The period of the fetus ________ (p. 83)
   a. is characterized by rapid prenatal changes.
   b. is the "growth and finishing" phase, when the organism increases rapidly in size.
   c. is the shortest prenatal period.
   d. takes place before most mothers know they are pregnant.

5. The age of viability occurs sometime between _________ weeks. (p. 84)
   a. 10 and 14
   b. 16 and 20
   c. 22 and 26
   d. 28 and 32

6. Between 30 and 34 weeks, fetuses show rhythmic alterations between sleep and wakefulness that gradually increase in organization. Around this time, synchrony between fetal heart rate and motor activity peaks. These are clear signs that ________ (p. 84)
   a. the brain's respiratory center is now mature.
   b. the cerebral cortex has finished growing.
   c. coordinated neural networks are beginning to form in the brain.
   d. neurological organization is complete.

7. The effects of teratogens ________ (p. 85)
   a. generally subside in the first six months of life.
   b. can lead to psychological consequences.
   c. are always obvious at birth.
   d. are usually reversible.

8. The __________ period is the time when serious defects are most likely to occur because the foundations for all body parts are being laid down. (p. 85)
   a. zygote
   b. embryonic
   c. fetal
   d. neural

9. What of the following statements about the prenatal environment and health in later life is true? (p. 89)
   a. Low birth weight is linked to an increased risk of developing certain types of cancer in adulthood.
   b. The prenatal environment has little effect on an individual's long-term health.
   c. High birth weight is linked to an increased risk of developing certain types of cancer in adulthood.
   d. Prenatally growth-stunted babies fail to gain sufficient weight in childhood and often remain short and thin throughout the lifespan.

10. As with heroine and cocaine, alcohol abuse is most common in ________ (p. 90)
    a. rural areas.
    b. young mothers.
    c. Caucasian women.
    d. poverty-stricken women.

11. Even tiny amounts of __________ in the paternal bloodstream cause a dramatic change in the sex ratio of offspring. (p. 91)
    a. dioxins
    b. mercury
    c. lead
    d. radiation

12. Pregnant women who eat undercooked meat or clean a cat's litter box are at risk for ________ (p. 92)
    a. toxoplasmosis.
    b. rubella.
    c. cytomegalovirus.
    d. tuberculosis.

13. Regular, moderate exercise during pregnancy is linked to ________ (p. 93)
    a. prematurity.
    b. miscarriage.
    c. low birth weight.
    d. increased birth weight.

14. Folic acid supplementation around the time of conception reduces the incidence of ________ (p. 93)
    a. low birth weight.
    b. genetic disorders.
    c. neural tube defects.
    d. anoxia.

15. Research consistently indicates that women in their thirties ________ (p. 94)
    a. have about the same rates of prenatal and birth complications as women in their twenties.
    b. actually have lower rates of prenatal and birth complications than women in their twenties.
    c. have significantly higher rates of prenatal and birth complications than women in their twenties.
    d. are less likely to seek early prenatal care than women in their twenties.

16. Prenatal health care is ________ (p. 95)
    a. an unnecessary medical expense for young, pregnant women.
    b. readily available to women from all socioeconomic backgrounds.
    c. only necessary for mothers who are at risk for health problems.
    d. particularly critical for women who are young, unmarried, or poor.

17. Dilation and effacement of the cervix occurs during the __________ stage of labor. (p. 96)
    a. first
    b. second
    c. third
    d. fourth

18. Doctors and nurses routinely use __________ to assess a baby's condition immediately after birth. (p. 98)
    a. fetal monitors
    b. the Apgar Scale
    c. the Lamaze method
    d. neuroimaging techniques

19. Women who have a companion with them during childbirth __________ than women who lack companionship. (pp. 99–100)
    a. have longer labors
    b. interact less positively with their babies
    c. are less likely to have cesarean deliveries
    d. are more likely to choose a home birth

20. Fetal monitors ________ (p. 100)
    a. reduce rates of infant brain damage and death in healthy pregnancies.
    b. save the lives of many babies in high-risk situations.
    c. reduce the rate of cesarean deliveries.
    d. are comfortable devices that ease the normal course of labor.

21. The use of epidural analgesia during childbirth ________ (p. 101)
    a. strengthens uterine contractions.
    b. often reduces the length of labor.
    c. can lead to prolonged labor.
    d. decreases the chances of a cesarean delivery.

22. "Kangaroo care" ________ (p. 103)
    a. provides a carefully controlled, isolated environment for the preterm infant.
    b. provides a preterm infant with gentle stimulation of all sensory modalities.
    c. is less effective and more expensive than hospital interventions.
    d. is unavailable in most developing countries due to hospital and resource shortages.

23. In the United States, the federal government mandates __________ for employees in businesses with at least 50 workers. (p. 104)
    a. 12 weeks of unpaid maternity and paternity leave
    b. 12 weeks of paid maternity and paternity leave at 100 percent of prior earnings
    c. 15 weeks of maternity leave at 55 percent of prior earnings
    d. one year of maternity leave at 80 percent of prior earnings

24. What do the Kauai study and similar investigations reveal about the long-term consequences of birth complications? (p. 106)
    a. Children born with moderate or severe birth complications nearly always display long-term negative outcomes, regardless of home environment.
    b. Babies born with mild birth complications are just as likely to experience long-term difficulties as babies born with moderate or severe complications.
    c. The impact of serious birth complications can be lessened by the child's personal characteristics and social experiences.
    d. The majority of children with both severe birth complications and troubled family environments fare well as adults.

25. Researchers believe that most newborn reflexes disappear during the first six months due to ________ (p. 108)
    a. a lack of environmental stimulation.
    b. a gradual increase in voluntary control over behavior as the cerebral cortex develops.
    c. a significant increase in muscle mass.
    d. the infant's inability to use reflexes to promote survival.

26. The leading cause of death for infants between 1 and 12 months of age in industrialized nations is ________ (p. 110)
    a. AIDS.
    b. malnourishment.
    c. automobile accidents.
    d. SIDS.

27. The most effective way to soothe a crying baby is to ________ (p. 109)
    a. lift the baby to the shoulder while walking or rocking.
    b. swaddle the baby.
    c. offer a pacifier.
    d. play rhythmic sounds.

28. Which of the following statements about infants' sensitivity to pain is true? (p. 112)
    a. Newborns are less sensitive to pain than older babies and toddlers.
    b. Because of central nervous system immaturity, male and preterm babies feel pain less intensely than other babies.
    c. When a baby suffers severe pain, stress hormones overwhelm the nervous system, which can lead to long-term difficulties.
    d. Physical touch relieves pain by causing the baby to release cortisol.

29. At birth, infants prefer __________ to __________. (p. 113)
    a. salty tastes; sweet tastes
    b. the smell of human milk; the smell of formula
    c. pure tones; complex tones
    d. nonspeech sounds; human speech

30. Unlike adults, newborns ________ (p. 113)
    a. have excellent visual acuity.
    b. can see nearby objects more clearly than distant ones.
    c. see unclearly across a wide range of distances.
    d. prefer to look at gray stimuli over colored stimuli.

CHAPTER 4
PHYSICAL DEVELOPMENT IN INFANCY AND TODDLERHOOD

BRIEF CHAPTER SUMMARY

During the first 2 years, body size increases dramatically—faster than at any other time after birth. Rather than steady gains, infants and toddlers grow in little spurts. Body fat is laid down quickly in the first 9 months, whereas muscle development is slow and gradual. As with all aspects of development, children vary in body size and muscle–fat makeup. The best way to estimate a child's physical maturity is by using skeletal age. Two growth patterns—cephalocaudal and proximodistal trends—describe changes in the child's body proportions.

At birth, the brain is nearer than any other physical structure to its adult size, and it continues to develop at an astounding pace throughout infancy and toddlerhood. Neurons, or nerve cells, that store and transmit information, develop and form an elaborate communication system in the brain. As neurons form connections, stimulation becomes necessary for their survival. The cerebral cortex is the largest, most complex brain structure—accounting for 85 percent of the brain's weight, containing the greatest number of neurons and synapses, and responsible for the unique intelligence of our species. At birth, the two hemispheres of the cerebral cortex have already begun to specialize, a process called lateralization. However, the brain is more plastic during the first few years than it will ever be again. Animal research and natural experiments with children who were victims of deprived early environments provide evidence for sensitive periods in brain development. Appropriate stimulation is key to promoting experience-expectant brain growth—the young brain's rapidly developing organization, which depends on ordinary experiences. Experience-dependent brain growth, in contrast, occurs throughout our lives as a result of specific learning experiences. Rapid brain growth means that the organization of sleep and wakefulness changes substantially between birth and 2 years, but the social environment also plays a role.

Physical growth, like other aspects of development, results from the continuous and complex interplay between genetic and environmental factors. Heredity, nutrition, and emotional well-being all affect early physical growth. Dietary diseases caused by malnutrition affect many children in developing countries. If allowed to continue, body growth and brain development can be permanently stunted. Breastfeeding provides many benefits to infants, especially for those in the developing world where safe, nutritious alternatives are not widely available. Breastfeeding also helps protect against later obesity. Babies who do not receive affection and stimulation may suffer from nonorganic failure to thrive, which has symptoms resembling those of malnutrition but has no physical cause.

Babies come into the world with built-in learning capacities that permit them to profit from experience immediately. Classical and operant conditioning, habituation and recovery, and imitation are all important mechanisms through which infants learn about their physical and social worlds.

Like physical development, motor development follows the cephalocaudal and proximodistal trends. Babies' motor achievements have a powerful effect on their social relationships. According to the dynamic systems theory of motor development, each new motor skill is a joint product of central nervous system development, movement capacities of the body, the child's goals, and environmental supports for the skill. Cultural differences in infant-rearing practices affect the timing of motor development.

Perception changes remarkably over the first year of life. Hearing and vision undergo major advances during the first 2 years as infants organize stimuli into complex patterns, improve their perception of depth and objects, and combine information across sensory modalities. From extensive everyday experience, babies gradually figure out how to use depth cues to detect the danger of falling. According to Eleanor and James Gibson's differentiation theory, perceptual development is a matter of detecting invariant features in a constantly changing perceptual world.

LEARNING OBJECTIVES

After reading this chapter, you should be able to:

4.1 Describe major changes in body growth over the first 2 years. (pp. 120–121)

4.2 Summarize changes in brain development during infancy and toddlerhood. (pp. 121–129)

4.3 Discuss the development and functions of neurons and glial cells. (pp. 121–123)

4.4 Describe the development of the cerebral cortex, and explain the concepts of brain lateralization and brain plasticity. (pp. 124–125, 126)

4.5 Describe how both heredity and early experience contribute to brain organization. (pp. 125, 127–128)

4.6 Discuss changes in the organization of sleep and wakefulness over the first 2 years. (pp. 128–129)

4.7 Cite evidence that heredity, affection, and stimulation contribute to early physical growth. (p. 130)

4.8 Discuss the nutritional needs of infants and toddlers, the advantages of breastfeeding, and the extent to which chubby babies are at risk for later overweight and obesity. (pp. 130–131)

4.9 Summarize the impact of severe malnutrition on the development of infants and toddlers, and cite two dietary diseases associated with this condition. (p. 132)

4.10 Describe the growth disorder known as nonorganic failure to thrive, noting symptoms and family circumstances associated with the disorder. (pp. 132–133)

4.11 Describe four infant learning capacities, the conditions under which they occur, and the unique value of each. (pp. 133–136)

4.12 Describe the general course of motor development during the first 2 years, along with factors that influence it. (pp. 137–138)

4.13 Explain dynamic systems theory of motor development, and discuss support for this approach stemming from cross-cultural research. (pp. 138–140)

4.14 Discuss changes in hearing, depth and pattern perception, and intermodal perception that occur during infancy. (pp. 140–147)

4.15 Explain differentiation theory of perceptual development. (pp. 147–148)

STUDY QUESTIONS

Body Growth

Changes in Body Size and Muscle–Fat Makeup

1. True or False: Infants and toddlers grow in spurts, wherein they may experience relatively long stretches without any growth and then add as much as half an inch in a 24-hour period. (pp. 120–121)

2. Why do infants experience an increase in body fat during the first year of life? (p. 121)

____

____

3. Muscle tissue increases (slowly / rapidly) during infancy. (p. 121)

Individual and Group Differences

1. (Boys / Girls) have a higher muscle-to-fat ratio during infancy. (p. 121)

2. True or False: Trends in body size are cross-culturally consistent. (p. 121)
3. The best way to estimate a child's physical growth is to use ________________________, a measure of bone development. (p. 121)
4. When skeletal age is examined, (African-American / Caucasian) children and (boys / girls) tend to be ahead. (p. 121)

Changes in Body Proportions

1. Briefly explain the *cephalocaudal* and *proximodistal* growth trends. (p. 121)

   Cephalocaudal: ____

   ____

   Proximodistal: ____

   ____

Brain Development

Development of Neurons

1. *Neurons* are _________ cells that store and transmit _____________. (p. 121)
2. Between neurons, there are tiny gaps, or _______________. Neurons release chemicals called ___________________, which cross these gaps. (pp. 121–122)
3. True or False: By the end of the second trimester of pregnancy, production and migration of neurons is largely complete. (p. 122)
4. Explain the process of *synaptic pruning*. (p. 122)

   ____

   ____

   ____

5. About half of the brain's volume is made up of _______________ *cells,* whose most important function is _______________, the coating of neural fibers with an insulating fatty sheath that improves the efficiency of message transfer. (p. 122)

Neurophysiological Methods

1. Match each measure of brain functioning with its descriptor. Measures and descriptors may have more than one match. (p. 123)

   ______ Electroencephalogram (EEG)
   ______ Event-related potentials (ERPs)
   ______ Functional magnetic resonance imaging (fMRI)
   ______ Positron emission tomography (PET)
   ______ Near-Infrared Optical Topography (NIROT)

   A. Yields three-dimensional images of the entire brain
   B. Detects changes in electrical activity in the cerebral cortex
   C. Depends on X-ray photography
   D. Especially useful with young children

Development of the Cerebral Cortex

1. The ___________________ is the largest, most complex brain structure, accounting for 85 percent of the brain's weight and containing the greatest number of neurons and synapses. (p. 124)
2. The ___________________ are responsible for thought and have the most extended developmental period of any cortical region. (p. 124)

3. Describe the different functions controlled by the left and right hemispheres of the brain. (p. 124)

   Left: ______________________________

   Right: ______________________________

4. Brain (*lateralization* / *plasticity*) refers to specialization of the two cortical hemispheres. In a brain that is highly (lateralized / plastic), many areas are not yet committed to specific functions, and learning capacity is high. (p. 124)

5. As the brain becomes increasingly lateralized with age, it grows (more / less) plastic. (pp. 124–125)

A Lifespan Vista: Brain Plasticity: Insights from Research on Brain-Damaged Children and Adults

1. Adults who suffered brain injuries in infancy and early childhood show (fewer / more) cognitive impairments than adults with later occurring injuries. (p. 126)

2. Describe the impact of brain injury on childhood language and spatial skills, noting how these outcomes relate to brain plasticity. (p. 126)

   Language: ______________________________

   ____

   ____

   Spatial Skills: ______________________________

   ____

   ____

3. Describe the negative consequences of high brain plasticity. (p. 126)

   ____

   ____

4. True or False: Brain plasticity is restricted to childhood. (p. 126)

Sensitive Periods in Brain Development

1. Explain how findings of the following natural experiments support or refute the existence of sensitive periods in development of the cerebral cortex. (pp. 125, 127)

   Children born with cataracts: ______________________________

   ____

   Orphanage children: ______________________________

   ____

2. True or False: Trying to prime infants with stimulation for which they are not ready, such as training with flash cards, can threaten their interest in learning. (p. 127)

3. Match each description and set of growth-promoting experiences with the appropriate type of brain growth. (p. 127)

Type of Brain Growth	Description	Experiences
___ ___*Experience-expectant*	A. Brain organization develops as a result of ordinary experiences, common to all cultures and individuals.	1. Reading and writing, playing an instrument, practicing athletic skills, learning to hunt
___ ___*Experience-dependent*	B. Additional brain refinement results from specific learning experiences that vary widely across individuals and cultures.	2. Seeing and touching objects, hearing language and other sounds, exploring one's environment

Changing States of Arousal

1. Describe major changes in the organization of sleep and wakefulness during the first 2 years. (p. 128)

   Total sleep time: ______

   Periods of sleep and wakefulness: ______

   Sleep-wake pattern: ______

2. Describe three ways in which changing arousal patterns can be affected by the social environment. (p. 128)

   A. ______

   B. ______

   C. ______

Cultural Influences: Cultural Variation in Infant Sleeping Arrangements

1. True or False: Although rare in the United States, parent–infant cosleeping is common in many other countries around the world. (p. 129)

2. Mothers in (collectivist / individualistic) cultures believe that cosleeping helps build a close parent–child bond. (Collectivist / Individualistic) mothers are more likely to sleep apart from their infants, concerned with instilling early independence, preventing bad habits, and protecting their own privacy. (p. 129)

3. Summarize several benefits of parent–infant cosleeping. (p. 129)

   ______

4. Discuss the criticisms and concerns surrounding parent–infant cosleeping. (p. 129)

   ______

Influences on Early Physical Growth

Heredity

1. True or False: When diet and health are adequate, height and rate of physical growth are largely determined by heredity. (p. 130)
2. What is catch-up growth? (p. 130)

____

____

____

Nutrition

1. Describe several nutritional and health benefits of breastfeeding. (pp. 130, 131)

____

____

____

____

2. Cite four ways in which breastfeeding benefits mothers and infants in poverty-stricken regions of the world. (p. 130)

   A. ____

   B. ____

   C. ____

   D. ____

3. Breastfeeding has become (less / more) common in industrialized nations, especially among well-educated women. Today, (few / most) American mothers breastfeed. (pp. 130–131)
4. True or False: The U.S. Department of Health and Human Services advises exclusive breastfeeding for the first 6 months. (p. 131)
5. True or False: Infants and toddlers can eat nutritious foods freely without the risk of becoming overweight. (p. 131)
6. List four ways that parents can prevent infants and toddlers from becoming overweight at later ages. (p. 131)

   A. ____

   B. ____

   C. ____

   D. ____

Malnutrition

1. Recent evidence indicates that about ________ of the world's children suffer from malnutrition before age 5. (p. 132)

2. Describe the causes of *marasmus* and *kwashiorkor,* two dietary diseases associated with severe malnutrition, and summarize the developmental outcomes associated with these extreme forms of malnutrition. (p. 132)

   Marasmus

   Causes: ______________________________

   ____

   Outcomes: ______________________________

   ____

   Kwashiorkor

   Causes: ______________________________

   ____

   Outcomes: ______________________________

   ____

3. Food ______________ is uncertain access to enough food for a healthy, active life. Identify groups in which it is especially high. (p. 132)

   ____

   ____

Emotional Well-Being

1. Children who suffer from (marasmus / *nonorganic failure to thrive)* display wasted bodies and are withdrawn and apathetic, even though they are offered enough food and have no serious illness. (p. 133)

2. Describe family circumstances surrounding nonorganic failure to thrive. (p. 133)

   ____

   ____

   ____

Learning Capacities

1. Define learning. (p. 133)

   ____

Classical Conditioning

1. Briefly explain how learning takes place through *classical conditioning*. (p. 133)

   ____

   ____

   ____

2. Why is classical conditioning of great value to infants? (p. 133)

   ____

   ____

3. Match the following terms to the appropriate definition. (p. 133)

______ Neutral stimulus that leads to a new response after learning has occurred	A. *Unconditioned stimulus (UCS)*
______ Learned response exhibited toward a previously neutral stimulus	B. *Conditioned stimulus (CS)*
______ Reflexive response	C. *Unconditioned response (UCR)*
______ Automatically leads to a reflexive response	D. *Conditioned response (CR)*

4. Using the definitions in question 3 as a guide, number the steps of classical conditioning in the order in which they occur. (p. 134)
   ______ A neutral stimulus is presented just before, or at about the same time as, the UCS.
   ______ The UCS must consistently produce the UCR.
   ______ The neutral stimulus becomes a CS once it elicits the CR.

5. In classical conditioning, if the CS is presented alone enough times without being paired with the UCS, the CR will no longer occur. This is referred to as ________________. (p. 133)

Operant Conditioning

1. Briefly explain how learning takes place through *operant conditioning.* (p. 134)
   ____
   ____
   ____

2. In operant conditioning, a (*punishment / reinforcer*) increases the occurrence of a response, and a (*punishment / reinforcer*) decreases the occurrence of a response. (p. 134)

3. Describe two important functions of operant conditioning in infancy. (p. 134)
   A. ____
   ____
   B. ____
   ____

Habituation

1. (*Habituation / Recovery*) is a gradual reduction in the strength of a response due to repetitive stimulation. The introduction of a new stimulus can lead to (*habituation / recovery*), a return to high levels of responsiveness. (pp. 134–135)

2. With passage of time, infants shift from a (novelty / familiarity) preference to a (novelty / familiarity) preference. By focusing on that shift, researchers can use habituation to assess ____________________________. (p. 135)

Imitation

1. True or False: The newborn's capacity to *imitate* certain gestures has been demonstrated in many ethnic groups and cultures. (p. 135)

2. Cite two reasons why some researchers are skeptical of the newborn imitative response. (pp. 135–136)
   A. ____
   ____
   B. ____
   ____

3. ____________ *neurons* are believed to be the biological basis of a variety of interrelated, complex social abilities, including imitation. (p. 136)

4. Summarize ways in which infants benefit from imitation. (p. 136)

____

____

____

Motor Development

The Sequence of Motor Development

1. (Gross- / Fine-) motor development refers to control over actions that help infants get around in the environment, while (gross- / fine-) motor development refers to smaller movements. Provide examples of each. (p. 137)

   Gross: ____

   Fine: ____

2. True or False: Large individual differences exist in the rate of motor development. (p. 137)

3. Describe the cephalocaudal and proximodistal trends in motor development. (pp. 137–138)

   Cephalocaudal trend: ____

   ____

   Proximodistal trend: ____

   ____

4. True or False: Motor development follows a fixed maturational timetable. (p. 138)

Motor Skills as Dynamic Systems

1. According to ________________________ *theory of motor development,* motor skills work as a system. Separate abilities cooperate to produce more effective ways of acting upon the environment. Provide an example of this cooperation of motor skills. (p. 138)

   ____

   ____

2. List four factors that contribute to the development of each new motor skill. (p. 138)

   A. ____

   B. ____

   C. ____

   D. ____

3. True or False: Dynamic systems theory regards motor development as a genetically determined process. (p. 138)

4. The order in which motor skills develop (follows a strict cephalocaudal pattern / depends on several variables). (p. 139)

5. Give at least one example of how cultural variations in infant-rearing practices affect motor development. (p. 139)

____

____

____

6. The current Western practice of having babies sleep on their backs to protect against SIDS (advances / delays) gross-motor milestones of rolling, sitting, and crawling. (p. 139)

Fine-Motor Development: Reaching and Grasping

1. Of all motor skills, (crawling / reaching / sitting upright) may play the greatest role in infant cognitive development. (p. 139)

2. Match the following terms to the appropriate definition. (pp. 139–140)

_______ Well-coordinated movement in which infants use the thumb and forefinger opposably A. Prereaching
_______ Poorly coordinated swipes or swings toward an object B. Ulnar grasp
_______ Clumsy motion in which the fingers close against the palm C. Pincer grasp

Perceptual Development

Hearing

1. Indicate which aspects of language development most children demonstrate within the first year of life. (p. 141)

_______ Sensitivity to native-language syllable stress patterns
_______ Production of two-word utterances
_______ Ability to divide the speech stream into wordlike units
_______ Recognition of familiar words in spoken passages
_______ Development of a 10,000-word vocabulary
_______ Capacity to "screen out" sounds not used in one's native language

2. Explain how infants' *statistical learning capacity* facilitates rapid progress in perceiving the structure of language. (p. 141)

____

____

____

Biology and Environment: "Tuning In" to Familiar Speech, Faces, and Music: A Sensitive Period for Culture-Specific Learning

1. Research indicates that 6-month-olds can discriminate individual faces of (humans only / monkeys only / both humans and monkeys equally well). By 9 months, infants can discriminate individual faces of (humans only / monkeys only / both humans and monkeys equally well). (p. 142)

2. True or False: Infants' perception of native and non-native musical rhythms follows a trend similar to language and face perception. (p. 142)

3. What do the above findings suggest about infants' perceptual development in the second half of the first year? (p. 142)

____

____

____

Vision

1. ___________ perception is the ability to judge the distance of objects from one another and from ourselves. Cite two ways in which it is important in infant development. (p. 142)

   A. ______________________________

   B. ______________________________

2. Using the visual cliff, Gibson and Walk discovered that around the time infants crawl, (few / most) distinguish deep and shallow surfaces and avoid drop-offs. Cite limitations for understanding infant depth perception through visual cliff findings. (pp. 142–143)

   ____

   ____

   ____

3. List and describe three cues for depth. (p. 143)

   A. ______________________________

   ____

   B. ______________________________

   ____

   C. ______________________________

   ____

4. True or False: Crawling promotes a new level of brain organization. (p. 144)

5. The principle of ___________________________, which accounts for early pattern preferences, states that if infants can detect the contrast between two or more patterns, they will prefer the one with (more / less) contrast. (p. 144)

6. In the early weeks of life, newborns respond to (patterns as unified wholes / separate parts of a pattern). (p. 144)

7. True or False: Around 2 months of age, infants recognize their mothers' detailed facial features, and prefer her face to that of an unfamiliar woman. (p. 146)

8. Three-month-old infants prefer and more easily discriminate among (female / male) faces. Those who have been exposed mostly to members of their own race prefer to look at faces of members of (their own race / other races). (p. 146)

Intermodal Perception

1. In *intermodal perception*, we perceive simultaneous streams of information from multiple sensory systems as (unified wholes / individual elements). (p. 146)

2. Babies perceive input from different sensory systems in a unified way by detecting ___________________ —information that overlaps two or more sensory systems. Provide an example. (p. 146)

   ____

3. Explain how infants' intermodal sensitivity is crucial for perceptual development. (p. 147)

   ____

   ____

Understanding Perceptual Development

1. In Eleanor and James Gibson's *differentiation theory,* infants actively search for __________________ features of the environment. Explain how this theory applies to two different perceptual modalities. (p. 147)

   A. ____

   ____

   B. ____

   ____

2. True or False: As described in differentiation theory, babies detect finer and finer invariant features among stimuli over time. (p. 147)

3. Explain how acting on the environment plays a vital role in perceptual differentiation. (p. 147)

   ____

   ____

   ____

ASK YOURSELF

For *Ask Yourself* questions for this chapter, along with feedback on the accuracy of your answers, please log on to MyDevelopmentLab (for registration and access, please visit mydevelopmentlab.com or follow the instructions on page ix).

(1) Select the Multimedia Library.

(2) Choose the explore option.

(3) Find your chapter from the drop down box.

(4) Click find now.

(5) Complete questions and choose "Submit answers for grading" or "Clear answers" to start over.

SUGGESTED READINGS

Doidge, N. (2007). *The brain that changes itself.* New York: Viking Penguin. Written by an expert in neuroscience, this book examines the amazing plasticity of the human brain throughout the lifespan. The author presents real-life examples of brain plasticity, as well as personal accounts from individuals who have overcome traumatic brain injury.

Marcus, C., Loughlin, G. M., Donnelly, D., & Carroll, J. L. (Eds.). (2008). *Sleep in children.* Boca Raton, FL: CRC Press. Examines developmental changes in sleep from infancy to adolescence. Topics include normal and abnormal sleep, maturational changes in sleep, and the relationship between sleep, growth, and neurocognitive development.

Posner, M. I., & Rothbart, M. K. (2006). *Educating the human brain.* Washington, DC: American Psychological Association. This book presents 25 years of research on early learning, including the development of attention and self-regulation, the relationship between emotion and cognition, and ways adults can foster healthy development from infancy to adolescence.

CROSSWORD PUZZLE 4.1

Across

4. Experience- ______ brain growth: brain organization depends on ordinary experiences
6. Nerve cells that store and transmit information to the brain
12. In classical conditioning, a new response produced by a CS that resembles the UCR (abbr.)
13. In classical conditioning, a neutral stimulus that, through pairing with an UCS, leads to a new response (abbr.)
14. A disease usually appearing in the first year of life, caused by a diet low in all essential nutrients
15. ______ cells are responsible for myelination of neural fibers.
16. Specialization of functions of the two hemispheres of the cortex

Down

1. Synaptic _____ is the loss of connective fibers by seldom-stimulated neurons.
2. Gaps between neurons, across which messages are sent
3. ______ trend: pattern of growth that proceeds from the center of the body outward
5. ______ trend: pattern of growth that proceeds from head to tail
7. A disease appearing between 1 and 3 years of age that is caused by a diet low in protein
8. Coating neural fibers with an insulating fatty sheath to improve message transfer
9. The largest structure of the human brain is the ______ cortex.
10. Experience- ______ brain growth: result of specific experiences that vary across individuals and cultures
11. Brain ______: ability of other parts of the brain to assume functions of damaged regions

CROSSWORD PUZZLE 4.2

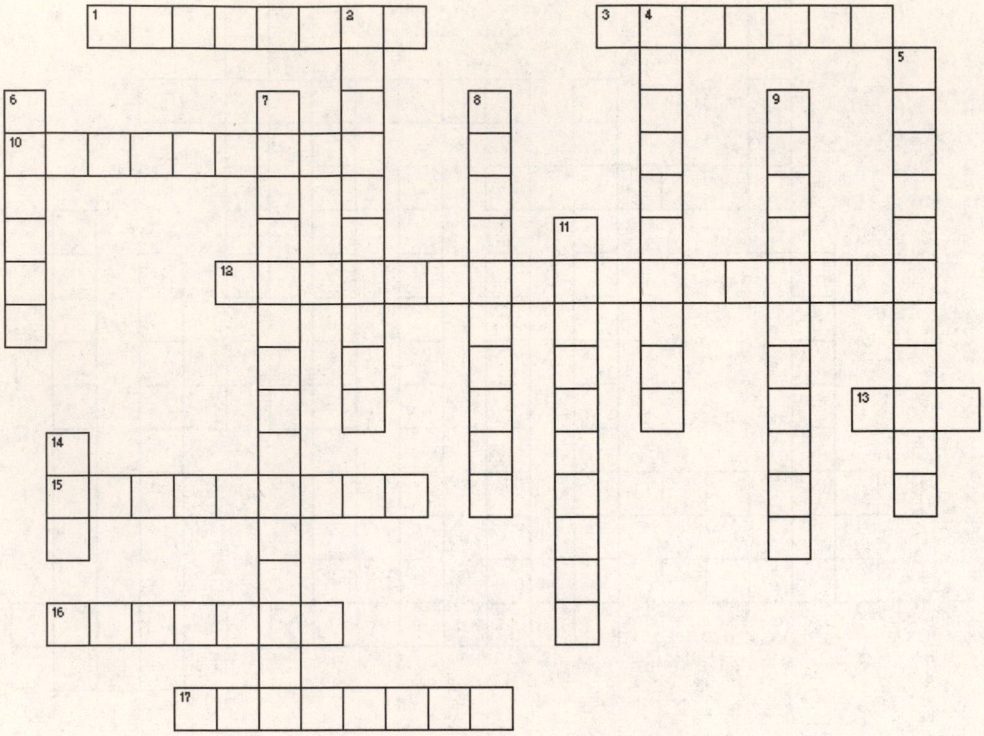

Across

1. Following habituation, an increase in responsiveness to a new stimulus
3. ______ conditioning: the recurrence of a behavior is altered by its resulting stimuli
10. Learning by copying the behavior of another person
12. Neurons send messages to one another by releasing chemicals called ______.
13. In classical conditioning, a reflexive response that is produced by an UCS (abbr.)
15. ______ conditioning: associating a neutral stimulus with a stimulus that elicits a reflexive response
16. ______ systems theory of motor development: reorganization of previously mastered skills yields new, more effective capacities
17. ______ sensitivity: ability to detect differences in light levels between adjacent regions in a pattern

Down

2. In operant conditioning, a(n) _____ increases the occurrence of a response.
4. In operant conditioning, ______ decreases the occurrence of a response.
5. Infants' ______ learning capacity allows them to analyze the speech stream for patterns.
6. ______ neurons enable us to observe another's behavior while simulating that behavior in our mind.
7. _____ theory: perceptual development involves detection of increasingly fine-grained, invariant features
8. ______ failure to thrive: growth disorder caused by lack of affection and stimulation
9. A gradual reduction in the strength of a response due to repetitive stimulation
11. ______ perception combines information from more than one sensory system.
14. In classical conditioning, a stimulus that leads to a reflexive response (abbr.)

PRACTICE TEST #1

1. Which of the following statements about early growth is true? (p. 120)
   a. Between birth and five months, an infant's height usually triples.
   b. The typical infant gains weight slowly until about one year of age, when weight gain accelerates.
   c. Infants and toddlers tend to grow slowly and steadily.
   d. Infants and toddlers tend to grow in little spurts.

2. In the synaptic pruning process, understimulated neurons ________ (p. 122)
   a. establish synapses quickly.
   b. disappear from the brain.
   c. lose their synapses.
   d. form a communication system with other neurons.

3. The dramatic increase in brain size from birth to age 2 is caused by ________ (p. 122)
   a. brain stimulation.
   b. gains in neural fibers and myelination.
   c. electrical activity in the cerebral cortex.
   d. the increase in neuron production.

4. Language areas of the brain are especially active ________ (p. 124)
   a. in the first 3 months of age.
   b. from late infancy through the preschool years.
   c. from ages 6 through 11.
   d. during adolescence.

5. Studies show that infants reared in orphanages and deprived of early stimulation ________ (pp. 125–126)
   a. have cortisol levels in the normal range.
   b. rarely exhibit long-term effects because they develop coping mechanisms to handle chronic stress.
   c. are likely to catch-up intellectually if they are enrolled in an intense academic curriculum by age 5.
   d. may catch-up intellectually by middle childhood if they are adopted before six months of age.

6. Brain plasticity ________ (p. 126)
   a. is restricted to early childhood.
   b. is more limited in children than in adults.
   c. is enhanced by synaptic pruning.
   d. can lead to a "crowding effect" after brain injury.

7. Which of the following is an example of experience-expectant brain growth? (p. 127)
   a. touching objects
   b. learning to read
   c. practicing the piano
   d. weaving a rug

8. Most parents across the world ________ (p. 129)
   a. struggle with their children at bedtime.
   b. cosleep with their babies.
   c. isolate babies during sleep.
   d. establish elaborate bedtime routines with their children.

9. Which of the following statements about breastfeeding during infancy is true? (p. 130)
   a. Breastfeeding is not recommended for women in developing countries because breast milk does not contain sufficient nutrients to protect against malnutrition and infection.
   b. Breastfeeding is rare among American mothers, and rates of breastfeeding have declined over the last two decades.
   c. Breastfeeding is essential for children's healthy psychological development.
   d. Breast milk provides infants with nutrients that are ideally suited for early rapid brain development.

10. Most chubby babies ________ (p. 131)
    a. have parents who promote unhealthy eating habits.
    b. would benefit from switching from breast milk to formula.
    c. will become obese adults.
    d. will thin out during the toddler and preschool years.

11. About 17 percent of U.S. children suffer from ________ (p. 132)
    a. marasmus.
    b. kwashiorkor.
    c. food insecurity.
    d. nonorganic failure to thrive.

12. Nonorganic failure to thrive ________ (p. 133)
    a. is associated with a known biological cause.
    b. is caused by a lack of stimulation and affection.
    c. results from an inadequate diet in early infancy.
    d. is usually inherited from the mother's side of the family.

13. As a result of classical conditioning, babies ________ (p. 133)
    a. learn to appreciate novel stimuli.
    b. begin to perceive their environment as orderly and predictable.
    c. learn that their actions can lead to predictable consequences.
    d. become fearful of neutral stimuli.

14. As 4-month-old Molly stares at her crib mobile over a period of several minutes, she gradually loses interest in it. This is an example of ________ (pp. 134–135)
    a. recovery.
    b. operant conditioning.
    c. extinction.
    d. habituation.

15. Although __________ is widely accepted, a few studies have failed to reproduce it, and some skeptics believe that it is an automatic response that declines with age. (p. 135)
    a. classical conditioning
    b. operant conditioning
    c. imitation
    d. a novelty preference

16. Scientists believe that __________ is/are the biological basis of a variety of interrelated, complex social abilities, including imitation and understanding others' intentions. (p. 136)
    a. myelination
    b. mirror neurons
    c. cortisol
    d. brain plasticity

17. A baby who has just learned to walk will likely ________ (p. 137)
    a. be uninterested in social interactions for a period of time.
    b. avoid exploration of an unfamiliar environment.
    c. become bored with her environment quickly.
    d. become especially attentive to social interactions.

18. Motor skills ________ (p. 138)
    a. follow a fixed developmental timetable.
    b. develop independently from each other.
    c. are influenced by both internal and external factors.
    d. develop from legs to head, in a reversal of the cephalocaudal trend.

19. According to the dynamic systems theory of motor development, ________ (p. 138)
    a. new skills are acquired by revising and combining earlier accomplishments.
    b. new skills are acquired independently of previously learned skills.
    c. motor development is a genetically determined process.
    d. children require extensive training and reinforcement to acquire new motor skills.

20. Of all motor skills, __________ may play the greatest role in infant cognitive development. (p. 139)
    a. rolling
    b. reaching
    c. sitting alone
    d. pulling to a stand

21. When 1-year-old Martine picks up pieces of cereal with her thumb and index finger, she is using a(n) ________ (p. 140)
    a. gross-motor skill.
    b. spontaneous reflex.
    c. pincer grasp.
    d. ulnar grasp.

22. Over the first year of life, the greatest change in hearing is the ability to ________ (p. 141)
    a. hear a wider range of tones.
    b. analyze complex sound patterns.
    c. turn the eyes and head in the direction of a sound.
    d. match voices to familiar people.

23. Eight-month-old Collin can identify English words by distinguishing syllables that often occur together, and he prefers to listen to new speech that preserves the familiar syllable patterns. This is known as ________ (p. 141)
    a. statistical learning capacity.
    b. intermodal perception.
    c. verbal perception.
    d. speech acuity.

24. Rosa is familiarized with the face of a human and the face of a primate. When she sees a picture of the familiar face next to a novel face of the same species, she looks longer at the novel face for both pairs. What is Rosa's likely age? (p. 142)
    a. 1 month
    b. 6 months
    c. 12 months
    d. 18 months

25. Research using the visual cliff shows that ________ (p. 143)
    a. babies and toddlers are unable to distinguish deep and shallow surfaces.
    b. newly crawling and walking infants and toddlers can be trusted to avoid drop-offs.
    c. infants begin to track moving objects at around 4 months of age.
    d. crawling and avoidance of drop-offs are linked.

26. Responsiveness to __________ cues develops first, followed by sensitivity to __________ cues, and then to __________ cues. (p. 143)
    a. binocular depth; motion; pictorial depth
    b. binocular depth; pictorial depth; motion
    c. motion; binocular depth; pictorial depth
    d. motion; pictorial depth; binocular depth

27. Newborn babies prefer to look at ________ (p. 144)
    a. nonfacelike stimuli over facelike stimuli.
    b. a female face than a male face.
    c. the internal features of a pattern over the edges of a pattern.
    d. simple high-contrast patterns over complex, detailed patterns.

28. From the start, infants expect sight, sound, and touch to go together, a capacity called _________ perception. (p. 146)
    a. intermodal
    b. sensory
    c. systematic
    d. integrative

29. Which of the following is an example of amodal sensory properties? (p. 146)
    a. the sound of a familiar voice in dialogue with an unfamiliar voice
    b. a black and white pattern
    c. the sight and sound of a bouncing ball
    d. the sensation of warm bath water

30. According to the Gibsons' differentiation theory, infants actively search for ________ (p. 147)
    a. binocular cues.
    b. familiar contexts.
    c. unstable relationships among stimuli.
    d. invariant features of the environment.

PRACTICE TEST #2

1. "Baby fat" ________ (p. 121)
   a. peaks at about 3 years of age.
   b. helps babies maintain a constant body temperature.
   c. decreases during the first six months of life.
   d. is an accurate predictor of childhood obesity.

2. __________ is the best way of estimating a child's physical maturity. (p. 121)
   a. Brain scanning
   b. Skeletal age
   c. Body mass
   d. Muscle density

3. Robert and Angela notice that their 1-year-old son Ethan's arms and legs are relatively short compared to the trunk of his body. This is an example of the __________ trend of growth. (p. 121)
   a. cephalocaudal
   b. proximodistal
   c. experience-dependent
   d. experience-expectant

4. Approximately how many neurons are there in the human brain? (p. 121)
   a. 10 to 20 million
   b. 100 to 200 million
   c. 10 to 20 billion
   d. 100 to 200 billion

5. Which of the following measures of brain functioning is suitable for infants and young children? (p. 124)
   a. functional magnetic resonance imaging (fMRI)
   b. electroencephalogram (EEG)
   c. Near-Infrared Optical Topography (NIROT)
   d. positron emission tomography (PET)

6. The right hemisphere of the brain is responsible for ________ (p. 124)
   a. spatial abilities.
   b. positive emotion.
   c. verbal abilities.
   d. inhibition of impulses.

7. Research on brain plasticity indicates that babies who suffer brain seizures or hemorrhages ________ (p. 126)
   a. are less likely to recover their mental capacities than adults with similar injuries.
   b. often recover language skills, but have other lasting cognitive deficits.
   c. tend to fully recover both language and spatial skills by middle childhood.
   d. easily recover spatial skills, but have lifelong difficulty with speech and language.

8. _____________ seem(s) to help protect the young brain from the potentially damaging effects of both excessive and inadequate stress-hormone exposure. (p. 127)
   a. Good parenting
   b. Low cortisol levels
   c. Experience-dependent brain growth
   d. Aggressive academic training

9. When Lisa reads books and plays peek-a-boo with Jade, her 11-month-old daughter, Lisa is building a foundation for the __________ that will occur later in Jade's life. (pp. 127–128)
   a. attachment bond
   b. sensitive period
   c experience-dependent brain growth
   d. experience-expectant brain growth

10. Infants develop an adultlike sleep–waking schedule ________ (p. 128)
    a. halfway through the first year, when melatonin levels decrease at night.
    b. at the end of the first year, when REM sleep declines.
    c. only when they have established independent sleeping habits.
    d. at around 3 months of age, when REM sleep increases.

11. What does research suggest about the safety of parent–infant cosleeping? (p. 129)
    a. SIDS occurs more frequently in Asian cultures where cosleeping is widespread.
    b. Children who cosleep with their parents are at risk for long-term emotional problems.
    c. Cosleeping infants tend to arouse frequently throughout the night, which can lead to infant stress and sleep deprivation.
    d. With appropriate precautions, parents and infants can cosleep safely.

12. Marasmus generally occurs ________ (p. 132)
    a. when a baby's diet is lacking in all essential nutrients.
    b. between 1 and 3 years, after a baby is weaned.
    c. when a baby suffers from emotional neglect.
    d. in obese babies and children.

13. Children who survive extreme malnutrition __________ when access to food is restored. (p. 132)
    a. tend to recover cognitively
    b. generally remain underweight
    c. easily catch up in height and head size
    d. often overeat and gain excessive weight

14. Which of the following is a common contributor to nonorganic failure to thrive? (p. 133)
    a. food insecurity
    b. lack of protein
    c. parental psychological disturbance
    d. prenatal stress

15. Babies are born with ________ (p. 133)
    a. a natural avoidance of novel stimulation.
    b. a strongly lateralized brain.
    c. learning capacities that permit them to profit from experience.
    d. conditioned responses to pleasant stimuli.

16. When baby Sam sees his mother, he gazes at her and smiles. Sam's mother looks and smiles back, and then Sam looks and smiles again. This is an example of ________ (p. 134)
    a. extinction.
    b. habituation.
    c. operant conditioning.
    d. classical conditioning.

17. Researchers use __________ to assess infants' remote memories. (p. 135)
    a. habituation
    b. imitation
    c. conditioned responses
    d. parent reports

18. When Isaiah's grandmother sticks out her tongue at him, 3-month-old Isaiah sticks out his tongue, too. This is an example of ________ (p. 135)
    a. recovery.
    b. imitation.
    c. remote memory.
    d. operant conditioning.

19. Mirror neurons ________ (p. 136)
    a. are unique to the human species.
    b. are present at birth, but disappear over the first year.
    c. help babies recognize their own image.
    d. are found in motor areas of the cerebral cortex.

20. Which of the following is an example of a fine-motor skill? (p. 137)
    a. reaching
    b. crawling
    c. standing
    d. walking

21. Dynamic systems theory shows us that ________ (p. 138)
    a. motor development is hardwired into the nervous system.
    b. culture and child-rearing practices have little impact on motor development.
    c. motor development is an inefficient system.
    d. motor development cannot be genetically determined because it is motivated by exploration and the desire to master new tasks.

22. Around 7 to 9 months, babies first learn to ________ (p. 141)
    a. distinguish nearly all sounds in human languages.
    b. divide the speech stream into wordlike units.
    c. recognize their native language over a foreign language.
    d. repeat recognizable words and phrases.

23. While playing with her 1-year-old daughter, Riley, Karen moves a stuffed dog from side to side and says "dog." She then helps Riley stroke the dog's fur and repeats the word "dog." This episode will ________ (p. 141)
    a. increase the likelihood that Riley will remember the word "dog" and its meaning.
    b. mean little to Riley, who is too young to grasp word-object associations.
    c. confuse Riley when she encounters other four-legged animals.
    d. result in sensory overload for Riley and may shut down her natural interest in learning.

24. Visual acuity reaches a near-adult level at approximately _____ months of age. (p. 141)
    a. 3
    b. 6
    c. 11
    d. 18

25. What does research suggest about the capacity to discriminate socially meaningful perceptual distinctions, such as musical rhythms of diverse cultures? (p. 142)
    a. A sensitive period for socially meaningful perceptual distinctions occurs during the second half of the first year.
    b. A sensitive period for socially meaningful perceptual distinctions occurs during middle childhood.
    c. When adults listen to non-Western music for several weeks, they are more likely to become fully sensitive to the range of sounds than 12-month-olds with similar experiences.
    d. No sensitive period seems to exist for socially meaningful perceptual distinctions.

26. Which of the following is an example of a pictorial depth cue? (p. 143)
    a. a moving object
    b. receding lines that create the illusion of perspective
    c. crawling or walking toward a stationary object
    d. each eye perceiving a slightly different image

27. __________ accounts for early pattern preferences. (p. 144)
    a. Intermodal perception
    b. Statistical learning capacity
    c. Contrast sensitivity
    d. Habituation

28. Research suggests that intermodal perception ________ (pp. 146–147)
    a. is a biologically primed capacity that is present at birth.
    b. emerges as a direct result of experience with the environment.
    c. develops as a result of independent locomotion.
    d. appears gradually over the first year of life.

29. According to the Gibsons' differentiation theory, infants constantly look ________ (p. 147)
    a. to adults for encouragement to explore the environment.
    b. for ways in which the environment affords possibilities for action.
    c. for unstable features in their environment.
    d. for experience-expectant learning opportunities.

30. The cognitive point of view holds that infants not only search for invariant features and possibilities for action, but also ________ (p. 148)
    a. remember their experiences.
    b. impose meaning on what they perceive.
    c. explore internal features of visual stimuli.
    d. detect patterns among stimuli.

CHAPTER 5
COGNITIVE DEVELOPMENT IN INFANCY AND TODDLERHOOD

BRIEF CHAPTER SUMMARY

According to Piaget, by acting directly on the environment, children move through four stages of cognitive development in which psychological structures, or schemes, achieve a better fit with external reality. The first stage, called the sensorimotor stage, spans the first two years of life and is divided into six substages. In this stage, infants make strides in intentional behavior and understanding of object permanence until, by the end of the second year, they become capable of mental representation, as seen in their sudden solutions to sensorimotor problems, mastery of object permanence, deferred imitation, and make-believe play. Recent research suggests that some infants display certain understandings earlier than Piaget believed, raising questions about the accuracy of his account of sensorimotor development.

Information-processing theorists, using computer-like flowcharts to describe the human cognitive system, focus on many aspects of thinking, from attention, memory, and categorization skills to complex problem solving. With age, infants attend to more aspects of the environment and take information in more rapidly. In the second year, as children become increasingly capable of intentional behavior, attention to novelty declines and sustained attention improves. As infants get older, they remember experiences longer and group stimuli into increasingly complex categories. Also, categorization shifts from a perceptual to conceptual basis. Information processing has contributed greatly to our view of young babies as sophisticated cognitive beings. However, its greatest drawback stems from its central strength—by analyzing cognition into its components, information processing has had difficulty putting them back together into a broad, comprehensive theory.

Vygotsky believed that complex mental activities have their origins in social interaction. Through joint activities with more mature members of their society, children come to master activities and think in ways that have meaning in their culture.

Infant intelligence tests primarily measure perceptual and motor responses and predict later intelligence poorly. Speed of habituation and recovery to visual stimuli, basic information-processing measures, are better predictors of future performance. Home and child-care environments, as well as early intervention for at-risk infants and toddlers, exert powerful influences on mental development.

As perception and cognition improve during infancy, they pave the way for an extraordinary human achievement: language. The behaviorist perspective regards language development as entirely due to environmental influences, whereas nativism assumes that children are prewired with an innate language acquisition device to master the intricate rules of their language. The interactionist perspective maintains that language development results from interactions between inner capacities and environmental influences.

Babies begin cooing around 2 months, followed by babbling, which gradually reflects the sound and intonation patterns of the child's language community. First words appear around 12 months, and two-word utterances between 18 and 24 months. However, substantial individual differences exist in the rate and style of early language progress. As toddlers learn words, they may apply them too narrowly (underextension) or too broadly (overextension), in part because their language comprehension develops ahead of their ability to produce language. Adults in many cultures speak to young children using child-directed speech, a simplified form of language that is well-suited to their learning needs. Deaf parents use a similar style of communication when signing to their deaf babies. Conversational give-and-take between adults and toddlers is one of the best predictors of early language development and academic success during the school years.

LEARNING OBJECTIVES

After reading this chapter, you should be able to:

5.1 Describe how schemes change over the course of development. (p. 152)

5.2 Identify Piaget's six sensorimotor substages, and describe the major cognitive achievements of the sensorimotor stage. (pp. 153–155)

5.3 Discuss recent research on sensorimotor development, noting its implications for the accuracy of Piaget's sensorimotor stage. (pp. 155–160)

5.4 Describe the information-processing view of cognitive development and the general structure of the information-processing system. (pp. 160–162)

5.5 Cite changes in attention, memory, and categorization during the first 2 years. (pp. 162–165)

5.6 Describe contributions and limitations of the information-processing approach, and explain how it contributes to our understanding of early cognitive development. (p. 165)

5.7 Explain how Vygotsky's concept of the zone of proximal development expands our understanding of early cognitive development. (pp. 165–166, 168)

5.8 Describe the mental testing approach and the extent to which infant tests predict later performance. (pp. 166, 167–169)

5.9 Discuss environmental influences on early mental development, including home, child care, and early intervention for at-risk infants and toddlers. (pp. 169–172)

5.10 Describe theories of language development, and indicate how much emphasis each places on innate abilities and environmental influences. (pp. 172–174)

5.11 Describe major milestones of language development in the first 2 years, noting individual differences, and discuss ways in which adults can support infants' and toddlers' emerging capacities. (pp. 174–179)

STUDY QUESTIONS

Piaget's Cognitive-Developmental Theory

1. During Piaget's ________________ *stage*, which spans the first 2 years of life, infants and toddlers "think" with their eyes, ears, and hands. (p. 152)

Piaget's Ideas About Cognitive Change

1. According to Piaget, specific psychological structures, or organized ways of making sense of experience called ________________, change with age. (p. 152)

2. Match the following terms with the appropriate description. (p. 152)

_______ Creating new schemes or adjusting old ones to fit the environment	A.	*Adaptation*
_______ Rearranging and linking schemes to create an interconnected cognitive system	B.	*Accommodation*
_______ Using current schemes to interpret the external world	C.	*Assimilation*
_______ Building schemes through direct interaction with the environment	D.	*Organization*

3. When children are not changing much, they assimilate more than they accommodate. Piaget called this a state of cognitive (disequilibrium / equilibrium). During rapid cognitive change, children are in a state of (disequilibrium / equilibrium), or cognitive discomfort. (p. 152)

The Sensorimotor Stage

1. True or False: Piaget based his sequence of sensorimotor substages on a large sample of children. (p. 153)

2. According to Piaget, the ________________ *reaction* allows infants to adapt their first schemes before they are capable of purposeful exploration. At first, the infant initiates a new experience (intentionally / accidentally). As the infant tries to ________________ the event, he develops a new scheme. (p. 153)

3. Match each sensorimotor substage with the appropriate description. (p. 153)

_______	Infants' primary means of adapting to the environment is through reflexes.	A.	Substage 1
_______	Infants engage in goal-directed behavior and begin to attain object permanence.	B.	Substage 2
_______	Toddlers explore properties of objects by acting on them in novel ways and begin to imitate unfamiliar behaviors.	C.	Substage 3
_______	Infants display simple motor habits centered on their own body with limited anticipation of events.	D.	Substage 4
_______	Infants' actions are aimed at repeating interesting effects in the environment and imitation of familiar behaviors.	E.	Substage 5
_______	Toddlers gain the ability to create mental representations and exhibit deferred imitation and make-believe play.	F.	Substage 6

4. Explain the differences among primary, secondary, and tertiary circular reactions. (pp. 153–154)

   Primary circular reaction: ______________________________

   ____

   Secondary circular reaction: ______________________________

   ____

   Tertiary circular reaction: ______________________________

   ____

5. Piaget regarded ______________ *behavior* as the foundation for all problem solving. (p. 154)

6. Describe the A-not-B search error. (p. 154)

   ____

   ____

7. List three new capacities that result from the ability to create *mental representations*. (pp. 154–155)

   A. ______________________________

   B. ______________________________

   C. ______________________________

Follow-Up Research on Infant Cognitive Development

1. True or False: Recent studies suggest that Piaget overestimated infants' capacities. (p. 155)

2. Explain how the *violation-of-expectation method* allows researchers to examine infants' grasp of *object permanence* and other aspects of physical reasoning. (pp. 155–156)

   ____

   ____

   ____

3. Violation-of-expectation studies by Baillargeon, movement-tracking studies, and ERP brain-wave analyses all indicate that young infants (are / are not) aware of object permanence. (p. 156)

4. Cite several reasons why 8- to 12-month-olds may make the A-not-B search error. (p. 156)

   ____

   ____

   ____

5. True or False: Studies show that infants exhibit *deferred imitation*, a form of representation, as early as 6 weeks of age. (p. 157)

6. True or False: Toddlers use deferred imitation to enrich their range of sensorimotor schemes. (p. 157)

7. By 10 to 12 months, infants can solve problems by _______________, or apply a solution strategy from one problem to other relevant problems. (p. 157)

Evaluation of the Sensorimotor Stage

1. True or False: Recent research indicates that the cognitive attainments of infancy follow the neat, stepwise fashion that Piaget assumed. (p. 158)

2. According to the ______________________________ *perspective*, babies are born with a set of innate knowledge systems, or core domains of thought. (p. 159)

3. Cite strengths and criticisms of the core knowledge perspective. (pp. 159–160)

   Strengths: ____

   ____

   Criticisms: ____

   ____

4. Briefly describe Piaget's contributions to our knowledge of infant cognition. (p. 160)

   ____

   ____

   ____

Information Processing

Structure of the Information-Processing System

1. Match each part of the mental system with its description, according to the information-processing approach. (p. 161)

   _______ *Sensory register*
   _______ *Working, or short-term, memory*
   _______ *Long-term memory*

   A. Represents sights and sounds directly; stores information briefly and monitors strategies
   B. Permanent knowledge base
   C. Where we actively apply *mental strategies* to a limited amount of information

2. Cite two ways in which mental strategies expand working memory. (p. 161)

   A. ____

   ____

   B. ____

   ____

3. The *central executive* is part of (the sensory register / working memory / long-term memory). Describe its functions. (p. 161)

   ____

   ____

   ____

4. We apply mental strategies in long-term memory to (increase memory capacity / aid retrieval). (p. 161)

5. According to the information-processing approach, with age, changes in the (basic structure / capacity) of the mental system facilitate more complex forms of thinking. (p. 161)

Attention

1. True or False: Habituation time decreases gradually within the first 5 months of life. (p. 162)
2. By 4 months, infants' attention becomes (more / less) flexible. (p. 162)
3. Summarize changes in attention from infancy to toddlerhood. (p. 162)

____

____

Memory

1. Operant conditioning studies reveal that duration of memory (decreases / increases) gradually over the first two years of life. (p. 162)
2. True or False: When infants forget an operant response, they need only a brief prompt or opportunity to reactivate the response to reinstate the memory. (p. 162)
3. What does habituation/recovery research reveal about the mechanisms through which infants learn and retain information? (p. 162)

____

____

4. A 3-month-old can remember unfamiliar (faces / movement of objects) significantly longer. (pp. 162–163)
5. ______________, the simplest form of memory, involves indicating whether a new experience is identical or similar to a previous one. ______________, on the other hand, is much more challenging because it involves remembering something not present. (p. 163)

A Lifespan Vista: Infantile Amnesia

1. Most of us cannot retrieve events that happened to us before age 3—a phenomenon called ________________________. (p. 164)
2. True or False: Passage of time is largely responsible for *infantile amnesia*. Explain your answer. (p. 164)

____

____

3. Summarize two theories of infantile amnesia. (p. 164)

Implicit memory: ____

____

Nonverbal processing: ____

____

4. Describe the biological and social developments that contribute to the end of infantile amnesia. (p. 164)

   Biological developments: ____

   ____

   ____

   Social developments: ____

   ____

   ____

Categorization

1. True or False: Research reveals that 6- to 12-month-olds categorize the physical world, but they cannot yet categorize their emotional and social worlds. (p. 163)
2. Babies' earliest categories are ________________, or based on similar overall appearance or prominent object part. By the end of the first year, more categories are ________________, or based on common function and behavior. (p. 163)
3. Describe two factors that contribute to the perceptual-to-conceptual change. (p. 165)

   A. ____

   ____

   B. ____

   ____

4. True or False: Infants develop categories in one uniform sequence across cultures. (p. 165)

Evaluation of Information-Processing Findings

1. Information-processing research underscores the (continuity / discontinuity) of human thinking from infancy into adult life. (p. 165)
2. In what way does information-processing research challenge Piaget's view of early cognitive development? (p. 165)

   ____

   ____

   ____

3. What is the greatest drawback of the information-processing approach to cognitive development? (p. 165)

   ____

   ____

   ____

The Social Context of Early Cognitive Development

1. According to Vygotsky's sociocultural theory, how do children come to master activities and think in culturally meaningful ways? (p. 165)

   ____

   ____

2. How do adults use scaffolding to foster children's development within their *zone of proximal development*? (pp. 165–166)

____

____

____

____

3. Provide an example of how cultural variations in social experiences affect mental strategies. (p. 166)

____

____

____

Cultural Influences: Social Origins of Make-Believe Play

1. Briefly contrast Piaget's and Vygotsky's views of the origins of make-believe play. (p. 167)

   Piaget: ____

   ____

   Vygotsky: ____

   ____

2. Why is adults' participation in toddlers' make-believe play so important? (p. 167)

____

____

3. True or False: In some cultures, such as Indonesia and Mexico, older siblings are toddlers' first play partners. (p. 167)
4. True or False: According to Vygotsky, providing a stimulating physical environment is sufficient to promote early cognitive development. (p. 167)

Individual Differences in Early Mental Development

1. How does the mental testing approach differ from the cognitive theories discussed earlier in this chapter? (pp. 166, 168)

____

____

Infant and Toddler Intelligence Tests

1. Most infant tests of intelligence tap ____________ and ____________ responses. (p. 168)
2. The Bayley Scales of Infant and Toddler Development are suitable for children between ___ month and ___ years. List the five subtests and scales of the Bayley-III. (p. 168)

   A. ______________________ D. ______________________

   B. ______________________ E. ______________________

   C. ______________________

3. Describe how intelligence tests are scored. (p. 168)

____

____

4. True or False: When intelligence tests are *standardized*, the mean *IQ* is set at 100. (p. 168)
5. True or False: Scores on infant intelligence tests are excellent predictors of later intelligence. (p. 169)
6. Why are the Bayley-III Cognitive and Language Scales better predictors of preschool mental test performance than other infant tests? (p. 169)

 ____

 ____

7. What are *developmental quotients,* and how do they differ from IQ scores? (p. 169)

 A. ____

 B. ____

 ____

8. Why do habituation and recovery predict later IQ more effectively than traditional infant tests? (p. 169)

 ____

 ____

Early Environment and Mental Development

1. What is the *Home Observation for Measurement of the Environment (HOME)*? (p. 169)

 ____

 ____

2. Cite ways in which both heredity and home environment contribute to mental test scores. (pp. 169–170)

 Heredity: ____

 Home Environment: ____

3. Today, (few / most) North American mothers with children under age 2 are employed. (p. 170)
4. Discuss the impact of low- versus high-quality child care on mental development. (p. 170)

 Low-quality: ____

 ____

 High-quality: ____

 ____

5. True or False: In the United States, child-care standards are nationally regulated and funded to ensure quality. (p. 170)
6. True or False: Most child-care centers and family child-care settings in the United States provide infants and toddlers with sufficiently positive, stimulating experiences to promote healthy psychological development. (p. 170)
7. Quality of child care tends to be lowest in (nonprofit centers / for-profit centers / family child care). (p. 170)
8. Indicate which of the following statements are consistent with standards for *developmentally appropriate practice*. (p. 171)

 _______ Play materials are stored out of children's reach.
 _______ In child-care centers, caregiver–child ratio is no greater than 1 to 3 for infants.
 _______ Staffing is consistent.
 _______ Daily schedule is highly structured and rigid.
 _______ Parents are welcome anytime.

Early Intervention for At-Risk Infants and Toddlers

1. True or False: In most early intervention programs, participating children score higher than untreated controls on mental tests by age 2. (p. 172)
2. Cite three characteristics of early intervention that promote cognitive and academic performance throughout childhood and adolescence. (p. 172)

   A. ______________________________

   B. ______________________________

   C. ______________________________
3. Describe differences between the treatment and control groups in the Carolina Abecedarian Project. (p. 172)

   Treatment: ______________________________

   Control: ______________________________

   ____
4. Briefly summarize the long-term benefits for children in the treatment group of the Carolina Abecedarian Project. (p. 172)

   ____

   ____

   ____

Language Development

1. On average, children say their first word at _______ months of age. (p. 172)

Theories of Language Development

1. Match each of the following terms with the appropriate description. (pp. 173–174)

   _______ Children acquire language through operant conditioning, imitation, and reinforcement.

   _______ Children are biologically primed to acquire language.

   _______ Language development reflects interactions between the child's inner capacities and environmental influences.

   A. Interactionist perspective
   B. Behaviorist perspective
   C. Nativist perspective
2. Why are reinforcement and imitation best viewed as supporting, rather than fully explaining, language development? (p. 173)

   ____

   ____
3. According to Chomsky, the ______________________ *device* enables children to speak and understand any language once they pick up enough words. (p. 173)
4. True or False: Research supports the idea that childhood is a sensitive period for language acquisition. (p. 173)
5. Summarize three challenges to Chomsky's theory. (p. 173)

   A. ______________________________

   B. ______________________________

   C. ______________________________

6. List two types of interactionist theories of language development. (p. 174)

   A. ______________________________

   B. ______________________________

Getting Ready to Talk

1. Around 2 months, babies begin to make vowel-like noises, called ________________. Around 6 months, ______________ appears, in which infants repeat consonant–vowel combinations in long strings. (p. 174)
2. Babies start *babbling* at (about the same age / vastly different ages). For *babbling* to develop further, infants must be able to ________________________. (p. 174)
3. ________________________ occurs when the child attends to the same object or event as the caregiver. Describe its effects on early language development. (p. 175)

   ____

4. True or False: Turn-taking games, such as pat-a-cake and peekaboo, contribute to infants' acquisition of language and communication skills. (p. 175)
5. How do preverbal gestures prepare children to use language? (pp. 175–176)

   ____

   ____

First Words

1. True or False: In their first 50 words, toddlers often name things that just sit there, like "table" or "vase." (p. 176)
2. When children apply words too narrowly, it is called (*underextension* / *overextension*). More commonly, children apply a word to a wider collection of objects and events than is appropriate—an error called (*underextension* / *overextension*). (p. 176)
3. Why do children often overextend deliberately? (p. 176)

   ____

   ____

4. True or False: At all ages, language comprehension develops ahead of language production. (p. 176)

The Two-Word Utterance Phase

1. True or False: Recent evidence indicates that most toddlers show a steady, continuous increase in rate of word learning that continues through the preschool years. (p. 176)
2. Explain *telegraphic speech*. (p. 176)

   ____

   ____

3. Two-word speech formulas indicate that young children first acquire (concrete pieces of language / grammatical rules). (p. 176)

Individual and Cultural Differences

1. Toddlers who are (boys / girls), (shy / outgoing), or temperamentally (negative / positive) tend to acquire language more slowly. (pp. 176–177)

2. Explain why the vocabularies of low-SES kindergartners are usually smaller than those of their higher-SES peers. (p. 177)

____

____

____

3. (*Expressive / Referential*)-style children's vocabularies consist mainly of words that refer to objects. Toddlers who use the (*expressive / referential*) style produce many more social formulas and pronouns. The vocabularies of (*expressive / referential*)-style children grow faster. (p. 177)

4. Cite factors that influence the development of referential and expressive communication styles. (p. 177)

   Referential style: ____

   ____

   Expressive style: ____

   ____

Supporting Early Language Development

1. Describe three ways caregivers can support early language learning. (p. 178)

   A. ____

   B. ____

   C. ____

2. Describe the characteristics of *child-directed speech (CDS)*. How does it promote language development? (pp. 177–178)

   A. ____

   ____

   B. ____

   ____

3. True or False: Parent–toddler conversation strongly predicts language development and academic success during the school years. (p. 178)

4. Explain how CDS and parent–child conversation create a zone of proximal development. (p. 178)

____

____

Biology and Environment: Parent–Child Interaction: Impact on Language and Cognitive Development of Deaf Children

1. True or False: The vast majority of deaf children have hearing parents who are fluent in sign language. (p. 179)

2. Describe outcomes for deaf children who have hearing parents not fluent in sign language. (p. 179)

____

____

____

3. True or False: The language (use of sign) and play maturity of deaf children with deaf parents is on par with hearing children's. (p. 179)

4. Describe differences in parent–child communication experienced by deaf children of hearing parents and deaf children of deaf parents. (p. 179)

____

____

____

____

ASK YOURSELF . . .

For *Ask Yourself* questions for this chapter, along with feedback on the accuracy of your answers, please log on to MyDevelopmentLab (for registration and access, please visit mydevelopmentlab.com or follow the instructions on page ix).

(1) Select the Multimedia Library.

(2) Choose the explore option.

(3) Find your chapter from the drop down box.

(4) Click find now.

(5) Complete questions and choose "Submit answers for grading" or "Clear answers" to start over.

SUGGESTED READINGS

Columbo, J., McCardle, P., & Freund, L. (Eds.). (2008). *Infant pathways to language.* New York: Psychology Press. Presents the latest research on early language development, including contemporary theories, genetic and environmental contributions, the importance of gestures, language disorders, and intervention strategies for young children with language delays.

Ensher, G. L., Clark, D. A., & Songer, N. S. (2008). *Families, infants, and young children at risk.* Baltimore, MD: Paul H. Brookes. Provides an extensive overview of early child development, from infancy to age 8. Topics include physical, cognitive, and social/emotional milestones; development of premature babies; early intervention for infants, toddlers, and preschool-age children; and cultural influences on development and child rearing.

Posner, M. I., & Rothbart, M. K. (2006). *Educating the human brain.* Washington, DC: American Psychological Association. Based on 25 years of research on early cognitive development, this book examines the development of attention and self-regulation, the relationship between emotion and cognition, and presents suggestions on how parents, child-care providers, and educators can foster early learning.

CROSSWORD PUZZLE 5.1

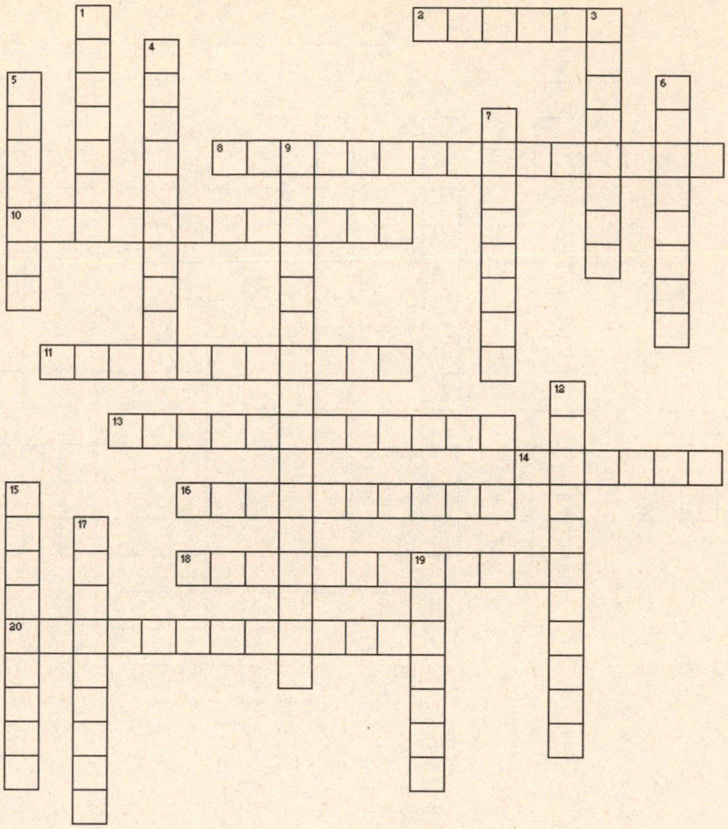

Across

2. Generating a mental representation of an absent stimulus
8. Using test results of a large, representative sample to interpret scores
10. Internal rearrangement and linking of schemes to form a strongly interconnected cognitive system
11. ______ behavior: schemes are deliberately combined to solve a problem
13. Piaget's first stage, during which infants and toddlers "think" with their eyes, ears, and hands
14. Specific structure, or way of understanding experience, that changes with age
16. Building schemes through direct interaction with the environment
18. Use of current schemes to interpret the external world
20. Creation of new schemes or adjustment of old ones to produce a better fit with the environment

Down

1. ______ memory: where we actively apply mental strategies to limited information
3. ______-______ memory contains our permanent knowledge base. (2 words, hyph.)
4. Object ______: understanding that objects continue to exist when they are out of sight
5. ______ register: represents information directly and holds it briefly
6. Children require the help of skilled partners to execute tasks within their zone of ______ development.
7. ______ reaction: infants try to repeat a chance event caused by their own motor activity
9. ______ memory: long-lasting representations of meaningful, one-time events
12. Noticing whether a stimulus is identical or similar to one previously experienced
15. ______-of-expectation method: uses habituation to examine infants' understanding of physical experience
17. Central ______: directs the flow of information
19. Infantile ______: the inability to remember events that occurred before age 3

CROSSWORD PUZZLE 5.2

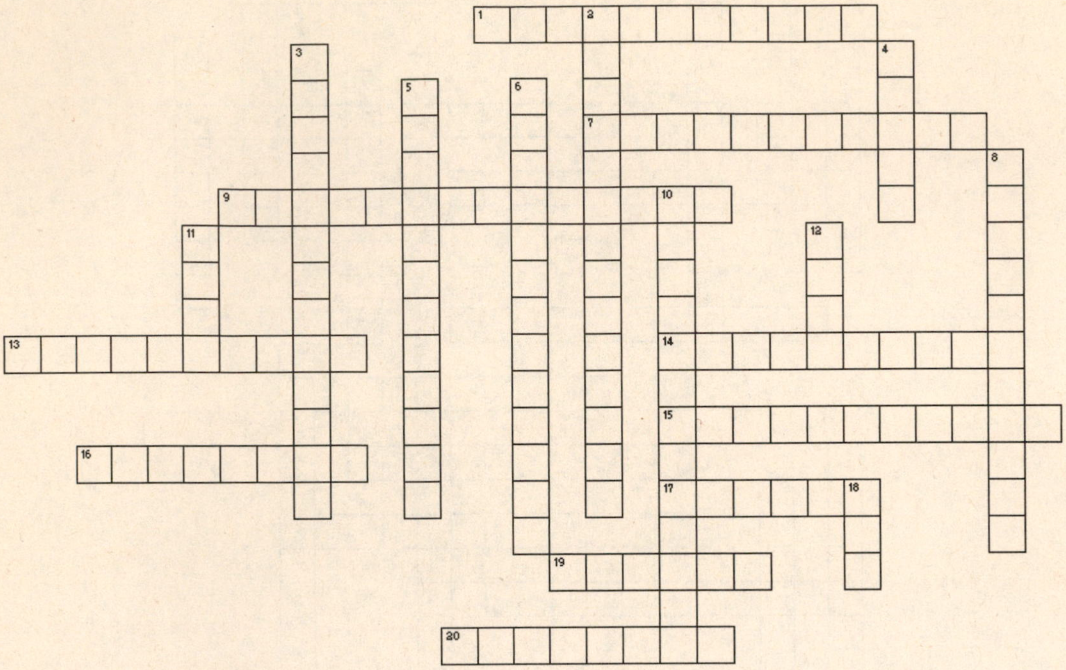

Across

1. Standards of developmentally ______ practice specify program characteristics to meet age-specific needs.
7. ______ style: toddlers use language mainly to label objects
9. Early vocabulary error in which a word is applied too narrowly
13. Mental ______: learned procedures that operate on and transform information
14. ______ style: toddlers produce many social formulas and pronouns
15 ______ speech: children's two-word utterances that omit smaller and less important words
16. ______ imitation: remembering and copying the behavior of models who are not present
17. ______ distribution: bell-shaped; most scores cluster around the average
19. Pleasant vowel-like noises made by infants beginning around 2 months of age
20. Repetition of consonant-vowel combinations in long strings

Down

2. Mental ______: an internal image of an absent object or past event
3. ______-______ speech: high-pitched, exaggerated expression, clear pronunciations, and repetition of new words (2 words, hyph.)
4. ______ attention: infants gaze in the same direction as adults
5. ______ quotient: indicates the extent to which a raw score deviates from agemates' averages
6. ______ quotient: score on an infant intelligence test, based primarily on perceptual and motor responses
8. ______-______ play: children act out everyday and imaginary activities (2 words, hyph.)
10. Early vocabulary error in which a word is applied too broadly
11. Checklist for gathering information about the quality of children's home lives (abbr.)
12. ______ knowledge perspective: babies are born with knowledge systems
18. Permits children to speak in a rule-oriented fashion, according to Chomsky (abbr.)

PRACTICE TEST #1

1. According to Piaget, during the sensorimotor stage, infants and toddlers __________ (p. 152)
   a. can carry out most activities inside their heads.
   b. primarily rely on reflexive schemes to make sense of their environment.
   c. develop highly sophisticated problem-solving skills.
   d. cannot yet carry out many activities inside their heads.

2. According to Piaget, children develop __________ to make sense of experience. (p. 152)
   a. object permanence
   b. mental strategies
   c. schemes
   d. a novelty preference

3. Piaget believed that during rapid cognitive change, children are in a state of __________, or cognitive discomfort. (p. 152)
   a. adaptation
   b. assimilation
   c. organization
   d. disequilibrium

4. In the second year, the circular reaction __________ (p. 153)
   a. disappears completely.
   b. centers on the toddler's own body.
   c. becomes experimental and creative.
   d. allows the toddler to imitate others' behavior.

5. Ten-month-old Adam understands that his pacifier continues to exist even when his father hides it under a blanket. Adam has begun to master __________ (p. 154)
   a. object permanence.
   b. a novelty preference.
   c. deferred imitation.
   d. the tertiary circular reaction.

6. To study infants' grasp of physical reasoning, researchers often use a violation-of-expectation method in which infants are __________ (p. 155)
   a. habituated to a physical event and then researchers determine whether they recover faster to a possible or impossible event.
   b. asked to seek an object after it has been moved from one hiding place to another.
   c. instructed to perform a response after seeing it modeled by an adult.
   d. asked to retrieve an object that has been hidden from their view.

7. Brain-wave research suggests that __________ (p. 156)
   a. young infants have some notion of object permanence.
   b. babies search for hidden objects as soon as they begin to reach.
   c. babies begin forming their first understanding of object permanence around 12 months of age.
   d. object permanence develops in a quick, stepwise fashion.

8. Which of the following cognitive attainments emerges earlier than Piaget expected? (p. 157)
   a. problem solving by analogy
   b. anticipating events
   c. searching for hidden objects
   d. engaging in make-believe play

9. Core knowledge researchers use controversial __________ findings to show that infants have a set of innate physical, linguistic, psychological, and numerical knowledge. (pp. 159–160)
   a. information-processing
   b. brain-wave
   c. case study
   d. violation-of-expectation

10. Like Piaget, information-processing researchers __________ (p. 160)
   a. view children as active, inquiring beings.
   b. propose a single, unified theory of cognitive development.
   c. emphasize general concepts, like assimilation or accommodation.
   d. believe that cognitive changes in infancy are abrupt and stagelike.

11. How does automatic processing expand working memory? (p. 161)
   a. It coordinates incoming information.
   b. It allows us to focus on different kinds of information simultaneously.
   c. It allows us to focus on one type of information at a time.
   d. It categorizes information to help with retrieval.

12. Information-processing theorists believe that information in __________ is categorized like a library. (p. 161)
   a. long-term memory
   b. working memory
   c. the central executive
   d. the sensory register

13. With the transition from infancy to toddlerhood, __________ (p. 162)
   a. attraction to novelty disappears.
   b. goal-directed behavior appears.
   c. sustained attention declines.
   d. sustained attention improves.

14. Which of the following experiences is a young infant likely to remember over several months? (pp. 162–163)
   a. an unfamiliar voice
   b. a toy swinging on the end of a string
   c. a book's colorful pictures
   d. the location of a hidden object

15. Which of the following statements best represents current understanding of infantile amnesia? (p. 164)
   a. Infantile amnesia occurs when young children can remember explicitly but not implicitly.
   b. Infantile amnesia occurs when meaningful events are held up in the sensory register.
   c. Infantile amnesia can be attributed mainly to the passage of time; we remember recent experiences more sharply than long-ago ones.
   d. Both biology and social experience contribute to the decline in infantile amnesia.

16. Three-year-old Max is unable to complete a jigsaw puzzle on his own, but when his preschool teacher guides and directs his learning, Max's competence at the task improves. This activity is within Max's __________ (p. 165)
   a. zone of proximal development.
   b. developmental quotient.
   c. cognitive scheme.
   d. sensory register.

17. Current research suggests that ________ (p. 167)
   a. make-believe play is discovered independently, when children are capable of representational schemes.
   b. the best way to encourage make-believe play is to provide a stimulating physical environment.
   c. make-believe play is first learned and initiated by parents and older siblings.
   d. children tend to engage in less mature forms of make-believe play when adults participate.

18. What is the mean IQ in a standardized intelligence test? (p. 168)
    a. 85
    b. 100
    c. 115
    d. 150

19. Which of the following statements accurately describes the stability of IQ? (p. 169)
    a. IQ scores are relatively stable throughout the lifespan.
    b. IQ scores obtained in infancy accurately predict IQ in early childhood.
    c. The majority of children show substantial IQ fluctuations between toddlerhood and adolescence.
    d. The younger the child at the time of the first testing, the better the prediction of later IQ.

20. Which of the following is an especially strong predictor of an infant's later IQ? (p. 169)
    a. speed of habituation and recovery to novel visual stimuli
    b. mother's IQ and mastery of object permanence
    c. the ability to follow simple directions
    d. motor progress and communication skills

21. Between 1½ and 2 years, toddlers begin to __________ (p. 172)
    a. form word–gesture combinations.
    b. add more adjectives than nouns to their vocabulary.
    c. combine words.
    d. engage in joint attention.

22. Behaviorist B. F. Skinner proposed that language is like any other behavior in that it is acquired through __________ (p. 173)
    a. classical conditioning.
    b. operant conditioning.
    c. imitation.
    d. a core knowledge system.

23. According to the nativist perspective, the early and rapid development of language in humans is due primarily to __________ (p. 173)
    a. adult reinforcement of children's communication attempts.
    b. an innate system that contains a set of rules common to all languages.
    c. children's ability to imitate others' speech.
    d. parents' use of child-directed speech.

24. Which of the following provides evidence that children are biologically primed to acquire language? (p. 173)
    a. Children's first word combinations do not appear to follow grammatical rules.
    b. Parental reinforcement results in rapid vocabulary acquisition.
    c. Children all over the world reach major language development milestones in a similar sequence.
    d. Language acquisition is a steady and gradual process.

25. Critics have challenged Chomsky's theory by pointing out that __________ (p. 173)
    a. nonhuman primates can learn to speak with minimal training.
    b. children acquire language more quickly than nativist theory suggests.
    c. language areas in the cortex develop as children acquire language.
    d. there is no evidence to support a sensitive period for language development.

26. One interactionist theory of language development applies the information-processing perspective, and a second theory emphasizes __________ (p. 174)
    a. biological maturation.
    b. classical conditioning.
    c. a language acquisition device.
    d. social interaction.

27. A toddler who uses the word "dog" to describe every furry animal is making the error of __________ (p. 176)
    a. overextension.
    b. underextension.
    c. referential speech.
    d. telegraphic speech.

28. "Daddy snack" and "more ball" are both examples of __________ (p. 176)
    a. telegraphic speech.
    b. expressive communication.
    c. underextension.
    d. overextension.

29. Child-directed speech __________ (p. 178)
    a. is only effective when combined with gestures.
    b. helps to create a zone of proximal development for expanding language skills.
    c. is mostly used by North American and European parents.
    d. is a form of "baby talk" and interferes with accurate pronunciation of common words and phrases.

30. Which of the following statements about deaf children's language acquisition is true? (p. 179)
    a. Deaf children of deaf parents usually have serious developmental and social delays due to early communication deficits.
    b. Deaf children of hearing parents experience more parental involvement and responsiveness than deaf children of deaf parents.
    c. Regardless of timing of intervention, deaf children remain significantly behind their hearing agemates in language, social, and cognitive functioning.
    d. When deaf children receive early intervention, their language, social, and cognitive functioning improve greatly.

PRACTICE TEST #2

1. For Piaget, the transition from sensorimotor to preoperational thought occurs when a child __________ (p. 152)
   a. turns 2.
   b. begins to act on objects.
   c. is in a state of equilibrium.
   d. shows evidence of thinking before she acts.

2. When children are not changing much, they mostly __________. Piaget called this a state of cognitive __________. (p. 152)
   a. adapt; disequilibrium
   b. assimilate; equilibrium
   c. accommodate; organization
   d. organize; dissonance

3. When 2-year-old Gabriela sees a green apple for the first time, she notices its color and adjusts her "apple" scheme to incorporate different colors of apples. This is an example of __________ (p. 152)
   a. accommodation.
   b. assimilation.
   c. organization.
   d. equilibrium.

4. According to Piaget, the process of organization occurs __________ (p. 152)
   a. internally.
   b. when a child is in direct contact with the environment.
   c. during assimilation.
   d. when adults model new schemes.

5. Tertiary circular reactions differ from primary and secondary circular reactions in that they are __________ (p. 154)
   a. less flexible action patterns.
   b. temporary and have little impact on learning.
   c. centered around the infant's own body.
   d. deliberately exploratory.

6. Ten-month-old Paul successfully finds a stuffed rabbit under a blanket several times. He then watches an adult put the rabbit inside a box, yet Paul continues to look for it under the blanket. This is an example of __________ (p. 154)
   a. a novelty error.
   b. the A-not-B search error.
   c. mental representation.
   d. deferred imitation.

7. A milestone of Substage 6, which occurs between 18 months and 2 years, is the ability to __________ (p. 154)
   a. anticipate events.
   b. engage in goal-directed behavior.
   c. create mental representations.
   d. recognize familiar people and environments.

8. Follow-up research on object permanence suggests that __________ (p. 156)
   a. babies are born with an awareness of object permanence.
   b. babies rarely make search errors.
   c. Piaget overestimated babies' cognitive abilities.
   d. mastery of object permanence is a gradual achievement.

9. Follow-up research suggests that deferred imitation is present at __________ (p. 157)
   a. birth.
   b. 6 weeks of age.
   c. 6 months of age.
   d. 18 months of age.

10. Today, most researchers believe that babies __________ (p. 159)
    a. construct all representations out of sensorimotor activity.
    b. are born with core domains of thought.
    c. have some built-in cognitive equipment for making sense of experience.
    d. have little, if any, built-in cognitive equipment for making sense of experience.

11. Critics of the core knowledge perspective point out that it __________ (p. 160)
    a. fails to acknowledge the importance of experience in cognitive development.
    b. ignores important violation-of-expectation findings.
    c. says little about how experiences advance children's thinking.
    d. incorrectly views development as abrupt and stagelike.

12. According to the information-processing approach, we use __________ to operate on and transform information. (p. 161)
    a. schemes
    b. assimilation
    c. mental strategies
    d. retrieval strategies

13. According to the information-processing approach, the longer we hold information in working memory, the more likely it will transfer to __________ (p. 161)
    a. short-term memory.
    b. long-term memory.
    c. the central executive.
    d. the sensory register.

14. Which of the following best reflects changes in attention from infancy to toddlerhood? (p. 161)
    a. With age, attraction to novelty improves and sustained attention declines.
    b. Toddlers have increasing difficulty disengaging their attention from interesting stimuli.
    c. With age, attraction to novelty declines and sustained attention improves.
    d. Because of their limited need for sustained attention, young children's efficiency at managing their attention changes very little from infancy to toddlerhood.

15. Using operant conditioning and habituation, researchers have determined that retention of visual events __________ (p. 162)
    a. decreases from infancy to toddlerhood.
    b. remains steady from infancy to toddlerhood.
    c. increases dramatically from infancy to toddlerhood.
    d. emerges around age 18 months.

16. Babies' earliest categories are __________, but around 18 months, more categories become __________. (pp. 163,165)
    a. perceptual; conceptual
    b. spatial; physical
    c. animate; inanimate
    d. functional; visual

17. Preschoolers __________ (p. 164)
    a. rarely produce accurate autobiographical memories.
    b. remember primarily through nonverbal techniques.
    c. experience a sharp decline in verbal recall between ages 3 and 4.
    d. require strong contextual cues to use language to refer to preverbal experiences.

18. The greatest drawback of the information-processing approach is that it __________ (p. 165)
    a. fails to account for the continuity of human thinking from infancy into adulthood.
    b. regards infants and toddlers as passive beings who are acted on by their environment rather than acknowledging them as active, inquiring beings.
    c. explains cognitive development in terms of discrete stages.
    d. analyzes cognition in terms of its components but has difficulty putting the components back together into a comprehensive theory.

19. Vygotsky believed that complex mental activities have their origins in __________ (p. 165)
    a. independent efforts to construct knowledge.
    b. core domains of knowledge.
    c. social interaction.
    d. evolutionary history.

20. A goal of intelligence tests is to __________ (pp. 166, 168)
    a. explain the process of mental development.
    b. measure cultural differences in mental ability.
    c. encourage behaviors that promote healthy development.
    d. predict future performance.

21. When parents participate in make-believe play with their toddlers, the play __________ (p. 167)
    a. becomes more elaborate.
    b. becomes less creative.
    c. is less spontaneous.
    d. has fewer cognitive benefits.

22. Which of the following is an especially strong predictor of a toddler's future intelligence and academic performance? (p. 169)
    a. having older siblings
    b. organization of the home environment
    c. early academic training
    d. extent of parent talking to the child

23. According to recent research, which child is most likely to experience the very worst child care? (p. 170)
    a. Brayden, who lives in New Zealand
    b. Carter, who comes from a middle-SES family
    c. Danica, who comes from a low-SES family
    d. Maurice, who is enrolled in Early Head Start

24. Gains in IQ and academic achievement among children living in poverty are greatest when early intervention __________ (p. 172)
    a. begins in the primary grades.
    b. includes home visits.
    c. is intense and long lasting.
    d. includes nutritional services.

25. Professor Cortez believes that language development is entirely due to environmental influences. Her belief is consistent with the __________ perspective. (p. 173)
    a. behaviorist
    b. nativist
    c. interactionist
    d. sociocultural

26. Which of the following suggests that children's language acquisition cannot be fully explained by reinforcement and imitation? (p. 173)
    a. Young children often repeat words that they hear at home.
    b. Young children spontaneously produce words and phrases, regardless of their exposure to language.
    c. Young children create many new word combinations, like "car bye bye now."
    d. Parents tend to respond to young children's attempts at language with smiles, praise, and affection.

27. Consistent with __________, people who learn a language in adolescence or adulthood never become as proficient as those who learned it in childhood. (p. 173)
    a. the behaviorist perspective
    b. brain-imaging research
    c. the information-processing perspective
    d. the sensitive period

28. Theorists who blend the information-processing view with Chomsky's nativist perspective believe that __________ (p. 174)
    a. infants and toddlers spontaneously produce language, regardless of environmental input.
    b. infants' innate capacities are not sufficient to account for mastery of higher-level language abilities.
    c. social skills are central to early language acquisition.
    d. attraction to novelty helps toddlers rapidly build their vocabularies.

29. When first learning to talk, Alex used words mostly to label objects, such as "doggie," "ball," "car," and "book." Alex's style of language learning is best categorized as __________ (p. 177)
    a. expressive.
    b. referential.
    c. concrete.
    d. attributional.

30. Why are deaf children of hearing parents more likely to experience academic and social difficulties than deaf children of deaf parents? (p. 179)
    a. because their hearing loss tends to be more profound and less responsive to intervention
    b. because they are more likely to be born with a number of other genetic traits that make social and academic pursuits more challenging
    c. because their parents tend to be less directive and more lenient, which contributes to low self-esteem and poor motivation
    d. because their early parent–child interaction is less rewarding and stimulating

CHAPTER 6
EMOTIONAL AND SOCIAL DEVELOPMENT IN INFANCY AND TODDLERHOOD

BRIEF CHAPTER SUMMARY

Although Freud's psychoanalytic theory is no longer in the mainstream of human development research, his emphasis on the importance of the parent–child relationship was accepted and elaborated on by other theorists, notably Erik Erikson. Erikson believed that the psychological conflict of the first year of life is basic trust versus mistrust, and that a healthy outcome depends on the quality of the parent–child relationship. During toddlerhood, the conflict of autonomy versus shame and doubt is resolved favorably when parents provide appropriate guidance and reasonable choices. If children emerge from the first few years without sufficient trust and autonomy, the seeds are sown for adjustment problems.

All humans and other primates experience basic emotions—happiness, interest, surprise, fear, anger, sadness, and disgust—that have an evolutionary history of promoting survival. Emotions play powerful roles in organizing social relationships, exploration of the environment, and discovery of the self. Cognitive and motor development, caregiver–infant communication, and cultural factors all affect the development and expression of emotions.

Infants' emotional expressions are closely tied to their ability to interpret the emotional cues of others. As toddlers become aware of the self as a separate, unique individual, self-conscious emotions—guilt, shame, embarrassment, envy, and pride—appear. Toddlers also begin to use emotional self-regulation strategies to manage their emotions. Rapid development of the cerebral cortex, sensitive caregiving, and growth in representation and language contribute to the development of effortful control, which is necessary for self-regulation.

Infants vary widely in temperament, including both reactivity (quickness and intensity of emotional arousal, attention, and motor activity) and self-regulation (strategies for modifying reactivity). Research findings have inspired a growing body of research on temperament, examining its stability, biological roots, and interaction with child-rearing experiences. The goodness-of-fit model explains how temperament and environment can together produce favorable outcomes when child-rearing practices match each child's temperament while encouraging more adaptive functioning.

Attachment refers to the strong affectionate tie we have with special people in our lives that leads us to feel pleasure when we interact with them and to be comforted by their nearness in times of stress. By the second half of the first year, infants have become attached to familiar people who have responded to their needs. Today, the ethological theory of attachment, which recognizes the infant's emotional tie to the caregiver as an evolved response that promotes survival, is the most widely accepted view. By the end of the second year, children develop an enduring affectionate tie to the caregiver that serves as an internal working model, a guide for future close relationships. Attachment security is influenced by opportunity for attachment, quality of caregiving, infant characteristics, and family circumstances. Babies form attachments to a variety of familiar people in addition to mothers—fathers, siblings, grandparents, and professional caregivers. Mounting evidence indicates that continuity of caregiving is the crucial factor that determines whether attachment security in early life is linked to later development. Children can recover from an insecure attachment history if caregiving improves.

During the first two years, knowledge of the self as a separate, permanent identity emerges, beginning with self-recognition—identification of the self as a physically unique being. Self-awareness is associated with the beginnings of empathy—the ability to feel with another person. Self-awareness also contributes to effortful control—the extent to which children can inhibit impulses, manage negative emotion, and behave in socially acceptable ways. Self-control allows toddlers to become compliant and acquire the ability to delay gratification.

LEARNING OBJECTIVES

After reading this chapter, you should be able to:

6.1 Discuss personality changes in the first two stages of Erikson's psychosocial theory—basic trust versus mistrust and autonomy versus shame and doubt. (pp. 184–185)

6.2 Describe changes in the expression of happiness, anger and sadness, and fear over the first year, noting the adaptive function of each. (pp. 185–188)

6.3 Summarize changes during the first two years in understanding others' emotions and expression of self-conscious emotions. (pp. 188–189)

6.4 Trace the development of emotional self-regulation during the first 2 years. (pp. 189–190)

6.5 Describe temperament, and identify the three temperamental styles elaborated by Thomas and Chess. (pp. 190–191)

6.6 Compare Thomas and Chess's model of temperament with that of Rothbart. (p. 191)

6.7 Explain how temperament is assessed, and distinguish inhibited, or shy, children from uninhibited, or sociable, children. (pp. 191–193)

6.8 Discuss the stability of temperament and the role of heredity and environment in the development of temperament. (pp. 193–194)

6.9 Summarize the goodness-of-fit model. (pp. 194–195)

6.10 Describe Bowlby's ethological theory of attachment, and trace the development of attachment during the first two years. (pp. 196–198)

6.11 Describe the Strange Situation and Attachment Q-Sort procedures for measuring attachment, along with the four patterns of attachment that have been identified using the Strange Situation. (pp. 198–199)

6.12 Discuss the factors that affect attachment security, including opportunity for attachment, quality of caregiving, infant characteristics, family circumstances, and parents' internal working models. (pp. 200–202, 203)

6.13 Discuss fathers' attachment relationships with their infants, and explain the role of early attachment quality in later development. (pp. 202, 204–205)

6.14 Describe and interpret the relationship between secure attachment in infancy and later development. (pp. 205–206)

6.15 Trace the emergence of self-awareness, and explain how it influences early emotional and social development, categorization of the self, and development of self-control. (pp. 206–209)

STUDY QUESTIONS

Erikson's Theory of Infant and Toddler Personality

Basic Trust versus Mistrust

1. Expanding on Freud's theory, Erikson believed that a healthy outcome during infancy depends on the (amount / quality) of food and caregiving offered. (p. 184)

2. Based on Erikson's theory, summarize the psychological conflict of the first year, *basic trust versus mistrust,* and explain how it can be resolved positively. (p. 184)

   A. ______________________________

   ____

   B. ______________________________

   ____

Autonomy versus Shame and Doubt

1. True or False: Like Freud, Erikson viewed toilet training as a critical milestone in the second year. (p. 184)
2. Explain how the psychological conflict of toddlerhood, *autonomy versus shame and doubt,* is resolved favorably. (pp. 184–185)

____

____

Emotional Development

1. (Body movements / Facial expressions / Vocalizations) offer the most reliable indicators of babies' emotions. (p. 185)

Development of Basic Emotions

1. ______________ *emotions* are universal in humans and other primates and have a long evolutionary history of promoting survival. Select which of the following emotions belong in this category. (p. 185)

____ guilt	____ interest	____ shame
____ embarrassment	____ happiness	____ sadness
____ pride	____ disgust	____ fear
____ anger	____ surprise	____ envy

2. True or False: At birth, infants are able to express all of the basic emotions. (p. 185)
3. The *social smile* develops between ___ and ___ weeks. How does this expression differ from babies' earlier smiles? (p. 185)

____

____

4. Laughter, which appears (before / after) the social smile, reflects (faster / slower) processing of information than does smiling. (p. 185)
5. How do expressions of happiness change between early infancy and the middle of the first year? (pp. 185–186)

____

____

6. The frequency and intensity of infants' angry reactions (increases / decreases) with age. __________________ and __________________ development contribute to this change. (p. 186)
7. The most frequent expression of fear in infancy is to unfamiliar adults, a response called _________________ *anxiety.* (p. 186)
8. True or False: To minimize stranger anxiety, an unfamiliar adult should hold and comfort the infant immediately. (p. 186)
9. Explain how the rise in fear after 6 months of age is adaptive. (p. 186)

____

____

10. Describe how cognitive development influences infants' fearful reactions. (pp. 186, 188)

____

____

A Lifespan Vista: Parental Depression and Children's Development

1. Approximately 8 to 10 percent of women experience ______________________________—mild to severe feelings of sadness and withdrawal that continue for months or years. (p. 187)
2. Depression that emerges or strengthens after childbirth but fails to subside is called ______________ depression. (p. 187)
3. Discuss how depression affects the mother's interactions with her infant. (p. 187)

   ____

   ____

   ____

4. Explain how persistent maternal depression and associated parenting behaviors affect the development of the child. (p. 187)

   ____

   ____

   ____

5. Describe how persistent paternal depression affects child development. (p. 187)

   ____

   ____

6. True or False: Early treatment of parental depression is vital to prevent the disorder from interfering with the parent–child relationship. (p. 187)

Understanding and Responding to the Emotions of Others

1. True or False: The ability to match the feeling tone of one's caregiver in face-to-face communication emerges around 3 to 4 months of age. (p. 188)
2. Beginning at 8 to 10 months, infants engage in *social* _________________—actively seeking emotional information from a trusted person in an uncertain situation. Cite several ways in which toddlers benefit from this capacity. (p. 188)

   ____

   ____

   ____

   ____

Emergence of Self-Conscious Emotions

1. *Self-conscious emotions* involve ________________ or ________________ our sense of self. (p. 188)
2. Self-conscious emotions develop (before / after) basic emotions. (p. 189)
3. Describe two factors that contribute to the development of self-conscious emotions. (p. 189)

   A. ____

   B. ____

4. True or False: Adults encourage children's expressions of self-conscious emotions in similar situations across cultures. (p. 189)

Beginnings of Emotional Self-Regulation

1. Define *emotional self-regulation*. (p. 189)

   ____

   ____

2. Briefly summarize three developments during the first year of life that contribute to infants' capacity for emotional regulation. (p. 189)

   A. ____

   B. ____

   C. ____

3. True or False: When parents do not respond to infants' emotional cues until infants are extremely agitated, infants tend to be less fussy and easier to soothe. (p. 189)

4. When toddlers experience temper tantrums, how can parents help them acquire more effective anger-regulation strategies and social skills? (pp. 189–190)

   ____

   ____

   ____

Temperament and Development

1. *Temperament* refers to early-appearing, stable individual differences in ______________ and ______________. (p. 190)

2. Cite two important findings from the New York Longitudinal Study of temperament. (p. 190)

   A. ____

   ____

   B. ____

   ____

The Structure of Temperament

1. Match each type of child with the appropriate description, according to Thomas and Chess. (p. 190)

_______	Quickly establishes regular routines in infancy, is generally cheerful, and adapts easily to new experiences	A.	*Slow-to-warm-up child*
_______	Is inactive, shows mild, low-key reactions to environmental stimuli, is negative in mood, and adjusts slowly to new experiences	B.	*Easy child*
_______	Is irregular is daily routines, is slow to accept new experiences, and tends to react negatively and intensely	C.	*Difficult child*

2. True or False: All children fit into one of the three categories of temperament described above. (p. 190)

3. The ("difficult" / "easy" / "slow-to-warm-up") pattern places children at highest risk for adjustment problems. (p. 190)

4. Cite three ways in which Rothbart's model of temperament differs from the model designed by Thomas and Chess. (p. 191)

   A. ____

   B. ____

   C. ____

5. According to Rothbart, individuals differ in their (reactivity / *effortful control* / reactivity and *effortful control*) on each dimension. (p. 191)

Measuring Temperament

1. Briefly cite several advantages and disadvantages of using parental reports and researcher observations to assess children's temperament. (p. 191)

Assessment Method	Advantages	Disadvantages
Parental reports		
Researcher observations		

2. Parental ratings are (weakly / moderately / strongly) related to observational measures of children's behavior. (p. 191)

3. Most physiological assessments of temperament have focused on ____________________ *children*, who react negatively to and withdraw from novel stimuli, and ____________________ *children*, who display positive emotion to and approach novel stimuli. (p. 191)

Biology and Environment: Development of Shyness and Sociability

1. True or False: Most children's dispositions become more extreme over time. (p. 192)

2. According to researcher Jerome Kagan, individual differences in arousal of the ____________________, an inner brain structure that controls avoidance reactions, contribute to children's styles of temperament. (p. 192)

3. Cite several physiological responses that distinguish shy versus sociable children. (p. 192)

____

____

____

4. Heritability research indicates that genes contribute (modestly / substantially) to shyness and sociability. (p. 192)

5. How can parents decrease the likelihood that an emotionally reactive baby will become a fearful child? (p. 192)

____

____

____

Stability of Temperament

1. Temperamental stability from one age period to the next is generally (low to moderate / moderate to high). (p. 193)

2. Provide an example of why a long-term prediction from early temperament is best achieved after age 3. (p. 193)

3. True or False: Experience can modify biologically based temperamental traits considerably. (p. 193)

Genetic Influences

1. True or False: Research shows that identical twins are no more similar than fraternal twins in temperament and personality. (p. 193)

2. What do comparisons of early temperaments between sexes and across ethnicities reveal about the influence of heredity upon temperament? (p. 193)

3. The role of heredity on temperamental traits is considerably (less / greater) in infancy than in childhood and later years. (p. 193)

Environmental Influences

1. Explain how parents' perceptions of their children can influence ethnic and sex differences in temperament. (pp. 193–194)

2. True or False: Research indicates that parents often regard siblings as having more distinct temperaments than observers do. How does this affect the children's developing temperaments? (p. 194)

Temperament and Child Rearing: The Goodness-of-Fit Model

1. According to the *goodness-of-fit model*, what two aspects of the child-rearing environment combine to produce a favorable outcome? (p. 194)

   A. ______

   B. ______

2. According to the goodness-of-fit model, why are difficult children at high risk for later adjustment problems? (pp. 194–195)

3. True or False: The fit between parenting and child temperament is cross-culturally consistent. (p. 195)

4. Describe parental behaviors that benefit children who exhibit the following styles of temperament. (p. 195)

   Difficult and shy children: ____

   ____

   Reserved, inactive children: ____

   ____

5. True or False: The same parenting approach that benefits reserved, inactive toddlers can have a negative impact on active children. (p. 195)

Development of Attachment

1. Define *attachment.* (p. 196)

   ____

   ____

2. True or False: Both psychoanalytic and behaviorist theories emphasize the important role of feeding in the development of attachment. (p. 196)

3. How did research on rhesus monkeys challenge the idea that attachment depends on hunger satisfaction? (p. 196)

   ____

   ____

Ethological Theory of Attachment

1. True or False: The *ethological theory of attachment* is the most widely accepted view of the infant's emotional tie to the caregiver. (p. 196)

2. According to Bowlby, attachment can best be understood in a(n) __________________ context in which ______________________________ is of utmost importance. (p. 196)

3. Match each phase of attachment with the appropriate description. (pp. 196–197)

   _______ Attachment to the familiar caregiver is evident, and infants display *separation anxiety*.

   _______ Infants are not yet attached to their mother and do not mind being left with an unfamiliar adult.

   _______ Separation anxiety declines as children gain an understanding of the parent's comings and goings and can predict her return.

   _______ Infants start to respond differently to a familiar caregiver than to a stranger, as they begin to develop a sense of trust.

   A. Preattachment phase
   B. "Attachment-in-the making" phase
   C. "Clear-cut" attachment phase
   D. Formation of a reciprocal relationship

4. According to Bowlby, children construct an *internal working model* based on their experiences during the four phases of attachment. Define this term and explain its importance. (pp. 197–198)

   ____

   ____

   ____

Measuring the Security of Attachment

1. The ______________________________, designed by Mary Ainsworth, is a widely used technique for measuring the quality of attachment between 1 and 2 years of age. (p. 198)

2. Indicate whether each set of reactions to the *Strange Situation* is typical of children who display *secure*, *avoidant*, *resistant*, or *disorganized/disoriented attachment*. (p. 198)

Type of Attachment	Infant's Reaction to Separation	Infant's Reaction to Reunion
____ Secure ____ Avoidant ____ Resistant ____ Disorganized/disoriented	Is not distressed; reacts to the stranger in much the same way as to the parent	Avoids or is slow to greet the parent; often fails to cling when picked up
____ Secure ____ Avoidant ____ Resistant ____ Disorganized/disoriented	Is distressed	Combines clinginess with angry, resistive behavior; cannot be comforted easily
____ Secure ____ Avoidant ____ Resistant ____ Disorganized/disoriented	May or may not cry; prefers the parent to the stranger	Actively seeks contact; crying reduces immediately
____ Secure ____ Avoidant ____ Resistant ____ Disorganized/disoriented	Displays confused, contradictory behaviors	Displays confused, contradictory behaviors

3. Briefly describe the *Attachment Q-Sort* method. (pp. 198–199)

____

____

4. Indicate which of the following are accurate descriptors of the Attachment Q-Sort. (p. 199)
   _______ Time-consuming
   _______ Indicates patterns of insecurity
   _______ May better reflect the everyday parent–infant relationship than the Strange Situation
   _______ Parent responses correspond well with babies' behavior in the Strange Situation
   _______ Expert responses correspond well with babies' behavior in the Strange Situation

Stability of Attachment

1. Match each family condition with its likely effects on infant attachment. (p. 199)
   _______ Middle-SES families experiencing favorable life conditions
   _______ Well-adjusted mothers who have positive social ties
   _______ Low-SES families with many daily stresses and little social support

   A. Infants may move from insecurity to security
   B. Quality of attachment is usually secure and stable
   C. Attachment generally moves away from security or changes from one secure pattern to another

2. (Insecurely / Securely) attached infants and those with (secure / avoidant / resistant / disorganized/disoriented) styles are most likely to maintain their attachment status. (p. 199)

3. True or False: Many young children show short-term instability in attachment quality. (p. 199)

Cultural Variations

1. Match each cultural parenting practice with its effects on infant attachment patterns. (p. 199)

______	German parents encourage their infants to be independent.	A.	Infants do not display avoidant attachment to their mothers.
______	Dogon mothers hold their babies close and nurse them promptly.	B.	Infants show considerably more avoidant attachment than do American babies.
______	Japanese mothers view attention seeking as a normal indicator of infant dependency.	C.	Many infants appear resistantly attached in the Strange Situation.

2. True or False: The secure pattern is the most common attachment quality in all societies studied. (p. 199)

Factors That Affect Attachment Security

1. Cite immediate and long-term consequences that may result when a baby lacks the opportunity to establish a close tie to a caregiver. (p. 200)

   Immediate consequences: ______________________________

   ____

   Long-term consequences: ______________________________

   ____

   ____

2. True or False: Research on adopted children indicates that children can develop a first attachment bond as late as 4 to 6 years of age. (p. 200)
3. True or False: Fully normal development depends on establishing close ties with caregivers early in life. (p. 200)
4. Describe differences in the sensitivity of caregiving experienced by securely attached and insecurely attached infants. (p. 200)

   Securely attached: ______________________________

   ____

   Insecurely attached: ______________________________

   ____

5. A special form of communication known as ______________________ appears to separate the experiences of securely and insecurely attached infants. Describe this pattern of communication. (pp. 200–201)

   ____

   ____

   ____

6. Compared with securely attached infants (avoidant / resistant) infants often receive overstimulating, intrusive care. (Avoidant / Resistant) babies often experience inconsistent care; their mothers are unresponsive to signals and interfere with infant exploration. (p. 201)
7. Among maltreated infants, ______________________ attachment is especially high. (p. 201)
8. What factors often combine to increase the likelihood that difficult children will develop later insecure attachments? (p. 201)

   ____

   ____

   ____

9. The heritability of attachment is (very strong / modest / virtually nil). This indicates that children's temperaments (do / do not) determine attachment quality. (p. 201)

10. Explain why infant characteristics do not show a strong relationship with attachment quality. (pp. 201–202)

____

____

____

11. Cite two ways in which family circumstances, such as job loss, a failing marriage, or financial difficulties, can undermine infant attachment. (p. 202)

 A. ______________________________

 B. ______________________________

12. Parents who discuss their childhoods with objectivity and balance tend to have (insecurely / securely) attached infants. Parents who speak dismissively or angrily of their early relationships usually have (securely / insecurely) attached babies. (p. 202)

13. True or False: The way parents view their childhood experiences is more influential than their actual experiences in determining how they rear their own children. (p. 202)

Social Issues: Does Child Care in Infancy Threaten Attachment Security and Later Adjustment?

1. True or False: North American infants placed in full-time child care before 12 months of age are more likely than infants who remain at home to display insecure attachments. (p. 203)

2. Cite two instances in which children's avoidance in the Strange Situation may represent healthy autonomy, not insecurity. (p. 203)

 A. ______________________________

 B. ______________________________

3. True or False: Research suggests that many children who attend child-care centers for full days show an increase in the stress hormone cortisol. (p. 203)

4. What characteristics of child care promote positive child–caregiver interactions and favorable child development? (p. 203)

 A. ______________________________

 B. ______________________________

 C. ______________________________

Multiple Attachments

1. True or False: When both parents are present and infants are anxious, unhappy, or distressed, they prefer to be comforted by their mother. (p. 202)

2. Describe differences in mothers' and fathers' interactions with babies. (pp. 202, 204)

 Mothers: ______________________________

 ____

 Fathers: ______________________________

 ____

3. How have parental roles in relating to infants changed in response to women's workforce participation? (p. 204)

____

____

____

4. Briefly summarize several factors that influence sibling relationships soon after the arrival of a new baby. (pp. 204–205)

____

____

____

____

Cultural Influences: The Powerful Role of Paternal Warmth in Development

1. True or False: Mothers' warmth is a better predictor of later cognitive, emotional, and social competence than is fathers' sustained affectionate involvement. (p. 204)
2. Cite positive outcomes associated with father–child play. (p. 204)

   ____

   ____

3. Summarize two factors that promote paternal warmth. (p. 204)

   A. ____

   B. ____

Attachment and Later Development

1. True or False: Research consistently shows that secure infants exhibit more favorable development than insecure infants. (pp. 205–206)
2. The __________________ attachment pattern is consistently related to both internalizing and externalizing problems in early and middle childhood. (p. 206)
3. Evidence suggests that continuity of caregiving determines whether attachment is linked to later development. Briefly explain this relationship. (p. 206)

   ____

   ____

   ____

4. Attachment can be fully understood only from a(n) __________________________________ perspective. (p. 206)

Self-Development During the First Two Years

Self-Awareness

1. True or False: At birth, infants sense that they are physically distinct from their surroundings. (p. 206)
2. Newborns' capacity for ______________ perception supports the beginnings of self-awareness. (p. 206)

3. ______________________, or identification of the self as a physically unique being, is well under way around age ___. Provide an example of this ability. (p. 207)

____

4. A ____________ parenting style, common in cultures that emphasize independence, contributes to Greek and German babies' (earlier / later) attainment of mirror *self-recognition.* Meanwhile, Nso children who experience a ____________ parenting style tend to attain mirror *self-recognition* (earlier / later). (p. 207)

5. Describe two ways in which self-awareness supports emotional and social development. (p. 208)

   A. ____

   ____

   B. ____

   ____

Categorizing the Self

1. List several characteristics upon which toddlers categorize themselves and others. (p. 208)

   ____

2. Children's ability to label their own gender is associated with a (sharp decline / gradual increase / sharp rise) in gender-stereotyped responses. (p. 208)

Self-Control

1. List two milestones that are essential for the development of self-control. (p. 208)

   A. ____

   B. ____

2. Toddlers 12 to 18 months of age are capable of ________________; they are aware of caregivers' wishes and can obey simple requests and commands. Opposition is far (less / more) common than *compliance.* (p. 208)

3. True or False: Children who are advanced in development of attention and language tend to have greater difficulty with *delay of gratification.* (pp. 208–209)

4. Describe ways that parents can help toddlers develop compliance and self-control. (p. 209)

   ____

   ____

   ____

ASK YOURSELF . . .

For *Ask Yourself* questions for this chapter, along with feedback on the accuracy of your answers, please log on to MyDevelopmentLab (for registration and access, please visit mydevelopmentlab.com or follow the instructions on page ix).

(1) Select the chapter of the *Ask Yourself.*

(2) Open the E-Book and select the Explore icon next to the *Ask Yourself.*

(3) Complete questions and choose "Submit answers for grading" or "Clear answers" to start over.

SUGGESTED READINGS

Grossmann, K. E., Grossmann, K., & Walters, E. (Eds.). (2006). *Attachment from infancy to adulthood: The major longitudinal studies*. New York: Guilford. Presents findings from some of the most well-known longitudinal studies of attachment. Each chapter highlights the importance of early relationships for favorable development throughout the lifespan.

Kopp, C. B., & Brownell, C. A. (Eds.). (2007). *Socioemotional development in the toddler years: Transitions and transformations.* New York: Guilford. A comprehensive look at social/emotional development in toddlerhood, this book examines the importance of language, early social relationships, the emergence of self-regulation, and individual differences in emotional understanding.

Strelau, J. (2008). *Temperament as a regulator of behavior: After fifty years of research.* New York: Percheron Press. Drawing on 50 years of research, this book examines the relationship between temperament and diverse aspects of behavior, including learning styles, physiological aspects of temperament, self-regulation, and the role of temperament in moderating the effects of stress. The author also provides an overview of assessment instruments used to measure temperament.

CROSSWORD PUZZLE 6.1

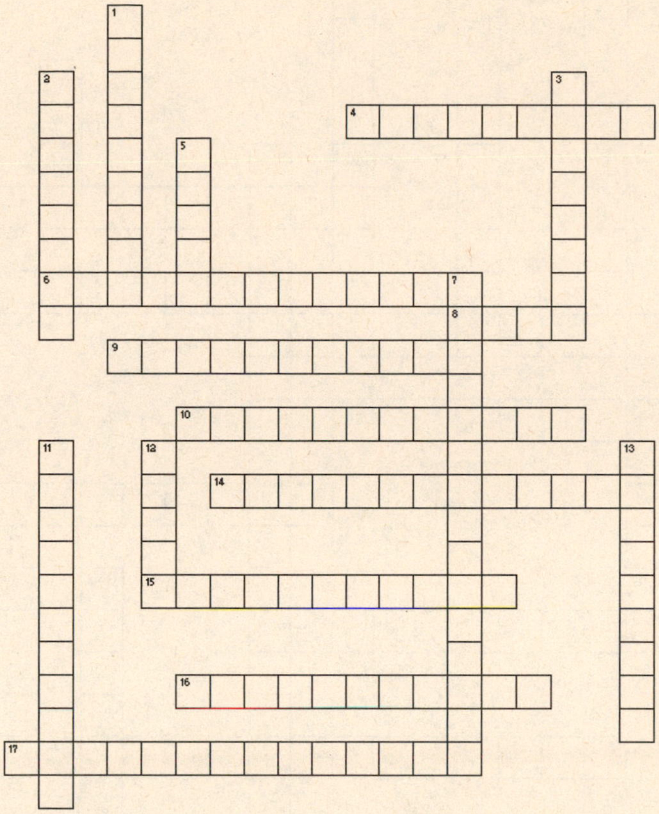

Across

4. ______ children exhibit irregular routines; slow acceptance of change; and negative, intense reactions.
6. ______ -______ emotions involve injury to or enhancement of the sense of self. (2 words, hyph.)
8. ______ children establish regular routines, are generally cheerful, and readily adapt to change.
9. ______ self: children classify themselves and others on characteristics such as age, sex, and physical traits
10. ______ children display inactivity, negative mood, and slow adjustment to change. (4 words, hyph.)
14. Delay of ______: waiting for an appropriate time and place to engage in a tempting act
15. Stable, individual differences in reactivity and self-regulation
16. Social ______: seeking emotional information from a trusted person in an uncertain situation
17. Emotional ______ - ______: adjusting one's emotional level to a comfortable level to accomplish goals (2 words, hyph.)

Down

1. ______ control: self-regulatory dimension of temperament
2. Basic trust versus ______: Erikson's psychological conflict of the first year
3. ______ versus shame and doubt: Erikson's psychological conflict of toddlerhood
5. ______ emotions are universal in humans and other primates.
7. Identification of the self as a physically unique being (2 words, hyph.)
11. A child who reacts positively to and approaches novel stimuli
12. Attachment ______: observer ratings are used to score attachment security (hyph.)
13. A child who reacts negatively to and withdraws from novel stimuli

CROSSWORD PUZZLE 6.2

Across

1. ______ smile: broad grin evoked by the parent's communication
7. Strong affectionate tie with special people in one's life
8. ______ attachment: infants are not distressed by separation and are slow to greet the parent upon reunion
9. ______ anxiety: infant's distressed reaction to the departure of a familiar caregiver
10. Awareness of and obedience to caregivers' requests and expectations
13. ______ attachment: infants respond in a confused, contradictory fashion when reunited with the parent
15. ______ theory of attachment: the infant's emotional tie to the caregiver evolved to promote survival
16. ______ model: temperament and environment together can produce favorable outcomes (3 words, hyph.)

Down

2. ______ working model: set of expectations about the availability of attachment figures
3. ______ caregiving involves prompt, consistent, and appropriate responses to infant signals.
4. ______ anxiety: infants' expressions of fear in response to unfamiliar adults
5. Infants use the caregiver as a secure ______ from which to explore, returning for emotional support.
6. Brief separations from and reunions with the parent reveal the quality of the attachment bond. (2 words)
9. ______ attachment: infants may be distressed at parental separation and are easily comforted upon reunion
11. Interactional ______: caregiver responds to infant signals in a well-timed, appropriate fashion
12. ______ attachment: infants remain close to the parent and react to separation with both angry and clingy behaviors
14. Ability to understand another's emotional state and feel with that person

PRACTICE TEST #1

1. In Erikson's theory, the psychological conflict of the first year, __________, is resolved positively when a baby experiences warm, responsive caregiving. (p. 184)
   a. autonomy vs. shame and doubt
   b. approach vs. withdrawal
   c. interest vs. fear
   d. basic trust vs. mistrust

2. A baby's first laughs occur __________ (p. 185)
   a. between 6 and 10 weeks, in response to an eye-catching object.
   b. between 6 and 10 weeks, in response to the mother's voice.
   c. around 3 to 4 months, in response to a subtle event.
   d. around 3 to 4 months, in response to a very active stimulus.

3. The most frequent expression of fear in older infants is to __________ (p. 186)
   a. unfamiliar adults.
   b. unfamiliar objects or places.
   c. animals.
   d. dark rooms.

4. Depressed mothers __________ (p. 187)
   a. view their infants more positively than independent observers do.
   b. view their infants more negatively than independent observers do.
   c. tend to use lax discipline.
   d. are unable to establish a secure attachment to their babies.

5. During a loud thunderstorm, 16-month-old Owen looks to his parents, who remain calm and relaxed. As a result, Owen does not appear afraid of the storm. This example illustrates __________ (p. 188)
   a. emotional contagion.
   b. a secure base.
   c. basic trust.
   d. social referencing.

6. Which of the following are examples of self-conscious emotions? (p. 188)
   a. happiness and sadness
   b. fear and anger
   c. interest and surprise
   d. shame and embarrassment

7. When 3-year-old Jorel sees his younger sister playing with his favorite toy train, he suppresses his desire to take the train out of her hands. Instead, he finds a toy car and coaxes his sister into trading toys with him. Jorel is demonstrating __________ (p. 189)
   a. effortful control.
   b. inhibition.
   c. reactivity.
   d. a slow-to-warm-up temperament.

8. Which of the following traits make up a person's temperament? (p. 190)
   a. mood and behavior
   b. empathy and self-confidence
   c. personality and intelligence
   d. reactivity and self-regulation

9. During her first visit to a farm, 22-month-old Jane fearlessly runs to a goat and laughs with delight as it licks her hands. Jane is a(n) __________ child. (p. 191)
   a. inhibited
   b. uninhibited
   c. difficult
   d. temperamental

10. Parents who __________ can reduce shy children's intense physiological reaction to novelty. (p. 192)
    a. ignore their children's emotional reactivity
    b. act fearful of new situations
    c. force their children into new experiences
    d. are warm and supportive

11. Research suggests that temperament __________ (p. 193)
    a. is highly stable from infancy to adulthood.
    b. is moderately stable from one age period to the next.
    c. is not at all stable from one age period to the next.
    d. can vary widely from one day to the next.

12. Research on environmental influences on temperament indicates that parents __________ (p. 193)
    a. tend to perceive newborn boys and girls similarly.
    b. usually deemphasize their children's differences.
    c. often view siblings as more distinct than researchers do.
    d. play a relatively minor role in children's temperamental style.

13. Temperament and personality can be understood only in terms of __________ (p. 194)
    a. parent–child interactions and physiological responses to novelty.
    b. genetic makeup.
    c. sociocultural influences.
    d. complex interdependencies between genetic and environmental factors.

14. Contemporary research on attachment indicates that __________ (p. 196)
    a. development is influenced by both early attachment experiences and the continuing parent–child relationship.
    b. the mother–infant bond is the foundation for all future development.
    c. attachment begins as an association with hunger satisfaction.
    d. fathers are more effective at establishing a secure attachment to their daughters than to their sons.

15. Formation of a reciprocal relationship usually occurs between __________ (p. 197)
    a. 6 and 9 months.
    b. 9 months and 1 year.
    c. 1 year and 18 months.
    d. 18 months and 2 years, and beyond.

16. According to Bowlby, children develop a(n) __________ out of their experiences during the four attachment phases that becomes a guide to all future close relationships. (p. 197)
    a. reciprocal relationship
    b. internal working model
    c. secure attachment
    d. temperament

17. About 65 percent of North American infants in middle-SES families show the __________ attachment pattern. (p. 198)
    a. secure
    b. avoidant
    c. resistant
    d. disorganized/disoriented

18. During the Strange Situation, 18-month-old Stefan seems unresponsive to his mother. He shows no reaction when his mother leaves the room, and he doesn't even look up when she returns. Stefan is displaying __________ attachment. (p. 198)
    a. secure
    b. resistant
    c. avoidant
    d. disorganized/disoriented

19. Research on the relationship between caregiving and attachment style shows that __________ (p. 200)
    a. sensitive caregiving distinguishes securely from insecurely attached infants.
    b. because attachment is primarily influenced by genetic factors, child rearing has little impact on attachment security.
    c. resistant infants tend to have mothers who are minimally involved in caregiving and unresponsive to infant signals.
    d. a disorganized/disoriented attachment style is an adaptive response to child abuse and neglect.

20. Interactional synchrony is best described as a(n) __________ (p. 200)
    a. eventful journey.
    b. guarded conversation.
    c. emotional dance.
    d. cognitive map.

21. About two-thirds of siblings—including identical and fraternal twins, nontwins, unrelated siblings, and foster infants—establish similar attachment patterns with their parents, even though they differ in temperament. What does this suggest about attachment? (p. 201)
    a. Attachment is moderately heritable.
    b. Temperament is less stable than attachment.
    c. Difficult babies rarely form secure attachments, even with sensitive caregiving.
    d. Most parents try to adjust their caregiving to each child's individual needs.

22. Research on child care suggests that __________ (p. 203)
    a. infants in full-time child care are more likely to display secure attachments than infants who remain at home.
    b. most young children in child care exhibit signs of stress and behavior problems, regardless of the quality of care.
    c. sensitive caregiving in the home cannot compensate for effects of poor quality child care.
    d. long periods of time spent in poor-quality care contributes to a higher likelihood of insecure attachment.

23. Which of the following fathers will probably spend the most amount of time engaged with his baby? (pp. 202–203)
    a. Jonah, who is from a middle-SES background
    b. Frankie, who is from a low-SES background
    c. Pablo, who is Hispanic
    d. Han, who is Japanese American

24. Through play, fathers seem to transfer to young children __________ (p. 204)
    a. a sense of confidence about parental support.
    b. their own gender stereotypes.
    c. empathy and self-control.
    d. autonomy and trustworthiness.

25. Newborns' capacity for intermodal perception supports the beginnings of __________ (p. 206)
    a. attachment security.
    b. cognition.
    c. self-awareness.
    d. effortful control.

26. When 2-year-old Elijah points to himself in a photo and says "me," he is demonstrating __________ (p. 207)
    a. sociability.
    b. intermodal perception.
    c. knowledge of the categorical self.
    d. self-recognition.

27. Many theorists believe that self-awareness develops as infants and toddlers realize that __________ (p. 207)
    a. their needs will be met by sensitive caregivers.
    b. their actions cause objects and people to react in predictable ways.
    c. other people have emotions similar to their own.
    d. they can organize their own behavior to comply with social categories.

28. Which of the following children is demonstrating empathy? (p. 208)
    a. Ten-month-old Zachary cries when his mother leaves the room.
    b. Two-year-old Enrique complies with his mother's request to pick up his toys.
    c. Three-year-old Haley yells out for her parents when she is frightened at night.
    d. Eighteen-month-old Kiri sees that her friend Tommy is upset and gives him a hug.

29. As soon as children develop the ability to categorize themselves, they exhibit a sharp increase in __________ (p. 208)
    a. their capacity to resist an impulse to engage in socially disapproved behavior.
    b. their ability to understand another's emotional state.
    c. sociable play with peers.
    d. gender-stereotyped responses.

30. When 3-year-old Malik resists taking a piece of chewing gum from his mother's purse, he is exhibiting __________ (p. 208)
    a. self awareness.
    b. compliance.
    c. self-control.
    d. empathy.

PRACTICE TEST #2

1. According to Erikson's theory, a mother who provides suitable guidance and reasonable choices is fostering her child's sense of __________ (p. 184)
   a. attachment.
   b. autonomy.
   c. trust.
   d. self.

2. Eight-week-old Zara flashes her first grin as her mother smiles and talks to her. Zara is exhibiting __________ (p. 185)
   a. spontaneous emotion.
   b. the social smile.
   c. a secure base.
   d. emotional self-regulation.

3. In infants, angry expressions __________ (p. 186)
   a. are less frequent than expressions of sadness.
   b. decrease after 4 months of age, as behavior becomes more intentional.
   c. are usually the result of stranger anxiety.
   d. increase in frequency as cognitive and motor skills develop.

4. During a play date, 11-month-old Casey toddles off to explore the new environment but returns to his mother frequently for hugs and reassurance. Casey is using his mother as a(n) __________ (p. 186)
   a. secure base.
   b. social reference.
   c. emotional control.
   d. internal working model.

5. Babies of chronically depressed parents __________ (p. 187)
   a. are just as happy and securely attached as other babies.
   b. tend to exhibit high levels of empathy toward those in distress.
   c. are at risk for a wide range of symptoms, including developmental delays, attachment difficulties, and future behavior problems.
   d. may exhibit irritability and other emotional symptoms, but rarely suffer from long-term deficits.

6. Which of the following is the best example of an infant engaging in social referencing? (p. 188)
   a. looking for home while riding in a stroller
   b. crying loudly when hungry
   c. taking a toy back from an older sibling
   d. searching for mother's face in a crowded market

7. To promote the early development of emotional self-regulation, parents can __________ (p. 189)
   a. safeguard infants from exposure to any unpleasant situation or stimuli.
   b. wait to intervene in a high-anxiety situation until the infant becomes extremely agitated.
   c. sympathetically respond to infants' emotional cues.
   d. adopt a strict zero-tolerance policy for negative emotional outbursts.

8. Temperament __________ (p. 190)
   a. first becomes apparent around age 2.
   b. is inherent, and cannot be modified by parenting practices.
   c. changes dramatically over an individual's life course.
   d. incorporates differences in reactivity and self-regulation.

9. During the first weeks of preschool, 4-year-old Daijah's teacher noticed that Daijah seemed withdrawn and less active than the other children. By the second month, Daijah had finally adjusted to preschool, but still displayed little reaction to events the other children found exciting, like a trip to the fire station. Daijah is a(n) __________ child. (p. 190)
   a. easy
   b. slow-to-warm-up
   c. difficult
   d. detached

10. Which of the following methods of measuring temperament allows researchers to control children's experiences and combine findings with physiological measures? (p. 191)
   a. parental reports
   b. behavior ratings by teachers and pediatricians
   c. home observations by researchers
   d. lab observations by researchers

11. Research on temperament shows that most children's dispositions __________ (p. 192)
   a. cannot be modified.
   b. are influenced primarily by early experiences.
   c. become more extreme over time.
   d. become less extreme over time.

12. Research on genetic and environmental influences on temperament shows that __________ (p. 193)
   a. identical twins are no more alike than fraternal twins across a wide range of temperament traits.
   b. about half of the individual differences in temperament and personality can be traced to differences in genetic makeup.
   c. environmental factors have little impact on temperament.
   d. environmental factors are primarily responsible for the development of temperament.

13. Girls' large advantage over boys in __________ contributes to their greater compliance, better school performance, and lower incidence of behavior problems. (p. 193)
   a. IQ
   b. goodness-of-fit
   c. temperamental stability
   d. effortful control

14. Two-year-old Gavin is a difficult and highly emotional toddler. Because his parents react to his outbursts with calmness, warmth, and sensitivity, Gavin is slowly learning to regulate his emotions. This is consistent with the __________ model. (p. 194)
   a. ethological
   b. internal working
   c. goodness-of-fit
   d. interactional synchrony

15. Today, the most widely accepted view of attachment is the __________ (p. 196)
   a. ethological theory of attachment.
   b. psychoanalytic perspective.
   c. behaviorist perspective.
   d. information-processing perspective.

16. In which of Bowlby's attachment phases does a baby begin to develop a sense of trust? (pp. 196–197)
   a. preattachment phase
   b. "attachment-in-the-making" phase
   c. "clear-cut" attachment phase
   d. formation of a reciprocal relationship

17. Separation anxiety __________ (p. 197)
   a. increases between 6 and 15 months.
   b. is a sign of an insecure attachment.
   c. is present within the first few weeks of life.
   d. peaks at age 2.

18. The Attachment Q-Sort __________ (pp. 198–199)
   a. simulates the Strange Situation but takes place in the child's home.
   b. is a laboratory procedure for assessing attachment.
   c. requires a nonparent observer to spend several hours observing the child at home.
   d. is widely used because of its efficiency.

19. The most stable attachment patterns are __________ (p. 199)
   a. secure and disorganized/disoriented.
   b. secure and resistant.
   c. resistant and disorganized/disoriented.
   d. avoidant and resistant.

20. Studies of institutionalized infants indicate that __________ (p. 200)
   a. regardless of when they are adopted, institutionalized babies rarely develop a secure attachment to their caregivers.
   b. when infants are adopted in early childhood, they easily form strong attachments to caregivers and rarely exhibit further social and emotional problems.
   c. children adopted as late as 4 to 6 years of age are able to form a first attachment bond, although they continue to display emotional and social problems.
   d. institutionalized children tend to develop normally, even in the absence of close attachment relationships.

21. Which attachment pattern is especially high among maltreated infants? (p. 201)
   a. avoidant
   b. resistant
   c. secure
   d. disorganized/disoriented

22. Research on parents' self-reports of their own childhood experiences suggest that __________ (p. 202)
   a. parents who discuss their childhoods with objectivity tend to have insecurely attached infants.
   b. the actual care parents received is more influential to their child rearing than the way they view their early childhoods.
   c. the way parents view their early childhoods is more influential to their childrearing than the actual care they received.
   d. parents' internal working models are directly transferred to their children.

23. Research suggests that the relationship between child care and a child's emotional well-being is determined by __________ (p. 203)
   a. the child's temperament.
   b. the number of hours spent in child care.
   c. both family and child-care experiences.
   d. the family's socioeconomic status.

24. Paternal warmth predicts __________ (p. 203)
   a. sibling rivalry in middle childhood.
   b. childhood behavior problems, particularly for boys.
   c. children's later cognitive, emotional, and social competence.
   d. children's long-term favorable development, but less strongly than maternal warmth does.

25. Ray and Jennifer just had their second child. How is their 3-year-old daughter, Hailey, likely to respond to the new baby? (p. 204)
   a. Hailey is likely to become demanding, clingy, and deliberately naughty for a time.
   b. Hailey will probably display characteristics of a disorganized/disoriented attachment style.
   c. Because of her age, Hailey will not experience a decline in attachment security.
   d. Hailey will develop a difficult temperament and is likely to experience long-term attachment difficulties.

26. Attachment builds within the intimacy of infant–caregiver interactions, but it can be fully understood only from a(n) __________ perspective. (p. 206)
    a. psychoanalytic
    b. behaviorist
    c. information-processing
    d. ecological systems

27. At what age do children become consciously aware of their own physical features? (p. 207)
    a. 6 months
    b. 9–11 months
    c. 1–2 years
    d. 2–3 years

28. In the Nso culture, which values interdependence, mothers engage in less face-to-face communication and object stimulation and more body contact and physical stimulation. This proximal parenting style predicts __________ than the distal parenting style. (p. 207)
    a. earlier attainment of self-recognition
    b. later attainment of self-recognition
    c. a resistant attachment style
    d. more frequent crying and signs of distress

29. An 18-month-old who obeys his mother's request to hold her hand is displaying __________ (p. 208)
    a. empathy.
    b. defiance.
    c. effortful control.
    d. compliance.

30. __________ tend to be better at delaying gratification than __________. (pp. 208–209)
    a. Girls; boys
    b. Toddlers; school-age children
    c. Uninhibited children; inhibited children
    d. Boys; girls

CHAPTER 7
PHYSICAL AND COGNITIVE DEVELOPMENT IN EARLY CHILDHOOD

BRIEF CHAPTER SUMMARY

While body growth slows during early childhood, the brain increases from 70 percent of its adult weight to 90 percent. Lateralization increases, and handedness develops. Myelination continues, and connections between parts of the brain increase, supporting motor and cognitive development. Heredity influences physical growth by controlling the release of hormones, but environmental factors also play important roles. Emotional deprivation and malnutrition can interfere with physical development, and illness can interact with malnutrition to undermine children's growth. In industrialized countries, unintentional injuries are the leading cause of childhood mortality.

In early childhood, an explosion of new motor skills occurs, with each building on the simpler movement patterns of toddlerhood. As the child's center of gravity shifts toward the trunk and balance improves, gross motor skills are performed with greater speed and endurance. Fine motor skills also advance dramatically as control of the hands and fingers improves. Drawing begins in the toddler years with scribbling and progresses to representational forms and then to more complex, realistic drawings at age 5 or 6. Both gross and fine motor skills are influenced by a combination of heredity and environment.

The beginning of Piaget's preoperational stage is marked by an extraordinary increase in representational, or symbolic, activity, including language, which is the most flexible means of mental representation. Make-believe play is another example of the development of representation. By around age 2, children engage in sociodramatic play—make-believe with others—which increases rapidly over the next few years as children display growing awareness that make-believe is a representational activity. Gradually, children become capable of dual representation—viewing a symbolic object as both an object in its own right and a symbol.

Piaget described preschoolers in terms of their limitations—for example, their egocentrism, animistic thinking, inability to conserve, irreversibility, and lack of hierarchical classification. Research has challenged this view, indicating that on simplified tasks based on familiar experiences, preschoolers do show the beginnings of logical thinking. Three educational principles derived from Piaget's theory continue to have a powerful influence on education: discovery learning, sensitivity to children's readiness to learn, and acceptance of individual differences.

In contrast to Piaget, Vygotsky's sociocultural theory, which emphasizes the social context of cognitive development, regards language as the foundation for all higher cognitive processes. As adults and more skilled peers provide children with verbal guidance on challenging tasks, children incorporate these dialogues into their own self-directed, or private, speech. In this view, children learn within a zone of proximal development, attempting tasks too difficult to do alone but possible with the help of adults and more skilled peers. A Vygotskian approach to education emphasizes assisted discovery, with teachers providing guidance within each child's zone of proximal development, as well as peer collaboration. In addition, Vygotsky saw make-believe play as the ideal social context for fostering cognitive development in early childhood. Guided participation, an expansion of Vygotsky's concept of scaffolding, refers to shared endeavors between more expert and less expert participants, allowing for variations across situations and cultures.

Information-processing theorists focus on children's use of mental strategies; during early childhood, advances in representation and children's ability to guide their own behavior lead to more efficient ways of attending, manipulating information, and solving problems. Preschoolers also become better at planning. Although young children's recognition memory is very accurate, their recall for listlike information is much poorer than that of older children and adults, mostly because preschoolers use memory strategies less effectively. Like adults, young children remember everyday experiences in terms of scripts. As children's cognitive and conversational skills improve, their descriptions of special events become better organized, detailed, and related to the larger context of their own lives. Improvements in representation, memory, and problem solving contribute to the young child's theory of mind, or metacognition. Through informal experiences with written symbols, preschoolers engage in emergent literacy, making active efforts to understand how these symbols, as well as math concepts, convey meaning.

Children with warm, affectionate parents who stimulate language and academic knowledge and who make reasonable demands for mature behavior score higher on mental tests, especially when they also have access to educational toys and books. At-risk children show long-term benefits from early intervention and high-quality child care. In contrast, poor-quality child care undermines the development of all children. Exposure to educational media—both television and computers—is extremely common in industrialized nations, and both media can have value for emergent literacy and other aspects of cognitive development. However, both media have a more controversial impact on social and emotional development due to the content of much entertainment programming.

Language development, including both word learning and grammar, proceeds rapidly in early childhood and is supported by conversational give-and-take. By the end of the preschool years, children have an extensive vocabulary, use most grammatical constructions competently, and are effective conversationalists.

LEARNING OBJECTIVES

After reading this chapter, you should be able to:

7.1 Describe major trends in body growth during early childhood. (pp. 216–217)

7.2 Discuss brain development in early childhood, including handedness and changes in the cerebellum, reticular formation, and the corpus callosum. (pp. 217–219)

7.3 Explain how heredity influences physical growth by controlling the production of hormones. (p. 219)

7.4 Describe the effects of emotional well-being, nutrition, and infectious disease on physical development. (pp. 219–222)

7.5 Summarize factors that increase the risk of unintentional injuries, and cite ways childhood injuries can be prevented. (pp. 222–223)

7.6 Cite major milestones of gross- and fine-motor development in early childhood, including individual and sex differences. (pp. 224–227)

7.7 Describe advances in mental representation during the preschool years. (pp. 227–229)

7.8 Describe limitations of preoperational thought, and summarize the implications of recent research for the accuracy of the preoperational stage. (pp. 229–233)

7.9 Describe educational principles derived from Piaget's theory. (pp. 233–234)

7.10 Describe Piaget's and Vygotsky's views on the development and significance of children's private speech, along with related evidence. (pp. 234–235)

7.11 Discuss applications of Vygotsky's theory to education, and summarize challenges to his ideas. (pp. 235–237)

7.12 Describe changes in attention and memory during early childhood. (pp. 237–239)

7.13 Describe the young child's theory of mind. (pp. 239–241)

7.14 Summarize children's literacy and mathematical knowledge during early childhood. (pp. 241–243)

7.15 Describe early childhood intelligence tests and the impact of home, educational programs, child care, and media on mental development in early childhood. (pp. 243–248)

7.16 Trace the development of vocabulary, grammar, and conversational skills in early childhood. (pp. 248–251)

7.17 Cite factors that support language learning in early childhood. (p. 251)

STUDY QUESTIONS

Physical Development

A Changing Body and Brain

1. True or False: Children gradually become thinner in early childhood. (p. 216)

Skeletal Growth

1. Doctors use X-rays of ________________, or growth centers in which cartilage hardens into bone, to estimate children's ___________________, or progress toward physical maturity. (p. 217)
2. Explain how heredity and environment influence the age at which children lose their primary, or "baby," teeth. (p. 217)

   Heredity: ____

   Environment: ____
3. True or False: Diseased baby teeth can affect the health of permanent teeth. (p. 217)
4. List three factors that can help to prevent tooth decay. (p. 217)

   A. ____

   B. ____

   C. ____

Brain Development

1. EEG and fMRI measures reveal especially rapid growth from early to middle childhood in frontal-lobe areas devoted to what two functions? (p. 217)

   A. ____

   B. ____
2. The (right / left) hemisphere is especially active between 3 and 6 years of age and then levels off. In contrast, activity in the (right / left) hemisphere increases steadily throughout early and middle childhood. (p. 217)
3. Differences in rate of development between the two hemispheres suggest that they are continuing to __________________. (p. 217)
4. A strong hand preference reflects the greater capacity of one side of the brain, or the ______________________________, to carry out skilled motor action. (p. 217)
5. True or False: For right-handed people, language is housed with hand control in the right hemisphere of the brain. (p. 217)
6. For left-handers, language is typically shared between both hemispheres, which indicates that their brains tend to be (less / more) strongly lateralized than those of right-handers. (pp. 217–218)
7. List three possible influences on handedness. (p. 218)

   A. ____

   B. ____

   C. ____
8. True or False: Most left-handers experience mental disabilities as a result of atypical lateralization. (p. 218)

9. Match each brain structure with the motor and cognitive skills it supports in early childhood. (p. 218)

_______ *Cerebellum* — A. Alertness, consciousness, and sustained attention
_______ *Reticular formation* — B. Balance and motor coordination
_______ *Hippocampus* — C. Motor coordination and integrated thinking
_______ *Corpus callosum* — D. Memory and spatial understanding

Influences on Physical Growth and Health

Biology and Environment: Low-Level Lead Exposure and Children's Development

1. Cite two environmental conditions under which children's blood levels of lead exceed the official "level of concern" today. (p. 220)

   A. ______________________________

   B. ______________________________

2. Summarize negative outcomes associated with lead exposure for children, according to recent studies. (p. 220)

   ____

   ____

3. True or False: Poorer mental test scores associated with lead exposure, even below the official "level of concern," appear to be permanent. (p. 220)

4. Cite two factors that may contribute to the greater cognitive consequences of lead exposure for low-SES children than for higher-SES children. (p. 220)

   A. ______________________________

   B. ______________________________

Heredity and Hormones

1. The ______________________________, located at the base of the brain, releases two hormones that induce growth. (p. 219)

2. What is the function of *growth hormone (GH)*? (p. 219)

   ____

   ____

3. ______________________________ stimulates the release of thyroxin, which is necessary for normal development of the nerve cells of the brain and for GH to have its full impact on body size. (p. 219)

Emotional Well-Being

1. True or False: Preschoolers with very stressful home lives suffer more respiratory and intestinal illnesses and unintentional injuries than their peers. (p. 219)

2. Summarize the cause and characteristics of *psychosocial dwarfism.* (p. 219)

   Cause: ______________________________

   Characteristics: ______________________________

   ____

3. True or False: Children diagnosed with psychosocial dwarfism are capable of rapid growth if removed from their emotionally inadequate environments. (p. 219)

Nutrition

1. True or False: During early childhood, many children become picky eaters. (p. 221)
2. Why does appetite decline in early childhood? What is the possible adaptive value of preschoolers' wariness of new foods? (p. 221)

   A. ______________________________

   ____

   B. ______________________________

   ____

3. Cite two factors that influence young children's food preferences. (p. 221)

   A. ______________________________

   B. ______________________________

4. List the four most common dietary deficiencies during the preschool years. (p. 221)

   A. ______________ C. ______________

   B. ______________ D. ______________

Infectious Disease

1. In what way does malnutrition contribute to infectious disease? (p. 221)

   ____

   ____

2. In what way does infectious disease contribute to malnutrition? (p. 221)

   ____

   ____

3. True or False: Due to their high cost, effective treatments for diarrhea reach very few children each year. (p. 222)
4. In the United States, a (lower / greater) percentage of preschoolers lack essential immunizations than in Denmark, Norway, Great Britain, Canada, the Netherlands, and Sweden. (p. 222)
5. What are some causes of inadequate immunization in the United States? (p. 222)

   ____

   ____

6. True or False: Large-scale studies show no association between the measles–mumps–rubella vaccine and a rise in the number of children diagnosed with autism. (p. 222)

Childhood Injuries

1. What is the leading cause of childhood mortality in industrialized countries? (p. 222)

   ____

2. List the three most common injuries during the early childhood years. (p. 222)

   A. ______________________________

   B. ______________________________

   C. ______________________________

3. Because of their higher activity level and greater willingness to take risks, (boys / girls) are 1.5 times more likely to be injured than (boys / girls). (pp. 222–223)

4. Cite three family characteristics associated with early childhood injuries. (p. 223)

   A. ______________________________

   B. ______________________________

   C. ______________________________

5. Provide reasons for the high childhood injury rates in the United States. (p. 223)

   ____

   ____

   ____

6. True or False: By age 2 or 3, preschoolers' ability to spontaneously remember safety rules contributes to a decline in home injuries. (p. 223)

7. Describe characteristics of programs that successfully prevent childhood injuries. (p. 223)

   ____

   ____

   ____

Motor Development

Gross-Motor Development

1. As children's center of gravity shifts (downward / upward), ________________ improves greatly, paving the way for new motor skills involving the large muscles of the body. (p. 224)

2. Match the following gross-motor developments with the ages at which they are typically acquired. (p. 225)

   _______ Walks up stairs with alternating feet; flexes upper body when jumping and hopping; throws with slight involvement of upper body; still catches against chest; pedals and steers tricycle

   _______ Walks downstairs with alternating feet; gallops; throws ball with transfer of weight on feet; catches with hands; rides tricycle rapidly, steers smoothly

   _______ Hurried walk changes to run; jumps, hops, throws, and catches with rigid upper body; pushes riding toy with feet, little steering

   _______ Engages in true skipping; displays mature throwing and catching style; rides bicycle with training wheels

   A. 2 to 3 years
   B. 3 to 4 years
   C. 4 to 5 years
   D. 5 to 6 years

Fine-Motor Development

1. To parents, fine-motor development is most apparent in what two areas? (p. 224)

   A. ______________________________

   B. ______________________________

2. Match the following fine-motor developments with the ages at which they are typically acquired. (p. 225)

_______	Draws first tadpole image of a person; copies vertical line and circle; uses scissors; fastens and unfastens large buttons	A. 2 to 3 years
_______	Draws a person with six parts; copies some numbers and words; ties shoes; uses knife	B. 3 to 4 years
_______	Copies triangle, cross, and some letters; cuts along line with scissors; uses fork effectively	C. 4 to 5 years
_______	Puts on and removes simple items of clothing; zips large zippers; uses spoon effectively	D. 5 to 6 years

3. Shoe tying illustrates the close connection between ________________ and ________________ development. (p. 224)

4. List and briefly describe the 3-step sequence in which drawing develops during early childhood. (pp. 224–225)

   A. ____

   ____

   B. ____

   ____

   C. ____

   ____

5. Research on the Jimi people, who have no indigenous pictorial art, reveals that the form of children's first drawings is (culture-specific / universal). (p. 226)

6. True or False: Between ages 4 and 6, children begin to realize that writing stands for language. (p. 226)

7. True or False: Until children start to read, they do not find it useful to distinguish between mirror-image written forms. (p. 226)

Individual Differences in Motor Skills

1. Due to their greater muscle mass, (boys / girls) tend to be ahead in skills that emphasize force and power, while (boys'/ girls') greater overall physical maturity contributes to their better balance and precision of movement. (p. 226)

2. Provide an example of how social pressures might exaggerate small, genetically based sex differences in motor skills. (p. 226)

   ____

   ____

3. True or False: Preschoolers exposed to formal lessons in motor skills are generally ahead in motor development. (p. 226)

4. How does the social climate created by adults affect preschoolers' motor development? (p. 226)

   ____

   ____

   ____

Cognitive Development

Piaget's Theory: The Preoperational Stage

1. As children move from the sensorimotor to the *preoperational stage,* the most obvious change is an extraordinary increase in ________________________________. (p. 227)

Mental Representation

1. According to Piaget, __________________ is the most flexible means of mental representation. (p. 227)
2. True or False: Piaget regarded language as the major ingredient in childhood cognitive development. (p. 227)

Make-Believe Play

1. List and provide an example of three important changes in make-believe play that take place in early childhood. (p. 228)
   A. ____
   Example: ____
   B. ____
   Example: ____
   C. ____
   Example: ____
2. In ______________________ *play*, children combine schemes with those of peers. (p. 228)
3. Summarize contributions of make-believe play to children's cognitive and social development. (p. 228)
   ____
   ____
   ____

Symbol–Real-World Relations

1. Around age 3, children begin to demonstrate ______________________, or the ability to view a symbolic object as both an object in its own right and a symbol. (p. 229)
2. Summarize two types of experiences that help children grasp the *dual representation* of symbolic objects. (p. 229)
   A. ____
   B. ____

Limitations of Preoperational Thought

1. Piaget described preschoolers in terms of what they (can / cannot) understand. (p. 229)
2. Piaget claimed that because young children are not capable of __________________, their thinking is rigid, limited to one aspect of a situation at a time, and strongly influenced by appearances. (p. 229)
3. Match Piaget's limitations of preoperational thought with their descriptions. (pp. 229–230)

_______	Failure to distinguish the symbolic viewpoints of others from one's own; the most fundamental deficiency of this stage	A. *Animistic thinking*
_______	Belief that inanimate objects have lifelike qualities, such as thoughts, wishes, feelings, and intentions	B. Inability to *conserve*
_______	Failure to understand that certain physical characteristics remain the same, despite changes in their appearance	C. *Irreversibility*
_______	Tendency to focus on one aspect of a situation, neglecting other important features	D. *Egocentrism*
_______	Inability to mentally go through a series of steps in a problem and then reverse direction, returning to the starting point	E. *Centration*
_______	Inability to organize objects into classes and subclasses on the basis of similarities and differences	F. Lack of *hierarchical classification*

Follow-Up Research on Preoperational Thought

1. True or False: Current research supports Piaget's view of preschoolers as cognitively deficient. (p. 230)
2. Cite an example of a nonegocentric response in preschoolers' everyday interactions. (pp. 230–231)

   ____

   ____
3. True or False: With respect to animistic beliefs, even babies can make categorical distinctions between living and nonliving things. (p. 231)
4. Between ages 4 and 8, as familiarity with physical events and principles increases, children's magical beliefs (decline / increase). (p. 231)
5. Children perform more logically than Piaget might have expected when tasks are altered in what two ways? (p. 231)

   A. ____

   B. ____
6. True or False: Three-year-olds are capable of moving back and forth between basic-level categories and general categories. (p. 231)
7. How can adults help guide children's inferences about categories? (p. 232)

   ____
8. Describe two reasons why preschoolers may struggle with appearance versus reality tasks. (p. 232)

   A. ____

   ____

   B. ____

   ____

Evaluation of the Preoperational Stage

1. Cite two indications that preschoolers attain logical operations gradually. (p. 232)

   A. ____

   B. ____
2. Some neo-Piagetian theorists combine Piaget's stage approach with the information-processing emphasis on task-specific change. Briefly describe this viewpoint. (pp. 232–233)

   ____

   ____

Piaget and Education

1. Briefly describe three educational principles derived from Piaget's theory. (p. 233)

   Discovery learning: ____

   ____

   Sensitivity to children's readiness to learn: ____

   ____

   Acceptance of individual differences: ____

   ____

Vygotsky's Sociocultural Theory

1. Vygotsky's sociocultural theory stresses the ______________ context of cognitive development. (p. 234)

Private Speech

1. Indicate whether the following statements about children's self-directed speech can be attributed to Piaget (P) or Vygotsky (V). (p. 234)

   Children's self-directed speech . . .
   ______ is the foundation for all higher cognitive processes.
   ______ results from poor perspective-taking.
   ______ declines as a result of disagreements with peers.
   ______ is a means of self-guidance.
   ______ becomes silent, inner speech as children get older.

2. Most research findings have supported (Piaget's / Vygotsky's) view of children's *private speech*. (p. 234)

3. Under what circumstances are children likely to use private speech? (p. 234)

   A. ____

   B. ____

   C. ____

Social Origins of Early Childhood Cognition

1. Vygotsky believed that children's learning takes place within a ____________________________, or range of tasks too difficult for the child to do alone but possible with the help of more skilled partners. (p. 235)

2. Describe features of effective *scaffolding*, according to Vygotsky. (p. 235)

   ____

   ____

3. How do children benefit from their parents' effective scaffolding? (p. 235)

   ____

   ____

Vygotsky and Education

1. What two features are emphasized in both Piagetian and Vygotskian classrooms? (p. 235)

   A. ____

   B. ____

2. Describe assisted discovery and peer collaboration in Vygotskian classrooms. (p. 235)

   Assisted discovery: ____

   ____

   Peer collaboration: ____

   ____

3. Vygotsky saw ________________ as the ideal social context for fostering cognitive development in early childhood. (p. 235)

4. Describe ways in which children benefit from make-believe play. (pp. 235–236)

____

____

Evaluation of Vygotsky's Theory

1. Vygotsky's theory underscores the vital role of (teaching / independent exploration) in cognitive development. (p. 236)
2. ______________________, a broader concept than scaffolding, accounts for children's diverse ways of learning through involvement with others. (p. 236)
3. (Piaget / Vygotsky) paid far more attention to the development of basic cognitive processes. (p. 237)

Cultural Influences: Children in Village and Tribal Cultures Observe and Participate in Adult Work

1. Describe differences in the daily lives of children in U.S. middle-SES suburbs compared to the Efe and Mayan children. (p. 236)

   U.S. suburban middle-SES: ____

   ____

   Efe and Mayan: ____

   ____

2. Yucatec Mayan preschoolers are highly competent at ______________, while their ______________ is limited. Describe how parenting influences this distinction. (p. 236)

   ____

   ____

   ____

Information Processing

Attention

1. What two abilities contribute to steady gains in preschoolers' capacity to sustain attention? (p. 237)

   A. ____

   B. ____

2. True or False: As early as age 3 to 5, children's ability to resist the "pull" of their attention toward a dominant stimulus predicts reading and math achievement through high school. (p. 237)
3. In ______________—a preschool curriculum inspired by Vygotsky's theory—scaffolding of attentional skills is woven into virtually all classroom activities. (p. 237)
4. What task characteristics facilitate preschoolers' ability to generate and follow a plan? (pp. 237–238)

   A. ____

   B. ____

5. Provide examples of activities that support and encourage preschoolers' developing ability to plan. (p. 238)

   ____

   ____

Memory

1. True or False: Preschoolers' recognition memory is much better than their recall memory. (p. 238)
2. In early childhood, ________________ development is associated with better recall, as it enhances long-lasting representations of past experiences. (p. 238)
3. True or False: Young children often use *memory strategies*. Explain why or why not. (p. 238)

    ____

    ____

4. Like adults, preschoolers remember familiar experiences in terms of ______________, general descriptions of what occurs and when it occurs in a particular situation. (p. 238)
5. True or False: Although young children's *scripts* begin as only a structure of main acts, they are almost always recalled in correct sequence. (p. 238)
6. How do preschoolers benefit from the use of scripts? (p. 238)

    ____

    ____

7. When adults use the (elaborative / repetitive) style to elicit children's autobiographical narratives, they follow the child's lead, adding information and volunteering their own recollections and evaluations of events. Those who use the (elaborative / repetitive) style provide little information and keep repeating the same questions. (p. 238)
8. How are children likely to benefit from elaborative, autobiographical reminiscence? (p. 239)

    ____

    ____

9. Explain how parent–child conversations contribute to differences between Asian and Western children's autobiographical narratives. (p. 239)

    Asian: ____

    ____

    Western: ____

    ____

The Young Child's Theory of Mind

1. A theory of mind, also called ______________________, is a coherent set of ideas about mental activities. (p. 239)
2. Indicate in what order children typically attain the following developments in *metacognition*. (p. 239)

    ______ Realize that beliefs and desires determine behavior.
    ______ First verbs include such words as "think," "remember," and "pretend."
    ______ View people as intentional beings who can influence one another's mental states.
    ______ Realize that thinking takes place inside their heads.

3. True or False: Across diverse cultural and SES backgrounds, false-belief understanding strengthens between ages 4 and 6, and becomes a good predictor of social skills. (pp. 239–240)
4. Briefly describe how the following factors contribute to preschoolers' theory of mind. (p. 240)

    Language: ____

    ____

Cognitive abilities: ____

____

Social experiences: ____

____

5. Indicate which of the following statements are true of preschoolers' awareness of mental activities. (p. 240)

   Preschoolers . . .
   ______ are aware that people continue to think while they wait or read books.
   ______ pay little attention to the process of thinking.
   ______ express confusion about subtle distinctions between mental states.
   ______ believe that all events must be directly observed to be known.
   ______ understand that mental inferences can be a source of knowledge.

6. True or False: Preschoolers greatly underestimate the amount of mental activity that people engage in and are poor at inferring what people know or are thinking about. (pp. 240–241)

Biology and Environment: "Mindblindness" and Autism

1. Cite three core areas of functioning that are deficient in children with autism. (p. 241)

   A. ____

   B. ____

   C. ____

2. True or False: Autism stems from abnormal brain functioning, usually due to genetic or prenatal environmental conditions. (p. 241)

3. Cite evidence that children with autism have a deficient theory of mind. (p. 241)

   ____

   ____

   ____

4. True or False: Researchers agree that impairment of innate, core brain functions leaves autistic children "mindblind." (p. 241)

5. How may impairment in executive processing affect children with autism? (p. 241)

   ____

   ____

   ____

Early Childhood Literacy

1. True or False: Preschoolers understand a great deal about written language long before they are able to read and write. (p. 242)

2. What is *emergent literacy*? (p. 242)

   ____

   ____

3. The ability to reflect on and manipulate the sound structure of spoken language, or ________________ *awareness*, is a (weak / strong) predictor of emergent literacy knowledge. (p. 242)

4. List ways adults can foster young children's literacy development. (p. 242)

____

____

Young Children's Mathematical Reasoning

1. In what order do children typically reach the following steps in the development of mathematical reasoning? (p. 243)
   ______ Use counting to solve arithmetic problems.
   ______ Display a beginning grasp of *ordinality*.
   ______ Grasp the principle of *cardinality*.
   ______ Begin to count.

2. (Cardinality / Ordinality) refers to order relationships between quantities. The principle of (cardinality / ordinality) states that the last number in a counting sequence indicates the quantity of items in a set. (p. 243)

3. Describe ways adults can promote preschoolers' mathematical skills. (p. 243)

____

____

Individual Differences in Mental Development

1. Why do low-SES and certain ethnic minority preschoolers often do poorly on intelligence tests? What steps can be taken to help improve their performance? (p. 244)

   A. ____

   B. ____

2. Intelligence tests (do / do not) sample all human abilities, and performance (is / is not) affected by cultural and situational factors. (p. 244)

3. True or False: By age 6 to 7, intelligence test scores are good predictors of later IQ and academic achievement. (p. 244)

Home Environment and Mental Development

1. Describe characteristics of homes that foster young children's intellectual growth. (p. 244)

____

____

____

2. True or False: When low-SES parents manage, despite daily pressures, to obtain high HOME scores, their preschoolers perform substantially better on tests of intelligence and emergent literacy skills. (p. 244)

Preschool, Kindergarten, and Child Care

1. Over the past several decades, the number of young children in preschool or child care has (decreased / increased). (p. 244)

2. A(n) ________________ is a program with planned educational experiences aimed at enhancing the development of 2- to 5-year-olds. In contrast, ________________ identifies a variety of arrangements for supervising children. (p. 244)

3. Describe the difference between *child-centered programs* and *academic programs*. (p. 245)

   Child-centered: ____

____

Academic: ____

____

4. How do formal academic programs affect preschoolers' motivation and emotional well-being? (p. 245)

____

____

____

5. ______________ education is a special type of (academic / child-centered) approach, which includes materials designed to promote exploration, child-chosen activities, and equal emphasis on academic and social development. (p. 245)
6. Describe the features of *Project Head Start*. (p. 245)

____

____

7. Describe the long-term benefits of exposure to cognitively enriching preschool. (pp. 245–246)

____

____

____

8. True or False: Gains in IQ and achievement scores from attending Head Start and other interventions are maintained across the school years. (p. 246)
9. Describe likely outcomes for children in substandard child care versus high-quality child care. (p. 246)

Substandard: ____

____

High quality: ____

____

Educational Media

1. Describe positive outcomes associated with watching children's educational television programs. (p. 247)

____

____

____

2. By age 2, (few / about half of / most) U.S. children regularly watch either TV or videos. (Low- / High-) SES children are more frequent viewers. (p. 247)
3. True or False: The more children watch prime-time shows and cartoons, the less time they spend reading and interacting with others and the poorer their academic skills. (p. 247)
4. How do computer word-processing programs support emergent literacy? (p. 248)

____

____

5. True or False: Computer programming experiences using simplified languages promote gains in preschoolers' problem-solving skills and metacognition. (p. 248)

Language Development

Vocabulary

1. Preschoolers learn an average of _____ new words each day, increasing their vocabulary from _____ words at age 2 to _______ at age 6. (p. 248)
2. Through ______________________, children connect new words with their underlying concepts after only a brief encounter. (p. 248)
3. Children in many language communities *fast-map* (labels for objects / verbs) especially rapidly, while (labels for objects / verbs) require more complex understandings. Modifiers expressing (general / specific) distinctions tend to appear earlier. (p. 248)
4. When learning new words, children may adopt a ___________________________ bias, in which they assume that words refer to entirely separate categories. They may also learn nouns based on the perceptual property of _______________. (pp. 248–249)
5. How do preschoolers differentiate objects that have more than one name? (p. 249)

   ____

   ____
6. True or False: Preschool children use social cues to identify word meanings. (p. 249)
7. Cite two criticisms of the view that children are innately biased to induce word meanings. (p. 249)

   A. ____

   B. ____
8. Some theorists believe that children draw on a coalition of ________________, ________________, and ________________ cues as they build vocabulary. (p. 249)

Grammar

1. True or False: All English-speaking children master grammatical markers in a regular sequence. (p. 249)
2. Once children acquire grammatical markers, they occasionally overextend the rules to words that are exceptions, a type of error called ________________________. (p. 250)
3. True or False: Most children demonstrate complete mastery of questions and passive sentences by age 2 or 3. (p. 250)
4. True or False: By the end of the preschool years, children use most of the grammatical constructions of their language competently. (p. 250)
5. How do information-processing theorists explain grammatical development? (p. 250)

   ____

   ____

Conversation

1. The practical, social side of language is called ___________________. (p. 250)
2. Cite evidence that at the beginning of early childhood, children are already skilled conversationalists. (p. 250)

   ____

   ____
3. By age 4, children (do / do not) adjust their speech to fit the age, sex, and social status of the listener. (p. 250)

4. Telephone talk provides an example of how preschoolers' competencies (are consistent throughout / depend upon the demands of) differing situations. (pp. 250–251)

Supporting Language Development in Early Childhood

1. True or False: When children make grammatical mistakes, overcorrection by adults can discourage children from freely using language. (p. 251)
2. Adults provide indirect feedback about grammar using two strategies. Briefly describe these strategies. (p. 251)

   Recasts: ____

   Expansions: ____

ASK YOURSELF . . .

For *Ask Yourself* questions for this chapter, along with feedback on the accuracy of your answers, please log on to MyDevelopmentLab (for registration and access, please visit mydevelopmentlab.com or follow the instructions on page ix).

(1) Select the Multimedia Library.

(2) Choose the explore option.

(3) Find your chapter from the drop down box.

(4) Click find now.

(5) Complete questions and choose "Submit answers for grading" or "Clear answers" to start over.

SUGGESTED READINGS

Clegg, J., & Ginsborg, J. (Eds.). (2006). *Language and social disadvantage: Theory into practice.* Hoboken, NJ: Wiley. A comprehensive look at language development in low-income children, this book explores the relationship between language and social and emotional development, including individual differences in language development, environmental influences on early language skills, processing of linguistic information, and the impact of language on academic achievement, self-esteem, self-regulation, and peer relationships.

Lillard, A. (2007). *Montessori: The science behind the genius.* New York: Oxford University Press. Presents an alternative to traditional educational practices by focusing on children's learning and cognition, their natural interest in learning, meaningful learning contexts, the importance of peers, and adult interaction styles and child outcomes.

Schneider, W., Schumann-Hengsteler, R., & Sodian, B. (2006). Young children's cognitive development: Interrelationships among executive functioning, working memory, verbal ability, and theory of mind. Mahwah, NJ: Erlbaum. Using research by leading experts in the field, this book examines how advances in information processing contribute to young children's cognitive development.

Singer, D. Hirsh-Pasek, K., & Golinkoff, R. (Eds.). (2006). *Play = Learning: How play motivates and enhances children's cognitive and social-emotional growth.* New York: Oxford University Press. A collection of chapters highlighting the diverse benefits of play for children's learning. The authors argue that in trying to create a generation of "Einsteins," many parents and educators are overlooking the importance of play in early child development.

CROSSWORD PUZZLE 7.1

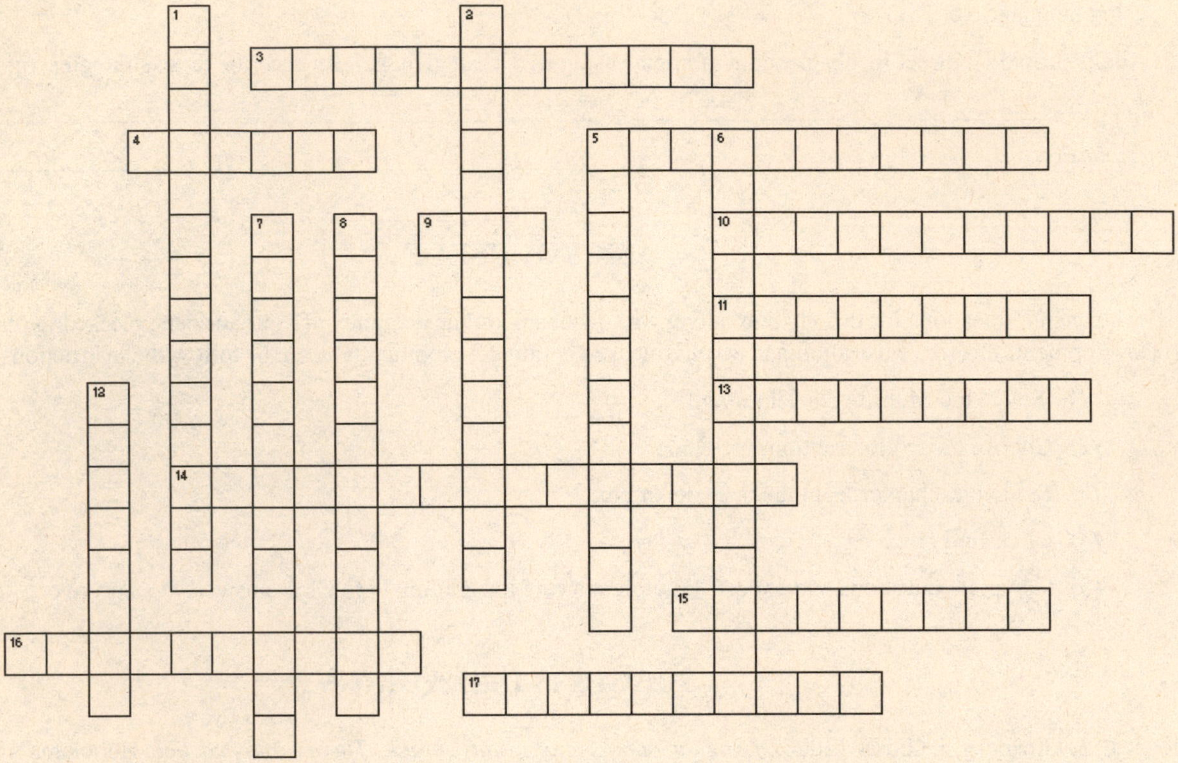

Across

3. ______ dwarfism: growth disorder caused by severe emotional deprivation
4. ______ hormone is necessary for development of nearly all body tissues.
5. Inner-brain structure which facilitates memory and images of space that help us find our way
9. Prompts the thyroid gland to produce thyroxine (abbr.)
10. The tendency to focus on one's own viewpoint and ignore others' perspectives
11. The ______ gland, located near the base of the brain, releases hormones that affect physical growth.
13. ______ formation: structure in the brain stem that maintains alertness and consciousness
14. Inability to mentally reverse a series of steps in a problem, returning to the starting point
15. ______ thinking: belief that inanimate objects have lifelike qualities
16. Tendency to focus on one aspect of a situation to the exclusion of other important features
17. Brain structure that aids in balance and control of body movements

Down

1. Dual ______ : viewing a symbolic object as both an object in its own right and as a symbol
2. Bundle of fibers that connects the two hemispheres of the brain (2 words)
5. ______ classification: organizing objects into classes and subclasses
6. Piaget's second stage; rapid development of representation takes place
7. ______ play: make-believe play with others
8. Understanding that certain physical properties remain the same, even when their appearance changes
12. The ______ cerebral hemisphere is responsible for skilled motor action.

CROSSWORD PUZZLE 7.2

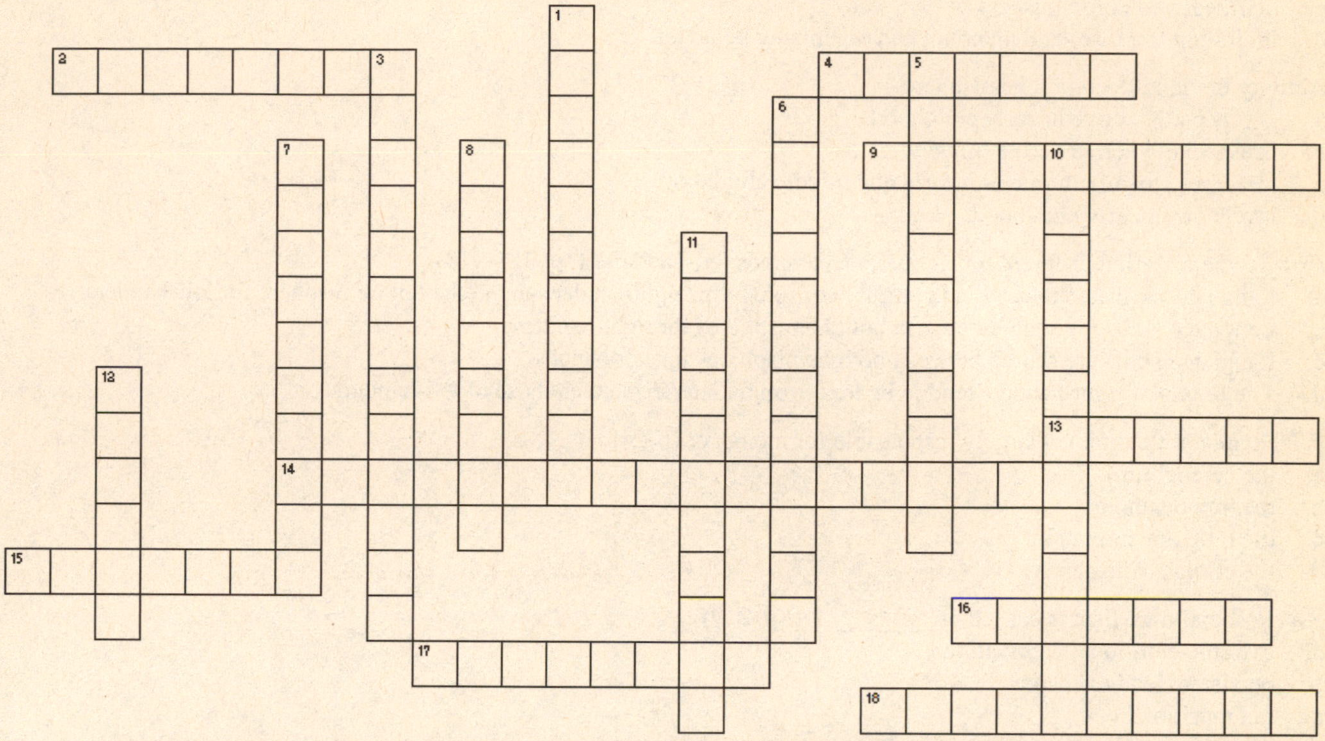

Across

2. ______ preschool programs are teacher-structured and promote and academic skills through repetition.
4. Adult responses that restructure children's incorrect speech into a more mature form
9. The practical, social side of language, concerned with effective and appropriate communication
13. ______ participation: shared endeavors between more expert and less expert participants
14. Extending grammatical rules to words that are exceptions
15. General descriptions of what occurs and when it occurs in a particular situation
16. ______ speech: self-directed speech that children use to plan and guide their own behavior
17. ______ literacy: attempts to figure out how written symbols convey meaning
18. Order relationships between quantities

Down

1. Adults adjust the assistance they provide to fit the child's current level of performance.
3. ______-______ preschool programs focus on free play and provide children with options. (2 words, hyph.)
5. The last number in a counting sequence indicates the quantity of items in the set.
6. ______ awareness: ability to reflect on and manipulate the sound structure of spoken language
7. Adult responses that elaborate on children's speech, increasing its complexity
8. Project _____: provides preschool for low-SES children and encourages parent involvement (2 words)
10. Thinking about thought; awareness of mental activities
11. Connecting a new word with an underlying concept after only a brief encounter (2 words, hyph.)
12 ______ strategies: deliberate mental activities that improve the likelihood of remembering

PRACTICE TEST #1

1. From early to middle childhood, the frontal-lobe areas devoted to __________ grow rapidly. (p. 217)
   a. spatial skills
   b. abstract thinking
   c. alertness and consciousness
   d. inhibiting impulses and planning and organizing behavior

2. Activity in the left cerebral hemisphere __________ (p. 217)
   a. is especially active in early childhood.
   b. is especially active during infancy.
   c. increases steadily throughout early and middle childhood.
   d. levels off in early childhood.

3. How is lateralization different for right-handers versus left-handers? (pp. 217–218)
   a. Language skills are housed in the right hemisphere for right-handers and in the left hemisphere for left-handers.
   b. Language skills are shared between both hemispheres for right-handers.
   c. Language skills are shared between both hemispheres for left-handers.
   d. The brains of right-handers tend to be less strongly lateralized than those of left-handers.

4. Which area of the brain is largely responsible for memory? (p. 218)
   a. the cerebellum
   b. the hippocampus
   c. the reticular formation
   d. the corpus callosum

5. Psychosocial dwarfism is caused by __________ (p. 219)
   a. extreme emotional deprivation.
   b. persistent lead exposure.
   c. malnutrition.
   d. overactive GH secretion.

6. Longitudinal research indicates that ____________________ seem(s) to heighten lead-induced damage. (p. 220)
   a. being overweight
   b. long hours in child care
   c. living in rural areas
   d. a stressed, disorganized home life

7. In developing countries, widespread diarrhea caused by __________ leads to growth stunting and death. (p. 221)
   a. unsafe water and contaminated foods
   b. poor nutrition
   c. infectious disease
   d. high zinc intake

8. Childhood immunizations __________ (p. 222)
   a. have contributed to the rising number of children diagnosed with autism.
   b. have led to a dramatic decline in childhood diseases in the past half century.
   c. are unnecessary for healthy and well-nourished children.
   d. have had little impact on rates of childhood diseases in industrialized nations.

9. What is the leading cause of childhood mortality in industrialized nations? (p. 222)
   a. child abuse
   b. infectious disease
   c. malnutrition
   d. unintentional injuries

10. Which of the following statements about sex differences in motor skills is true? (p. 226)
    a. By age 5, boys are ahead of girls in skills that emphasize force and power.
    b. Sex differences in motor skills are not yet evident in early childhood.
    c. Girls' overall physical maturity explains why they can jump slightly farther and run slightly faster than boys.
    d. Boys' overall physical maturity explains why they are ahead of girls in all fine and gross motor skills.

11. Research shows that make-believe play __________ (p. 228)
    a. is mainly valuable as practice of representational schemes.
    b. is less important for overall development than academic training.
    c. reflects, but does not contribute to, children's social and cognitive skills.
    d. strengthens a wide variety of mental abilities.

12. Children master dual representation through __________ (p. 229)
    a. hearing stories about supernatural or magical events.
    b. practice with counting.
    c. experiences with diverse symbols, including photos and maps.
    d. opportunities to practice fine motor skills, such as cutting with scissors.

13. Piaget believed that the most fundamental deficiency of preoperational thinking is __________ (p. 229)
    a. trouble with dual representation.
    b. magical thinking.
    c. egocentrism.
    d. centration.

14. Piaget's famous class inclusion problem demonstrated the difficulty preschoolers have with __________ (p. 230)
    a. egocentrism.
    b. conservation.
    c. centration.
    d. hierarchical classification.

15. Contemporary researchers have challenged Piaget's belief that young children are wholly egocentric, pointing out that __________ (p. 230)
    a. preschoolers rarely adapt their speech to fit the needs of their listeners.
    b. when the three-mountains problem includes familiar objects, 4-year-olds show awareness of others' vantage points.
    c. toddlers are unable to infer others' intentions.
    d. preschoolers are only egocentric in face-to-face conversations.

16. Preschoolers categorize objects by __________ (p. 231)
    a. texture.
    b. location.
    c. appearance.
    d. function or behavior.

17. Between ages 4 and 7, children __________ (p. 233)
    a. show the beginnings of abstract thinking.
    b. believe that magic can alter everyday experiences.
    c. replace magical beliefs with more plausible explanations.
    d. spend less time in make-believe play than toddlers.

18. In a Piagetian classroom, __________ (p. 233)
    a. teachers speed up development by imposing new skills.
    b. teachers evaluate students based on normative standards and average performance.
    c. children are encouraged to discover for themselves.
    d. children are presented with ready-made knowledge.

19. As 3-year-old Kylene builds a tower of blocks, she says to herself, "Here is a big block. That goes there. And on the top, I put the square one. What block next?" Piaget called these utterances __________ speech. (p. 234)
    a. egocentric
    b. inner
    c. private
    d. self-guided

20. Adult emotional support during difficult tasks predicts gains in children's __________ (p. 235)
    a. private speech.
    b. effort.
    c. abstract reasoning.
    d. anxiety.

21. Yucatec Mayan parents conclude that their children are ready for more responsibility __________ (p. 236)
    a. once they complete elementary school.
    b. when the children seem bored and disengaged with their current roles.
    c. when they see the children imitate adult tasks.
    d. when the children verbally express their desire to tackle harder tasks.

22. Which of the following statements about preschoolers' memory is true? (p. 238)
    a. Both recognition and recall memory are remarkably good during the preschool years.
    b. Preschoolers perform poorly on both recognition and recall tasks.
    c. Preschoolers' recall is far greater than their recognition.
    d. Preschoolers' recognition is far greater than their recall.

23. When asked the question, "Can you tell me what happens when you go to the doctor's office?" Yvonne answers, "The nurse gives you a shot, the doctor checks your heart, you get a lollipop, and then you go home." This is an example of a(n) __________ (p. 238)
    a. verbatim memory.
    b. autobiographical memory.
    c. script.
    d. semantic memory.

24. Most 3-year-olds understand that __________ (p. 239)
    a. both desires and beliefs affect people's behavior.
    b. a person can think about something without seeing, touching, or talking about it.
    c. false beliefs can guide people's actions.
    d. other people have different beliefs and knowledge than their own.

25. Which of the following is a characteristic of autism? (p. 241)
    a. absorption in make-believe play
    b. advanced language skills
    c. early mastery of false-belief tasks
    d. narrow, intense interests

26. By age 4, most children grasp the principle of __________, which increases the efficiency of their counting. (p. 243)
    a. ordinality
    b. cardinality
    c. phonological awareness
    d. emergent mathematics

27. Research on the effectiveness of Head Start consistently shows that __________ (p. 246)
    a. children who attend Head Start score lower than controls in IQ and achievement during the first two years of elementary school.
    b. children who attend Head Start are as likely as controls to drop out of high school.
    c. gains in IQ and achievement test scores from attending Head Start quickly dissolve.
    d. children who attend Head Start demonstrate greater gains in IQ and achievement than children who attend university-based intervention programs.

28. Research shows that children are able to build their vocabularies quickly through a process called __________ (p. 248)
    a. metacognition.
    b. fast-mapping.
    c. scripting.
    d. ordinality.

29. Information-processing theorists believe that children __________ (p. 250)
    a. learn language in an abrupt, stagelike fashion.
    b. have a universal language-processing device.
    c. search for consistencies and patterns in language, as in all cognitive development.
    d. learn grammar mainly through direct instruction.

30. Which of the following is consistently related to preschoolers' language progress? (p. 251)
    a. adults' correction of children's grammatical mistakes
    b. children's interaction with more skilled speakers
    c. attending an academic preschool program
    d. early phonics instruction

PRACTICE TEST #2

1. Between ages 2 to 6, __________ (p. 216)
   a. brain growth tapers off, whereas body growth increases rapidly.
   b. children acquire more fat than muscle.
   c. children gradually become thinner.
   d. girls become slightly more muscular than boys.

2. Which of the following provides evidence that the two brain hemispheres continue to lateralize during early and middle childhood? (p. 217)
   a. Between ages 2 and 6, the brain increases to 90 percent of its adult weight.
   b. By age 4, many parts of the cerebral cortex have overproduced synapses.
   c. Both spatial skills and language skills improve rapidly in early childhood.
   d. The two hemispheres develop at different rates in early childhood.

3. Which of the following skills is typically housed in the left cerebral hemisphere? (p. 217)
   a. using language
   b. drawing pictures
   c. giving directions
   d. recognizing geometric shapes

4. The cerebellum __________ (p. 218)
   a. connects the two cerebral hemispheres.
   b. maintains alertness and consciousness.
   c. aids in balance and control of body movement.
   d. provides spatial images to help us find our way.

5. An absence of thyroxine at birth __________ (p. 219)
   a. results in mental retardation and stunted growth.
   b. results in cardiac distress.
   c. causes anoxia.
   d. causes physical deformities and blindness.

6. Research shows that persistent childhood lead exposure __________ (p. 220)
   a. leads to temporary cognitive deficits.
   b. contributes to cognitive and behavior problems, particularly in low-SES children.
   c. primarily affects children in rural areas.
   d. affects all children similarly, regardless of diet or quality of home life.

7. Worldwide, 70 percent of deaths of children under age 5 are due to __________ (p. 221)
   a. anemia.
   b. accidents.
   c. infectious diseases.
   d. starvation.

8. Childhood injuries __________ (p. 222)
   a. are highest in rural areas.
   b. primarily occur in child-care centers.
   c. are much less frequent in the United States than in other industrialized nations.
   d. occur within a complex ecological system.

9. Children are first able to draw representational forms, such as a picture of a person, at age __________ (p. 225)
   a. 1 to 2.
   b. 3 to 4.
   c. 5 to 6.
   d. 7 to 8.

10. Three-year-old Jenna holds up a spoon, pretending that it is a flower. Her 18-month-old sister Maggie grabs the spoon, holds it to her mouth, and says "yum, yum." What accounts for this difference in the sisters' play? (p. 228)
    a. Until age 2, toddlers are incapable of pretending.
    b. After age 2, children's play becomes more self-centered.
    c. Children younger than age 2 are unable to detach play from real-life associations.
    d. Children begin to experiment with sociodramatic play around age 3.

11. Piaget's three-mountains problem demonstrates that preoperational children __________ (p. 229)
    a. have poor planning skills.
    b. are easily distracted by the perceptual appearance of objects.
    c. focus on one aspect of a situation, neglecting other important features.
    d. fail to distinguish the symbolic viewpoints of others from one's own.

12. When 3-year-old Farid tells his mother that his blanket will be lonely without him, he is demonstrating __________ (p. 229)
    a. animistic thinking.
    b. egocentrism.
    c. irreversibility.
    d. illogical thought.

13. When water is poured from a tall glass into a short, wide container, a preoperational child is likely to __________ (p. 229)
    a. believe that the amount of water has remained the same.
    b. believe that the amount of water has changed.
    c. ignore the perceptual differences between the two containers.
    d. point out the dynamic transformation between the glass and the container.

14. Preschoolers seem to reason logically when considering __________ (p. 231)
    a. an overwhelming amount of information.
    b. contradictory facts they cannot reconcile.
    c. unfamiliar topics.
    d. familiar objects or contexts.

15. Follow-up research on Piaget's stage concept suggests that __________ (p. 232)
    a. preschoolers cannot be trained to perform well on Piagetian problems.
    b. operational thinking develops rapidly during the preschool years.
    c. operational thinking develops gradually during the preschool years.
    d. children move from the preoperational to the concrete operational stage around age 5.

16. Piaget believed that children learn __________ (p. 233)
    a. through acting on the environment.
    b. through observing the environment.
    c. through social dialogues.
    d. best when adults provide highly-structured, academic tasks.

17. Vygotsky believed that children use private speech __________ (p. 234)
    a. to ease anxiety.
    b. to relieve boredom.
    c. to ask for adult assistance.
    d. for self-guidance.

18. In Virgil's classroom, the teacher creates mixed ability groups and encourages all students to participate and help one another with projects and assignments. This classroom style is consistent with Vygotsky's concept of __________ (p. 235)
    a. scaffolding.
    b. intersubjectivity.
    c. peer collaboration.
    d. peer–teacher collaboration.

19. Research reveals that children in village and tribal cultures who spend their days in contact with adult work __________ (p. 236)
    a. rely on conversation to learn new tasks.
    b. rarely engage in make-believe play.
    c. are unable to sit still for long periods.
    d. are less self-sufficient than Western children.

20. Piaget paid far more attention than Vygotsky to the __________ (p. 237)
    a. development of basic cognitive processes.
    b. role of language in children's development.
    c. social context of cognitive development.
    d. importance of teacher-directed learning activities.

21. Research on planning indicates that __________ (pp. 237–238)
    a. as early as age 3, children are skilled at generating and following complex plans.
    b. even when young children design effective plans, they often forget to implement important steps.
    c. on tasks with several steps, preschoolers are able to decide what to do first and what to do next in an orderly fashion.
    d. most preschoolers can generate but cannot follow a plan.

22. Even preschoolers with good language skills recall poorly because they are not yet skilled at using __________ (p. 238)
    a. categorization.
    b. inference.
    c. recognition.
    d. memory strategies.

23. Which of the following questions illustrates the elaborative style of eliciting children's autobiographical narratives? (p. 238)
    a. "Do you remember what we did at the playground today?"
    b. "Who did you see at the playground?"
    c. "I was scared when you went so high on the swing! How did you feel?"
    d. "Did you have fun going down the slide?"

24. Preschoolers typically believe that __________ (p. 240)
    a. events must be directly observed to be known.
    b. people continue to think even when there are no obvious cues that they are thinking.
    c. mental inferences can be a source of knowledge.
    d. the mind is an active, constructive agent.

25. Researchers agree that autism __________ (p. 241)
    a. can be cured if treated aggressively in early childhood.
    b. is caused by immunizations given in infancy and toddlerhood.
    c. results from maternal illness during pregnancy and malnutrition in infancy and toddlerhood.
    d. stems from abnormal brain functioning, usually due to genetic or prenatal environmental causes.

26. Research suggests that children in academic preschool and kindergarten programs __________ than children in child-centered programs. (p. 245)
    a. are more confident in their abilities
    b. display more stress behaviors
    c. make more academic gains
    d. are more socially advanced

27. What kind of television programs have been linked to gains in early literacy and math skills? (p. 247)
    a. *Sesame Street* and similar educational programs
    b. programs with a rapid-paced format
    c. programs designed for babies under 1 year of age
    d. No television programs have been linked to gains in early literacy or math.

28. Two-year-old Mei often utters sentences like "I *eated* my breakfast." Why does Mei make such grammatical errors? (p. 250)
    a. She is mimicking the incorrect English grammar she hears at home.
    b. She has not yet mastered the passive form.
    c. She is overregularizing the past-tense marker.
    d. She is incapable of pronouncing the words correctly.

29. A 5-year-old who is able to adjust his speech depending on whether the listener is his baby brother, a classmate, or a teacher understands the __________ of language. (p. 250)
    a. complex grammatical structures
    b. pragmatics
    c. categories
    d. origins

30. Young Colleen says, "I go school, too." Her mother says, "Yes, you are going to school, too." Her mother's response would be classified as __________ (p. 251)
    a. repetition and correction.
    b. correction and reflection.
    c. rejection and restatement.
    d. recast and expansion.

CHAPTER 8
EMOTIONAL AND SOCIAL DEVELOPMENT IN EARLY CHILDHOOD

BRIEF CHAPTER SUMMARY

Erikson identified the psychological conflict of the preschool years as initiative versus guilt. Through play, children practice using new skills and cooperating to achieve common goals. Conscience development prompts children to feel guilt for disobeying society's standards; excessive guilt interferes with initiative.

As preschoolers think more intently about themselves, they construct a self-concept, or set of beliefs about their own characteristics, that consists largely of observable characteristics and typical emotions and attitudes. Through conversations with adults, children develop autobiographical memory—a life-story narrative that is more coherent and lasting than the isolated memories of the first few years. By age 4, children develop several separate self-judgments based on performance in different areas; together, these make up self-esteem, which affects long-term psychological adjustment.

Between ages 2 and 6, children make gains in emotional competence, experiencing self-conscious emotions, such as pride and shame, as well as empathy. By age 4 or 5, children can correctly judge the causes of many basic emotions and understand that thinking and feeling are related. Emotional outbursts decline as children use effortful control to achieve emotional self-regulation. Temperament plays a role, as do children's observations of adult strategies for handling their own feelings. To induce adaptive levels of shame and pride, parents should focus on how to improve performance and should avoid labeling the child.

The capacity for empathy, an important motivator of prosocial behavior, increases as children develop the ability to take another's perspective. Preschoolers form first friendships with peers and move from nonsocial activity to parallel play and then to social interaction. The beginnings of moral development are evident by age 2, when children can evaluate behavior as good or bad. Conscience gradually comes to be regulated by inner standards. Children whose parents discipline with physical punishment or withdrawal of affection tend to misbehave more often and feel little guilt. A more effective disciplinary approach is induction, in which an adult supports conscience formation and encourages empathy and sympathy by pointing out the effects of misbehavior on others.

According to social learning theory, morality is acquired through reinforcement and modeling—observing and imitating people who behave appropriately. Children are most willing to imitate models who exhibit warmth and responsiveness, competence and power, and consistency. Punishment is an ineffective disciplinary tactic, promoting momentary compliance but not lasting change. Positive alternatives, such as time out and withdrawal of privileges, are more effective. Unfortunately, use of corporal punishment is common in North America.

All children occasionally display aggression. Proactive aggression occurs when a child wants something and attacks a person who is in the way, while reactive aggression is intended to hurt another person. Proactive and reactive aggression come in at least three forms: physical, verbal, or relational. A conflict-ridden family atmosphere and exposure to media violence promote aggressive behavior, leading children to see the world from a violent perspective. Treatment for aggressive children should begin early to break the cycle of hostilities between family members and promote effective ways of relating to others, while also teaching parents effective techniques for interacting with an aggressive child.

Gender typing develops rapidly in the preschool years. Heredity, through prenatal hormones, contributes to boys' higher activity level and overt aggression and to children's preference for same-sex playmates. At the same time, parents, teachers, peers, and the broader social environment encourage many gender-typed responses. Masculine and androgynous identities are linked to better psychological adjustment. Neither cognitive-developmental theory nor social learning theory provides a complete account of the development of gender identity. Gender schema theory is an information-processing approach to gender typing that combines social learning and cognitive developmental features. It emphasizes that both environmental pressures and children's cognitions combine to shape gender-role development. Parents and teachers help children avoid gender stereotyping by modeling and providing alternatives to traditional gender.

Child-rearing styles can be distinguished on the basis of three features: acceptance and involvement, control, and autonomy granting. The most successful style is authoritative child rearing, which combines high acceptance and involvement, adaptive control techniques, and appropriate autonomy granting. Authoritarian child rearing is low in acceptance, involvement, and autonomy granting, and high in coercive control. The permissive style is warm and accepting, but uninvolved. Uninvolved parenting is low in acceptance, involvement, and control; at the extreme, it can be considered neglect.

Child maltreatment, which can take the form of neglect or physical, sexual, or emotional abuse, is the result of many interacting variables at the family, community, and cultural levels. Interventions at all of these levels are essential for preventing it.

LEARNING OBJECTIVES

After reading this chapter, you should be able to:

8.1 Describe Erikson's stage of initiative versus guilt, noting major personality changes of early childhood. (p. 256)

8.2 Discuss preschoolers' self-understanding, including characteristics of self-concepts and the emergence of self-esteem. (pp. 256–258)

8.3 Cite changes in the understanding and expression of emotion during early childhood, along with factors that influence those changes. (pp. 258–259)

8.4 Explain how language and temperament contribute to the development of emotional self-regulation during the preschool years. (p. 259)

8.5 Discuss the development of self-conscious emotions, empathy, sympathy, and prosocial behavior during early childhood, noting the influence of parenting. (pp. 259–261)

8.6 Describe advances in peer sociability and in friendship in early childhood, along with cultural and parental influences on early peer relations. (pp. 261–264)

8.7 Compare psychoanalytic, social learning, and cognitive-developmental approaches to moral development, and cite child-rearing practices that support or undermine moral understanding. (pp. 264–269)

8.8 Describe the development of aggression in early childhood, noting the influences of family and television, and cite strategies for controlling aggressive behavior. (pp. 269–272)

8.9 Discuss genetic and environmental influences on preschoolers' gender-stereotyped beliefs and behavior. (pp. 273–276)

8.10 Describe and evaluate the accuracy of major theories of gender identity, including ways to reduce gender stereotyping in young children. (pp. 276–278)

8.11 Describe the impact of child-rearing styles on child development, explain why authoritative parenting is effective, and note cultural variations in child-rearing beliefs and practices. (pp. 278–281)

8.12 Discuss the multiple origins of child maltreatment, its consequences for development, and effective prevention. (pp. 281–283)

STUDY QUESTIONS

1. True or False: In the preschool years, cooperative exchanges are more common than grabbing, hitting, and pushing. (p. 255)

Erikson's Theory: Initiative versus Guilt

1. Describe Erikson's psychological conflict of the preschool years, *initiative versus guilt*. (p. 256)

____

____

____

2. Summarize two ways in which children learn about themselves and their social world through play, according to Erikson. (p. 256)

   A. ____

   B. ____

3. According to Erikson, what leads to a negative resolution of initiative versus guilt? (p. 256)

____

____

____

Self-Understanding

1. As self-awareness strengthens, preschoolers focus more intently on qualities that make the self unique, and they begin to develop a ________________. (p. 256)

Foundations of Self-Concept

1. Preschoolers' *self-concepts* are very (abstract / concrete). (p. 256)
2. Check all of the following that are likely to be included in preschoolers' self-descriptions. (p. 256)
   _____ Observable characteristics, such as name and possessions
   _____ Typical emotions and attitudes
   _____ Direct references to personality traits
3. The stronger children's self-definition, the (less / more) possessive they tend to be. Given this information, how can adults promote friendly peer interaction? (p. 257)

____

____

Cultural Influences: Cultural Variations in Personal Storytelling: Implications for Early Self-Concept

1. How do Chinese and Irish-American parents differ in their personal storytelling with young children? (p. 257)

   Chinese: ____

   ____

   Irish-American: ____

   ____

2. How do early narratives about the child launch preschoolers' self-concepts on culturally distinct paths? (p. 257)

   Chinese: ____

   ____

   Irish-American: ____

   ____

Emergence of Self-Esteem

1. Cite an example of a common self-judgment in early childhood. (p. 258)

____

2. True or False: When making self-evaluations, preschoolers tend to rate their own ability as extremely low and often overestimate task difficulty. (p. 258)

3. List three ways adults can avoid promoting low *self-esteem* and self-defeating reactions in preschoolers. (p. 258)

   A. ______________________________

   B. ______________________________

   C. ______________________________

Emotional Development

1. List three developmental gains that support emotional development in early childhood. (p. 258)

   A. ______________________________

   B. ______________________________

   C. ______________________________

Understanding Emotion

1. Preschoolers' explanations of basic emotions tend to emphasize (external / internal) factors over (external / internal) states, a balance that changes with age. (p. 258)

2. Check all of the following statements that accurately characterize preschoolers' emotional understanding. (pp. 258–259) Preschoolers . . .

   _____ can predict what a playmate expressing a certain emotion might do next.
   _____ do not realize that thinking and feeling are interconnected.
   _____ skillfully interpret situations that offer conflicting cues about how a person is feeling.
   _____ focus on the most obvious aspect of an emotional situation, neglecting other relevant information.

3. What can parents do to foster their child's ability to interpret others' emotions? (p. 259)

   ____

   ____

4. True or False: Attachment security is unrelated to preschoolers' emotional understanding. (p. 259)

5. Explain the relationship between emotion talk and peer interaction during the preschool years. (p. 259)

   ____

   ____

   ____

Emotional Self-Regulation

1. True or False: Language contributes to preschoolers' improved emotional self-regulation. (p. 259)

2. List three strategies that preschoolers use to blunt emotions. (p. 259)

   A. ______________________________

   B. ______________________________

   C. ______________________________

3. How are preschoolers likely to benefit from emotional self-regulation and effortful control? (p. 259)

____

____

____

4. True or False: Emotionally reactive children are more likely to be anxious and fearful. (p. 259)

5. Explain how parents influence the development of emotional self-regulation in early childhood. (p. 259)

____

____

6. Cite two reasons why fears are common in early childhood. (p. 259)

A. ______________________________

B. ______________________________

Self-Conscious Emotions

1. Indicate which of the following statements are accurate characterizations of preschoolers' self-conscious emotions. (p. 259)

Preschoolers . . .
_____ are not yet sensitive to praise and blame.
_____ do not display a clear link between self-conscious emotions and self-evaluation.
_____ depend on the messages of adults to know when to feel proud, ashamed, or guilty.
_____ often view adult expectations as obligatory rules.

2. Explain the role of parental feedback in the development of shame and pride. (pp. 259–260)

____

____

____

3. Among Western children, intense (guilt / shame) is associated with feelings of personal inadequacy. In contrast, (guilt / shame), as long as it occurs in appropriate circumstances, is related to good adjustment, perhaps because it helps children resist harmful impulses. (p. 260)

Empathy

1. Empathy serves as an important motivator of ______________________ *behavior*, or actions that benefit another person without any expected reward for the self. (p. 260)

2. True or False: In some children, empathizing with an upset peer or adult escalates into personal distress. (p. 260)

3. (Empathy / *Sympathy*) is feeling with another person and responding emotionally in a similar way, while (empathy / *sympathy*) involves feelings of concern or sorrow for another's plight. (p. 260)

4. Explain how temperament affects empathy and sympathy. (p. 261)

____

____

____

5. Describe the differential impact of warm parenting and punitive parenting on the development of empathy and sympathy. (p. 261)

   Warm parenting: ______________________________

   ____

   Punitive parenting: ______________________________

   ____

Peer Relations

Advances in Peer Sociability

1. Match Parten's stages of social development with the appropriate descriptions. (p. 261)

   _____ Children engage in separate activities but exchange toys and comment on one another's behavior
   _____ An advanced type of interaction in which children orient toward a common goal
   _____ A child plays near other children with similar materials but does not try to influence their behavior
   _____ Unoccupied, onlooker behavior and solitary play

   A. *Nonsocial activity*
   B. *Parallel play*
   C. *Associative play*
   D. *Cooperative play*

2. Longitudinal research shows that Parten's play types (do / do not) emerge in a developmental sequence. Later-appearing play types (do / do not) replace earlier ones. (p. 261)

3. True or False: The type, rather than the amount, of solitary and parallel play changes during early childhood. (p. 262)

4. Cite three types of nonsocial activity in preschoolers that are cause for concern. (p. 262)

   A. ______________________________

   B. ______________________________

   C. ______________________________

5. True or False: Most preschoolers with low rates of peer interaction simply like to play alone, and their solitary activities are positive and constructive. (p. 262)

6. True or False: Peer sociability takes essentially the same form in collectivist and individualistic cultures. (p. 262)

7. Provide an example of how cultural beliefs influence early peer associations. (p. 263)

   ____

   ____

   ____

First Friendships

1. Check all of the following statements that accurately describe preschoolers' understanding of friendship. (p. 263)
   Preschoolers view friendship as . . .
   _____ pleasurable play and sharing of toys.
   _____ a relationship with someone "who likes you."
   _____ having a long-term, enduring quality.
   _____ based on mutual trust.

2. Describe three unique qualities of preschoolers' interactions with friends. (p. 263)

   A. ______________________________

   B. ______________________________

   C. ______________________________

3. True or False: Social maturity in early childhood contributes to academic performance. (p. 263)

Parental Influences on Early Peer Relations

1. Explain how parents directly influence children's peer sociability. (pp. 263–264)

   ____

   ____

   ____

2. What social outcomes are linked with secure attachments to parents? (p. 264)

   ____

   ____

3. Research suggests that mothers' play is more strongly linked to (daughters' / sons') social competence, and fathers' play to (daughters' / sons') social competence. (p. 264)

Foundations of Morality

1. Cite three points on which most major theories of moral development agree. (p. 264)

   A. ______________________________

   B. ______________________________

   C. ______________________________

2. Match each of the following theories of moral development with its emphasis. (p. 264)

_____	Emotional side of conscience development, with emphasis on identification and guilt as motivators of good conduct	A. Social learning theory
_____	Thinking, specifically children's ability to reason about justice and fairness	B. Psychoanalytic theory
_____	Moral behavior is learned through reinforcement and modeling	C. Cognitive-developmental theory

The Psychoanalytic Perspective

1. Summarize Freud's psychoanalytic theory of moral development. (p. 264)

   ____

   ____

   ____

2. True or False: Most researchers agree with Freud's assertion that fear of punishment and loss of parental love motivates conscience formation. (p. 264)

3. A type of discipline called ____________ supports conscience development. Why is this form of discipline successful? (p. 265)

____

____

____

4. Why is discipline that relies too heavily on threats of punishment less effective than *induction*? (p. 265)

____

____

5. Mild, patient tactics are sufficient to prompt guilt reactions in (anxious, fearful / fearless, impulsive) children. (p. 265)

6. How can parents of impulsive children foster conscience development? (p. 265)

____

____

7. True or False: Freud was incorrect in his assertion that guilt is an important motivator of moral action. (p. 265)

8. ____________________ guilt reactions are associated with stopping harmful actions, repairing damage caused by misdeeds, and engaging in future prosocial behavior. (p. 265)

Social Learning Theory

1. Why is operant conditioning insufficient for children to acquire moral responses? (pp. 265–266)

____

____

2. Social learning theorists believe that children learn to behave morally largely through ____________—observing and imitating people who demonstrate appropriate behavior. (p. 266)

3. List three characteristics of models that affect children's willingness to imitate them. (p. 266)

   A. ____

   B. ____

   C. ____

4. Models are most influential in (early / middle) childhood. (p. 266)

5. Indicate which of the following are true of harsh punishment. (pp. 266–267)
   Harsh punishment . . .
   _____ promotes immediate compliance.
   _____ fosters lasting changes in behavior.
   _____ often models aggression.
   _____ encourages a sympathetic orientation to others' needs.
   _____ decreases opportunities to teach desirable behaviors.
   _____ provides adults with immediate relief, and thus may spiral into serious abuse.
   _____ rarely transfers to future generations.

6. Describe two alternatives to harsh punishment. (p. 268)

   A. ____

   B. ____

7. Describe three ways that parents can increase the effectiveness of punishment. (p. 268)
   A. ______________________________
   B. ______________________________
   C. ______________________________

8. List three ways parents can effectively encourage good conduct, reducing the need for punishment. (p. 268)
   A. ______________________________
   B. ______________________________
   C. ______________________________

Cultural Influences: Ethnic Differences in the Consequences of Physical Punishment

1. True or False: Use of physical punishment is highest among low-SES ethnic minority parents. (p. 267)

2. How is physical punishment in early and middle childhood related to adolescent outcomes in Caucasian- and African-American families? (p. 267)

   Caucasian-American: ______________________________

   ____

   African-American: ______________________________

   ____

3. How do Caucasian-American and African-American beliefs about physical punishment differ? (p. 267)

   Caucasian-American: ______________________________

   ____

   African-American: ______________________________

   ____

4. True or False: According to one study, spanking is associated with a rise in behavior problems if parents are cold and rejecting, but not if they are warm and supportive. (p. 267)

The Cognitive-Developmental Perspective

1. The (cognitive-developmental / psychoanalytic and behaviorist) approach(es) focus(es) on how children acquire ready-made standards of good conduct. The (cognitive-developmental / psychoanalytic and behaviorist) approach(es) regard(s) children as active thinkers about social rules. (p. 269)

2. Match the following terms with their descriptions. (p. 269)

_____ Protect people's rights and welfare	A. *Social conventions*
_____ Do not violate rights and are up to the individual	B. *Matters of personal choice*
_____ Are determined solely by consensus	C. *Moral imperatives*

3. True or False: Preschool and young school-age children tend to reason rigidly within the moral domain. (p. 269)

4. Explain how young children learn to make distinctions between moral imperatives and social conventions. (p. 269)

   ____

   ____

The Other Side of Morality: Development of Aggression

1. Match each type of aggression with its appropriate description. (p. 269)

_____	Children act to fulfill a need or desire and unemotionally attack a person to achieve their goal	A.	*Relational aggression*
_____	Angry, defensive response to provocation or a blocked goal; meant to hurt another person	B.	*Verbal aggression*
_____	Harms others through physical injury—pushing, hitting, kicking, punching others, or destroying another's property	C.	*Proactive aggression*
_____	Damages another's peer relationships through social exclusion, malicious gossip, or friendship manipulation	D.	*Reactive aggression*
_____	Harms others through threats of physical aggression, name-calling, or hostile teasing	E.	*Physical aggression*

2. Destroying property is an example of (direct / indirect) aggression, while hitting is an example of (direct / indirect) aggression. (pp. 269–270)

3. In early childhood, (physical / verbal) aggression is gradually replaced by (physical / verbal) aggression. (p. 270)

4. In early childhood, proactive aggression (declines / increases), while reactive aggression (declines / increases). (p. 270)

5. Summarize three reasons why boys are more physically aggressive than girls. (p. 270)

   A. ______________________________

   B. ______________________________

   C. ______________________________

6. True or False: Rates of verbal and relational aggression are much higher for girls than for boys. (p. 270)

7. Describe family interactions that create a conflict-ridden atmosphere and an "out-of-control" child. (p. 270)

   ____

   ____

   ____

8. (Boys / Girls) are more likely to be targets of harsh, inconsistent discipline. (p. 270)

9. True or False: Children's television programming typically contains far less violence than other programming. (p. 271)

10. Explain why preschoolers and young school-age children are especially likely to imitate TV violence. (p. 271)

    ____

    ____

11. Describe the lasting negative consequences of childhood exposure to violent television. (p. 271)

    ____

    ____

    ____

12. True or False: TV violence hardens children to aggression, making them more willing to tolerate it in others. Briefly explain your answer. (p. 271)

    ____

    ____

13. Describe how Canada and the United States have intervened to regulate children's television programming. (pp. 271–272)

    Canada: ______

    United States: ______

14. List several strategies parents can use to regulate children's media exposure. (p. 272)

    A. ______

    B. ______

    C. ______

15. To reduce children's aggression, list several ways of intervening with both parents and children. (p. 272)

    Parents:

    A. ______

    B. ______

    C. ______

    Children:

    A. ______

    B. ______

    C. ______

Gender Typing

1. Define *gender typing*. (p. 273)

Gender-Stereotyped Beliefs and Behavior

1. True or False: Preschoolers associate toys, clothing, tools, household items, games, occupations, and colors (pink or blue) with one sex or the other. (p. 273)
2. Describe gender differences in the development of personality traits. (p. 273)

    Boys: ______

    Girls: ______

3. During early childhood, children's gender-stereotyped beliefs become (stronger / weaker), operating more like (blanket rules / flexible guidelines). (p. 273)

4. What two factors are responsible for preschoolers' one-sided judgments about violations of gender stereotypes? (p. 273)

   A. ______________________________

   B. ______________________________

Genetic Influences on Gender Typing

1. How does the evolutionary perspective explain gender typing of males and females? (p. 273)

   Males: ______________________________

   Females: ______________________________

2. True or False: According to evolutionary theorists, family and cultural forces cannot eradicate certain aspects of gender typing. (p. 273)

3. Describe Eleanor Maccoby's argument that hormonal differences between males and females have important consequences for gender typing, including play styles in early childhood. (p. 274)

A Lifespan Vista: David: A Boy Who Was Reared as a Girl

1. True or False: After sex reassignment surgery, Bruce—renamed Brenda—readily adopted feminine social and personality characteristics. (p. 275)

2. Explain how David Reimer's development confirms the impact of genetic sex and prenatal hormones on a person's sense of self as male or female. (p. 275)

3. What does David Reimer's childhood reveal about the importance of environmental influences on gender typing? (p. 275)

Environmental Influences on Gender Typing

1. How do parenting practices encourage gender-stereotyped beliefs and behaviors in boys and girls? (p. 274)

   Boys: ______________________________

   Girls: ______________________________

2. True or False: Evidence suggests that children pick up many generic utterances about gender from parental speech. (p. 274)

3. Of the two sexes, (boys / girls) are more gender-typed. Why might this be so? (pp. 274–275)

____

____

4. Discuss ways that preschool teachers promote gender typing within the classroom. How does this affect children's social behaviors? (pp. 275–276)

   A. _______________

   ____

   B. _______________

   ____

5. Peer rejection is greater for (girls / boys) who engage in "cross-gender" activities. (p. 276)

6. Discuss the different styles of social influence within gender-segregated peer groups. (p. 276)

   Boys: _______________

   ____

   Girls: _______________

   ____

7. As boys and girls separate, _______________, or more positive evaluation of members of one's own gender, becomes another factor that sustains the separate social worlds of boys and girls. (p. 276)

Gender Identity

1. _______________ is an image of oneself as relatively masculine or feminine in characteristics. Describe how researchers measure this concept. (p. 276)

____

____

2. _______________ refers to a *gender identity* in which the person scores high on both masculine and feminine personality characteristics. (p. 276)

3. How is gender identity related to psychological adjustment? (p. 276)

____

____

____

4. Contrast social learning and cognitive-developmental accounts of the emergence of gender identity. (p. 276)

   Social Learning: _______________

   ____

   Cognitive-Developmental: _______________

   ____

5. _______________ refers to the understanding that sex is biologically based and remains the same even if clothing, hairstyles, and play activities change. (p. 276)

6. Cite evidence supporting the notion that cognitive immaturity is largely responsible for preschoolers' difficulty grasping the permanence of sex. (p. 277)

____

____

____

7. Evidence that *gender constancy* is responsible for children's gender-typed behavior is (weak / moderate / strong). Briefly explain your answer. (p. 277)

____

____

8. *Gender* __________ *theory* is a(n) (information-processing / psychoanalytic) approach to gender typing that combines social learning and cognitive-developmental features. It explains how environmental pressures and children's cognitions work together to shape gender-role development. (p. 277)

9. What are gender schemas? (p. 277)

____

10. Explain how gender schemas contribute to children's behavior. (p. 277)

____

____

____

11. True or False: When children see others behaving in "gender inconsistent" ways, they often cannot remember the information or distort it to make it "gender-consistent." (p. 278)

Reducing Gender Stereotyping in Young Children

1. True or False: Most aspects of gender typing are built into human nature. (p. 278)

2. How do cognitive limitations contribute to preschoolers' gender typing? (p. 278)

____

____

3. Cite several ways that adults can reduce gender stereotyping in young children. (p. 278)

____

____

____

____

Child Rearing and Emotional and Social Development

Styles of Child Rearing

1. True or False: *Child-rearing styles* occur over a wide range of situations, creating an enduring child-rearing climate. (p. 278)

2. Using research findings of Baumrind and others, list three features that consistently differentiate an effective child-rearing style from less effective ones. (p. 278)

   A. ______________________________

   B. ______________________________

   C. ______________________________

3. Match each child-rearing style with the appropriate description and associated child outcomes. (pp. 278–280)

Child-Rearing Style	Description	Associated Child Outcomes
___ ___ *Uninvolved*	A. High acceptance and involvement, adaptive control techniques, and appropriate autonomy granting	1. Anxiety, low self-esteem and self-reliance, hostile reactions to frustration, high anger, dependence in girls, poor school performance
___ ___ *Authoritative*	B. Warmth and acceptance combined with overindulgence or inattention	2. Poor emotional self-regulation, poor school achievement, antisocial behavior
___ ___ *Permissive*	C. Low acceptance and involvement, little control, and general indifference to autonomy	3. Upbeat mood, self-control, persistence, cooperativeness, high self-esteem, academic success
___ ___ *Authoritarian*	D. Low acceptance and involvement, high coercive control, and low autonomy granting	4. Impulsivity, disobedience, rebellion, dependent and nonachieving, antisocial behavior

4. In addition to unwarranted direct control, authoritarian parents engage in a more subtle type called ______________ *control*, in which they intrude on and manipulate children's verbal expression, individuality, and attachment to parents. (p. 279)

5. At its extreme, uninvolved parenting is a form of child maltreatment called ____________. (p. 280)

What Makes Authoritative Child Rearing Effective?

1. How does authoritative child rearing create an emotional context for positive parental influence? (p. 280)

   A. ______________________________

   B. ______________________________

   C. ______________________________

   D. ______________________________

Cultural Variations

1. Match the following cultural groups with the ways in which their child-rearing practices differ from typical Western child rearing. (pp. 280–281)

_____	More controlling; withhold praise, use shame, withdraw love, and use physical punishment more often	A.	Low-SES African-American parents
_____	Firm insistence on respect for parental authority paired with high parental warmth, greater paternal involvement	B.	Chinese parents
_____	Expect immediate obedience, use physical punishment sparingly and combine it with warmth and reasoning	C.	Hispanic, Asian Pacific Island, and Caribbean parents

2. True or False: The desire of mothers and fathers to be good parents is sufficient to sustain effective child rearing. (p. 281)

Child Maltreatment

1. Match the following descriptions with the corresponding type of child maltreatment. (p. 281)

_____	Social isolation, repeated unreasonable demands, ridicule, humiliation, intimidation, or terrorizing	A. Neglect
_____	Fondling, intercourse, exhibitionism, commercial exploitation through prostitution or production of pornography	B. Physical abuse
_____	Failure to meet a child's basic needs for food, clothing, medical attention, or supervision	C. Sexual abuse
_____	Assaults on children, such as kicking, biting, shaking, punching, or stabbing, that inflict physical injury	D. Emotional abuse

2. True or False: (Parents / Nonparent relatives / Unrelated adults) commit most abusive incidents. (p. 281)

3. Which types of child maltreatment are more often committed by mothers, and which by fathers? (p. 281)

   Mothers: ______________________________

   Fathers: ______________________________

4. True or False: Researchers have identified a single "abusive" personality type. (pp. 281–282)

5. List child, parent, and family environment characteristics that increase the likelihood of child maltreatment. (p. 282)

   Child: ______________________________

   ____

   ____

   Parent: ______________________________

   ____

   ____

   Family environment: ______________________________

   ____

6. Cite two reasons why most abusive parents are isolated from supportive ties to their communities. (p. 282)

   A. ______________________________

   B. ______________________________

7. Societies that view violence as an appropriate way to solve problems set the stage for child abuse. These conditions (do / do not) exist in the United States. (p. 282)

8. True or False: The United States prohibits corporal punishment in schools. (p. 282)

9. List five consequences of child maltreatment. (p. 283)

   A. ______________________________

   B. ______________________________

   C. ______________________________

   D. ______________________________

   E. ______________________________

10. Explain why maltreated children present serious discipline problems at school. (p. 283)

____

____

11. True or False: Repeated child abuse is not associated with central nervous system damage. (p. 283)
12. True or False: Providing social supports to families effectively reduces child maltreatment. (p. 283)
13. What is the most important factor in preventing mothers with childhood histories of abuse from repeating the cycle with their own children? (p. 283)

____

14. List several strategies for preventing child maltreatment. (p. 283)

____

____

____

ASK YOURSELF . . .

For *Ask Yourself* questions for this chapter, along with feedback on the accuracy of your answers, please log on to MyDevelopmentLab (for registration and access, please visit mydevelopmentlab.com or follow the instructions on page ix).

(1) Select the Multimedia Library.

(2) Choose the explore option.

(3) Find your chapter from the drop down box.

(4) Click find now.

(5) Complete questions and choose "Submit answers for grading" or "Clear answers" to start over.

SUGGESTED READINGS

Colapinto, J. (2006). *As nature made him: The boy who was raised as a girl.* New York: HarperCollins. Presents the tragic story of David Reimer, an identical twin who was raised as a girl following a botched circumcision. This book highlights the impact of genetic sex and prenatal hormones on one's sense of self as male or female, while also emphasizing the importance of experience.

Hirsh-Pasek, K., Golinkoff, R. M., Berk, L. E., & Singer, D. G. (2009). *A mandate for playful learning in preschool: Presenting the evidence.* New York: Oxford University Press. Using the latest research on early child development, this book examines the importance of play for academic and social development. Although some parents and educators favor academic training over playtime, scientific evidence shows that unstructured free time and opportunities for play are ideal for fostering cognitive and social/emotional development in preschool-age children.

Nelsen, J., Erwin, C., & Duffy, R. (2007). *Positive discipline for preschoolers.* New York: Random House. Using the latest research in child development, this book presents the most common challenges in raising young children. In addition, instead of focusing on punitive discipline, the authors describe strategies for preventing behavior problems while promoting maturity and moral development in preschoolers.

Perry, D. F., Knitzer, J., & Kaufmann, R. (Eds.). (2007). *Social and emotional health in early childhood: Building bridges between services and systems.* Baltimore, MD: Paul H. Brookes. A collection of chapters examining the link between social/emotional development and cognitive development in young children. The book highlights the importance of social skills and emotional well-being for school readiness, peer relations, and favorable mental health across the school years.

CROSSWORD PUZZLE 8.1

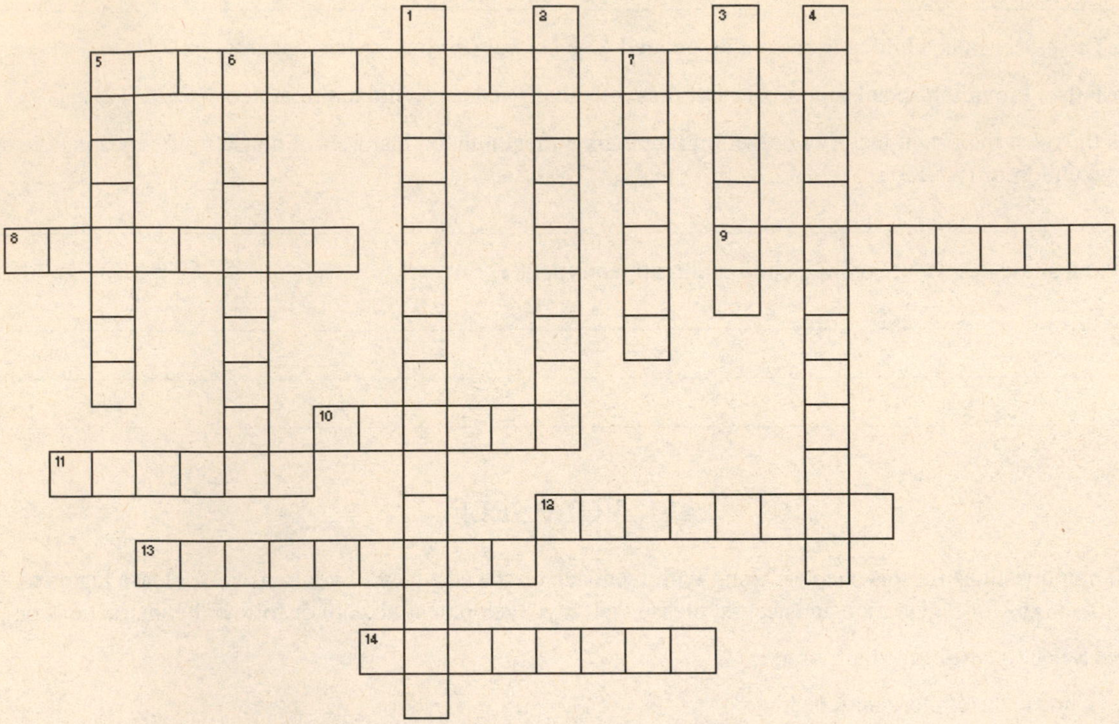

Across

5. Customs determined solely by consensus, such as table manners (2 words)
8. ______ aggression: angry response to provocation or frustration, meant to hurt someone
9. ______ aggression: children unemotionally attack to fulfill a need or desire
10. ______ aggression: threats of physical aggression, name-calling, or hostile teasing
11. Self-______: judgments that we make about our own worth and associated feelings
12. ______ aggression harms others through physical injury.
13. ______, or altruistic, behavior: actions that benefit another without any expected reward for the self
14. Matters of ______ choice do not violate rights and are up to the individual.

Down

1. Protect people's rights and welfare (2 words)
2. ______ aggression damages another's peer relationships.
3. Self-______: attributes, abilities, attitudes, and values that an individual believes defines who she is
4. ______ control: authoritarian parents manipulate children's verbal expression, individuality, and attachment
5. Feelings of concern or sorrow for another's plight
6. ______ versus guilt: Erikson's psychological conflict of the preschool years
7. Removing children from the immediate setting until they are ready to act appropriately (2 words)

CROSSWORD PUZZLE 8.2

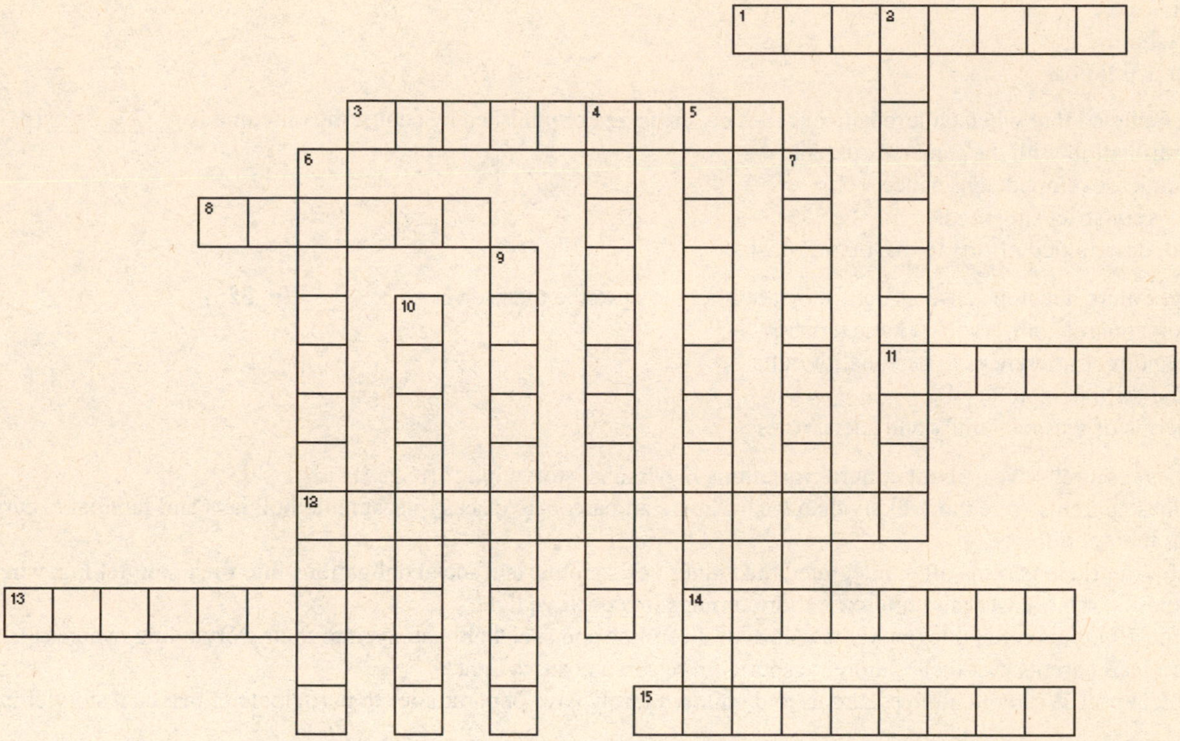

Across

1. ______ play: child plays near others, with similar materials, but does not interact or influence their behavior
3. ______ activity: unoccupied, onlooker behavior and solitary play
8. Gender ______ theory: information-processing approach to gender typing, combines social learning and cognitive-developmental features
11. Gender ______: culturally stereotyped association of objects, activities, etc. with one sex
12. ______ child-rearing style: high acceptance and involvement, adaptive control techniques, and appropriate autonomy granting
13. Discipline in which an adult points out the effects of the child's misbehavior on others
14. Gender ______: image of oneself as relatively masculine or feminine in characteristics
15. Gender identity high in both masculine and feminine personality characteristics

Down

2. ______ play: children engage in separate activities but exchange toys and comment on one another's behavior
4. ______ play: advanced interaction in which children orient toward a common goal
5. ______ child-rearing style: low acceptance and involvement, high coercive control, low autonomy granting
6. ______-______ styles: combinations of parenting behaviors that occur over a wide range of situations (2 words, hyph.)
7. ______ child-rearing style: high acceptance, overindulging or inattentive, low control, lax autonomy granting
9. ______ child-rearing style: low acceptance and involvement, little control, indifference to autonomy
10. Gender ______: understanding of the biologically based permanence of one's gender

PRACTICE TEST #1

1. According to Erikson, __________ creates a small social organization of children who must cooperate to achieve common goals. (p. 256)
   a. play
   b. child care
   c. preschool
   d. peer affiliation

2. Erikson believed that when children are excessively criticized or punished by adults, the outcome is __________ (p. 256)
   a. identification with the same-sex parent.
   b. an underdeveloped conscience.
   c. an overly strict superego.
   d. bold, determined efforts to master new tasks.

3. As preschoolers develop self-concepts, they are likely to describe themselves__________ (p. 256)
   a. using concrete, observable characteristics.
   b. using direct references to personality traits.
   c. in the third person.
   d. in terms of various family and social roles.

4. What does research reveal about cultural variations in personal storytelling? (p. 257)
   a. Chinese parents were more likely than Irish-American parents to discuss pleasurable holidays and familiar excursions with their children.
   b. Irish-American parents often integrated the values of discipline and social obligations into their storytelling, whereas Chinese parents cast their children's shortcomings in a positive light.
   c. Chinese parents often integrated the values of discipline and social obligations into their storytelling, whereas Irish-American parents cast their children's shortcomings in a positive light.
   d. In most non-Western cultures, parents and children rarely have opportunities to participate in personal storytelling.

5. Preschoolers __________ (p. 259)
   a. can identify many emotions but are unable to correctly judge their causes.
   b. are incapable of predicting what a friend displaying a certain emotion might do next.
   c. can interpret situations that offer conflicting cues about how a person is feeling.
   d. can think of effective ways to relieve others' negative emotions, such as patting a playmate's back to reduce sadness.

6. Three-year-old Charles is an emotionally reactive child. When he is frustrated, he becomes very angry and aggressive. What can his parents do to promote the development of emotional self-regulation? (p. 259)
   a. Avoid expression of any emotion, positive or negative.
   b. Ignore Charles's emotional outbursts.
   c. Punish Charles's emotional outbursts through withholding of privileges.
   d. Model appropriate methods of emotional management.

7. Among Western children, __________ is associated with feelings of personal inadequacy and maladjustment. (p. 260)
   a. intense shame
   b. empathy
   c. guilt
   d. pride

8. In early childhood, empathy __________ (p. 260)
   a. declines sharply.
   b. motivates altruistic behavior.
   c. always leads to sympathetic behavior.
   d. often escalates into personal distress.

9. Follow-up research on Parten's three-step sequence of peer sociability indicates that __________ (p. 261)
   a. frequent solitary play is a sign of maladjustment.
   b. Parten's play forms emerge in a different order from what she suggested.
   c. later-appearing play forms coexist with earlier ones.
   d. few children reach the advanced level of cooperative play.

10. Which type of nonsocial activity in preschoolers may be a cause for concern? (p. 262)
   a. hovering near peers
   b. solitary play with art materials
   c. reading alone
   d. preference for talking to adults over other children

11. Preschoolers view friendship as __________ (p. 263)
   a. a mutual relationship of understanding and caring.
   b. a special, pleasant relationship.
   c. temporary interaction with any acquaintance.
   d. a relationship that will survive conflict and endure over time.

12. Julio, 3, begins to cry after Manny, 4, takes away his paintbrush. Manny's father, Raoul, says, "Manny, Julio is crying because you took away his paintbrush." Raoul's response is an example of __________ (p. 265)
   a. inductive discipline.
   b. withdrawal of love.
   c. punitive discipline.
   d. withdrawal of privileges.

13. Research shows that guilt __________ (p. 265)
   a. is the only force that compels us to act morally.
   b. can be a strong motivator of moral action.
   c. has a similar effect on children as harsh discipline.
   d. rarely compels us to act morally.

14. Frequent harsh punishment __________ (p. 266)
   a. promotes positive, lasting changes in behavior when combined with induction.
   b. causes children to be overly sympathetic toward adults and peers.
   c. is more effective than induction in reducing children's misbehavior.
   d. increases the likelihood that a preschooler will develop serious, lasting mental health problems.

15. Low-SES ethnic minority parents are more likely than middle-SES white parents to __________ (p. 267)
   a. advocate physical discipline of children.
   b. view spanking as abusive.
   c. scream and curse at their children.
   d. adopt a permissive child-rearing style.

16. Which approach to morality regards children as active thinkers about social rules? (p. 269)
   a. psychoanalytic
   b. social learning
   c. behaviorist
   d. cognitive-developmental

17. When 5-year-old Brittany's older brother refuses to let her play in his room, Brittany yells, "You're mean and ugly and I hate you!" What type of aggression is Brittany displaying? (p. 269)
   a. proactive verbal aggression
   b. proactive relational aggression
   c. reactive verbal aggression
   d. reactive relational aggression

18. TV violence __________ (p. 271)
    a. hardens children to aggression, making them more willing to tolerate it in others.
    b. teaches children that violence is socially unacceptable and has harsh negative consequences.
    c. rarely causes violent behavior, even among highly aggressive children.
    d. is uncommon in children's programming, particularly cartoons.

19. Evolutionary theorists claim that __________ (p. 273)
    a. stereotypical sex differences are primarily seen in humans and primates.
    b. females are genetically primed for dominance, which motivates them to protect offspring.
    c. family and cultural forces have no influence on biologically based sex differences.
    d. family and cultural forces can influence the intensity of biologically based sex differences.

20. Research on gender typing shows that __________ (p. 274)
    a. from birth, parents hold similar perceptions and expectations of their sons and daughters.
    b. of the two sexes, girls are more gender-stereotyped than boys.
    c. of the two sexes, boys are more gender-stereotyped than girls.
    d. mothers are less tolerant of cross-gender behavior in their children than fathers.

21. The case of David, who underwent a sex reassignment as an infant, illustrates that __________ (p. 275)
    a. females develop more favorably after gender reassignment than males.
    b. genetic and prenatal hormones have a large impact on a person's sense of self as male or female.
    c. males develop more favorably after gender reassignment than females.
    d. environmental factors have a greater impact on gender identity than genetic factors.

22. Androgynous individuals __________ (p. 276)
    a. report lower self-esteem than "feminine" individuals.
    b. tend to display "masculine" behavior at work and "feminine" behavior at home.
    c. have higher suicide rates than "feminine" individuals.
    d. are often well-adjusted and adaptable.

23. Gender schema theory __________ (p. 277)
    a. maintains that genetic factors are more powerful on gender typing than environmental factors.
    b. emphasizes development of gender-stereotyped beliefs through identification with the same-sex parent.
    c. focuses on the role of modeling and reinforcement in gender identity development.
    d. emphasizes how environmental pressures and children's cognitions work together to shape gender-role development.

24. Which child-rearing style is linked to an upbeat mood, high self-esteem, social maturity, and other aspects of competence? (p. 279)
    a. authoritative
    b. authoritarian
    c. permissive
    d. uninvolved

25. __________ parents engage in both direct control and psychological control. (p. 279)
    a. Authoritative
    b. Authoritarian
    c. Permissive
    d. Uninvolved

26. Research on cultural influences in child rearing shows that African-American parents who use more controlling strategies tend to have __________ (p. 281)
    a. children with high rates of antisocial behavior.
    b. more cognitively and socially competent children.
    c. children with low self-esteem and poor academic achievement.
    d. more demanding and controlling children.

27. Research on child maltreatment shows that infants and young children are most at-risk for __________ (p. 281)
    a. physical abuse.
    b. emotional abuse.
    c. sexual abuse.
    d. neglect.

28. When maltreating parents see their child misbehaving, they are likely to __________ (p. 282)
    a. blame themselves for their child's behavior.
    b. feel confident and powerful in handling the situation.
    c. attribute the misbehavior to the child's "bad" disposition.
    d. minimize or ignore the child's transgressions.

29. Over time, the impact of persistent abuse __________ (p. 283)
    a. causes children to be overly sympathetic toward peers.
    b. leads to central nerve damage.
    c. motivates children to bond with other adults, such as teachers or coaches.
    d. decreases, as children develop effective coping strategies.

30. What is the most important factor in preventing at-risk mothers from abusing their children? (p. 283)
    a. monthly visits with a social worker
    b. books and other reading materials about child maltreatment
    c. a trusting relationship with another person
    d. a child development course

PRACTICE TEST #2

1. According to Erikson's theory, the psychological conflict of the preschool years is __________ (p. 256)
   a. introversion versus extroversion.
   b. initiative versus guilt.
   c. trust versus mistrust.
   d. autonomy versus shame and doubt.

2. Erikson regarded play as __________ (p. 256)
   a. a source of entertainment that has little impact on child development.
   b. a critical context for physical, cognitive, and moral development.
   c. a means through which young children learn about themselves and their social world.
   d. a way for children to overcome an overly strict superego.

3. When parents engage in personal storytelling with their preschoolers, the events they discuss and the interpretation of these events __________ (p. 257)
   a. are largely dictated by the children.
   b. affect the way children view themselves.
   c. are often harsh and hurtful to children, particularly in Asian cultures.
   d. are similar across cultures.

4. Why do very young preschoolers frequently assert their rights to objects with phrases like "That's mine!"? (p. 257)
   a. They have weak self-definitions that lead to a sense of possessiveness.
   b. They have had limited opportunities to practice sharing or compromise.
   c. They are egocentric and often behave in a selfish manner.
   d. Their self-concepts are bound up with specific possessions and actions.

5. Which of the following factors is probably the strongest influence on a preschooler's emotional competence? (p. 258)
   a. parenting
   b. mental health
   c. peer relationships
   d. the child's personality

6. Four-year-old Marisol covers her eyes when she sees a scary event on television. This is an example of __________ (p. 259)
   a. a reactive attachment.
   b. empathy.
   c. emotional self-regulation.
   d. prosocial behavior.

7. Three-year-olds who engage in effortful control __________ (p. 259)
   a. prefer to play alone than with peers.
   b. rarely feel strong emotions.
   c. tend to become cooperative school-age children.
   d. often have anxious, fearful temperaments.

8. In preschool children, guilt __________ (p. 260)
   a. is related to good adjustment.
   b. is associated with feelings of personal inadequacy.
   c. often causes a sharp drop in self-esteem.
   d. often leads to sympathetic actions.

9. As 4-year-old Liza builds a house with blocks, her friend Luis plays with cars nearby. "Can I use a car for my house?" Liza asks. Luis hands her a red car. A few minutes later, Luis tells Liza that he likes her house and asks for a few blocks to build a ramp for the cars. Liza and Luis are engaged in __________ (p. 261)
   a. nonsocial activity.
   b. parallel play.
   c. associative play.
   d. cooperative play.

10. Sociodramatic play seems particularly important for social development in __________ (p. 263)
    a. collectivist societies.
    b. cultures that emphasize task persistence.
    c. societies with distinct adult and child worlds.
    d. societies with little distinction between adult and child worlds.

11. Children first acquire skills for interacting with peers within __________ (p. 263)
    a. a child-care or preschool setting.
    b. the family.
    c. informal play groups.
    d. highly-structured, adult-directed activities.

12. Most theories of moral development agree that a child's morality is first __________ and gradually becomes __________. (p. 264)
    a. guided by emotion; guided by reason
    b. motivated by guilt; motivated by empathy
    c. externally controlled; regulated by internal standards
    d. regulated by internal standards; externally controlled

13. According to Freud, young children obey ____________ to avoid __________. (p. 264)
    a. the ego; punishment
    b. the superego; guilt
    c. the id; the superego
    d. adults; the ego

14. Professor Cooper is interested in moral development and believes that children learn to behave morally through modeling and reinforcement. Professor Cooper's belief is consistent with __________ theory. (p. 265)
    a. psychoanalytic
    b. social learning
    c. cognitive-developmental
    d. ecological systems

15. In African-American families, spanking __________ (p. 267)
    a. is usually mild and delivered in a context of parental warmth.
    b. occurs only when the parent is very angry.
    c. is more effective than time outs.
    d. usually leads to long-term behavior problems.

16. Preschoolers judge ________ as more wrong than ________. (p. 269)
    a. violations of personal choice; violations of social conventions
    b. moral violations; violations of social conventions
    c. violations of social conventions; moral violations
    d. violations of personal choice; moral violations

17. Frankie says to James, "Do what I say, or I won't be your friend anymore!" Frankie is engaging in __________ aggression. (p. 269)
    a. moral
    b. verbal
    c. indirect
    d. relational

18. Which of the following statements about sex differences in aggressive behavior is true? (p. 270)
    a. By age 17 months, boys are more physically aggressive than girls.
    b. Parents respond more negatively to physical fighting in boys than in girls.
    c. Girls are far more verbally and relationally aggressive than boys.
    d. Boys engage in indirect relational aggression more often than girls do.

19. A preschooler who thinks that boys always have short hair and girls always have long hair is demonstrating __________ (p. 273)
    a. relational aggression.
    b. a gender schema.
    c. gender typing.
    d. gender appropriateness.

20. Eleanor Maccoby's research on play indicates that __________ (p. 274)
    a. preference for same-sex playmates is rarely found in cultures outside of the United States, suggesting that hormones exert little influence on play behavior.
    b. hormonal differences lead boys to prefer rough, noisy play and girls to prefer calm, gentle actions.
    c. preference for same-sex playmates declines sharply during the preschool years.
    d. hormonal differences lead girls to prefer large group activities, whereas boys prefer to play in pairs.

21. David Reimer's gender reassignment failed because __________ (p. 275)
    a. he was not allowed to experiment with "feminine" activities and behaviors.
    b. he lacked support from his family.
    c. his male biology overwhelmingly demanded a consistent sexual identity.
    d. doctors waited too long to inject him with female hormones.

22. Gabe believes that if a woman dresses up like a man, she becomes a man. Gabe has yet to develop gender __________ (p. 276)
    a. identity.
    b. schema.
    c. stereotyping.
    d. constancy.

23. Research on gender constancy shows that __________ (p. 277)
    a. social experience, not cognitive immaturity, is largely responsible for preschoolers' difficulty grasping the permanence of sex.
    b. gender constancy is responsible for children's gender-typed behavior.
    c. understanding of gender constancy leads to a reduction in gender-stereotyped behaviors.
    d. cognitive immaturity, not social experience, is largely responsible for preschoolers' difficulty grasping the permanence of sex.

24. Four-year-old Gisele's mother often tells her that "cars and trucks are for boys." According to gender schema theory, Gisele is likely to __________ (pp. 277–278)
    a. avoid playing with cars and trucks.
    b. ask her father to play cars and trucks with her.
    c. be resentful when she sees other girls playing with cars and trucks.
    d. seek out opportunities to play with boys who are playing with cars and trucks.

25. The permissive child-rearing style is warm and accepting __________ (p. 279)
    a. but uninvolved.
    b. but psychologically controlling.
    c. but authoritarian.
    d. and highly successful with most children.

26. Which of the following statements about ethnic differences in child rearing is true? (p. 281)
    a. Compared to Chinese parents, Western parents are more likely to withhold praise, be directive, and shame their children.
    b. Physical punishment is associated with a reduction of antisocial behavior among Caucasian youths but an increase of antisocial behavior among African-American youths.
    c. Physical punishment is associated with a reduction of antisocial behavior among African-American youths but an increase of antisocial behavior among Caucasian youths.
    d. Compared to Western fathers, Hispanic fathers spend very little time with their children and are less warm and sensitive.

27. __________ commit more than 80 percent of abusive incidents with children. (p. 281)
    a. Parents
    b. Teachers and other school officials
    c. Siblings
    d. Strangers

28. Which of the following is an example of a cultural factor in child maltreatment? (p. 282)
    a. Maltreating parents view their child's transgressions as worse than they are.
    b. Abusive parents react to stressful situations with high emotional arousal.
    c. The United States recently passed a federal law that bans parents and caregivers from using physical force with children.
    d. In the United States, widespread support exists for use of physical force with children.

29. Which of the following family characteristics is strongly associated with child maltreatment? (p. 283)
    a. having a single "abusive personality type"
    b. authoritarian child rearing
    c. partner abuse
    d. having 3 or more young children in the home

30. When the Healthy Families program added a(n) __________ to their intervention, physical punishment and abuse dropped sharply. (p. 283)
    a. home visit
    b. cognitive component
    c. evaluative appraisal
    d. community contact

CHAPTER 9
PHYSICAL AND COGNITIVE DEVELOPMENT IN MIDDLE CHILDHOOD

BRIEF CHAPTER SUMMARY

Physical growth during the school years continues at the slow, regular pace of early childhood. Bones of the body lengthen and broaden, and primary teeth are replaced with permanent teeth.

Although most children appear to be at their healthiest in middle childhood, a variety of health problems do occur, especially in children who live in poverty. Nearsightedness may develop, while ear infections become less common. Over the past several decades, a rise in overweight and obesity has occurred in many Western nations, putting many children at risk for lifelong health problems. Children experience a somewhat higher rate of illness during the first two years of elementary school than they will later, because of exposure to sick children and an immune system that is still developing. The frequency of injury fatalities increases from middle childhood into adolescence, especially for boys.

Gains in flexibility, balance, agility, and force contribute to school-age children's advances in gross-motor development. Steady gains in reaction time also occur. Fine-motor development improves over the school years, and sex differences in motor skills that appeared in the preschool years continue and, in some instances, become more pronounced in middle childhood. School-age boys' genetic advantage in muscle mass is not sufficient to account for their gross-motor superiority; the social environment plays a larger role. Games with rules become common in the school years, as does rough-and-tumble play, which helps children, especially boys, establish a dominance hierarchy. High-quality physical education classes that focus on individual exercise rather than competitive sports help ensure that all children have access to the benefits of regular exercise and play.

During Piaget's concrete operational stage, children's thought becomes far more logical, flexible, and organized than in early childhood. A limitation of concrete operational thought is that children's mental operations work poorly with abstract ideas. Specific cultural and school practices affect children's mastery of Piagetian tasks. Some neo-Piagetian theorists argue that the development of operational thinking can best be understood in terms of gains in information-processing speed rather than a sudden shift to a new stage.

In contrast to Piaget's focus on overall cognitive change, the information-processing perspective examines separate aspects of thinking. Brain development contributes to an increase in information-processing speed and capacity and gains in cognitive inhibition. In addition, attention becomes more selective, adaptable, and planful. As attention improves, so do memory strategies. School-age children's theory of mind, or metacognition, expands, as does their understanding of sources of knowledge and of false belief. However, they are not yet good at cognitive self-regulation. Fundamental discoveries about the development of information processing have been applied to children's learning of reading and mathematics.

Around age 6, IQ becomes more stable than it was at earlier ages, and it correlates well with academic achievement. Intelligence tests provide an overall score (the IQ), which represents general intelligence, as well as an array of scores measuring specific mental abilities. Sternberg's triarchic theory of successful intelligence identifies three broad, interacting intelligences: analytical intelligence, creative intelligence, and practical intelligence. Gardner's theory of multiple intelligences identifies at least eight mental abilities, each with a distinct biological basis and course of development. SES accounts for some, but not all, of the black–white IQ difference, and many experts acknowledge that IQ scores can underestimate the intelligence of culturally different children.

Vocabulary, grammar, and pragmatics continue to develop in middle childhood, although less obviously than at earlier ages. In addition, school-age children develop language awareness. Many children throughout the world grow up bilingual; as with first-language development, a sensitive period for second-language development exists. Research shows that bilingualism has positive consequences for development, but the question of how to educate bilingual children continues to be hotly debated.

Schools are vital forces in children's cognitive development, with class size, educational philosophies, teacher–student relationships, and the larger cultural context all playing a role. Teaching children with learning disabilities, as well as those with special gifts and talents, presents unique challenges. U.S. students fare poorly when their achievement is compared to that of children in other industrialized nations. Families, schools, and the larger society must work together to upgrade U.S. education.

LEARNING OBJECTIVES

After reading this chapter, you should be able to:

9.1 Describe major trends in body growth during middle childhood. (p. 290)

9.2 Identify common vision and hearing problems in middle childhood. (p. 291)

9.3 Describe the causes and consequences of serious nutritional problems in middle childhood, giving special attention to obesity. (pp. 291–293)

9.4 Identify factors that contribute to illness during the school years, and describe ways to reduce these health problems. (pp. 293–294)

9.5 Describe changes in unintentional injuries in middle childhood. (p. 294)

9.6 Cite major changes in motor development and play during middle childhood, including sex differences and the importance of physical education. (pp. 294–299)

9.7 Describe major characteristics of concrete operational thought. (pp. 299–301)

9.8 Discuss follow-up research on concrete operational thought, noting the importance of culture and schooling. (pp. 301–302)

9.9 Cite basic changes in information processing and describe the development of attention and memory in middle childhood. (pp. 303–305)

9.10 Describe the school-age child's theory of mind, noting the importance of mental inferences and understanding of false belief and capacity to engage in self-regulation. (pp. 306–307)

9.11 Discuss applications of information processing to academic learning, including current controversies in teaching reading and mathematics to elementary school children. (pp. 307–309)

9.12 Describe major approaches to defining and measuring intelligence. (pp. 309–310)

9.13 Summarize Sternberg's triarchic theory and Gardner's theory of multiple intelligences, noting how these theories explain the limitations of current intelligence tests in assessing the diversity of human intelligence. (pp. 310–312)

9.14 Describe evidence indicating that both heredity and environment contribute to intelligence. (pp. 312–317)

9.15 Summarize findings on emotional intelligence, including implications for the classroom. (p. 313)

9.16 Describe changes in school-age children's vocabulary, grammar, and pragmatics, and cite advantages of bilingualism. (pp. 316–319)

9.17 Explain the impact of class size and educational philosophies on children's motivation and academic achievement. (pp. 319–321)

9.18 Discuss the role of teacher-student interaction and grouping practices in academic achievement. (pp. 321–322)

9.19 Explain the conditions that contribute to successful placement of children with mild mental retardation and learning disabilities in regular classrooms. (p. 322)

9.20 Describe the characteristics of gifted children, including creativity and talent, and current efforts to meet their educational needs. (pp. 323–324)

9.21 Compare the academic achievement of North American children with children in other industrialized nations. (pp. 324–325)

STUDY QUESTIONS

Physical Development

Body Growth

1. During middle childhood, children add about _______ inches in height and _______ pounds in weight each year. (p. 290)
2. True or False: Between ages 6 and 8, girls are slightly shorter and lighter than boys. By age 9, this trend reverses. (p. 290)
3. List two factors that account for unusual flexibility of movement in middle childhood. (p. 290)

   A. ______________________________

   B. ______________________________
4. Between the ages of _______ and _______, all primary teeth are lost and replaced by permanent teeth. (p. 290)

Common Health Problems

1. Cite three factors that lead many children from economically advantaged homes to be at their healthiest in middle childhood. (p. 291)

   A. ______________________________

   B. ______________________________

   C. ______________________________
2. True or False: During the school years, poverty is no longer a powerful predictor of ill health. (p. 291)

Vision and Hearing

1. The most common vision problem in middle childhood is _______________, or nearsightedness. (p. 291)
2. Cite evidence indicating that both heredity and environment contribute to myopia. (p. 291)

   Heredity: ______________________________

   ____

   Environment: ______________________________

   ____
3. True or False: Myopia is one of the few health conditions that increases with SES. (p. 291)
4. Middle ear infections become (less / more) frequent in middle childhood. (p. 291)
5. True or False: Repeated ear infections can lead to permanent hearing loss. (p. 291)

Nutrition

1. The percentage of children eating dinner with their families (rises / drops) sharply between ages 9 and 14. (p. 291)
2. List four consequences of serious, prolonged malnutrition in middle childhood. (p. 291)

   A. ______________________________

   B. ______________________________

   C. ______________________________

   D. ______________________________

3. True or False: Malnutrition that persists from infancy or early childhood into the school years usually leads to permanent physical and mental damage. (p. 291)

Obesity

1. During the past several decades, overweight and *obesity* have (decreased / increased) in the United States. (p. 292)
2. Why are obesity rates increasing rapidly in developing countries? (p. 292)

____

____

3. List several health problems associated with childhood overweight and obesity. (p. 292)

____

____

____

4. How do heredity and environment contribute to childhood obesity? (p. 292)

Heredity: ____

____

Environment: ____

____

5. (Low- / Middle-)SES children are more likely to be overweight. (p. 292)
6. List parental feeding practices that contribute to obesity, along with their consequences for children's eating habits. (p. 292)

Parenting Practices: ____

____

Consequences: ____

____

7. True or False: The more TV children watch, the more body fat they add. Explain. (p. 293)

____

____

____

8. Summarize the consequences of childhood obesity for emotional and social development. (p. 293)

____

____

____

9. The most effective interventions for childhood obesity focus on the (family / individual) and work to change (behaviors / environments). (p. 293)
10. How can schools help reduce childhood obesity? (p. 293)

____

____

Illnesses

1. What accounts for the somewhat higher rate of illness during the first two years of elementary school than in the later school years? (p. 293)

   ____

2. The most common chronic illness, representing the most frequent cause of school absence and childhood hospitalization, is ______________. (pp. 293–294)

3. Cite five factors that place children at risk for developing asthma. (p. 294)

   A. ____

   B. ____

   C. ____

   D. ____

   E. ____

4. Which environmental factors contribute to the higher rate and greater severity of asthma among African-American and poverty-stricken children? (p. 294)

   A. ____

   B. ____

   C. ____

5. True or False: Childhood obesity is related to asthma in middle childhood. (p. 294)

6. Why are children with serious chronic illnesses at risk for academic, emotional, and social difficulties? (p. 294)

   ____

   ____

7. Briefly describe effective interventions for chronically ill children and their families. (p. 294)

   ____

   ____

   ____

Unintentional Injuries

1. ______________________________ is/are the leading cause of injury in middle childhood. (p. 294)

2. Cite three characteristics of effective school-based safety education programs. (p. 294)

   A. ____

   B. ____

   C. ____

3. Describe characteristics of children who are at greatest risk for injury in middle childhood. (p. 294)

   ____

   ____

Motor Development and Play

Gross-Motor Development

1. Improvements in motor skills over middle childhood reflect gains in what four basic motor capacities? (p. 295)

   A. ______________________________

   B. ______________________________

   C. ______________________________

   D. ______________________________

2. Body growth, as well as more efficient ______________________, plays a vital role in improved motor performance in middle childhood. (p. 295)

Fine-Motor Development

1. Describe typical gains in writing and drawing during middle childhood. (p. 295)

   Writing: ______________________________

   ____

   Drawing: ______________________________

   ____

Sex Differences

1. How do girls and boys differ in motor-skill development during middle childhood? (pp. 295–296)

   Girls: ______________________________

   ____

   Boys: ______________________________

   ____

2. True or False: School-age boys' genetic advantage in muscle mass fully accounts for their superiority in most gross-motor skills. (p. 296)

3. Parents hold higher expectations for (boys' / girls') athletic performance. Children (do / do not) readily absorb these messages. (p. 296)

4. List two strategies for increasing girls' participation and self-confidence in athletics. (p. 296)

   A. ______________________________

   B. ______________________________

Games with Rules

1. What cognitive capacity facilitates the transition to rule-oriented games in middle childhood? (p. 296)

   ____

2. Briefly describe how child-organized games contribute to emotional and social development. (p. 296)

   ____

   ____

   ____

3. List two reasons why today's children devote less time to informal outdoor play. (pp. 296–297)

   A. ______________________________

   B. ______________________________

4. Under what conditions may youth sports fail to provide children with positive learning experiences? (p. 297)

____

____

____

Shadows of Our Evolutionary Past

1. Friendly chasing and play-fighting in childhood are called ______________________________. (p. 297)
2. Why was *rough-and-tumble play* important in our evolutionary past? (p. 298)

____

3. Rough-and-tumble play helps children establish a ______________________________, or a stable ordering of group members that predicts who will win when a conflict arises. (p. 298)
4. Once school-age children establish a *dominance hierarchy*, hostility is (rare / common). (p. 298)

Physical Education

1. Cite several aspects of children's development supported by physical activity. (p. 298)

____

____

2. (Few / Most) U.S. elementary and middle schools provide students with physical education at least three days a week. (Few / Most) boys and girls are active enough for good health. (pp. 298–299)
3. How can physical education programs reach the least physically fit children? (p. 299)

____

____

4. What are some long-term benefits of being physically fit in childhood? (p. 299)

____

____

____

Social Issues: School Recess—A Time to Play, a Time to Learn

1. In recent years, recess has (diminished / increased) in U.S. elementary schools. (p. 298)
2. True or False: Recess periods subtract from classroom learning. Why or why not? (p. 298)

____

____

3. Explain the link between peer socialization at recess and academic achievement. (p. 298)

____

____

Cognitive Development

Piaget's Theory: The Concrete Operational Stage

Concrete Operational Thought

1. During Piaget's *concrete operational stage,* thought is far more ____________, ____________, and ____________ than it was earlier. (p. 299)

2. Match each of the following terms with its appropriate description. (p. 299)

______	Ability to order items along a quantitative dimension, such as length or weight	A. *Seriation*
______	Focusing on several aspects of a problem and relating them, rather than focusing on just one	B. Decentration
______	Ability to think through a series of steps and then mentally reverse direction, returning to the starting point	C. *Reversibility*

3. True or False: During middle childhood, children develop the ability to focus on relations between a general category and two specific categories at the same time. (p. 299)

4. Describe *transitive inference,* and provide an example of this ability. (p. 300)

   Description: ____

   Example: ____

5. ______________________ are mental representations of familiar large-scale spaces. (p. 300)

6. Cite evidence that spatial reasoning improves in middle childhood. (p. 300)

   ____

   ____

   ____

   ____

7. How do cultural frameworks influence children's *cognitive maps*? (p. 300)

   ____

   ____

   ____

Limitations of Concrete Operational Thought

1. Cite the major limitation of concrete operational thought. (p. 300)

   ____

   ____

2. School-age children master Piaget's concrete operational tasks (all at once / step by step). (p. 300)

Follow-Up Research on Concrete Operational Thought

1. Children (do / do not) master conservation tasks around the same age across cultures. Children who have been in school longer (perform better / show no special advantage) on transitive inference problems. What does this suggest about the impact of culture and schooling on concrete operational thought? (p. 301)

   ____

   ____

2. True or False: Researchers agree that the forms of logic required by Piagetian tasks emerge spontaneously during childhood. (p. 302)

3. How might gains in processing speed facilitate the development of operational thinking? (p. 302)

____

____

4. Information-processing theorists believe that children integrate concrete operational schemes into _______________ structures, or broadly applicable principles. How does this affect reasoning? (p. 302)

____

5. Describe two ways Case's theory helps explain unevenness in cognitive development during middle childhood. (p. 302)

A. ____

B. ____

Evaluation of the Concrete Operational Stage

1. Piaget's theory assumes that school-age children develop rational thought due to (continuous improvement in logical skills / discontinuous restructuring of thinking). (p. 302)

2. Describe the qualitative change in children's thought during the school years. (p. 302)

____

____

Information Processing

1. The information-processing perspective examines (overall cognitive change / separate aspects of thinking). (p. 303)

2. Summarize two basic changes in information processing that facilitate diverse aspects of thinking. (p. 303)

A. ____

B. ____

Attention

1. Describe three ways that attention changes in middle childhood. (p. 303)

A. ____

____

B. ____

____

C. ____

____

2. True or False: The demands of school tasks, and teachers' explanations of how to plan, contribute to gains in planning. (p. 303)

Biology and Environment: Children with Attention-Deficit Hyperactivity Disorder

1. (Boys / Girls) are diagnosed with *ADHD* about four times as often as children of the opposite sex. (p. 304)

2. Describe two common characteristics of children with ADHD. (p. 304)

   A. ____

   B. ____

3. True or False: All children with ADHD are hyperactive. (p. 304)

4. Researchers agree that deficient ______________________ underlies ADHD symptoms. (p. 304)

5. Cite evidence that ADHD is influenced by both genetic and environmental factors. (pp. 304–305)

   Genetic: ____

   ____

   Environmental: ____

   ____

6. The most common treatment for ADHD is ______________________. List two additional interventions for children with ADHD. (p. 305)

   A. ____

   B. ____

7. Describe social factors that influence community differences in the incidence of ADHD. (p. 305)

   ____

   ____

   ____

8. True or False: Usually ADHD does not persist into adulthood. (p. 305)

Memory Strategies

1. (*Organization / Rehearsal*), or repeating information to be remembered, first appears in the early grade school years. Soon after, (*organization / rehearsal*), or grouping related items together, becomes common. (p. 303)

2. True or False: The more memory strategies children apply simultaneously and consistently, the better they remember. (p. 303)

3. By the end of middle childhood, children start to use ______________________, creating a relationship between pieces of information that do not belong to the same category. Why does this memory strategy develop later than others? (p. 304)

   ____

4. Why are organization and *elaboration* especially effective memory strategies? (p. 304)

   ____

   ____

The Knowledge Base and Memory Performance

1. How does an expanding long-term knowledge base affect children's ability to remember? (p. 304)

   ____

   ____

2. Explain how motivation contributes to children's strategic memory processing. (p. 305)

____

____

Culture, Schooling, and Memory Strategies

1. True or False: People in non-Western cultures who have no formal schooling are likely to use and benefit from instruction in memory strategies. (p. 305)
2. How do task demands and cultural circumstances influence the development of memory strategies? (p. 305)

____

____

____

The School-Age Child's Theory of Mind

1. (Preschoolers / School-age children) view the mind as a passive container of information, while (preschoolers / school-age children) regard it as an active, constructive agent. (p. 306)
2. School-age children realize that people can extend their knowledge not only by directly observing events and talking to others, but also by making ____________________________. This enables knowledge of ______________________ to expand. (p. 306)
3. Appreciation of _________________ false belief enables children to pinpoint the reasons that another person arrived at a certain belief. (p. 306)
4. How does schooling contribute to the school-age child's theory of mind? (pp. 305–306)

____

____

Cognitive Self-Regulation

1. Although metacognition expands, school-age children are not yet good at ______________________________, the process of continuously monitoring progress toward a goal, checking outcomes, and redirecting unsuccessful efforts. (p. 307)
2. True or False: By second grade, the more children know about memory strategies, the more they recall. (p. 307)
3. Explain why *cognitive self-regulation* develops gradually. (p. 307)

____

____

4. How can parents and teachers foster self-regulation during middle childhood? (p. 307)

____

____

____

5. Children who acquire effective self-regulatory skills develop a sense of academic ____________________, or confidence in their own ability, which supports future self-regulation. (p. 307)

Applications of Information Processing to Academic Learning

1. Reading taxes (few / all) aspects of our information-processing systems. (Few / Most) of the skills involved in reading must be done automatically. (p. 307)

2. Cite three capacities or information-processing activities that facilitate the transition from emergent literacy to conventional reading. (p. 307)

   A. ____________________

   B. ____________________

   C. ____________________

3. According to the (*phonics* / *whole-language*) *approach*, children should first be coached on basic rules for translating written symbols into sounds. The (*phonics* / *whole-language*) *approach* argues that children should first experience complete texts so they can appreciate the communicative function of language. (p. 307)

4. Children learn best with (the phonics / the whole-language / a mixture of whole-language and phonics) approach(es). (p. 307)

5. Explain why it is important for children to learn to decipher relationships between letters and sounds and to utilize reading strategies. (pp. 307–308)

   ____

   ____

   ____

   ____

6. School-age children acquire basic math facts through a combination of what types of experiences? (p. 308)

   A. ____________________

   B. ____________________

   C. ____________________

   D. ____________________

7. When teaching mathematics, the most beneficial approaches emphasize (drill in computing / "number sense" / a blend of drill in computing and "number sense"). (p. 308)

8. True or False: When children are taught mathematics by rote memorization, they easily apply procedures to new problems. (p. 308)

9. Cite three learning opportunities that reduce the likelihood of children making mathematical errors. (p. 308)

   A. ____________________

   B. ____________________

   C. ____________________

10. Describe five factors that support the acquisition of mathematical knowledge in Asian countries. (p. 308)

    A. ____________________

    B. ____________________

    C. ____________________

    D. ____________________

    E. ____________________

Individual Differences in Mental Development

1. Around age _____, IQ becomes (less / more) stable than it was at earlier ages, and it correlates moderately well with academic achievement. (p. 309)

Defining and Measuring Intelligence

1. True or False: Current IQ tests can accurately assess all aspects of intelligence. (p. 309)
2. Why do intelligence test designers use factor analysis? (p. 309)

____

____

3. Explain why group-administered tests are useful. (p. 309)

____

____

4. How do examiners determine if individually administered tests accurately reflect children's abilities? (p. 309)

____

____

5. In addition to general intelligence, list the five intellectual factors measured by the Stanford-Binet Intelligence Scales, Fifth Edition. (p. 310)

A. ______________________ D. ______________________

B. ______________________ E. ______________________

C. ______________________

6. In addition to general intelligence, list the four broad factors measured by the Wechsler Intelligence Scale for Children (WISC-IV*)*. (p. 310)

A. ______________________ D. ______________________

B. ______________________ E. ______________________

7. The (Stanford-Binet Intelligence Scale / Wechsler Intelligence Scale for Children) was the first test to be standardized on children representing the total population of the United States, including ethnic minorities. (p. 310)

Recent Efforts to Define Intelligence

1. Investigators use ________________ analyses to examine relationships between aspects of information processing and children's intelligence test scores. (p. 310)
2. True or False: Individuals whose nervous systems function efficiently appear to have an edge in intellectual skills. (p. 310)
3. What is one major shortcoming of the componential approach? (p. 310)

____

____

____

4. Match the three interacting intelligences identified in Sternberg's *triarchic theory of successful intelligence* with the appropriate descriptions. (p. 310)

_______ Application of intellectual skills in everyday situations
_______ Information-processing skills
_______ The capacity to solve novel problems

A. Analytical intelligence
B. Creative intelligence
C. Practical intelligence

5. How does Sternberg's theory help explain cultural differences in mental test scores? (p. 311)

____

____

____

6. True or False: Gardner's *theory of multiple intelligences* dismisses the idea of general intelligence. (p. 311)

7. List Gardner's eight independent intelligences. (p. 311)

A. ______________________ E. ______________________

B. ______________________ F. ______________________

C. ______________________ G. ______________________

D. ______________________ H. ______________________

A Lifespan Vista: Emotional Intelligence

1. ______________________ refers to a set of emotional abilities that enable individuals to process and adapt to emotional information. How is this trait measured? (p. 313)

____

____

2. *Emotional intelligence* is (weakly / modestly / highly) related to IQ. (p. 313)

3. Cite some positive outcomes associated with emotional intelligence. (p. 313)

____

____

4. What experiences can teachers provide to meet students' social and emotional needs? (p. 313)

____

____

____

Explaining Individual and Group Differences in IQ

1. How does SES relate to IQ in childhood? What do these findings reveal about the black–white IQ gap? (p. 312)

A. ____

____

B. ____

____

2. Arthur Jensen and his followers argue that (environment / heredity) is largely responsible for individual, ethnic, and SES variations in intelligence. (p. 312)

3. The IQ scores of identical twins are (less / more) similar than those of fraternal twins. About ________ of the differences in IQ among children can be traced to their genetic makeup. (p. 312)

4. What do adoption studies reveal about the contribution of environmental factors to IQ? (pp. 312–313)

____

____

5. Cite two types of testing conditions that result in test bias. (pp. 313–314)

   A. ____

   B. ____

6. Explain why some experts reject the idea that intelligence tests are biased. (p. 314)

____

____

7. Describe the types of questions that low-SES African-American parents typically ask their children. How do these experiences affect children's verbal skills? (p. 314)

   Questions: ____

____

   Verbal skills: ____

____

8. Match each of the following descriptions to either the collaborative (C) or hierarchical (H) style of communication. (p. 314)

   _____ Preferred by many parents without extensive schooling.
   _____ Becomes more common with increasing education.
   _____ The parent directs each child to carry out an aspect of the task independently.
   _____ Parent and child collaborate, each focused on the same aspect of the problem.

9. True or False: Because low-income ethnic minority children grow up in "object-oriented" homes, they often lack opportunities to use games and objects that promote certain intellectual skills. (p. 314)

10. The fear of being judged on the basis of a negative stereotype, or ______________________________, can trigger anxiety that interferes with performance. (p. 314)

11. Why is assessment of adaptive behavior especially important for minority children? (p. 315)

____

____

12. In ________________________, an adult uses purposeful teaching to find out what the child can attain with social support. This approach is consistent with Vygotsky's ______________________. (p. 315)

Social Issues: High-Stakes Testing

1. Explain how the U.S. No Child Left Behind Act has promoted high-stakes testing in schools. (p. 316)

____

____

____

2. According to proponents of high-stakes testing, how does this practice benefit students? (p. 316)

____

____

____

3. Evidence indicates that high-stakes testing often (undermines / upgrades) the quality of education. (p. 316)
4. List groups of students whose educational needs are especially likely to be neglected as a result of high-stakes testing. (p. 316)

____

5. True or False: Punishments associated with high-stakes testing have sparked unprecedented levels of educationally detrimental behaviors in adults. (p. 316)
6. How has high-stakes testing affected minority youths living in poverty? (p. 317)

____

____

7. True or False: High-stakes testing has led to an increased emphasis on teaching for deeper understanding. (p. 317)

Language Development

Vocabulary

1. Children's rate of vocabulary growth during the elementary years is (slower / faster) than in early childhood. (p. 316)
2. Describe two ways in which school-age children add new words to their vocabulary. (p. 317)

   A. ____

   B. ____

3. Summarize two advances in vocabulary that take place during the school-age years. (p. 317)

   A. ____

   B. ____

4. Provide an example that illustrates the school-age child's ability to appreciate the multiple meanings of words. (p. 317)

____

Grammar

1. Cite two grammatical achievements of middle childhood. (p. 317)

   A. ____

   B. ____

Pragmatics

1. Pragmatics refers to the ______________________ side of language. (p. 317)
2. How do the narratives of school-age children differ from those of preschoolers? (p. 317)

____

____

3. Most North American school-age children use a (topic-associating / topic-focused) narrative style, describing an experience from beginning to end. African-American children often use a (topic-associating / topic-focused) style in which they blend several similar anecdotes. As a result, (African-American / Caucasian-American) children's narratives are usually longer and more complex. (p. 318)

Learning Two Languages at a Time

1. List two ways that children can become bilingual. (p. 318)

   A. ______________________________

   B. ______________________________

2. True or False: Children of bilingual parents who teach them both languages in infancy and early childhood attain early language milestones according to a typical timetable. (p. 318)

3. True or False: Mastery of a second language must begin sometime in childhood for most second-language learners to attain full proficiency. (p. 318)

4. List several positive developmental consequences of bilingualism. (p. 318)

   ____

   ____

   ____

5. Describe Canada's language immersion programs, noting outcomes for students. (p. 318)

   Description: ______________________________

   ____

   Outcomes: ______________________________

   ____

6. Summarize the current debate in the United States regarding how best to educate ethnic minority children with limited English proficiency. (p. 318)

   English-only instruction: ______________________________

   ____

   Native-language instruction: ______________________________

   ____

7. True or False: In the United States, current public opinion and educational practice favor English-only instruction. (p. 318)

Learning in School

Class Size

1. Cite research indicating that class size influences children's learning. (p. 319)

   ____

   ____

   ____

2. Why is small class size beneficial to students? (p. 319)

   ____

   ____

Educational Philosophies

1. Indicate whether the following statements depict *constructivist* (C) or *traditional* (T) *classrooms*. (pp. 319–320)
   _____ Students are relatively passive.
   _____ The teacher is the sole authority for knowledge.
   _____ Students are evaluated by comparison with their own prior achievement.
   _____ Progress is evaluated by how well students keep pace with uniform standards for their grade.
   _____ Children are active agents, building their own knowledge.
   _____ Teachers provide support in response to children's needs.

2. (Constructivist / Traditional) instruction is prevalent today. (p. 320)

3. List several benefits associated with constructivist classrooms. (p. 320)

   ____

   ____

4. True or False: Research reveals many advantages, both academic and social, of delaying kindergarten entry. (p. 320)

5. Describe *social-constructivist classrooms*. (p. 320)

   ____

   ____

   ____

6. Cite three educational themes inspired by Vygotsky's sociocultural theory. (pp. 320–321)

   A. ____

   B. ____

   C. ____

7. In ___________________________, small groups of classmates work toward common goals. Children profit more from this experience when their partner is a(n) ("novice" / "expert"). (p. 321)

8. True or False: Western cultural-majority children typically require extensive guidance to succeed at *cooperative learning*. (p. 321)

Teacher–Student Interaction

1. True or False: Students in more academically demanding classrooms show better attendance and larger gains in math achievement. (p. 321)

2. How does teacher interaction with well-behaved, high-achieving students differ from teacher interaction with unruly students? (p. 321)

   Well-behaved: ____

   Unruly: ____

3. Define *educational self-fulfilling prophecies*. (p. 321)

   ____

   ____

4. Teacher expectations have a greater impact on (low / high) achievers. (p. 321)

Grouping Practices

1. In schools that practice (homogenous / heterogeneous) grouping, children of similar ability levels are taught together. How can this practice promote self-fulfilling prophecies? (p. 322)

____

____

2. List the benefits associated with multigrade classrooms. (p. 322)

____

____

Teaching Children with Special Needs

1. True or False: U.S. legislation mandates that schools place children who require special supports for learning in the "least restrictive" environments that meet their educational needs. (p. 322)
2. In ____________________, students with learning difficulties are placed in regular classrooms for all or part of the school day. Students placed full-time in regular classrooms experience ______________ inclusion. (p. 322)
3. Describe characteristics of students who have mild mental retardation. (p. 322)

____

____

4. A large number of students in *inclusive classrooms* have ________________________________, or great difficulty with one or more aspects of learning, usually reading. Their achievement is (considerably behind / on track with) what would be expected on the basis of their IQ. (p. 322)
5. Cite three factors that influence whether children with *learning disabilities* will benefit from inclusion. (p. 322)

   A. ____

   B. ____

   C. ____

6. Under what conditions do students with special needs often do best? (p. 322)

____

____

7. What steps can be taken to promote peer relations in inclusive classrooms? (p. 322)

____

____

8. __________ children display exceptional intellectual strengths. (p. 323)
9. Match each of the following terms with its definition. (p. 323)

_______	Outstanding performance in a specific field	A. *Creativity*
_______	The ability to produce work that is original yet appropriate	B. *Divergent thinking*
_______	Arriving at a single correct answer; emphasized on intelligence tests	C. *Convergent thinking*
_______	The generation of multiple and unusual possibilities when faced with a task or problem	D. *Talent*

10. True or False: Researchers agree that tests of divergent thinking are strong predictors of creative accomplishment in everyday life. (p. 323)

11. True or False: Individuals designated as *gifted* by virtue of high IQ are usually equally skilled across academic subjects. (p. 323)

12. Cite parental characteristics that help nurture talented children. (p. 323)

____

____

____

13. Describe two reasons why many gifted children and adolescents are socially isolated. (pp. 323–324)

A. _______________

B. _______________

14. The extent to which programs foster creativity and talent depends on whether they (provide enrichment in regular classrooms / pull children out for special instruction / advance brighter students to a higher grade / provide opportunities to acquire relevant skills). (p. 324)

How Well-Educated Are North American Children?

1. Cite four factors, both within and outside schools, that affect children's learning. (p. 324)

A. _______________ C. _______________

B. _______________ D. _______________

2. Provide two reasons why U.S. youths fall behind in academic accomplishment. (p. 324)

A. _______________

B. _______________

3. List three social forces that combine to foster a strong commitment to learning in Asian families and schools. (p. 325)

A. _______________

B. _______________

C. _______________

4. Describe characteristics of parents whose children consistently show superior academic achievement. (p. 325)

____

____

ASK YOURSELF . . .

For *Ask Yourself* questions for this chapter, along with feedback on the accuracy of your answers, please log on to MyDevelopmentLab (for registration and access, please visit mydevelopmentlab.com or follow the instructions on page ix).

(1) Select the Multimedia Library.

(2) Choose the explore option.

(3) Find your chapter from the drop down box.

(4) Click find now.

(5) Complete questions and choose "Submit answers for grading" or "Clear answers" to start over.

SUGGESTED READINGS

Fiese, B. H. (2006). *Family routines and rituals*. New Haven: Yale University Press. Examines the importance of family routines, such as shared mealtimes, for favorable child and adolescent development. The author presents research showing how family routines and rituals contribute to physical, cognitive, and social/emotional well-being.

Heinberg, L. J., & Thompson, J. K. (2009). *Obesity in youth: Causes, consequences, and cures.* Washington, DC: American Psychological Association. Presents leading research on the obesity epidemic among American children, including genetic and environmental contributions; psychological consequences, such as teasing and poor body image; treatment options; and strategies for preventing overweight and obesity.

Johnson, A. W. (2009). *Objectifying measures: The dominance of high-stakes testing and the politics of schooling.* Philadelphia, PA: Temple University Press. A compelling look at the high-stakes testing movement, this book examines the effects of standardized testing on educational quality in the United States. The author also presents research how high-stakes testing affects minority students from low-SES backgrounds.

Stewart-Brown, S., & Edmunds, L. (2007). *Educating people to be emotionally intelligent.* Westport, CT: Praeger. Highlights the importance of emotional intelligence for favorable adjustment throughout the lifespan. The authors also present strategies for enhancing emotional development in both children and adults.

CROSSWORD PUZZLE 9.1

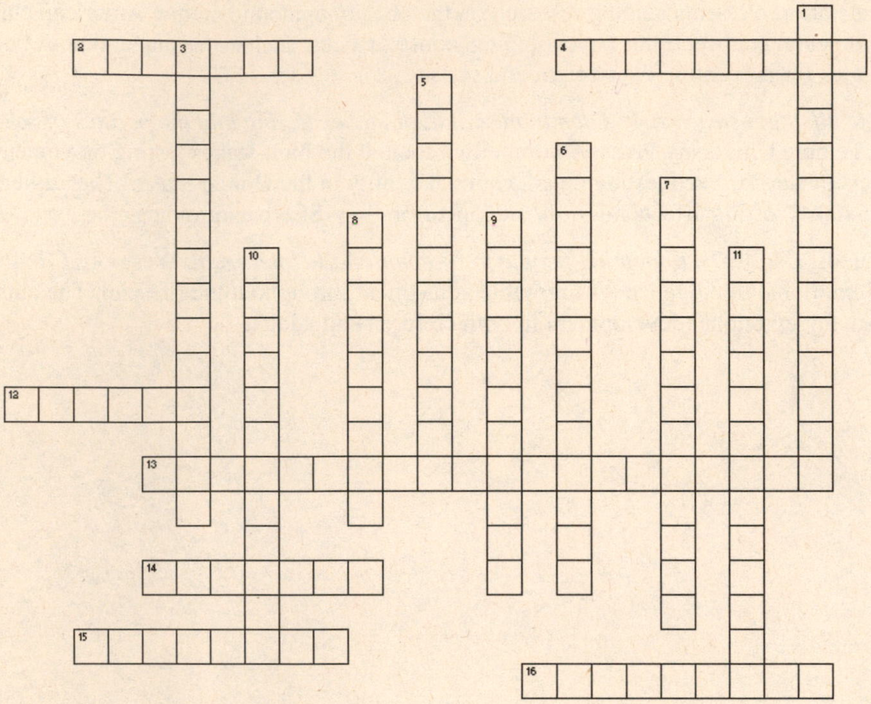

Across

2. Greater-than-20-percent increase over healthy weight, based on body mass index
4. Ability to order items along a quantitative dimension
12. Stereotype ______: fear of being judged on the basis of a negative stereotype
13. ______-______ classroom: children develop understandings jointly with teachers and peers (2 words, hyph.)
14. ______ approach: children should first learn the basic rules for translating text into sounds
15. ______ operational stage: Piaget's third stage; thought becomes more logical, flexible, and organized
16. Memory strategy of repeating information to oneself

Down

1. ______ classrooms encourage students to build their own knowledge.
3. Cognitive ______-______: monitoring progress toward a goal, redirecting unsuccessful efforts (2 words, hyph.)
5. Memory strategy of grouping related items together
6. ______-______ approach: parallels natural language learning, exposing children to complete texts (2 words, hyph.)
7. Ability to mentally reverse a series of steps, returning to the starting point
8. Transitive ______: the ability to seriate mentally
9. Memory strategy of relating pieces of information that do not belong to the same category
10. Emotional ______: ability to process and adapt to emotional information
11. Mental representations of familiar large-scale spaces (2 words)

CROSSWORD PUZZLE 9.2

Across

1. ______ classrooms: students with learning difficulties attend regular classrooms for all or part of the school day
3. Outstanding performance in a specific field
6. Displaying exceptional intellectual strengths
9. Sternberg's ______ theory of successful intelligence involves balancing three intelligences to achieve success.
12. Play involving friendly chasing and play-fighting (3 words, hyph.)
13. Gardner's theory of ______ intelligences involves distinct sets of processing operations.
14. ______ assessment uses individualized teaching to see what the child can attain with social support.
15. ______ thinking: generation of multiple unusual solutions
16. Ability to produce work that is original yet appropriate

Down

2. Educational ______-______ prophecies: children may start to live up to teachers' attitudes towards them (2 words, hyph.)
4. ______ classroom: the teacher is the sole authority for knowledge; students are relatively passive
5. Learning ______: involve great difficulty with learning; achievement considerably behind expectations for IQ
7. ______ thinking involves arriving at a single correct solution to a problem.
8. Involves inattention, impulsivity, and excessive motor activity, resulting in academic and social problems (abbr.)
10. ______ learning: small groups of classmates work toward common goals
11. _____ hierarchy: stable ordering of group members that predicts who will win in conflicts

PRACTICE TEST #1

1. In all cultures, children from ages 6 to 11 __________ (p. 289)
   a. take on new responsibilities.
   b. undergo rapid growth spurts.
   c. begin formal schooling.
   d. experience a significant decline in appetite.

2. During middle childhood, __________ (p. 290)
   a. children's bodies become less flexible than in the preschool years.
   b. boys tend to be shorter and lighter than girls.
   c. boys have more muscle and more body fat than girls.
   d. the lower portion of the body grows fastest.

3. Family dinnertimes __________ (p. 291)
   a. occur with increased frequency between ages 9 and 14.
   b. often take place at fast food restaurants, especially in the United States.
   c. lead to diets higher in fruits and vegetables.
   d. are associated with a higher rate of childhood obesity.

4. Which of the following is the most effective treatment for overweight and obese children? (p. 293)
   a. healthy school-lunch options
   b. family-based intervention
   c. a strict diet and exercise regimen
   d. a nutrition and lifestyle course

5. What is the most common chronic disease in childhood? (p. 293)
   a. asthma
   b. ear infections
   c. diabetes
   d. myopia

6. Compared to girls, school-age boys are __________ (p. 296)
   a. less positive about their athletic ability.
   b. held to higher expectations in athletics.
   c. more skilled in fine-motor capacities.
   d. more skilled in tasks requiring balance and agility.

7. In middle childhood, gains in perspective taking permit the transition to __________, which contribute(s) greatly to emotional and social development. (p. 296)
   a. rough-and-tumble play
   b. child-led, rule-oriented games
   c. organized sports
   d. make-believe play

8. What does research suggest about school recess? (p. 298)
   a. Most school-age children get at least 40 minutes of daily recess.
   b. Elementary school students are less attentive after recess than before recess.
   c. Recess can boost social maturity when adults direct, rather than supervise, games.
   d. Students' engagement in peer conversation and games during recess leads to gains in academic achievement.

9. Most school-age children in the United States __________ (p. 299)
   a. have at least three hours of physical education per week.
   b. are not active enough for good health.
   c. are overweight or obese.
   d. engage in aggressive rough-and-tumble play.

10. Nine-year-old Tomas can easily sort sticks of different lengths from smallest to largest. This ability is called __________ (p. 299)
    a. seriation.
    b. classification.
    c. cognitive mapping.
    d. conservation.

11. Preschoolers and young school-age children are likely to __________ (p. 300)
    a. include landmarks on the maps they draw.
    b. give clear, well-organized directions.
    c. have a general mental map of a large area.
    d. omit landmarks on the maps they draw.

12. Compared with Piaget's theory, Case's neo-Piagetian theory __________ (p. 302)
    a. completely dismisses a stage approach to cognitive development.
    b. dismisses the importance of information processing in cognitive development.
    c. better accounts for unevenness in cognitive development.
    d. maintains that development of operational thinking reflects a sudden shift to a new stage.

13. Gains in cognitive inhibition help school-age children __________ (p. 303)
    a. prevent their minds from straying to irrelevant thoughts.
    b. retrieve information from long-term memory.
    c. retrieve information from short-term memory.
    d. understand their own mental processes.

14. Which of the following statements about ADHD is true? (p. 304)
    a. A gender bias explains why many boys with ADHD are often overlooked.
    b. To be diagnosed with ADHD, children must have symptoms that appear before age 10 as a persistent problem.
    c. Research consistently shows that a stressful home life often causes ADHD.
    d. Children with ADHD score 7 to 10 points lower than other children on intelligence tests.

15. Quentin needs to remember the words *tree* and *toaster*. If he uses the memory strategy of elaboration, he will __________ (p. 304)
    a. think of words that rhyme with both.
    b. imagine a tree with toasters growing out of it.
    c. write the words several times on a piece of paper.
    d. say the words over and over to himself.

16. Although 9-year-old Vivian knows that she should reread a complicated passage in her science book to make sure she understands the information, she instead moves on to the next passage. What does this demonstrate about Vivian's thinking? (p. 307)
    a. Vivian has yet to acquire metacognitive understanding.
    b. Vivian has a sense of academic self-efficacy.
    c. Vivian is a learned-helpless child.
    d. Vivian has not yet mastered cognitive self-regulation.

17. Many studies show that children best learn how to read __________ (p. 307)
    a. through a whole-language approach.
    b. through a phonics approach.
    c. with a mixture of phonics and whole language.
    d. through exposure to educational media.

18. Most intelligence tests __________ (p. 309)
    a. address cultural and situational factors that affect children's thinking.
    b. provide a general intelligence score and scores for separate intellectual factors.
    c. provide both a developmental quotient (DQ) and a general intelligence score (IQ).
    d. are poor predictors of academic performance.

19. What is the major limitation of the componential approach to defining intelligence? (p. 310)
    a. It is more concerned with analyzing test data than learning how to improve performance.
    b. It is unable to identify relationships between information-processing abilities and intelligence test scores.
    c. It regards intelligence as entirely due to causes within the child.
    d. It regards intelligence as entirely caused by cultural and situational factors.

20. According to Sternberg's triarchic theory of successful intelligence, ___________ intelligence reminds us that intelligent behavior is never free of cultural influence. (p. 311)
    a. analytical
    b. creative
    c. practical
    d. emotional

21. Ten-year-old Arjun senses that a fellow classmate is feeling sad, and he makes a point to be especially kind to her throughout the day. Arjun is demonstrating __________ (p. 313)
    a. emotional intelligence.
    b. cognitive self-regulation.
    c. divergent thinking.
    d. convergent thinking.

22. Eleven-year-old Sarah's performance on her state's standardized test is adversely affected by her worries that she, as an African-American student, is not expected to do well on the test. This anxiety she feels is known as __________ (p. 314)
    a. dynamic assessment.
    b. in-group bias.
    c. stereotype threat.
    d. cultural negativity.

23. Which of the following statements about high-stakes testing is true? (p. 316)
    a. High-stakes testing leads to greater rigor in the classroom.
    b. High-stakes testing improves student motivation and achievement.
    c. When high-stakes testing is introduced in high school, fewer low-income minority students drop out.
    d. High-stakes testing often undermines, rather than upgrades, the quality of education.

24. School-age children learn words __________ (p. 316)
    a. at a slower rate than toddlers and preschoolers.
    b. at a faster rate than toddlers and preschoolers.
    c. mainly through rote memorization.
    d. through trial-and-error and adult correction.

25. When asked which shirt he wanted to wear, 9-year-old Vaughn said, "the blue shirt with the baseball on the sleeve. You know, the one grandma bought for me." Vaughn's description illustrates which of the following language developments in middle childhood? (p. 317)
    a. vocabulary
    b. grammar
    c. a reflective approach to language
    d. pragmatics

26. Which of the following statements accurately describes the sensitive period in acquiring a second language? (p. 318)
    a. There is a gradual decrease from childhood to adulthood in the ability to acquire a second language.
    b. After age 6, there is a dramatic decline in the ability to acquire a second language.
    c. Adults can master a second language nearly as easily as a school-age child.
    d. Unlike first-language development, there is no sensitive period for second-language development.

27. Research on bilingual development indicates that __________ (p. 318)
    a. bilingual children have difficulty transferring their language skills in one language to the other.
    b. adolescents and adults acquire a second language more easily than school-age children.
    c. there is no sensitive period for second-language learning.
    d. bilingual children are advanced in cognitive flexibility.

28. In a constructivist classroom, students __________ (p. 320)
    a. are relatively passive.
    b. are evaluated against a uniform set of standards.
    c. solve self-chosen problems.
    d. rarely work in groups.

29. What does research indicate about cooperative learning? (p. 321)
    a. Western cultural-majority children require very little teacher guidance to succeed at cooperative learning.
    b. Children benefit most from cooperative learning when they are grouped with peers of the same ability.
    c. The quality of children's collaborative discussions predicts gains in cognitive skills that last for weeks.
    d. In multigrade classrooms, cooperative learning often promotes educational self-fulfilling prophecies.

30. Educational self-fulfilling prophecies __________ (p. 321)
    a. have a greater impact on high than low achievers.
    b. are especially likely to occur in classrooms that emphasize competition.
    c. are common in social-constructivist classrooms.
    d. are usually positive, particularly for low achievers.

PRACTICE TEST #2

1. A 6-year-old child's brain __________ (p. 289)
   a. is similar in size to a toddler's brain.
   b. has reached 90 percent of its adult weight.
   c. first begins to lateralize.
   d. follows the same growth trends as her body.

2. During the school years, physical growth __________ (p. 290)
   a. is much faster in boys than girls.
   b. slows down considerably from the rapid pace of early childhood.
   c. continues at the slow, regular pace of early childhood.
   d. continues to occur in rapid, dramatic bursts.

3. Which of the following is one of the few health conditions that increases with SES? (p. 291)
   a. hearing loss
   b. myopia
   c. asthma
   d. obesity

4. Obesity __________ (p. 292)
   a. is increasing in developing nations.
   b. is an inherited trait.
   c. tends to decrease with age.
   d. is decreasing in industrialized nations.

5. Which of the following parenting practices leads to healthy eating habits in children? (p. 293)
   a. enforcing a strict, low-calorie diet
   b. frequently monitoring the child's weight
   c. using treats as a reward for trying new foods
   d. eating regular family meals at home

6. Most 6-year-olds can __________ (p. 295)
   a. produce letters of uniform height and spacing.
   b. write their first and last names.
   c. create drawings that suggest three dimensions.
   d. write in cursive.

7. In which of the following activities do school-age girls tend to outperform boys? (p. 295)
   a. throwing
   b. kicking
   c. hopping
   d. running

8. Rough-and-tumble play __________ (p. 298)
   a. helps children form a dominance hierarchy.
   b. is equally common in girls and boys.
   c. emerges in middle childhood and peaks in puberty.
   d. leads to aggression and hostility in school-age children.

9. In a series of studies, elementary school students were __________ (p. 298)
   a. especially hyper after morning recess periods.
   b. less attentive in the classroom before recess than after it.
   c. more attentive in the classroom after recess than before it.
   d. more agitated and irritable after recess than before it.

10. In first grade, Caleb began collecting baseball cards. Now that he's older, Caleb spends a great deal of time sorting his cards, arranging them by team, and putting them into albums. Which of Piaget's concepts is Caleb demonstrating? (p. 299)
    a. conservation
    b. centration
    c. classification
    d. spatial reasoning

11. In school-age children, concrete operational thought is limited in that they __________ (p. 301)
    a. have difficulty with reversibility tasks.
    b. are unable to focus on more than one aspect of a problem.
    c. do not consider the perspectives of others.
    d. do not come up with general logical principles.

12. Research on the impact of culture and schooling on concrete operational thought indicates that __________ (p. 301)
    a. specific cultural practices, especially formal schooling, affect children's mastery of these tasks.
    b. children master concrete operational tasks at about the same age everywhere, regardless of life experiences.
    c. formal schooling has little impact on children's mastery of concrete operational tasks.
    d. children in tribal and village societies master concrete operational tasks earlier than children in industrialized nations.

13. According to Case's neo-Piagetian theory, with practice, cognitive schemes become more automatic, freeing up space in children's __________ (p. 302)
    a. central conceptual structures.
    b. sensory register.
    c. working memory.
    d. cerebral cortex.

14. Unlike Piaget, information-processing theorists __________ (p. 303)
    a. focus on overall cognitive change.
    b. examine separate aspects of thinking.
    c. fail to consider biological contributions to cognitive development.
    d. view development as a discontinuous restructuring of children's thinking.

15. ADHD is __________ (p. 304)
    a. highly heritable.
    b. often caused by a stressful home life.
    c. a temporary condition, rarely extending into adulthood.
    d. often overlooked in boys.

16. What memory strategy is 9-year-old Nithya using when she repeats the state capitals to herself over and over again before a test? (p. 303)
    a. elaboration
    b. organization
    c. rehearsal
    d. planning

17. At age 7, children __________ (p. 306)
    a. view the mind as a passive container of information.
    b. understand second-order false belief.
    c. excel at cognitive self-regulation.
    d. cannot yet make mental inferences.

18. How can parents and teachers foster cognitive self-regulation? (p. 307)
    a. by regularly assessing and monitoring students' learning outcomes
    b. by explaining the effectiveness of mental strategies
    c. by requiring students to complete schoolwork on their own
    d. by assigning tasks below students' actual ability level

19. Which of the following statements about mathematics teaching is true? (p. 308)
    a. Calculators and computer programs are the most effective methods for teaching mathematics to school-age children.
    b. For most school-age children, experimentation in mathematical strategies leads to frustration and an increase in errors.
    c. Compared with Asian parents, North American parents are more likely to provide their preschoolers with extensive practice in counting and adding.
    d. Compared with North American students, Asian students spend more time exploring math concepts and less to drill and repetition.

20. The __________ was the first intelligence test to be standardized on children representing the total population of the United States, including ethnic minorities, and was designed to downplay culturally dependent knowledge. (p. 310)
    a. Stanford-Binet
    b. WISC-IV
    c. Sternberg
    d. Bayley

21. Gardner's theory __________ (p. 311)
    a. dismisses the idea of general intelligence.
    b. dismisses the idea of independent intelligences.
    c. ignores the effects of culture on mental development.
    d. overlooks biological contributions to intelligence.

22. Emotional intelligence __________ (p. 313)
    a. is unrelated to IQ.
    b. predicts success in the workplace.
    c. can now be measured using traditional IQ tests.
    d. is highly heritable.

23. Adoption studies reveal that __________ (p. 313)
    a. an advantaged home life does little to increase IQ test performance.
    b. children of low-IQ biological mothers show a steady decline in IQ over middle childhood.
    c. heredity is a more powerful predictor of IQ test performance than environmental factors.
    d. IQ test performance can be greatly improved by an advantaged home life.

24. Dynamic assessment __________ (p. 315)
    a. is a component of high-stakes testing.
    b. often underestimates the IQs of ethnic minority children.
    c. is an innovation consistent with Piaget's notion of discovery learning.
    d. introduces purposeful teaching to find out what the child can attain with social support.

25. The U.S. No Child Left Behind Act mandates that __________ (p. 316)
    a. dynamic assessment be included in high-stakes testing.
    b. each state evaluate every public school's performance through annual achievement testing.
    c. gifted children be offered specialized academic programs to meet their unique needs.
    d. "failing" schools be given government funding to increase students' test performance.

26. Because African-American children often use a _________ style of communication, their narratives are usually longer and more complex than those of white children. (p. 318)
    a. topic-associating
    b. topic-focused
    c. pragmatic
    d. repetitive

27. Non-English-speaking children in North America are more involved in learning and acquire English more easily __________ (p. 319)
    a. in English-only classrooms.
    b. in segregated classrooms where only their native language is spoken.
    c. in classrooms that integrate both languages.
    d. when they receive English instruction outside of the regular classroom.

28. In Gerald's classroom, there are richly equipped learning centers, and small groups and individuals solve self-chosen problems. Students are evaluated based on their own prior development. Gerald is in a(n) _______________ classroom. (pp. 319–320)
    a. traditional
    b. social-constructivist
    c. inclusive
    d. constructivist

29. Gifted students are best served by __________ (p. 324)
    a. educational programs that build on their strengths.
    b. ample opportunities to improve their convergent thinking skills.
    c. self-contained classrooms.
    d. traditional, teacher-directed instruction.

30. In international studies of reading, mathematics, and science achievement, children in the United States generally perform __________ (p. 324)
    a. above children in Hong Kong, Korea, and Japan.
    b. far below the international average.
    c. far above the international average.
    d. at the international average.

CHAPTER 10
EMOTIONAL AND SOCIAL DEVELOPMENT IN MIDDLE CHILDHOOD

BRIEF CHAPTER SUMMARY

According to Erikson, the combination of adult expectations and children's drive toward mastery sets the stage for the psychosocial conflict of middle childhood—industry versus inferiority—which is resolved positively when experiences lead children to develop a sense of competence at useful skills and tasks. Psychological traits and social comparisons appear in children's self-concepts, and a hierarchically organized self-esteem emerges. Children who make mastery-oriented attributions credit success to ability and failure to controllable factors, but children who receive negative feedback about their ability are likely to develop learned helplessness, attributing success to external factors, such as luck, and failure to low ability. Greater self-awareness and social sensitivity support emotional development in middle childhood. Gains take place in experience of self-conscious emotions, understanding of emotional states, and emotional self-regulation. Cognitive maturity and experiences in which adults and peers encourage children to take note of another's viewpoint support gains in perspective-taking skill. By middle childhood, children have internalized rules for good conduct. They clarify and link moral imperatives and social conventions, considering the purpose of the rule, people's intentions, and the context of their actions.

By the end of middle childhood, children form peer groups, which give them insight into larger social structures. Friendship becomes more complex and psychologically based, providing children with a context for the development of trust and sensitivity. Peer acceptance becomes a powerful predictor of current and future psychological adjustment.

School-age children extend their awareness of gender stereotypes to personality traits and academic subjects. Boys' masculine gender identities strengthen, whereas girls' identities become more flexible. Cultural values and parental attitudes influence these trends.

In middle childhood, the amount of time children spend with parents declines dramatically. Child rearing shifts toward coregulation as parents grant children more decision-making power. Sibling rivalry tends to increase in middle childhood, and in response, siblings often strive to be different from one another. When children experience divorce—often followed by entry into blended families as a result of remarriage—child, parent, and family characteristics all influence how well they fare. Growing up in dual-earner families can have many benefits for school-age children, particularly when mothers enjoy their work, when work settings and communities support their child-rearing responsibilities, and when high-quality child care is available, including appropriate after-school activities for school-age children.

Fears and anxieties in middle childhood are directed toward new concerns, including physical safety, media events, academic performance, parents' health, and peer relations. Child sexual abuse has devastating consequences for children and is especially difficult to treat. Personal characteristics of children, a warm parental relationship, and social supports outside the immediate family are related to the development of resilience: the ability to cope with stressful life conditions.

LEARNING OBJECTIVES

After reading this chapter, you should be able to:

10.1 Describe Erikson's stage of industry versus inferiority, noting major personality changes in middle childhood. (p. 330)

10.2 Describe school-age children's self-concept and self-esteem, and discuss factors that affect their achievement-related attributions. (pp. 330–334)

10.3 Cite changes in understanding and expression of emotion in middle childhood, including the importance of problem-centered coping and emotion-centered coping for managing emotion. (pp. 335–336)

10.4 Trace the development of perspective taking in middle childhood, and discuss the relationship between perspective taking and social skills. (pp. 336–337)

10.5 Describe changes in moral understanding during middle childhood, and note the extent to which children hold racial and ethnic biases. (pp. 337–339)

10.6 Summarize changes in peer sociability during middle childhood, including characteristics of peer groups and friendships. (pp. 339–341)

10.7 Describe four categories of peer acceptance, noting how each is related to social behavior, and discuss ways to help rejected children. (pp. 341–342, 343)

10.8 Describe changes in gender-stereotyped beliefs and gender identity during middle childhood, including sex differences and cultural influences. (pp. 342–345)

10.9 Discuss changes in parent–child communication and sibling relationships in middle childhood, and describe the adjustment of only children. (pp. 345–346)

10.10 Discuss factors that influence children's adjustment to divorce and blended families, highlighting the importance of parent and child characteristics, as well as social supports within the family and surrounding community. (pp. 347–350)

10.11 Explain how maternal employment and life in dual-earner families affect school-age children, noting the influence of social supports within the family and surrounding community, including child care for school-age children. (pp. 350–351)

10.12 Cite common fears and anxieties in middle childhood, with particular attention to school phobia. (pp. 352, 353)

10.13 Discuss factors related to child sexual abuse and its consequences for children's development. (pp. 352–354, 355)

10.14 Cite factors that foster resilience in middle childhood. (p. 354)

STUDY QUESTIONS

Erikson's Theory: Industry versus Inferiority

1. According to Erikson, what two factors set the stage for *industry versus inferiority*? (p. 330)

   A. ______________________________

   B. ______________________________

2. What must children develop in order to positively resolve Erikson's industry versus inferiority conflict? (p. 330)

   ____

3. In industrialized nations, the beginning of ____________________ marks the transition to middle childhood. (p. 330)

4. List two factors that contribute to a sense of inferiority during middle childhood. (p. 330)

   A. ______________________________

   B. ______________________________

5. Erikson's concept of industry combines the following four developments: (p. 330)

   A. ____________________ C. ____________________

   B. ____________________ D. ____________________

Self-Understanding

1. List three improvements in self-understanding that occur during middle childhood. (p. 330)

   A. ______________________________

   B. ______________________________

   C. ______________________________

Self-Concept

1. In middle childhood, children's self-descriptions emphasize (competencies / specific behaviors). Older school-age children are far (less / more) likely than younger children to describe themselves in extreme, all-or-none ways. (p. 330)

2. How do older children's *social comparisons* differ from those of younger children? (p. 330)

____

____

3. Describe factors that are responsible for revisions in the structure of self-concept during middle childhood. (p. 330)

____

____

4. Discuss the relationship between perspective-taking skills and the development of self-concept. (pp. 330–331)

____

____

____

5. True or False: As children move into adolescence, self-concept is increasingly vested in feedback from close friends. (p. 331)

Development of Self-Esteem

1. List four broad self-evaluations that develop by the age of 6 to 7. (p. 331)

   A. ______________________ C. ______________________

   B. ______________________ D. ______________________

2. During middle childhood and adolescence, perceived ______________________ correlates more strongly with overall self-worth than any other self-esteem factor. (pp. 331–332)

3. For most children, self-esteem (declines / increases) during the first few years of elementary school and then (declines / increases) from fourth to sixth grade. (p. 332)

Influences on Self-Esteem

1. Match each type of self-esteem with its associated outcomes in middle childhood. (p. 332)

   _______ Anxiety, depression, and increasing antisocial behavior
   _______ Increased investment and performance in sports
   _______ Children who are consistently better-liked by classmates
   _______ Predicts how important, useful, and enjoyable children find school subjects, their willingness to try hard, and their achievement

   A. High academic self-esteem
   B. High social self-esteem
   C. High athletic self-esteem
   D. Low self-esteem in all areas

2. Chinese and Japanese children score (lower / higher) in self-esteem than North American children. Briefly explain this finding. (p. 332)

____

____

____

3. True or False: Boys' overall sense of self-worth is much higher than girls'. (p. 332)

4. Compared to Caucasian children, African-American children tend to have slightly (lower / higher) self-esteem. Briefly explain this finding. (p. 332)

____

____

5. Match the following child-rearing practices with their effects on self-esteem in middle childhood. (p. 332)

_______ Authoritative style; warm, positive parenting; appropriate expectations with explanations	A. Promotes unrealistically high self-esteem
_______ Controlling parenting; repeated disapproval and insults	B. Promotes high self-esteem
_______ Indulgent parenting	C. Promotes low self-esteem

6. True or False: Although the self-esteem of U.S. youths rose sharply from the 1970s to the 1990s, American youths are achieving less well and displaying more antisocial behavior than previous generations. Cite parenting practices that may contribute to this trend. (pp. 332–333)

____

____

____

7. _____________ are common, everyday explanations for the causes of behavior. (p. 333)

8. Attribute the following characteristics to either children who make *mastery-oriented attributions* (M) or those who develop *learned helplessness* (L). (p. 333)

_______ Credit successes to external factors
_______ Credit successes to internal factors
_______ Attribute failures to factors that can be changed or controlled
_______ Attribute failures to ability
_______ Take an industrious, persistent approach to learning
_______ Often give up without really trying

9. True or False: Over time, the ability of learned-helpless children no longer predicts their performance. Explain your response. (p. 333)

____

____

____

10. Describe parental responses to children's failures and successes that promote learned helplessness in children. (p. 333)

Failures: ____

____

Successes: ____

____

11. Teachers who are caring and helpful and emphasize learning over getting good grades tend to have (learned-helpless / mastery-oriented) students. Students with unsupportive teachers often face outcomes that lead to (learned-helpless / mastery-oriented) attributions. (p. 333)

12. (Boys / Girls) and (low / high)-SES ethnic minority students are especially likely to be undermined by negative adult feedback. (p. 333)

13. ______________________ is an intervention that encourages learned-helpless children to believe that they can overcome failure by exerting more effort. Describe this technique. (p. 334)

____

____

____

Emotional Development

Self-Conscious Emotions

1. Describe changes in how children experience pride and guilt during middle childhood. (p. 335)

   Pride: ____

   ____

   Guilt: ____

   ____

Emotional Understanding

1. Describe three ways in which school-age children's ability to appreciate mixed emotions contributes to their emotional understanding. (p. 335)

   A. ____

   B. ____

   C. ____

2. What factors lead to a rise in empathy during middle childhood? (p. 335)

   ____

   ____

Emotional Self-Regulation

1. In ______________*-centered coping*, children appraise the situation as changeable, identify the difficulty, and decide what to do about it. When little can be done about an outcome, children engage in ______________*-centered coping*, which is internal, private, and aimed at controlling distress. (p. 335)

2. In middle childhood, children increasingly prefer (aggression / crying / sulking / verbal strategies) to regulate their negative emotions. (p. 336)

3. Describe parenting practices experienced by emotionally well-regulated children versus children with poor emotional self-regulation. (p. 336)

   Well-regulated: ____

   ____

   Poorly regulated: ____

   ____

Understanding Others: Perspective Taking

1. Match each of Selman's stages of *perspective taking* with the appropriate description. (p. 336)

_______ Understands that third-party perspective taking can be influenced by larger societal values

_______ Recognizes that self and others can have different perspectives but frequently confuses the two

_______ Understands that different perspectives may result from access to different information

_______ Can imagine how the self and others are viewed from the perspective of an impartial third party

_______ Can view own thoughts, feelings, and behavior from others' perspectives; recognizes that others can do the same

A. Undifferentiated
B. Social-informational
C. Self-reflective
D. Third-party
E. Societal

2. How do social skills and experiences contribute to individual differences in children's perspective taking? (pp. 336–337)

____

____

____

____

Moral Development

Moral and Social-Conventional Understanding

1. During the school years, children interpret moral rules (less / more) flexibly. How do cultural values influence these evaluations? (p. 337)

____

____

2. Cite three ways in which children clarify and link moral imperatives and social conventions in middle childhood. (p. 337)

A. ____

B. ____

C. ____

3. True or False: Children in Western and non-Western cultures reason similarly about moral and social-conventional concerns. (p. 337)

Understanding Individual Rights

1. When children in diverse cultures challenge adult authority, they typically do so within the (moral / personal / social-conventional) domain. (p. 337)

2. How do notions of personal choice enhance children's moral understanding? (p. 338)

____

____

____

3. How do changes in the understanding of individual rights among older school-age children contribute to declines in prejudice? (p. 338)

____

____

____

Understanding Diversity and Inequality

1. Children pick up associations about white people and people of color from (parents and friends / societal attitudes and environmental messages). (p. 338)
2. Describe research findings on white and minority children's evaluations of their own and other racial groups during the early school years. (p. 338)

   White children: ____

   ____

   Minority children: ____

   ____

3. What capacity contributes to a decline in voicing of negative attitudes toward minorities? (p. 338)

   ____

4. List factors that influence the extent to which children hold racial and ethnic biases. (pp. 338–339)

   A. ____

   B. ____

   C. ____

5. True or False: The positive effects of assignment to diverse cooperative learning groups typically generalize to relationships beyond the group. (p. 339)
6. Briefly summarize two additional methods of reducing childhood prejudice. (p. 339)

   A. ____

   B. ____

Peer Relations

Peer Groups

1. ____________________ are collectives that generate unique values and standards for behavior and a social structure of leaders and followers. (p. 339)
2. Describe the function of "peer culture," and discuss positive influences of group identity. (p. 340)

   A. ____

   B. ____

3. True or False: Most school-age children believe it is wrong to exclude a child from a *peer group*. (p. 340)
4. Describe outcomes for school-age children who are socially excluded from a peer group. (p. 340)

   ____

   ____

Friendships

1. Summarize children's view of friendship in middle childhood. (p. 340)

____

____

____

2. True or False: School-age children are less selective in their choice of friends than they were at younger ages. (p. 340)
3. In what ways do school-age friends resemble one another? (p. 340)

____

____

4. Friendships (do / do not) tend to remain stable over middle childhood. (p. 340)
5. Describe qualities of aggressive girls' and boys' friendships. (p. 341)

Aggressive girls: ____

____

Aggressive boys: ____

____

Peer Acceptance

1. ____________________ refers to likability—the extent to which a child is viewed by a group of agemates as a worthy social partner. How does this concept differ from friendship? (p. 341)

____

____

2. Match each category of *peer acceptance* with its description. (p. 341)

_______	Get many positive peer votes	A.	*Controversial children*
_______	Get many negative peer votes	B.	*Neglected children*
_______	Get a large number of positive and negative peer votes	C.	*Popular children*
_______	Are seldom mentioned, either positively or negatively	D.	*Rejected children*

3. True or False: All school-age children fit into one of the categories of peer acceptance described in Question 2. (p. 341)
4. Briefly summarize the emotional and social consequences of peer rejection. (p. 341)

____

____

____

____

5. What two early influences may largely explain the link between peer acceptance and adjustment? (p. 341)

A. ____

B. ____

6. Match the following subtypes of popular and rejected children to the appropriate description. (pp. 341–342)

_______	Show high rates of conflict; physical and relational aggression; and hyperactive, inattentive, and impulsive behavior	A. *Popular-prosocial children*
_______	Combine academic and social competence	B. *Rejected-aggressive children*
_______	"Tough" boys and relationally aggressive children	C. *Rejected-withdrawn children*
_______	Timid children who are passive and socially awkward	D. *Popular-antisocial children*

7. With age, peers like popular-antisocial children (less / more). (p. 342)

8. True or False: Controversial children are hostile and disruptive but also engage in high rates of positive, prosocial acts. (p. 342)

9. True or False: Neglected children are more poorly adjusted and display less socially competent behavior than their "average" counterparts. (p. 342)

10. Summarize three interventions designed to help rejected children. (p. 342)

    Social-skills training: ____

    ____

    Perspective taking and solving social problems: ____

    ____

    Parenting: ____

    ____

Biology and Environment: Bullies and Their Victims

1. Through ______________________________, certain children become targets of verbal and physical attacks or other forms of abuse. (p. 343)

2. Describe characteristics of bullies. (p. 343)

   ____

   ____

3. Describe biologically based traits and family characteristics of victimized children. (p. 343)

   Biological: ____

   ____

   ____

   Family: ____

   ____

   ____

4. List adjustment difficulties associated with chronic victims of bullying. (p. 343)

   ____

   ____

5. True or False: Passive victims of bullying are more despised by peers than aggressive bully victims. (p. 343)

6. Describe individual and school-based interventions for *peer victimization*. (p. 343)

   Individual: ____

   ____

   School-based: ____

   ____

Gender Typing

Gender-Stereotyped Beliefs

1. Stereotyping of personality traits (decreases / increases) steadily in middle childhood. (p. 342)
2. Explain how adult treatment of boys and girls contributes to children's gender-stereotyped beliefs. (pp. 342–343)

   Boys: ____

   ____

   Girls: ____

   ____

3. Indicate which of the following academic subjects and skills children typically stereotype as masculine (M) or feminine (F). (p. 343)

   _____ Reading skills _____ Spelling _____ Mechanical
   _____ Mathematics _____ Art and music _____ Athletics

4. True or False: As school-age children extend their awareness of gender stereotypes, they become more closed-minded about what males and females can do. (p. 344)

Gender Identity and Behavior

1. Indicate whether the following descriptors are typical of boys' (B) or girls' (G) gender identity development during middle childhood. (p. 344)

   _____ Strengthen their identification with gender-stereotyped personality traits
   _____ Often describe themselves as having some other-gender characteristics
   _____ More often consider traditionally other-gender future work roles
   _____ Usually stick to gender-stereotyped pursuits

2. Cite two factors that influence the changes described in Question 1. (p. 344)

   A. ____

   B. ____

3. List and define three self-evaluations included in school-age children's gender identity. (p. 344)

   A. ____

   B. ____

   C. ____

4. Gender-typical and gender-contented children (decline / increase) in self-esteem in middle childhood. In contrast, gender-atypical and gender-discontented children's self-esteem (declines / increases). (p. 344)

5. Summarize two approaches to helping children who feel gender-atypical. (pp. 344–345)

   A. ______________________________

   ____

   B. ______________________________

   ____

Family Influences

Parent–Child Relationships

1. True or False: In middle childhood, the amount of time that children spend with parents declines dramatically. (p. 345)
2. During the school years, child rearing becomes easier for those parents who established a(n) ______________ parenting style during the early years. (p. 345)
3. In *coregulation* (children / parents) exercise general oversight and (children / parents) take charge of moment-by-moment decision making. What makes this form of supervision effective? (p. 345)

   ____

   ____

4. Indicate whether the following statements characterize father (F) or mother (M) involvement during the school years. (p. 345)

   _____ Are more concerned with ensuring that children meet responsibilities
   _____ Focus on achievement-related and recreational pursuits
   _____ Are more knowledgeable about children's everyday activities
   _____ Spend more time with school-age children
   _____ Are more concerned with caregiving

Siblings

1. In middle childhood, sibling rivalry tends to (decrease / increase). (p. 345)
2. Cite sibling and family characteristics associated with frequent parental comparisons, noting the consequences of these comparisons for children. (p. 345)

   Sibling and family characteristics: ______________________________

   ____

   ____

   Consequences: ______________________________

   ____

3. True or False: To reduce rivalry, siblings often strive to be different from one another. (p. 345)
4. Under what conditions are younger siblings more likely to reap increased academic and social competence from older siblings? (p. 346)

   ____

   ____

Only Children

1. True or False: Sibling relationships are essential for healthy development. (p. 346)
2. True or False: Research supports the commonly held belief that only children are spoiled. (p. 346)

3. Discuss the developmental advantages and disadvantages of being an only child. (p. 346)

   Advantages: ____

   ____

   Disadvantages: ____

   ____

Divorce

1. True or False: The United States has the highest divorce rate in the world. (p. 347)
2. Divorce is a (single event / transition) in the lives of parents and children. (p. 347)
3. Summarize ways that divorce has an immediate impact on the home environment. (p. 347)

   ____

   ____

   ____

   ____

4. Explain how younger and older children react to divorce. (pp. 347–348)

   Younger: ____

   ____

   ____

   Older: ____

   ____

   ____

5. Indicate whether boys (B), girls (G), or both sexes (BG) are most likely to experience the following outcomes of divorce. (p. 348)

   _____ Tend to receive less emotional support from mothers, teachers, and peers than the opposite sex
   _____ Display internalizing reactions, such as crying, self-criticism, and withdrawal
   _____ Show demanding, attention-getting, acting-out behavior
   _____ In mother-custody families, are at greater risk for serious adjustment problems than the opposite sex

6. Most children show improved adjustment by ______ year(s) after their parents' divorce. (p. 348)
7. (Boys / Girls) and children with ________________ temperaments are especially likely to drop out of school and display antisocial behavior in adolescence following a parental divorce. (p. 348)
8. True or False: Divorce is linked to problems with adolescent sexuality and development of intimate ties. (p. 348)
9. What is the overriding factor in children's positive adjustment following parental divorce? (p. 348)

   ____

10. Explain why a good father–child relationship is important for both girls and boys following a parental divorce. (p. 348)

    Girls: ____

    ____

    Boys: ____

    ____

11. True or False: Transitioning to a low-conflict, single-parent household is better for children than staying in a high-conflict, intact family. (p. 348)

12. Cite three ways in which children and families benefit from *divorce mediation*. (p. 348)

    A. ______________________________

    B. ______________________________

    C. ______________________________

13. ______________________, the practice of granting both parents equal say in important decisions regarding the child's upbringing, is becoming (decreasingly / increasingly) common. (p. 348)

14. True or False: All U.S. states have procedures for withholding wages from parents who fail to make child support payments. (pp. 348–349)

Blended Families

1. List two reasons why *blended families* present adjustment difficulties for most children. (p. 349)

   A. ______________________________

   B. ______________________________

2. (Older / Younger) children and (girls / boys) have the hardest time adjusting to a blended family. (p. 349)

3. The most frequent form of blended family is a (father–stepmother / mother–stepfather) arrangement. Indicate how boys (B) and girls (G) tend to adjust to this type of family. (p. 349)

   _____ Often react with sulky, resistant behavior
   _____ Experience decreased friction with mothers
   _____ Adjust quickly

4. Cite two reasons why older children and adolescents of both sexes living in mother–stepfather families may display more irresponsible, acting-out behavior than agemates who are not in stepfamilies. (pp. 349–350)

   A. ______________________________

   ____

   B. ______________________________

   ____

5. Remarriage of noncustodial fathers often leads to (reduced / increased) contact with their biological children. (p. 350)

6. Cite two reasons why children tend to react negatively to the remarriage of custodial fathers. (p. 350)

   A. ______________________________

   ____

   B. ______________________________

   ____

7. (Girls / Boys) have an especially hard time getting along with stepmothers. Explain this finding. (p. 350)

   ____

   ____

   ____

8. Cite two ways in which family life education and therapy can help parents and children adapt to the complexities of blended families. (p. 350)

   A. ______________________________

   B. ______________________________

Maternal Employment and Dual-Earner Families

1. True or False: Single mothers are far more likely than their married counterparts to enter the workforce. (p. 350)
2. Summarize positive outcomes for children whose mothers enjoy their work and remain committed to parenting. (p. 350)

   ____

   ____

   ____

3. Cite three parenting practices that contribute to the benefits described in Question 2. (p. 350)

   A. ______________________________

   B. ______________________________

   C. ______________________________

4. Discuss the risks of stressful maternal employment on child adjustment. (pp. 350–351)

   ____

   ____

5. List four work-setting and community supports that can help parents juggle the demands of work and child rearing. (p. 351)

   A. ______________ C. ______________

   B. ______________ D. ______________

6. True or False: Self-care increases with age and also with SES. (p. 351)
7. Describe factors associated with positive versus poor adjustment for *self-care children*. (p. 351)

   Positive adjustment: ______________________________

   ____

   Poor adjustment: ______________________________

   ____

8. Before age _____ or ______, most children need supervision because they are not yet competent to handle emergencies. (p. 351)

Some Common Problems of Development

Fears and Anxieties

1. Indicate which of the following are likely to emerge as new fears and anxieties in middle childhood. (p. 352)

   Fears of . . .

   _____ the dark
   _____ supernatural beings
   _____ media events
   _____ parents' illness
   _____ the possibility of physical harm
   _____ academic failure
   _____ thunder and lightning
   _____ peer rejection

2. What is the most common self-reported source of children's fears in Western nations? (p. 352)

___

3. Fears (decline / increase) with age, especially for (boys / girls). (p. 352)
4. Children with ___ temperaments are at high risk for developing *phobias*. (p. 352)
5. Describe two common symptoms of school phobia. (p. 352)

   A. ___

   B. ___

6. Most cases of school phobia appear around age ___ to ___. Describe effective methods of reducing this fear. (p. 352)

___

___

___

A Lifespan Vista: Impact of Ethnic and Political Violence on Children

1. Discuss children's adjustment to war and social crises, noting differences between situations involving temporary crises and those involving chronic danger. (p. 353)

   Temporary crises: ___

   ___

   Chronic danger: ___

   ___

   ___

2. What is the best safeguard against lasting problems for children encountering war and social crises? (p. 353)

   ___

3. Describe the "trauma curriculum" used to help children from Public School 31 in Brooklyn, New York, in the wake of the September 11 attack on the World Trade Center. (p. 353)

   ___

   ___

   ___

Child Sexual Abuse

1. Sexual abuse is committed against children of both sexes, but more often against (girls / boys). (p. 352)
2. Describe general and psychological characteristics that are common among sexual abusers. (p. 352)

   General: ___

   ___

   Psychological: ___

   ___

3. What type of children do abusers often target? (p. 352)

   ___

   ___

4. Discuss the adjustment problems of sexually abused children, noting differences between younger children and adolescents. (p. 353)

   Younger children: ____

   ____

   Adolescents: ____

   ____

5. True or False: Repeated sexual abuse is associated with central nervous system damage. (p. 353)

6. Explain how the harmful impact of sexual abuse is often transmitted to the next generation. (p. 353)

   ____

   ____

   ____

7. What is the best way to reduce the suffering of victims of child sexual abuse? (pp. 353–354)

   ____

8. Cite two characteristics of educational programs that help reduce the risk of child sexual abuse. (p. 354)

   A. ____

   B. ____

9. True or False: Most U.S. schools provide intervention programs to educate children about sexual abuse. (p. 354)

Social Issues: Children's Eyewitness Testimony

1. Describe conditions that can compromise the accuracy of children's eyewitness recall. (p. 355)

   ____

   ____

   ____

   ____

2. Summarize aspects of children's eyewitness testimony that improve with age. (p. 355)

   ____

   ____

   ____

3. True or False: When adults lead children by suggesting incorrect information, they increase the likelihood of incorrect reporting among preschool and school-age children alike. (p. 355)

4. Describe ways that children can easily be misled into providing false information. (p. 355)

   ____

   ____

   ____

5. True or False: Interviewing methods involving the use of anatomically correct dolls prompt more accurate recall of sexual abuse experiences among preschoolers. (p. 355)

6. Summarize three types of interventions that can be used to increase accurate eyewitness testimony in children. (p. 355)

   "Court schools": ______________________________

   Interviewing procedures: ______________________________

   Protective procedures: ______________________________

Fostering Resilience in Middle Childhood

1. List four broad factors that protect children against maladjustment. (p. 354)

   A. ______________________________

   B. ______________________________

   C. ______________________________

   D. ______________________________

2. True or False: Resilience is a (capacity that develops / preexisting attribute). (p. 354)

ASK YOURSELF . . .

For *Ask Yourself* questions for this chapter, along with feedback on the accuracy of your answers, please log on to MyDevelopmentLab (for registration and access, please visit mydevelopmentlab.com or follow the instructions on page ix).

(1) Select the Multimedia Library.

(2) Choose the explore option.

(3) Find your chapter from the drop down box.

(4) Click find now.

(5) Complete questions and choose "Submit answers for grading" or "Clear answers" to start over.

SUGGESTED READINGS

Clarke-Stewart, A., & Dunn, J. (Eds.). (2006). *Families count: Effects on child and adolescent development.* New York: Cambridge University Press. Written and edited by leading experts, this book explores the importance of family for child development. Topics include the link between family and peers, the effects of work on parenting, divorce, child care, the role of grandparents and extended family, and gay and lesbian families.

Feerick, M. M., & Silverman, G. B. (Eds.). (2006). *Children exposed to violence*. Baltimore, MD: Paul H. Brookes. With an emphasis on domestic violence, community violence, and war and terrorism, this book explores the effects of violence on all aspects of child development, including physical health, psychological well-being, academic achievement, and social competence.

Marquardt, E. (2006). *Between two worlds: The inner lives of children of divorce.* New York: Crown Publishing. Based on extensive longitudinal research, this book examines the effects of divorce on children, including emotional reactions, resilience, and adjusting to blended families.

CROSSWORD PUZZLE 10.1

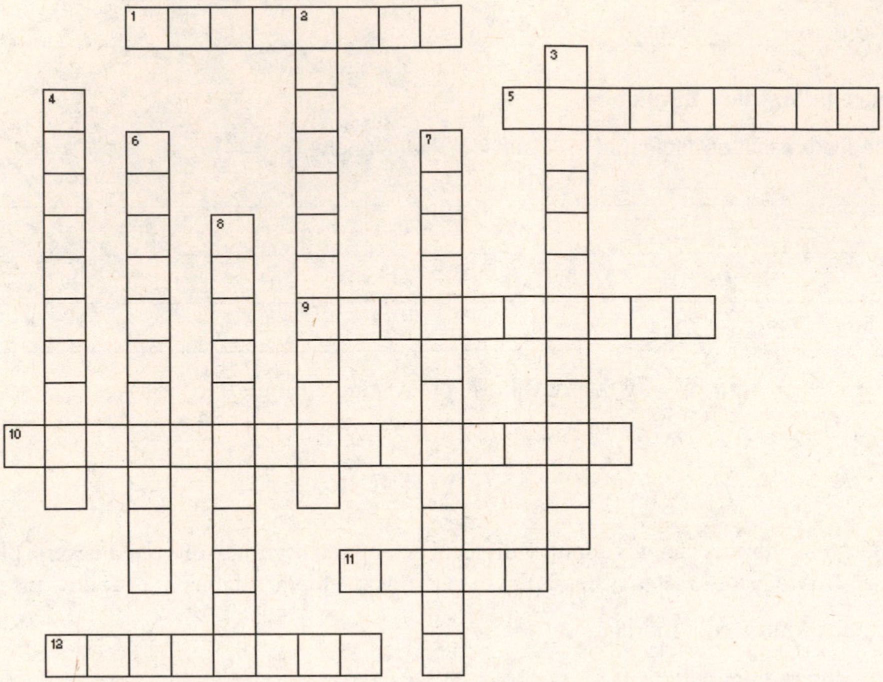

Across

1. ______-______ children are without adult supervision for some period of time after school. (2 words, hyph.)
5. Divorce ______: meetings between divorcing adults and a trained professional aimed at reducing family conflict
9. Rejected-______ children show high rates of conflict, aggression, and inattentive, impulsive behavior.
10. ______-______ children credit their successes to ability and their failures to factors that can be changed or controlled. (2 words, hyph.)
11. In ______ custody, the court grants both parents equal say in important decisions about the child's upbringing.
12. ______ versus inferiority: Erikson's psychological crisis of middle childhood

Down

2. Parents exercise general oversight while letting children make moment-by-moment decisions.
3. Children who develop learned ______ attribute their failures to ability and their successes to external factors.
4. Popular-______ children: "tough" boys who are antisocial and athletically skilled, but poor students; relationally aggressive children
6. ______ taking: the capacity to imagine what other people may be thinking and feeling
7. ______ children get a large number of positive and negative votes from peers.
8. Social ______: judging one's appearance, abilities, and behavior in relation to those of others

CROSSWORD PUZZLE 10.2

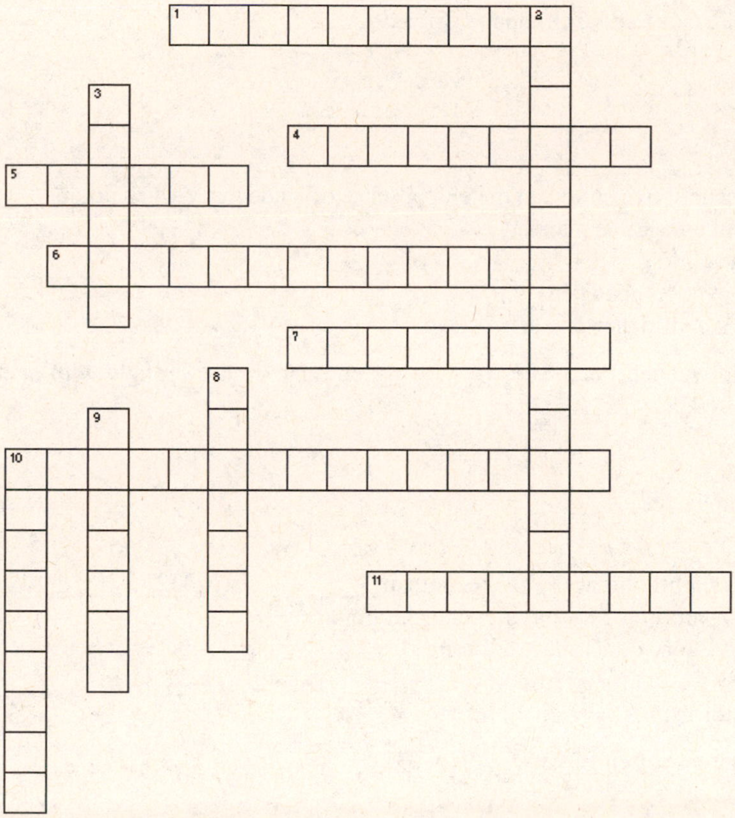

Across

1. Peer ______ refers to likability, the extent to which a child is viewed by agemates as a worthy social partner.
4. ______ children are seldom mentioned, either positively or negatively, on peers' self-reports.
5. Peer ______: collectives that generate unique values and standards for behavior and a social structure
6. Peer ______: certain children become targets of verbal and physical attacks or other forms of abuse
7. ______ children are actively disliked and get many negative votes on peers' self-reports.
10. In ______-______ coping, children deem the situation changeable, identify the difficulty, and find a solution. (2 words, hyph.)
11. Rejected-______ children are passive and socially awkward.

Down

2. ______-______ coping: controlling distress internally when little can be done about an outcome (2 words, hyph.)
3. An intense, unmanageable fear
8. ______, or reconstituted, families are comprised of the parent, stepparent, and children.
9. ______ children get many positive votes from peers.
10. Popular-______ children combine academic and social competence.

PRACTICE TEST #1

1. By striving to do well on an exam, working to improve soccer skills, or auditioning for a school play, a child shows __________, a major change of middle childhood. (p. 329)
   a. inferiority
   b. industriousness
   c. perspective taking
   d. self-esteem

2. According to Erikson, a school-age child can develop a sense of inadequacy when adults __________ (p. 330)
   a. respond to the child in a negative manner.
   b. make demands on the child.
   c. emphasize behavior over competence.
   d. overinflate the child's confidence and self-esteem.

3. During childhood and adolescence, perceived __________ correlates more strongly with overall self-worth than any other self-esteem factor. (pp. 331–332)
   a. academic competence
   b. social competence
   c. physical/athletic competence
   d. physical appearance

4. __________ tend to have slightly higher self-esteem than __________. (p. 332)
   a. Chinese and Japanese children; North American children
   b. African-American children; Caucasian children
   c. Girls; boys
   d. Caucasian children; African-American children

5. Children of controlling parents often __________ (p. 332)
   a. feel inadequate.
   b. are advanced in moral understanding.
   c. have unrealistically high self-esteem.
   d. become high achievers.

6. Children who develop mastery-oriented attributions __________ (p. 333)
   a. are highly competitive and believe that grades are more important than learning.
   b. attribute failures to lack of ability, which they regard as a fixed trait.
   c. believe they can succeed at challenging tasks by increasing their effort.
   d. tend to have parents who use an authoritarian style of child rearing.

7. In a learning environment, __________ children focus on obtaining positive and avoiding negative evaluations. (p. 333)
   a. mastery-oriented
   b. high-achieving
   c. learned-helpless
   d. self-aware

8. Attribution research suggests that __________ (p. 334)
   a. well-intended messages from adults can undermine children's competence.
   b. learned-helpless children will fail at most tasks even if they exert the required effort.
   c. over time, the ability of learned-helpless children predicts how well they will do.
   d. learned-helpless children can be retrained through continuous praise from adults.

9. Which of the following statements about children's emotional understanding is true? (p. 335)
   a. School-age children are likely to explain emotion by referring to external events rather than internal states.
   b. Around age 8 or 9, children can reconcile contradictory cues to determine another's feelings.
   c. School-age children tend to become overwhelmed by other people's distress.
   d. School-age children believe that people can experience only one emotion at a time.

10. When 9-year-old Lataesha's best friend is angry with her, Lataesha decides to call her friend to talk about the issue. Lataesha is engaging in __________ (p. 335)
    a. problem-centered coping.
    b. emotion-centered coping.
    c. self-understanding.
    d. perspective taking.

11. Why do children whose parents react to their distress in hostile or dismissive ways tend to be less emotionally well-regulated than other children? (p. 336)
    a. They are overempathetic to others' distress.
    b. They are overwhelmed by negative emotion.
    c. They have a high sense of emotional self-efficacy.
    d. They are unable to understand others' perspectives.

12. A North American child is more likely than a Chinese child to __________ (p. 337)
    a. consider lying about antisocial acts to be appropriate.
    b. say that lying is always bad and truth telling is always good.
    c. rate lying favorably when the intention is modesty.
    d. rate lying favorably to support the individual at the group's expense.

13. Which of the following children is most likely to hold racial prejudices? (p. 338)
    a. Aiden, who has below-average self-esteem
    b. Gram, who has very high self-esteem
    c. Tia, who believes that personality traits are changeable
    d. Li, who has regular contact with other races

14. Which of the following declines dramatically in middle childhood? (p. 339)
    a. verbal aggression
    b. relational aggression
    c. physical aggression
    d. prosocial acts

15. Which of the following is true of school-age children's peer groups? (p. 340)
    a. When ousted by their peer group, socially anxious children often reach out to older peers who help them acquire socially competent behavior.
    b. Once children begin to form peer groups, relational and overt aggression toward "outgroup" members declines dramatically.
    c. Peer groups often direct their hostilities toward no longer "respected" children within their own group.
    d. Formal group ties, such as 4-H, are ineffective for meeting school-age children's desire for group belonging.

16. Research on peer acceptance indicates that __________ (p. 342)
    a. all children fit into one of the four categories of peer acceptance—popular, rejected, neglected, or controversial.
    b. rejected children, in particular, are at risk for poor school performance, absenteeism, dropping out, and antisocial behavior.
    c. neglected children tend to be socially maladjusted and are at risk for long-term psychological problems.
    d. controversial children have few friends and are typically unhappy with their peer relationships.

17. As a group, neglected children _________ (p. 342)
    a. have as many friends as popular children.
    b. are at risk for peer harassment.
    c. are eventually rejected by their peers.
    d. are just as socially skilled as average children.

18. The best way to reduce bullying is to __________ (p. 343)
    a. teach victimized children to be passive when interacting with bullies to avoid a physical confrontation.
    b. encourage bullies and victims to work out their problems with minimal adult intervention.
    c. teach victims how to fight off their attackers.
    d. change youth environments, promoting prosocial attitudes and behaviors.

19. From third to sixth grade, __________ (p. 344)
    a. boys strengthen their identification with "masculine" traits, whereas girls' identification with "feminine" traits declines.
    b. girls strengthen their identification with "feminine" traits, whereas boys' identification with "masculine" traits declines.
    c. children are especially intolerant when girls engage in "cross-gender" acts, which they regard nearly as bad as moral transgressions.
    d. many children feel dissatisfied with their gender assignment, although they rarely share their feelings with adults or peers.

20. Coregulation __________ (p. 345)
    a. is more effective with boys than girls.
    b. is more effective with preschoolers than school-age children.
    c. helps prepare children for adolescence.
    d. is used as a form of psychological control.

21. Compared with agemates who have siblings, only children __________ (p. 347)
    a. exhibit higher rates of hyperactive, inattentive, and impulsive behavior.
    b. tend to be more popular with peers.
    c. have lower self-esteem.
    d. do better in school and attain higher levels of education.

22. In mother-custody families, __________ (p. 348)
    a. boys are at greater risk for serious adjustment problems.
    b. girls are at greater risk for serious adjustment problems.
    c. boys tend to display more mature behavior, willingly taking on household tasks.
    d. boys and girls are at equal risk for serious adjustment problems.

23. What is the overriding factor in positive adjustment following divorce? (p. 348)
    a. the child's temperament
    b. financial security
    c. effective parenting
    d. a caring network of family and friends

24. Children of joint custody arrangements __________ (p. 348)
    a. are more poorly adjusted than children in sole-maternal-custody homes.
    b. are better-adjusted than children in sole-maternal-custody homes.
    c. tend to resent one parent, usually the mother.
    d. eventually choose to live with one parent, usually the more permissive one.

25. Which of the following statements about maternal employment is true? (p. 350)
    a. Children show favorable adjustment when their mothers work, regardless of their mothers' employment conditions.
    b. Employed mothers who value their parenting role are less likely to use authoritative child rearing and coregulation.
    c. Daughters of employed mothers are more achievement- and career-oriented, but only in high-SES families.
    d. Maternal employment leads fathers to take on greater child-rearing responsibilities, and this involvement is linked to favorable adjustment.

26. Most cases of school phobia __________ (p. 352)
    a. are actually a fear of maternal separation.
    b. are mild and easily overcome.
    c. appear in kindergarten or first grade.
    d. appear around age 11 to 13.

27. Research on child sexual abuse indicates that __________ (p. 352)
    a. boys and girls are equally likely to be victimized.
    b. reported cases are highest in early childhood and adolescence.
    c. the abuser is most often a parent or someone the child knows well.
    d. the abuser is most often a stranger.

28. When exposed to temporary war violence and social crises, most children __________ (p. 353)
    a. escape long-term emotional difficulties.
    b. become excessively shy and suicidal.
    c. become more aggressive and antisocial.
    d. permanently lose their sense of personal safety.

29. Which of the following questioning methods reduces suggestibility in child witnesses? (p. 355)
    a. repeating questions with which the child does not agree
    b. asking leading questions
    c. asking yes-or-no questions
    d. asking open-ended questions

30. Why is long-term therapy with both parents and children usually needed in treatment of sexual abuse? (p. 353)
    a. Parents are most often the perpetrators of the abuse.
    b. Sexual abuse typically appears in the midst of other family problems.
    c. Family therapy is required by most courts, regardless of the circumstances surrounding the abuse.
    d. Parents rarely believe their children's claims of abuse.

PRACTICE TEST #2

1. According to Erikson, the psychological conflict of middle childhood is __________ (p. 330)
   a. autonomy versus shame and doubt.
   b. initiative versus guilt.
   c. industry versus inferiority.
   d. identity versus role confusion.

2. When describing themselves, older school-age children are far more likely than younger children to __________ (p. 330)
   a. compare themselves to one peer rather than multiple peers.
   b. describe themselves in extreme, all-or-none ways.
   c. emphasize specific behaviors rather than competencies.
   d. describe themselves in terms of competencies and personality traits.

3. George Herbert Mead proposed that a well-organized psychological self emerges when __________ (p. 330)
   a. children adopt a view of the self that resembles others' attitudes toward the child.
   b. there is a large discrepancy between the child's real self and ideal self.
   c. children adopt a view of the self that is independent of others' attitudes toward the child.
   d. teachers and peers provide feedback that helps children adjust their self-esteem to a more realistic level.

4. Which of the following statements accurately describes changes in self-esteem throughout childhood? (p. 332)
   a. Self-esteem tends to be fairly low in the preschool years and gradually rises throughout middle childhood.
   b. Self-esteem is fairly high in the preschool years and gradually decreases throughout middle childhood.
   c. Self-esteem is fairly high in the preschool years, peaks around second grade, then decreases.
   d. Self-esteem is extremely high in the preschool years, declines during the first few years of elementary school, then rises from fourth grade on.

5. Over the past few decades, the self-esteem of American young people has __________ (p. 332)
   a. dropped sharply.
   b. dropped slightly.
   c. risen sharply.
   d. remained stable.

6. Children who develop learned helplessness __________ (p. 333)
   a. think that ability can be changed through increased effort.
   b. tend to attribute their failures, but not their successes, to ability.
   c. often persevere on difficult tasks in an effort to overcome feelings of incompetence.
   d. have parents who set unusually high standards.

7. Low-SES ethnic minority students in __________ are more likely to receive unfavorable feedback from teachers, which results in a drop of academic self-esteem and achievement. (p. 333)
   a. homogeneous groups
   b. heterogeneous groups
   c. gifted programs
   d. constructivist classrooms

8. Attribution retraining __________ (p. 334)
   a. often undermines academic competence, especially in low-SES children.
   b. often results in an inflated sense of self-esteem.
   c. requires children to complete tasks without adult feedback on their performance.
   d. is best begun early, before children's views of themselves become hard to change.

9. A child who experiences intense shame is likely to __________ (p. 335)
   a. have feelings of withdrawal, depression, or anger.
   b. make amends for any transgression.
   c. strive for self-improvement.
   d. show high rates of empathy toward distressed peers.

10. According to Selman's stages of perspective taking, children ages 7 to 12 are in the __________ (p. 336)
    a. undifferentiated perspective-taking stage, often confusing the thoughts and feelings of themselves and others.
    b. third-party perspective-taking stage, able to imagine how a third, impartial party may view a two-person situation.
    c. societal perspective taking stage, understanding that societal values can influence third-party perspective taking.
    d. self-reflective stage, able to view themselves from another person's perspective.

11. After age 7 or 8, __________ (p. 338)
    a. children are more likely to voice negative attitudes toward minorities.
    b. minority children express in-group favoritism, whereas majority children express out-group bias.
    c. both minority and majority children express in-group favoritism.
    d. most children abandon prejudiced beliefs entirely.

12. What is the best way to reduce prejudice in children? (p. 339)
    a. organizing cross-race, cooperative learning groups
    b. creating opportunities for long-term intergroup contact
    c. including discussions of ethnic stereotypes in public education
    d. highlighting group distinctions

13. School-age children's informal peer groups __________ (pp. 339–340)
    a. are often characterized by aggression and competition.
    b. are typically diverse in sex and ethnicity.
    c. are necessary for satisfying children's desire for group membership.
    d. organize based on proximity and similarities.

14. Which of the following statements about school-age children's friendships is true? (p. 340)
    a. Trust is the defining feature of friendships in middle childhood.
    b. School-age children's friendships are less selective than preschoolers' friendships.
    c. Boys are more exclusive in their friendships than girls.
    d. As in early childhood, school-age children's friendships are highly unstable.

15. Rejected-aggressive children are __________ (p. 342)
    a. often "tough" boys who are athletically skilled but poor students.
    b. deficient in perspective taking and regulation of negative emotion.
    c. passive and socially awkward.
    d. hostile and disruptive but also engage in positive, prosocial acts.

16. Which of the following statements about peer victimization is true? (p. 343)
    a. Girls are just as likely as boys to bully vulnerable peers.
    b. Chronic victims of bullying tend to be active when passive behavior is expected.
    c. Peer onlookers rarely intervene to help victims of bullying.
    d. Most bullies are "tough" boys who are athletically skilled but poor students.

17. By the end of middle childhood, children __________ (p. 344)
    a. dismiss most gender stereotypes.
    b. regard gender typing as socially, rather than biologically, based.
    c. are open-minded about violations of gender roles.
    d. are rigid in their view of what males and females can do.

18. Why are some researchers opposed to making gender-atypical children gender-typical through therapy? (p. 344)
    a. Gender-atypical children are often well-adjusted and secure in their gender identity.
    b. Therapy makes gender-atypical children feel like there is something wrong with them.
    c. Gender-atypical children need to come to terms with their gender identity on their own.
    d. Gender-atypical children who feel intense pressure to conform experience serious difficulties.

19. Sibling rivalry tends to be especially strong __________ (p. 345)
    a. among siblings who are close in age.
    b. when siblings strive to be different from one another.
    c. among other-sex siblings.
    d. among adopted siblings.

20. In response to divorce, boys are more likely than girls to __________ (p. 348)
    a. receive emotional support.
    b. withdraw from others.
    c. develop serious adjustment problems.
    d. blame themselves.

21. Which of the following statements about divorce is true? (p. 348)
    a. Residing in a low-conflict single-parent household is better for children than remaining in an intact but high-conflict family.
    b. Following divorce, declines in well-being are greatest for mothers of older children.
    c. Children's contact with noncustodial fathers tends to increase as they get older.
    d. In mother-custody families, girls are at greater risk for serious adjustment problems than boys.

22. __________ have the hardest time adjusting to blended-family relationships. (pp 349–350)
    a. Older children and boys
    b. Older children and girls
    c. Younger children and boys
    d. Younger children and girls

23. Child self-care __________ (p. 351)
    a. decreases with age and SES.
    b. is a form of neglect and can result in long-term adjustment difficulties for many children.
    c. is inappropriate for children under the age of 9.
    d. is associated with positive outcomes for children who have a history of permissive parenting.

24. Which of the following statements about fears in middle childhood is true? (p. 352)
    a. Most school-age children can handle their fears constructively if they are not too intense.
    b. Fears increase with age, as children begin to understand the realities of the world.
    c. Boys express more fears than girls throughout childhood and adolescence.
    d. Approximately 40 percent of children experience school phobia during middle childhood.

25. What is the best safeguard against lasting problems for children living in chronic danger? (p. 353)
    a. education and high-quality child care
    b. individual and family therapy
    c. parental affection and reassurance
    d. drawing and writing about traumatic experiences

26. __________ is the only country with a national, school-based sexual-abuse prevention program. (p. 354)
    a. The United States
    b. Canada
    c. France
    d. New Zealand

27. Compared to 30 years ago, cases of sexual abuse today are __________ (p. 354)
    a. prosecuted more vigorously.
    b. taken less seriously.
    c. less frequently reported.
    d. primarily committed by strangers.

28. A __________ relationship exists between stressful life experiences and psychological disturbance in childhood. (p. 354)
    a. negative
    b. weak
    c. moderate
    d. strong

29. Resilience is best viewed as a(n) __________ (p. 354)
    a. biologically based attribute.
    b. capacity that develops out of internal and external resources.
    c. outcome of effective parenting.
    d. third-party influence.

30. Research on children's eyewitness testimony indicates that preschool-age children __________ (p. 355)
    a. recall information accurately when presented with yes/no questions.
    b. are rarely able to recall events accurately, regardless of questioning techniques.
    c. are more resistant to leading questions than older children.
    d. can recall recent events accurately when properly questioned.

CHAPTER 11
PHYSICAL AND COGNITIVE DEVELOPMENT IN ADOLESCENCE

BRIEF CHAPTER SUMMARY

The beginning of adolescence is marked by puberty: biological changes leading to physical and sexual maturity. Modern research has shown that adolescence is a product of biological, psychological, and social forces.

Genetically influenced hormonal processes regulate pubertal growth. On average, girls reach puberty two years earlier than boys. As the body enlarges, girls' hips and boys' shoulders broaden, girls add more fat, and boys add more muscle. Puberty is accompanied by steady improvement in gross motor performance, but whereas girls' gains are slow and gradual, leveling off by age 14, boys show a dramatic spurt in strength, speed, and endurance that continues through the teenage years.

Menarche, or first menstruation, occurs late in the girl's sequence of pubertal events, following the rapid increase in body size. Among boys, spermarche (first ejaculation) occurs around age 13½, as the sex organs and body enlarge and pubic and underarm hair appear. Heredity, nutrition, and overall health contribute to the timing of puberty. A secular trend toward earlier menarche has occurred in industrialized nations as physical well-being has increased. Brain development continues in adolescence, supporting cognitive advances as well as more intense reactions to stimuli.

Puberty is related to a rise in parent–child conflict, but this is usually mild. Parent–child distancing seems to be a modern substitute for the physical departure of young people in nonindustrialized cultures and among nonhuman primates. Reactions to pubertal changes are influenced by prior knowledge, support from family members, and cultural attitudes toward puberty and sexuality. Besides higher hormone levels, negative life events and adult-structured situations are associated with adolescents' negative moods. Early-maturing boys and late-maturing girls, whose appearance closely matches cultural standards of physical attractiveness, have a more positive body image and usually adjust well in adolescence. In contrast, early-maturing girls and late-maturing boys experience emotional and social difficulties.

The arrival of puberty is accompanied by new health issues related to the young person's striving to meet physical and psychological needs. As the body grows, nutritional requirements increase; however, because of poor eating habits, many adolescents suffer from vitamin and mineral deficiencies. Eating disorders, sexually transmitted diseases, adolescent pregnancy and parenthood, and substance abuse are some of the most serious health concerns of the teenage years.

During Piaget's formal operational stage, young people develop the capacity for systematic, scientific thinking, arriving at new, more general logical rules through internal reflection. Piaget believed that adolescents become capable of hypothetico-deductive reasoning, in which they begin with a hypothesis, or prediction, from which they deduce logical inferences. Piaget used the term propositional thought to refer to adolescents' ability to evaluate the logic of verbal statements without referring to real-world circumstances. Recent research indicates that adolescents are capable of a much deeper grasp of scientific principles than are school-age children. However, even well-educated adults have difficulty with formal operational reasoning, indicating that Piaget's highest stage is affected by specific, school-learning opportunities. Information-processing theorists agree with the broad outlines of Piaget's description of adolescent cognition. But they refer to a variety of specific mechanisms for cognitive change, with metacognition regarded as central to adolescent cognitive development. By coordinating theories with evidence, adolescents develop advanced scientific reasoning skills.

The development of formal operations leads to dramatic revisions in the way adolescents see themselves, others, and the world in general. Using their new cognitive powers, teenagers become more argumentative, idealistic, and critical. Although they show gains in self-regulation, adolescents often have difficulty making decisions in everyday life.

Boys and girls do not differ in general intelligence, but they do vary in specific mental abilities. Females have a slight advantage in verbal ability, while boys do better in mathematical reasoning. Although heredity is involved in these differences, the gender gap is also affected by environmental factors.

School transitions create adjustment problems for adolescents, especially girls. Teenagers who must cope with added stressors are at greatest risk for adjustment problems following school change. Enhanced support from parents, teachers, and peers eases the strain of school transition.

Adolescent achievement is the result of a long history of cumulative effects. Early on, positive educational environments, both family and school, lead to personal traits that support achievement. The more hours students devote to a part-time job, the poorer their school attendance, academic performance, and extracurricular participation. However, when work experiences are specially designed to meet educational and vocational goals, teenagers experience positive school and work attitudes and improved achievement. The dropout rate in the United States is particularly high among low-SES ethnic minority youths and is affected by family and school experiences.

LEARNING OBJECTIVES

After reading this chapter, you should be able to:

11.1 Discuss changing conceptions of adolescence over the past century. (pp. 362–363)

11.2 Describe pubertal changes in body size, proportions, sleep patterns, motor performance, and sexual maturity. (pp. 363–366)

11.3 Cite factors that influence the timing of puberty. (pp. 366–367)

11.4 Describe brain development in adolescence. (pp. 367–368)

11.5 Discuss adolescents' reactions to the physical changes of puberty, including sex differences, and describe the influence of family and culture. (pp. 368–370)

11.6 Discuss the impact of pubertal timing on adolescent adjustment, noting sex differences. (pp. 370–371)

11.7 Describe the nutritional needs of adolescents, and cite factors that contribute to serious eating disorders. (pp. 371–373)

11.8 Discuss social and cultural influences on adolescent sexual attitudes and behavior. (pp. 373–376)

11.9 Describe factors involved in the development of gay, lesbian, and bisexual orientations, and discuss the unique adjustment problems of these youths. (pp. 376, 377)

11.10 Discuss factors related to sexually transmitted diseases and to teenage pregnancy and parenthood, including interventions for adolescent parents. (pp. 376, 378–380)

11.11 Cite personal and social factors that contribute to adolescent substance use and abuse, and describe prevention and treatment programs. (pp. 380–382)

11.12 Describe the major characteristics of formal operational thought. (pp. 382–384)

11.13 Discuss recent research on formal operational thought and its implications for the accuracy of Piaget's formal operational stage. (pp. 384–385)

11.14 Explain how information-processing researchers account for cognitive change in adolescence, emphasizing the development of scientific reasoning. (pp. 385–386)

11.15 Summarize cognitive and behavioral consequences of adolescents' newfound capacity for advanced thinking. (pp. 386–388)

11.16 Note sex differences in mental abilities at adolescence, along with biological and environmental factors that influence them. (pp. 389–390, 391)

11.17 Discuss the impact of school transitions on adolescent adjustment, and cite ways to ease the strain of these changes. (pp. 390, 392–393)

11.18 Discuss family, peer, school, and employment influences on academic achievement during adolescence. (pp. 393–395)

11.19 Describe personal, family, and school factors related to dropping out, and cite ways to prevent early school leaving. (pp. 396–397)

STUDY QUESTIONS

Physical Development

Conceptions of Adolescence

The Biological Perspective

1. Match each theorist with his or her major contributions to the biological perspectives of *adolescence*. (p. 362)
   A. G. Stanley Hall ______ Adolescence is a universal "developmental disturbance."
   B. Anna Freud ______ Reawakened sexual impulses trigger conflict in adolescence.
   C. Sigmund Freud ______ Adolescence resembles human evolution from savages into civilized beings.

The Social Perspective

1. True or False: Rates of psychological disturbance increase dramatically in adolescence, supporting the storm-and-stress view of this period. (p. 362)
2. Describe Margaret Mead's view of adolescent development. (p. 362)

____

____

____

A Balanced Point of View

1. (Biological / Social) forces in adolescence are universal. The length of adolescence varies (little / greatly) among cultures. (p. 362)
2. List and define the three phases of adolescence. (p. 362)
   A. ____
   B. ____
   C. ____

Puberty: The Physical Transition to Adulthood

Hormonal Changes

1. Secretions of ________________ and ________________ increase during *puberty*, leading to tremendous gains in body size and attainment of skeletal maturity. (p. 363)
2. Cite ways that estrogens and androgens contribute to pubertal development in both sexes. (p. 363)

	Estrogens	Androgens
Males		
Females		

3. Pubertal changes can be divided into two broad types: (p. 363)

   A. ______________________________ B. ______________________________

Body Growth

1. The first outward sign of puberty is the rapid gain in height and weight known as the ____________________. (p. 363)
2. On average, the North American adolescent *growth spurt* begins and ends (earlier / later) for girls than for boys. (p. 363)
3. True or False: During adolescence, the cephalocaudal growth trend of infancy and childhood reverses. (p. 363)
4. Briefly describe sex differences in body proportions and muscle–fat makeup during adolescence. (pp. 363–364)

   Boys: ______________________________

   ____

   Girls: ______________________________

   ____

Motor Development and Physical Activity

1. How does motor development differ between adolescent girls and boys? (p. 364)

   Adolescent girls: ______________________________

   ____

   Adolescent boys: ______________________________

   ____

2. Among adolescent boys, athletic competence is (modestly / strongly) related to peer admiration and self-esteem. (p. 364)
3. In high school, (boys / girls) are more likely to take performance-enhancing drugs. Check all side-effects that may result from these drugs. (p. 364)

   _____ Brain seizures
   _____ High blood pressure
   _____ Muscle tissue disease
   _____ Liver damage
   _____ Heart irregularities
   _____ Acne and excess body hair
   _____ Mood swings
   _____ Damage to reproductive organs

4. Physical activity rates of U.S. youths (rise / decline) in adolescence. (p. 365)
5. Cite the benefits of sports and exercise in adolescence. (p. 365)

   ____

   ____

   ____

Sexual Maturation

1. Distinguish between *primary* and *secondary sexual characteristics*. (p. 365)

   Primary: ______________________________

   Secondary: ______________________________

2. On average, American girls tend to reach __________________, or first menstruation, (earlier / later) than boys experience __________________, or first ejaculation. (p. 366)

Individual Differences in Pubertal Growth

1. Cite evidence that the following factors influence the timing of puberty. (pp. 366–367)

   Heredity: ______________________________

   Nutrition and exercise: ______________________________

   SES: ______________________________

2. In industrialized nations, African-American girls reach *menarche* (earlier / later), on average, than Caucasian-American girls. This difference is likely influenced by (heredity / environment / both heredity and environment). (p. 367)

3. Threats to emotional health (accelerate / delay) puberty, whereas threats to physical health (accelerate / delay) it. (p. 367)

4. Industrialized nations have experienced a *secular trend* toward (earlier / later) age of menarche from 1900 to 1970. This trend supports the role of (physical / emotional) well-being in pubertal development. Explain your answer. (p. 367)

   ____

   ____

Brain Development

1. Explain how the following brain changes affect adolescents' cognition and behavior. (p. 367)

   Pruning, growth, and myelination of neural fibers: ______________________________

   ____

   Increased neural sensitivity to chemical messages: ______________________________

   ____

2. True or False: The brain changes much less during adolescence than researchers once believed. (p. 368)

Changing States of Arousal

1. Explain the adolescent sleep "phase delay." (p. 368)

   ____

   ____

   ____

2. True or False: Adolescents need much less sleep than school-age children. (p. 368)

3. List three consequences of sleep deprivation in adolescence. (p. 368)

   A. ______________________________

   B. ______________________________

   C. ______________________________

The Psychological Impact of Pubertal Events

Reactions to Pubertal Changes

1. Both girls and boys report (mostly positive / mostly negative / mixed) feelings toward the onset of puberty. Those who learn about menarche and *spermarche* ahead of time tend to respond (more / less) favorably. (p. 368)

2. Overall, (boys / girls) get much less social support for the physical changes of puberty. (p. 368)

3. How does cultural context influence the experience of puberty? (p. 368)

____

____

____

Pubertal Change, Emotion, and Social Behavior

1. Adolescents report (less / more) favorable moods than school-age children and adults. (p. 369)
2. Younger adolescents' moods are (less / more) stable than those of older adolescents and adults. (p. 369)
3. Indicate whether the following events tend to coincide with adolescents' emotional highs (+) or lows (–). (p. 369)

_____ School classes
_____ Time spent with peers
_____ Friday and Saturday evenings
_____ Self-chosen leisure activities
_____ Religious services
_____ Time spent at work

4. How might parent–child conflict during adolescence be adaptive? (p. 370)

____

____

5. True or False: Parent–child disputes are often severe in adolescence. (p. 370)

Pubertal Timing

1. Describe the effects of maturational timing on boys and girls. (p. 370)

	Early Maturation	Late Maturation
Boys		
Girls		

2. Cite two factors that contribute to boys' and girls' adjustment to early versus late pubertal maturation. (p. 370)

A. ____

B. ____

3. Images in popular culture favor the (early- / late-) maturing female and the (early- / late-) maturing male. (Early- / Late-) maturing (African-American / Caucasian / Hispanic) females tend to report a less positive *body image* than their agemates. (pp. 370–371)
4. True or False: Early-maturing girls experience more lasting difficulties than do early-maturing boys. Describe the long-term consequences of early maturation. (p. 371)

____

____

Health Issues

Nutritional Needs

1. True or False: Of all age groups, adolescents are the most likely to skip breakfast, consume empty calories, and eat on the run. (pp. 371–372)
2. The most common nutritional problem of adolescence is ______________________. How does this affect teenagers' behavior? (p. 372)

   ____

3. What factor strongly predicts healthy eating in teenagers? (p. 372)

   ____

Eating Disorders

1. __________________________ is the strongest predictor of the onset of an eating disorder in adolescence. (p. 372)
2. Describe characteristics of *anorexia nervosa.* (p. 372)

   ____

   ____

   ____

3. Cite forces within the individual, the family, and the larger culture that give rise to anorexia nervosa. (pp. 372–373)

   Individual: ____

   ____

   Family: ____

   ____

   Culture: ____

   ____

4. Because anorexic girls tend to (deny or minimize / exaggerate) the seriousness of their disorder, it is difficult to treat. (p. 373)
5. Describe characteristics of *bulimia nervosa.* (p. 373)

   ____

   ____

   ____

6. True or False: Bulimia nervosa is far less common than anorexia nervosa. (p. 373)
7. How are bulimics similar to anorexics? How are they different? (p. 373)

   Similar: ____

   ____

   Different: ____

   ____

Sexuality

1. The production of ________________ during adolescence leads to an increased sex drive. (p. 373)
2. True or False: Sexual attitudes in North America are relatively restrictive, and typically parents give children little or no information about sex. (p. 374)
3. Contrast the messages about sexuality that adolescents receive from parents and the media. How do these contradictory messages influence adolescents' understanding of sex? (p. 374)

   Parents: ____

   ____

   Media: ____

   ____

   Influence: ____

   ____

4. True or False: The sexual attitudes of North American adolescents and adults have become less liberal over the past 40 years. (p. 374)
5. While rates of extramarital sex among U.S. young people have (increased / decreased) for the past several decades, recently these rates have (risen / declined). (p. 375)
6. Adolescents in the United States tend to begin sexual activity at a(n) (younger / older) age than their Canadian and Western European counterparts. (p. 375)
7. Check the personal, family, peer, and educational variables that are linked with early and frequent teenage sexual activity. (p. 375)

   _____ Childhood inhibition
   _____ Early pubertal timing
   _____ Parental divorce
   _____ Weak sense of personal control
   _____ Poor school performance
   _____ Childhood impulsivity
   _____ Low-SES family background
   _____ Sexually active friends
   _____ High religious involvement
   _____ Low religious involvement
   _____ Late pubertal timing
   _____ Drug abuse and delinquency

8. Why do many sexually active adolescents fail to use contraception consistently? (p. 375)

   Cognitive Factors: ____

   ____

   Social Factors: ____

   ____

9. What two factors increase the likelihood that teenagers will use birth control? (p. 376)

   A. ____

   B. ____

10. Explain how heredity and the prenatal environment might contribute to homosexuality. (p. 376)

    Heredity: ____

    ____

    Prenatal Environment: ____

    ____

11. True or False: Most gay, lesbian, and bisexual youths are "gender-deviant" in dress or behavior, meaning they dress and behave quite differently from their heterosexual peers. (p. 376)

Social Issues: Gay, Lesbian, and Bisexual Youths: Coming Out to Oneself and Others

1. In North America, homosexuals are largely (accepted / stigmatized / unnoticed). (p. 377)
2. In what order do many adolescents experience the three phases of coming out to themselves and others? (p. 377)
   _____ Confusion
   _____ Self-Acceptance
   _____ Feeling Different
3. For most gay and lesbian individuals, a first sense of their sexual orientation appears during (infancy and toddlerhood / childhood / adolescence). In what context does this commonly occur? (p. 377)

   ____

   ____

4. What are some potential outcomes for adolescents who are extremely troubled or guilt-ridden about their sexual orientation? (p. 377)

   ____

   ____

5. What factors increase the likelihood that gay and lesbian youths will adjust favorably? (p. 377)
   A. ____
   B. ____
6. Explain how coming out can enhance development of gay and lesbian adolescents. (p. 377)

   ____

   ____

Sexually Transmitted Diseases

1. True or False: Adolescents have the highest rates of sexually transmitted diseases (STDs) of all age groups. (p. 376)
2. Describe characteristics of teenagers who are in greatest danger of contracting STDs. (p. 376)

   ____

   ____

3. By far the most serious STD is ____________. (p. 376)
4. True or False: It is at least twice as easy for a female to infect a male with any STD, including AIDS, as it is for a male to infect a female. (p. 376)

Adolescent Pregnancy and Parenthood

1. True or False: The adolescent pregnancy rate in the United States is similar to that of most other industrialized nations. (p. 378)

2. List three factors that heighten the incidence of adolescent pregnancy. (p. 378)

   A. ______________________________

   B. ______________________________

   C. ______________________________

3. Adolescent pregnancy is a (less / more) significant problem today than it was 50 years ago, because adolescents are (less / more) likely to marry before childbirth (p. 378)

4. Describe common background characteristics of teenage parents. (p. 378)

   ____

   ____

   ____

5. Indicate whether adolescent parents are more (+) or less (–) likely than their peers who postpone childbearing to experience the following outcomes. (p. 378)

   _____ Finishing high school
   _____ Divorce
   _____ Unsatisfying, low-paying jobs
   _____ Single parenthood
   _____ Marriage
   _____ Welfare support

6. ______________________________ is a common birth complication among babies of teenage mothers. (p. 379)

7. True or False: Children of adolescent mothers tend to exhibit average school performance and social behavior for their age group. (p. 379)

8. What factors help to minimize long-term difficulties for adolescent parents and their children? (p. 379)

   ____

   ____

   ____

9. List three components of effective sex education programs. (p. 379)

   A. ______________________________

   B. ______________________________

   C. ______________________________

10. Teenagers' access to __________________________ is the most controversial aspect of adolescent pregnancy prevention. (p. 379)

11. True or False: Academic and social competence have little effect on rates of adolescent pregnancy and parenthood. (p. 379)

12. Explain why older adolescent mothers often display more effective parenting when they establish their own residence with the help of relatives. (p. 379)

    ____

    ____

13. Nearly half of young fathers visit their children during the first few years after birth, and contact usually (diminishes / increases) over time. (p. 380)

A Lifespan Vista: Like Parent, Like Child: Intergenerational Continuity in Adolescent Parenthood

1. First-generation mothers' age at first childbirth (weakly / moderately / strongly) predicts the age at which second-generation young people become parents. (p. 380)
2. Summarize three unfavorable family conditions linked with adolescent parenthood. (p. 380)

   A. ______________________________

   ____

   B. ______________________________

   ____

   C. ______________________________

   ____

3. True or False: Unmarried fathers are more likely to remain in contact with their daughters than with their sons. (p. 380)

Substance Use and Abuse

1. By tenth grade, most U.S. young people have tried (cigarette smoking / drinking / at least one illegal drug). There has been a substantial (increase / decline) in adolescent substance use since the mid-1990s. (p. 381)
2. Cite factors that may explain recent trends in adolescent substance use. (p. 381)

   ____

   ____

   ____

3. True or False: Teenagers who experiment with alcohol, tobacco, and marijuana are headed for a life of addiction. (p. 381)
4. Explain how adolescent experimenters differ from abusers. (pp. 381–382)

   ____

   ____

   ____

5. What environmental factors are associated with adolescent drug abuse? (p. 382)

   ____

   ____

   ____

6. List three lifelong consequences of adolescent drug abuse. (p. 382)

   A. ______________________________

   B. ______________________________

   C. ______________________________

7. Successful drug experimentation prevention programs: (check all that apply) (p. 382)

   _____ promote effective parenting.

   _____ teach skills for resisting peer pressure.

   _____ emphasize health and safety risks of drug use.

   _____ elicit a commitment to not using drugs.

Cognitive Development

Piaget's Theory: The Formal Operational Stage

1. Summarize the basic differences between concrete and *formal operational* reasoning. (p. 383)

____

____

____

Hypothetico-Deductive Reasoning

1. What is *hypothetico-deductive reasoning?* (p. 383)

____

____

____

2. True or False: Adolescents approach Piaget's pendulum problem by varying one factor at a time while holding the others constant. (p. 383)

Propositional Thought

1. ____________________ involves evaluating the logic of verbal statements without referring to real-world circumstances. (p. 383)

2. True or False: Piaget maintained that language plays a more central role in children's than in adolescents' cognitive development. (p. 384)

Follow-Up Research on Formal Operational Thought

1. Cite examples illustrating that school-age children show signs of hypothetico-deductive reasoning and *propositional thought* but are not as competent as adolescents. (p. 384)

   Hypothetico-deductive reasoning: ____

   ____

   Propositional thought: ____

   ____

2. True or False: Hypothetico-deductive reasoning and propositional thought appear suddenly, around the time of puberty. (p. 384)

3. What is one reason that many adults are not fully formal operational? (pp. 384–385)

____

____

____

4. True or False: Research in villages and tribal societies suggests that formal operational thought results from independent efforts to make sense of the world, as Piaget claimed. (p. 385)

An Information-Processing View of Adolescent Cognitive Development

1. Using research on information processing, list and briefly describe the seven mechanisms that underlie cognitive change in adolescence. (p. 385)

   A. ____________________

   B. ____________________

   C. ____________________

   D. ____________________

   E ____________________

   F ____________________

   G. ____________________

2. Which of the above mechanisms is central to the development of abstract thought? (p. 385)

   ____

Scientific Reasoning: Coordinating Theory with Evidence

1. How does scientific reasoning change from childhood into adolescence and adulthood? (p. 385)

   ____

   ____

How Scientific Reasoning Develops

1. Identify three factors that support adolescents' skill at coordinating theory with evidence. (p. 386)

   A. ____________________

   B. ____________________

   C. ____________________

2. Scientific reasoning is (weakly / strongly) influenced by years of schooling. (p. 386)

3. True or False: Like Piaget, information-processing theorists maintain that scientific reasoning results from an abrupt, stagewise change. Briefly explain your response. (p. 386)

   ____

   ____

Consequences of Adolescent Cognitive Change

Self-Consciousness and Self-Focusing

1. True or False: Adolescents' ability to reflect on their own thoughts, combined with physical and psychological changes, leads them to think less about themselves. (p. 386)

2. According to Piaget's followers, the (*imaginary audience / personal fable*) refers to adolescents' belief that they are the focus of everyone else's attention. The (*imaginary audience / personal fable*) describes adolescents' feeling that they are special and unique. (p. 387)

3. The imaginary audience and personal fable result from (egocentrism / advances in perspective taking). (p. 387)

4. Describe positive, protective functions of the imaginary audience and personal fable in adolescence. (p. 387)

____

____

Idealism and Criticism

1. How are idealism and criticism advantageous to teenagers? (p. 388)

____

____

Decision Making

1. List four components of rational decision making. (p. 388)

   A. ____

   B. ____

   C. ____

   D. ____

2. True or False: When making decisions, adolescents, more often than adults, fall back on well-learned, intuitive judgments. (p. 388)

3. Why is decision making so challenging for adolescents? (p. 388)

____

____

____

____

Sex Differences in Mental Abilities

Verbal Abilities

1. (Boys / Girls) score higher on tests of verbal ability in every country in which assessments have been conducted. This gender advantage (increases / decreases) in adolescence. (p. 389)

2. True or False: Gender differences in reading and writing achievement are believed to be a major contributor to the widening gender gap in college enrollments. (p. 389)

3. Describe three explanations for the gender gap in verbal ability. (p. 389)

   A. ____

   B. ____

   C. ____

Mathematics

1. As coursework becomes more difficult around early adolescence, (boys / girls) show a clear advantage in math and science abilities. (p. 389)

2. What hereditary factors and social pressures contribute to the gender gap in mathematics? (p. 390)

   Heredity: ______________________________

   ____

   Social Pressures: ______________________________

   ____

3. True or False: Boys and girls reach advanced levels of high school math and science study in equal proportions. (p. 390)

4. What steps can be taken to promote girls' interest in and confidence at math and science? (p. 390)

   ____

   ____

   ____

Biology and Environment: Sex Differences in Spatial Abilities

1. Indicate whether males (M) or females (F) tend to perform better on measures of each ability or whether performance is roughly equal (=) between genders. (p. 391)
   ___ Mental rotation
   ___ Spatial perception
   ___ Spatial visualization

2. Cite evidence suggesting that biology contributes to sex differences in spatial abilities. (p. 391)

   ____

   ____

   ____

3. Why might a biologically based sex difference in spatial abilities be evolutionarily adaptive? (p. 391)

   ____

   ____

   ____

4. What environmental experiences affect children's spatial performance? (p. 391)

   ____

   ____

5. True or False: Research confirms that superior spatial skills contribute to the greater ease with which males solve complex math problems. (p. 391)

Learning in School

School Transitions

1. With each school change, adolescents' grades (decline / increase). Why is this so? (p. 390)

   ____

   ____

   ____

2. The transition to junior high has an especially negative impact on girls' self-esteem because it coincides with the onset of ____________ and ____________. (p. 390)

3. What factors place adolescents at greatest risk for developing self-esteem and academic difficulties during school transitions? (p. 390)

____

____

____

4. List four environmental changes during school transitions that fit poorly with adolescents' developmental needs. (p. 392)

   A. ____

   B. ____

   C. ____

   D. ____

5. Discuss ways that parents, teachers, and peers can ease the strain of school transitions. (pp. 392–393)

____

____

____

Academic Achievement

1. How do authoritative, authoritarian, permissive, and uninvolved child-rearing styles contribute to adolescent academic achievement? Which style is the most effective, and why? (p. 393)

   Authoritative: ____

   Authoritarian: ____

   Permissive: ____

   Uninvolved: ____

   Most effective: ____

2. Explain how parent–school partnerships foster academic achievement. (pp. 393–394)

____

____

3. True or False: Peers play a minor role in academic achievement. (p. 394)

4. How does the surrounding peer climate and social order influence ethnic minority youths' academic achievement? (p. 394)

____

____

____

5. In classrooms high in teacher support, student interaction, and mutual respect, students show (gains / declines) in motivation and self-regulation. The (same / opposite) is true for classrooms emphasizing competition and public comparison of students. (p. 394)

6. Why does some grouping become unavoidable during the high school years? (p. 395)

    ____

    ____

7. Assignment to a __________ track accelerates academic progress, whereas assignment to a __________ or __________ track decelerates it. (p. 395)

8. True or False: Most students who work part-time jobs are low-income teenagers who need to contribute to family income or support themselves. (p. 395)

9. How does a heavy commitment to part-time work affect adolescents' academic achievement? Under what circumstances are work experiences beneficial? (p. 395)

    A. ______________________________

    ____

    B. ______________________________

    ____

Dropping Out

1. Describe several consequences of dropping out of school. (p. 396)

    ____

    ____

    ____

2. Describe personal characteristics, family characteristics, and school experiences of students who are at risk for dropping out of high school. (p. 396)

    Personal Characteristics: ______________________________

    ____

    Family Characteristics: ______________________________

    ____

    School Experiences: ______________________________

    ____

3. List four strategies for helping teenagers who are at risk for dropping out of high school. (pp. 396–397)

    A. ______________________________

    B. ______________________________

    C. ______________________________

    D. ______________________________

4. Over the past half century, the percentage of U.S. young people completing high school has (increased / decreased) steadily. (p. 397)

ASK YOURSELF . . .

For *Ask Yourself* questions for this chapter, along with feedback on the accuracy of your answers, please log on to MyDevelopmentLab (for registration and access, please visit mydevelopmentlab.com or follow the instructions on page ix).

(1) Select the Multimedia Library.

(2) Choose the explore option.

(3) Find your chapter from the drop down box.

(4) Click find now.

(5) Complete questions and choose "Submit answers for grading" or "Clear answers" to start over.

SUGGESTED READINGS

Blyth, D., & Simmons, R. G. (2008). *Moving into adolescence: The impact of pubertal change and school context.* Piscataway, NJ: Rutgers. Examines the pubertal experience for young people in Western societies. The authors discuss the developmental milestones associated with the transition to adulthood, including how parents and schools can support adolescents during this exciting and challenging time of life.

Borkowski, J. G., Whitman, T. L., Weed, K., Keogh, D. A., & Farris, J. R. (Eds.). (2007). *Risk and resilience: Adolescent mothers and their children grow up.* Mahwah, NJ: Erlbaum. In 1984, the University of Notre Dame began a longitudinal study to examine the social and psychological consequences of adolescent parenthood. This edited volume presents findings from that study, highlighting the long-term consequences of adolescent parenthood for both parents and children.

Kirke, D. M. (2006). *Teenagers and substance use: Social networks and peer influence.* New York: Palgrave Macmillan. An insightful look at teenagers who abuse alcohol and drugs, this book explores how adolescents' peer groups and social networks contribute to or buffer against substance abuse.

Wing, Y., & Noguera, P. A. (Eds.). (2008). *Closing the racial achievement gap in our schools.* Hoboken, NJ: Wiley. A compelling look at racial inequalities in public education, this book examines racial and academic segregation in U.S. high schools. Topics include factors contributing to academic inequality, the importance of parent involvement, student reflections on the high school experience, and strategies for increasing academic engagement in minority students.

CROSSWORD PUZZLE 11.1

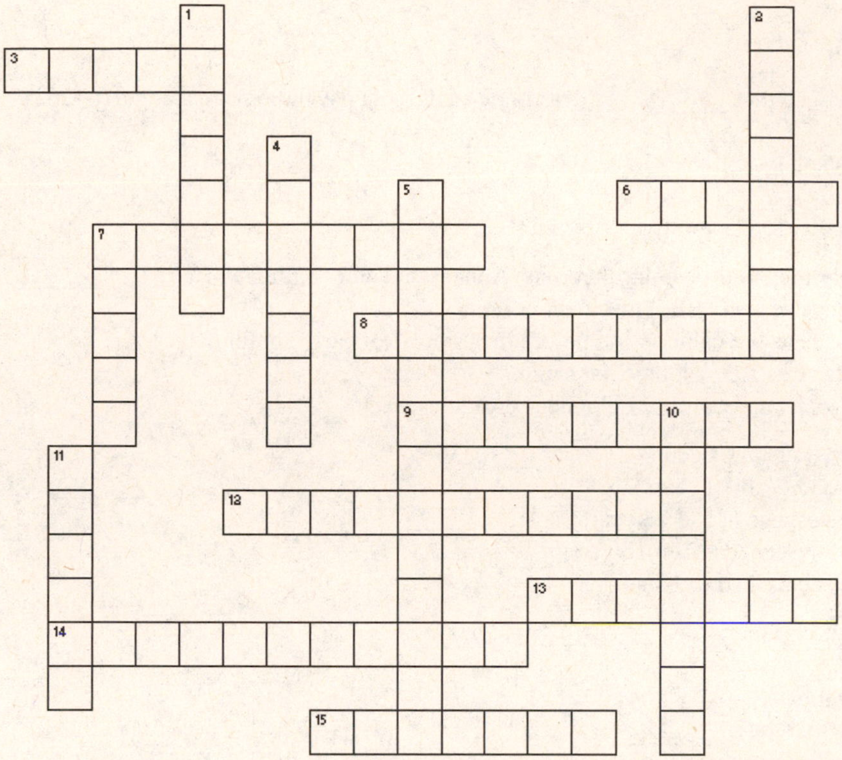

Across

3. Personal ______: adolescents' belief that they are unique and others cannot understand them
6. Growth ______: rapid gain in height and weight during adolescence
7. ______ audience: adolescents' belief that they are the focus of everyone else's attention
8. First ejaculation of seminal fluid
9. ______ sexual characteristics: externally visible features, do not involve reproductive organs
12. ______-deductive reasoning begins with a theory and tests all variables systematically.
13. Biological changes that lead to an adult-sized body and sexual maturity
14. Period of development; crossing the division between childhood and adulthood
15. ______ nervosa involves eating binges followed by deliberate purging and strict dieting.

Down

1. ______ trend: generational change
2. First menstruation
4. ______ sexual characteristics involve the reproductive organs.
5. ______ thought: evaluating a statement's logic without referring to real-world circumstances
7. Body ______: conception of and attitude toward one's physical appearance
10. ______ nervosa: individuals starve themselves because of a compulsive fear of getting fat
11. Piaget's ______ operational stage: the capacity for abstract, scientific thinking develops

PRACTICE TEST #1

1. __________ marks the beginning of adolescence. (p. 361)
   a. The transition to high school
   b. Intellectual maturity
   c. Puberty
   d. An identity crisis

2. Researchers today believe that __________ determine adolescent psychological change. (p. 362)
   a. sexual impulses
   b. biological forces solely
   c. social forces solely
   d. biological and social forces jointly

3. Along with other early twentieth-century theorists, Anna Freud and G. Stanley Hall __________ (p. 362)
   a. viewed adolescence as a stressful, turbulent period.
   b. viewed adolescence as the calm period before the "storm" of early adulthood.
   c. ignored adolescence as a developmental stage.
   d. emphasized the social and cultural influences on adolescence.

4. The most rapid pubertal change occurs __________ (p. 362)
   a. in middle childhood (7 to 10 years).
   b. during early adolescence (11 to 14 years).
   c. during middle adolescence (14 to 16 years).
   d. during late adolescence (16 to 18 years).

5. The first outward sign of puberty is __________ (p. 363)
   a. voice deepening.
   b. body and/or facial hair.
   c. menarche or spermarche.
   d. rapid growth.

6. During puberty, __________ accelerate first, reversing the cephalocaudal trend of infancy and childhood. (p. 363)
   a. the head and shoulders
   b. facial features
   c. hands, legs, and feet
   d. torsos

7. Research on adolescent exercise shows that __________ (p. 365)
   a. from age 9 to age 15, the amount of time youths exercise nearly doubles.
   b. at age 15, most youths do not exercise the recommended 60 minutes per day.
   c. at all ages, girls spend more time exercising than boys.
   d. from age 9 to age 15, boys increase in physical activity, whereas girls show a decline.

8. Which of the following is an example of a secondary sexual characteristic? (p. 365)
   a. breast development
   b. testes
   c. ovaries
   d. menarche

9. Research on brain development in adolescence indicates that __________ (p. 367)
   a. neurons become less responsive to excitatory neurotransmitters.
   b. neurons become more responsive to excitatory neurotransmitters.
   c. the brain becomes highly plastic, similar to that of early childhood.
   d. communication between the left and right hemispheres slows dramatically.

10. Adolescent sleep deprivation __________ (p. 368)
    a. is more common in girls than boys.
    b. tends to be caused by alcohol and drug abuse.
    c. can be overcome by "catch-up" sleep on weekends.
    d. is eased but not eliminated by later school start times.

11. Today, girls __________ (p. 368)
    a. rarely talk to their friends about menarche.
    b. report predominantly negative feelings about menarche.
    c. get more social support than boys for the physical changes of puberty.
    d. are usually uninformed and unprepared for menarche.

12. Adolescent moodiness is __________ (p. 369)
    a. most apparent on weekends.
    b. usually the result of alcohol or drug abuse.
    c. often a sign of serious emotional disturbance.
    d. linked to negative life events.

13. Which of the following statements about parent–adolescent conflict is true? (pp. 369–370)
    a. In most cultures, parent–son conflict is more intense than parent–daughter conflict.
    b. Parent–adolescent conflict is rare in cultures that value respect for parental authority.
    c. Across various cultures, parents and teenagers often disagree on core values.
    d. Across various cultures, there is a rise in parent–child conflict during puberty.

14. Compared with African-American and Hispanic girls, Caucasian girls are more likely to __________ (p. 371)
    a. mature early.
    b. want to fit the cultural ideal of thinness.
    c. have a positive body image.
    d. abuse drugs and alcohol.

15. Anorexia nervosa is equally common in __________ (p. 372)
    a. boys and girls.
    b. all ethnicities.
    c. all SES groups.
    d. all age groups.

16. In North America, most young people __________ (p. 374)
    a. receive contradictory messages about sex from society.
    b. discuss sex openly with their parents.
    c. consistently use contraception during sexual activity.
    d. have three or more sexual partners by the end of high school.

17. Most gay teenagers __________ (p. 377)
    a. are rejected by their parents when they come out.
    b. come to terms with their sexual identity with little internal struggle.
    c. transition to a heterosexual orientation by early adulthood.
    d. eventually accept their sexual identity.

18. Why do adolescents have higher rates of STDs than any other age group? (p. 378)
    a. Most teenagers are poorly informed about STDs and how to protect themselves.
    b. Overall, teenagers are highly susceptible to all forms of illness, including STDs.
    c. Many public schools have cut sex education programs, leaving teenagers without knowledge of safe contraceptive use.
    d. Contraceptives are not available to most teenagers.

19. Intergenerational continuity in adolescent parenthood __________ (p. 380)
    a. is inevitable in most cases.
    b. is a stereotype that has yet to be verified by research.
    c. results from related, unfavorable family conditions and personal characteristics.
    d. results from a lack of sex education classes in public schools.

20. Which of the following programs is most likely to prevent teenage pregnancies? (pp. 379–380)
    a. a sex education course that relates facts about anatomy and reproduction over several sessions
    b. a long-term program that provides specific information, access to contraceptives, and a community connection
    c. a year-long abstinence-based program geared toward younger adolescents
    d. a sex education course geared toward older adolescents who have already engaged in sexual activity

21. Research on adolescent drug use and abuse shows that __________ (p. 381)
    a. use of inhalants, sedatives, and OxyContin has declined dramatically since the mid-1990s.
    b. well-adjusted, curious youth often engage in limited drug and alcohol experimentation.
    c. drug experimentation usually leads to long-term abuse and dependency.
    d. like drug abusers, drug experimenters tend to be seriously troubled young people.

22. A researcher hides a poker chip in her hand and asks participants to indicate whether the following statement is true, false, or uncertain: "Either the chip in my hand is green or it is not green." The researcher is assessing __________ (p. 384)
    a. hypothetico-deductive reasoning.
    b. propositional reasoning.
    c. concrete operational thought.
    d. metacognition.

23. Information-processing findings confirm that scientific reasoning __________ (p. 386)
    a. results from abrupt, stagewise change.
    b. develops gradually out of different experiences.
    c. is possible even without sophisticated metacognitive understanding.
    d. is a biological capacity that first appears at adolescence, regardless of experiences.

24. Sixteen-year-old Michael feels that his experiences are extraordinary and that he is special and unique. He tells his parents, "You'll never understand what it's like to be me!" This is an example of __________ (p. 387)
    a. the personal fable.
    b. the imaginary audience.
    c. hypothetico-deductive reasoning.
    d. idealism.

25. Which of the following statements about gender differences in math abilities is true? (p. 389)
    a. Beginning in elementary school, boys consistently outperform girls in math achievement.
    b. The gender gap between boys and girls in math scores has grown in the past quarter-century.
    c. In most non-Western nations, adolescent girls outperform their male counterparts in math achievement.
    d. Boys start to outperform girls in math during early adolescence, when math concepts become more abstract and spatial.

26. Sex differences in spatial abilities ___________ (p. 391)
    a. emerge in early childhood, persist through the lifespan, and are evident in many cultures.
    b. first appear in early adolescence and strengthen across the lifespan.
    c. are caused by biological differences between boys and girls and cannot be modified with experience or training.
    d. are primarily due to boys' interest in playing video games that require rapid mental rotation of visual images.

27. Young adolescents often feel __________ in middle school than in elementary school. (p. 390)
    a. more motivated
    b. more popular
    c. less motivated
    d. less anonymous

28. To help ease the strain of school transition, parents __________ (p. 392)
    a. should enroll their adolescent in a private high school.
    b. can encourage their adolescent to seek a vocational track.
    c. should emphasize grades over mastery of subject matter.
    d. can gradually grant their adolescents more autonomy.

29. Teenagers who are heavily committed to low-level jobs __________ than their peers. (p. 395)
    a. have better school attendance
    b. report more drug and alcohol use
    c. are less likely to drop out of high school
    d. have closer relationships with their parents

30. To help prevent students from dropping out, school districts can __________ (p. 396)
    a. retain more students at each grade level.
    b. offer the GED to low-achieving students.
    c. increase opportunities for personalized remedial instruction.
    d. assign more students to a vocational track.

PRACTICE TEST #2

1. Which of the following is an experience particular to young people of industrialized nations? (p. 362)
   a. acceptance of the full-grown body
   b. attainment of independence from family
   c. identity construction
   d. extended adolescence

2. G. Stanley Hall based his ideas about development, including the "storm-and-stress" view, on __________ (p. 362)
   a. Margaret Mead's emphasis on the social environment.
   b. Charles Darwin's theory of evolution.
   c. Sigmund Freud's genital stage.
   d. Jean Piaget's cognitive developmental theory.

3. Contemporary research suggests that the storm-and-stress notion of adolescence is __________ (p. 362)
   a. necessary for mature identity development.
   b. an inevitable part of growing up.
   c. greatly exaggerated.
   d. responsible for a drastic increase in psychological disturbance among teens.

4. Which of the following statements about sex hormones is true? (p. 363)
   a. Sex hormones control sexual maturation in boys and girls.
   b. Estrogens are exclusively a female hormone, but androgens are found in both sexes.
   c. Boys' testes release large quantities of estrogen, which contributes to gains in body size.
   d. Sex hormones have little effect on body growth for either sex.

5. Around age ____, boys surpass girls in height and weight. (p. 363)
   a. 9
   b. 11
   c. 14
   d. 17

6. Which of the following is a sex difference in adolescents' physical development? (p. 364)
   a. During puberty, cephalocaudal growth continues for girls but reverses for boys.
   b. In industrialized nations, boys experience a growth spurt two years before girls.
   c. Throughout adolescence, boys gain far more muscle than girls.
   d. Boys and girls gain similar amounts of fat and muscle during the adolescent growth spurt.

7. Adolescent exertion during exercise is __________ (p. 365)
   a. a strong predictor of adult exercise.
   b. discouraged by most health professionals.
   c. a strong indicator of anorexia.
   d. a leading cause of serious injury.

8. A typical puberty lasts ________ years. (p. 365)
   a. two
   b. three
   c. four
   d. six

9. The first sign of puberty in boys is __________ (p. 366)
   a. spermarche.
   b. the enlargement of the testes.
   c. the appearance of facial hair.
   d. significant weight gain.

10. Girls who __________ usually experience later puberty. (p. 367)
    a. are obese
    b. are of African descent
    c. live in high-conflict families
    d. eat very little

11. Parent–adolescent conflicts typically focus on __________ (p. 370)
    a. substance abuse.
    b. mundane, day-to-day matters.
    c. early sexual activity.
    d. long-term goals.

12. Early-maturing boys __________ (p. 370)
    a. tend to be popular with agemates.
    b. are often viewed as anxious and attention-seeking.
    c. tend to be rejected by agemates.
    d. often lack self-confidence.

13. The most common nutritional problem of adolescence is __________ (p. 372)
    a. protein deficiency.
    b. iron deficiency.
    c. anorexia.
    d. bulimia.

14. Both anorexics and bulimics __________ (p. 373)
    a. feel depressed about their eating habits and desperately want help.
    b. usually require hospitalization to treat.
    c. engage in deviant behaviors, including shoplifting and alcohol abuse.
    d. are influenced by heredity.

15. Which of the following sequences do most homosexual youth move through before coming out to themselves and others? (p. 377)
    a. confusion, self-hatred, questioning
    b. feeling different, confusion, self-acceptance
    c. self-awareness, pretending, sexual questioning
    d. internalized homophobia, choice of sexuality, social acceptance

16. The rate of adolescent pregnancy in the United States __________ (p. 378)
    a. has changed very little over the past six decades.
    b. is higher than it was 50 years ago.
    c. is higher than that of other industrialized nations.
    d. is similar to that of other industrialized nations.

17. Which of the following factors is related to becoming a second-generation teenage parent? (p. 380)
    a. father absence
    b. lack of sex education in public schools
    c. assignment to a general education track in high school
    d. being adopted

18. U.S. adolescents are more likely to __________ than European adolescents. (p. 381)
    a. drink alcohol
    b. use illegal drugs
    c. smoke cigarettes
    d. use contraceptives

19. Piaget's pendulum problem, in which participants separate and test different variables in order to arrive at a solution, illustrates his belief that __________ begins in adolescence. (p. 383)
    a. hypothetico-deductive reasoning
    b. concrete operational thinking
    c. propositional thought
    d. logical thinking

20. Seven-year-old Xiaohan is presented with the following set of statements: "If dogs can fly and Banjo is a dog, then Banjo can fly." Xiaohan believes this statement to be false because dogs do not fly in real life. In this example, Xiaohan is unable to __________ (p. 384)
    a. understand the content of the statements.
    b. explain why a pattern of observations supports a hypothesis.
    c. understand second-order false beliefs.
    d. grasp the logical necessity of propositional thinking.

21. Follow-up research on formal operational thought shows that __________ (p. 384)
    a. school-age children are as competent as adolescents in hypothetico-deductive reasoning.
    b. the capacity for formal operational thought appears at puberty.
    c. schooling and practice lead to gains in formal operational thinking.
    d. nearly all adults are fully formal operational.

22. Which of the following statements reflects the imaginary audience? (p. 387)
    a. "I don't care if my new haircut is bad. I'm going to the party anyway."
    b. "I can't go to the party with a huge pimple on my cheek! Everyone will make fun of me!"
    c. "My parents don't understand how hard school is for me!"
    d. "No one will care if I can't afford a new dress for the prom. I'll just wear the same one I wore last year."

23. Fifteen-year-old Kate seems to find fault with everything; she is critical of the way her parents dress, the food they buy, the cars they drive, and the manner in which they spend their free time. Kate's fault-finding results from adolescent __________ (p. 388)
    a. idealism.
    b. realism.
    c. egocentrism.
    d. perspective taking.

24. Which of the following statements about adolescent decision making is true? (p. 388)
    a. Adolescents are just as skilled as adults in day-to-day decision making.
    b. Adolescents are more likely than adults to seek advice in solving real-world problems.
    c. Adolescents are more likely than adults to fall back on well-learned intuitive judgments.
    d. Adolescents rarely consider their options or think about the consequences of their decisions.

25. Which of the following statements about gender differences in reading and writing achievement is true? (p. 389)
    a. Girls attain higher scores in reading and writing until adolescence, when boys start to outperform girls.
    b. The area of the brain where language is localized develops earlier in girls than in boys.
    c. Despite receiving more verbal stimulation from their mothers, boys lag behind girls in reading and writing achievement.
    d. The area of the brain where language is localized develops earlier in boys than in girls.

26. Kristiana, an eighth grader, believes that her peers will judge her negatively if she does well in math. This is an example of __________ (p. 390)
    a. a self-fulfilling prophecy.
    b. propositional thought.
    c. metacognitive understanding.
    d. stereotype threat.

27. Research on school transitions shows that __________ (p. 390)
    a. the earlier the transition occurs, the more dramatic and long-lasting its negative impact on psychological well-being, especially for girls.
    b. earlier transitions are associated with negative outcomes for boys, whereas later transitions are associated with negative outcomes for girls.
    c. the transition from junior high to high school is relatively problem-free for most adolescents and rarely has an effect on academic achievement.
    d. adolescents with multiple life strains, such as the onset of puberty together with family disruption, tend to display resilience during the transition to high school.

28. Sex differences in spatial abilities __________ (p. 391)
    a. emerge in early childhood.
    b. emerge in adolescence.
    c. are evident only in Western cultures.
    d. are primarily determined by biological factors.

29. Which of the following child-rearing styles is associated with high academic achievement in adolescence? (p. 393)
    a. authoritarian
    b. authoritative
    c. permissive
    d. uninvolved

30. Compared with many Western European nations, the United States __________ (p. 396)
    a. has a much higher high school dropout rate.
    b. has a much lower high school dropout rate.
    c. rarely assigns high school students to vocational tracks.
    d. allocates more resources to the education of low-income minority students.

CHAPTER 12
EMOTIONAL AND SOCIAL DEVELOPMENT IN ADOLESCENCE

BRIEF CHAPTER SUMMARY

Erikson was the first to recognize identity as the major personality achievement of adolescence and as a crucial step toward becoming a productive, happy adult. Young people who successfully resolve the psychological conflict of identity versus role confusion construct a solid self-definition based on self-chosen values and goals. During adolescence, cognitive changes transform the young person's vision of the self into a more complex, well-organized, and consistent picture. For most young people, self-esteem rises over the teenage years and is influenced by family, school, and the larger social environment. Among older adolescents, personal and moral values become key themes.

Adolescents' well-organized self-descriptions and differentiated sense of self-esteem provide the cognitive foundation for identity development. Researchers have derived four identity statuses that reflect adolescents' progress toward developing a mature identity. Two of these—identity achievement and moratorium—are psychologically healthy routes to a mature self-definition. Adolescents who remain in one of the other statuses—identity foreclosure or identity diffusion—tend to have adjustment difficulties.

Lawrence Kohlberg, inspired by the research of Piaget, identified three levels of moral development, each with two stages. According to Kohlberg, moral development is a gradual process that occurs as the individual actively grapples with moral issues and achieves gains in perspective taking. Child-rearing practices, schooling, peer interaction, and culture all contribute to moral development. Maturity of moral reasoning is only modestly related to moral behavior. Moral action is also influenced by the individual's empathy and guilt, temperament, and history of morally relevant experiences.

Biological, social, and cognitive factors all play a role in making early adolescence a period of gender intensification—increased gender stereotyping of attitudes and behavior, and movement toward a more traditional gender identity, especially for girls. Development at adolescence involves striving for autonomy—a sense of oneself as a separate, self-governing individual. Over the adolescent years, relationships with parents and siblings change as teenagers strive to establish a healthy balance between connection to and separation from the family. As adolescents spend more time with peers, intimacy and loyalty become central features of friendship. Adolescent peer groups tend to be organized into tightly knit groups called cliques, or into crowds—larger, more loosely organized groups. Although it rises in adolescence, most peer pressure is not in conflict with important adult values.

Although most young people move through adolescence with little difficulty, some encounter major disruptions, such as premature parenthood, substance abuse, and school failure. The most common psychological problem of the teenage years, depression, is influenced by a diverse combination of biological and environmental factors. The suicide rate increases dramatically at adolescence. Many teenagers become involved in some delinquent activity, but only a few are serious or repeat offenders. Family, school, peer, and neighborhood factors contribute to delinquency.

LEARNING OBJECTIVES

After reading this chapter, you should be able to:

12.1 Discuss Erikson's theory of identity development. (p. 402)

12.2 Describe changes in self-concept and self-esteem during adolescence. (pp. 402–403)

12.3 Describe the four identity statuses, the adjustment outcomes of each status, and factors that promote identity development. (pp. 403–406)

12.4 Discuss Kohlberg's theory of moral development, and evaluate its accuracy. (pp. 407–409)

12.5 Summarize research on Gilligan's claim that Kohlberg's theory underestimated the moral maturity of females. (pp. 409–410)

12.6 Describe influences on moral reasoning and its relationship to moral behavior. (pp. 410–414)

12.7 Explain why early adolescence is a period of gender intensification, and cite factors that promote the development of an androgynous gender identity. (pp. 414–415)

12.8 Discuss changes in parent–child and sibling relationships during adolescence. (pp. 415–417)

12.9 Describe adolescent friendships, peer groups, and dating relationships and their consequences for development. (pp. 417–421)

12.10 Discuss conformity to peer pressure in adolescence, noting the importance of authoritative child rearing. (p. 421)

12.11 Discuss factors related to adolescent depression and suicide, along with approaches for prevention and treatment. (pp. 421–423)

12.12 Summarize factors related to delinquency, and describe strategies for prevention and treatment. (pp. 423–426)

STUDY QUESTIONS

Erikson's Theory: Identity versus Role Confusion

1. What three aspects of the self do adolescents define as they construct an *identity*? (p. 402)

   A. ______________________

   B. ______________________

   C. ______________________

2. Describe the identity crisis experienced by teenagers in complex societies, according to Erikson. (p. 402)

   ____

   ____

   ____

3. Explain how a negative resolution of Erikson's psychological conflict of adolescence, *identity versus role confusion*, might affect teenagers. (p. 402)

   ____

   ____

4. True or False: Current theorists agree with Erikson that the process of identity development constitutes a "crisis." (p. 402)

Self-Understanding

Changes in Self-Concept

1. True or False: Young adolescents often provide contradictory self-descriptions—for example, describing themselves as both shy and outgoing. Explain. (p. 402)

   ____

   ____

2. Compared with school-age children, teenagers place (less / more) emphasis on social virtues, such as being friendly, considerate, kind, and cooperative. Why is this so? (p. 402)

   ____

   ____

Changes in Self-Esteem

1. List three new dimensions of self-evaluation that emerge during adolescence. (p. 402)

   A. ______________________________

   B. ______________________________

   C. ______________________________

2. Although some adolescents experience declines associated with ________________, self-esteem rises for most young people. (p. 402)

3. True or False: Individual differences in self-esteem become increasingly stable in adolescence. (p. 403)

4. Describe self-esteem factors associated with adjustment difficulties in adolescence. (p. 403)

   ____

   ____

   ____

Paths to Identity

1. Match each identity status with its appropriate description. (p. 403)

______	Commitment to values and goals without exploration	A.	*Identity achievement*
______	Exploration of alternatives without having reached commitment	B.	*Identity moratorium*
______	Commitment to beliefs and goals following a period of exploration	C.	*Identity foreclosure*
______	An apathetic state lacking both exploration and commitment	D.	*Identity diffusion*

2. Most adolescents start out at "lower" identity statuses, such as ________________ and ________________. By the time they reach their mid-twenties, most have moved toward "higher" statuses, including ________________ and ________________. (p. 403)

3. True or False: Most adolescent girls postpone the task of establishing an identity, focusing instead on intimacy development. (p. 403)

Identity Status and Psychological Well-Being

1. Indicate whether each of the following identity statuses is a healthy route (+) or a maladaptive route (–) to a mature self-definition. (p. 403)

______	Identity achievement	______	Identity foreclosure
______	Identity diffusion	______	Identity moratorium

2. Cite several ways in which adolescents in moratorium resemble identity-achieved individuals. (p. 404)

   ____

   ____

   ____

3. Describe the cognitive styles of foreclosed versus diffused adolescents. (p. 404)

   Foreclosed: ______________________________

   ____

   Diffused: ______________________________

   ____

4. Long-term (diffused / foreclosed) individuals are the least mature in identity development. (p. 404)

Factors Affecting Identity Development

1. Match each identity status with its associated characteristics. Characteristics may apply to more than one identity status. (p. 404)

______	Assumes that absolute truth is always attainable	A.	Identity achievement
______	Doubts that she will ever feel certain about anything	B.	Identity moratorium
______	Appreciates that he can use rational criteria to select alternatives	C.	Identity foreclosure
______	Feels attached to parents but also free to voice her own opinions	D.	Identity diffusion
______	Has close bonds with parents but lacks healthy separation		
______	Reports the lowest levels of warm, open family communication		

2. How do close friendships help adolescents explore their identity options? (pp. 404–405)

____

____

3. In what ways can schools and communities support adolescent identity development? (p. 405)

____

____

____

4. Explain how Native Canadian and cultural-majority youths differ in their sense of self-continuity. (p. 405)

Native Canadian: ____

____

Cultural-majority: ____

____

Cultural Influences: Identity Development Among Ethnic Minority Adolescents

1. ____________________ refers to a sense of ethnic-group membership and attitudes and feelings associated with that membership. (p. 406)

2. Some immigrant adolescents experience *acculturative stress*, psychological distress resulting from conflict between the ______________ and the ______________ culture. (p. 406)

3. True or False: Discrimination can interfere with the formation of a positive *ethnic identity*. (p. 406)

4. Describe the extra challenges to identity development faced by young people with parents of different ethnicities. (p. 406)

____

____

____

5. List three ways society can help minority adolescents resolve identity conflicts constructively. (p. 406)

A. ____

B. ____

C. ____

6. How do minority adolescents benefit from the development of a *bicultural identity*? (p. 406)

____

____

Moral Development

Kohlberg's Theory of Moral Development

1. Kohlberg's moral ______________ are stories presenting a conflict between two moral values. (p. 407)
2. Kohlberg emphasized that the (individual's reasoning about a dilemma / content of the response) determines moral maturity. (p. 407)
3. List two factors that promote moral reasoning, according to Kohlberg. (p. 407)

   A. ______________________________

   B. ______________________________
4. Explain the basic characteristics of moral reasoning at each of Kohlberg's three levels. (pp. 407–409)

   Preconventional: ______________________________

   ____

   Conventional: ______________________________

   ____

   Postconventional: ______________________________

   ____
5. Match each of the following moral orientations with its appropriate description. (pp. 407–409)

   ______ Laws must always be obeyed; rules must be enforced evenly for everyone; members of society have a personal duty to uphold rules
   ______ Right action is defined by universally applicable, self-chosen ethical principals, regardless of law and social agreement
   ______ Overlooks people's intentions, focusing on fear of authority and avoidance of punishment as reasons for moral behavior
   ______ Obeys rules to maintain others' affection and approval
   ______ Rules and laws are flexible; emphasizes fair evaluation of the law to protect individual rights and the interests of the majority
   ______ Right action flows from self-interest; reciprocity is understood as equal exchange of favors

   A. Punishment and obedience
   B. Instrumental purpose
   C. "Good boy–good girl"
   D. Social-order-maintaining
   E. Social contract
   F. Universal ethical principal
6. True or False: Longitudinal research suggests that Kohlberg incorrectly predicted the order in which people move through his first four stages. (p. 409)
7. True or False: The development of moral understanding is slow and gradual. (p. 409)
8. Few people move beyond Kohlberg's Stage ____. What does this reveal about the accuracy of Kohlberg's theory? (p. 409)

   ____

   ____

   ____
9. Moral reasoning about real-life problems tends to fall (below / above) a person's actual moral capacity. Why is this? (p. 409)

   ____

   ____

   ____
10. True or False: Kohlberg's stages develop in a neat, stepwise fashion. (p. 409)

Are There Sex Differences in Moral Reasoning?

1. Carol Gilligan believes that feminine morality emphasizes a(n) ______________________ that is devalued in Kohlberg's system. According to Gilligan, a concern for others is a (less valid / different) basis for moral judgment than a focus on impersonal rights. (p. 409)
2. True or False: Most research suggests that Kohlberg's approach underestimates females' moral maturity. (p. 409)
3. In their moral judgments, (females / males) tend to emphasize care, whereas (females / males) either stress justice or focus equally on justice and care. (p. 409)

Coordinating Moral, Social-Conventional, and Personal Concerns

1. True or False: In diverse Western and non-Western cultures, teenagers express great concern with matters of personal choice. (p. 410)
2. By tenth grade, young people indicate that exclusion of another peer (is / is not) okay. How do adolescents justify this response? (p. 410)

   ____

   ____

3. Discuss adolescents' mindfulness of moral imperatives and social conventions. (p. 410)

   ____

   ____

   ____

Influences on Moral Reasoning

1. Summarize child-rearing practices that promote gains in moral understanding. (p. 411)

   ____

   ____

   ____

2. Cite two aspects of higher education that promote moral development. (p. 411)

   A. ____

   B. ____

3. Cite two aspects of peer discussions that stimulate moral development. (p. 411)

   A. ____

   B. ____

4. True or False: Cross-cultural research shows that individuals in industrialized nations move through Kohlberg's stages more quickly and advance to higher levels than individuals in village societies. Briefly explain your answer. (p. 411)

   ____

   ____

   ____

Moral Reasoning and Behavior

1. A (weak / modest / strong) connection exists between mature moral reasoning and action. (p. 412)

2. Besides cognition, what factors influence moral behavior in adolescence? (p. 412)

____

____

3. ____________________ refers to the degree to which morality is central to self-concept. (p. 412)

4. Cite two ways in which schools can foster adolescents' sense of *moral self-relevance*. (p. 412)

A. ____

____

B. ____

____

Social Issues: Development of Civic Responsibility

1. List three components of civic responsibility. (p. 413)

A. ____

B. ____

C. ____

2. Briefly summarize family, school, and community influences that contribute to adolescents' civic responsibility. (p. 413)

Family: ____

____

School and Community: ____

____

3. Youths who endorse (individual / situational and societal) causes of unemployment and poverty tend to have more altruistic life goals and to engage in more civic activities. (p. 413)

4. Cite two aspects of involvement in extracurricular activities and youth organizations that account for their lasting impact. (p. 413)

A. ____

B. ____

Religious Involvement and Moral Development

1. (Few / Most) Americans report being religious. Formal religious involvement tends to (decline / increase) in adolescence. (p. 412)

2. Teenagers who belong to a religious community are (less / more) involved in community service activities and show (lower / higher) levels of drug and alcohol use, early sexual activity, and delinquency than nonaffiliated youths. (p. 412)

3. How do religious communities promote adolescents' moral values and behaviors? (pp. 412, 414)

____

____

____

Further Challenges to Kohlberg's Theory

1. Summarize the pragmatic approach to morality. (p. 414)

____

____

2. List three cognitive-developmental objections to the pragmatic approach. (p. 414)

   A. ____

   B. ____

   C. ____

3. True or False: Most researchers have rejected the idea that with age, humans everywhere construct deeper understandings that guide moral action. (p. 414)

Gender Typing

1. *Gender* ____________________ refers to increased gender stereotyping of attitudes and behavior and movement toward a more traditional gender identity. (p. 414)

2. Gender intensification is stronger for (boys / girls). (p. 414)

3. Cite biological, social, and cognitive factors associated with gender intensification. (pp. 414–415)

   Biological: ____

   ____

   Social: ____

   ____

   Cognitive: ____

   ____

4. Gender intensification (declines / increases) by middle to late adolescence. (p. 415)

5. (Androgynous / Gender-typed) adolescents tend to be psychologically healthier. (p. 415)

The Family

1. Adolescents strive for ________________—a sense of oneself as a separate, self-governing individual. (p. 415)

Parent–Child Relationships

1. Indicate which of the following parenting practices foster adolescent *autonomy* and other positive outcomes. (p. 415)

   ______ Permitting young people to explore ideas and social roles
   ______ Using coercion
   ______ Attempting to psychologically control the adolescent
   ______ Consistently, cooperatively monitoring the young person's daily activities

2. How can parents' development contribute to friction with teenagers? (p. 416)

____

____

____

3. The quality of the ________________________ is the most consistent predictor of mental health throughout adolescence. (p. 416)

4. Explain how mild parent–child conflict is beneficial during adolescence. (p. 416)

5. True or False: The drop in time spent with family during adolescence is universal. Briefly explain your response. (p. 416)

Family Circumstances

1. Cite factors that can make it easier for parents to grant teenagers appropriate autonomy and reduce parent-adolescent conflict. (p. 416)

2. List three factors that help teenagers to develop well despite family stresses. (p. 416)

   A. ________________________

   B. ________________________

   C. ________________________

Siblings

1. During adolescence, teenagers invest (less / more) time and energy in siblings. Why is this? (p. 417)

2. Sibling relationships become (less / more) intense during adolescence, in both positive and negative feelings. (p. 417)

3. True or False: In adolescence, mild sibling differences in perceived parental affection no longer trigger jealousy but, instead, predict greater sibling warmth. (p. 417)

Peer Relations

Friendships

1. Cite three important characteristics of adolescent friendships. (p. 417)

   A. ________________________ C. ________________________

   B. ________________________

2. Summarize ways in which adolescent friends are likely to resemble one another. (p. 417)

3. Adolescents are (less / more) possessive of their friends than they were in childhood. (p. 417)

4. Indicate whether the following statements describe boys' (B) or girls' (G) close friendships in adolescence. (p. 417)

______	Characterized by emotional closeness	______	Often gather for sports or competitive games
______	Discussions focus on accomplishments	______	Frequently get together to "just talk"
______	Interactions contain more self-disclosure	______	Focus on communal concerns
______	Focus on achievement and status	______	Conversations focus on competition and conflict

5. (Androgynous / Highly "masculine") boys are more likely to form intimate same-sex ties. (p. 418)

6. When can closeness in friendship be problematic? (p. 418)

____

____

7. As the amount of instant messaging between preexisting friends increases, adolescents' perceptions of intimacy and well-being in the relationship (decrease / increase). (p. 418)

8. Describe potential dangers adolescents face when developing friendships over the Internet. (p. 418)

____

____

9. Cite four reasons why adolescent friendships are related to psychological health and competence into early adulthood. (p. 419)

A. ____

B. ____

C. ____

D. ____

Cliques and Crowds

1. Indicate whether the following statements describe *cliques* (L) or *crowds* (R). (p. 419)

______ Typically consist of about five to seven members
______ Larger, more loosely organized groups
______ Membership is based on reputation and stereotype
______ Members resemble one another in family background, attitudes, and values

2. Provide some examples of typical high school crowds. (p. 419)

____

____

3. True or False: Peer group values are often an extension of values learned in the home. Explain your answer. (p. 419)

____

____

____

4. Describe the function of mixed-sex cliques in early adolescence. (pp. 419–420)

____

____

____

5. True or False: By late adolescence, mixed-sex cliques disappear. (p. 420)

6. True or False: Crowds increase in importance from early to late adolescence. (p. 420)

Dating

1. Indicate whether the following reasons for dating are more typical of younger (Y) or older (O) adolescents. (p. 420)

   ______ Recreation ______ Companionship and affection
   ______ Social support ______ Achieving peer status

2. How does early parental attachment influence the quality of adolescents' friendships and romantic relationships? (p. 420)

   ____
   ____
   ____

3. True or False: Early dating is associated with positive outcomes for adolescents. (p. 420)

4. What factors increase the likelihood of dating violence? (p. 420)

   ____
   ____

5. True or False: Gay and lesbian youths' relationships tend to be short-lived and to involve little emotional commitment. Explain your answer. (p. 420)

   ____

6. Describe the benefits of close romantic relationships among older teenagers. (p. 420)

   ____
   ____

Peer Conformity

1. True or False: Conformity to peer pressure is greater during adolescence than during childhood or young adulthood. (p. 421)

2. To what aspects of peer culture do U.S. youths feel the greatest pressure to conform? (p. 421)

   ____

3. (Parents / Peers) exert more influence on teenagers' day-to-day personal choices. (Parents / Peers) have more impact on basic life values and educational plans. (p. 421)

4. Match the following parenting practices with their associated outcomes for adolescents. Practices may apply to more than one outcome. (p. 421)

   ______ Greater reliance on friends for advice
   ______ Resistance to peer pressure
   ______ Tendency to be highly peer-oriented
   ______ Greater willingness to engage in problem behaviors

   A. Authoritative child rearing
   B. Too much or too little parental control

Problems of Development

Depression

1. ____________________ is the most common psychological problem of adolescence. (p. 421)

2. Depression is much more prevalent in (childhood / adolescence). More (boys / girls) display adolescent-onset depression. (p. 422)

3. Explain why adolescents' depressive symptoms tend to be overlooked by parents and teachers. (p. 422)

____

____

4. True or False: Kinship studies reveal that heredity plays an important role in depression. (p. 422)

5. Explain how biology and experience contribute to depression. (p. 422)

   Biology: ____

   ____

   Experience: ____

   ____

6. Biological changes associated with puberty (can / cannot) account for sex differences in depression. Explain your answer. (p. 422)

____

____

____

7. Describe factors that are responsible for girls' higher rates of depression. (p. 422)

____

____

____

Suicide

1. The suicide rate (decreases sharply / increases gradually / jumps sharply) at adolescence. (p. 422)

2. True or False: Adolescent suicide rates are roughly equivalent in all industrialized countries. (p. 422)

3. Indicate whether the following statements describe adolescent boys (B) or girls (G). (p. 422)

   ______ Are more likely to kill themselves
   ______ Make more unsuccessful suicide attempts
   ______ Tend to choose techniques that lead to instant death
   ______ Experience less tolerance for feelings of helplessness and failed efforts

4. Compared with their Caucasian American peers, African-American and Hispanic adolescents have (lower / higher) suicide rates. (pp. 422–423)

5. Cite factors that may contribute to the high suicide rates among African-American adolescent males and Native-American youths. (p. 423)

____

____

6. True or False: Gay, lesbian, and bisexual youths are more likely than other adolescents to attempt suicide. (p. 423)

7. Describe two types of young people who tend to commit suicide. (p. 423)

   A. ____

   ____

   B. ____

   ____

8. Describe family characteristics and life events associated with adolescent suicide. (p. 423)

____

____

____

9. Cite two reasons why suicide increases in adolescence. (p. 423)

A. ____

B. ____

10. What types of interventions are available for depressed and suicidal adolescents? (p. 423)

____

____

____

11. True or False: Teenage suicides often take place in clusters. (p. 423)

Delinquency

1. Juvenile delinquents are children or adolescents who engage in ____________ acts. (p. 423)
2. Explain why delinquency rises during early adolescence, remains high in middle adolescence, and then declines into young adulthood. (p. 424)

   ____

   ____

   ____

3. True or False: For most adolescents, a brush with the law forecasts long-term antisocial behavior. (p. 424)
4. Adolescent (girls / boys) commit more violent crimes than the other gender. The violent offenses of adolescent (girls / boys) are largely limited to simple assault. (p. 424)
5. True or False: Authorities are more likely to arrest, charge, and punish low-SES minority youths than their higher-SES white and Asian counterparts. (p. 424)
6. List personal, family, neighborhood, and school factors associated with delinquency. (p. 424)

   Personal: ____

   ____

   Family: ____

   ____

   Neighborhood: ____

   ____

   School: ____

   ____

7. Indicate which of the following are characteristics of effective treatment programs for adolescent delinquency. (pp. 424, 426)

   ______ Starts early
   ______ Utilizes a zero tolerance policy
   ______ Promotes cognitive and social skills
   ______ Takes place at multiple levels
   ______ Includes parent training
   ______ Disengages youths from deviant peers

A Lifespan Vista: Two Routes to Adolescent Delinquency

1. Persistent adolescent delinquency follows two paths of development, one with an onset of ______________________ problems in childhood, the second with an onset in ______________. (p. 425)

2. Indicate whether the following statements describe early-onset (E) or late-onset (L) delinquent youths. (p. 425)

   ______ Are far more likely to develop a life-course pattern of aggression and criminality
   ______ Conduct problems arise from peer context
   ______ Inherit traits that predispose them to aggressiveness
   ______ Show subtle deficits in cognitive functioning

3. What factor combines with biological risks to set early-onset juvenile delinquents on the life-course path of aggression and criminality? (p. 425)

   ____

ASK YOURSELF . . .

For *Ask Yourself* questions for this chapter, along with feedback on the accuracy of your answers, please log on to MyDevelopmentLab (for registration and access, please visit mydevelopmentlab.com or follow the instructions on page ix).

(1) Select the Multimedia Library.

(2) Choose the explore option.

(3) Find your chapter from the drop down box.

(4) Click find now.

(5) Complete questions and choose "Submit answers for grading" or "Clear answers" to start over.

SUGGESTED READINGS

Brandt, D., & Kazdin, A. E. (2007). *Delinquency, development, and social policy*. New Haven: Yale University Press. An ecological approach to understanding antisocial behavior in adolescence, this book examines the origins and pathways of delinquency. The authors argue that early intervention that addresses the developmental needs of children and adolescents is more effective in preventing antisocial behavior than referral to juvenile courts or incarceration.

Deutsch, N. (2008). *Pride in the projects: Teens building identities in urban contexts*. New York: New York University Press. Based on four years of field research, this book examines identity development in inner-city youth. Although many of these young people encounter significant obstacles in their daily life, such as exposure to gangs and violence, discrimination, and poverty, having access to community resources and high-quality after-school programs can help foster resilience and favorable identity development.

Jamieson, P. E. (2008). *The changing portrayal of adolescents in the media since 1950*. New York: Oxford University Press. Presents a compelling look at how adolescents have been portrayed in the media for the past 60 years, including how these portrayals contribute to adolescent behavior. The author contends that a drastic increase in media consumption—from television to music to the Internet—has contributed to current trends in gender and ethnic representation, sexuality, substance use, violence, and even suicidal behavior among teens.

Sylwester, R. (2007). *The adolescent brain: Reaching for autonomy*. Thousand Oaks, CA: Sage. A comprehensive review of adolescent development, this book presents the milestones and challenges young people face as they transition into adulthood. The book illustrates how brain development contributes to adolescent identity, autonomy, morality, risk taking, sexuality, and emotional well-being.

CROSSWORD PUZZLE 12.1

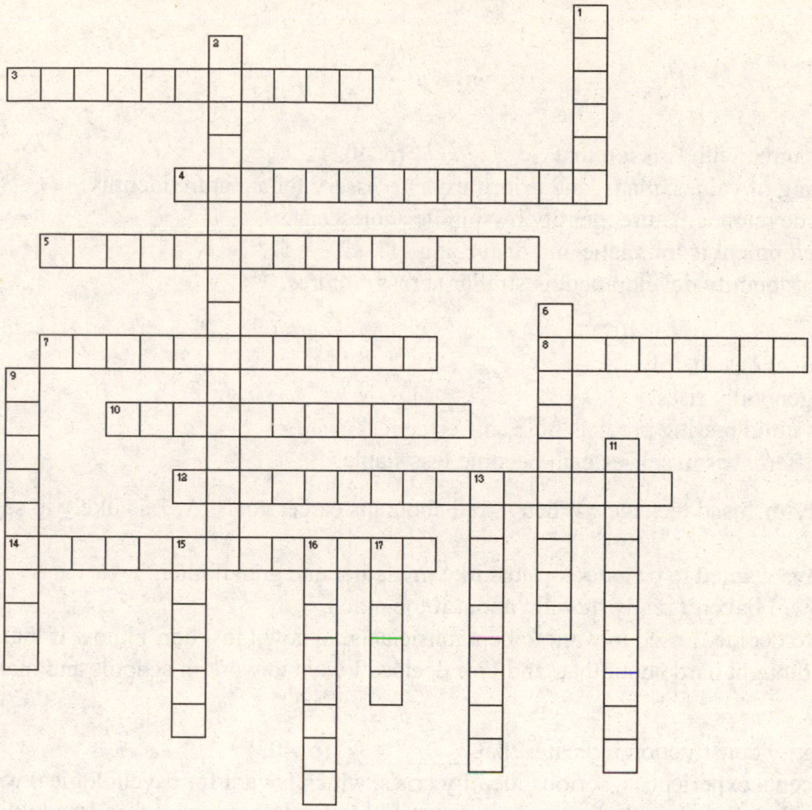

Across

3. Identity ______: commitment to values and goals without exploration
4. ______ stress: psychological distress resulting from conflict between the minority and the host culture
5. Kohlberg's first moral level; morality is externally controlled
7. Kohlberg's second moral level; individuals follow rules to maintain the current social system
8. Encompasses who you are, what you value, and the directions you choose to pursue in life
10. Identity ______: commitment to beliefs and goals following a period of exploration
12. Gender ______: increased stereotyping of attitudes and behavior; movement toward a traditional gender identity
14. Moral ______-______: degree to which morality is central to one's self-concept (2 words, hyph.)

Down

1. Five to seven peers who are friends and typically resemble one another
2. Kohlberg's highest moral level; morality is defined in terms of abstract, universal principles and values
6. ______ identity: includes values from both one's subculture and the dominant culture
9. Identity ______: apathetic state lacking both exploration and commitment
11. Identity ______: exploration of identity alternatives without having reached commitment
13. Identity versus role ______: Erikson's psychological conflict of adolescence
15. ______ identity: sense of cultural-group membership and associated attitudes and feelings
16. Sense of oneself as a separate, self-governing individual
17. Large, loosely organized peer group; membership is based on reputation and stereotype

PRACTICE TEST #1

1. Erikson was the first to recognize __________ as the major personality achievement of adolescence. (p. 402)
   a. intimacy
   b. rationality
   c. self-esteem
   d. identity

2. Current theorists agree with Erikson that __________ (p. 402)
   a. the questioning of values, plans, and priorities is necessary for a mature identity.
   b. most people develop a mature identity by middle adolescence.
   c. identity development is traumatic and disturbing.
   d. the process of identity development is similar across cultures.

3. In adolescence, __________ (p. 402)
   a. self-esteem declines sharply.
   b. self-esteem generally rises.
   c. authoritarian child rearing predicts high self-esteem.
   d. individual differences in self-esteem become less stable.

4. A. J. is an identity-diffused teenager. When asked about his career goals, A. J. is likely to say, __________ (pp. 403, 404)
   a. "I have always wanted to be a doctor, just like my father and grandfather."
   b. "I don't know. I haven't really thought about it too much."
   c. "I'm trying to decide. I used to want to be a musician, and now I just don't know if that's practical."
   d. "I've really thought hard about that, and I've decided I want to work in schools and make them better places for children."

5. Research on identity construction indicates that __________ (p. 403)
   a. most adolescents experience a serious identity crisis, which is vital for psychological well-being.
   b. adolescents typically retain the same identity status across adolescence and early adulthood.
   c. adolescents who go to work after high school settle on an identity status later than college-bound youths.
   d. adolescents who go to work after high school settle on an identity status earlier than college-bound youths.

6. Identity-foreclosed teenagers usually __________ (p. 404)
   a. feel attached to their parents but also free to voice their own opinions.
   b. report low levels of parental support.
   c. have close bonds with their parents.
   d. have ample opportunities for healthy separation from their parents.

7. Thanh's family immigrated to the United States from Vietnam when she was 5. Now, at age 15, Thanh identifies with American culture and resists her parents' efforts to keep her from full assimilation. The conflict between Thanh and her parents is an example of __________ (p. 406)
   a. acculturative stress.
   b. bicultural identity.
   c. ethnic-identity diffusion.
   d. in-group discrimination.

8. When confronted with the Heinz dilemma, 14-year-old Andrew reasons, "Heinz should obey the law and not steal the medicine because if everybody just stole whenever they wanted, our whole society would break down." According to Kohlberg's theory of moral development, Andrew's answer reflects __________ (p. 408)
   a. a postconventional level of moral reasoning.
   b. a conventional level of moral reasoning.
   c. the instrumental purpose orientation.
   d. the universal ethical principle orientation.

9. When faced with moral dilemmas, adolescent girls and women __________ (p. 409)
   a. tend to emphasize justice, whereas males tend to emphasize care.
   b. emphasize care over justice in hypothetical situations, but not in real life.
   c. display reasoning at a lower stage than male agemates, regardless of culture.
   d. display reasoning at the same stage and often at a higher stage than male agemates.

10. Which of the following statements about cultural differences in moral development is true? (p. 411)
    a. Individuals in village societies move through Kohlberg's stages more quickly and advance to a higher level than individuals in industrialized nations.
    b. In both village cultures and industrialized nations that value interdependency, people commonly view the individual as highly connected to society.
    c. Individuals in collectivist societies value justice over caring, whereas individuals in Western societies value caring over justice.
    d. Research consistently shows that only Western individuals predictably progress through Kohlberg's first four stages.

11. When asked about the causes of social problems, such as unemployment or poverty, adolescents with a strong sense of civic responsibility __________ (p. 413)
    a. usually stress individual factors.
    b. usually stress situational and societal factors.
    c. are more interested in solving the problems than understanding their causes.
    d. refuse to speculate on the causes of individual hardship.

12. Which of the following statements about religious involvement in adolescence is true? (p. 412)
    a. Religious teenagers are no more advanced in moral values and behavior than their nonreligious peers.
    b. Religious involvement promotes responsible academic and social behavior and discourages misconduct.
    c. As adolescents search for a personally meaningful identity, formal religious involvement increases.
    d. In adolescence, many young people reject religion as a way to rebel against their parents.

13. Critics of the pragmatic approach to morality point out that __________ (p. 414)
    a. sometimes people use moral judgments for immoral purposes.
    b. people tend to act first, and then make a retrospective moral judgment.
    c. automatic moral judgments are extremely rare.
    d. people frequently rise above self-interest to defend others' rights.

14. During early adolescence, gender intensification __________ (p. 414)
    a. is stronger for boys.
    b. is stronger for girls.
    c. is equally strong for both boys and girls.
    d. declines sharply.

15. An improved ability to reason about social relationships leads teenagers to __________ (p. 415)
    a. bend to parental authority.
    b. resist opportunities for autonomy.
    c. deidealize their parents.
    d. deidealize their friends.

16. Throughout adolescence, the most consistent predictor of mental health is __________ (p. 416)
    a. the quality of the parent–child relationship.
    b. extracurricular or religious involvement.
    c. popularity and social status.
    d. high academic achievement.

17. Which of the following statements about parent–child relationships in adolescence is true? (p. 416)
    a. Less than 10 percent of families with adolescents have seriously troubled relationships.
    b. About half of families with adolescents have seriously troubled relationships.
    c. A sharp decline in family time during adolescence is universal.
    d. In Western societies, parents and young teenagers usually agree on the appropriate age of granting certain privileges like dating.

18. When asked about the meaning of friendship, teenagers stress three characteristics: __________ (p. 417)
    a. generosity, sincerity, and trust.
    b. helpfulness, proximity, and shared goals.
    c. fun, compatibility, and opportunity for growth or change.
    d. intimacy, mutual understanding, and loyalty.

19. Corumination __________ (p. 418)
    a. decreases intimacy among friends.
    b. triggers anxiety and depression.
    c. is a common feature of boys' friendships.
    d. is a common feature of adolescent dating relationships.

20. Clique membership __________ (p. 419)
    a. predicts academic and social competence among girls.
    b. predicts academic and social problems for both sexes.
    c. is equally important to boys and girls in early adolescence.
    d. becomes increasingly important throughout adolescence.

21. Between tenth and twelfth grade, __________ (p. 420)
    a. mixed-sex cliques begin to form.
    b. crowds increase in importance.
    c. deviant high school crowds lose members.
    d. cliques begin to form into crowds.

22. In early adolescence, dating __________ (p. 420)
    a. is done for recreational purposes, as well as to achieve status among agemates.
    b. is focused on psychological intimacy and shared interests.
    c. fosters social maturity, particularly for youths with authoritarian parents.
    d. protects teens against drug use, delinquency, and poor school performance.

23. Research suggests that __________ predicts secure romantic relationships in high school seniors. (p. 420)
    a. early dating experience
    b. peer status
    c. secure parental attachment
    d. sexual intimacy

24. Which of the following statements about peer conformity is true? (p. 421)
    a. In adolescence, peer pressure to engage in prosocial, proadult behavior is strong.
    b. Parents can control teenagers' day-to-day choices, but peers have more impact on their life values.
    c. In adolescence, peer pressure to engage in antisocial behavior is strong.
    d. Teenagers whose parents exert excessive control over them tend to resist negative peer pressure.

25. Teenage girls are __________ boys to report persistent depressed mood. (p. 422)
    a. much less likely than
    b. as likely as
    c. twice as likely as
    d. four times as likely as

26. Suicide rates __________ (p. 422)
    a. peak at adolescence, then stabilize.
    b. peak at adolescence, then decline.
    c. are higher for adolescent girls than boys.
    d. increase over the lifespan, jumping sharply at adolescence.

27. Teenagers who have committed a law-breaking offense __________ (p. 424)
    a. account for a small minority of the adolescent population.
    b. are more commonplace now than in any previous generation.
    c. often become recurrent offenders.
    d. overwhelmingly become law-abiding citizens.

28. Which of the following youths is most at risk for a life-course pattern or aggression and criminality? (p. 425)
    a. Victor, age 16, who has been arrested 4 times since the age of 12
    b. Ali, age 17, who tried alcohol and marijuana last year and suffers from depression
    c. Carlos, age 16, who is part of the "party crowd" and was recently arrested for shoplifting after a dare from his friends
    d. Mariah, age 15, who is socially awkward and easily influenced by peers

29. Which of the following statements about adolescent delinquency is true? (p. 424)
    a. Adolescent boys and girls are equally likely to commit violent crimes.
    b. Due to public awareness, SES and ethnicity are no longer strong predictors of adolescent arrests.
    c. By the late teenage years, boys' offenses are largely limited to simple assaults.
    d. Girls' offenses are largely limited to simple assaults.

30. Treatment for serious juvenile offenders is most effective when interventions are __________ (p. 426)
    a. carried out in a residential facility so that the adolescent is removed from his home and community during treatment.
    b. intense but brief so as not to interfere with school, extracurricular activities, and family life.
    c. lengthy and use problem-focused strategies to teach cognitive and social skills for addressing social and academic difficulties.
    d. focused on improving ineffective parenting practices instead of directly addressing the adolescent's aggressive behavior.

PRACTICE TEST #2

1. According to Erikson, the development of identity in adolescence is __________ (p. 402)
   a. similar across cultures.
   b. rarely experienced as a "crisis."
   c. experienced as a "crisis" in complex societies.
   d. resolved positively in societies that limit personal choices.

2. Compared with younger children, adolescents __________ when describing themselves. (p. 402)
   a. are more critical and negative
   b. more often mention contradictory traits
   c. are less likely to use qualifiers, such as fairly or kind of
   d. place less emphasis on social virtues

3. When asked whether he ever had doubts about his religious beliefs, Cody said, "No. I have gone to the same church my whole life, and I know what the truth is and what my values are." Cody is __________ (pp. 403, 404)
   a. identity-achieved.
   b. in moratorium.
   c. identity-foreclosed.
   d. identity-diffused.

4. Young people who are identity-achieved or in moratorium tend to __________ (p. 404)
   a. be advanced in moral reasoning.
   b. display a dogmatic cognitive style.
   c. bend easily to peer pressure.
   d. be immature in identity development.

5. Identity development is __________ (p. 404)
   a. a relatively short process in most cultures.
   b. primarily influenced by schools and communities.
   c. primarily influenced by family values.
   d. influenced by a wide variety of factors.

6. Which group of adolescents is most likely to achieve a strong, secure ethnic identity? (p. 406)
   a. biracial adolescents who interact with peers of different ethnicities
   b. majority adolescents who interact frequently with same-ethnicity peers
   c. monoracial minority adolescents who interact frequently with same-ethnicity peers
   d. monoracial minority adolescents who interact mainly with majority peers

7. If Danica's moral reasoning stems from self-interest, which stage of Kohlberg's theory would best characterize her level of moral understanding? (p. 408)
   a. Stage 2: The instrumental purpose orientation
   b. Stage 3: The "good boy-good girl" orientation
   c. Stage 4: The social-order-maintaining orientation
   d. Stage 6: The universal ethical principle orientation

8. Follow-up research on Kohlberg's stages of moral understanding reveals that __________ (p. 409)
   a. boys and men tend to reason at a lower stage than girls and women.
   b. contrary to Kohlberg's belief, most adults reach Stage 6 of moral reasoning.
   c. Kohlberg's moral stages are loosely organized and overlapping.
   d. Kohlberg's moral stages are rarely affected by situational factors.

9. Teenagers who __________ show little or no change in moral reasoning over time. (p. 411)
   a. have warm, demanding, and communicative parents
   b. have parents who lecture or threaten
   c. often seek advice from friends instead of family
   d. interact with peers who have differing viewpoints

10. The connection between moral reasoning and moral action is __________ (p. 412)
    a. weak.
    b. modest.
    c. strong.
    d. mostly affected by gender and SES.

11. Which of the following statements about youth involvement in community service is true? (p. 413)
    a. Compared with youths in other developed nations, U.S. youths are less likely to engage in community service.
    b. When adolescents are required to serve their communities, they are unlikely to continue their involvement once they have met their requirements.
    c. Low-SES, inner-city youths are far less likely than higher-SES youth to express interest in community service participation.
    d. Low-SES, inner-city youths express interest in community service but score substantially lower than higher-SES youths in civic knowledge and participation.

12. Androgynous adolescents, particularly girls, tend to be __________ (p. 415)
    a. identity-foreclosed.
    b. psychologically healthy.
    c. self-loathing.
    d. rejected by their peers.

13. Research suggests that in adolescence, urban low- and middle-SES African-American youths __________ (p. 416)
    a. show no decline in hours spent with family.
    b. show an especially sharp decline in hours spent with family.
    c. adjust more favorably when parents maintain loose control over them.
    d. have less trusting relationships with their parents than white youths do.

14. In adolescence, sibling relationships __________ (p. 417)
    a. become more intense in positive feelings.
    b. become less intense in both positive and negative feelings.
    c. are often defined by jealousy.
    d. tend to dissolve.

15. Self-disclosure to __________ (p. 418)
    a. friends declines steadily in adolescence.
    b. romantic partners rises in adolescence.
    c. parents rises in early adolescence, then declines.
    d. parents remains stable throughout adolescence.

16. Which of the following is true of gender differences in adolescent friendships? (p. 417)
    a. Boys' closest same-sex friendships tend to be more intense but of shorter duration than girls'.
    b. Girls' friendships tend to focus on achievement and status, and boys' friendships tend to focus on communal concerns.
    c. Boys' friendships tend to focus on achievement and status, and girls' friendships tend to focus on communal concerns.
    d. Highly masculine boys are more likely than highly feminine girls to form intimate same-sex ties.

17. Which of the following teenagers' Internet use poses the most danger? (p. 418)
    a. Morgan constantly instant messages her friends, sometimes ignoring her family.
    b. Kaley, who suffers from bulimia, frequents a message board about eating disorders.
    c. Scott has conflict with his family and spends a lot of time on the Internet.
    d. Omar has encountered racial slurs in an unmonitored chat room he occasionally visits.

18. In early adolescence, cliques __________ (p. 419)
    a. are used by boys to establish a dominance hierarchy.
    b. primarily serve as a context for relational aggression.
    c. are used by girls to express emotional closeness.
    d. often lead to delinquency.

19. "Jocks," "brains," and "partyers" are examples of __________ (p. 419)
    a. typical high school crowds.
    b. traditional cliques.
    c. mixed-sex cliques.
    d. negative peer networks

20. Which of the following statements about adolescent peer groups is true? (p. 419)
    a. Many peer-group values are extensions of ones acquired at home.
    b. Clique membership is based on reputation and stereotype.
    c. Clique and crowd membership usually has negative implications for teenagers' futures.
    d. Mixed-sex clique membership pressures teenagers into premature romantic intimacy.

21. __________ determine when and how adolescent dating begins. (p. 420)
    a. Media influences
    b. Hormonal changes
    c. Peer group values
    d. Cultural expectations

22. The first dating relationships of homosexual youths tend to be short-lived and involve little emotional commitment. This is largely because they __________ (p. 420)
    a. are often less mature than their heterosexual peers.
    b. fear peer harassment and rejection.
    c. are still questioning their sexual identity.
    d. are looking for relationships that are fun and recreational.

23. Research on peer conformity indicates that __________ (p. 421)
    a. adolescents are less likely to conform to peer pressure than school-age children and young adults.
    b. peers exert more influence on teenagers' basic life values and educational plans than parents do.
    c. adolescents feel the greatest pressure to conform to obvious aspects of the peer culture, such as style of dress.
    d. adolescents with authoritative parents are more likely than their peers to turn to friends for advice on important decisions.

24. Teenagers who follow parental rules and resist peer pressure tend to have parents who __________ (p. 421)
    a. put strict limits on their free time.
    b. exert oversight within a supportive environment.
    c. permit independent decision making in most areas of adolescent life.
    d. use authoritarian child rearing.

25. What is the most common psychological problem of adolescence? (p. 421)
    a. gender confusion
    b. delinquency
    c. anxiety
    d. depression

26. Teenage girls who __________ are especially prone to depression. (p. 422)
    a. live in developing nations
    b. are androgynous
    c. identify with "feminine" traits
    d. are late-maturing

27. Which of the following is true of suicide among teenagers? (p. 422)
    a. Boys are three to four times more likely to kill themselves than girls.
    b. African Americans have higher suicide rates than Caucasian Americans.
    c. Rates of teenage suicide are similar among all industrialized nations.
    d. Boys make more unsuccessful suicide attempts than girls.

28. Which of the following is a major reason for the decline in delinquency after middle adolescence? (p. 424)
    a. The desire for peer approval becomes stronger in late adolescence.
    b. Moral reasoning improves in late adolescence.
    c. Teenage lawbreakers are usually incarcerated by late adolescence.
    d. Older adolescents rarely draw attention to their crimes.

29. Among boys who follow a life-course path of delinquency and criminality, __________ tends to transform their biologically based difficulties into defiance and persistent aggression. (p. 425)
    a. low self-esteem
    b. peer pressure
    c. inept parenting
    d. academic failure

30. Which of the following is a consistent finding in research on juvenile delinquency? (p. 424)
    a. Low-SES and minority youths are much more likely to commit violent crimes than higher-SES white and Asian youths.
    b. Violent crime is equally common among adolescent boys and girls, though boys' violent crimes are of a more serious nature.
    c. Families of delinquent youths tend to be have harsh, inconsistent discipline tactics and low monitoring.
    d. Delinquent youths are usually identity-foreclosed and have controlling, authoritarian parents.

CHAPTER 13
PHYSICAL AND COGNITIVE DEVELOPMENT IN EARLY ADULTHOOD

BRIEF CHAPTER SUMMARY

Once body structures reach maximum capacity and efficiency, biological aging begins. The combined result of many causes, it can be modified through behavioral and environmental interventions. In early adulthood, gradual changes occur in physical appearance and body functioning, including declines in athletic skills, in the immune system's protective function, and in reproductive capacity.

Economically advantaged, well-educated individuals tend to sustain good health over most of their adult lives, whereas the health of lower-income individuals with limited education declines. SES differences in health-related living conditions and habits are largely responsible. Overweight and obesity, strongly associated with serious health problems, have increased dramatically in many Western nations. Young adults are more likely than younger or older people to smoke cigarettes, use marijuana, take stimulants, or engage in binge drinking.

Monogamous, emotionally committed relationships are more typical than casual sex among young adults, and attitudes toward homosexuality have become more accepting as a result of greater exposure and interpersonal contact. Many Americans will contract a sexually transmitted disease (STD) at some point in their lives; the deadliest STD, AIDS, is the sixth-leading cause of death among U.S. young adults. A significant percentage of American women have endured rape; many more have experienced other forms of sexual aggression, sometimes with lasting psychological effects. Women's menstrual cycle presents unique health concerns, including premenstrual syndrome, an array of symptoms preceding the monthly period. The unique challenges of early adulthood make it a particularly stressful time of life. Social support can provide a buffer against psychological stress, which is related to unfavorable health outcomes, including both unhealthy behaviors and direct physical consequences.

The cognitive-developmental changes of childhood and adolescence extend into adulthood, as seen in the development of epistemic cognition (reflection on one's own thinking process); a movement from dualistic, right-or-wrong thinking toward relativistic thinking; and a shift from hypothetical to pragmatic thought, with greater use of logic to solve real-world problems. These cognitive changes of early adulthood are supported by further development of the cerebral cortex, especially the frontal lobes.

Expertise develops in adulthood as individuals master specific complex domains. College serves as a formative environment in which students can devote their attention to exploring alternative values, roles, and behaviors. Personality, family influences, teachers, and gender stereotypes all influence vocational choice as young adults explore possibilities and eventually settle on an occupation. Non-college-bound young people have a particular need for apprenticeships and other forms of preparation for productive, meaningful lives.

LEARNING OBJECTIVES

After reading this chapter, you should be able to:

13.1 Describe current theories of biological aging, including those at the level of DNA and body cells, and those at the level of organs and tissues. (pp. 432–434)

13.2 Describe the physical changes of aging, paying special attention to the cardiovascular and respiratory systems, motor performance, the immune system, and reproductive capacity. (pp. 434–438)

13.3 Describe the impact of SES, nutrition, obesity, and exercise on health in adulthood. (pp. 438–444)

13.4 Describe trends in substance abuse in early adulthood, and discuss the health risks of each. (pp. 444–445)

13.5 Summarize sexual attitudes and behaviors in young adults, including sexual orientation, sexually transmitted diseases, sexual coercion, and premenstrual syndrome. (pp. 445–449)

13.6 Explain how psychological stress affects health. (pp. 449–451)

13.7 Summarize prominent theories on the restructuring of thought in adulthood, including those of Perry and Labouvie-Vief. (pp. 451–453)

13.8 Discuss the development of expertise and creativity in adulthood. (pp. 453–454)

13.9 Describe the impact of a college education on young people's lives, and discuss the problem of dropping out. (pp. 454–455)

13.10 Trace the development of vocational choice, and note factors that influence it. (pp. 455–458)

13.11 Discuss vocational preparation of non-college-bound young adults, including the challenges these individuals face. (pp. 458–459)

STUDY QUESTIONS

1. List several common tasks of early adulthood. (pp. 431–432)

____

____

____

Physical Development

1. Describe *biological aging*, or *senescence*. (p. 432)

____

____

2. List four contextual factors that influence biological aging. (p. 432)

   A. ______________________________

   B. ______________________________

   C. ______________________________

   D. ______________________________

3. True or False: Biological aging is fixed and immutable. (p. 432)

Biological Aging Is Under Way in Early Adulthood

1. The ______________ *theory of aging* states that the body wears out from use. Cite a major weakness of this theory. (p. 432)

____

____

Aging at the Level of DNA and Body Cells

1. List two current explanations of biological aging at the level of DNA and body cells. (p. 432)

   A. ______________________________

   B. ______________________________

2. The heritability of longevity is (weak / modest / strong). (p. 432)

3. Explain how *telomere* shortening contributes to aging. (p. 433)

____

____

____

____

4. Briefly summarize the "random events" theory of biological aging. (p. 433)

____

____

____

5. One probable cause of age-related DNA and cellular abnormalities is the release of ____________ —naturally occurring, highly reactive chemicals that form in the presence of oxygen. (p. 434)

Biology and Environment: Telomere Length: A New Marker of the Impact of Life Circumstances on Biological Aging

1. True or False: Telomeres shorten at a uniform rate across individuals. Explain your answer. (p. 433)

____

____

2. Explain the relationship between telomere length and illness. (p. 433)

____

____

____

3. Describe the effects of unfavorable health conditions and psychological stress on telomeres. (p. 433)

Unfavorable health conditions: ____________________________

____

Psychological stress: ____________________________

____

4. True or False: When adults make healthy lifestyle changes, telomeres respond positively. (p. 433)

Aging at the Level of Tissues and Organs

1. According to the ____________ *theory of aging,* protein fibers that make up the body's connective tissue form bonds with one another over time. When these normally separate fibers link, tissue becomes (less / more) elastic, leading to many negative outcomes. (p. 434)

2. Cite two examples of how gradual failure of the endocrine system leads to aging. (p. 434)

A. ____________________________

____

B. ____________________________

____

3. True or False: Declines in immune system functioning contribute to many conditions of aging. (p. 434)

Physical Changes

Cardiovascular and Respiratory Systems

1. The rate of death from heart disease among (African Americans / Caucasian Americans) is much higher than among (African Americans / Caucasian Americans). (pp. 434–435)

2. True or False: In healthy individuals, the heart's ability to meet the body's oxygen needs under typical conditions does not change during adulthood. (pp. 435–436)

3. ____________________ is a serious cardiovascular disease in which heavy deposits of plaque containing cholesterol and fats collect on the walls of the main arteries. How does this disease develop and progress? (p. 436)

____

____

4. Cite three reasons why rates of heart disease have declined considerably since the mid-twentieth century. (p. 436)

   A. ____________________

   B. ____________________

   C. ____________________

5. Cite two ways in which lung functioning changes with age. (p. 436)

   A. ____________________

   ____

   B. ____________________

   ____

Motor Performance

1. Many athletic skills peak between the ages of ______ and ______ and then gradually decline. (p. 436)

2. Indicate which of the following athletic skills typically peak in the early twenties (E) and which typically peak in the late twenties and early thirties (L). (p. 436)

___ Speed of movement	___ Endurance	___ Aiming
___ Sprinting	___ Golf	___ Gross-motor coordination
___ Jumping	___ Tennis	___ Arm-hand steadiness
___ Long-distance running	___ Baseball	

3. What does research on outstanding athletes reveal about the upper biological limit of motor capacity? (p. 436)

____

____

4. True or False: Age-related declines in athletic skill are almost entirely attributable to biological aging. (p. 437)

Immune System

1. (B cells / T cells) attack antigens directly, while (B cells / T cells) secrete antibodies that capture antigens and permit the blood system to destroy them. (p. 437)

2. Shrinkage of the ____________ results in decreased production of certain hormones and reduced immune system capacities. (p. 437)

3. True or False: Stress can weaken the immune response. Explain your answer. (p. 437)

____

____

____

Reproductive Capacity

1. Explain why many women experience a decline in fertility across early and middle adulthood. (pp. 437–438)

____

____

____

2. True or False: Male reproductive capacity is unaffected by age. (p. 438)

Health and Fitness

1. U.S. death rates for all causes in early adulthood are (lower / higher) than for other industrialized nations. Cite several factors that contribute to this difference. (pp. 438–439)

____

____

2. Briefly summarize SES variations in health during adulthood, noting factors responsible for these differences. (p. 438)

   Variations: ____

   ____

   Factors responsible: ____

   ____

3. Cite three reasons why SES disparities in health and mortality are larger in the United States than in other industrialized nations. (p. 438)

   A. ____

   B. ____

   C. ____

Nutrition

1. ______ percent of American adults are obese. More (men / women) suffer from obesity. (p. 439)
2. True or False: Most Americans are overweight or obese. (pp. 439–440)
3. Weight gain in adulthood most often occurs between ages ___ and ___. (p. 440)
4. What factors contribute to the rising rates of obesity in the United States and other industrialized countries? (p. 440)

____

____

____

5. *Basal metabolic rate (BMR)* refers to the amount of energy the body uses (at complete rest / during vigorous exercise). How does it affect body weight in adulthood? (p. 440)

____

____

____

6. List several health problems associated with being overweight or obese. (p. 440)

____

____

7. Describe five elements of effective treatment for obesity. (pp. 440–441)

   A. ____

   B. ____

   C. ____

   D. ____

   E. ____

8. Summarize the detrimental effects of excess dietary fat consumption, noting specific consequences of saturated fat. (p. 441)

____

____

____

9. True or False: Excess fat consumption is a major contributor to the high rate of heart disease in the U.S. black population. (p. 441)

A Lifespan Vista: The Obesity Epidemic: How Americans Became the Heaviest People in the World

1. Summarize five societal factors that have encouraged widespread, rapid weight gain. (pp. 442–443)

   A. ____

   B. ____

   C. ____

   D. ____

   E. ____

2. List five societal efforts that may help to combat obesity. (p. 443)

   A. ____

   B. ____

   C. ____

   D. ____

   E. ____

Exercise

1. True or False: Most Americans engage in at least moderate leisure-time physical activity for 20 minutes or more at least five times a week. (pp. 441, 443)
2. Cite several health benefits of exercise. (pp. 441, 443)

   ____

   ____

3. List five ways that exercise helps prevent serious illnesses. (pp. 443–444)

   A. ____

   B. ____

   C. ____

   D. ____

   E. ____

4. How much exercise is recommended for a healthier and longer life? (p. 444)

   ____

   ____

Substance Abuse

1. True or False: Drug taking peaks among 19- to 22-year-olds and then declines throughout the twenties. (p. 444)
2. What are the two most commonly abused substances in early adulthood? (p. 444)

   A. ____

   B. ____

3. Smoking rates have declined (slowly / rapidly) over the past 40 years. (p. 444)
4. Discuss the health consequences of smoking. (p. 444)

   ____

   ____

   ____

5. True or False: One out of every three young people who become regular smokers will die from a smoking-related disease. (p. 444)
6. Summarize the benefits of quitting smoking. (p. 444)

   ____

   ____

7. True or False: Those who enter treatment programs or use cessation aids to quit smoking often fail. Explain your answer. (p. 444)

   ____

   ____

8. Describe gender differences in the development of alcoholism. (p. 445)

   Men: ____

   Women: ____

9. True or False: Twin studies support a genetic contribution to alcoholism. (p. 445)
10. List personal and cultural factors associated with alcoholism. (p. 445)

Personal: ______________________________

____

Cultural: ______________________________

____

11. List several health problems associated with chronic alcohol use. (p. 445)

____

____

12. Describe components of successful treatment programs for alcoholism. (p. 445)

____

____

Sexuality

1. Indicate whether the following statements about sexuality and dating are true or false. (pp. 445–446)
(T / F) Compared with earlier generations, contemporary adults display a wider range of sexual choices and lifestyles.
(T / F) Sexual partners tend to be alike in age, education, ethnicity, and religion.
(T / F) Internet dating services have higher success rates than conventional dating practices.
(T / F) Americans today have more sexual partners than they did a generation ago.
2. Contemporary men and women differ (little / greatly) in average number of lifetime sexual partners. Why is this? (p. 446)

____

____

3. What explains the current trend toward more relationships in the context of sexual commitment? (p. 446)

____

____

____

4. List three factors that affect frequency of sexual activity. (p. 446)

A. ______________________________

B. ______________________________

C. ______________________________

5. True or False: As the number of sexual partners increases, satisfaction with one's sex life also increases. (p. 446)
6. List the two sexual difficulties most frequently reported by men and by women. (pp. 446–447)

Men: ______________________________

Women: ______________________________

7. True or False: The majority of Americans support civil liberties and equal employment opportunities for gay men, lesbians, and bisexuals. (p. 447)
8. Heterosexual (men / women) judge homosexuals more harshly. (p. 447)

9. Explain how homosexual sex follows many of the same rules as heterosexual sex. (p. 447)

____

____

10. Describe the living arrangements and education level typical of homosexuals. (p. 447)

A. ____

B. ____

11. Why is the incidence of sexually transmitted diseases (STDs) especially high in adolescence and early adulthood? (p. 447)

____

____

12. The overall rate of STDs is higher among (men / women). Explain your answer. (p. 447)

____

____

13. True or False: The incidence of HIV is higher in the United States than in any other industrialized nation. (p. 447)

14. In what U.S. population is AIDS spreading most rapidly? (p. 447)

____

____

15. Cite three ways that AIDS can be contained or reduced. (p. 447)

A. ____

B. ____

C. ____

16. An estimated _____to ____ percent of North American women have endured rape. (p. 448)

17. Women are most often raped by (strangers / acquaintances / men they know well). (p. 448)

18. Describe common personal characteristics of men who commit sexual assault. (p. 448)

____

____

____

19. Describe three cultural forces that contribute to sexual coercion. (p. 448)

A. ____

____

B. ____

____

C. ____

____

20. True or False: Authorities rarely recognize female-initiated forced sex as illegal. (p. 448)

21. Summarize the immediate and long-term consequences of rape. (p. 448)

    Immediate: ______________________________

    ____

    Long-term: ______________________________

    ____

22. Cite three critical features in the treatment of rape victims that help foster recovery. (p. 448)

    A. ______________________________

    B. ______________________________

    C. ______________________________

23. List five ways to prevent sexual coercion. (p. 449)

    A. ______________________________

    B. ______________________________

    C. ______________________________

    D. ______________________________

    E. ______________________________

24. List common symptoms of *premenstrual syndrome (PMS)*. (p. 449)

    ____

    ____

    ____

25. About ______ percent of women worldwide experience some form of PMS, but only ______ percent of women experience symptoms severe enough to interfere with academic, occupational, or social functioning. (p. 449)

26. List common treatments for PMS. (p. 449)

    ____

    ____

Psychological Stress

1. Describe several physical consequences of chronic psychological stress. (p. 450)

   ____

   ____

   ____

2. Explain why young adults more often report depressive feelings than middle-aged people. (p. 450)

   ____

   ____

Cognitive Development

1. Cite several factors that promote cognitive development in early adulthood. (p. 451)

____

____

____

Changes in the Structure of Thought

1. Cognitive development beyond Piaget's formal operational stage is known as ______________. (p. 451)

Perry's Theory: Epistemic Cognition

1. ______________ refers to our reflections on how we arrived at facts, beliefs, and ideas. (p. 451)
2. (Older / Younger) college students engage in ______________ thinking, dividing information, values, and authority into right and wrong or good and bad. Meanwhile, (older / younger) students engage in ______________ thinking, viewing all knowledge as embedded in a framework of thought. Cite additional characteristics of younger and older college students' thinking. (pp. 451–452)

   Younger students: ____

   ____

   Older students: ____

   ____

3. Define *commitment within relativistic thinking,* and provide an example. (p. 452)

   Definition: ____

   ____

   Example: ____

4. True or False: Almost all college students reach commitment within relativistic thinking. (p. 452)
5. How does peer interaction facilitate advanced reasoning in early adulthood? (p. 452)

   ____

   ____

Labouvie-Vief's Theory: Pragmatic Thought and Cognitive-Affective Complexity

1. According to Labouvie-Vief, adulthood marks a shift from hypothetical to ______________ *thought*—a structural advance in which logic becomes a tool for solving real-world problems. What motivates this change? (p. 452)

   ____

   ____

2. From adolescence through middle adulthood, people (decline / gain) in ______________________, or awareness of positive and negative feelings and coordination of them into a complex, organized structure. Describe the benefits of this capacity. (p. 453)

Expertise and Creativity

1. How does *expertise* develop in early adulthood? (p. 453)

2. How does experts' reasoning differ from that of novices? (p. 453)

3. The creative products of (childhood / adulthood) are not just original but also directed at a social or aesthetic need. (p. 453)

4. Describe general trends in the development of creativity across adulthood. (pp. 453–454)

5. In addition to expertise, what other personal qualities foster the development of creativity? (pp. 453–454)

The College Experience

Psychological Impact of Attending College

1. Describe psychological changes that take place during the college years. (pp. 454–455)

2. Cite two factors that jointly contribute to the impact of college. (p. 455)

   A. ______________________

   B. ______________________

Dropping Out

1. True or False: Most U.S. students who drop out of college do so within the first year. (p. 455)

2. Summarize personal and institutional characteristics that contribute to young people's decision to drop out of college. (p. 455)

   Personal: ______________________________

   ____

   Institutional: ______________________________

   ____

3. Describe ways to prepare young people for college success. (p. 455)

   ____

   ____

4. Discuss ways college communities can support the young person's transition to the college environment. (p. 455)

   ____

   ____

   ____

Vocational Choice

Selecting a Vocation

1. Match each characteristic with the correct period of vocational development. (p. 456)

   _______ Occurs between ages 11 and 16
   _______ Occurs during the late teens and early twenties
   _______ Occurs in early and middle childhood
   _______ Preferences are guided by familiarity, glamour, and excitement
   _______ Involves exploration and crystallization
   _______ Careers are considered in terms of interests, abilities, and values

   A. *Fantasy period*
   B. *Tentative period*
   C. *Realistic period*

Factors Influencing Vocational Choice

1. Match each of the following personality types that affect vocational choice with the appropriate description. (p. 456)

   _______ Likes well-structured tasks and values social status; tends to choose business occupations
   _______ Prefers real-world problems and work with objects; tends to choose mechanical occupations
   _______ Is adventurous, persuasive, and a strong leader; drawn toward sales and supervisory positions or politics
   _______ Enjoys working with ideas; drawn toward scientific occupations
   _______ Has a high need for emotional and individual expression; drawn to artistic fields
   _______ Likes interacting with people; drawn toward human services

   A. Investigative
   B. Social
   C. Realistic
   D. Artistic
   E. Conventional
   F. Enterprising

2. Research confirms a (weak / moderate / strong) relationship between Holland's personality types and vocational choice in diverse cultures. (p. 456)

3. Identify several reasons why young people's vocational aspirations correlate strongly with the jobs of their parents. (p. 456)

4. True or False: Over the past three decades, young women's career preferences have remained strongly gender stereotyped. Explain your answer. (p. 457)

5. Women's progress in entering and excelling at male-dominated professions has been (slow / rapid). (p. 457)

6. True or False: Sex differences in vocational achievement can be directly attributed to differences in ability. Explain your response. (p. 457)

7. True or False: The educational and career aspirations of academically talented females often decline during the college years. (p. 457)

8. List four experiences common to young women who show high achievement during college. (p. 458)

A. ______

B. ______

C. ______

D. ______

Social Issues: Masculinity at Work: Men Who Choose Nontraditional Careers

1. How do men who choose traditionally feminine occupations tend to differ from those who choose traditionally masculine jobs? (p. 458)

2. Indicate whether the following statements are true or false. (pp. 458–459)

Men in traditionally feminine careers …
(T / F) are often assumed to be more knowledgeable than they actually are.
(T / F) have opportunities to move quickly into supervisory positions.
(T / F) often report that they do not feel socially accepted.
(T/ F) express anxiety about being stigmatized for their career choice by other men.

Vocational Preparation of Non-College-Bound Young Adults

1. Non-college-bound high school graduates have (fewer / more) work opportunities than high school graduates of several decades ago. (p. 458)

2. Describe the types of jobs that high school graduates typically hold. (p. 458)

3. Describe Germany's work–study apprenticeship system. (p. 459)

4. Summarize the challenges of implementing an apprenticeship program for non-college-bound young adults. (p. 459)

ASK YOURSELF . . .

For *Ask Yourself* questions for this chapter, along with feedback on the accuracy of your answers, please log on to MyDevelopmentLab (for registration and access, please visit mydevelopmentlab.com or follow the instructions on page ix).

(1) Select the Multimedia Library.

(2) Choose the explore option.

(3) Find your chapter from the drop down box.

(4) Click find now.

(5) Complete questions and choose "Submit answers for grading" or "Clear answers" to start over.

SUGGESTED READINGS

Crawford, D., & Jeffrey, R. W. (Eds.). (2006). *Obesity prevention and public health*. New York: Oxford. A comprehensive overview of the obesity epidemic in both children and adults, this book addresses factors that contribute to obesity, individual and social consequences of obesity, increasing rates of obesity in developing nations, and prevention strategies.

Massey, D. S., Lundy, G., Charles, C. Z., & Fischer, M. J. (2006). *The source of the river: The social origins of freshmen at America's selective colleges and universities*. New Jersey: Princeton University Press. Using findings from the National Longitudinal Survey of Freshmen, this book examines racial and ethnic differences in academic success, how experiences within the family, peer group, and community contribute to college performance, and how racial stereotypes of intellectual inferiority influence the life chances of many ethnic minority college students.

Settersten, R., Furstenberg, F. F., & Rumbart, R. G. (Eds.). (2008). *On the frontier of adulthood*. Chicago, IL: University of Chicago Press. Presents leading research on early adult development, including factors related to substance use, the college experience, selecting a vocation, and public policies aimed at helping young people with the transition to adulthood.

CROSSWORD PUZZLE 13.1

Across

3. ______ thinking: dividing information, values, and authority into right and wrong, good and bad, we and they
7. ______ within relativistic thinking: synthesizing contradictions instead of choosing between opposing views
8. ______ thinking: viewing all knowledge as embedded in a framework of thought; favoring multiple truths relative to their context
9. ______ cognition refers to our reflections on how we arrived at facts, beliefs, and ideas.
11. Cognitive development beyond Piaget's formal operations is referred to as ______ thought.
12. ______ aging: species-wide genetically influenced declines in the functioning of organs and systems
14. ______ -______ theory of aging: the formation of bonds between protein fibers decreases elasticity of connective tissue (2 words, hyph.)
16. During the ______ period, children's career preferences are guided largely by familiarity, glamour, and excitement.
17. Acquisition of extensive knowledge in a field or endeavor

Down

1. Free ______: naturally occurring, highly reactive chemicals that form in the presence of oxygen
2. ______ thought: logic becomes a tool for solving real-world problems
4. ______ -______ complexity: coordination of positive and negative feelings into a complex, organized structure (2 words, hyph.)
5. Physical and psychological symptoms that usually appear 6 to 10 days prior to menstruation (abbr.)
6. The amount of energy the body uses at complete rest (abbr.)
10. With each duplication, a special type of DNA called ______ shortens, eventually leading the cells to no longer duplicate at all.
13. During the ______ period, adolescents weigh vocational options against their interests, abilities, and values.
15. During the ______ period, individuals focus on a general career category and eventually settle on one occupation.

PRACTICE TEST #1

1. Which of the following statements provides evidence against the "wear-and-tear" theory? (p. 432)
   a. Moderate-to-vigorous exercise predicts health problems in later life.
   b. No relationship exists between physical activity and early death.
   c. People reach their peak athletic performance in early adulthood.
   d. Individual differences in biological aging are great.

2. The heritability of longevity is __________ (p. 432)
   a. nil.
   b. modest.
   c. strong.
   d. unknown.

3. Research examining the influence of life circumstances on telomere length indicates that __________ (p. 433)
   a. cigarette smoking and physical inactivity prevent telomeres from shortening.
   b. chronic illnesses hasten telomere shortening, which, in turn, hastens disease progression.
   c. stress accelerates the production of telomarese, which, in turn, accelerates telomere shortening.
   d. normal-birth-weight preschoolers have shorter telomeres than low-birth-weight preschoolers.

4. According to the ______________ theory of aging, organs are negatively affected when protein fibers form links and become less elastic. (p. 434)
   a. cross-linkage
   b. "genetic programming"
   c. "random events"
   d. "wear-and-tear"

5. A probable cause of age-related DNA and cellular abnormalities is the release of __________ (p. 434)
   a. growth hormone.
   b. telomerase.
   c. free radicals.
   d. senescent cells.

6. Heart disease __________ (p. 435)
   a. has nearly doubled since 1950 in the United States.
   b. is significantly lower in blacks than in whites.
   c. is a leading cause of death throughout adulthood.
   d. is higher in females than males throughout early adulthood.

7. Most of the age-related decline in athletic performance can be attributed to __________ (p. 436)
   a. decreased heart and lung functioning.
   b. loss of body coordination.
   c. gradual muscle loss.
   d. lower activity levels.

8. What does research indicate about the relationship between health and SES? (p. 438)
   a. SES factors, such as income and education level, predict most diseases.
   b. After early adulthood, there is only a weak relationship between health and SES.
   c. The influence of childhood health on adult health is very strong, even if SES improves.
   d. SES differences widen over the lifespan, peaking in old age.

9. Fat consumption __________ (p. 441)
   a. in the U.S. has declined in the past decade.
   b. is linked to breast cancer and colon cancer.
   c. is highest in early adulthood.
   d. rarely predicts cancer in early or middle adulthood.

10. Between the 1970s and the 1990s, Americans increased __________ (p. 442)
    a. their involvement in regular exercise.
    b. their daily calorie intake.
    c. their consumption of organic foods.
    d. the number of meals eaten at home.

11. In the United States, drug taking __________ (p. 444)
    a. peaks between ages 25 to 30, then declines over the decade of the thirties.
    b. peaks between ages 19 to 22, then declines over the decade of the twenties.
    c. leads to permanent cognitive impairment in the majority of users.
    d. is rare in early adulthood, with only 1 percent of 20-year-olds reporting drug use.

12. Which of the following statements about U.S. smoking trends is true? (p. 444)
    a. Prevalence of smoking increased from 24 percent of people in 1965 to 40 percent in 2007.
    b. In recent decades, there has been virtually no change in smoking rates among college graduates.
    c. More women than men smoke, though the gender gap is narrower today than it was in the past.
    d. More men than women smoke, though the gender gap is narrower today than it was in the past.

13. Alcohol abuse and dependency occur more often in __________ (p. 445)
    a. cultures where access to alcohol is loosely controlled.
    b. cultures where alcohol is a traditional part of religious ceremony.
    c. cultures where alcohol is viewed as a sign of adulthood.
    d. young people who cohabitate before marriage.

14. What is likely the main reason for the decline in sexual activity around age 30? (p. 446)
    a. decreased hormone levels
    b. demands of daily life
    c. more people in committed relationships
    d. performance anxiety

15. Most adults in committed relationships __________ (p. 446)
    a. are less sexually fulfilled than single adults.
    b. lose interest in sex shortly after cohabitation.
    c. have sexual intercourse twice a week or more.
    d. report feeling physically and emotionally satisfied.

16. The majority of Americans __________ (p. 447)
    a. are accepting of sexual relations between adults of the same sex.
    b. do not support civil liberties for homosexuals and bisexuals.
    c. are highly critical of sexual relations between adults of the same sex.
    d. judge homosexual women more harshly than homosexual men.

17. __________ Americans is/are likely to contract a sexually transmitted disease (STD) during their lifetime. (p. 447)
    a. One out of every ten
    b. One-quarter of
    c. One-half of
    d. Three-quarters of

18. AIDS is spreading most rapidly through __________ (p. 447)
    a. homosexual contact in large urban areas.
    b. homosexual contact on college campuses.
    c. heterosexual contact in the suburban white population.
    d. heterosexual contact in impoverished minority groups.

19. Men who engage in sexual assault __________ (p. 448)
    a. are less likely to endorse traditional gender roles.
    b. have difficulty accurately interpreting women's social behavior.
    c. usually acknowledge their own responsibility.
    d. are most likely to be from low-SES, ethnic minority groups.

20. Postformal thought __________ (p. 451)
    a. is necessary for creativity.
    b. often prevents young people from accepting another's reasoning.
    c. is generally well-developed by adolescence.
    d. reflects a flexible way of thinking that varies across situations.

21. Which of the following statements reflects relativistic thinking? (p. 452)
    a. "In order to evaluate these theories, we must come up with criteria."
    b. "It must be true because it's written in this book."
    c. "Her belief system is different from mine, but is equally valid."
    d. "Candidate Foley is right on all issues, and Candidate Alvarez is wrong."

22. Which of the following activities is likely to advance students' epistemic cognition? (p. 452)
    a. active note taking during a series of lectures
    b. reflection on the learning process through journal writing
    c. collaborating with others on a realistic, ambiguous problem
    d. independently solving a challenging logic problem

23. Individuals high in cognitive-affective complexity view events and people __________ (p. 453)
    a. in a tolerant, open-minded fashion.
    b. through a "rose-colored lens."
    c. in a negative, defensive way.
    d. as incapable of change.

24. Compared with novices, experts __________ (p. 453)
    a. are more likely to solve problems than to find them.
    b. tend to be less creative and original.
    c. more often use trial and error to arrive at solutions.
    d. remember and reason more quickly and effectively.

25. When looking back at their lives, many people view the college years as __________ (p. 454)
    a. stress-free.
    b. formative.
    c. restrictive.
    d. unrewarding.

26. Psychological changes during the college years are most dramatic in students who __________ (p. 455)
    a. attend private liberal arts colleges.
    b. attend large four-year institutions.
    c. interact with like-minded peers of similar backgrounds.
    d. are involved in academic and extracurricular activities.

27. Twenty-year-old Dominic explored the possibility of becoming a teacher by tutoring in an after-school program and interviewing several of his previous teachers about their career choice. He then decided to major in education. Dominic is in the __________ period of vocational development. (p. 456)
    a. fantasy
    b. tentative
    c. realistic
    d. acquisition

28. Occupational choice is _________ (p. 456)
    a. the result of dynamic interaction between person and environment.
    b. a rational, linear process for most young people.
    c. almost exclusively influenced by the individual's personality type.
    d. an especially long, difficult process for low-SES youths.

29. Non-college-bound North American students are _________ (p. 458)
    a. even less likely to find employment than students who drop out of high school.
    b. typically well-prepared for skilled business and industrial occupations.
    c. better able to find skilled jobs than their counterparts in western Europe.
    d. typically unable to find a job better than the ones they held as students.

30. Men who choose traditionally female occupations, such as nursing or teaching, often _________ (p. 459)
    a. express regret about their choice.
    b. quit within the first year.
    c. express anxiety about being stigmatized.
    d. have few opportunities for advancement.

PRACTICE TEST #2

1. Biological aging __________ (p. 432)
   a. varies widely across all parts of the body.
   b. begins before body structures reach maximum capacity.
   c. is influenced solely by genetic factors.
   d. leads to increases in organ and system functioning.

2. Which of the following provides support for the "programmed" effects of "aging genes"? (p. 432)
   a. Human cells that are allowed to divide in the laboratory have a lifespan of 50 divisions, plus or minus 10.
   b. DNA in body cells is gradually damaged through spontaneous or externally caused mutations.
   c. Free radicals released by the body's cells destroy nearby cellular material.
   d. A decrease in the number of senescent cells contributes to loss of function and early mortality.

3. Telomeres __________ (p. 433)
   a. lengthen with each cell duplication.
   b. respond to lifestyle changes.
   c. are unresponsive to lifestyle changes.
   d. shorten at a predetermined, biological rate.

4. During the twenties and thirties, changes in physical appearance and declines in body functioning __________ (p. 435)
   a. occur only in those with chronic illnesses, such as diabetes.
   b. are rare, occurring mainly in those who are obese or smoke heavily.
   c. are gradual and barely noticeable.
   d. occur more rapidly than at any other time during the lifespan.

5. Which of the following types of exercise peaks in the late twenties and early thirties? (p. 436)
   a. tennis
   b. jumping
   c. long-distance running
   d. sprinting

6. Why do people get more colds and other illnesses during times of stress? (p. 437)
   a. Most stressful events occur after age 20, when the immune system is in a decline.
   b. The thymus reduces hormone production when the body is under stress.
   c. B cells release more antibodies than T cells during stressful times.
   d. The immune response is fostered by reduced body activity.

7. Between 1970 and 2007, birth rates __________ (p. 438)
   a. increased for women of all ages.
   b. increased for women 20 to 24 years of age.
   c. doubled for women in their thirties.
   d. decreased for women in their twenties and thirties.

8. Some weight gain between the ages of 25 and 50 is normal, due to __________ (p. 440)
   a. decline of the basal metabolic rate.
   b. accumulation of dense muscle.
   c. social isolation and high rates of depression.
   d. the body's increased need for fat and calories.

9. Which nation has the world's highest rate of overweight and obesity, with more than 75 percent of people affected? (p. 442)
   a. Germany
   b. China
   c. United States
   d. Samoa

10. Which of the following statements about exercise is true? (p. 443)
    a. Regular exercise is associated with substantially lower death rates from all causes.
    b. Vigorous exercise in adulthood is associated with bone breaks and muscle sprains.
    c. Exercise predicts longevity mainly because inactive people often have preexisting illnesses.
    d. Adults who exercise moderately reap more health benefits than adults who engage in intense exercise.

11. _____________ is the single most important preventable cause of death in industrialized nation. (p. 444)
    a. Alcohol or drug abuse
    b. Obesity
    c. Poor nutrition
    d. Cigarette smoking

12. __________ heavy drinkers are alcoholics. (p. 445)
    a. Very few
    b. About one-third of
    c. About one-half of
    d. Nearly all

13. Today, most adults __________ (p. 446)
    a. prefer cohabitation over marriage.
    b. have fewer sexual partners than in previous generations.
    c. are far less sexually active than is commonly believed.
    d. meet in formerly unconventional ways, such as through online dating services.

14. When Americans of any age are asked how many partners they have had in the past year, the usual reply is __________ (p. 446)
    a. "zero."
    b. "one."
    c. "two."
    d. "I don't know."

15. People who identify as gay or lesbian tend to __________ (p. 447)
    a. have more partners than heterosexuals.
    b. live in isolated rural communities.
    c. not "come out" until their mid-20s.
    d. be well-educated.

16. Why are women more likely to contract a sexually transmitted disease (STD) than men? (p. 447)
    a. Women typically have their first sexual experience earlier than men.
    b. Women are less likely than men to take precautions to prevent STDs.
    c. It is much easier for a man to infect a woman than for a woman to infect a man.
    d. During their teens and twenties, women have more sexual partners than men.

17. Which of the following statements about rape in the United States is true? (p. 448)
    a. Less than half of rape victims are under age 30.
    b. In most rape cases, the victims know their abusers well.
    c. The vast majority of rapes occur when the victim is intoxicated.
    d. In most cases, the abuser is a stranger.

18. Premenstrual syndrome (PMS) __________ (p. 449)
    a. is primarily limited to low-SES women.
    b. affects women in all nations and SES levels.
    c. occurs at higher rates in industrialized nations.
    d. increases sharply after childbirth.

19. Compared to middle-aged adults, young adults __________ (p. 450)
    a. more often report depressive feelings.
    b. are better-equipped to control their own stress.
    c. experience fewer stressful life events.
    d. are less prone to the physical effects of stress.

20. With regard to epistemic cognition, __________ (p. 451)
    a. it often prevents students from accepting differing viewpoints.
    b. students typically move from relativistic thinking toward dualistic thinking.
    c. it strengthens in early adulthood, regardless of educational experiences.
    d. the most mature students eventually progress to commitment within relativistic thinking.

21. Adulthood involves movement from __________ to __________. (p. 452)
    a. relativistic thinking; dualistic thinking
    b. cognitive-affective complexity; hypothetical thought
    c. hypothetical thought; pragmatic thought
    d. pragmatic thought; emotional intelligence

22. Which of the following statements about expertise and creativity is true? (p. 453)
    a. Experts and novices show remarkably similar reasoning and problem-solving skills.
    b. Creativity takes essentially the same form in childhood and adulthood.
    c. Creativity tends to peak in early adulthood, approximately five years after initial exposure to a field.
    d. Although expertise is necessary for creativity, not all experts are creative.

23. Those who get an early start in creativity tend to peak and drop off sooner, whereas "late bloomers" reach their full stride at older ages. This suggests that creativity is more a function of ____________ than of chronological age. (p. 454)
    a. "actual age"
    b. "career age"
    c. "adult age"
    d. "old age"

24. Cognitive growth during the college years is promoted when students __________ (p. 455)
    a. take online and independent study classes.
    b. choose a major during their freshman year.
    c. live in college residence halls.
    d. live at home during their freshman year.

25. Students who __________ are especially likely to graduate from college. (p. 455)
    a. are emotionally dependent on their parents
    b. come from low-SES backgrounds
    c. feel part of a college community
    d. attended public high schools

26. The relationship between personality and vocational choice is __________ (p. 456)
    a. weak, because people rarely choose occupations that complement their personality.
    b. moderate, because people are a blend of personality types and could succeed at many occupations.
    c. strong, because career choice is almost entirely attributable to personality factors.
    d. inconclusive, with research findings varying widely on this topic.

27. A low-SES parent is more likely to emphasize __________ than a high-SES parent. (p. 457)
    a. obedience
    b. nonconformity
    c. self-direction
    d. curiosity

28. Over the past three decades, the number of women in male-dominated professions has __________ (p. 457)
    a. remained unchanged, despite efforts to increase equality in these fields.
    b. declined, even though young women express interest in these fields.
    c. exploded, with a substantial number of women surpassing the achievements of men.
    d. increased, but representation is still far from equal.

29. Compared to men who choose traditionally masculine careers, men in nontraditional careers tend to be __________ (p. 458)
    a. more gender-typed.
    b. more focused on the social status of their work.
    c. less interested in working with people.
    d. more interested in working with people.

30. Unlike many European nations, the United States has __________ (p. 459)
    a. a high number of non-college-bound high school graduates.
    b. a wide range of work opportunities for non-college-bound youths.
    c. no widespread training program for non-college-bound youths.
    d. a national vocational apprenticeship program for high school graduates.

CHAPTER 14
EMOTIONAL AND SOCIAL DEVELOPMENT IN EARLY ADULTHOOD

BRIEF CHAPTER SUMMARY

In emerging adulthood, young adults from about age 18 to 25 are released from parental oversight but have not yet taken on adult roles. During these years of extended exploration, young people prolong identity development as they explore alternatives in breadth and depth.

Erikson described the psychological conflict of early adulthood as intimacy versus isolation. In his view, successful resolution of this conflict prepares the individual for the middle adulthood stage, which focuses on generativity, or caring for the next generation and helping to improve society. Levinson suggested that development consists of a series of qualitatively distinct "seasons" in which individuals revise their life structure to meet changing needs. Vaillant refined Erikson's stages, confirming Erikson's stages but filling in the gaps between them.

Although societal expectations have become less rigid, conformity to or departure from the social clock—age-graded expectations for major life events—can be a major source of personality change in adulthood. Following a social clock fosters confidence in young adults, whereas deviating from it can lead to psychological distress.

Although young adults are especially concerned with romantic love and the establishment of an intimate tie with another person, they also satisfy the need for intimacy through relationships with friends, siblings, and co-workers that involve mutual commitment. Romantic partners tend to resemble one another in age, ethnicity, SES, religion, and various personal and physical attributes. Loneliness, as long as it is not overwhelming, can be a motivating factor in healthy personality development.

The family life cycle is a sequence of phases characterizing the development of most families around the world, but wide variation exists in the sequence and timing of these phases. Departure from the parental home is a major step toward assuming adult responsibilities, although nearly half of young adults return home for a brief time after initial leaving. Young adults also delay marriage more today than a half-century ago. Same-sex marriages are recognized in Canada, Belgium, South Africa, and several other countries, and in the states of Massachusetts, Vermont, Iowa, and Connecticut; evidence suggests that the factors contributing to happiness for cohabiting same-sex couples are similar to those in other-sex marriages. Women's workplace participation affects both traditional and egalitarian marriages in defining marital roles, with most couplings arriving at a form of marriage somewhere between traditional and egalitarian. Modern couples are having fewer children and postponing parenthood longer than in past generations. Marriages that are gratifying and supportive tend to remain so after childbirth, while troubled marriages usually become more distressed. Parent education programs can help parents clarify their child-rearing values and use more effective strategies.

Today, more adults are single than in the past, and cohabitation without marriage is much more common. The number of couples who choose to remain childless has risen as well. Although childlessness may be distressing when it is involuntary, adults who are childless by choice are just as satisfied with their lives as are parents who have good relationships with their children. Nearly half of all marriages end in divorce, and many people later remarry, often creating blended families that pose their own unique challenges. Never-married parenthood has increased and, for low-SES women, often increases financial hardship. Gay and lesbian parents are as committed to and effective at child rearing as heterosexual parents.

Men's career paths are usually continuous, while women's are often discontinuous because of child rearing and other family demands. Although women and ethnic minorities have entered nearly all professions, they still tend to be concentrated in occupations that are less well-paid and that offer little opportunity for advancement. Couples in dual-earner marriages, now the norm, often face complex career decisions and challenges in meeting both work and family responsibilities. When dual-earner couples cooperate to surmount difficulties, they benefit from higher earnings, a better standard of living, and women's self-fulfillment and improved well-being.

LEARNING OBJECTIVES

After reading this chapter, you should be able to:

14.1 Define emerging adulthood, and explain how cultural change has contributed to the emergence of this period. (pp. 464–466)

14.2 Explain how emerging adulthood may present risks for some, and why this may not be a universally distinct period of development. (pp. 466–467)

14.3 Describe Erikson's stage of intimacy versus isolation, noting personality changes that take place during early adulthood. (pp. 468–469)

14.4 Summarize Levinson's and Vaillant's psychosocial theories of adult personality development, including how they apply to both men's and women's lives and their limitations. (pp. 469–471)

14.5 Describe the social clock and how it relates to adjustment in adulthood. (p. 471)

14.6 Discuss factors that affect mate selection, and explain the role of romantic love in young adults' quest for intimacy. (pp. 472, 474)

14.7 Explain how culture influences the experience of love. (p. 475)

14.8 Cite characteristics of adult friendships and sibling relationships, including differences between same-sex, other-sex, and sibling friendships. (pp. 475–476)

14.9 Cite factors that influence loneliness, and explain the role of loneliness in adult development. (pp. 476–477)

14.10 Trace phases of the family life cycle that are prominent in early adulthood, noting factors that influence these phases. (pp. 478–485)

14.11 Discuss the diversity of adult lifestyles, focusing on singlehood, cohabitation, and childlessness. (pp. 486–488)

14.12 Discuss trends in divorce and remarriage, along with factors that contribute to them. (pp. 488–489)

14.13 Summarize challenges associated with variant styles of parenthood, including stepparents, never-married single parents, and gay and lesbian parents. (pp. 489–491)

14.14 Describe patterns of career development, and cite difficulties faced by women, ethnic minorities, and couples seeking to combine work and family. (pp. 491–495)

STUDY QUESTIONS

A Gradual Transition: Emerging Adulthood

1. True or False: Most 18- to 25-year-olds believe they have reached adulthood. (p. 464)
2. The transitional period extending from the late teens to the mid-twenties is called ____________________. (p. 464)

Unprecedented Exploration and Advances in Identity

1. Cite several changes that contribute to advances in identity during *emerging adulthood.* (pp. 464–465)

____

____

____

2. During the college years, young people explore their identity in (breadth / depth), weighing multiple possibilities. They also explore in (breadth / depth), evaluating existing commitments. (p. 465)

3. Describe the dual-cycle model of identity development. (p. 465)

4. College students who spend more time exploring their identity in (depth / breadth) are better adjusted. (p. 465)

5. A set of qualities called ______________________ consists of a sense of purpose, self-efficacy, determination to overcome obstacles, and responsibility for outcomes. Describe outcomes associated with these qualities. (p. 465)

Cultural Change, Cultural Variation, and Emerging Adulthood

1. Cite two cultural changes that have contributed to the recent appearance of emerging adulthood. (p. 465)

   A. ______________________

   B. ______________________

2. True or False: Emerging adulthood is limited to cultures that postpone entry into adult roles until the twenties. (p. 465)

3. Cite examples of varying beliefs about what it means to become an adult. (p. 466)

4. True or False: Virtually all researchers agree that emerging adulthood is a distinct period of development. (p. 466)

Risk and Resilience in Emerging Adulthood

1. List several resources that foster resilience in emerging adulthood. (p. 466)

2. Cite several ways in which emerging adults benefit from secure bonds with parents. (p. 466)

Erikson's Theory: Intimacy versus Isolation

1. According to Erikson, in what area of life is the psychological conflict of early adulthood, *intimacy versus isolation*, most prominent? (p. 468)

2. Explain how a secure identity fosters attainment of intimacy. (p. 468)

____

____

____

3. Describe the characteristics of individuals who have achieved a sense of intimacy versus those affected by isolation. (pp. 468–469)

Intimacy: ____

____

Isolation: ____

____

Other Theories of Adult Psychosocial Development

Levinson's Seasons of Life

1. The ____________________ is the underlying design of a person's life, consisting of relationships with significant others. Which of its components are usually central? (p. 469)

____

2. True or False: Like Erikson, Levinson regarded development as a sequence of qualitatively distinct eras. (p. 470)
3. List the three phases involved with Levinson's eras. (pp. 469–470)

A. ____

B. ____

C. ____

4. Indicate whether the following are more typical of men's (M) or women's (W) life dreams during the early adult transition. (p. 470)

_____ Emphasize an independent achiever in an occupational role
_____ Display "split dreams" involving both marriage and career
_____ Define the self in terms of relationships with spouse, children, and colleagues
_____ Are usually more individualistic

5. Finding a supportive mentor is easier for (men / women). (p. 470)
6. Explain how young people reevaluate their *life structure* during the age-30 transition. (p. 470)

____

____

____

7. Cite conditions under which the age-30 transition can be a time of crisis, conflict, or instability. (p. 470)

____

____

8. Compare and contrast men's and women's experiences with "settling down" during their thirties. (p. 470)
   Men: ____

   ____

   Women: ____

   ____

Vaillant's Adaptation to Life

1. Cite one way in which Vaillant's theory is similar to Levinson's and one way in which they differ. (p. 470)
   Similar: ____
   Different: ____
2. Using Vaillant's theory, indicate how men alter themselves and their social world to adapt to life at the following ages. (p. 470)

______	Focus on career consolidation	A. Twenties
______	Become more spiritual and reflective	B. Thirties
______	Focus on intimacy concerns	C. Forties
______	Pull back from individual achievement and become more generative	D. Fifties and Sixties
______	Become guardians of their culture, concerned with values and society	E. Seventies

Limitations of Levinson's and Vaillant's Theories

1. Identify three limitations of Levinson's and Vaillant's theories. (p. 471)
   A. ____
   B. ____
   C. ____

The Social Clock

1. The ____________________ refers to age-graded expectations for major life events, such as beginning a first job or buying a home. (p. 471)
2. How does the *social clock* affect self-esteem? (p. 471)

   ____

   ____
3. Match the following personality changes with college women born in the 1930s who followed a "feminine" social clock, a "masculine" social clock, or no social clock. Items may have more than one match. (p. 471)

______	Suffered from self-doubt, feelings of incompetence, and loneliness	A. Feminine
______	Became more responsible, self-controlled, tolerant, and caring	B. Masculine
______	Became more dominant, sociable, independent, and intellectually effective	C. No social clock
______	Declined in self-esteem and felt more vulnerable as their lives progressed	

4. Why is it beneficial to follow a social clock during early adulthood? (p. 471)

   ____

   ____

Close Relationships

Romantic Love

1. True or False: In selecting a mate, research suggests that "opposites attract." Explain your answer. (p. 472)

____

____

2. Indicate whether the following characteristics tend to be more important to men (M) or women (W) when selecting a long-term partner. (p. 472)

______ Intelligence	______ Younger than oneself
______ Physical attractiveness	______ Financial status
______ Domestic skills	______ Moral character
______ Ambition	______ Same age or slightly older

3. Describe how evolutionary theory and the social learning perspective explain the differences mentioned in the previous question. (p. 472)

   Evolutionary: ____

   ____

   Social learning: ____

   ____

4. True or False: Both men and women value relationship satisfaction over good looks, earning power, and mate's age relative to their own. (p. 472)

5. Match each component of Sternberg's *triangular theory of love* with its description. (pp. 472–473)

   _____ Desire for sexual activity and romance; the physical- and psychological-arousal component

   _____ Involves warm communication, concern for the other, and a desire for the partner to reciprocate; the emotional component

   _____ Leads partners to decide that they are in love and to maintain that love; the cognitive component

   A. Intimacy
   B. Passion
   C. Commitment

6. Explain the roles of *passionate love* and *companionate love* in the development of a relationship. (p. 474)

   Passionate love: ____

   ____

   Companionate love: ____

   ____

7. During the first year of marriage, husbands and wives reported they gradually felt (less / more) "in love" and (less / more) pleased with married life. Cite three factors that contributed to this change. (p. 474)

   A. ____

   B. ____

   C. ____

8. In the transformation of romantic involvements from passionate to companionate, ______________ may be the aspect of love that determines whether a relationship survives. (p. 474)

9. Describe important features of communication that contribute to high-quality intimate relationships. (p. 474)

____

____

____

10. Cite differences between Western and Eastern views of love. (p. 475)

Western: ____

____

Eastern: ____

____

11. When selecting an intimate partner, college students of Asian heritage place more emphasis on (physical attraction and deep emotion / companionship and practical matters) than students of American or European descent. (p. 475)

A Lifespan Vista: Childhood Attachment Patterns and Adult Romantic Relationships

1. According to Bowlby's ethological theory of attachment, early attachment bonds lead to the construction of a(n) ______________________________, or set of expectations about attachment figures, that serve as a guide for close relationships. (p. 473)

2. Indicate whether the following relationship characteristics are more common among adults who recall secure (S), avoidant (A), or resistant (R) childhood attachment patterns. Attachment patterns may correspond with more than one item. (p. 473)

_____ Seek to merge completely with another and fall in love quickly
_____ Stress independence, mistrust, and anxiety about people getting too close
_____ Often deny attachment needs through excessive work and brief sexual encounters
_____ View themselves as likeable and easy to get to know and are comfortable with intimacy
_____ Display empathic and supportive behaviors toward their partner
_____ Believe that others dislike them and that romantic love is hard to find and rarely lasts
_____ Are quick to express fear and anger
_____ Report mutually initiated, enjoyable sexual activity
_____ Endorse many unrealistic beliefs about relationships
_____ Provide support that fits poorly with their partner's needs

3. In addition to child attachment patterns, what other factors contribute to later internal working models and intimate ties? (p. 473)

____

____

Friendships

1. Cite three benefits of adult friendship. (p. 475)

A. ____

B. ____

C. ____

2. (Female / Male) friends see one another more often and experience greater friendship continuity. (p. 475)

3. Compare characteristics of women's same-sex friendships with those of men. (pp. 475–476)

   Women: ____

   ____

   Men: ____

   ____

4. Cite two factors that contribute to individual differences in friendship quality. (pp. 475–476)

   A. ____

   B. ____

5. What group of adults has the largest number of other-sex friends? (p. 476)

   ____

6. What are some benefits of other-sex friendships? (p. 476)

   ____

   ____

7. (Men / Women) are more likely to feel sexually attracted to an other-sex friend. (p. 476)

8. In what ways do adult sibling ties resemble friendships? (p. 476)

   ____

   ____

9. In Vaillant's study of well-educated men, what was the best predictor of emotional health at age 65? (p. 476)

   ____

Loneliness

1. Explain why *loneliness* peaks during the late teens and early twenties and then declines steadily into the seventies. (p. 477)

   ____

   ____

   ____

2. Under what conditions are adults more likely to experience loneliness? (p. 477)

   ____

   ____

3. When not involved in a romantic relationship, (men / women) feel lonelier, perhaps because they have fewer alternatives for satisfying intimacy needs. (p. 477)

4. Describe personal characteristics of lonely people. (p. 477)

   ____

   ____

   ____

5. Describe potential positive outcomes of loneliness, as long as it is not overwhelming. (p. 477)

____

____

The Family Life Cycle

1. The ____________________ is a sequence of phases characterizing the development of most families around the world. (p. 478)

2. True or False: The *family life cycle* is a fixed progression. (p. 478)

Leaving Home

1. The average age of leaving the family home has (decreased / increased) in recent years. (p. 478)

2. Nearly ______ percent of young adults return home for a brief time after initial leaving. Those who departed to marry are (least / most) likely to return. Those who left because of family conflict (rarely / often) return. (p. 478)

3. How do SES and ethnicity contribute to early departure from the family home? (p. 478)

____

____

____

Joining of Families in Marriage

1. Currently, the average age of marriage in the United States is ____ for women and ____ for men. (p. 478)

2. The number of first and second marriages in the United States and Canada has (declined / increased) over the last few decades. Explain your answer. (p. 478)

____

____

3. True or False: Most Americans marry at least once. (p. 478)

4. True or False: The same factors that contribute to happiness in other-sex marriages do so in same-sex unions. (p. 479)

5. True or False: "Mixed" marriages are increasingly common today. (p. 479)

6. ____________________ is the most consistent predictor of marital stability. Explain why. (p. 479)

____

____

7. Cite differences between *traditional marriages* and *egalitarian marriages*. (p. 479)

Traditional: ____

____

Egalitarian: ____

____

8. In Western nations, men in dual-earner marriages participate much (less / more) in child care than in the past. (p. 479)

9. True or False: In North America, women spend nearly twice as much time as men on housework. (p. 479)

10. True or False: Equal power in the relationship and sharing of family responsibilities usually enhances both men's and women's satisfaction. (p. 480)

11. Cite three marital myths endorsed by many young adults. (p. 480)

 A. ______________________________

 B. ______________________________

 C. ______________________________

12. Young people who hold a religious view of marriage as sacred are (less / more) likely to enter marriage with unrealistic expectations and (less / more) able to cope with disagreement. (p. 480)

13. Indicate whether the following factors contribute to a happy (+) or unhappy (–) marriage. (p. 481)
 _____ Marriage before age 23
 _____ Stable marital patterns in extended family
 _____ Courtship of at least six months
 _____ Family responsibilities largely fall to the woman
 _____ First pregnancy before or within first year of marriage

14. True or False: Most couples spend little time before their wedding day reflecting on the decision to marry. (p. 481)

Social Issues: Partner Abuse

1. Partner abuse in which (husbands / wives) are perpetrators and (husbands / wives) are physically injured is the type most likely to be reported to authorities. Why might this not accurately reflect true rates of abuse? (p. 482)

____

____

2. True or False: Partner abuse occurs at about the same rate in same-sex relationships as in heterosexual relationships. (p. 482)

3. True or False: American men and women are equally likely to "strike first." (p. 482)

4. Describe factors that contribute to partner abuse. (pp. 482–483)

 Psychological: ______________________________

____

____

 Family: ______________________________

____

____

 Cultural: ______________________________

____

____

5. List reasons why many people do not leave destructive relationships before abuse escalates. (p. 483)

6. Describe treatment for victims and perpetrators of partner abuse. (p. 483)

   Victims:

   Perpetrators:

7. True or False: Most existing treatments for male batterers are effective at dealing with relationship difficulties and alcohol abuse. (p. 483)

Parenthood

1. Family size in industrialized nations has (declined / increased). (p. 481)
2. List three factors that affect the decision to have children. (p. 481)

   A.

   B.

   C.
3. True or False: Women with high-status, demanding careers less often choose parenthood and, when they do, more often delay it than women with less time-consuming jobs. (p. 481)
4. List reasons for having children that are most important to all groups of people. (p. 481)

5. Cite two disadvantages of parenthood mentioned most often by young adults. (pp. 481–482)

   A.

   B.
6. After the arrival of a new baby, the gender roles of husbands and wives become (less / more) traditional. (pp. 482–483)
7. True or False: For most new parents, the arrival of a baby causes significant marital strain. (p. 483)
8. List factors that contribute to marital satisfaction after childbirth. (p. 483)

9. How does postponing childbearing ease the transition to parenthood? (pp. 483–484)

10. Describe typical changes in fathers' roles and responsibilities after the birth of a second child. (p. 484)

____

____

____

11. True or False: Couples' groups led by counselors are effective in easing the transition to parenthood. Describe characteristics of these interventions. (p. 484)

____

____

12. True or False: Generous, paid employment leave after the birth of a child is widely available in industrialized nations but not in the United States. (p. 484)

13. True or False: Men and women today are more certain about how to rear children than they were in previous generations. (p. 484)

14. How do families benefit when parents work together as a coparenting team? (p. 484)

____

____

____

15. Describe additional struggles faced by employed parents. (pp. 484–485)

____

____

____

16. Identify some benefits of child rearing for adult development. (p. 485)

____

____

17. Briefly describe how adolescence brings changes in parental roles. (p. 485)

____

____

18. Cite differences in the way mothers and fathers seek information and learn about child rearing. (p. 485)

Mothers: ____

____

Fathers: ____

____

19. Parent education courses exist to help parents with what four tasks? (p. 485)

A. ____

B. ____

C. ____

D. ____

The Diversity of Adult Lifestyles

Singlehood

1. Cite two factors that have contributed to the growing numbers of single adults. (p. 486)

   A. ______________________________

   B. ______________________________

2. Because they marry later, more young adult (men / women) are single. But (men / women) are far more likely than (men / women) to remain single for many years or their entire life. Why is this? (p. 486)

   ____

   ____

3. True or False: In early adulthood, the percentage of never-married African Americans is nearly twice as great as that of Caucasian Americans. (p. 486)

4. Single (men / women) have more physical and mental health problems than single (men / women). Explain your answer. (p. 486)

   ____

   ____

5. List the two most often mentioned advantages of singlehood, as well as drawbacks of singlehood. (pp. 486–487)

   Advantages: ______________________________

   ____

   Drawbacks: ______________________________

   ____

6. True or False: Overall, people who have always been single are content with their lives. (p. 487)

Cohabitation

1. ________________ refers to the lifestyle of unmarried couples who have a sexually intimate relationship and who share a residence. Which group of young people has experienced an especially dramatic rise in this lifestyle? (p. 487)

   ____

2. True or False: Most North American couples in their twenties choose *cohabitation.* (p. 487)

3. List two different functions of cohabitation. (p. 487)

   A. ______________________________

   B. ______________________________

4. How do Western European attitudes toward cohabitation differ from those of North Americans? (p. 487)

   ____

   ____

   ____

5. American couples who cohabit before they are engaged to be married are (less / more) prone to divorce than married couples who wait to live together until they have made a commitment. Cite several possible reasons for this. (p. 487)

____

____

6. Identify three types of couples who do not experience the negative outcomes of cohabitation. (pp. 487–488)

A. ____

B. ____

C. ____

7. Cite advantages and drawbacks of cohabitation. (p. 488)

Advantages: ____

____

Drawbacks: ____

____

Childlessness

1. Childlessness in the United States has (declined / increased) steadily since 1975. (p. 488)
2. List reasons why couples may choose to remain childless. (p. 488)

____

____

3. (Involuntarily / Voluntarily) childless adults are just as content with their lives as parents who have warm relationships with their children. However, (involuntarily / voluntarily) childless adults are likely to be dissatisfied. (p. 488)

Divorce and Remarriage

1. Cite two reasons why divorce rates have stabilized since the mid-1980s. (p. 488)

A. ____

B. ____

2. During which two periods of adult life are divorces especially likely to occur? (p. 488)

A. ____

B. ____

3. Describe maladaptive communication and problem-solving patterns that contribute to divorce. (pp. 488–489)

____

____

____

4. Cite four background factors that increase the chances of divorce. (p. 489)

A. ______________________ C. ______________________

B. ______________________ D. ______________________

5. True or False: Parental divorce elevates the risk of divorce in at least two succeeding generations. (p. 489)

6. When a woman's workplace status and income exceed her husband's, the risk of divorce (decreases / is unaffected / increases). (p. 489)

7. Identify several immediate reactions to divorce. (p. 489)

____

____

8. Indicate whether the following statements describe men's (M), women's (W), or men's and women's (MW) adjustment to divorce. (p. 489)

_____ Adjust less well to living on their own
_____ Negative reactions subside within two years
_____ Tend to bounce back more easily
_____ Finding a new partner improves life satisfaction

9. On average, people remarry within ___ years of divorce. (Women / Men) do so somewhat faster. (p. 489)

10. List four reasons that remarriages are especially vulnerable to breakup. (p. 489)

A. ____
B. ____
C. ____
D. ____

11. Blended families generally take _____ to _____ years to develop the connectedness and comfort of intact biological families. (p. 489)

Variant Styles of Parenthood

1. (First-marriage / Remarried) parents typically report higher levels of tension and disagreement, most centering on _______________ issues. (p. 490)

2. Cite three reasons why stepmothers are especially likely to experience conflict. (p. 490)

A. ____
B. ____
C. ____

3. Cite three reasons why stepfathers with children of their own establish positive bonds with stepchildren relatively quickly. (p. 490)

A. ____
B. ____
C. ____

4. True or False: After making several overtures that are ignored or rebuffed, stepfathers without biological children often withdraw from parenting. (p. 490)

5. What are three crucial ingredients of positive stepparent adjustment? (p. 490)

A. ____
B. ____
C. ____

6. In the United States, ______________________________ make up the largest group of never-married parents. Explain this finding. (p. 490)

____

____

____

7. True or False: Never-married mothers are far less likely than divorced mothers to receive paternal child support payments. (p. 490)

8. Discuss the pros and cons of father involvement for children of never-married mothers. (p. 490)

   Pros: ______________________________

   ____

   Cons: ______________________________

   ____

9. True or False: Gay and lesbian parents are as committed to and effective at child rearing as heterosexual parents. (p. 490)

10. Overall, families headed by homosexuals can be distinguished from other families only by issues related to ______________________________. (p. 491)

Career Development

Establishing a Career

1. Men typically have ____________ career lives, from completion of formal education to retirement. Many women have ____________ career paths—ones that were interrupted or deferred by child rearing and other family needs. (p. 492)

2. Cite several reasons why entry into the workforce can be discouraging, even for those who enter their chosen field. (p. 492)

   ____

   ____

3. How does self-efficacy affect career progress? (p. 492)

   ____

   ____

   ____

4. Access to an effective mentor is jointly affected by what two factors? (p. 492)

   A. ______________________________

   B. ______________________________

Women and Ethnic Minorities

1. True or False: Women generally remain concentrated in occupations that offer little opportunity for advancement. (p. 492)

2. Cite three reasons for the considerable difference between men's and women's earnings in the United States. (p. 492)

   A. ______________________________

   B. ______________________________

   C. ______________________________

3. Between the ages of 18 and 34, the typical (man / woman) has been out of the labor force more than twice as long as the other gender. How does this affect career development? (p. 492)

____

4. Describe several challenges faced by women in male-dominated fields. (p. 493)

____

____

____

5. Cite examples of racial bias in the labor market. (p. 494)

____

____

____

Social Issues: Women in "Fast-Track" Careers Who Opt to Stay Home

1. True or False: Women with professional degrees opt out of the labor force at three to four times the rate of similarly accomplished men. (p. 493)
2. True or False: Most women who left prestigious, well-paid careers are ambivalent about quitting. (p. 493)
3. Describe reasons why accomplished women opt to stay home, focusing on work, spouses, and children. (p. 493)

Work: ____

____

Spouses ____

____

Children: ____

____

Combining Work and Family

1. The dominant family form today is the ______________________, in which both husband and wife are employed. What are the main sources of strain in these families? (p. 494)

____

____

2. Role overload is greater for (men / women). (p. 494)
3. Explain how dual-earner couples can combine work and family roles in ways that promote mastery and pleasure in both spheres of life. (pp. 494–495)

____

____

____

ASK YOURSELF . . .

For *Ask Yourself* questions for this chapter, along with feedback on the accuracy of your answers, please log on to MyDevelopmentLab (for registration and access, please visit mydevelopmentlab.com or follow the instructions on page ix).

(1) Select the Multimedia Library.

(2) Choose the explore option.

(3) Find your chapter from the drop down box.

(4) Click find now.

(5) Complete questions and choose "Submit answers for grading" or "Clear answers" to start over.

SUGGESTED READINGS

Arnett, J. J. (2006). *Emerging adulthood: The winding road from the late teens through the twenties.* New York: Oxford University Press. Provides a thorough and compelling look at the experiences, challenges, and unique opportunities associated with emerging adulthood.

Clarke-Stewart, A., & Brentano, C. (2006). *Divorce: Causes and consequences.* New Haven: Yale University Press. Presents the latest research on divorce, including factors that contribute to it, adult and child adjustment, issues surrounding custody and child support, and remarriage. Includes recommendations for policymakers on how to help protect both adults and children from the detrimental effects of divorce.

Watt, H. M., & Eccles, J. S. (Eds.). (2008). *Gender and occupational outcomes.* Washington, DC: American Psychological Association. Examines longitudinal trends in gender inequality in the workplace. Although women have made great strides in entering traditionally male-dominated professions, gender-related disparities in math, science, and technology careers persist, with women rarely sharing the salary and status of men in similar positions. An excellent resource for students, educators, policymakers, and anyone interested in vocational development.

CROSSWORD PUZZLE 14.1

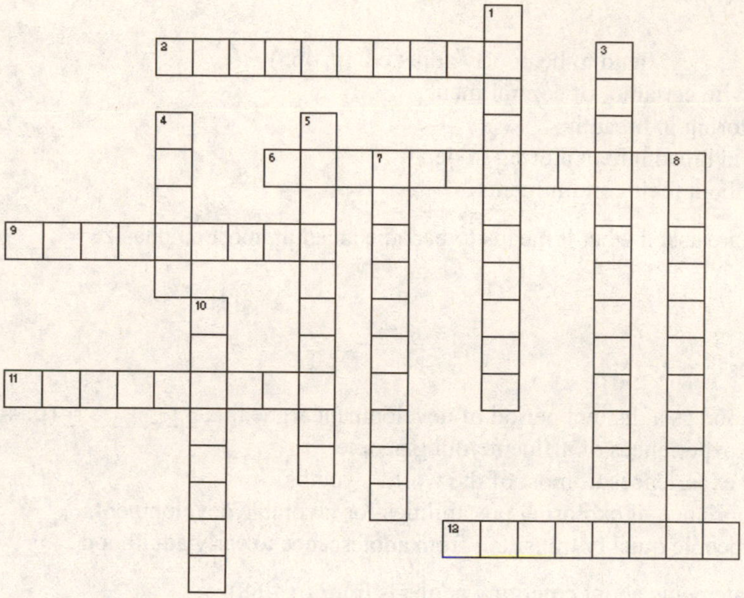

Across

2. Sternberg's ______ theory of love involves intimacy, passion, and commitment.
6. ______ love entails warm, trusting affection and caregiving.
9. Family ______ ______: sequence of phases characterizing the development of most families (2 words)
11. Life ______: in Levinson's theory, the underlying design of a person's life
12. ______ adulthood: transitional period extending from the late teens to the mid-twenties

Down

1. ______ marriage involves a clear division of husband's and wife's roles.
3. Lifestyle of unmarried couples who share a sexually intimate relationship and a residence
4. Social ______: age-graded expectations for major life events
5. Unhappiness resulting from a gap between actual and desired social relationships
7. ______ love is intense sexual attraction.
8. In ______ marriages, partners relate as equals, sharing power and authority.
10. ______ versus isolation: Erikson's psychological conflict of early adulthood

PRACTICE TEST #1

1. Twenty- to 29-year-olds report a greater sense of __________ than they ever will again. (p. 464)
   a. certainty
   b. fulfillment
   c. community
   d. control

2. College students who __________ tend to be poorly adjusted. (p. 465)
   a. explore in depth and with certainty of commitment
   b. spend much time exploring in breadth
   c. move from exploring in breadth to exploring in depth
   d. fluctuate in certainty about their commitments

3. When 18- to 25-year-olds are asked what it means to become an adult, most emphasize __________ (p. 466)
   a. career goals.
   b. family goals.
   c. physical qualities.
   d. psychological qualities.

4. Critics of emerging adulthood as a distinct period of development argue that __________ (p. 467)
   a. it fails to describe the experiences of affluent young people.
   b. it fails to describe the experiences of most of the world's youths.
   c. it exaggerates the importance of exploring possibilities for favorable development.
   d. in most cases, young people quickly transition from adolescence to early adulthood.

5. Which of the following statements about emerging adults is true? (p. 468)
   a. Positive relationships with parents have an especially wide-ranging influence in the emerging adult years.
   b. The psychological distancing between parents and adolescents often continues into the emerging adult years.
   c. Emerging adults with only a few cognitive, emotional, and social resources experience a rocky transition to adulthood.
   d. Exposure to multiple negative life events offers emerging adults the chance to overcome adversity and promotes successful development.

6. The conflict of intimacy versus isolation is successfully resolved when a young adult __________ (p. 468)
   a. establishes a committed, mutually gratifying close relationship.
   b. finds a mentor in his or her field of study.
   c. explores a variety of romantic relationships without yet committing to just one person.
   d. establishes autonomy from his or her parents.

7. What did Levinson's research reveal about sex differences in early adulthood? (p. 470)
   a. Men construct dreams in early adulthood, whereas women construct dreams much later or not at all.
   b. Young women tend to construct individualistic dreams, whereas young men display "split dreams."
   c. Women's career development is more likely than men's to extend into middle age.
   d. Young women usually "settle down" into a stable niche, while men remain unsettled into middle adulthood.

8. During the age-30 transition, young people reevaluate their __________ (p. 470)
   a. childhood.
   b. sexuality.
   c. life structure.
   d. physical health.

9. Departure from the social clock often results in increased __________ (p. 471)
   a. self-esteem.
   b. psychological distress.
   c. dependence on others.
   d. social stability.

10. Which of the following statements about gender roles and preferences provides support for the social learning perspective? (p. 472)
    a. In cultures with greater gender equity, men and women are more alike in their mate preferences.
    b. Both men and women value traits that will lead to relationship satisfaction, such as caring and dependability.
    c. In nearly all cultures, men and women are more alike than different in their mate preferences.
    d. Traditional gender differences in mate selection also characterize the preferences of gay and lesbian adults.

11. Adults who report an avoidant attachment history tend to __________ (p. 473)
    a. have more stable and fulfilling relationships than adults who report a resistant attachment history.
    b. have realistic views about the fleeting nature of relationships.
    c. overwhelm their partners with demands for love and reassurance.
    d. deny their own attachment needs and distrust their partners.

12. Couples who report having higher-quality long-term relationships __________ (p. 474)
    a. tend to value traditional gender roles.
    b. often choose to cohabitate before marriage.
    c. credit their success to being very different, because opposites attract.
    d. consistently communicate their commitment to each other.

13. Compared to male friendships, friendships between women __________ (p. 475)
    a. are more intimate at every age.
    b. are more likely to be defined by competitiveness.
    c. are usually of shorter duration and more superficial.
    d. more often involve "doing something" than "just talking."

14. Loneliness __________ (p. 477)
    a. rises steadily throughout the lifespan.
    b. peaks in the late teens and early twenties.
    c. is lowest during the late teens and early twenties.
    d. decreases steadily throughout the lifespan.

15. Most young adults who return to the parental home after initial leaving __________ (p. 478)
    a. bring a spouse and young children with them.
    b. remain there for several years.
    c. report maladaptive behaviors, such as drug addiction.
    d. are undergoing role transitions, such as the end of college.

16. North American women in dual-earner marriages __________ (p. 479)
    a. spend nearly twice as much time as men on housework.
    b. spend approximately the same amount of time on housework as their husbands.
    c. often feel alone, as most Western marriages are still traditional.
    d. report less satisfaction than women in single-earner marriages.

17. Young people most often mention __________ when discussing the disadvantages of parenthood. (p. 481)
    a. financial strain
    b. loss of freedom
    c. role overload
    d. loss of privacy

18. Which of the following statements about domestic violence is true? (p. 482)
    a. Domestic violence occurs primarily in low-SES households in industrialized nations.
    b. Partner abuse is more common in heterosexual relationships than in same-sex relationships.
    c. Women are far more likely than men to experience physical assault and emotional abuse.
    d. Partner abuse is particularly high in impoverished countries that sanction gender inequality.

19. Parents who __________ are more likely to have a warm relationship and use effective child-rearing techniques. (p. 484)
    a. work as a coparenting team
    b. adopt traditional gender roles
    c. have two or more children
    d. both work outside the home

20. About __________ of American adults will remain single throughout their lives. (p. 486)
    a. 8 to 10 percent
    b. 18 to 20 percent
    c. one-third
    d. one-half

21. Compared to their counterparts in Western Europe, cohabitating American couples __________ (p. 487)
    a. are more devoted to each other.
    b. are just as likely to break up.
    c. face less discrimination.
    d. are more prone to divorce after they marry.

22. Childlessness interferes with adjustment and life satisfaction only when __________ (p. 488)
    a. a person feels ambivalence about it.
    b. marriages dissolve and loneliness sets in.
    c. it is beyond a person's control.
    d. close friends begin having children.

23. Which of the following factors increases the chance of divorce? (p. 488)
    a. family history of divorce
    b. having children
    c. older ages at marriage
    d. an egalitarian view of marriage

24. Which of the following statements about the aftermath of divorce is true? (p. 490)
    a. Finding a new partner is more crucial to life satisfaction for men than for women.
    b. Divorce for second marriages tends to be much lower than for first marriages.
    c. Both men and women experience an increase in social support after a divorce.
    d. Men tend to bounce back more easily from divorce than women do.

25. In the United States, the largest group of never-married parents is young __________ (p. 490)
    a. Asian women.
    b. Mexican-American men.
    c. African-American women.
    d. Caucasian men.

26. Children of __________ are at the greatest risk for conduct problems. (p. 490)
    a. never-married black mothers
    b. never-married white mothers
    c. gay and lesbian families
    d. families that include an antisocial biological father

27. Which of the following statements about differences in men and women's work lives is true? (p. 491)
    a. Men's career paths are typically continuous, whereas women's are discontinuous.
    b. Men's career paths are typically discontinuous, whereas women's are continuous.
    c. In all fields, women are far more engaged in their daily work lives than men are.
    d. In all fields, men are far more engaged in their daily work lives than women are.

28. According to a national survey, most women who left high-powered careers to raise a family say that the most significant factor in their decision was __________ (p. 493)
    a. spousal pressure.
    b. a desire for a new identity.
    c. lack of high-quality child care.
    d. the work environment.

29. Women who enter nontraditional, male-dominated fields __________ (p. 493)
    a. are better adjusted and more productive than women who enter traditionally "feminine" careers.
    b. are typically more confident in their career paths than male co-workers.
    c. report uncertainty about their ability to overcome barriers to success.
    d. tend to maintain job satisfaction and productivity, even in sexist work climates.

30. Studies indicate that workplace supports in balancing career and family, such as time-flexible policies, __________ (p. 495)
    a. result in a more productive workforce.
    b. are more common in the U.S. than other Western nations.
    c. are linked to favorable adjustment in women but not men.
    d. contribute to favorable adjustment but have little impact on productivity.

PRACTICE TEST #2

1. When asked whether they have reached adulthood, the majority of 18- to 25-year-old Americans answered __________ (p. 464)
   a. "yes."
   b. "no."
   c. "yes and no."
   d. "I don't know."

2. The prolonged period of emerging adulthood __________ (p. 464)
   a. is seen in nearly every culture throughout the world.
   b. follows a predictable route to adult responsibilities.
   c. helps to advance identity development.
   d. interferes with identity development.

3. Low-SES young people in Western nations who do not move on to higher education __________ (p. 466)
   a. experience a particularly extended period of emerging adulthood.
   b. find alternate routes to personal expansion and identity development.
   c. report a high level of personal agency and commitment.
   d. encounter a "floundering period" of unemployment and dead-end jobs.

4. Proponents of the concept of emerging adulthood point out that __________ (p. 467)
   a. the trend of emerging adulthood is universal, occurring at similar rates in industrialized and developing nations.
   b. in the past two decades, age-graded influences have become less important for early adult development than nonnormative influences.
   c. the concept reminds us of the need to clarify the factors contributing to the unique circumstances of young adults.
   d. young people have always reached adult status earlier in some domains and later in others, and may reverse direction.

5. Research confirms Erikson's belief that __________ fosters attainment of intimacy. (p. 468)
   a. generativity
   b. fidelity
   c. identity moratorium
   d. identity achievement

6. Like Erikson, Levinson saw development as a __________ (p. 469)
   a. process of developing professional skills and values.
   b. sequence of qualitatively distinct eras.
   c. series of crises in a quest for personal fulfillment.
   d. lifelong process of trial and error.

7. Both Vaillant and Levinson agree that __________ (p. 470)
   a. men become more generative, and women less so, with age.
   b. quality of important relationships shape the life course.
   c. there is a strict, universal, age-related schedule of change.
   d. adult development is characterized more by losses than gains.

8. Ellie's same-age friends all seemed to be getting married and starting families, while Ellie was still single. As a consequence, Ellie felt lonely, had a negative opinion of herself, and questioned her future. The best explanation of Ellie's situation is the __________ (p. 471)
   a. life structure.
   b. social clock.
   c. age-30 transition.
   d. family life cycle.

9. Research on mate selection indicates that __________ (p. 472)
   a. "opposites" tend to attract and stay together longer than partners who are similar to one another.
   b. people usually select partners who resemble themselves in a variety of ways.
   c. men assign greater weight to potential partners' moral character than women do.
   d. men and women place equal importance on the physical attractiveness of potential partners.

10. __________ is the emotional component of the triangular theory of love. (p. 472)
    a. Passion
    b. Intimacy
    c. Commitment
    d. Conflict

11. Research suggests that adults' evaluations of their early attachment experiences __________ (p. 473)
    a. predict internal working models and romantic relationships.
    b. are often biased and inaccurate.
    c. are unrelated to their own parenting behaviors.
    d. tend to focus more on negative than positive experiences.

12. Compared to Eastern cultural perspectives, Western views of mature love are more likely to focus on __________ (p. 475)
    a. lifelong dependence on one's chosen partner.
    b. obligations to others, particularly parents.
    c. companionship and practical matters, such as similarity of background.
    d. autonomy, appreciation of the partner's unique qualities, and intense emotion.

13. In a study of well-educated men, a close sibling tie in early adulthood __________ (p. 476)
    a. was the single best predictor of emotional health at age 65.
    b. was the single best predictor of marital stability at age 65.
    c. was important for short-term emotional health but showed no long-term benefits.
    d. did little to alleviate feelings of loneliness.

14. The average age of leaving the parental home __________ (p. 478)
    a. is 18, the same age it was in 1940.
    b. is 22, the same age it was in 1940.
    c. has decreased in recent years.
    d. has increased in recent years.

15. What is the most consistent predictor of marital stability? (p. 479)
    a. similarity of background
    b. age at the time of marriage
    c. religious affiliation
    d. educational attainment

16. The quality of the marital relationship __________ (p. 480)
    a. is especially high among couples who assume traditional gender roles.
    b. has a greater impact on women's psychological well-being than men's.
    c. has a greater impact on men's psychological well-being than women's.
    d. predicts mental health similarly for both genders.

17. Which of the following young couples is most likely to establish a well-functioning relationship? (p. 480)
    a. Keisha and Marty agree that the quality of a couple's sex life is the best predictor of marital happiness.
    b. Greta and Scott differ in many ways but believe that "opposites attract."
    c. Jenae and Bradley are both deeply religious and view marriage as a sacred bond.
    d. Melissa and Tomas have high expectations for marital bliss and believe spouses complete each other.

18. In the United States, the average number of children per couple is __________ (p. 481)
   a. 1.2.
   b. 1.8.
   c. 2.5.
   d. 3.1.

19. Most domestic abuse treatments __________ (p. 482)
   a. are effective in dealing with substance-abuse issues.
   b. lead to dramatic, lasting improvements in relationships.
   c. teach communication, problem solving, and anger control.
   d. acknowledge that both men and women are victims.

20. After the birth of the first child, couples often __________ (p. 483)
   a. take on more traditional gender roles.
   b. divide housekeeping and child-care responsibilities equally.
   c. report a significant decline in marital satisfaction, even in previously satisfying marriages.
   d. report high satisfaction, even in previously troubled marriages.

21. At which point in the family life cycle do people most often seek family therapy? (p. 484)
   a. in the newlywed stage
   b. after the birth of the first child
   c. when children are in the preschool and school-age years
   d. when children are adolescents

22. Most single adults __________ (p. 487)
   a. have more frequent and satisfying sex than married adults.
   b. are men in their late twenties or early thirties.
   c. were open to marriage, but life choices took them in a different direction.
   d. report greater happiness and life satisfaction than married adults.

23. Voluntarily childless adults __________ (p. 488)
   a. are just as content as parents who have warm relationships with their children.
   b. are less content than parents who have warm relationships with their children.
   c. generally find that their marriages become increasingly unhappy over time.
   d. almost never change their minds about having children later in life.

24. Compared to wives, husbands __________ (p. 488)
   a. place less importance on marriage.
   b. are more in tune to their spouse's emotions.
   c. are more likely to report marital problems.
   d. are less likely to report marital problems.

25. Which of the following stepparents is most likely to quickly establish positive bonds with their stepchildren? (p. 490)
   a. stepfathers with no children of their own
   b. stepfathers with children of their own
   c. stepmothers with no children of their own
   d. stepmothers with children of their own

26. Studies indicate that children in gay and lesbian families __________ (p. 490)
   a. do not differ from other children in adjustment and gender-role preferences.
   b. are at increased risk for mental health problems in adulthood.
   c. are more likely to assume a homosexual orientation in adolescence.
   d. typically report stressful peer relations in adolescence.

27. Among men, "work disengagement" __________ (p. 492)
    a. occurs around midlife in all occupations.
    b. is most common among highly successful men.
    c. occurs early with few opportunities for advancement.
    d. is rare at all ages and in all occupations.

28. Most women who leave high-powered careers to stay home with their children __________ (p. 493)
    a. are unable to reestablish their careers once their children begin school.
    b. report ambivalence about quitting their jobs.
    c. were dissatisfied with their jobs long before they had children.
    d. have husbands who pressured them to devote more time to family responsibilities than work.

29. Career-oriented, successful ethnic minority women __________ (p. 493)
    a. face racial but not gender discrimination.
    b. rarely receive support from other women.
    c. tend to have mothers who had low expectations for them.
    d. often display unusually high self-efficacy.

30. __________ are most likely to experience role overload. (p. 494)
    a. Men in dual-earner marriages
    b. Women in dual-earner marriages
    c. Stay-at-home mothers
    d. Stay-at-home fathers

CHAPTER 15
PHYSICAL AND COGNITIVE DEVELOPMENT IN MIDDLE ADULTHOOD

BRIEF CHAPTER SUMMARY

Physical development in midlife is a continuation of the gradual changes under way in early adulthood. Age-related deterioration in vision, hearing, and the condition of the skin becomes more apparent. Weight gain coupled with loss of lean body mass is a concern for both men and women, as is a loss of bone mass. Dietary changes and regular exercise that includes resistance training can offset these effects of aging.

The climacteric, or decline in fertility, occurs gradually over a 10-year period for women, concluding with menopause—the end of menstruation and of reproductive capacity. Doctors may prescribe hormone therapy to reduce the discomforts of menopause and to protect women from other impairments due to estrogen loss, but research also shows some potential risks of this therapy. The wide variation in physical symptoms and attitudes indicates that menopause is not merely a hormonal event but is also affected by societal beliefs and practices. Men also experience a climacteric, but the change is less dramatic, limited to a decrease in quantity of semen and sperm after age 40.

Frequency of sexual activity among married couples declines only slightly in middle adulthood and is associated with marital happiness. Cancer and cardiovascular disease are the leading causes of death in middle age. Unintentional injuries continue to be a major health threat, although they occur at a lower rate than in early adulthood, largely because of a decline in motor vehicle collisions. When age-related bone loss is severe, a disabling condition called osteoporosis develops. In both men and women, expressed hostility predicts heart disease and other health problems.

Stress management in middle adulthood can limit the age-related rise in illness and, when disease strikes, reduce its severity. Heredity, diet, exercise, social support, coping strategies, and hardiness contribute to middle-aged adults' ability to cope with stress. Although negative stereotypes of aging discourage older adults of both sexes, middle-aged women are more likely to be viewed unfavorably, especially by men. The double standard seems to be declining as both genders view middle age more positively.

Although declines in cognitive development occur in some areas, most middle-aged people display cognitive competencies, especially in familiar contexts, and some attain outstanding accomplishment. Consistent with the lifespan perspective, cognitive change in middle adulthood is viewed as multidimensional, multidirectional, and plastic. Crystallized intelligence (which depends on accumulated knowledge and experience) gains steadily through middle adulthood, while fluid intelligence (which depends on basic information-processing skills) begins to decline in the twenties. Research shows that using intellectual skills seems to affect the degree to which they are maintained.

Speed of cognitive processing slows with age, making it harder for middle-aged people to divide their attention, focus on relevant stimuli, and switch from one task to another as the situation demands. With age, the amount of information people can retain in working memory diminishes, but general factual knowledge, procedural knowledge, and knowledge related to one's occupation either remain unchanged or increase into midlife. Middle-aged adults in all walks of life often become good at practical problem solving, largely as a result of development of expertise, and creativity in midlife becomes more deliberately thoughtful.

At all ages and in different cultures, a reciprocal relationship exists between vocational life and cognitive development. Stimulating, complex work and flexible, abstract, autonomous thinking support each other. Often motivated by life transitions, adults are returning to undergraduate and graduate study in record numbers. The majority of adult learners are women, who are often pulled in conflicting directions by role demands outside of school. Social supports for returning students can make the difference between continuing in school and dropping out.

LEARNING OBJECTIVES

After reading this chapter, you should be able to:

15.1 Describe the physical changes of middle adulthood, paying special attention to vision, hearing, the skin, muscle–fat makeup, and the skeleton. (pp. 502–504, 505)

15.2 Summarize reproductive changes experienced by middle-aged men and women, and discuss the symptoms of menopause, the benefits and risks of hormone therapy, and women's psychological reactions to menopause. (pp. 504, 506–509)

15.3 Discuss sexuality in middle adulthood. (p. 509)

15.4 Discuss cancer, cardiovascular disease, and osteoporosis, noting sex differences, risk factors, and interventions. (pp. 509–513)

15.5 Explain how hostility and anger affect health. (pp. 513–514)

15.6 Discuss the benefits of stress management, exercise, and an optimistic outlook in adapting to the physical challenges of midlife. (pp. 514–517)

15.7 Explain the double standard of aging. (p. 517)

15.8 Describe changes in crystallized and fluid intelligence during middle adulthood, and discuss individual and group differences in intellectual development. (pp. 518–520)

15.9 Describe changes in information processing in midlife, paying special attention to speed of processing, attention, and memory. (pp. 520–523)

15.10 Discuss the development of practical problem solving, expertise, and creativity in middle adulthood. (pp. 523–525)

15.11 Describe the relationship between vocational life and cognitive development. (pp. 525–526)

15.12 Discuss the challenges of adult learners, ways to support returning students, and benefits of earning a degree in midlife. (pp. 526–527)

STUDY QUESTIONS

Physical Development

Physical Changes

Vision

1. Around age 60, the lens of the eye loses its capacity to adjust to objects at varying distances entirely, a condition called ______________________________. (p. 502)

2. Place a check mark by each structural change in the eye that is common during middle adulthood. (p. 502)

_______ Pupil enlarges
_______ Pupil shrinks
_______ Lens gradually thins
_______ Lens becomes yellowed
_______ Vitreous develops opaque areas
_______ Vitreous becomes less dense

3. Cite four ways in which the changes mentioned above can affect vision in midlife. (pp. 502–503)

A. ____

B. ____

C. ____

D. ____

4. Describe three neural changes in the visual system that occur in midlife. (p. 503)

   A. ______________________________

   B. ______________________________

   C. ______________________________

5. Middle-aged adults are at increased risk of ____________________—a disease in which poor fluid drainage leads to a buildup of pressure within the eye, damaging the optic nerve. (p. 503)

Hearing

1. Most adult-onset hearing impairments are (age-related / hereditary), a condition called ____________________. (p. 503)

2. Cite two physical changes that lead to age-related hearing loss. (p. 503)

   A. ______________________________

   B. ______________________________

3. (Men's / Women's) hearing tends to decline earlier and more rapidly. Explain your answer. (p. 503)

   ____

   ____

Skin

1. Match the three skin layers below with their descriptions and typical age-related changes. Some changes may apply to more than one layer. (p. 503)

Layer of Skin	Description	Age-Related Change
____ ____ Epidermis	A. Middle supportive layer	1. Becomes less firmly attached
____ ____ Dermis	B. Inner fatty layer	2. Cells decline in water content
____ ____ Hypodermis	C. Outer protective layer	3. Fibers thin
		4. Fat diminishes

2. Describe changes in the skin at the following ages: (p. 503)

   Thirties: ______________________________

   Forties: ______________________________

   Fifties: ______________________________

Muscle–Fat Makeup

1. In middle adulthood, it is common for body fat to (decrease / increase) and lean body mass to (decrease / increase). The (limbs / torso) are more likely to show an increase in fat. (p. 504)

2. Describe gender differences in fat distribution during middle adulthood. (p. 504)

   Men: ______________________________

   Women: ______________________________

3. Explain how weight gain and muscle loss can be prevented. (p. 504)

   ____

   ____

   ____

Biology and Environment: Anti-Aging Effects of Dietary Calorie Restriction

1. True or False: In nonhuman animals, dietary calorie restriction slows aging and maintains good health. (p. 505)
2. Summarize the three most powerful physiological processes mediating the benefits of calorie restriction in monkeys. (p. 505)

   A. ______________________________

   B. ______________________________

   C. ______________________________
3. Briefly describe two natural experiments that have provided information about the effects of calorie restriction in humans. (p. 505)

   A. ______________________________

   ____

   B. ______________________________

   ____
4. What factors make it difficult to study the impact of reduced caloric intake in humans? (p. 505)

   ____

   ____

   ____

Skeleton

1. What change leads to a substantial reduction in bone density during adulthood? (p. 505)

   ____
2. (Men / Women) are especially susceptible to loss in bone mass in middle adulthood. Why is this? (p. 505)

   ____

   ____
3. True or False: Loss of bone strength causes bones to fracture more easily and heal more slowly. (p. 505)
4. List several lifestyle factors that can slow bone loss in postmenopausal women. (p. 505)

   ____

   ____

Reproductive System

1. (*Climacteric* / *Menopause*) is the midlife transition in which fertility declines. This transition concludes with (*climacteric* / *menopause*), the end of menstruation and reproductive capacity. This occurs, on average, around age ______ among North American, European, and East Asian women. (p. 504)
2. Summarize gradual changes that precede menopause, as well as the physical changes that occur after menopause. (pp. 504, 506)

   Preceding menopause: ______________________________

   ____

   ____

After menopause: ____

3. True or False: Research reveals that menopause is linked to changes in the quantity and quality of sleep. (p. 506)
4. Describe characteristics of women who are likely to experience depressive episodes during climacteric. (p. 506)

____

5. Describe two types of *hormone therapy*. (p. 506)

   Estrogen replacement therapy: ____

   Hormone replacement therapy: ____

6. Briefly summarize the benefits and risks associated with hormone replacement therapy. (p. 506)

   Benefits: ____

   Risks: ____

7. Cite several alternative treatments to hormone therapy. (p. 506)

____

8. Describe factors that affect women's psychological reactions to menopause. (p. 507)

____

9. True or False: Compared with previous generations, the baby boom generation is more accepting of menopause. (p. 507)
10. Research suggests that women of ____________ and ____________ ethnicities hold especially favorable views of menopause. (p. 507)
11. True or False: Men lose their reproductive capacity during midlife and can no longer father children. (p. 507)
12. Summarize reproductive changes in middle-aged men. (p. 507)

____

Cultural Influences: Menopause as a Biocultural Event

1. Summarize the differing views of menopause held by individuals in Western industrialized nations compared with their non-Western counterparts. (p. 508)

   Western: ______________________________

   ____

   Non-Western: ______________________________

   ____

2. True or False: Japanese women and doctors consider menopause to be a significant marker of female middle age. (p. 508)

3. Compare Mayan and Greek perspectives on menopause, noting similarities and differences. (p. 508)

   Similarities: ______________________________

   ____

   Differences: ______________________________

   ____

Health and Fitness

1. True or False: In midlife, most Americans rate their health as either "excellent" or "good." (p. 509)

Sexuality

1. Frequency of sexual activity declines (slightly / dramatically) in middle adulthood. (p. 509)
2. What is the best predictor of sexual frequency in midlife? (p. 509)

   ____

3. The intensity of sexual response (declines / remains constant / increases) during middle adulthood. (p. 509)
4. During middle adulthood, more (men / women) report having no sexual partners in the previous year. What factors are responsible for this gender difference in sexual activity? (p. 509)

   ____

   ____

   ____

Illness and Disability

1. List the two leading causes of death in midlife. (p. 509)

   A. ______________________________

   B. ______________________________

2. Overall, middle-aged (men / women) are more vulnerable to most health problems. (p. 509)
3. As in earlier decades, ______________________ is a strong predictor of poor health and premature death in midlife. (p. 510)
4. In the last 15 years, the incidence of lung cancer dropped in (men / women), but it has increased in (men / women). (p. 510)

5. Describe the three main types of mutations that contribute to cancer. (p. 510)

   A. ______________________________

   B. ______________________________

   C. ______________________________

6. True or False: Cancer death rates increase sharply as SES decreases and are especially high among low-income ethnic minorities. (p. 510)

7. Provide an example of the complex interaction of heredity, biological aging, and environment on cancer. (p. 511)

   ____

   ____

   ____

8. Among individuals affected with cancer, _____ percent are cured. (p. 511)

9. Place a check mark by each true statement below. (p. 511)

   _____ A physically active lifestyle offers protection against cancers of the breast and colon.
   _____ Warning signs of cancer include indigestion, unusual bleeding, and nagging cough.
   _____ Women should have a mammogram and Pap test once every five years.
   _____ If detected early, breast and testicular cancers usually can be cured.
   _____ Estrogen replacement therapy decreases risk of uterine and breast cancers.

10. List three indicators of cardiovascular disease that are known as "silent killers" because they often have no symptoms. (p. 513)

    A. ______________________________

    B. ______________________________

    C. ______________________________

11. List three symptoms of cardiovascular disease. (p. 512)

    A. ______________________________

    B. ______________________________

    C. ______________________________

12. Place a check mark by each proven way to reduce risk of heart attack. (p. 512)

    _____ Abstain from alcohol consumption.
    _____ Reduce hostility and psychological stress.
    _____ Avoid drug therapy for blood cholesterol.
    _____ Take low-dose aspirin.
    _____ Exercise regularly.
    _____ Quit smoking.

13. Accurate diagnosis of cardiovascular disease is of special concern to (women / men), since doctors frequently overlook their symptoms. (p. 513)

14. More (men / women) are diagnosed with *osteoporosis*, a condition involving severe age-related bone loss. (p. 513)

15. True or False: Osteoporosis affects the majority of people of both sexes over age 70. (p. 513)

16. True or False: A slumped-over posture, shuffling gait, and a "dowager's hump" are common symptoms of osteoporosis. (p. 513)

17. Place a check mark by the factors below that increase an individual's risk of developing osteoporosis. (p. 513)

    _____ Family history of osteoporosis
    _____ African-American ethnicity
    _____ Menopausal decline in estrogen
    _____ Physical inactivity
    _____ High bone density
    _____ Thin, small-framed body
    _____ In men, age-related decrease in testosterone
    _____ Cigarette smoking

18. True or False: Men are far less likely than women to be screened and treated for osteoporosis. Explain your answer. (p. 513)

19. List several interventions for treating osteoporosis. (p. 513)

Hostility and Anger

1. Describe characteristics of the *Type A behavior pattern.* (p. 514)

2. What is the "toxic" ingredient of the Type A behavior pattern? (p. 514)

3. Explain the link between expressed hostility and health problems. (p. 514)

4. True or False: A socially dominant style predicts heart disease. (p. 514)
5. True or False: Suppressing anger is a healthier way of dealing with negative feelings than expressing anger. (p. 514)

Adapting to the Physical Challenges of Midlife

Stress Management

1. Describe qualities of effective versus ineffective coping with stress. (p. 514)

   Effective coping: ____________________

   Ineffective coping: ____________________

2. Identify five ways to manage stress. (p. 515)

   A. ____________________
   B. ____________________
   C. ____________________
   D. ____________________
   E. ____________________

3. Cite several constructive approaches to anger reduction. (p. 515)

4. Summarize changes in coping with stress from early to middle adulthood. (p. 515)

5. Communities provide (fewer / more) social supports to middle-aged individuals relative to young adults and senior citizens. (p. 515)

Exercise

1. True or False: Most U.S. middle-aged adults are sedentary. (p. 516)
2. Define self-efficacy, and describe the link between self-efficacy and exercise. (p. 516)

   Definition:

   Link to exercise:

3. Identify whether beginning exercisers with the following characteristics are more likely to persist in group exercise classes (G) or home-based routines (H). (p. 516)

   _____ Normal-weight adults
   _____ Overweight adults
   _____ Adults with highly stressful lives

4. List barriers to exercise often mentioned by low-SES adults. (p. 516)

An Optimistic Outlook

1. Briefly describe the three personal qualities that contribute to *hardiness*. (p. 516)

   Control:

   Commitment:

   Challenge:

2. Cite several benefits associated with hardiness. (p. 517)

3. (Low- / High-) hardy individuals are more likely to use active, problem-centered coping strategies in situations they can control. (Low-/High-) hardy people more often use emotion-centered and avoidant coping strategies. (p. 517)

4. Describe the link between hardiness and physiological arousal. (p. 517)

____

____

____

Gender and Aging: A Double Standard

1. Unfavorable stereotypes about aging are more often applied to (men / women), who are rated as less attractive and as having more negative characteristics. (p. 517)

2. What factor may be at the heart of the double standard of aging? (p. 517)

____

3. Explain how societal forces exaggerate unfavorable stereotypes about aging women. (p. 517)

____

____

4. New evidence suggests that the double standard of aging is (increasing / declining). (p. 517)

Cognitive Development

Changes in Mental Abilities

Cohort Effects

1. Schaie's Seattle Longitudinal Study examined adult development of intellectual abilities using a ______________ design, which combines cross-sectional and longitudinal approaches. (p. 518)

2. The Seattle Longitudinal Study's (cross-sectional / longitudinal) component revealed a drop in five mental abilities after the mid-thirties. Meanwhile, (cross-sectional / longitudinal) trends revealed modest gains in midlife, sustained into the fifties and early sixties. (p. 518)

3. What two factors are largely responsible for the discrepancies mentioned in the previous question? (p. 518)

   A. ____

   ____

   B. ____

   ____

Crystallized and Fluid Intelligence

1. __________ *intelligence* depends on basic information-processing abilities, whereas ________ *intelligence* relies on accumulated knowledge and experience, good judgment, and mastery of social conventions. (p. 519)

2. Many cross-sectional studies show that (crystallized / fluid) intelligence increases steadily throughout middle adulthood, whereas (crystallized / fluid) intelligence begins to decline in the twenties. (p. 519)

3. Indicate whether the following factors show gains (+) or declines (–) through early and middle adulthood. (pp. 519–520)

   ______ Inductive reasoning
   ______ Verbal memory
   ______ Verbal ability
   ______ Spatial orientation
   ______ Perceptual speed
   ______ Numeric ability

4. List three reasons why middle-aged adults show stability in crystallized abilities despite a much earlier decline in fluid intelligence. (p. 520)

   A. ______________________________

   B. ______________________________

   C. ______________________________

Individual and Group Differences

1. List factors associated with the maintenance of intellectual skills in middle adulthood. (p. 520)

   ____

   ____

2. During early and middle adulthood, (men / women) excel at spatial skills, while (men / women) perform better on verbal tasks and perceptual speed. (p. 520)

3. Compared with the previous generation at the same age, middle-aged baby boomers show substantially (worse / better) verbal memory, inductive reasoning, and spatial orientation. Cite four reasons for this cohort difference. (p. 520)

   A. ______________________________

   B. ______________________________

   C. ______________________________

   D. ______________________________

Information Processing

Speed of Processing

1. Response time on both simple and complex reaction time tasks (decreases / remains stable / increases) from early to late adulthood. (pp. 520–521)

2. Describe two explanations for age-related declines in speed of processing. (p. 521)

   Neural network view: ______________________________

   ____

   Information-loss view: ______________________________

   ____

3. How does processing speed affect adults' performance on many complex tasks? (p. 521)

   ____

   ____

   ____

4. Processing speed is a (weak / strong) predictor of the skill with which older adults perform complex, familiar tasks in everyday life. (p. 521)

5. True or False: Knowledge and experience help older adults compensate for declines in processing speed. (p. 521)

Attention

1. Studies of attention focus on the following four changes: (p. 522)

   A. ______________________________

   B. ______________________________

   C. ______________________________

   D. ______________________________

2. Explain the link between attention and information processing during midlife. (p. 522)

   ____

   ____

3. As adults get older, inhibition becomes (easier / more difficult). How does this affect adults in everyday life? (p. 522)

   ____

   ____

4. True or False: Practice and experience with attentional skills can help midlifers compensate for age-related declines. (p. 522)

Memory

1. From early to middle adulthood, the amount of information people can retain in working memory (increases / diminishes). What explains this change? (p. 522)

   ____

   ____

2. Memory strategies, such as organization and elaboration, are applied (less / more) often and (less / more) effectively with age. What explains these changes? (pp. 522–523)

   ____

   ____

   ____

3. Cite three ways in which memory tasks can be designed to help older people compensate for age-related declines in working memory. (p. 523)

   A. ______________________________

   B. ______________________________

   C. ______________________________

4. List three types of knowledge that remain unchanged or show improvement during midlife. (p. 523)

   A. ______________________________

   B. ______________________________

   C. ______________________________

5. True or False: Aging has little impact on metacognition. (p. 523)

Practical Problem Solving and Expertise

1. What is practical problem solving? (p. 524)

____

____

2. Expertise (peaks / declines) in midlife. (p. 524)
3. True or False: Advances in expertise are found only among highly educated individuals and business executives. (p. 524)
4. Briefly describe advances in practical problem solving during middle adulthood. (p. 524)

____

____

Creativity

1. Indicate which of the following changes in creativity occur in middle adulthood. (p. 525)

______ Is often spontaneous and intensely emotional
______ Appears more deliberately thoughtful
______ Combines extensive knowledge and experience into unique ways of thinking
______ Focuses on generating unusual products
______ Reflects a largely egocentric concern with self-expression
______ Reflects altruistic goals

Information Processing in Context

1. In what areas are middle-aged adults most likely to experience cognitive gains? (p. 525)

____

____

2. True or False: When given a challenging real-world problem related to their expertise, middle-aged adults are likely to outperform younger adults in both efficiency and quality of thinking. (p. 525)

Vocational Life and Cognitive Development

1. Summarize the relationship between vocational life and cognition. (p. 525)

____

____

____

2. Cross-cultural findings (support / refute) the notion that complex work leads to gains in cognitive flexibility. (p. 525)
3. True or False: The impact of challenging work on cognition is greater in early adulthood than in middle adulthood. (p. 526)

Adult Learners: Becoming a Student in Midlife

1. List several reasons why middle-aged adults may decide to enroll in undergraduate and graduate programs. (p. 526)

____

____

____

Characteristics of Returning Students

1. (Men / Women) represent the majority of adult learners. (p. 526)
2. Describe common feelings of women during their first-year reentry as a student. What factors influence these feelings? (p. 526)

   Common feelings: ____________________

   Influences: ____________________

3. Describe common characteristics of returning women who report high psychological stress. (p. 526)

   ____

4. What is the most common reason women do not complete their degree in middle adulthood? (p. 526)

   ____

Supporting Returning Students

1. List social supports and institutional services that facilitate adult reentry into college. (pp. 526–527)

   Social supports: ____________________

   Institutional services: ____________________

2. Summarize the benefits of adult reentry to college. (p. 527)

   ____

ASK YOURSELF

For *Ask Yourself* questions for this chapter, along with feedback on the accuracy of your answers, please log on to MyDevelopmentLab (for registration and access, please visit mydevelopmentlab.com or follow the instructions on page ix).

(1) Select the Multimedia Library.

(2) Choose the explore option.

(3) Find your chapter from the drop down box.

(4) Click find now.

(5) Complete questions and choose "Submit answers for grading" or "Clear answers" to start over.

SUGGESTED READINGS

Chodzko-Zajko, W., Poon, L. W., & Kramer, A. F. (Eds.). (2009). *Enhancing cognitive functioning and brain plasticity.* Champaign, IL: Human Kinetics Publishing. Using up-to-date research, this book examines the importance of exercise and physical activity for favorable brain development in middle-aged and older adults. It also emphasizes the benefits of cognitive training and intellectual engagement for the aging adult.

Rutter, M. (Ed.). (2008). *Genetic effects on environmental vulnerability to disease*. Hoboken, NJ: John Wiley & Sons. Examines the relationship between biological aging, individual heredity, and environmental vulnerability to illness and disease in older adults. A range of health problems are discussed, including cancer, metabolic disorders, and depression.

Schulkin, J. (2007). *Medical decisions, estrogen and aging*. New York: Springer-Verlag. Based on two large-scale studies of women's health, this book presents findings on menopause and the use of hormone therapy (HT). The author also addresses recent controversies surrounding HT, including advice to women who are considering this option.

CROSSWORD PUZZLE 15.1

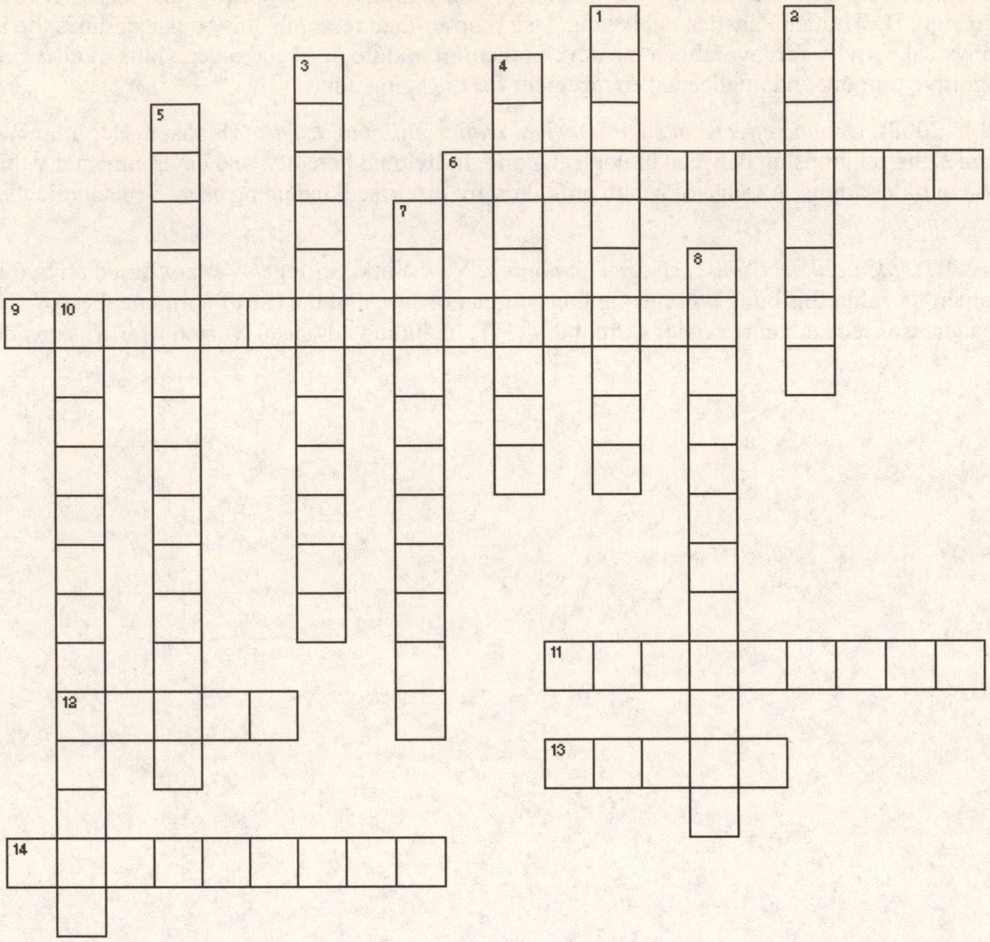

Across

6. Age-related hearing loss
9. ______-______ view: older adults experience greater loss of information as it moves through the cognitive system (2 words, hyph.)
11. The end of menstruation and reproductive capacity in women
12. ______ behavior pattern: competitiveness, ambition, impatience, angry outbursts, and sense of time pressure (2 words)
13. ______ intelligence: largely depends on basic information processing
14. ______ problem solving: sizing up real-world situations and analyzing how best to achieve highly uncertain goals

Down

1. Around age 60, the optic lens loses its capacity to adjust to objects at varying distances.
2. Poor fluid drainage leads to a buildup of pressure within the eye, damaging the optic nerve.
3. ______ intelligence: depends on accumulated knowledge, good judgment, and mastery of social conventions
4. Comprised of commitment, control, and challenge
5, Low daily doses of estrogen (2 words)
7. Midlife transition in which fertility declines
8. Condition associated with severe age-related bone loss
10. ______ view: as neurons die, the brain forms less efficient bypasses (2 words)

PRACTICE TEST #1

1. Throughout adulthood, the size of the pupil __________ and the lens __________. (p. 502)
   a. grows; shrinks
   b. grows; thins
   c. shrinks; thickens
   d. shrinks; yellows

2. Most adult-onset hearing impairments are __________ (p. 503)
   a. age-related.
   b. hereditary.
   c. unpreventable.
   d. untreatable.

3. Which of the following statements about sex differences in muscle-fat makeup in midlife is true? (p. 504)
   a. Women experience a "middle-age spread," whereas men tend to maintain or lose weight.
   b. Men lose lean body mass and weight, and women gain both muscle power and weight.
   c. Men accumulate fat on the waist and upper arms, women on the back and upper abdomen.
   d. Women accumulate fat on the waist and upper arms, men on the back and upper abdomen.

4. Studies on menopause reveal that __________ (p. 504)
   a. complaints about sexual functioning decrease during menopause.
   b. hot flashes and night sweats accompanying menopause are often debilitating.
   c. most women experience episodes of depression during menopause.
   d. complaints about sexual functioning increase during menopause.

5. Animal research suggests that calorie restriction combined with limited consumption of __________ may lead to increased longevity. (p. 505)
   a. iron
   b. protein
   c. fiber
   d. caffeine

6. One large-scale study revealed that hormone replacement therapy (HRT) caused a mild increase in __________, among other conditions. (p. 506)
   a. irritability
   b. depression
   c. heart attacks
   d. migraines

7. What is one likely reason that Western women's experience with menopause differs from that of Asian women? (p. 508)
   a. Asian cultures tend to view menopause as a syndrome requiring treatment, whereas most Western doctors dismiss women's symptoms.
   b. Asian women view menopause as a significant marker of middle age, whereas Western women rarely attribute meaning to menopause.
   c. Because Western women gain respect and social status with age, they report less menopausal distress than Asian women.
   d. Because Asian women gain respect and social status with age, they report less menopausal distress than Western women.

8. Longitudinal research reveals that __________ (p. 509)
   a. frequency of sexual activity drops dramatically in middle adulthood.
   b. frequency of sexual activity typically stabilizes rather than changes dramatically.
   c. intensity of sexual response increases among women, but not men, in middle age.
   d. both intensity and frequency of sexual activity remain stable from early to middle adulthood.

9. In middle age, __________ is the leading cause of death for both men and women. (p. 509)
   a. cardiovascular disease
   b. stroke
   c. cancer
   d. unintentional injury

10. Which indicator of cardiovascular disease is referred to as a "silent killer"? (p. 512)
   a. atherosclerosis—a buildup of plaque in the coronary arteries
   b. heart attack—blockage of normal blood supply to an area of the heart
   c. arrhythmia—an irregular heartbeat
   d. angina pectoris—indigestion-like or crushing chest pains

11. Which of the following can help to treat osteoporosis? (p. 513)
   a. a diet high in protein
   b. a diet enriched with calcium and vitamin D
   c. hormone therapy
   d. angioplasty

12. Robert, a 58-year-old man, has a dominant personality type. In conversation with others, he often interrupts or talks over them, and he regularly lashes out angrily at neighbors, family members, and service people. Because of his hostile emotional style, Robert __________ (p. 514)
   a. may be at reduced risk of heart disease compared to those who "bottle up" their emotions.
   b. likely utilizes a problem-centered coping style.
   c. is at increased risk for heart disease, high blood pressure, and stroke.
   d. is only at increased risk for health problems if he also smokes and/or is overweight.

13. Compared to younger adults, middle-aged adults __________ (p. 515)
   a. are less realistic about their ability to change situations.
   b. are more likely to use emotion-centered coping.
   c. have more difficulty coping with stress.
   d. tend to cope with stress more effectively.

14. Which three personal qualities define a hardy individual? (p. 516)
   a. ambition, competitiveness, and intensity
   b. control, commitment, and challenge
   c. organization, industriousness, and versatility
   d. sensitivity, tolerance, and creativity

15. Which of the following responses to a stressful situation is most consistent with the attitude of a hardy individual? (p. 516)
   a. "I wish I could change how I feel about this."
   b. "I'm just not going to think about it."
   c. "I will do what I can to make this situation better."
   d. "This is going to end badly, and there's nothing I can do."

16. Studies on the double standard of gender and aging reveal that __________ (p. 517)
   a. women tend to judge aging women more harshly than men do.
   b. in recent years, the double standard has become more pronounced.
   c. the double standard is declining as attitudes toward middle age change.
   d. the double standard is a biological, rather than a social, construct.

17. Schaie's sequential design revealed that early cross-sectional research showing a drop-off in intelligence after age 35 resulted largely from __________ (p. 518)
   a. cohort effects.
   b. brain deterioration.
   c. age-related verbal declines.
   d. test bias.

18. Which of the following is associated with fluid intelligence? (p. 519)
    a. good judgment
    b. speed of analyzing information
    c. mastery of social conventions
    d. expertise in a particular subject

19. Many cross-sectional studies show that _____________ increases steadily through middle adulthood, whereas _____________ begins to decline in the twenties. (p. 519)
    a. crystallized intelligence; fluid intelligence
    b. fluid intelligence; general intelligence
    c. problem solving; crystallized intelligence
    d. fluid intelligence; crystallized intelligence

20. What did the Seattle Longitudinal Study reveal about individual differences in intellectual decline? (p. 520)
    a. Age-related declines in intellect were delayed for people who were well-educated, healthy, and economically well-off.
    b. Age related declines occurred at similar rates among middle-aged adults, regardless of educational attainment or SES.
    c. Compared with men, women experienced a more rapid and dramatic drop-off in mental abilities beginning in middle age.
    d. People of all ages scored lower on mental tests than same-age individuals of previous generations.

21. According to the neural network view, what causes age-related slowing of cognitive processing? (p. 521)
    a. Neurons increase in size, resulting in a crowding effect.
    b. Neurons die, resulting in the formation of less efficient connections.
    c. The neural network is adversely affected by changes in the balance of neurotransmitters.
    d. Information loss increases as it moves through the cognitive system.

22. Processing speed __________ (p. 521)
    a. tends to increase in middle adulthood.
    b. is a poor predictor of performance on memory tasks.
    c. contributes to decrements in attention and memory.
    d. tends to decline much earlier in women than men.

23. Angelo, a 60-year-old office manager, finds it hard to ignore outside distractions, such as a ringing telephone, while working. Angelo is experiencing difficulty with __________ (p. 522)
    a. metacognition.
    b. working memory.
    c. problem solving.
    d. cognitive inhibition.

24. With respect to memory in midlife, __________ (p. 522)
    a. the amount of information people can retain in working memory diminishes.
    b. adults more often use memory strategies of rehearsal, organization, and elaboration.
    c. the amount of information people can retain in working memory increases.
    d. adults have great difficulty compensating for memory problems.

25. Donna, a college professor, prepares for lectures by making extensive notes and reviewing them before class. Donna is relying on __________ to maximize her performance. (p. 523)
    a. factual knowledge
    b. procedural knowledge
    c. metacognitive knowledge
    d. practical intelligence

26. Expertise __________ (p. 524)
    a. is negatively affected by declines in processing speed.
    b. is limited to high-SES individuals.
    c. declines sharply in middle adulthood.
    d. is found in adults of all occupations.

27. In middle adulthood, creativity _________ (p. 525)
    a. declines.
    b. increases.
    c. is primarily found in women.
    d. takes new forms.

28. Research on the relationship between vocational life and cognitive development indicates that _________ (p. 526)
    a. the impact of challenging work on cognitive growth is greatest for young adults.
    b. middle-aged adults show as many cognitive gains from complex work as do young adults.
    c. because of declines in attention and memory, middle-aged adults tend to perform poorly on complex work tasks.
    d. cognitive ability affects vocational choice in early adulthood, but not in middle adulthood.

29. About 60 percent of middle-aged adults who return to college are _________ (p. 526)
    a. men.
    b. women.
    c. minorities.
    d. divorced.

30. What is the most common reason that older adults who enroll in college do not finish their degrees? (p. 526)
    a. role overload
    b. lack of motivation
    c. lack of intellectual ability
    d. financial concerns

PRACTICE TEST #2

1. Prominent concerns among middle-aged adults include __________ (p. 502)
   a. getting divorced.
   b. getting a fatal disease.
   c. losing financial stability.
   d. not performing well at work.

2. Glaucoma __________ (p. 503)
   a. is present in most older adults.
   b. is untreatable.
   c. runs in families.
   d. literally means "old eyes."

3. The first sign of presbycusis is __________ (p. 503)
   a. hearing loss at high frequencies.
   b. hearing loss at low frequencies.
   c. difficulty making out human speech.
   d. ringing in the ears.

4. Why does women's skin tend to age more quickly than men's skin? (p. 504)
   a. Women have a thinner dermis than men.
   b. Women have more fat in the hypodermis than men do.
   c. Women have more exaggerated facial expressions than men do.
   d. Women tend to smoke more than men.

5. What do natural experiments, such as studies of Okinawans, suggest about the relationship between calorie intake and longevity? (p. 505)
   a. Heredity plays a larger role in length of lifespan than diet or exercise.
   b. Low-calorie, low-protein diets may actually reduce the lifespan by 5 to 10 years.
   c. Calorie-limited, healthy diets reduce deaths due to cancer and cardiovascular disease.
   d. Calorie restriction in early life or middle age has no apparent health benefits.

6. The period leading up to and following menopause is often accompanied by __________ (p. 504)
   a. memory problems and severe anxiety.
   b. excessive sleep.
   c. a sharp rise in estrogen levels.
   d. mood fluctuations.

7. Despite the potential risks, __________ currently provide(s) the most reliable relief from menopausal symptoms. (p. 506)
   a. hormone therapy
   b. antidepressant medication
   c. vitamin–mineral supplements
   d. a high-protein diet

8. When viewed in a __________ context, attitudes toward menopause tend to be negative. (p. 508)
   a. medical
   b. transitional
   c. social
   d. cultural

9. Which of the following is an accurate description of the climacteric in men? (p. 507)
   a. Some middle-aged men experience erectile dysfunction, but sperm is unchanged in quantity and motility.
   b. Testosterone production declines dramatically after age 40, particularly in sexually active men.
   c. Both testosterone and sperm production decline with age but continue throughout the lifespan.
   d. Testosterone production doubles, while sperm production declines dramatically.

10. In middle age, deaths from __________ occur at a lower rate than in early adulthood. (p. 509)
    a. cancer
    b. falls
    c. cardiovascular disease
    d. motor vehicle collisions

11. Cancer death rates __________ (p. 510)
    a. have increased over the past decade.
    b. increase sharply as SES decreases.
    c. remain stable from early to middle adulthood.
    d. are especially high among high-SES whites.

12. __________ cancer is the most common type of cancer for men, and __________ is the most common type for women. (p. 511)
    a. Lung; breast
    b. Prostate; breast
    c. Prostate; colon
    d. Colon; lung

13. Which of the following interventions reduces risk of heart attack? (p. 512)
    a. treating high blood pressure
    b. drinking 3–4 alcoholic beverages per day
    c. avoiding unnecessary X-ray exposure
    d. a diet high in carbohydrates and protein

14. Which Type A behavior predicts heart disease and other heart problems? (p. 514)
    a. competitiveness
    b. impatience
    c. ambition
    d. hostility

15. When Kathy and her husband divorced after 25 years of marriage, Kathy felt depressed and overwhelmed by the life changes brought on by the divorce. To get through the difficult time, she began to meditate, write in a journal, and take long, solitary walks. Kathy's behavior is an example of __________ coping. (p. 514)
    a. ineffective
    b. escapist
    c. emotion-centered
    d. problem-centered

16. __________ is vital in adopting, maintaining, and exerting oneself in an exercise regimen. (p. 516)
    a. Self-efficacy
    b. Access to a fitness center
    c. A low-stress lifestyle
    d. A group-exercise program

17. High-hardy individuals __________ (p. 516)
    a. more often use emotion-centered or avoidant coping strategies.
    b. more often use active, problem-centered coping strategies.
    c. tend to respond pessimistically to life changes.
    d. report feeling detached from or indifferent toward daily activities.

18. Why might a steep, age-related decline in intelligence appear in cross-sectional, but not longitudinal, studies? (p. 518)
    a. Cross-sectional studies are especially vulnerable to researcher bias.
    b. Cross-sectional studies show the improved health and education of each new generation.
    c. Longitudinal studies reveal the more rigorous education of earlier generations.
    d. Cross-sectional studies are more likely to be affected by cohort effects.

19. .Which of these tasks most clearly makes use of crystallized intelligence? (p. 519)
    a. pressing a button quickly in response to a green light
    b. finding hidden figures in a drawing
    c. expressing ideas and information articulately
    d. creating novel pieces of art work

20. Which of the following abilities decrease steadily from the twenties to the late eighties? (p. 519)
    a. perceptual speed
    b. inductive reasoning
    c. verbal memory
    d. spatial orientation

21. Women outperform men on __________, whereas men outperform women on __________. (p. 520)
    a. inductive reasoning; verbal memory
    b. numeric ability; verbal memory and inductive reasoning
    c. verbal tasks; perceptual speed
    d. verbal tasks and perceptual speed; spatial skills

22. On reaction-time tasks, older adults __________ (p. 521)
    a. perform best on highly complicated tasks.
    b. do best on tasks that require focusing on two activities at the same time.
    c. outperform younger adults in simple, but not complex, situations.
    d. become more disadvantaged as tasks increase in complexity.

23. The information-loss view explains the __________ in middle age by suggesting that older adults lose information with each step of thinking. (p. 521)
    a. ability of the brain to accommodate
    b. loss of creativity
    c. slowdown of cognitive processing
    d. loss of expertise

24. Studies of attention during midlife indicate that __________ (p. 522)
    a. cognitive inhibition improves during middle adulthood.
    b. middle-aged adults have greater difficulty engaging in two activities at the same time.
    c. attention problems are caused by sensory impairments, such as diminished vision and hearing.
    d. practice with attention-related tasks does little to improve attention skills.

25. Declines in working memory in midlife largely result from __________ (p. 523)
    a. changes in the structure of the brain.
    b. declines in metacognitive knowledge.
    c. decreased motivation to learn and remember new information.
    d. infrequent and ineffective use of memory strategies.

26. In which of the following circumstances would an older adult likely perform poorly? (p. 523)
    a. in a self-paced testing condition
    b. in a pressurized testing condition
    c. when asked to relay factual knowledge
    d. when asked to describe a known procedure

27. Why might older adults be particularly adept at practical problem solving? (p. 524)
    a. They are skilled at engaging in two activities at the same time.
    b. They have more expertise from which to draw.
    c. They display superior performance in high-pressure situations.
    d. They can retain a large amount of information in their working memories.

28. Creativity in middle adulthood frequently reflects a transition from __________ (p. 525)
    a. deliberately thoughtful work to more spontaneous expression.
    b. combining knowledge in new ways to generating unusual products.
    c. making new discoveries to summing up or integrating ideas.
    d. altruistic goals to a concern with self-expression.

29. Cognitive flexibility is responsive to vocational experience __________ (p. 526)
    a. only in early adulthood.
    b. primarily in Western cultures.
    c. well into middle adulthood and perhaps beyond.
    d. only when jobs provide minimal stimulation and challenge.

30. The most important factor in the success of returning students is __________ (p. 526)
    a. social support.
    b. high intellectual ability.
    c. financial support.
    d. access to stimulating classes.

CHAPTER 16
EMOTIONAL AND SOCIAL DEVELOPMENT IN MIDDLE ADULTHOOD

BRIEF CHAPTER SUMMARY

Generativity begins in early adulthood but expands greatly as middle-aged adults face Erikson's psychological conflict of midlife: generativity versus stagnation. Highly generative people find fulfillment as they make contributions to society through parenthood, other family relationships, the workplace, volunteer activities, and many forms of productivity and creativity. From Levinson's perspective, middle-aged adults go through a transition in which they reassess their relation to themselves and the world. They confront four developmental tasks, each requiring them to reconcile two opposing tendencies within the self: young–old, destruction–creation, masculinity–femininity, and engagement–separateness. Rebuilding the life structure depends on supportive social contexts. Vaillant added that middle-aged adults become guardians of their culture, and the most successful and best adjusted enter a calmer, quieter time of life. Only a minority experience a midlife crisis characterized by intense self-doubt and stress that lead to drastic life alterations.

Midlife changes in self-concept and personality reflect growing awareness of a finite lifespan, longer life experience, and generative concerns. But certain aspects of personality remain stable, revealing that individual differences established during earlier phases persist. Possible selves become fewer and more realistic. Midlifers also become more introspective, and self-acceptance, autonomy, environmental mastery, and coping strategies improve. Both men and women become more androgynous in middle adulthood—a change that results from a complex combination of social roles and life conditions. Although adults change in overall organization and integration of personality, they do so on a foundation of basic, enduring dispositions.

Because of a declining birthrate and longer life expectancy, the midlife phase of the family life cycle, called "launching children and moving on," has greatly lengthened over the past century. The changes of midlife prompt many adults to focus on improving their marriages, but when divorce occurs, midlifers seem to adapt more easily than do younger people. Gains in practical problem solving and effective coping strategies may reduce the stressful impact of divorce. Most middle-aged parents adjust well to departure of children, especially if the parents have a strong work orientation and if parent–child contact and affection are sustained. When family relationships are positive, grandparenthood is an important means of fulfilling personal and societal needs. A growing number of North American children live apart from their parents in households headed by grandparents, a situation that can create great emotional and financial strain.

Compared with earlier generations, today's adults spend more years not only as parents and grandparents, but also as children of aging parents. The burden of caring for aging parents can be great. Many middle-aged adults become "sandwiched" between the needs of aging parents and assisting young-adult children. Although middle-aged adults often become more appreciative of their parents' strengths and generosity, caring for chronically ill or disabled parents is highly stressful. Sibling contact and support generally declines from early to middle adulthood, although many siblings feel closer, often in response to major life events, such as parental illness. Friendships become fewer and more selective in midlife. Viewing a spouse as a best friend can contribute greatly to marital happiness.

Work continues to be a salient aspect of identity and self-esteem in middle adulthood. More so than in earlier or later years, people attempt to increase the personal meaning and self-direction of their vocational lives. Job satisfaction has both psychological and economic significance. Overall job satisfaction improves during midlife, but burnout has become a greater problem in recent years. Vocational development is less available to older workers, and many women and ethnic minorities leave the corporate world to escape the "glass ceiling," which limits their advancement. Still, radical career changes are rare in middle adulthood. Unemployment is especially difficult for middle-aged individuals, and retirement is an important change that is often stressful, making effective planning important for positive adjustment.

LEARNING OBJECTIVES

After reading this chapter, you should be able to:

16.1 Describe Erikson's stage of generativity versus stagnation, noting major personality changes of middle adulthood and related research findings. (pp. 532–535)

16.2 Discuss Levinson's and Vaillant's views of psychosocial development in middle adulthood, noting gender similarities and differences. (pp. 535–536)

16.3 Summarize research examining the question of whether most middle-aged adults experience a midlife crisis. (pp. 536–537)

16.4 Characterize middle adulthood using a life events approach and a stage approach. (p. 537)

16.5 Describe stability and change in self-concept and personality in middle adulthood. (pp. 538–539)

16.6 Describe changes in gender identity in midlife. (pp. 540–542)

16.7 Discuss stability and change in the "big five" personality traits in adulthood. (pp. 542–543)

16.8 Describe the middle adulthood phase of the family life cycle, and discuss midlife marital relationships and relationships with adult children, grandchildren, and aging parents. (pp. 543–551)

16.9 Describe midlife sibling relationships and friendships. (pp. 551–553)

16.10 Discuss job satisfaction and career development in middle adulthood, paying special attention to gender differences and experiences of ethnic minorities. (pp. 553–555)

16.11 Describe career change and unemployment in middle adulthood. (p. 556)

16.12 Discuss the importance of planning for retirement, noting various issues that middle-aged adults should address. (pp. 556–557)

STUDY QUESTIONS

1. Summarize the aim and research methods of the Midlife Development in the United States (MIDUS) study. (p. 532)

Aim: ____

____

Research Methods: ____

____

Erikson's Theory: Generativity versus Stagnation

1. ______________ involves reaching out to others in ways that give to and guide the next generation. Cite characteristics of adults who possess this trait. (p. 532)

____

____

2. In addition to parenting, list four ways adults can be generative. (p. 533)

A. ______________________ C. ______________________

B. ______________________ D. ______________________

3. Explain how *generativity* brings together personal desires and cultural demands. (p. 533)

   Personal desires: ______________________________

   ____

   Cultural demands: ______________________________

   ____

4. Cite characteristics of adults who develop a sense of *stagnation*. (p. 533)

   ____

   ____

5. Indicate whether the following statements about generativity are true (T) or false (F). (pp. 533–534)

   ______ Generativity tends to increase in midlife.
   ______ Highly generative people are especially well-adjusted.
   ______ Having children seems to foster generative development more in men than in women.
   ______ Religiosity and spirituality are linked to greater generativity.

A Lifespan Vista: Generative Adults Tell Their Life Stories

1. Cite themes commonly found in the narratives of highly generative people. (p. 534)

   ____

   ____

   ____

2. True or False: Less generative adults tell stories in which good scenes turn bad. (p. 534)

3. True or False: Adults high and low in generativity do not differ in the number of positive and negative events included in their narratives. (p. 534)

4. Cite positive outcomes linked with redemptive events in one's life stories. (p. 534)

   ____

   ____

Other Theories of Psychosocial Development in Midlife

Levinson's Seasons of Life

1. According to Levinson, what four developmental tasks do midlifers confront in order to reassess their relation to themselves and to the external world? (p. 535)

   A. ______________________________

   B. ______________________________

   C. ______________________________

   D. ______________________________

2. True or False: Middle-aged men do not express concern about appearing less attractive as they grow older. (p. 535)

3. Cite several ways in which the desire for a legacy can be satisfied in midlife. (p. 535)

____

____

4. Explain how men and women reconcile masculine and feminine parts of the self in middle age. (pp. 535–536)

   Men: ____

   ____

   Women: ____

   ____

5. True or False: Midlife requires that men and women with highly active, successful careers reduce their concern with ambition and achievement and focus on themselves. (p. 536)

6. Describe several social contexts that restrict midlifers' ability to adjust to age-related changes. (p. 536)

____

____

____

7. True or False: Opportunities for advancement ease the transition to middle adulthood. (p. 536)

Vaillant's Adaptation to Life

1. According to Vaillant, what is unique about midlife for the most-successful and best-adjusted individuals? (p. 536)

____

____

2. What personal changes occur as people approach the end of middle age? (p. 536)

____

____

Is There a Midlife Crisis?

1. What characteristics are implied by the term *midlife crisis*? (p. 536)

____

____

2. True or False: Turning points in midlife are often negative, resembling midlife crises. (p. 536)

3. Explain the connection between midlife regrets and well-being. (p. 537)

____

____

____

4. What are some characteristics of adults who experience a midlife crisis? (p. 537)

____

____

Stage or Life Events Approach

1. Cite evidence that emotional and social development is characterized by both continuity and stagewise change. (p. 537)
   Continuity: ____
   ____
   ____
   Stagewise change: ____
   ____
   ____

Stability and Change in Self-Concept and Personality

Possible Selves

1. ______________________ are future-oriented representations of what one hopes to become and what one is afraid of becoming. (p. 538)

2. Indicate whether the following descriptions are typical of *possible selves* in early (E) or middle (M) adulthood. (p. 538)
   _____ Many possible selves
   _____ More modest and concrete
   _____ Concerned with current roles and responsibilities
   _____ Fewer possible selves
   _____ Lofty, idealistic visions
   _____ Reflect a desire to be the best

3. How do possible selves differ from self-concept? (p. 538)
   ____
   ____

Self-Acceptance, Autonomy, and Environmental Mastery

1. Three traits have been found to increase from early to middle adulthood and then level off in well-educated adults. Match each trait with its description. (p. 539)
   _____ Acknowledging both good and bad qualities and feeling positively about oneself
   _____ Seeing oneself as capable of mastering a complex array of tasks
   _____ Feeling less concerned about others' evaluations and more concerned with following self-chosen standards

   A. Self-acceptance
   B. Autonomy
   C. Environmental mastery

2. True or False: Prevailing social expectations have little impact on psychological well-being. (p. 539)

3. Why do Korean middle-aged adults report lower levels of well-being than their North American counterparts? (p. 539)
   ____
   ____
   ____

Biology and Environment: What Factors Promote Psychological Well-Being in Midlife?

1. Explain how exercise promotes well-being in midlife. (p. 540)
   ____
   ____

2. _______________ refers to the psychological state of being so engrossed in a demanding, meaningful activity that one loses all sense of time and self-awareness. Why does this state increase in middle adulthood? (p. 540)

____

____

____

3. Cite two factors in early adulthood that are among the best predictors of midlife well-being. (p. 540)

A. ____

B. ____

4. True or False: Friendships are more effective than a good marriage in boosting psychological well-being in midlife. (p. 541)

5. Adults who occupy (one or two / multiple) roles and who also report (low / high) control score especially high in well-being. (p. 541)

Coping with Daily Stressors

1. Midlife brings a(n) (decrease / increase) in effective coping strategies. (p. 539)

2. Indicate which of the following statements are true of middle-aged adults' coping strategies. (pp. 539–540)

Compared with young adults, middle-aged adults are more likely to…
_____ act quickly and decisively.
_____ identify the positive side of difficult situations.
_____ postpone action to permit evaluation of alternatives.
_____ use humor to express themselves without offending others.
_____ rely mostly upon emotion-centered coping.
_____ anticipate and plan ways to handle future discomforts.

3. Cite three possible reasons why effective coping strategies increase in middle adulthood. (p. 540)

A. ____

B. ____

C. ____

Gender Identity

1. Gender identity becomes (less / more) androgynous in midlife. Explain your answer. (p. 541)

____

____

2. How does *parental imperative theory* explain androgyny in later life? (p. 541)

____

____

____

3. True or False: Longitudinal studies show that children's departure from the home is responsible for midlife androgyny in both men and women. (p. 542)

4. How do social roles influence gender identity in midlife? (p. 542)

____

____

Individual Differences in Personality Traits

1. Below are descriptions of individuals who are each high in one of the *"big five" personality traits*. Match each description with the correct trait. (p. 542)

_____ Soft-hearted, trusting, generous, lenient, and good-natured	A. Neuroticism
_____ Hardworking, well-organized, ambitious, and persevering	B. Extroversion
_____ Worrying, temperamental, self-pitying, and self-conscious	C. Openness to experience
_____ Affectionate, talkative, active, fun-loving, and passionate	D. Agreeableness
_____ Imaginative, creative, original, curious, and liberal	E. Conscientiousness

2. Which "big five" personality traits show modest declines in midlife? Which ones increase? (p. 542)

Decline: ____

Increase: ____

3. How do theorists who emphasize change in personality during midlife differ from those who emphasize stability? (pp. 542–543)

Change: ____

____

Stability: ____

____

Relationships at Midlife

1. True or False: People tend to have a larger number of close relationships during midlife than at any other period. (p. 543)

Marriage and Divorce

1. True or False: Middle-aged adults are more likely than younger or older adults in other age groups to experience financial difficulty. (p. 544)
2. True or False: Midlifers seem to adapt more easily to divorce than younger people. (p. 544)
3. Highly educated middle-aged adults are (less / more) likely to divorce. (p. 544)
4. Marital breakup is a strong contributor to the *feminization of poverty*. Explain what this means. (p. 544)

____

____

____

5. List outcomes for middle-aged women who weather divorce successfully. (p. 544)

____

____

____

Changing Parent–Child Relationships

1. True or False: Most parents adjust well to their children's departure. (p. 545)
2. Cite factors that affect adjustment to changing parent–child relationships in midlife. (p. 545)

   ____

   ____
3. True or False: The social clock for children's departure is fairly consistent across cultures. (p. 545)
4. Parents who are warm and supportive in middle childhood and adolescence are (less / more) likely to experience contact and closeness with their child in early adulthood. (p. 545)
5. Throughout middle adulthood, parents give (less / more) assistance to children than they receive. (p. 545)
6. Once young adults strike out on their own, members of the middle generation, especially mothers, usually take on the role of ____________________, gathering the family for celebrations and making sure everyone stays in touch. (p. 545)

Grandparenthood

1. On average, American adults become grandparents in their ____________. (p. 545)
2. List four commonly mentioned gratifications of grandparenthood. (p. 546)

   A. ______________________ C. ______________________

   B. ______________________ D. ______________________
3. How do grandparent–grandchild relationships change with the grandchild's age? (pp. 546–547)

   ____

   ____

   ____
4. Cite several factors that impact grandparents' bond and face-to-face interaction with grandchildren. (pp. 546–547)

   ____

   ____

   ____
5. Typically, (same-sex / other-sex) grandparents and grandchildren are closer, especially (maternal / paternal) (grandfathers / grandmothers) and (granddaughters / grandsons). (p. 547)
6. Explain how SES and ethnicity influence grandparent–grandchild ties. (p. 547)

   SES: ____

   ____

   Ethnicity: ____

   ____
7. True or False: All 50 U.S. states currently permit grandparents to seek legal visitation judgments. (p. 547)

Social Issues: Grandparents Rearing Grandchildren: The Skipped-Generation Family

1. What are *skipped-generation families*? (p. 548)

2. The number of grandparents raising grandchildren has (decreased / remained constant / increased) over the past two decades. (p. 548)

3. Cite several reasons why grandparents step in and rear grandchildren. (p. 548)

4. Describe challenges grandparents encounter when they raise grandchildren. (p. 548)

5. True or False: Custodial grandparents report less satisfaction with the grandparent role than typical grandparents. (p. 548)

Middle-Aged Children and Their Aging Parents

1. True or False: Adults of past generations were more devoted to their aging parents than adults of the present generation. (p. 549)

2. In midlife, the (father / mother)–(daughter / son) relationship tends to be closer than other parent–child ties. (p. 549)

3. True or False: In collectivist cultures, older adults often live with their married children. (p. 549)

4. Why are today's middle-aged adults called the *sandwich generation*? (p. 550)

5. Why are women more often principal caregivers of aging parents? (p. 550)

6. True or False: The care sons and daughters provide for their aging parents tends to be divided along gender-role lines. (p. 550)

7. Explain why caring for a chronically ill or disabled parent is radically different from caring for a young child. (p. 550)

8. What emotional and physical health consequences are associated with parental caregiving? (p. 551)

9. List four ways to relieve the stress of caring for an aging parent. (pp. 551–552)

   A.

   B.

   C.

   D.

Siblings

1. Sibling contact and support (decline / increase) from early to middle adulthood, yet siblings often feel (less / more) close in midlife. (p. 551)
2. True or False: As siblings get older, good relationships often strengthen and poor relationships often worsen. (p. 551)
3. Explain how sibling relationships in village societies differ from those in industrialized nations. (p. 552)

____

____

____

Friendships

1. Indicate whether the following descriptions are more typical of men's (M) or women's (W) midlife friendships. (p. 552)

_____ Are less intimate
_____ Report a greater number of close friends
_____ Most are couple-based
_____ Focus on feelings and life problems
_____ Tend to discuss sports, politics, and business
_____ Provide friends with more emotional support

2. Number of friends (declines / remains constant / increases) with age. (p. 552)
3. Describe different aspects of psychological well-being supported by family relationships and friendships. (p. 553)

Family: ____________________

____

Friendships: ____________________

____

Vocational Life

1. True or False: Work continues to be a salient aspect of identity and self-esteem in middle adulthood. (p. 553)
2. Cite aspects of job performance that improve in midlife. (p. 553)

____

____

3. The number of older workers will (decline / rise) dramatically over the next few decades. What two factors are responsible for this? (p. 553)

A. ____________________

B. ____________________

Job Satisfaction

1. Research shows that job satisfaction (decreases / increases) in midlife at all occupational levels. (p. 553)
2. Describe one aspect of job satisfaction that rises with age and one that remains stable. (pp. 553–554)

Rises: ____________________

Remains stable: ____________________

3. Under what occupational conditions is *burnout* likely to occur? (p. 554)

4. True or False: Burnout is a serious occupational hazard. (p. 554)
5. How can employers prevent burnout? (p. 554)

Career Development

1. Training and on-the-job career counseling are (less / equally / more) available to older workers. (p. 554)
2. List characteristics of the person and the work environment that influence employees' willingness to engage in job training and updating. (p. 554)

   Personal characteristics:

   Workplace characteristics:

3. How do age-balanced work groups foster on-the-job learning? (p. 554)

4. List four workplace factors that contribute to a *glass ceiling* effect for women and ethnic minorities. (p. 555)

   A.

   B.

   C.

   D.

5. (Few / Most) start-up businesses in the United States are owned and operated by women, and (few / most) of those achieve or exceed their business goals. (p. 556)

Career Change at Midlife

1. What kind of midlife career changes are most common? (p. 556)

2. True or False: When an extreme career shift occurs, it usually signals a personal crisis. (p. 556)

Unemployment

1. True or False: As companies downsize and jobs are eliminated, the majority of people affected are middle-aged and older. (p. 556)
2. Unemployment affects middle-aged adults (less / more) negatively than younger adults. Explain your answer. (p. 556)

3. Which forms of social support are most effective for reducing stress and reassuring middle-aged job seekers of their worth? (p. 556)

____

____

Planning for Retirement

1. The average age of retirement (declined / increased) during the past several decades. (p. 557)
2. What are some benefits of retirement planning? (p. 557)

____

____

3. True or False: In the United States, the federal government offers a pension system that guarantees an adequate standard of living. (p. 557)
4. (Financial planning / Planning for an active life) has a greater impact on happiness after retirement than (financial planning / planning for an active life). (p. 557)
5. True or False: Less well-educated people with lower lifetime earnings are least likely to attend retirement preparation programs. (p. 557)

ASK YOURSELF . . .

For *Ask Yourself* questions for this chapter, along with feedback on the accuracy of your answers, please log on to MyDevelopmentLab (for registration and access, please visit mydevelopmentlab.com or follow the instructions on page ix).

(1) Select the Multimedia Library.

(2) Choose the explore option.

(3) Find your chapter from the drop down box.

(4) Click find now.

(5) Complete questions and choose "Submit answers for grading" or "Clear answers" to start over.

SUGGESTED READINGS

Hedge, J. W., Borman, W. C., & Lammlein, S. E. (2006). *The aging workforce: Realities, myths, and implications for organizations.* Washington, DC: American Psychological Association. Examines the strengths, limitations, expertise, and unique needs of workers over age 60. The authors also address myths and stereotypes about the aging workforce, age discrimination, and strategies for attracting and retaining older workers.

Waldron, V. R., & Kelley, D. L. (2009). *Marriage at midlife.* New York: Springer. Using hundreds of interviews with couples who have been married between 20 and 50 years, this book describes the highlights and challenges of midlife marriage. The authors emphasize the importance of communication and renegotiating the marital relationship following significant events, such as children leaving the home and retirement.

Whitbourne, S., & Willis, S. L. (Eds.). (2006). *The baby boomers grow up: Contemporary perspectives on midlife.* Mahwah, NJ: Erlbaum. Examines development among baby boomers, including how this generation has influenced our perceptions of midlife. Topics include physical and mental health issues, identity development, intergenerational relationships, and work and retirement.

CROSSWORD PUZZLE 16.1

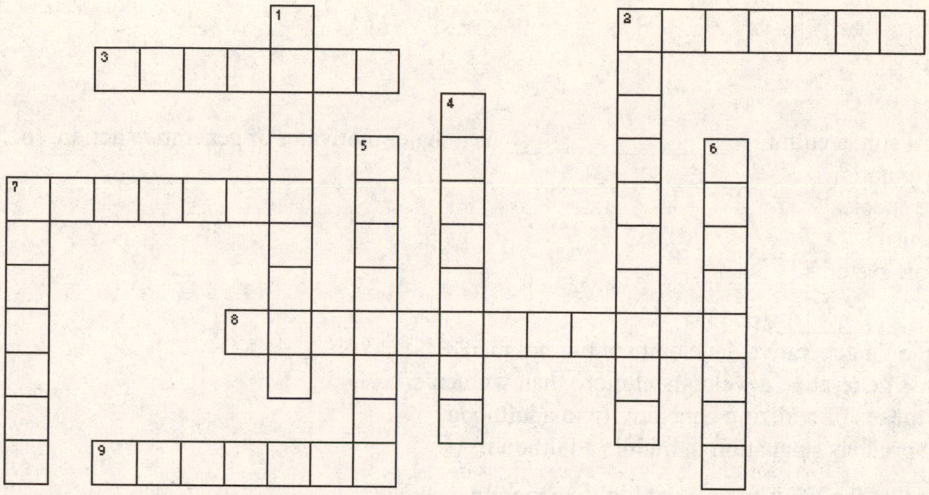

Across

2. ______-generation family: children live with grandparents but apart from parents
3. Glass _____: invisible barrier to advancement up the corporate ladder faced by women and ethnic minorities
7. "______ ______" personality traits: neuroticism, extroversion, openness to experience, agreeableness, and conscientiousness
8. ______ of poverty: self-supporting women constitute most of the adult population living in poverty
9. ______ crisis: time of self-doubt and stress, prompting major restructuring of the personality

Down

1. Person who gathers the family for celebrations and makes sure everyone stays in touch
2. Generativity versus ______: Erikson's psychological conflict of midlife
4. ______ generation: middle-aged adults must care for multiple generations above and below them simultaneously
5. ______ selves: future-oriented representations of what one hopes or is afraid to become
6. ______ imperative theory: traditional gender roles are maintained throughout active parenting to ensure children's survival
7. Long-term job stress leads to mental exhaustion, a sense of loss of personal control, and feelings of reduced accomplishment.

PRACTICE TEST #1

1. Erikson's psychological conflict of midlife is called generativity versus __________ (p. 532)
   a. isolation.
   b. obligation.
   c. deprivation.
   d. stagnation.

2. According to Erikson, a culture's _________________ is a major motivator of generative action. (p. 533)
   a. religious orientation
   b. belief in the species
   c. sense of security
   d. set of support systems

3. Having children __________ (p. 533)
   a. fosters women's generative development but not men's.
   b. fosters men's generative development more than women's.
   c. is the only means of realizing generativity in adulthood.
   d. moderately predicts stagnation in middle adulthood.

4. Research shows that the life narratives of highly generative people __________ (p. 534)
   a. gloss over negative events and emphasize positive ones.
   b. are often told in a disorderly sequence.
   c. often include subtle moral lessons.
   d. typically contain both blessing and suffering.

5. A middle-aged person who feels regret about her past hurtful acts and who wants to leave a positive legacy is involved in Levinson's developmental task of __________ (p. 535)
   a. young–old.
   b. masculinity–femininity.
   c. destruction–creation.
   d. engagement–separateness.

6. As people approach the end of middle age, they focus on __________ (p. 536)
   a. short-term personal goals, such as reuniting with an old friend.
   b. short-term professional goals, such as a work promotion.
   c. long-term, less personal goals, such as the state of human relations.
   d. achieving fundamental change through challenging society's beliefs.

7. Levinson reported that during the transition to middle adulthood, most men and women in his samples experienced __________ (p. 536)
   a. substantial inner turmoil.
   b. slow, steady changes.
   c. smooth acceptance of aging.
   d. personal and financial gratification.

8. Most MIDUS respondents who reported a midlife crisis __________ (p. 537)
   a. attributed the crisis to fears of growing older.
   b. attributed the crisis to challenging life events.
   c. were emotionally unstable in adolescence and early adulthood.
   d. were between ages 45 and 50 at the time of the crisis.

9 At lunch, Louisa tells a colleague, "I'm thinking about changing jobs. I feel like I'm doing the same thing day after day. Or maybe I can save some money and start a small business in a few years. I've always wanted to do that, and if I don't do it soon, it will never happen." Louisa is discussing __________ (p. 538)
   a. possible selves.
   b. emotion-centered coping.
   c. environmental mastery.
   d. self-acceptance.

10. Studies reveal that self-esteem in older adults equals or surpasses that of younger adults. How do researchers explain this trend? (p. 538)
    a. Middle-aged adults receive more positive feedback from others.
    b. Middle-aged adults tend to focus more on themselves than other people.
    c. Middle-aged adults adjust possible selves in response to life disappointments.
    d. Middle-aged adults are more likely to utilize emotion-centered coping strategies.

11. Which of the following statements about the relationship between marriage and mental health is true? (p. 540)
    a. The role of marriage in mental health decreases throughout the lifespan.
    b. The role of marriage in mental health increases throughout the lifespan.
    c. Close friendships are more powerful predictors of mental health than marriage.
    d. Marriage predicts well-being, but only among highly educated, affluent couples.

12. Compared with young adults, middle-aged adults are more likely to __________ (p. 540)
    a. perceive their stressors as disruptive and unpleasant.
    b. report frequent stress due to role overload.
    c. act quickly when confronted with a problem.
    d. cope effectively with difficult situations.

13. Critics of parental imperative theory point out that __________ (p. 541)
    a. in early adulthood, women take on a nurturing role.
    b. people become more androgynous after their children reach adulthood.
    c. even women without children display "masculine" traits in middle adulthood.
    d. men with grown children tend to become more independent and assertive as they age.

14. The middle adulthood phase of the family life cycle is known as __________ (p. 543)
    a. "launching children and moving on."
    b. "breaking down and building anew."
    c. the "goodbye phase."
    d. the "empty nest."

15. In inner cities, welfare recipients often include a large number of single mothers. This trend is an example of __________ (p. 544)
    a. the parental imperative theory.
    b. the feminization of poverty.
    c. environmental mastery.
    d. the glass ceiling.

16. Which of the following statements about gender differences in midlife divorce is true? (p. 544)
    a. Women who initiate a divorce are more likely than male initiators to have another relationship to turn to.
    b. Newly divorced women are far more likely than men to say they value equal friendship over passionate love.
    c. Men tend to mention their own desire for autonomy as a reason for divorce, whereas women admit they were emotionally inattentive.
    d. Women are more likely than men to initiate divorce, and those who do tend to fare better psychologically.

17. Which of the following is linked to a decline in life satisfaction in midlife? (p. 546)
    a. departure of children when little or no communication is sustained
    b. providing emotional and financial support to adult children
    c. prolonged intimacy with adult children and an enlarged family network
    d. adult children's lack of success in meeting educational or occupational goals

18. What is one way that middle-aged parents can promote positive ties with their adult children? (p. 546)
    a. Encourage adult children to follow family traditions and lifestyles.
    b. Step in to help adult children fix their personal problems.
    c. Avoid comments that are a holdover from childhood.
    d. Hold adult children to high standards of achievement.

19. What is the strongest predictor of frequent interaction between grandparents and their young grandchildren? (p. 546)
    a. the grandchildren's gender
    b. grandparents' financial stability
    c. grandparents living near their grandchildren
    d. grandparents' lack of work or social commitments

20. After a parental divorce, grandparents __________ (p. 547)
    a. are permitted to seek legal visitation judgments in all 50 U.S. states.
    b. have no legal recourse if parents refuse to grant them contact with grandchildren.
    c. nearly always take on the role of "constructive helper" in custody disputes.
    d. often lose touch with their grandchildren, even if they are related to the custodial parent.

21. In about half of skipped-generation families, grandparents take on custody of their grandchildren because the parents __________ (p. 548)
    a. are no longer living.
    b. have substance abuse problems.
    c. returned to college or started a new career.
    d. abandoned the children.

22. Mother–daughter relationships __________ (p. 549)
    a. are less close than other parent–child bonds.
    b. are often characterized by competition and conflict.
    c. become less complex as the daughter moves into middle age.
    d. become more complex as the daughter moves into middle age.

23. Adult caregivers of aging parents experience the most stress when __________ (p. 550)
    a. they also have full-time jobs.
    b. they must live apart from their parents.
    c. their parents have mentally deteriorated.
    d. they must help parents with day-to-day activities.

24. Compared with middle-aged men, middle-aged women __________ (p. 552)
    a. are more likely to view their spouse as their best friend.
    b. have more couple-based, rather than independent, friendships.
    c. are less likely to view their friendships as pleasurable.
    d. have a greater number of close friends.

25. In middle age, productivity at work __________ (p. 553)
    a. declines, partly due to slower decision making.
    b. declines, due to a high rate of absenteeism.
    c. equals or exceeds that of younger workers.
    d. remains stable, despite workers' increased unhappiness.

26. Research shows that job satisfaction increases in midlife __________ (p. 553)
    a. for men, but not for women.
    b. for white-collar, but not blue-collar, workers.
    c. only for those in helping professions.
    d. in diverse nations and at all occupational levels.

27. Which of the following is a powerful predictor of employees' efforts to develop their career skills? (p. 554)
    a. routine tasks at work
    b. a solitary work environment
    c. self-efficacy
    d. age-segregated work groups

28. When an extreme career shift occurs, it is usually __________ (p. 556)
    a. a positive step toward career advancement.
    b. an indication of a personal crisis.
    c. the result of unemployment.
    d. due to discrimination in the workplace.

29. Compared with younger people, middle-aged workers who lose their jobs __________ (p. 556)
    a. are more likely to return to college.
    b. show a sharper decline in physical and mental health.
    c. are more likely to find another job quickly.
    d. tend to more readily embrace their new freedom.

30. Which of the following statements about retirement in the U.S. is true? (p. 556)
    a. Social Security guarantees an adequate income after retirement.
    b. The retirement age in the United States is much higher than other nations.
    c. Baby boomers are likely to retire earlier than the previous generation.
    d. Today, the average age of retirement in the United States is 62.

PRACTICE TEST #2

1. At middle age, Donald's thoughts focus mainly on what he can get or preserve for himself. He takes little interest in his grown children or his new grandchild, and in conversations with neighbors and co-workers, he seems disengaged unless they have something specific to offer him. Donald has a sense of __________ (p. 532)
   a. obligation.
   b. stagnation.
   c. generativity.
   d. incompetence.

2. Which of the following tends to increase in midlife? (p. 532)
   a. stagnation
   b. emotion-centered coping
   c. self-absorption
   d. generativity

3. In the 1990s, the aim of the MIDUS study was to __________ (p. 533)
   a. promote self-efficacy in middle-aged adults.
   b. identify factors contributing to exceptional longevity.
   c. generate new knowledge on the challenges of middle-aged adults.
   d. identify middle-aged adults who were at risk for emotional or physical illness.

4. A major theme of the commitment stories told by generative adults is __________ (p. 534)
   a. redemption.
   b. fear.
   c. contamination.
   d. justice.

5. Which of the following groups reports the greatest rise in sensitivity to the physical changes of aging in middle age? (p. 535)
   a. non-college-educated women
   b. college-educated women
   c. non-college-educated men
   d. college-educated men

6. Yolanda stayed home for many years to raise her children and then care for her aging mother. At age 46, she felt a strong desire to launch a career. Over the next few years, she earned a college degree and became a nurse. Yolanda's experience illustrates one example of Levinson's __________ task. (p. 536)
   a. destruction–creation
   b. engagement–separateness
   c. young–old
   d. masculinity–femininity

7. __________ middle-aged adults experience a midlife crisis that results in drastic life alterations. (p. 537)
   a. A minority of
   b. Ethnic minority
   c. Low-SES
   d. Nearly all

8. Studies on regret in midlife show that compared with those who modify their lives due to regrets, women who acknowledge regrets without making life changes __________ (p. 537)
   a. report less favorable psychological well-being.
   b. have fewer financial and social resources.
   c. are more confident and assertive.
   d. report greater life satisfaction and better health.

9. With age, possible selves become __________ (p. 538)
   a. greater in number.
   b. less important.
   c. more modest.
   d. more idealistic.

10. Middle age is referred to as "the prime of life," but middle-aged adults of different cohorts and cultures __________ (p. 539)
   a. vary widely on the factors that contribute to well-being.
   b. often experience a midlife crisis in their late twenties or early thirties.
   c. describe their twenties and thirties as a period of transitions and uncertainty.
   d. rate their children's success above all other factors.

11. When Max is engrossed in his work, he loses all sense of time and self-awareness. Max is experiencing the enjoyable psychological state known as __________ (p. 540)
   a. self-efficacy.
   b. generativity.
   c. flow.
   d. absorption.

12. For both sexes, gender identity in middle adulthood becomes more __________ (p. 541)
   a. feminine.
   b. masculine.
   c. androgynous.
   d. traditional.

13. Which of the "big five" personality traits increase from the teenage years through middle age? (p. 542)
   a. neuroticism and openness to experience
   b. extroversion and openness to experience
   c. conscientiousness and agreeableness
   d. extroversion and agreeableness

14. Studies show that 9 out of 10 middle-aged people __________ (p. 543)
   a. live with families, usually with a spouse.
   b. live alone after their children are grown.
   c. are or will eventually be divorced.
   d. come from families that have experienced divorce.

15. Which of the following statements about divorce in midlife is true? (p. 544)
   a. Most divorces occur after 20 years or more of marriage.
   b. Middle-aged adults have extreme difficulty adapting to life after divorce.
   c. Middle-aged adults who are highly educated are more likely to divorce.
   d. After a midlife divorce, women fare better than men.

16. After "launching" their children, most parents __________ (p. 545)
   a. go through an extended grieving process.
   b. lose interest in the parental role.
   c. adapt well, especially if they have a strong work orientation.
   d. adapt poorly, especially if close contact with children is sustained.

17. Marcia's ability to keep her family of grown children together by holding bimonthly parties and get-togethers at her home shows that she has __________ (p. 545)
   a. mastered her femininity.
   b. become more androgynous.
   c. adopted the parental imperative theory.
   d. taken on the role of kinkeeper.

18. Which pair typically has the closest relationship? (p. 547)
    a. maternal grandmother and granddaughter
    b. paternal grandfather and grandson
    c. maternal grandfather and granddaughter
    d. paternal grandmother and grandson

19. Which of the following accurately describes an influence of SES or ethnicity on grandchild–grandparent ties? (p. 547)
    a. In low-income families, the grandparent role takes a variety of forms, whereas in high-income families, the grandparent role is usually central to family maintenance.
    b. In low-income families, grandparents often perform specific, essential functions, whereas in high-income families, the grandparent role is more unstructured.
    c. Nonminority parents are more likely than ethnic-minority parents to place young children in grandparents' care while they are at work.
    d. Chinese, Korean, Mexican-American, and Native-American grandparents tend to be less involved in the grandparent role than nonminority grandparents.

20. In most skipped-generation families, grandparents __________ (p. 548)
    a. were pressured by child welfare authorities to take in the grandchildren.
    b. experience both emotional and financial strains.
    c. are financially well-off and, therefore, rarely experience money problems after taking in a grandchild.
    d. welcome a second chance at raising children.

21. Compared to adult children of past generations, today's adult children __________ (p. 549)
    a. are less likely to visit or call their aging parents.
    b. spend less time in physical proximity to their parents.
    c. are more likely to live with their aging parents.
    d. are more likely to resent having to care for a sick parent.

22. Because they must often care for multiple generations at the same time, middle-aged adults are often referred to as the __________ generation. (p. 550)
    a. glass ceiling
    b. kinkeeper
    c. burnout
    d. sandwich

23. Which of the following statements about caring for aging parents is true? (p. 550)
    a. In Asian cultures, daughters usually care for aging parents, while in most Western cultures, sons and daughters take on equal responsibility.
    b. In all ethnic groups, responsibility for providing care for aging parents falls more on daughters than on sons.
    c. Because of physical proximity, fewer commitments, and parental preference, sons take on more responsibility for their aging parents than daughters do.
    d. As adults move from early to later middle age, the sex difference in parental caregiving increases.

24. Caregivers who __________ tend to best cope with stress. (p. 551)
    a. have social support
    b. take a leave of absence from work
    c. feel a cultural obligation toward their parents
    d. use emotion-centered coping strategies

25. During middle adulthood, many siblings __________ (p. 551)
    a. feel less close than they did in early adulthood.
    b. report strained relations.
    c. feel closer than they did in early adulthood.
    d. provide each other with more support than at any other time of life.

26. Which of the following is true of friendships in middle age? (p. 552)
    a. For both men and women, the number of friends declines with age.
    b. Middle-aged people attach less value to friendships than younger people.
    c. In middle age, men's friendships become as intimate as women's friendships.
    d. Viewing one's spouse as a best friend predicts depression and low life satisfaction.

27. Job burnout __________ (p. 554)
    a. occurs less often in the United States than in Western Europe.
    b. is unpreventable in most occupations.
    c. occurs more often in helping professions.
    d. is associated with psychological well-being in middle age.

28. Women face a glass ceiling in their careers because __________ (p. 555)
    a. they are less effective managers than men.
    b. modern businesses realize that the best managers display "masculine" traits.
    c. they have less access to mentors, role models, and informal networks than men.
    d. they are less committed to their careers than men.

29. Research shows that job loss __________ (p. 556)
    a. can disrupt major tasks of midlife, such as generativity.
    b. has more negative consequences for younger adults than middle-aged adults.
    c. often prompts middle-aged workers to return to college.
    d. often prompts older adults to reappraise life goals and accomplishments.

30. Financial planning in preparation for retirement is __________ (p. 557)
    a. required by most public and private organizations in the U.S.
    b. especially important for individuals in high-status positions.
    c. primarily geared toward early retirees, who often underestimate the costs associated with growing older.
    d. especially important for women and low-income retirees.

CHAPTER 17
PHYSICAL AND COGNITIVE DEVELOPMENT IN LATE ADULTHOOD

BRIEF CHAPTER SUMMARY

Vastly different rates of aging are apparent in late adulthood. A complex array of genetic and environmental factors combine to determine longevity. Dramatic gains in average life expectancy—the number of years that an individual born in a particular year can expect to live—provide powerful support for the multiplicity of factors that slow biological aging, including improved nutrition, medical treatment, sanitation, and safety. Although most Americans over age 65 can live independently, some need assistance with activities of daily living or, more commonly, with instrumental activities of daily living, such as shopping and paying bills.

The programmed effects of specific genes, as well as the random cellular events believed to underlie biological aging, make physical declines more apparent in late adulthood. Although aging of the nervous system affects a wide range of complex activities, research reveals that the brain can respond adaptively to some of these age-related cognitive declines. Changes in sensory functioning become increasingly noticeable in late life: Older adults see and hear less well, and taste, smell, and touch sensitivity may also decline. Hearing impairments are far more common than visual impairments and affect many more men than women.

Aging of the cardiovascular and respiratory systems becomes more apparent in late adulthood. As at earlier ages, not smoking, reducing dietary fat, avoiding environmental pollutants, and exercising can slow the effects of aging on these systems. A less competent immune system can increase the elderly person's risk for a variety of illnesses, including infectious diseases, cardiovascular disease, certain forms of cancer, and a variety of autoimmune disorders.

As people age, they have more difficulty falling asleep, staying asleep, and sleeping deeply—a trend that begins earlier for men than for women. Outward signs of aging, such as white hair, wrinkled and sagging skin, age spots, and decreases in height and weight, become more noticeable in late adulthood. Problem-centered coping strategies yield improved physical functioning in the elderly, and assistive technology is increasingly available to help older people cope with physical declines.

Physical and mental health are intimately related in late life. The physical changes of late life lead to an increased need for certain nutrients, and exercise continues to be a powerful health intervention. Although sexual desire and frequency of sexual activity decline in older people, longitudinal evidence indicates that most healthy older married couples report continued, regular sexual enjoyment. Illness and disability climb as the end of the lifespan approaches. Cardiovascular disease, cancer, stroke, and emphysema claim many lives, while arthritis and type 2 diabetes increase substantially. At age 65 and older, the death rate from unintentional injuries is at an all-time high.

Dementia refers to a set of disorders occurring almost entirely in old age in which many aspects of thought and behavior are so impaired that everyday activities are disrupted. Alzheimer's disease, the most common form of dementia, can be either familial (which runs in families) or sporadic (where there is no obvious family history). With no cure available, family interventions ensure the best adjustment possible for the Alzheimer's victim, spouse, and other relatives. Careful diagnosis is crucial because other disorders can be misidentified as dementia. Family members provide most long-term care, especially among ethnic minorities with close-knit extended families.

Individual differences in cognitive functioning are greater in late adulthood than at any other time of life. According to one view, elders who sustain high levels of functioning select personally valued activities to optimize returns from their diminishing energy and come up with new ways to compensate for cognitive losses. Research shows that language and memory skills are closely related. Although language comprehension changes very little in late life, retrieving words from long-term memory and planning what to say become more difficult. Finally, traditional problem solving, in the absence of real-life context, shows declines.

Cultures around the world assume that age and wisdom go together. Older adults with the cognitive, reflective, and emotional qualities that make up wisdom tend to be better educated and physically healthier and to forge more positive relations with others. As in middle adulthood, a mentally active life—above average education, stimulating leisure pursuits, community participation, and a flexible personality—predicts maintenance of mental abilities into advanced old age. And interventions that train the elderly in cognitive strategies can partially reverse age-related declines in mental ability. Elders who participate in continuing education through university courses, community offerings, and programs like Elderhostel are enriched by new knowledge, new friends, a broader perspective on the world, and an image of themselves as more competent.

LEARNING OBJECTIVES

After reading this chapter, you should be able to:

17.1 Distinguish between chronological age and functional age, and discuss changes in life expectancy over the past century. (pp. 564–566)

17.2 Explain age-related changes in the nervous system during late adulthood. (pp. 566–567, 568–569)

17.3 Summarize changes in sensory functioning during late adulthood, including vision, hearing, taste, smell, and touch. (pp. 567–570)

17.4 Describe cardiovascular, respiratory, and immune system changes in late adulthood. (pp. 570–571)

17.5 Discuss sleep difficulties in late adulthood. (pp. 571–572)

17.6 Summarize changes in physical health and mobility in late adulthood, including elders' adaptation to the physical changes, and reactions to stereotypes of aging. (pp. 572–575, 576)

17.7 Discuss health and fitness in late life, paying special attention to nutrition, exercise, and sexuality. (pp. 575–579)

17.8 Discuss common physical disabilities in late adulthood, with special attention to arthritis, adult-onset diabetes, and unintentional injuries. (pp. 580–582)

17.9 Describe mental disabilities common in late adulthood, including Alzheimer's disease, cerebrovascular dementia, and misdiagnosed and reversible dementia. (pp. 582–588)

17.10 Discuss health-care issues that affect senior citizens. (pp. 589–590)

17.11 Describe changes in crystallized and fluid abilities in late adulthood, and explain how older adults can make the most of their cognitive resources. (pp. 590–591)

17.12 Summarize memory changes in late life, including implicit, associative, remote, and prospective memories. (pp. 591–594)

17.13 Discuss changes in language processing in late adulthood. (pp. 594–595)

17.14 Explain how problem solving changes in late life. (p. 595)

17.15 Discuss the capacities that contribute to wisdom, noting how it is affected by age and life experience. (pp. 595–596)

17.16 Discuss factors related to cognitive change in late adulthood. (pp. 596–597)

17.17 Describe the effectiveness of cognitive interventions in late adulthood. (p. 597)

17.18 Describe the types of continuing education programs available to the elderly, and summarize the benefits of participation in such programs. (pp. 597–599)

STUDY QUESTIONS

Physical Development

1. ____________________ refers to a person's actual competence and performance. (p. 564)
2. True or False: Researchers have identified a single biological measure that predicts rate of aging. (p. 564)

Life Expectancy

1. *Average life expectancy* refers to the number of years that an individual (born in a particular year / with certain health characteristics) can expect to live, starting at (any given age / birth). (p. 564)
2. In 2008, average life expectancy reached age _________ in the United States. (p. 564)

3. Cite factors that contributed to twentieth-century gains in life expectancy. (p. 564)

____

____

Variations in Life Expectancy

1. On average, (men / women) can expect to live 4 to 7 years longer than their other-sex counterparts—a difference found in almost all cultures. What accounts for this gender gap in life expectancy? (p. 564)

____

____

2. True or False: Over the past several decades, the gender gap in life expectancy has narrowed in industrialized nations. (p. 564)
3. List factors that contribute to SES and ethnic differences in life expectancy. (pp. 564–565)

____

____

____

4. _______________ refers to the number of years a person born in a particular year can expect to live in full health. How does the United States rank internationally on this measure? (p. 565)

____

Life Expectancy in Late Adulthood

1. The number of people age 65 and older has (declined / risen) dramatically in the industrialized world. (p. 565)
2. Cite two segments of the population that are growing the fastest. (p. 565)

   A. _______________

   B. _______________

3. Life expectancy is greater for older (men / women). (p. 566)
4. True or False: With advancing age, gender and SES differences in life expectancy increase. (p. 566)
5. Describe the life expectancy crossover. (p. 566)

____

____

6. Indicate whether the following characteristics describe *activities of daily living (ADLs)* or *instrumental activities of daily living (IADLs)*. (p. 566)

   _______ Basic self-care tasks required to live on one's own
   _______ Tasks necessary to conduct the business of daily life, which also require some cognitive competence
   _______ Include telephoning, shopping, food preparation, housekeeping, and paying bills
   _______ Include bathing, dressing, getting in and out of bed or a chair, and eating
   _______ About 9 percent of adults over age 75 have difficulty carrying out these tasks
   _______ About 17 percent of adults over age 75 cannot carry out these tasks

7. Summarize evidence that heredity affects longevity. (p. 566)

____

____

____

8. True or False: Twin studies suggest that once people pass age 75 to 80, the contribution of heredity to length of life decreases in favor of environmental factors. (p. 566)

A Lifespan Vista: What Can We Learn About Aging from Centenarians?

1. The past 40 years have seen a sizeable (decrease / increase) in centenarians in the industrialized world. This trend is expected to (decelerate / accelerate). (p. 568)
2. Centenarians are more likely to be (men / women). (p. 568)
3. True or False: Most centenarians have physical and mental impairments that interfere with independent functioning. (p. 568)
4. True or False: Longevity runs in the families of centenarians. (p. 569)
5. Describe the health, personality, and activities of robust centenarians. (p. 569)

   Health: ______________________________

   ____

   Personality: ______________________________

   ____

   Activities: ______________________________

   ____

Maximum Lifespan

1. ______________________ refers to the genetic limit to length of life for a person free of external risk factors. Describe current estimates of this measure. (p. 566)

   ____

   ____

2. Cite evidence to support both sides of the debate over whether current figures for *maximum lifespan* represent the upper bound of human longevity or whether lifespan can be extended even further. (p. 566)

   Upper bound: ______________________________

   ____

   Lifespan can be extended: ______________________________

   ____

Physical Changes

Nervous System

1. Cite two factors responsible for declines in brain weight in older adults. (p. 567)

   A. ______________________________

   B. ______________________________

2. Cite four components of the cerebral cortex that experience marked declines in late adulthood. (p. 567)

   A. ______________________ C. ______________________

   B. ______________________ D. ______________________

3. True or False: In healthy older adults, growth of neural fibers takes place at the same rate as in middle-aged adults. (p. 567)

4. Cite two changes in autonomic nervous system functioning in old age. (p. 567)

   A. ______________________________

   B. ______________________________

Sensory Systems

1. ______________ are cloudy areas in the lens of the eye. How do they affect vision? (p. 567)

   ____

   ____

2. True or False: The number of individuals with *cataracts* increases sharply from middle to late adulthood. (p. 567)
3. Cite two factors that largely account for visual impairments in late adulthood. (p. 567)

   A. ______________________________

   B. ______________________________

4. Dark adaptation, depth perception, and visual acuity (decline / remain stable / improve) in late life. (p. 568)
5. When light-sensitive cells in the central region of the retina break down, older adults may develop ______________ ______________, in which central vision blurs and is gradually lost. (p. 568)
6. (Cataracts / *Macular degeneration*) are/is the leading cause of blindness in older adults. (p. 568)
7. Describe the impact of visual difficulties on elders' self-confidence and everyday behavior. (p. 568)

   ____

   ____

8. List three changes in the ear that cause hearing to decline in late adulthood. (p. 569)

   A. ______________________________

   B. ______________________________

   C. ______________________________

9. Hearing decrements in late life are greatest at (low / high) frequencies. Cite several additional hearing declines. (p. 569)

   ____

   ____

10. What hearing difficulty has the greatest impact on life satisfaction? (p. 569)

    ____

11. True or False: Most older adults suffer hearing loss great enough to disrupt their daily lives. (p. 570)
12. List several ways in which older adults can compensate for hearing loss. (p. 570)

    ____

    ____

13. True or False: Age-related reductions in taste sensitivity are caused by changes in the number and distribution of taste buds. (p. 570)
14. List several factors that contribute to declines in taste sensitivity. (p. 570)

    ____

    ____

15. Summarize changes in smell during late adulthood. (p. 570)

____

____

16. True or False: After age 70, nearly all elders experience a decline in touch perception on the hands. (p. 570)

17. What two factors likely account for age-related declines in touch sensitivity? (p. 570)

A. ____

B. ____

Cardiovascular and Respiratory Systems

1. List five ways in which the heart muscle changes with advancing age. (p. 570)

A. ____

B. ____

C. ____

D. ____

E. ____

2. Describe changes in the cardiovascular and respiratory systems that reduce oxygen supply to body tissues. (pp. 570–571)

Cardiovascular: ____

____

Respiratory: ____

____

Immune System

1. What is an *autoimmune response*? (p. 571)

____

____

2. True or False: Most illnesses among elderly adults are caused by age-related declines in immune functioning. (p. 571)

3. Summarize the relationship among stress hormones, immune functioning, and aging. (p. 571)

____

____

4. Name two factors that protect the immune response in old age. (p. 571)

A. ______________________ B. ______________________

Sleep

1. True or False: Older adults require about as much total sleep as younger adults. (p. 571)

2. Describe sleep difficulties common in older adults, and cite two factors that are largely responsible for these problems. (p. 571)

   Sleep difficulties: ______________________________

   ____

   Factors responsible: ______________________________

   ____

3. Until age 70 or 80, (men / women) experience more sleep disturbances. List three reasons for this. (pp. 571–572)

   A. ______________________________

   B. ______________________________

   C. ______________________________

4. Describe ways to foster restful sleep in late adulthood. (p. 572)

   ____

   ____

   ____

Physical Appearance and Mobility

1. Describe changes in the skin in late adulthood. (p. 572)

   ____

   ____

2. The __________ is especially likely to show signs of aging. What factors contribute to this change? (p. 572)

   ____

3. Describe facial changes that occur in late adulthood. (p. 572)

   ____

   ____

4. True or False: Both height and weight tend to decline in late adulthood. (p. 573)

5. List three age-related changes that affect mobility. (p. 573)

   A. ______________________________

   B. ______________________________

   C. ______________________________

Adapting to Physical Changes of Late Adulthood

1. True or False: Outward signs of aging, such as graying hair, facial wrinkles, and baldness, are closely related to sensory, cognitive, and motor functioning, as well as longevity. (p. 573)

2. Explain how problem-centered coping strategies help older adults adjust to the physical changes of late life. (p. 573)

   ____

   ____

   ____

3. ______________________ includes an array of devices that permit people with disabilities to improve their functioning. Provide several examples of devices that help older adults cope with physical declines. (pp. 573–574)

____

____

____

4. True or False: Many older adults report experiencing prejudice and discrimination. (p. 574)

5. Describe the effects of negative versus positive age stereotypes for seniors. (p. 574)

Negative stereotypes: ______________________

____

Positive stereotypes: ______________________

____

6. Describe ways in which the Inuit and Japanese cultures display deference and respect toward the elderly. (p. 575)

____

____

____

Cultural Influences: Cultural Variations in Sense of Usefulness in Late Life

1. How do the Herero of Botswana, Africa, treat the elderly? (p. 576)

____

____

____

2. Explain why elders in Momence, Illinois, a small working-class town, are able to maintain social participation and positions of authority. (p. 576)

____

____

____

3. Describe two negative outcomes associated with frequent feelings of uselessness in late adulthood. (p. 576)

A. ______________________

B. ______________________

4. True or False: Providing elders with opportunities to assume important roles readily combats harmful self-perceptions. (p. 576)

Health, Fitness, and Disability

1. The majority of older adults rate their health (unfavorably / favorably). (p. 575)

2. Explain how physical and mental health are intimately related in late life. (p. 576)

____

____

____

3. Summarize SES and ethnic variations in physical functioning during late life, noting reasons for these differences. (pp. 576–577)

   SES: ____

   ____

   Ethnic variations: ____

   ____

4. True or False: Beyond age 85, women are more impaired than men and are less able to remain independent. (p. 577)

5. Ideally, as life expectancy extends, the average period of diminished vigor before death should decrease—a public health goal called the ______________________________. Over the past two decades, this (has / has not) occurred in industrialized nations. (p. 577)

6. Describe evidence indicating that *compression of morbidity* can be greatly extended. (p. 577)

   ____

   ____

   ____

Nutrition and Exercise

1. Briefly describe the physical and environmental conditions that lead to increased risk of dietary deficiencies in late life. (p. 577)

   Physical: ____

   Environmental: ____

2. Place a check mark by each true statement below. (p. 578)

   Vitamins and minerals…

   ______ enhance immune response.
   ______ decrease days of infectious illness.
   ______ improve elders' cognitive functioning.
   ______ reduce the incidence of cardiovascular disease.
   ______ reduce the incidence of cancer.
   ______ prevent or slow Alzheimer's disease.

3. Describe ways in which the body and brain benefit from physical exercise in late life. (p. 578)

   Body: ____

   ____

   Brain: ____

   ____

4. True or False: Elders who value the intrinsic benefits of exercise are likely to engage in it regularly. (p. 578)

Sexuality

1. Cross-sectional studies report (declines / maintenance / increases) in frequency of sexual activity in old age. (p. 579)

2. True or False: Most healthy married couples report diminished sexual enjoyment in late adulthood. (p. 579)

3. (Men / Women) are more likely to withdraw from sexual activity in late life. Explain your answer. (p. 579)

   ____

   ____

   ____

Physical Disabilities

1. List the four leading causes of death in late adulthood. (p. 580)

   A. ______________________________

   B. ______________________________

   C. ______________________________

   D. ______________________________

2. (*Primary* / *Secondary*) *aging* refers to genetically influenced declines that affect all humans, even in overall good health. (*Primary* / *Secondary*) *aging* describes declines due to hereditary defects and negative environmental influences. (p. 580)

3. Define *frailty*, and list factors that contribute to it. (p. 580)

   Definition: ______________________________

   ____

   ____

   Contributing factors: ______________________________

   ____

   ____

4. Indicate whether the following statements describe *osteoarthritis* (O) or *rheumatoid arthritis* (R). (pp. 580–581)

   ______ Limited to certain joints

   ______ Caused by an autoimmune response

   ______ Cartilage on the ends of bones deteriorates

   ______ Most common type of arthritis

   ______ Involves the whole body

   ______ Results from frequent use of joints

   ______ Connective tissue becomes inflamed

   ______ Affects about 2 percent of older adults

5. Older (men / women) show higher incidence and sharper increase of arthritis. (p. 581)

6. Cite evidence that both hereditary and environmental factors contribute to arthritis. (p. 581)

   Hereditary: ______________________________

   Environmental: ______________________________

7. How can older adults manage arthritis? (p. 581)

   ____

   ____

8. What risks are associated with type 2 diabetes? (p. 581)

   ____

   ____

9. What factors increase a person's risk for developing type 2 diabetes? (p. 581)

   ____

   ____

10. What treatments are used to control type 2 diabetes? (pp. 581–582)

    ____

    ____

11. The death rate from unintentional injuries is highest during (adolescence and early adulthood / late adulthood). (p. 582)

12. Describe statistical data on older adult drivers. (p. 582)

____

____

13. List three factors that contribute to driving difficulties in older adults. (p. 582)

    A. ____

    B. ____

    C. ____

14. True or False: The elderly account for more than 30 percent of all pedestrian deaths. (p. 582)

15. ____________________ is/are the leading type of unintentional injury among the elderly. (p. 582)

16. List factors that place older adults at increased risk for falling. (p. 582)

____

____

17. True or False: Fear of falling impairs health indirectly. Explain your answer. (p. 582)

____

____

18. Cite three ways to reduce the risk of unintentional injuries among the elderly. (p. 582)

    A. ____

    B. ____

    C. ____

Mental Disabilities

1. Define *dementia.* (p. 582)

____

____

2. Dementia (declines / rises) sharply with age, striking men and women (disproportionately / equally). (p. 582)

3. The most common form of dementia is ______________________________, in which structural and chemical brain deterioration is associated with gradual loss of many aspects of thought and behavior. (p. 583)

4. True or False: *Alzheimer's disease* is a leading cause of mortality in late life. (p. 584)

5. What is usually the first symptom of Alzheimer's disease? (p. 584)

____

6. Cite several additional symptoms associated with Alzheimer's disease. (p. 584)

____

____

____

7. Explain how Alzheimer's disease is diagnosed. (p. 584)

____

____

8. In people with Alzheimer's, the cerebral cortex often contains ______________________________, or bundles of twisted threads that result from collapsed neural structures and contain abnormal forms of a protein. Also present are ______________________, or dense deposits of a deteriorated protein, surrounded by clumps of dead nerve and glial cells. (p. 584)

9. (Abnormal breakdown of amyloid within neurons / *amyloid plaques*) contribute(s) to the neuronal damage of Alzheimer's. (p. 585)

10. Cite two ways in which amyloid is believed to damage neurons. (p. 585)

    A. ____

    B. ____

11. True or False: As Alzheimer's progresses, declining levels of neurotransmitters lead to impairments in many complex functions, such as memory and reasoning. (p. 585)

12. Indicate whether the following statements describe familial (F) or sporadic (S) Alzheimer's disease. (p. 585)

    ______ Runs in families
    ______ Has an early onset
    ______ Has no obvious family history
    ______ Progresses more rapidly

13. An abnormality of the ______________ gene is the most common known risk factor for sporadic Alzheimer's disease and is present in 50 percent of cases. (p. 585)

14. List several factors that play a role in susceptibility to Alzheimer's. (p. 585)

    ____

    ____

    ____

15. Cite evidence that Alzheimer's results from combinations of genetic and environmental factors. (p. 585)

    ____

    ____

    ____

16. Describe four factors that protect against Alzheimer's disease. (p. 586)

    A. ____

    B. ____

    C. ____

    D. ____

17. True or False: Alzheimer's is a curable disease. (p. 587)

18. ________________ interventions ensure the best possible adjustment for Alzheimer's victims and their families. (p. 587)

19. In ______________________________, a series of strokes leaves areas of dead brain cells, producing step-by-step degeneration of mental ability, with each step occurring abruptly after a stroke. (p. 588)

20. Summarize genetic and environmental influences on *cerebrovascular dementia*. (p. 588)

    Genetic: ____

    ____

    Environmental: ____

    ____

21. More (men / women) have cerebrovascular dementia by their late sixties. Prevalence of the disease (is roughly constant / varies) among countries. (p. 588)

22. True or False: Most cases of cerebrovascular dementia are caused by atherosclerosis. (p. 588)

23. List the warning signs of a stroke. (p. 588)

____

____

24. ____________________ is most often misdiagnosed as dementia. Describe one key difference between adults with this disorder and those with dementia. (p. 588)

____

____

25. Cite three additional factors that can lead to side effects resembling dementia. (p. 588)

A. ____

B. ____

C. ____

Social Issues: Interventions for Caregivers of Elders with Dementia

1. Explain how Alzheimer's disease affects caregivers. (p. 586)

____

____

____

2. Briefly describe four caregiver needs that are addressed by effective interventions. (pp. 586–587)

Knowledge: ____

____

Coping strategies: ____

____

Caregiving skills: ____

____

Respite: ____

____

3. Describe typical characteristics of "active" intervention programs that make a substantial difference in caregivers' lives. (p. 587)

____

____

4. Caregivers with greater care responsibility—(men / women), (lower- / higher-)SES, (spouses / nonspouses)—benefit most from active intervention. (p. 587)

Health Care

1. True or False: The cost of government-sponsored health insurance for the elderly is expected to double by the year 2025 and triple by the year 2050. (p. 589)

2. True or False: In the United States, Medicare funds 100 percent of older adults' medical expenses. (p. 589)
3. Which disorders of aging most often lead to nursing home placement? (p. 589)

4. True or False: Older adults in the United States are less likely to be institutionalized than elders in other industrialized nations. Explain your answer. (p. 589)

5. (Caucasian / African) Americans are more likely to be placed in nursing homes. Why is this so? (p. 589)

6. Describe two recommendations for reducing institutionalized care for the elderly and its associated costs. (p. 589)

   A.

   B.

7. Briefly summarize ways to improve the quality of nursing home services. (p. 590)

Cognitive Development

1. The more a mental ability depends on (crystallized / fluid) intelligence, the earlier it starts to decline. Mental abilities that rely on (crystallized / fluid) intelligence are sustained longer. (p. 590)
2. True or False: Individual differences in cognitive functioning are greater during late adulthood than at any other time of life. (pp. 590–591)
3. Explain how older adults can use *selective optimization with compensation* to sustain high levels of cognitive functioning in late life. (p. 591)

4. Compared with younger adults, older adults' goals are more likely to accentuate (maintaining and preventing loss of / gaining) abilities. (p. 591)

Memory

Deliberate versus Automatic Memory

1. Describe the link between declines in working memory and the ability to retrieve memories. (p. 592)

2. (Recall / Recognition) memory shows fewer declines in late adulthood. (p. 592)
3. ______________________ refers to memory without conscious awareness. (p. 592)
4. Age differences are greater for (*implicit* / deliberate) *memory*. Explain your answer. (p. 592)

____

____

Associative Memory

1. What are *associative memory deficits*? (p. 592)

____

____

2. Older adults have more difficulty (recognizing single pieces of information / forming associations between multiple pieces of information). (p. 592)
3. Cite a factor that greatly affects elders' associative memory deficits. (p. 593)

____

____

Remote Memory

1. True or False: Research shows that memory for recent events is clearer than *remote memory* in late life. (p. 593)
2. Explain why older adults recall their adolescent and early adulthood experiences more easily than their midlife experiences. (p. 593)

____

____

Prospective Memory

1. ____________________________ involves remembering to engage in planned actions in the future. (p. 593)
2. In the laboratory, older adults do better on (event-based / time-based) *prospective memory* tasks. Explain your answer. (p. 594)

____

____

3. Explain why prospective memory difficulties in the laboratory setting do not always appear in real-life contexts. (p. 594)

____

____

Language Processing

1. Language comprehension changes very little in late life, as long as what two factors are in place? (p. 594)

   A. ____

   B. ____

2. Describe two aspects of language production that show age-related declines. (p. 594)

   A. ____

   B. ____

3. What factors contribute to the changes mentioned in the previous question? (p. 594)

4. List several ways that older adults often compensate for difficulties with language production. (p. 595)

Problem Solving

1. What types of everyday problems are of concern to most older adults? (p. 595)

2. True or False: As long as they perceive problems of daily living as under their control and as important, elders are active and effective in solving them. (p. 595)

3. Older adults are (slower / faster) than younger adults to make decisions about seeking health care. (p. 595)

4. True or False: Older couples are less likely than younger couples to collaborate in everyday problem solving. (p. 595)

Wisdom

1. Cite several characteristics often used to describe *wisdom*. (p. 595)

2. True or False: Cultures around the world assume that age and wisdom go together. Provide examples to support your answer. (p. 595)

3. Research shows that (age / life experience) is more important in the development of wisdom. (p. 596)

4. In addition to age and life experience, what other factor contributes to late-life wisdom? (p. 596)

5. Cite several positive outcomes associated with wisdom. (p. 596)

Factors Related to Cognitive Change

1. List several factors that predict maintenance of mental abilities in late life. (p. 596)

2. True or False: As baby boomers enter late adulthood, the elderly are likely to show improved preservation of cognitive functions. Explain your answer. (p. 596)

____

____

3. Explain how retirement can affect cognitive change both positively and negatively. (p. 597)

   Positively: ____

   ____

   Negatively: ____

   ____

4. ____________________ refers to marked acceleration in deterioration of cognitive functioning prior to death. Its average length is ______________. (p. 597)

Cognitive Interventions

1. For most of late adulthood, cognitive declines are (gradual / rapid). (p. 597)
2. Briefly summarize findings from the Adult Development and Enrichment Project (ADEPT) and from the Advanced Cognitive Training for Independent and Vital Elderly (ACTIVE). (p. 597)

   ADEPT: ____

   ____

   ACTIVE: ____

   ____

3. True or False: Many cognitive skills can be enhanced in old age. (p. 597)

Lifelong Learning

1. Elders' participation in continuing education has (declined / increased) over the past few decades. (p. 598)

Types of Programs

1. Describe characteristics of the following learning programs for older adults. (p. 598)

   Elderhostel: ____

   ____

   Osher Lifelong Learning Institute: ____

   ____

   University of the Third Age: ____

   ____

2. True or False: Participants in the above programs tend to be active, well-educated, and financially well-off. (p. 598)
3. Summarize three ways to increase the effectiveness of instruction for older adults. (p. 598)

   A. ____

   B. ____

   C. ____

Benefits of Continuing Education

1. List five benefits of elders' participation in continuing education programs. (p. 599)

   A. ______________________________

   B. ______________________________

   C. ______________________________

   D. ______________________________

   E. ______________________________

ASK YOURSELF . . .

For *Ask Yourself* questions for this chapter, along with feedback on the accuracy of your answers, please log on to MyDevelopmentLab (for registration and access, please visit mydevelopmentlab.com or follow the instructions on page ix).

(1) Select the Multimedia Library.

(2) Choose the explore option.

(3) Find your chapter from the drop down box.

(4) Click find now.

(5) Complete questions and choose "Submit answers for grading" or "Clear answers" to start over.

SUGGESTED READINGS

Ballenger, J. F. (2006). *Self, senility, and Alzheimer's disease in modern America: A history.* Baltimore, MD: Johns Hopkins University Press. Based on current research in psychiatry and gerontology, this book provides an extensive overview of Alzheimer's disease, including health concerns, neurological changes, cultural perceptions of cognitive decline, and treatment options.

Buettner, D. (2009). *The blue zones: Lessons for living longer from people who've lived the longest.* Washington, DC: National Geographic Society. A compelling look at optimal aging, this book features elders and centenarians from all over the world, including a 102-year-old Sardinian man who hikes six miles a day. Through candid interviews, the author presents lifestyle characteristics that are associated with exceptional longevity.

Nordstrom, N., & Merz, J. F. (2006). *Learning later, living greater.* Boulder, CO: Sentient Publications. Written by the former director of the Elderhostel Institute Network and an expert in gerontology, this book examines the importance of maintaining physical health in middle and late adulthood, the benefits of continuing education and lifelong learning, and ways to enhance health and well-being through travel and volunteerism.

Vaarama, M., Pieper, R., & Sixsmith, A. (Eds.). (2007). *Care-related quality of life in old age: Concepts, models, and empirical findings.* New York: Springer-Verlag. Using up-to-date research from various countries throughout the world, this book examines the importance of health care in late adulthood, especially among fragile elders who require external supports for day-to-day functioning.

CROSSWORD PUZZLE 17.1

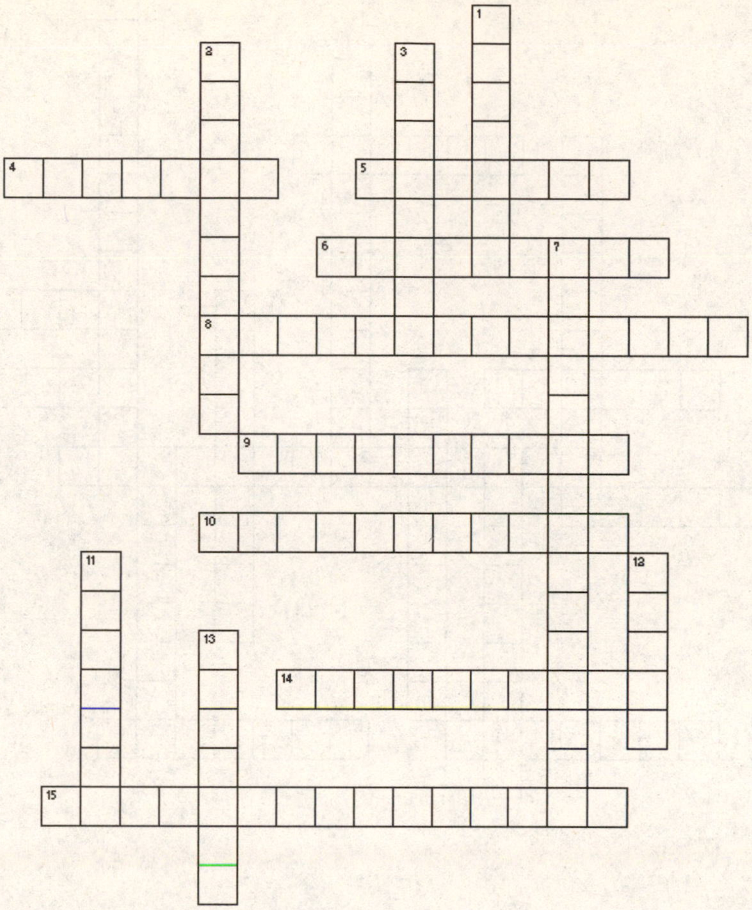

Across

4. ______ lifespan: genetic limit to length of life for a person free of external risk factors
5. Average ______ life expectancy: years a person born in a particular year can expect to live in full health
6. Cloudy areas in the lens of the eye that result in foggy vision and eventual blindness
8. Arthritis characterized by deteriorating cartilage on the ends of bones in frequently used joints
9. ______ disease: most common form of dementia; brain deterioration accompanies loss of thought and behavior
10. ______ memory deficits involve difficulty creating and retrieving links between pieces of information.
14. ______ response: the immune system malfunctions and turns against normal body tissues
15. ______ tangles: bundles of twisted threads that are the product of collapsed neural structures

Down

1. ______ degeneration: blurring and eventual loss of central vision due to a break-down of light-sensitive cells
2. ______ arthritis: immune system attacks the body, resulting in inflammation of connective tissue
3. Disorders occurring mostly in old age; impairments in thought and behavior disrupt everyday activities
7. ______ dementia: a series of strokes kills brain cells, producing step-by-step degeneration of mental ability
11. ______ life expectancy: years that a person born in a particular year can expect to live, starting at any given age
12. Sleep ______: breathing stops for 10 seconds or longer, resulting in many brief awakenings
13. ______ plaques: dense deposits of a deteriorated protein surrounded by clumps of dead cells

CROSSWORD PUZZLE 17.2

Across

4. Summed up by one group of researchers as "expertise in the conduct and meaning of life"
6. Basic self-care tasks required to live on one's own, such as dressing or eating (abbrev.)
7. ______ memory: very long-term recall
9. Tasks necessary to conduct the business of daily life and that require some cognitive competence (abbrev.)
10. Housing for seniors who cannot be cared for at home but who do not require nursing home care (2 words)
13. ______ decline: marked acceleration in deterioration of cognitive functioning prior to death
14. ______ aging: genetically influenced age-related declines that affect all humans, even in overall good health
15. Weakened body functioning interferes with everyday competence, leaving the older adult highly vulnerable.

Down

1. Selective ______ with compensation: choosing personally valued activities to maximize returns
2. ______ memory: remembering to engage in planned actions in the future
3. ______ age: actual competence and performance
5. Compression of ______: public health goal of reducing the average period of diminished vigor before death
8. ______ technology: devices that permit people with disabilities to improve their functioning
11. ______ aging: declines due to hereditary defects and environmental influences
12. Memory without conscious awareness

PRACTICE TEST #1

1. A 75-year-old who looks and acts much younger may have a(n) __________ age of 60. (p. 564)
   a. chronological
   b. average
   c. functional
   d. imagined

2. What life expectancy crossover occurs around age 85? (p. 566)
   a. Men live longer than women.
   b. Women live longer than men.
   c. Whites live longer than ethnic minorities.
   d. Low-SES ethnic minorities live longer than high-SES whites.

3. An example of an instrumental activity of daily living (IADL) is __________ (p. 566)
   a. bathing.
   b. shopping.
   c. dressing.
   d. eating.

4. Research on aging of the central nervous system indicates that __________ (p. 567)
   a. brain weight can decline by as much as 5 to 10 percent by age 80.
   b. neuron loss is restricted to the temporal lobes.
   c. the brain is incapable of overcoming declines in late adulthood.
   d. glial cells increase in size and number throughout late adulthood.

5.. Longitudinal studies reveal that centenarians are __________ (p. 568)
   a. generally white, college-educated females.
   b. generally financially successful males.
   c. mostly of African or Asian descent.
   d. diverse in education, economic well-being, and ethnicity.

6. Ellen is worried about developing cataracts or macular degeneration. To reduce her risk of developing these conditions, she can __________ (p. 568)
   a. spend fewer hours working at the computer.
   b. wear glasses for reading.
   c. take a daily multivitamin.
   d. eat a diet rich in green, leafy vegetables.

7. Among hearing-impaired elders, a decline in __________ leads to the greatest impact on life satisfaction. (p. 569)
   a. detection of high frequencies
   b. detection of soft sounds
   c. speech perception
   d. responsiveness to startling noises

8. Aging of the cardiovascular system causes the __________ (p. 570)
   a. heart muscle to become less rigid, so it pumps less efficiently.
   b. cells within the heart to shrink and multiply.
   c. artery walls to stiffen and accumulate some plaque.
   d. heart muscle to enlarge, which puts excessive pressure on the arteries and veins.

9. Older adults __________ (p. 571)
   a. require about 7 hours of sleep per night—the same amount as younger adults.
   b. fall asleep more easily and sleep more soundly than younger adults.
   c. require at least 10 hours of sleep per night for favorable health.
   d. rarely experience the problem of "restless legs" common in young adults.

10. Research shows that graying hair, wrinkles, and other outward signs of aging __________ (p. 573)
    a. can be delayed by taking dietary supplements.
    b. occur earlier in men than women.
    c. cause extreme distress for most older adults.
    d. bear no relationship to functioning or longevity.

11. The majority of disabled elders who use assistive technology __________ (p. 574)
    a. have cognitive impairments that prevent them from effectively using the devices.
    b. resent the privacy invasion of such devices.
    c. believe the benefits outweigh privacy concerns.
    d. report no improvement in life quality.

12. __________ Western older adults report feeling useless most or all of the time. (p. 576)
    a. A minority of
    b. About half of
    c. Both low- and high-SES
    d. Nearly all

13. Studies show that over the past two decades, compression of morbidity has __________ (p. 577)
    a. primarily occurred in developing nations.
    b. failed to occur in industrialized nations despite medical advances.
    c. occurred in industrialized nations despite rising rates of obesity.
    d. declined sharply, mostly due to soaring rates of obesity.

14. Which of the following statements about sex in late adulthood is true? (p. 579)
    a. Most older couples report no decline in frequency of sexual activity.
    b. Most older adults feel that sex is important.
    c. Most older couples feel that sex is unimportant in late life.
    d. Older women report more extended and frequent sexual activity than men.

15. Which of the following causes of death in late adulthood is more prevalent among women than men? (p. 580)
    a. emphysema
    b. cardiovascular disease
    c. cancer
    d. stroke

16. Osteoarthritis__________ (p. 581)
    a. results from an autoimmune response.
    b. involves the whole body.
    c. is unresponsive to medication.
    d. is the most common type of arthritis.

17. Dementia __________ (p. 583)
    a. usually appears around age 65.
    b. is more common in women than men.
    c. is usually irreversible and incurable.
    d. results from normal age-related cell death.

18. Which of the following statements about Alzheimer's disease is true? (p. 584)
    a. It can result in coma and, eventually, death.
    b. Many forms of the disease can now be cured.
    c. Memory problems usually present themselves at the end stages of the disease.
    d. The disease follows the same course in nearly all individuals.

19. __________ is/are linked to a significant reduction in the incidence of Alzheimer's, as well as slower Alzheimer's progression and a reduction in cerebrovascular dementia. (p. 586)
    a. Hormone therapy
    b. Vitamins B and E
    c. A Mediterranean diet
    d. Anti-inflammatory drugs

20. Which of the following interventions has been found to substantially reduce caregiver depressive symptoms? (p. 587)
    a. weekly leisure activities with other caregivers
    b. family therapy in the home
    c. information and referral to community agencies
    d. classes on effective caregiver coping strategies

21. What disorder is most often misdiagnosed as dementia? (p. 588)
    a. atherosclerosis
    b. psychosis
    c. depression
    d. calcium deficiency

22. U.S. Medicare funds __________ of older adults' medical needs. (p. 589)
    a. about 10 percent
    b. about half
    c. almost 80 percent
    d. all

23. What is a likely reason that an elder or elder's family would opt for nursing home care over assisted living? (p. 590)
    a. Nursing home care is less expensive than assisted living.
    b. The elder prefers to maintain a high degree of independence.
    c. The elder highly values socialization and community involvement.
    d. The elder requires a higher level of care than assisted living can provide.

24. Research on cognitive development in late adulthood reveals __________ (pp. 590–591)
    a. greater individual variation than at any other time of life.
    b. less individual variation than at any other time of life.
    c. greater plasticity than in midlife due to increased efforts to sustain high levels of functioning.
    d. only a modest decline in fluid intelligence.

25. Research shows that in late adulthood, personal goals focus on __________ (p. 591)
    a. acquiring new skills.
    b. building new social relationships.
    c. maintenance and loss prevention.
    d. regaining lost skills or abilities.

26. Which of the following is an example of temporal memory? (p. 592)
    a. where a birthday party took place
    b. when a birthday party occurred
    c. who was present at a birthday party
    d. what food was served at a birthday party

27. Age differences in __________ are much smaller than in __________. (p. 592)
    a. recall; recognition
    b. temporal memory; recognition
    c. implicit memory; explicit memory
    d. deliberate memory; working memory

28. Which of the following statements about memory in late adulthood is true? (p. 594)
    a. Age differences in implicit memory are much greater than in explicit, or deliberate, memory.
    b. When asked to recall an important event from the past, elders provide considerably more details than younger adults.
    c. In trying to remember a future activity, older adults rely more on strategies like external memory aids, younger adults on rehearsal.
    d. In trying to remember a future activity, older adults rely more on strategies like rehearsal, younger adults on external memory aids.

29. Which of the following statements about the link between health status and intellectual performance is true? (p. 597)
    a. Educated elders are no more likely than their uneducated counterparts to engage in health-protective behaviors that postpone the onset of serious disease.
    b. SES is a stronger predictor of intellectual functioning in late life than health status.
    c. This link may be exaggerated by the fact that brighter adults are more likely to engage in health-protective behaviors that postpone the onset of serious disease.
    d. Contrary to popular belief, health status is a poor predictor of cognitive functioning in late adulthood.

30. Elderly participants in continuing education programs like Elderhostel ____________ (p. 598)
    a. tend to be well-educated and financially well-off.
    b. tend to come from low-SES backgrounds.
    c. usually drop out after a few months.
    d. learn best when they already have a solid knowledge base.

PRACTICE TEST #2

1. In average healthy life expectancy, __________ ranks first and __________ ranks twenty-ninth. (p. 565)
   a. the United States; China
   b. Canada; China
   c. Japan; the United States
   d. the United States; Canada

2. With age, differences in average life expectancy between the sexes __________ (p. 566)
   a. decline.
   b. increase slightly.
   c. increase dramatically.
   d. remain stable.

3. The __________ varies between 70 and 110 for most people, with 85 being the average. (p. 566)
   a. average life expectancy
   b. average healthy life expectancy
   c. minimum lifespan
   d. maximum lifespan

4. Declines in brain weight throughout adulthood largely result from __________ (p. 567)
   a. shrinkage of the ventricles within the brain.
   b. death of neurons.
   c. myelination of neural fibers.
   d. increased incidence of stroke.

5. Why are the elderly at higher risk than younger adults during heat waves and cold spells? (p. 567)
   a. Changes in sensory function occur with age.
   b. Macular degeneration is common among the elderly.
   c. Higher levels of stress hormones are released in old age.
   d. The autonomic nervous system performs less well in old age.

6. Most centenarians __________ (p. 569)
   a. live in North America.
   b. have relatives who reached very old age.
   c. have age-related chronic diseases.
   d. feel pessimistic or depressed.

7. Age-related declines in immune functioning __________ (p. 571)
   a. permit a variety of diseases to progress.
   b. occur earlier in women than men.
   c. are dramatic for nearly all older adults.
   d. are reversible with vitamin–mineral supplements.

8. Why is the face especially likely to show signs of aging, such as creasing, sagging, and moles? (p. 572)
   a. The face is especially vulnerable to the effects of hot and cold temperatures.
   b. People tend to wait until middle adulthood to take adequate care of their face.
   c. The face is frequently exposed to the sun.
   d. The muscles of the face are the first to lose their strength.

9. Lawrence feels depressed about his aging body and believes that there is little he can do about age-related declines. When Lawrence's hearing worsens, he is most likely to __________ (p. 573)
   a. utilize problem-centered coping strategies.
   b. deny that he is having problems.
   c. take active measures to reverse his hearing loss.
   d. take a passive approach in dealing with his hearing loss.

10. Research confirms that older adults fare best when they __________ (p. 576)
    a. are excused from important decision-making roles.
    b. have opportunities to participate in their community.
    c. accept their limited usefulness to their families and communities.
    d. live with adult children or other close family members.

11. Older adults are generally _______________ about their own health. (p. 577)
    a. optimistic
    b. pessimistic
    c. indifferent
    d. oblivious

12. In late adulthood, exercise __________ (p. 578)
    a. is discouraged, as it often leads to serious injury.
    b. is not recommended for those with chronic disease.
    c. can help boost mood, but does little to improve overall health.
    d. is an especially powerful health intervention.

13. The two leading causes of death in old age are __________ (p. 580)
    a. stroke and pneumonia.
    b. cardiovascular disease and cancer.
    c. type 2 diabetes and cardiovascular disease.
    d. stroke and emphysema.

14. Which of these is the best example of primary aging? (p. 580)
    a. farsightedness resulting from stiffening of the lenses of the eye
    b. lung cancer caused by smoking cigarettes
    c. weight gain resulting from a sedentary lifestyle
    d. high blood pressure resulting from prolonged stress in the workplace

15. Of the following factors, which is the greatest contributor to frailty in old age? (p. 580)
    a. pessimistic outlook
    b. impaired mental health
    c. primary aging
    d. secondary aging

16. Because excessive blood glucose reduces blood flow to the hippocampus, type 2 diabetes can lead to __________ (p. 581)
    a. severe motor impairments.
    b. cognitive declines.
    c. secondary aging.
    d. hearing loss.

17. After age 65, the death rate from unintentional injuries __________ (p. 582)
    a. approaches that of adolescents and young adults.
    b. is similar to that of middle adulthood.
    c. reaches an all-time high.
    d. reaches an all-time low.

18. Which of the following is most likely to be an early symptom of Alzheimer's disease? (p. 584)
    a. forgetting an appointment
    b. inability to recall a long-ago event
    c. paranoia
    d. change in personality

19. At present, __________ is the most commonly known risk factor for sporadic Alzheimer's. (p. 585)
    a. poor nutrition
    b. mercury exposure
    c. low-SES
    d. the abnormal ApoE4 gene

20. Research on respite shows that it __________ (p. 587)
    a. boosts caregivers' sense of self-efficacy.
    b. is more cost-effective than other forms of community assistance, such as classes.
    c. improves caregivers' physical and mental health.
    d. does little to improve caregivers' physical and mental health.

21. Which of the following statements about cerebrovascular dementia and Alzheimer's is true? (p. 588)
    a. Cerebrovascular dementia results from environmental factors, whereas Alzheimer's is hereditary.
    b. Unlike Alzheimer's, cerebrovascular dementia results from a series of strokes.
    c. Unlike Alzheimer's, there is no way to prevent or stave off cerebrovascular dementia.
    d. Cerebrovascular dementia is incurable, whereas Alzheimer's can be managed with medication and diet.

22. In most cases, older adults must pay for nursing home care until they no longer have the financial resources, at which point Medicaid takes over. What is the result of this policy? (p. 589)
    a. Very poor families are especially reluctant to place elders in nursing homes.
    b. Only middle-class elders can afford nursing home placement.
    c. Nursing homes tend to be populated with elders who do not need special care.
    d. The largest users of nursing homes are very high-income and very low-income people.

23. The more a mental ability depends on __________, the earlier it starts to decline. (p. 590)
    a. implicit memory
    b. remote memory
    c. fluid intelligence
    d. crystallized intelligence

24. According to one view, selective optimization with compensation allows elders to __________ (p. 591)
    a. sustain high levels of functioning.
    b. learn to accept their poor health.
    c. maintain the energy levels of their youth.
    d. acquire emotion-centered coping skills.

25. An elder struggling to associate names with faces would benefit from __________ (p. 593)
    a. access to assistive technology devices.
    b. a daily vitamin–mineral supplement.
    c. repeated practice in various implicit memory tasks.
    d. memory strategies like elaboration during study and retrieval.

26. Research on memory capacity in late adulthood shows that __________ (pp. 592–593)
    a. recall memory suffers less in late adulthood than recognition memory.
    b. recognition memory suffers less in late adulthood than recall memory.
    c. older adults recall remote personal experiences more easily than recent ones.
    d. older adults perform better on time-based than event-based prospective memory tasks.

27. Which of the following is a compensatory strategy that elders with language production problems often use in conversation? (p. 594)
    a. simplification of grammatical structures
    b. elaboration of grammatical structures
    c. animated gestures
    d. emphasis of details over gist

28. Why do older adults make quicker decisions when confronted with health problems than younger people do? (p. 595)
    a. They have more anxiety about becoming ill.
    b. They rely less on consultation with others when solving problems.
    c. They perceive health problems as outside of their own control.
    d. They have accumulated more health-related knowledge.

29. Wisdom __________ (p. 595)
    a. tends to increase as a function of age, regardless of life experiences.
    b. is more common in early and middle adulthood than in late adulthood.
    c. is linked to life experiences, particularly the overcoming of adversity.
    d. shows no relationship to life satisfaction.

30. The Adult Development and Enrichment Project (ADEPT) and Advanced Cognitive Training for Independent and Vital Elderly (ACTIVE) study found that cognitive interventions in late adulthood __________ (p. 597)
    a. are more effective with women than men.
    b. can enhance cognitive functioning in the long-term.
    c. can maintain, but not enhance, cognitive functioning.
    d. offer no measurable cognitive benefits.

CHAPTER 18
EMOTIONAL AND SOCIAL DEVELOPMENT IN LATE ADULTHOOD

BRIEF CHAPTER SUMMARY

The final psychological conflict of Erikson's theory, ego integrity versus despair, involves coming to terms with one's life. Adults who arrive at a sense of integrity feel whole, complete, and satisfied with their achievements, whereas despair occurs when elders feel they have made many wrong decisions. In Peck's theory, ego integrity requires that older adults move beyond their life's work, their bodies, and their separate identities. Joan Erikson, widow of Erik Erikson, believed that older people can arrive at a psychosocial stage she calls gerotranscendence—a cosmic, transcendent perspective directed beyond the self. Labouvie-Vief addresses the development of adults' reasoning about emotion, pointing out that older, more psychologically mature adults develop affect optimization, the ability to maximize positive emotion and dampen negative emotion. Although researchers do not yet have a full understanding of why older people reminisce more than younger people do, current theory and research indicate that reflecting on the past can be positive and adaptive.

Older adults have accumulated a lifetime of self-knowledge, leading to more secure and complex conceptions of themselves than at earlier ages. During late adulthood, resilience is fostered by gains in agreeableness and acceptance of change. While U.S. elders generally become more religious or spiritual as they age, this trend is not universal: Some elders decline in religiosity.

In patterns of behavior called the dependency–support script and independence–ignore script, older adults' dependency behaviors are attended to immediately, while their independent behaviors are ignored, encouraging elders to become more dependent than they need or want to be. Physical declines and chronic disease can be highly stressful, leading to a sense of loss of personal control—a major factor in adult mental health. In late adulthood, social support continues to play a powerful role in reducing stress, thereby promoting physical health and psychological well-being.

In late adulthood, extroverts continue to interact with a wider range of people than introverts and people with poor social skills. Disengagement theory, activity theory, continuity theory, and socioemotional selectivity theory offer varying explanations for the changes in the amount of social interaction in late adulthood. The physical and social contexts in which elders live affect their social experiences and, consequently, their development and adjustment. Most elders prefer to age in place, remaining in a familiar setting where they have control over everyday life, but different communities, neighborhoods, and housing arrangements (including congregate housing and life-care communities) vary in the extent to which they enable aging residents to satisfy their social needs.

The social convoy is an influential model of changes in our social networks as we move through life. Marital satisfaction rises from middle to late adulthood as perceptions of fairness in the relationship increase, couples engage in joint leisure activities, and communication becomes more positive. Most gay and lesbian elders also report happy, highly fulfilling relationships. Couples who divorce in late adulthood constitute a very small proportion of all divorces in any given year. Compared to divorced younger adults, divorced elders find it harder to separate their identity from that of their former spouse, and they suffer more from a sense of personal failure. Wide variation in adaptation to widowhood exists, with age, social support, and personality making a difference. Today, more older adults who enter a new relationship choose to cohabit rather than remarrying.

Siblings, friends, and adult children provide important sources of emotional support and companionship to elders. In addition, older adults with adult grandchildren and great-grandchildren benefit from a wider potential network of support. Although the majority of older adults enjoy positive relationships with family members, friends, and professional caregivers, some suffer maltreatment at the hands of these individuals.

Financial and health status, opportunities to pursue meaningful activities, and societal factors (such as early retirement benefits) affect the decision to retire. Retirement also varies with gender and ethnicity. Most elders adjust well to retirement. Involvement in satisfying leisure activities is related to better physical and mental health and reduced mortality. Elders who experience optimal aging have developed many ways to minimize losses and maximize gains. Social contexts that permit elders to manage life changes effectively foster successful aging.

LEARNING OBJECTIVES

After reading this chapter, you should be able to:

18.1 Describe Erikson's stage of ego integrity versus despair. (p. 604)

18.2 Discuss Peck's tasks of ego integrity, Joan Erikson's gerotranscendence, and Labouvie-Vief's emotional expertise. (pp. 604–605)

18.3 Describe the functions of reminiscence and life review in older adults' lives. (pp. 606, 607)

18.4 Summarize stability and change in self-concept and personality in late adulthood. (pp. 606–608)

18.5 Discuss spirituality and religiosity in late adulthood. (pp. 608–609)

18.6 Discuss contextual influences on psychological well-being as older adults respond to increased dependency, declining health, and negative life changes. (pp. 609–611, 612)

18.7 Summarize the role of social support and social interaction in promoting physical health and psychological well-being in late adulthood. (p. 611)

18.8 Describe social theories of aging, including disengagement theory, activity theory, continuity theory, and socioemotional selectivity theory. (pp. 612–615, 616)

18.9 Explain how communities, neighborhoods, and housing arrangements affect elders' social lives and adjustment. (pp. 615–619)

18.10 Describe changes in social relationships in late adulthood, including marriage, gay and lesbian partnerships, divorce, remarriage, cohabitation, and widowhood, and discuss never-married, childless older adults. (pp. 619–623)

18.11 Explain how sibling relationships and friendships change in late life. (pp. 624–625)

18.12 Describe older adults' relationships with adult children, adult grandchildren, and great-grandchildren. (pp. 625–626)

18.13 Summarize elder maltreatment, including risk factors and strategies for prevention. (pp. 627–628)

18.14 Discuss the decision to retire, adjustment to retirement, and involvement in leisure and volunteer activities. (pp. 628–632)

18.15 Discuss the meaning of optimal aging. (pp. 632–633)

STUDY QUESTIONS

Erikson's Theory: Ego Integrity versus Despair

1. Cite characteristics of elders who arrive at a sense of *ego integrity* and those who experience *despair*. (p. 604)

   Integrity: ____

   ____

   Despair: ____

   ____

2. True or False: Ego integrity is associated with favorable psychological well-being. (p. 604)

Other Theories of Psychosocial Development in Late Adulthood

Peck's Tasks of Ego Integrity and Joan Erikson's Gerotranscendence

1. Match Peck's three tasks towards attaining ego integrity with their descriptions. (pp. 604–605)

_______	Surmounting physical limitations by emphasizing other rewarding capacities	A. Ego differentiation
_______	Finding ways to affirm self-worth beyond one's career	B. Body transcendence
_______	Facing the reality of death constructively through efforts to improve life for younger generations	C. Ego transcendence

2. Research suggests that body transcendence and ego transcendence (decrease / increase) as elders grow older. (p. 605)
3. Joan Erikson's psychosocial stage of ____________________ is a cosmic and transcendent perspective directed forward and outward, beyond the self. (p. 605)
4. True or False: Additional research is needed to confirm the existence of a distinct, transcendent late-life stage, such as *gerotranscendence*. (p. 605)

Labouvie-Vief's Emotional Expertise

1. ______________________________, the ability to maximize positive emotion and dampen negative emotion, contributes to elders' remarkable resilience. (p. 605)
2. Many middle-aged and elderly individuals give more vivid accounts of emotional experiences than those of younger people—evidence that they are (less / more) in touch with their feelings. (p. 605)
3. Explain how older adults' emotional perceptiveness influences their coping strategies. (p. 605)

   ____

   ____
4. Elders tend to focus on emotionally (negative / positive) features of past and current experiences. (p. 605)
5. True or False: A significant late-life psychosocial attainment is becoming expert at processing emotional information and regulating negative affect. (p. 605)

Reminiscence

1. True or False: *Reminiscence* can be positive and adaptive. (p. 606)
2. ________________________ involves reconsidering past experiences with the goal of achieving greater self-understanding. Explain why it is an important form of reminiscence. (p. 606)

   ____

   ____

   ____
3. True or False: Research suggests that older adults inevitably focus on the past and wish to be young again. (p. 606)
4. Besides life review, list three other types of reminiscence. (p. 606)

   A. ______________________________ C. ______________________________

   B. ______________________________

A Lifespan Vista: The New Old Age

1. Describe the *Third Age*. (p. 607)

2. True or False: Most older Americans self-identify as retired. Explain your answer. (p. 607)

3. Cite three ways in which today's Third Agers contribute to society. (p. 607)

   A.

   B.

   C.

Stability and Change in Self-Concept and Personality

Secure and Multifaceted Self-Concept

1. True or False: Elders' accumulated self-knowledge leads to more secure and complex conceptions of themselves than at earlier ages. (p. 606)
2. Explain how a firm, secure, and multifaceted self-concept relates to psychological well-being. (p. 606)

3. In what areas do elders continue to mention hoped-for selves? (pp. 606–607)

4. True or False: Possible selves reorganize well into old age. (p. 607)

Resilience: Agreeableness and Acceptance of Change

1. Indicate whether elders tend to show declines (–) or gains (+) in the following personality traits. (p. 608)

   ______ Agreeableness
   ______ Openness to experience
   ______ Extraversion
   ______ Acceptance of change

2. True or False: Older adults' general cheerfulness strengthens their physiological resistance to stress. (p. 608)

Spirituality and Religiosity

1. Older adults attach (little / moderate / great) value to religious beliefs and behaviors. (p. 608)
2. North American elders generally become (less / more) religious or spiritual as they age—a trend that (is / is not) universal. Explain your answer. (p. 608)

3. True or False: Involvement in religious activities is especially high among low-SES ethnic minority elders. (p. 608)
4. (Men / Women) are more likely to be involved in religion. What might explain this trend? (p. 609)

5. Briefly summarize the benefits of religious involvement. (p. 609)

Contextual Influences on Psychological Well-Being

Control versus Dependency

1. Describe two complementary behavior patterns people often use when interacting with older adults. (p. 609)

   Dependency–support script:

   Independence–ignore script:

2. What factors determine whether assistance from others undermines elders' well-being? (pp. 609–610)

3. True or False: A stereotype of the elderly as passive and incompetent causes caregivers to respond to elders in ways that promote excess dependency. (p. 610)
4. In (Western / non-Western) societies, many elders fear becoming dependent on others. (p. 610)

Physical Health

1. (Degree of physical limitation / Perceived negative physical health) predicts depressive symptoms more strongly. (p. 610)
2. Explain how the relationship between physical and mental health problems can become a vicious cycle in older adults. (p. 610)

3. True or False: People age 65 and older have the highest suicide rate of any age group. (p. 610)
4. Cite factors that help elders surmount physical impairment. (pp. 610–611)

5. True or False: Most nursing home residents receive regular mental health intervention. (p. 611)

Social Issues: Elder Suicide

1. The suicide rate (decreases / increases) over the lifespan. More (males / females) take their own lives. Compared with the white majority, most ethnic minority elders have (low / high) suicide rates. (p. 612)

2. Describe factors that contribute to low suicide rates for certain elders mentioned in the previous question. (p. 612)

3. List two reasons why elder suicides tend to be underreported. (p. 612)

   A.

   B.

4. What two types of events often prompt suicide in late life? (pp. 612–613)

   A.

   B.

5. Cite several warning signs of elder suicide. (p. 613)

6. Describe the most effective treatment for depressed, suicidal elders. (p. 613)

7. Rates of elder suicide have (declined / increased) during the past 50 years. List several reasons why this is so. (p. 613)

Negative Life Changes

1. Negative life changes are greater for (men / women) in very old age. Explain your answer. (p. 611)

2. True or False: Women of very advanced age tend to report a lower sense of psychological well-being than men. (p. 611)

Social Support

1. Summarize the benefits of social support in late adulthood. (p. 611)

2. True or False: When elders receive assistance that is excessive or cannot be returned, it often results in psychological distress. (p. 611)

3. Under what circumstance are ethnic minority elders more likely to accept formal support? (p. 611)

____

4. Describe forms of assistance that are likely to have negative versus positive effects for the elderly. (p. 611)

   Negative effects: ____

   ____

   Positive effects: ____

   ____

5. True or False: Perceived social support is associated with a positive outlook in older adults with disabilities, whereas the amount of help from family and friends has little impact. (p. 611)

A Changing Social World

1. True or False: Size of social networks and amount of social interaction declines with age for virtually everyone. (p. 612)

Social Theories of Aging

1. Match the following social theories of aging with their descriptions. (pp. 612–613)

   _______ Aging adults strive to maintain a personal system that ensures consistency between their past and future.
   _______ Mutual withdrawal between elders and society takes place in anticipation of death.
   _______ Social interaction extends lifelong selection processes.
   _______ Social barriers to engagement cause declining rates of interaction.

   A. Socioemotional selectivity theory
   B. Disengagement theory
   C. Activity theory
   D. Continuity theory

2. Explain the argument against disengagement theory. (p. 613)

   ____

   ____

   ____

3. True or False: Consistent with activity theory, studies show that simply offering older adults opportunities for social contact leads to greater social activity. (p. 614)

4. Research on the daily lives of older adults confirms a (low / moderate / high) degree of continuity in everyday pursuits and relationships. (p. 614)

5. Describe ways that reliance on continuity benefits older adults. (p. 614)

   ____

   ____

   ____

6. According to socioemotional selectivity theory, how do the functions of social interaction change in late adulthood? (pp. 614–615)

   ____

   ____

   ____

7. How do older adults apply their emotional expertise to promote harmony in social interactions? (p. 615)

____

____

____

Biology and Environment: Aging, Time Perception, and Social Goals

1. True or False: Socioemotional selectivity theory underscores that our time perspective plays a crucial role in the social goals we select and pursue. (p. 616)
2. How do the social perspectives of men with AIDS support socioemotional selectivity theory? (p. 616)

   ____

   ____

   ____

3. True or False: The preference for close partners when time is short stems from a need for social support, not meaningful interactions. (p. 616)

Social Contexts of Aging: Communities, Neighborhoods, and Housing

1. True or False: U.S. ethnic minority elders are more likely than Caucasian elders to live in cities. (p. 615)
2. The majority of senior citizens reside in ____________________, where they moved earlier in their lives and usually remain after retirement. (p. 615)
3. Summarize differences between suburban, inner-city, and small-town and rural elders. (pp. 615–616)

   Suburban: ____

   Inner-city: ____

   Small-town and rural: ____

4. What aspects of smaller communities foster gratifying relationships for older adults? (p. 616)

   ____

   ____

5. True or False: Presence of family members is not as crucial to older adults' well-being if they have neighbors and nearby friends who can provide support. (p. 616)
6. Cite a major reason why older adults in quiet neighborhoods in small and midsized communities are more satisfied with life than their peers in urban areas. (p. 617)

   ____

7. Older adults are (less / more) often targets of crime, especially violent crime, than other age groups. (p. 617)
8. How can fear of and experiences with crime affect older adults? (p. 617)

   ____

   ____

9. Elders' housing preferences reflect a strong desire to ____________________, or remain in a familiar setting where they have control over their everyday lives. (p. 617)

10. Cite several factors that prompt elder relocations. (p. 617)

____

____

____

11. Which setting affords the greatest possible personal control for the majority of elders? Under what conditions does this setting pose risks? (p. 617)

A. ____

B. ____

12. Although increasing numbers of ethnic minority elders want to live on their own, ________________ often prevents them from doing so. (p. 617)

13. During the past half-century, the number of unmarried, divorced, and widowed elders living alone has (declined / risen) rapidly. This trend (is / is not) evident in all segments of the elderly population. (p. 618)

14. Cite factors that contribute to high poverty rates among elderly widowed women. (p. 618)

____

____

15. Match the following types of residential communities for seniors with their descriptions. (p. 618)

_______ Has been modified to suit elders' capacities; otherwise resembles ordinary homes

_______ Offers many housing alternatives, guarantees that elders' needs will be met within the same facility as they age

_______ Provides a variety of support services, including common meals and watchful oversight of residents

A. *Congregate housing*
B. Housing development for the aged
C. *Life-care community*

16. Discuss the positive effects of residential communities on physical and mental health. (p. 618)

____

____

____

17. Summarize physical designs and support services that enable elders to *age in place* and facilitate residents' well-being. (p. 618)

____

____

____

18. Americans age 65 and older who live in (congregate housing / life-care communities / nursing homes) experience the most extreme restriction of autonomy and social integration. (p. 619)

19. Cite aspects of the Green House nursing home that promote elders' quality of life. (p. 619)

____

____

Relationships in Late Adulthood

1. How does the *social convoy* support adaptation to old age? (pp. 619–620)

____

____

Marriage

1. Provide four reasons why marital satisfaction increases from middle to late adulthood. (p. 620)

   A. ____

   B. ____

   C. ____

   D. ____

2. True or False: Compared to their single agemates, married elders generally have smaller social networks, with whom they interact less frequently. (p. 620)

3. When marital dissatisfaction is present, it often takes a greater toll on (men / women), who tend to confront marital problems and try to solve them. (p. 620)

Gay and Lesbian Partnerships

1. True or False: Most elderly gay and lesbian couples report happy, highly fulfilling relationships. (p. 620)

2. What unique challenges do aging gays and lesbians face? (p. 621)

____

____

____

Divorce, Remarriage, and Cohabitation

1. What reasons do men and women give for initiating divorce in late life? (p. 621)

   Men: ____

   Women: ____

2. Following divorce, (younger / older) adults find it harder to separate their identity from that of their former spouse, and they suffer (less / more) from a sense of personal failure. (p. 621)

3. Overall, (men / women) suffer more after a late-life divorce. Why is this? (p. 621)

____

____

4. List three reasons why late adulthood remarriages are more common among divorced than widowed elders. (p. 621)

   A. ____

   B. ____

   C. ____

5. True or False: Rather than remarrying, today many older adults who enter a new relationship choose cohabitation. What explains this trend? (p. 621)

____

____

____

Widowhood

1. Widows make up about ______________ of the elderly population. More U.S. (men / women) age 65 and over are widowed. Ethnic minorities with high rates of poverty and chronic disease are (less / more) likely to be widowed. (p. 622)

2. When widowed elders relocate due to financial or physical difficulties, they usually choose to move (closer to / in with) family. Explain your answer. (p. 622)

____

____

3. The greatest problem for recently widowed elders is ______________________________. (p. 622)

4. True or False: Widowed elders have fewer lasting problems than younger individuals who are widowed. (p. 622)

5. (Men / Women) find it more difficult to adjust to widowhood. Cite three reasons for this gender difference. (p. 622)

   A. ____

   B. ____

   C. ____

6. Describe factors that can help older people manage the challenges of widowed life. (p. 623)

____

____

____

Never-Married, Childless Older Adults

1. Cite examples of alternative, meaningful relationships formed by adults who remain single and childless throughout life. (p. 623)

____

____

2. Indicate whether the following traits are common among nonmarried, childless men (M) or women (W). (p. 623)

   _______ Are more likely to feel lonely and depressed
   _______ Report a level of well-being equivalent to that of married elders
   _______ Often state that they avoided many problems associated with marriage and parenthood
   _______ Report poorer physical and mental health than their married counterparts

Siblings

1. Both men and women perceive bonds with (sisters / brothers) to be closer. (p. 624)

2. Elderly siblings in industrialized nations are more likely to (provide direct assistance for / socialize with) one another. (p. 624)

3. __________________ and __________________ elders have more contacts with siblings and are more likely to receive sibling support during illness. (p. 624)

Friendships

1. List four functions of elder friendships. (pp. 624–625)

   A. ______________________________

   B. ______________________________

   C. ______________________________

   D. ______________________________

2. True or False: Friendship formation continues throughout life. (p. 625)

3. Describe characteristics of older adult friendships. (p. 625)

   ____

   ____

4. Older (men / women) have more ______________________________, or people who are not intimate ties but with whom they spend time occasionally. (p. 625)

5. Why do elders with physical limitations whose social networks consist mainly of friends tend to report low psychological well-being? (p. 625)

   ____

   ____

Relationships with Adult Children

1. As with other ties, the (quality / quantity) of interactions between elders and their adult children affects older adults' life satisfaction. (p. 625)

2. True or False: Elders in Western nations give more than they receive. (p. 625)

3. For adults age 75 and over, help received from adult children most often takes the form of ______________________________. (p. 625)

4. What type of support from adult children is linked to poor well-being in older adults? (p. 626)

   ____

5. Older adults are more likely to describe their family as (solely close / ambivalent). (p. 626)

Relationships with Adult Grandchildren and Great-Grandchildren

1. The majority of grandchildren (do /do not) feel obligated to assist grandparents in need. Grandparents often expect (affection / practical help) from grandchildren. (p. 626)

2. True or False: As grandparents and grandchildren move through life, contact declines. (p. 626)

3. Why does grandparents' affection for their grandchildren strengthen with age, often exceeding grandchildren's expressed closeness toward their grandparents? (p. 626)

   ____

   ____

Elder Maltreatment

1. Match each type of elder maltreatment with its description. (p. 627)

______	Verbal assaults, humiliation, and intimidation	A. Physical abuse
______	Exploitation of property or financial resources	B. Physical neglect
______	Intentional or unintentional failure to fulfill Caregiving obligations	C. Emotional abuse
______	Intentional infliction of pain, discomfort, or injury	D. Sexual abuxe
______	Unwanted sexual contact of any kind	E. Financial abuse

2. What forms of elder maltreatment are most frequently reported? (p. 627)

____

____

3. Perpetrators of elder abuse usually (are / are not) family members. (p. 627)

4. Describe a type of neglect the media refers to as "granny dumping." (p. 627)

____

____

5. List five risk factors that increase the likelihood of elder abuse. (pp. 627–628)

A. ____

B. ____

C. ____

D. ____

E. ____

6. Why is preventing elder maltreatment by family members especially challenging? (p. 628)

____

____

7. Identify several components of elder maltreatment prevention programs. (p. 628)

____

____

____

8. Cite two ways in which societal efforts can help to reduce the incidence of elder abuse. (p. 628)

A. ____

B. ____

Retirement

1. What social changes have led to a blurring of the distinction between work and retirement? (p. 628)

____

____

2. Cite two reasons why the trend toward earlier retirement may soon reverse. (p. 628)

   A. ______________________________

   B. ______________________________

The Decision to Retire

1. What is usually the first consideration in the decision to retire? List some additional considerations. (p. 629)

   First: ______________________________

   Additional: ______________________________

   ____

   ____

2. Provide an illustration of how societal factors affect older adults' retirement decisions. (p. 629)

   ____

   ____

3. (Men / Women) tend to retire earlier. Why is this? Cite an exception to this trend. (pp. 629–630)

   A. ______________________________

   B. ______________________________

Adjustment to Retirement

1. True or False: For most people, mental health and perceived quality of life are fairly stable from the pre- to postretirement years. (p. 630)

2. Indicate whether the following factors predict adjustment difficulties (–) or retirement satisfaction (+). (p. 630)

   _______ Sense of personal control over life events
   _______ Moving out of a high-stress job
   _______ Leaving a pleasant job before one is ready
   _______ Retirement heavily encouraged by husbands
   _______ Financial worries and having to give up one's job
   _______ High education, leaving a high-status career
   _______ For women, a continuous work life
   _______ Retirement encouraged by wives

3. How can retirement enhance marital satisfaction? How does marital satisfaction, in turn, influence adjustment to retirement? (p. 630)

   A. ______________________________

   B. ______________________________

Leisure and Volunteer Activities

1. What is the best preparation for leisure in late life? (pp. 630–631)

   ____

2. List several benefits of involvement in leisure activities. (p. 631)

   ____

   ____

3. True or False: With age, the frequency and variety of leisure pursuits tend to decline. (p. 631)

4. List four characteristics of elders who become involved in volunteer work. (p. 631)

   A. ______________________ C. ______________________

   B. ______________________ D. ______________________

5. Older adults report (less / more) awareness of public affairs and vote at a (lower / higher) rate than other adults. (pp. 631–632)

Optimal Aging

1. In ______________, gains are maximized and losses are minimized. Cite characteristics associated with this form of aging. (p. 632)

   ____

   ____

2. Recent views of a contented, fulfilling late adulthood have turned (away from / toward) specific achievements and (away from / toward) processes people use to reach valued goals. (p. 632)

3. True or False: Vaillant's findings reveal that factors people can control to some degree far outweigh uncontrollable factors in predicting a happy, active old age. (p. 632)

4. Describe three ways that older adults realize their goals. (p. 632)

   A. ____

   B. ____

   C. ____

5. Cite societal contexts that permit elders to manage life changes effectively. (pp. 632–633)

   ____

   ____

ASK YOURSELF . . .

For *Ask Yourself* questions for this chapter, along with feedback on the accuracy of your answers, please log on to MyDevelopmentLab (for registration and access, please visit mydevelopmentlab.com or follow the instructions on page ix).

(1) Select the Multimedia Library.

(2) Choose the explore option.

(3) Find your chapter from the drop down box.

(4) Click find now.

(5) Complete questions and choose "Submit answers for grading" or "Clear answers" to start over.

SUGGESTED READINGS

Ash, I., & Ask, I. (2009). *Aging is living: Myth-breaking stories from long-term care*. Toronto: Dundurn Press. Using research and personal interviews with elders and their families, the authors highlight the many positive aspects of aging, even among individuals residing in nursing homes. Contrary to popular belief, the majority of North American elders do not spend most of their time focused on death. For many, late adulthood is a fulfilling time of life with continued hopes and dreams for the future.

Connidis, I. A. (2009). *Family ties and aging*. Thousand Oaks, CA: Sage. A comprehensive approach to understanding changes in family relationships across middle and late adulthood, this book presents up-to-date research on marriage, sibling relationships, gay and lesbian couples, childlessness, parenthood and grandparenthood, and elder abuse and neglect.

Eyetsemitan, F. E. & Gire, J. T. (2006). *Aging and adult development in the developing world: Applying western theories and concepts*. West Point, CT: Greenwood Publishing. A collection of chapters highlighting the influence of environmental contexts on the aging process. According to the authors, Western theories of aging may be inappropriate for understanding the experiences of elders in developing societies.

CROSSWORD PUZZLE 18.1

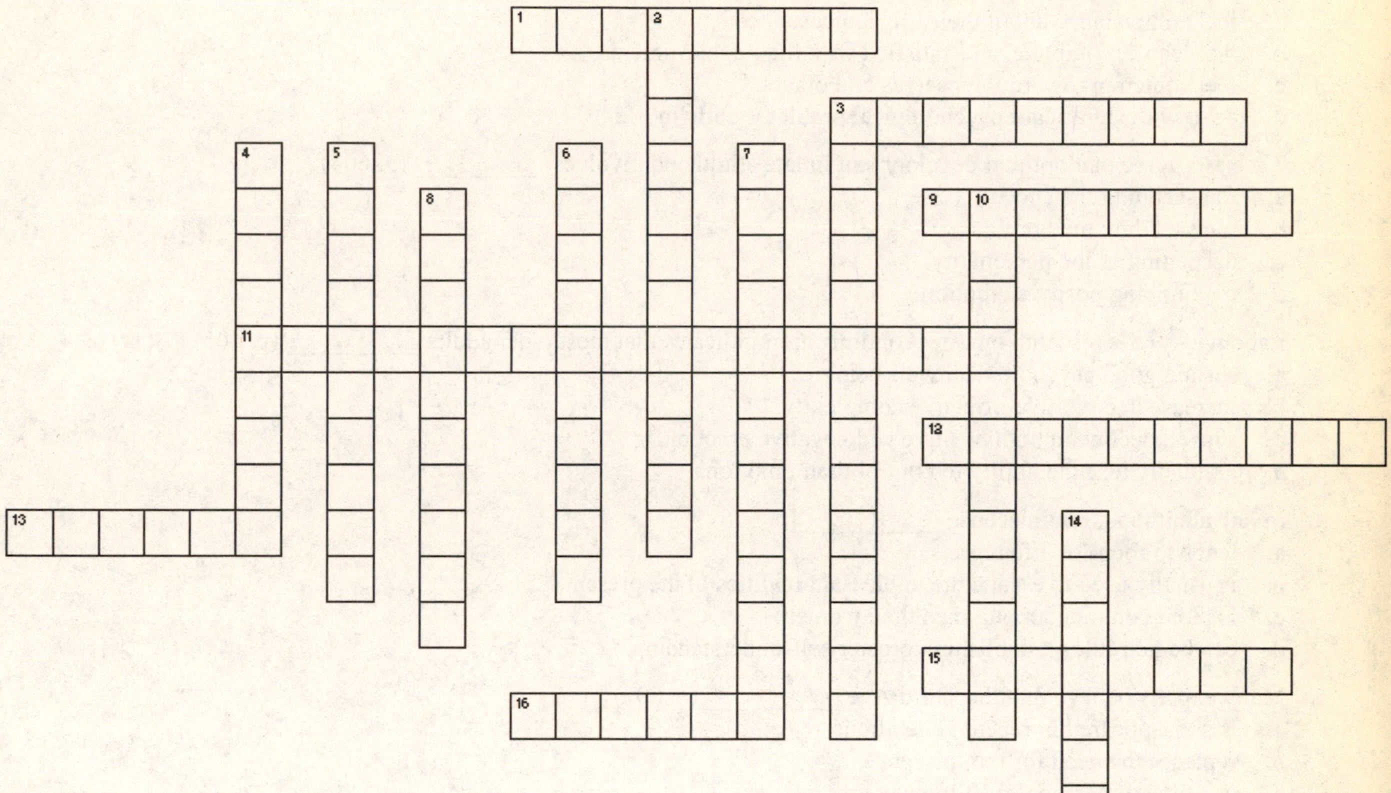

Across

1. Time of personal fulfillment extending from ages 65 to 79 and sometimes longer (2 words)
3. ______ friends: people who are not intimates but with whom one spends time occasionally
9. ______-______communities offer many options, from independent housing to nursing home care. (2 words, hyph.)
11. Joan Erikson's psychological stage; a cosmic and transcendent perspective directed beyond the self
12. ______-support script: requests for help are attended to immediately
13. Social ______: views the individual within a cluster of relationships moving throughout life
15. ______ theory: social barriers to engagement, not elders' desires, cause declining rates of interaction
16. ______ optimization: the ability to maximize positive and dampen negative emotions

Down

2. Telling stories about the past and reporting associated thoughts and feelings
3. ______ selectivity theory: social interaction extends lifelong selection processes
4. Ego ______ versus despair: Erikson's psychological conflict of late adulthood
5. ______ housing provides support services such as common meals and oversight.
6. Elders desire to ______, or remain in a familiar setting in which they have control. (3 words)
7. ______ theory: mutual withdrawal between elders and society takes place in anticipation of death
8. ______ theory: most aging adults strive for consistency between their past and anticipated future
10. ______-ignore script: autonomous behaviors are mostly ignored
14. ______ aging: gains are maximized and losses are minimized

PRACTICE TEST #1

1. According to Erikson, adults who arrive at a sense of integrity __________ (p. 604)
   a. feel ambivalence about their life choices.
   b. feel whole, complete, and satisfied with their achievements.
   c. feel contempt toward themselves and others.
   d. dealt with significant psychological problems early in life.

2. Theorists agree that optimal development in late adulthood involves __________ (p. 604)
   a. transcending the ego.
   b. transcending the body.
   c. deepening of the personality.
   d. maximizing positive emotion.

3. Labouvie-Vief's research on affect optimization indicates that most older adults __________ (p. 605)
   a. sustain good psychological well-being.
   b. increase in cognitive-affective complexity.
   c. show a decline in both positive and negative emotion.
   d. gradually lose the ability to control their emotions.

4. In late adulthood, reminiscence __________ (p. 606)
   a. tends to focus on life regrets.
   b. is usually used to escape the unpleasant realities of the present.
   c. is more common among men than women.
   d. can be helpful in establishing greater self-understanding.

5. Many experts believe that the Third Age __________ (p. 607)
   a. has disappeared in recent generations.
   b. replaces the need for reminiscence.
   c. is a time of personal fulfillment.
   d. occurs only in collectivist cultures.

6. Which of the following statements about elder spirituality and religiosity is true? (p. 608)
   a. In the United States, elders are more likely than other age groups to say religion is very important to them.
   b. In late adulthood, spirituality tends to decline, while religiosity increases sharply.
   c. Throughout the world, most elders become less religious or spiritual as they age.
   d. In nearly all cultures, elders become more religious or spiritual as they age.

7. Elders who have trouble performing daily activities generally __________ (p. 609)
   a. report especially gratifying social interaction.
   b. report less positive social interaction.
   c. reject any type of family support.
   d. adapt well to a dependency-support script.

8. Which of the following statements about the relationship between physical health and psychological well-being in late adulthood is true? (p. 610)
   a. Feelings of hopelessness tend to decline sharply in late adulthood, regardless of physical disability.
   b. There is a stronger physical impairment–depression relationship among higher-SES elders than low-SES elders.
   c. Actual physical health is a stronger predictor of depression than perceived physical health.
   d. Perceived negative physical health is an especially strong predictor of depression.

9. Elder suicide attempts __________ (p. 612)
   a. are often underreported.
   b. are very difficult to predict.
   c. have increased in recent years.
   d. are rarely successful.

10. Which of the following is strongly associated with a positive outlook in elders? (p. 611)
    a. the amount of help received from friends and family members
    b. the perceived social support from friends and family members
    c. a sense of independence, even in areas where help is needed
    d. a sense of dependence, even in areas where help is not needed

11. Which of the following provides a challenge to disengagement theory? (p. 613)
    a. Older people often decrease their activity levels.
    b. Older people become more preoccupied with their inner lives.
    c. Society frees elders from employment and family responsibilities.
    d. Older people often maintain satisfying social ties.

12. Despite a recent move to an assisted living facility, 82-year-old Eleanor strives to maintain familiar relationships and activities; she continues to play cards with her sister and shops at the same supermarket. Eleanor's actions are consistent with __________ theory. (p. 614)
    a. activity
    b. disengagement
    c. continuity
    d. Third Age

13. Contact with acquaintances and willingness to form new social ties __________ from middle to late adulthood. (p. 615)
    a. fall off steeply
    b. remain constant
    c. increase slightly
    d. increase sharply

14. Socioemotional selectivity theory considers the influence of __________ on our social goals. (p. 616)
    a. personality traits
    b. emotions
    c. time perspective
    d. political affiliation

15. A major reason that older adults in smaller communities are more satisfied with life than their urban counterparts is __________ (p. 617)
    a. they enjoy greater access to social services.
    b. their neighborhoods have lower crime rates.
    c. they tend to live closer to family members.
    d. they are more likely to live in their own homes or with relatives.

16. The majority of older adults in Western nations want to live __________ (p. 617)
    a. in their own homes and neighborhoods, and 90 percent of them do.
    b. in their own homes and neighborhoods, but only 50 percent do.
    c. in a warmer climate like that found in Florida and Arizona.
    d. with their children or other family members.

17. During the past half-century, the number of Western elders living alone has __________ (p. 618)
    a. declined dramatically.
    b. remained stable.
    c. risen dramatically.
    d. risen for men, but declined for women.

18. Age-segregated living __________ (p. 618)
    a. appeals to elders in all cultures.
    b. is gratifying for those who choose it.
    c. often leads to social disengagement.
    d. is rare in Western cultures.

19. Which of the following would improve the well-being of elders in nursing homes? (p. 619)
    a. removing or limiting aging-in-place features
    b. lifting or easing federal regulations of facilities
    c. requiring that residents interact with each other
    d. making institutions more homelike

20. Marital satisfaction __________ (p. 620)
    a. declines steadily from early to late adulthood.
    b. rises from early to middle adulthood, then declines.
    c. peaks in middle adulthood.
    d. peaks in late adulthood.

21. Elderly gay and lesbian couples typically __________ (p. 620)
    a. have great difficulty achieving a sense of integrity.
    b. report negative, unfulfilling relationships.
    c. report happy, highly fulfilling relationships.
    d. turn to family members and friends instead of their partners for social support.

22. After a divorce in late adulthood, women __________ than men. (p. 621)
    a. more often find happiness in new relationships
    b. suffer more severe financial consequences
    c. experience less depression and guilt
    d. criticize their former spouse more often

23. What is the greatest problem for recently widowed elders? (p. 622)
    a. ineffective problem-solving skills
    b. difficulty completing daily tasks
    c. profound loneliness
    d. conflict with adult children

24. Which of the following statements about elder friendships is true? (p. 624)
    a. Compared with younger people, fewer elders report other-sex friendships.
    b. Elderly women tend to have a few intimate friends, whereas elderly men have a larger circle of secondary friends.
    c. In late life, close friends rely on each other for ongoing assistance with daily living tasks.
    d. Older adults prefer the companionship of new acquaintances over established friends.

25. The kind of assistance that elders most often receive from their adult children is __________ (p. 625)
    a. emotional support.
    b. help with day-to-day living tasks.
    c. financial assistance.
    d. assistance with medical care.

26. Which of the following is the most frequently reported type of elder maltreatment? (p. 627)
    a. physical abuse
    b. financial abuse
    c. sexual abuse
    d. racial discrimination

27. __________ are more likely to delay retirement than __________. (p. 630)
    a. Women; men
    b. Blue-collar workers; white-collar workers
    c. African-American women; Caucasian women
    d. People in poor health; people in good health

28. In accord with socioemotional selectivity theory, older adults who volunteer __________ (p. 631)
    a. often quit after retirement in favor of other leisure pursuits.
    b. remain loyal to their favored organizations and rarely consider new opportunities.
    c. tend to commit a large number of hours shortly after retirement, then abandon volunteering.
    d. eventually narrow their volunteering to the few roles that mean the most to them.

29. Elders who experience optimal aging have __________ (p. 632)
    a. ways of minimizing losses and maximizing gains.
    b. excellent physical fitness and absence of disability.
    c. large networks of close friends.
    d. creative endeavors and accomplishments.

30. Recent views of successful aging focus on the __________ (p. 632)
    a. achievements of individuals with outstanding life accomplishments.
    b. processes people use to reach personally valued goals.
    c. social lives of successful and unsuccessful agers.
    d. leisure activities of retired elders.

PRACTICE TEST #2

1. What is the final psychological conflict in Erikson's theory? (p. 604)
   a. self-acceptance versus self-rejection
   b. differentiation versus transcendence
   c. ego stability versus change
   d. ego integrity versus despair

2. Family members of 91-year-old Lois notice that she seems to have reached a spiritual state of inner calm, spending many hours in quiet reflection. Lois's contemplative state is consistent with Joan Erikson's psychosocial stage of _________ (p. 605)
   a. affect optimization.
   b. gerotranscendence.
   c. reminiscence.
   d. body transcendence.

3. Elders experience improved _________, which contribute(s) to their resilience. (p. 605)
   a. information-processing skills
   b. cognitive-affective complexity
   c. affect optimization
   d. emotional distance

4. Which type of reminiscence is linked to adjustment problems? (p. 606)
   a. life review
   b. knowledge-based
   c. other-focused
   d. self-focused

5. During late adulthood, self-concept becomes _________ (p. 606)
   a. more insecure.
   b. more complex and multifaceted.
   c. less self-accepting.
   d. simpler and more streamlined.

6. What can societies do to expand elders' social and economic contributions? (p. 607)
   a. Restrict access to social security and Medicare
   b. Provide service incentives and opportunities
   c. Enforce a mandatory retirement age
   d. Raise the average age of retirement

7. Eighty-year-old Carlos tells his children that he wants to learn to play the harmonica. Carlos probably _________ (p. 607)
   a. has a tendency to ruminate.
   b. has unrealistic goals for someone his age.
   c. will take concrete steps to attain his goal.
   d. is unsatisfied with his life accomplishments.

8. Modest age-related dips in _________ occur in late adulthood. (p. 608)
   a. openness to experience
   b. general cheerfulness
   c. neuroticism
   d. religiosity

9. In the United States, _________ are more involved in religious activities than _________. (p. 608)
   a. young adults; older adults
   b. African-American elders; Caucasian elders
   c. high-SES elders; low-SES elders
   d. older men; older women

10. Which of the following is an example of the dependency–support script? (p. 609)
    a. A caregiver rushes to help an elder get a glass of water.
    b. An elder receives special attention when he crosses the room without his walker.
    c. An elder who takes care of her own basic needs is neglected by caregivers.
    d. A caregiver provides an elder with conversation but neglects his immediate needs.

11. Which of the following statements about elder suicide is true? (p. 612)
    a. In all cultures, suicide is at its lowest rate in late adulthood.
    b. In all cultures, suicide is at its highest rate in late adulthood.
    c. Older men are more likely than older women to commit suicide.
    d. Ethnic minority elders have higher suicide rates than white majority elders.

12. According to disengagement theory, declining rates of interaction in late adulthood are caused by __________ (p. 613)
    a. social barriers to engagement.
    b. life-long selection processes.
    c. the desire of elders to reduce social interaction.
    d. mutual withdrawal between elders and society in anticipation of death.

13. Activity theory fails to acknowledge __________ (p. 614)
    a. the social barriers to engagement faced by many elders.
    b. the psychological changes in old age.
    c. elders' desire to stay active and busy.
    d. the increased happiness of socially active elders.

14. By the time he was in his late eighties, Curtis's circle of friends had diminished, and he favored the companionship only of his wife and one other close friend. According to socioemotional selectivity theory, Curtis's reduced social network __________ (p. 615)
    a. will lead to increased physical fragility.
    b. may lengthen his life expectancy.
    c. is the result of changing life conditions.
    d. signals depression or another mental disorder.

15. Why do people with a short time left to live prefer the company of familiar friends and family members? (p. 616)
    a. They want to confront and resolve past conflicts with the people close to them.
    b. They need social support to cope with the dying process.
    c. Their desire for emotionally meaningful interactions increases.
    d. Their tendency to ruminate makes them sentimental about close relationships.

16. Older adults __________ (p. 617)
    a. are less often targets of violent crime than other age groups.
    b. are more often targets of violent crime than other age groups.
    c. are rarely concerned about the possibility of becoming victims of violent crime.
    d. rarely change their habits out of fear of violent crime, even if victimization occurs.

17. In the United States, assisted-living facilities __________ (p. 618)
    a. are regulated by the federal government.
    b. are not regulated by the federal government.
    c. must allow residents to stay when their health declines.
    d. are used primarily by low-income ethnic minority elders.

18. Older Americans experience the most extreme restriction of autonomy if they live in __________ (p. 619)
    a. a nursing home.
    b. their own home.
    c. congregate housing.
    d. a life-care community.

19. The social convoy is an influential model of change in our __________ as we move through life. (p. 619)
    a. desire for sociability
    b. intimate relationships
    c. goals and values
    d. social networks

20. The impact of marital dissatisfaction __________ (p. 620)
    a. can be negated through close friendships.
    b. has similar outcomes for both men and women.
    c. is more profound for women than for men.
    d. is more profound for men than for women.

21. Compared with younger adults, older adults who divorce are more likely to __________ (p. 621)
    a. enter new relationships.
    b. feel guilt and depression.
    c. be unsatisfied in new relationships.
    d. be future-oriented.

22. Compared to widowed women, widowed men ____________ (p. 622)
    a. are less likely to remarry.
    b. receive more social support.
    c. have a greater risk of mortality.
    d. adjust more favorably.

23. Nonmarried, childless women ____________ (p. 623)
    a. are at high risk for suicide.
    b. have larger social networks than married people.
    c. often suffer from loneliness and depression.
    d. usually develop alternative meaningful relationships.

24. Elderly siblings __________ (p. 624)
    a. report a decline in contact between middle and late adulthood.
    b. provide each other with an important "insurance policy" in late adulthood.
    c. more often provide one another with assistance than social support.
    d. usually live long distances from each other and rarely communicate.

25. Elders with adult children __________ (p. 625)
    a. usually feel ambivalent toward them.
    b. are more likely to engage in volunteer activities.
    c. give more financial support and practical assistance than they receive.
    d. rely on their children for assistance with household chores and errands.

26. Longitudinal research reveals that as grandparents and grandchildren move through life, contact __________ (p. 626)
    a. and affection decline.
    b. and affection increase.
    c. declines but affection increases.
    d. increases but affection declines.

27. When elder abuse is extreme, __________, though rare, offers the best protection. (p. 628)
    a. legal action
    b. caregiver counseling
    c. a volunteer "buddy" system
    d. elder education

28. What does research suggest about elders' adjustment to retirement? (p. 630)
    a. Retirement often leads to a decline in marital satisfaction.
    b. Retirement leads to an increase in mental health problems among older adults.
    c. Older adults adapt especially well to retirement if the decision was externally motivated.
    d. Most older adults adapt well to life after retirement.

29. Involvement in leisure activities __________ (p. 631)
    a. is related to better physical and mental health and reduced mortality.
    b. is related to better physical health but has relatively little impact on mental health.
    c. does not change much over the course of late adulthood.
    d. is greater for elders in ordinary homes than retirement communities.

30. Societies that permit older adults to manage life changes effectively foster __________ (p. 632)
    a. dependency.
    b. reminiscence.
    c. optimal aging.
    d. social networks.

CHAPTER 19
DEATH, DYING, AND BEREAVEMENT

BRIEF CHAPTER SUMMARY

When asked how they would like to die, most people say they want death with dignity—either a quick, agony-free end during sleep or a clear-minded final few moments in which they can say farewell and review their lives. In reality, death is long and drawn out for three-fourths of people—many more than in times past, as a result of medical advances that prolong life.

In general, dying takes place in three phases: the agonal phase, clinical death, and mortality. In most industrialized nations, brain death is accepted as the definition of death, but thousands of patients who remain in a persistent vegetative state reveal that the brain-death standard does not always solve the dilemma of when to halt treatment for the incurably ill. Because most people will not experience an easy death, we can best ensure death with dignity by supporting dying patients through their physical and psychological distress, being candid about death's certainty, and helping them learn enough about their condition to make reasoned choices about treatment.

Most children attain an adultlike concept of death in middle childhood, gradually mastering concepts of permanence, inevitability, cessation, applicability, and causation. Experiences with death and religious teachings affect children's understanding. While parents often worry that discussing death candidly with children will fuel their fears, children with a good grasp of the facts of death have an easier time accepting it. Adolescents often fail to apply their understanding of death to everyday life. Though aware that death happens to everyone and can occur at any time, teenagers nevertheless seek alternative views, are high risk takers, and do not take death personally. Candid discussions with adolescents can help them build a bridge between death as a logical concept and their personal experiences. In early adulthood, many people brush aside thoughts of death, perhaps prompted by death anxiety or relative disinterest in death-related issues. Overall, fear of death declines with age, reaching its lowest level in late adulthood and in adults with deep faith in some form of higher being.

According to Kübler-Ross, dying people typically express five responses, which she initially proposed as "stages": denial, anger, bargaining, depression, and acceptance. Rather than stages, these five reactions are best viewed as coping strategies that anyone may call on in the face of threat. A host of contextual variables—nature of the disease; personality and coping style; family members' and health professionals' truthfulness and sensitivity; and spirituality, religion, and cultural background—affect the way people respond to their own dying and, therefore, the extent to which they attain an appropriate death.

Although most people want to die at home, caring for a dying patient is highly demanding. Hospital dying takes many forms, each affected by the physical state of the dying person, the hospital unit in which it takes place, and the goal and quality of care. Whether a person dies at home or in a hospital, the hospice approach strives to meet the dying person's physical, emotional, social, and spiritual needs by providing palliative care focused on protecting the quality of remaining life rather than on prolonging life.

The same medical procedures that preserve life can prolong inevitable death, diminishing the quality of life and personal dignity. In the absence of national consensus on passive euthanasia, people can best ensure that their wishes will be followed by preparing an advance medical directive—a written statement of desired medical treatment should they become incurably ill. Although the practice has sparked heated controversy, public support for voluntary euthanasia is high; less public consensus exists for assisted suicide.

Although many theorists regard grieving as taking place in orderly phases of avoidance, confrontation, and restoration, in reality, people vary greatly in behavior and timing and often alternate between these reactions. Like dying, grieving is affected by many factors, including personality, coping style, and religious and cultural background. Circumstances surrounding the death—whether it is sudden and unanticipated or follows a prolonged illness—also shape mourners' responses. When a parent loses a child or a child loses a parent or sibling, grieving is generally very intense and prolonged. People who experience several deaths at once or in close succession are at risk for bereavement overload that may leave them emotionally overwhelmed and unable to resolve their grief.

Preparatory steps can be taken to help people of all ages cope with death more effectively. Today, instruction in death, dying, and bereavement can be found in colleges and universities; training programs for doctors, nurses, and helping professionals; adult education programs; and even a few elementary and secondary schools.

LEARNING OBJECTIVES

After reading this chapter, you should be able to:

19.1 Describe the physical changes of dying, along with their implications for defining death and the meaning of death with dignity. (pp. 640–642)

19.2 Discuss age-related changes in conception of and attitudes toward death, including ways to enhance child and adolescent understanding. (pp. 642–644)

19.3 Cite factors that influence death anxiety, including personal and cultural variables that contribute to the fear of death. (p. 643)

19.4 Describe and evaluate Kübler-Ross's theory of typical responses to dying, citing factors that influence dying patients' responses. (pp. 647–648)

19.5 List goals associated with an appropriate death, and summarize contextual factors that influence a person's adaptation to death. (pp. 648–650)

19.6 Evaluate the extent to which homes, hospitals, and the hospice approach meet the needs of dying people and their families. (pp. 650–653)

19.7 Discuss controversies surrounding euthanasia and assisted suicide. (pp. 654–659)

19.8 Describe bereavement and the phases of grieving, indicating factors that underlie individual variations in grief responses. (pp. 659–660)

19.9 Explain the concept of bereavement overload, and describe bereavement interventions. (pp. 663, 665)

19.10 Explain how death education can help people cope with death more effectively. (p. 665)

STUDY QUESTIONS

1. The interdisciplinary field of *thanatology* is devoted to the study of ______________________. (p. 640)

How We Die

Physical Changes

1. Describe physical and behavioral changes in the days or hours before death. (p. 640)

____

____

____

2. Match each phase of dying with its description. (p. 640)

_____	Permanent death. Within a few hours, the body appears shrunken.	1. *Agonal phase*
_____	As the regular heartbeat disintegrates, gasps and muscle spasms occur.	2. *Clinical death*
_____	Heartbeat, circulation, breathing, and brain functioning stop, but resuscitation is still possible.	3. *Mortality*

3. True or False: Most people experience a quick, agony-free death. Explain your answer. (p. 641)

____

____

Defining Death

1. What definition of death is currently used in most industrialized nations? (pp. 640–641)

____

____

2. In Japan, doctors rely on (absence of heartbeat and respiration / *brain death*) to signify death. What cultural factors may have influenced this? (p. 641)

____

____

3. For individuals in a ______________________, the cerebral cortex no longer registers electrical activity, but the brain stem remains active. Explain why this complicates the dilemma of when to halt treatment. (p. 641)

____

____

____

Death with Dignity

1. Summarize three ways to foster dignity in death. (pp. 641–642)

   Support: ____

   ____

   Honesty: ____

   ____

   Personal control: ____

   ____

Understanding of and Attitudes Toward Death

1. Compared with earlier generations, today (fewer / more) young people reach adulthood without having experienced the death of someone they know well. (p. 642)

Childhood

1. Match the following components of death understanding with their descriptions. (p. 642)

_____	Only living things can die.	A. Permanence
_____	Death results from a breakdown of bodily functioning.	B. Inevitability
_____	Once a living thing dies, it cannot be brought back to life.	C. Cessation
_____	All living things eventually die.	D. Applicability
_____	All living functions stop at death.	E. Causation

2. Describe two concepts children must grasp before they can understand death. (p. 642)

   A. ____

   ____

   B. ____

   ____

3. Before children have acquired the concepts described in the previous question, how do they interpret death? (p. 642)

____

____

4. Of the following, indicate which three components of the death concept are most challenging for children to understand. (p. 642)

_____ Permanence _____ Inevitability _____ Cessation
_____ Applicability _____ Causation _____ Agency

5. Cite evidence that experience with death and religious teachings affect children's conception of death. (p. 643)

Experience: ____

____

Religious teachings: ____

____

6. Describe several ways that parents and teachers can help to alleviate children's fears and confusion about death. (p. 643)

____

____

____

____

Adolescence

1. True or False: Adolescents' understanding of death is not yet fully mature. (p. 643)

2. How do teenagers often describe death? (p. 643)

____

____

3. True or False: Teenagers rarely take death personally. (p. 643)

4. List three reasons why adolescents may have difficulty integrating logic and reality in the domain of death. (pp. 643–644)

A. ____

____

B. ____

____

C. ____

____

5. Most 12- to 15-year-olds want to talk with (parents / peers) about the "meaning of life and death" and "what happens when you die." (p. 644)

Adulthood

1. Trace changes in conceptions of death from early to late adulthood. (p. 645)

Early adulthood: ____

____

Middle adulthood: ______

Late adulthood: ______

Death Anxiety

1. What is *death anxiety*? (p. 645)

2. Research reveals (few / large) individual and cultural differences in the anxiety-provoking aspects of death. (p. 645)
3. Identify two personal factors that minimize death anxiety. (p. 645)

   A. ______

   B. ______
4. Death anxiety (declines / increases) with age, reaching its (lowest / highest) level in late adulthood. What accounts for this trend? (p. 645)

5. Explain how death anxiety can motivate people in positive ways. (pp. 645–646)

6. Regardless of age, cross-cultural studies show that (men / women) are more anxious about death. (p. 646)
7. Explain the link between death anxiety and mental health. (p. 646)

8. Children (rarely / frequently) display death anxiety. Cite exceptions to this trend. (p. 646)

Thinking and Emotions of Dying People

Do Stages of Dying Exist?

1. Briefly summarize Kübler-Ross's five typical responses to dying. (p. 647)

   Denial: ______

   Anger: ______

   Bargaining: ______

   Depression: ______

   Acceptance: ______

2. Match Kübler-Ross's typical responses to dying with recommended ways for family members and health-care providers to help patients experiencing each response. (p. 647)

_____ Tolerate rather than lash out at the patient's behavior.
_____ Provide health care that responds humanely to the patient's wishes.
_____ Listen sympathetically.
_____ Do not distort the truth about the person's condition.

A. Denial
B. Anger
C. Bargaining
D. Depression

3. True or False: Kübler-Ross viewed the responses listed in question 1 as a fixed sequence that is universally experienced by all individuals. (p. 647)

4. Summarize criticisms of Kübler-Ross's theory. (pp. 647–648)

____

____

____

Contextual Influences on Adaptations to Dying

1. Describe an *appropriate death*. (p. 648)

____

____

____

2. Cite five goals that patients mention when asked about a "good death." (p. 648)

A. ____

B. ____

C. ____

D. ____

E. ____

3. True or False: Dying people display similar reactions, regardless of the nature of their disease. (p. 648)

4. True or False: Poorly adjusted individuals are usually more distressed by a terminal diagnosis. (p. 649)

5. Denying a patient's impending death makes dying (less / more) difficult. (p. 649)

6. Provide reasons why withholding information about a patient's prognosis is common in some cultures. (p. 649)

____

____

7. Cite three factors that are key to nurses' success in meeting the needs of dying patients and their families. (p. 649)

A. ____

B. ____

C. ____

8. Describe how a dying patient's hopes may change over time. (pp. 649–650)

____

____

9. Match the following cultures and belief systems with their attitudes toward death. (p. 650)

_____ The relationship between life and death is circular. Death is met with stoic self-control.

_____ Dying leads to rebirth in a heaven of peace and relaxation. It is possible to reach a state beyond the world of suffering.

_____ After a prayer ceremony, the patient is encouraged to discuss important matters with loved ones.

_____ Family members unite in caregiving. The patient remains active within the family for as long as he or she is able.

A. Buddhists
B. Native Americans
C. African Americans
D. Maori of New Zealand

A Place to Die

Home

1. (Few / Most) Americans would prefer to die at home. (Few / Most) Americans experience home death. (p. 651)

2. Summarize the advantages and disadvantages of dying at home. (p. 651)

   Advantages: ____

   ____

   Disadvantages: ____

   ____

3. True or False: After a home death, family members report more psychological stress than do family members whose loved one died elsewhere. (p. 651)

Hospital

1. How can emergency room staff help family members cope with the sudden loss of a loved one? (p. 651)

   ____

   ____

2. ________________ patients account for most cases of prolonged dying. (p. 651)

3. Explain the conflict of values between dying patients and health professionals in hospital settings. (p. 651)

   ____

   ____

4. True or False: The majority of U.S. hospitals have comprehensive treatment programs to ease physical, emotional, and spiritual pain at the end of life. (p. 651)

5. Most doctors and nurses (are / are not) specially trained in managing pain in dying patients. (p. 652)

Nursing Home

1. Nursing homes emphasize (high-quality terminal care / rehabilitation). (p. 652)

2. What did an investigation of two large North Carolina nursing homes reveal about what death is like in such settings? (p. 652)

   ____

   ____

   ____

The Hospice Approach

1. What is *hospice*? (p. 652)

____

____

2. Place a check mark by each feature of the hospice approach. (p. 652)

_____ The patient and family as a unit of care
_____ Emphasis on the patient's emotional needs
_____ Striving to keep the patient in the hospital
_____ *Palliative*, or *comfort, care*
_____ Focus on prolonging life above all else
_____ Care provided by an interdisciplinary team
_____ Emphasis on curing the patient's illness
_____ Striving to keep the patient in a homelike setting
_____ On-call services available at all times
_____ Bereavement services for families

3. Palliative care (prolongs life / relieves pain and other symptoms). (p. 652)

4. Cite several ways in which hospice care can be applied. (p. 652)

____

____

5. True or False: Hospice care is affordable for most dying patients and their families. (p. 653)

6. How does hospice affect family functioning? (p. 653)

____

____

7. The majority of North Americans (are / are not) familiar with the philosophy of the hospice approach. (p. 653)

Biology and Environment: Music as Palliative Care for Dying Patients

1. ______________________________ is an emerging specialty in music therapy that focuses on providing palliative care to the dying through music. (p. 653)

2. Describe the effects of music vigils for patients. (p. 653)

____

____

3. True or False: Since hearing typically functions longer than other senses, an individual may be responsive to music until his or her final moments. (p. 653)

The Right to Die

1. True or False: A uniform right-to-die policy exists in the United States. (p. 654)

2. What is *euthanasia*? (p. 654)

____

Passive Euthanasia

1. Define *passive euthanasia*. (p. 654)

____

____

2. True or False: When there is no hope of recovery, the majority of North Americans support the patient's or family members' right to end treatment. (p. 655)
3. Passive euthanasia (is / is not) widely practiced as part of ordinary medical procedure in the United States. (p. 655)
4. (Religion / Ethnicity) strongly contributes to people's views of passive euthanasia. (p. 655)
5. Without a national consensus on passive euthanasia, people can best ensure that their wishes will be followed by preparing a(n) ____. Describe this document. (p. 655)

   ____

   ____

6. Match the two types of *advance medical directives* recognized in the United States with their definitions. (p. 655)

   _____ Authorizes another person to make health care decisions on one's behalf

   _____ Specifies the treatments one does or does not want in case of a terminal illness, coma, or near-death situation

   A. *Living will*

   B. *Durable power of attorney for health care*

7. Cite two reasons why living wills do not guarantee personal control over treatment. (p. 655)

   A. ____

   ____

   B. ____

   ____

8. The durable power of attorney for health care is (less / more) flexible than the living will. Explain your answer. (p. 656)

   ____

   ____

   ____

9. True or False: Most Americans have executed a living will or durable power of attorney. (p. 656)

Voluntary Active Euthanasia

1. In ____, doctors or others act directly, at a patient's request, to end suffering before a natural end to life. (p. 656)
2. True or False: *Voluntary active euthanasia* is a criminal offense in most countries, including almost all U.S. states. (p. 656)
3. (Few / Most) people in Western nations approve of voluntary active euthanasia. (pp. 656–657)
4. Cite arguments for and against the legalization of voluntary active euthanasia. (p. 657)

   For: ____

   ____

   ____

   Against: ____

   ____

   ____

Social Issues: Voluntary Active Euthanasia: Lessons from Australia and the Netherlands

1. Explain two criticisms of the euthanasia statute in Australia's Northern Territory. (p. 658)

   A. ____

   ____

   B. ____

   ____

2. List the conditions under which voluntary active euthanasia is legal in the Netherlands. (p. 658)

   ____

   ____

   ____

3. True or False: Some Dutch doctors have admitted to actively causing death in patients who did not ask for it. (p. 658)

Assisted Suicide

1. True or False: Assisted suicide is legal or tacitly accepted in many Western European countries. (p. 657)
2. Describe Oregon's Death with Dignity Act. (p. 657)

   ____

   ____

   ____

3. True or False: Most Americans approve of assisted suicide. (p. 657)
4. According to the American Academy of Hospice and Palliative Medicine, which of the following conditions should be met before doctors engage in assisted suicide? (p. 659)

   _____ All reasonable, patient-accepted alternatives have been considered and implemented.
   _____ The patient is unable to handle the financial burden of his or her illness.
   _____ The patient has access to the best possible palliative care throughout the dying process.
   _____ If the patient is unable to make decisions, a proxy requests assisted suicide on his or her behalf.
   _____ The patient has full decision-making capacity and requests assisted suicide voluntarily.
   _____ The practice is consistent with the doctor's fundamental values.
   _____ The patient feels weary of life.

5. Public opinion favors (assisted suicide / voluntary active euthanasia) more. Why do some experts disagree with this opinion? (p. 659)

   ____

   ____

Bereavement: Coping with the Death of a Loved One

1. Match each term with its definition. (p. 659)

   _____ Intense physical and psychological distress
   _____ The experience of losing a loved one by death
   _____ The culturally specified expression of a person's thoughts and feelings in response to the loss of a loved one by death

   A. *Bereavement*
   B. *Grief*
   C. *Mourning*

Grief Process

1. Grief is more accurately described as a (roller-coaster ride with many ups and downs and gradual resolution / sequence of three universal phases). (p. 660)

2. List four tasks of the grieving process that help people recover and return to a fulfilling life. (p. 660)

   A. ______________________________

   B. ______________________________

   C. ______________________________

   D. ______________________________

3. Match each of the following grief reactions with the appropriate description. Grief reactions may correspond with more than one description. (p. 660)

   _____ The bereaved individual must balance dealing with emotional consequences of loss and attending to life changes.
   _____ A numbed feeling serves as "emotional anesthesia."
   _____ The mourner confronts the reality of the loss and experiences a cascade of emotional reactions.
   _____ The bereaved individual obsessively reviews the circumstances of the death.
   _____ The mourner may show a variety of behavioral changes, including absentmindedness, poor concentration, and self-destructive behavior.
   _____ Emotional energy shifts toward life-restoring pursuits.
   _____ The bereaved person experiences shock followed by disbelief.

   1. Avoidance
   2. Confrontation
   3. Restoration

4. Describe the *dual-process model of coping with loss*. (p. 660)

   ____

   ____

   ____

Personal and Situational Variations

1. Compared with women, bereaved men typically express distress and depression (less / more) directly and seek (less / more) social support. These factors may contribute to the much higher mortality rate among bereaved (men / women). (p. 660)

2. Explain differences in grieving when death is sudden and unexpected versus prolonged and expected. (pp. 660–661)

   Sudden and unexpected: ______________________________

   ____

   Prolonged and expected: ______________________________

   ____

3. ______________________________ involves acknowledging that a loss is inevitable and preparing emotionally for it. (p. 661)

4. Compared with survivors of other sudden deaths, people grieving a suicidal loss are (less / more) likely to blame themselves for what happened. (p. 661)

5. List three reasons why the death of a child is the most difficult loss an adult can face. (p. 661)

   A. ______________________________

   B. ______________________________

   C. ______________________________

6. True or False: A child's death typically leads to marital breakup, regardless of prior marital satisfaction. (p. 661)

7. Why is the loss of a family member likely to have long-standing consequences for children? (p. 662)

____

____

____

8. List the physical, behavioral, and emotional symptoms often displayed by children who are grieving the loss of a parent or sibling. (p. 662)

Physical: ____

Behavioral: ____

Emotional: ____

9. True or False: When children maintain mental contact with a deceased parent or sibling by dreaming about or speaking to the loved one, this hinders the child's ability to cope with the loss. (p. 662)

10. Describe how adults can tailor their explanations to help young children better understand a loved one's death. (p. 662)

____

____

____

11. Grief-stricken (school-age children / adolescents) tend to keep their grieving from both adults and peers, often leading to depression and attempts to escape the grief through acting-out behavior. (p. 662)

12. Younger adults display (fewer / more) negative outcomes than older adults following the death of a spouse. Cite several reasons for this trend. (p. 662)

____

____

____

13. Describe the unique challenges that gay and lesbian partners face when they experience the death of an intimate partner, including disenfranchised grief. (p. 662)

____

____

____

14. When a person experiences several deaths at once or in close succession, ____________________ ____________________ can occur. Note how this influences ability to cope with grief. (pp. 662–663)

____

____

15. Identify three groups of individuals who are at risk for bereavement overload. (p. 663)

A. ____

B. ____

C. ____

Cultural Influences: Cultural Variations in Mourning Behavior

1. Cite common goals of many cultural ceremonies for commemorating a death. (p. 664)

____

____

2. Match the following religious and cultural groups with their typical mourning behaviors and beliefs. (p. 664)

_____	Grief is expressed freely, triggered by music and eulogies.	A. Jews
_____	Calmness is emphasized so that the gods can hear their prayers.	B. Quakers
_____	The wooden coffin remains closed through a day-and-night vigil.	C. African Americans
	Loved ones shovel dirt onto the coffin and light a memorial candle.	D. Balinese of Indonesia
_____	The body is cremated promptly. At the memorial service, mourners worship silently, rising to speak when they feel moved.	

3. Summarize the benefits of Internet memorials. (p. 664)

____

____

____

Bereavement Interventions

1. Cite two of the best ways to help a grieving person. (p. 663)

   A. ______________________________

   B. ______________________________

2. True or False: Self-help groups that bring together mourners who have experienced the same type of loss seem highly effective for reducing stress. (p. 663)

3. List three characteristics of effective bereavement interventions for children and adolescents following violent deaths. (p. 665)

   A. ______________________________

   B. ______________________________

   C. ______________________________

4. Cite four instances in which bereaved people may find it harder to overcome their loss. (p. 665)

   A. ______________________________

   B. ______________________________

   C. ______________________________

   D. ______________________________

Death Education

1. List four goals of death education. (p. 665)

   A. ______________________________

   B. ______________________________

   C. ______________________________

   D. ______________________________

2. Compared to lecture-style programs, experiential programs that help people confront their own mortality are (less / more) likely to heighten death anxiety. (p. 665)

ASK YOURSELF . . .

For *Ask Yourself* questions for this chapter, along with feedback on the accuracy of your answers, please log on to MyDevelopmentLab (for registration and access, please visit mydevelopmentlab.com or follow the instructions on page ix).

(1) Select the Multimedia Library.

(2) Choose the explore option.

(3) Find your chapter from the drop down box.

(4) Click find now.

(5) Complete questions and choose "Submit answers for grading" or "Clear answers" to start over.

SUGGESTED READINGS

Hansson, R. O., & Stroebe, M. S. (Eds.). (2007). *Bereavement in late life: Coping, adaptation, and developmental influences.* Washington, DC: American Psychological Association. A collection of chapters examining death and bereavement in late adulthood, including current research and theories, assessment of grief, individual differences in coping styles, and factors that contribute to resilience in bereaved elders.

Lloyd-Williams, M. (Ed.). (2008). *Psychosocial issues in palliative care.* New York: Oxford University Press. Examines the social and emotional needs of terminally ill patients and their families. Topics include cultural influences associated with end-of-life care, the importance of honest communication, spirituality and religion, and family-based interventions.

Pappas, D. M. (2009). *Euthanasia/assisted suicide debate.* Westport, CT: Greenwood Publishing. A historical approach to understanding the right to die controversy, this book presents the ethical, legal, and social concerns surrounding euthanasia and assisted suicide. The author uses examples from some of the most notorious cases of euthanasia and assisted suicide in the United States, including Terri Schiavo and Dr. Jack Kevorkian.

CROSSWORD PUZZLE 19.1

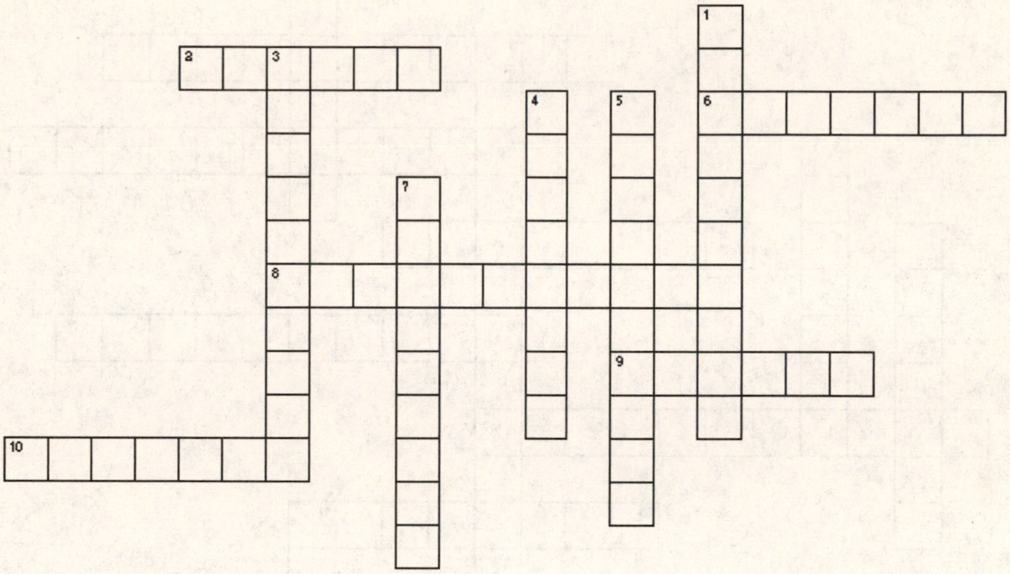

Across

2. ______ will: specifies one's treatment preferences in case of terminal illness, coma, or other near-death situation
6. ______ medical directive: statement of desired medical treatment should a person become incurably ill
8. A(n) ______ death matches one's lifestyle and values, honors significant relationships, and is as free of suffering as possible.
9. Voluntary ______euthanasia: ending a patient's suffering, at the patient's request, before a natural end to life
10. ______ euthanasia: withholding or withdrawing life-sustaining treatment, permitting the patient to die naturally

Down

1. Irreversible cessation of all activity in the brain and brain stem (2 words)
3. Persistent ______ state: the cerebral cortex no longer registers electrical activity, but the brain stem remains active
4. Durable power of ______ for health care: authorizes another person to make health care decisions on one's behalf
5. Ending the life of a person suffering from an incurable condition
7. Phase in which an individual passes into permanent death

CROSSWORD PUZZLE 19.2

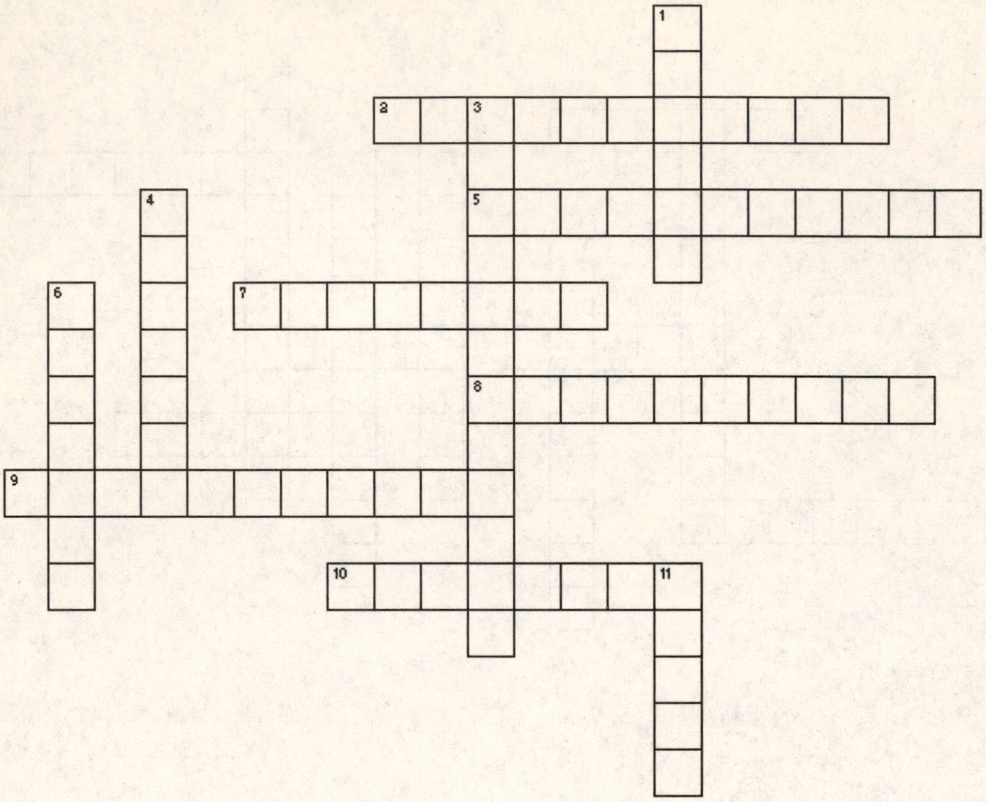

Across

2. ______-______ model of coping with loss: oscillation between dealing with emotions and attending to life changes (2 words, hyph)
5. Interdisciplinary field devoted to the study of death and dying
7. ______ death: heartbeat, circulation, breathing, and brain functioning stop, but resuscitation is still possible
8. ______ care relieves pain and other symptoms, rather than prolonging life.
9. The experience of losing a loved one by death
10. Culturally specified expression of a person's thoughts and feelings regarding the death of a loved one

Down

1. ______ phase: gasps and muscle spasms occur as the regular heartbeat disintegrates
3. ______ grieving: acknowledging that the loss is inevitable and preparing emotionally
4. Support services to help terminally ill people and their families prepare for death in satisfying ways
6. Death ______: fear and apprehension of death
11. Intense physical and psychological distress

PRACTICE TEST #1

1. A dying person moves through three phases when death is imminent: __________, clinical death, and mortality. (p. 640)
   a. acceptance
   b. loss of circulation
   c. the agonal phase
   d. brain death

2. The definition of death that is currently used in most industrialized nations is __________ (p. 641)
   a. loss of heartbeat and respiration.
   b. lack of activity in the cerebral cortex, even if the brain stem remains active.
   c. irreversible cessation of all activity in the brain and the brain stem.
   d. muscle spasms indicating that the body can no longer sustain life.

3. What can we do to help people die with dignity and integrity? (p. 641)
   a. Be candid and truthful about death's imminence.
   b. Ensure that their last moments are peaceful and easy.
   c. Protect them from difficult decision making.
   d. Be evasive about death's imminence.

4. The aspect of the death concept that is hardest for children to comprehend is that __________ (p. 642)
   a. people die at different ages and from different causes.
   b. dead people can no longer think or feel.
   c. dead people will not wake up or come back to life.
   d. all living things will eventually die.

5. How can parents best foster younger children's understanding of death? (p. 643)
   a. Use indirect explanations, such as "went to sleep for a long time."
   b. Present the scientific facts and negate religious beliefs.
   c. Avoid discussion of death, which tends to fuel children's fears.
   d. Offer direct, truthful, and reassuring explanations.

6. In middle age, people typically __________ (p. 645)
   a. adopt a vague, avoidant mindset about death.
   b. conclude that they are beyond death's reach.
   c. begin to take stock of their time left to live.
   d. ponder the practical circumstances of dying.

7. Throughout the world, death anxiety __________ (p. 645)
   a. declines throughout the lifespan, reaching its lowest level in late adulthood.
   b. increases throughout the lifespan, reaching its highest level in late adulthood.
   c. peaks in middle adulthood, then gradually declines.
   d. peaks in adolescence, reaches its lowest level in middle adulthood, then increases.

8. What is the most serious drawback to Kübler-Ross's theory? (p. 647)
   a. It overemphasizes multidimensional influences on the dying process.
   b. It looks at dying patients' thoughts and feelings outside of meaningful contexts.
   c. It inaccurately claims that dying people often come to acceptance shortly before death.
   d. It fails to acknowledge the importance of an appropriate death.

9. Recent theorists believe that __________ (p. 648)
   a. family and friends should avoid discussing death with terminally ill individuals.
   b. terminally ill individuals move through a fixed sequence of death acceptance.
   c. maintaining a strong personal identity, or ego, interferes with a "good death."
   d. an appropriate death is one that makes sense for the individual.

10. Many Mexican Americans and Korean Americans believe that informing patients about death __________ (p. 649)
    a. fosters death with dignity.
    b. is the responsibility of doctors and spiritual advisers.
    c. helps them to deal with fears and regrets.
    d. is wrong and will hasten death.

11. Which of the following statements about cultural influences on dying is true? (p. 650)
    a. In most cultures, death is met with stoic self-control.
    b. A sense of spirituality actually heightens death anxiety in many cultures.
    c. The notion of multidimensional, multidirectional development is as relevant to dying as to earlier periods of life.
    d. Though different cultural beliefs shape external dying experiences, thoughts and emotions during the dying process are universal.

12. Today, about half of deaths take place __________, though the overwhelming preference is for death __________. (p. 650)
    a. at home; in a hospital
    b. in a hospital; at home
    c. in a nursing home; in a hospital
    d. in a nursing home; at home

13. Why might there be a "conflict of values" in a hospital ward or intensive care setting when it comes to a dying patient? (p. 651)
    a. Hospital management tends to put the demands of staff members above the needs of patients.
    b. Hospital staff often value communication with the family over treatment of the patient.
    c. Hospital staff often avoid candid discussions about death, leaving patients poorly informed about what to expect.
    d. Hospital staff, who must perform their tasks efficiently, may neglect patients' physical and emotional needs.

14. Which of the following statements about hospice care is true? (p. 652)
    a. The hospice approach focuses on palliative care.
    b. Hospice programs attempt to prolong life by any means available.
    c. Hospice care is unaffordable for most dying patients and their families.
    d. Ethnic minorities are more likely than whites to participate in hospice care.

15. Research shows that when dying patients listen to music, __________ (p. 653)
    a. they undergo a spiritual transformation.
    b. their breathing becomes slower and deeper.
    c. their pain is mostly eliminated.
    d. they often feel increased agitation and discomfort.

16. An example of __________ is a doctor knowingly enabling a patient to end her own life by providing her with a lethal dose of drugs. (p. 654)
    a. passive euthanasia
    b. voluntary active euthanasia
    c. assisted suicide
    d. involuntary active euthanasia

17. The best way for people to ensure that they will have access to passive euthanasia should they desire it is by __________ (p. 656)
    a. asking their doctors to record their wishes in their medical file.
    b. informing a close friend or relative.
    c. preparing and signing a living will.
    d. preparing and signing a durable power of attorney.

18. If a patient is in a permanent vegetative state, and no advance medical directive exists, some U.S. states permit appointment of a __________ (p. 656)
    a. spiritual adviser.
    b. living will.
    c. health care proxy.
    d. thanatologist.

19. Which of the following is a common argument among supporters of the legalization of active euthanasia? (p. 658)
    a. Individuals have the right to control their own life course.
    b. Only "natural" deaths are truly dignified.
    c. Dying patients are often mentally impaired and unstable.
    d. Doctors may exert undue pressure on a patient's decision.

20. Why do some experts maintain that legalizing assisted suicide is preferable to legalizing voluntary active euthanasia? (p. 659)
    a. The public is more accepting of assisted suicide than of active euthanasia.
    b. In active euthanasia, doctors are more likely to be sued by surviving family members.
    c. Doctors are less likely to experience guilt or moral opposition in cases of assisted suicide.
    d. In assisted suicide, the final act is solely the patient's.

21. Theorists formerly believed that bereaved individuals moved through three phases of grieving. A more accurate account, however, compares grief to a __________ (p. 660)
    a. roller-coaster ride, with many ups and downs.
    b. pinwheel, with many points of spinning emotions.
    c. washing machine, with anger, fear, and frustration all mixing together.
    d. rocket launch, with a huge surge of emotion followed by a settling-down period.

22. Martha, who recently lost her teenage son to a car accident, is fixated on the details of his death. She eats and sleeps very little and seems unable to concentrate on topics other than her lost son. Martha's behavior is consistent with the __________ stage of the grieving process. (p. 660)
    a. awareness
    b. restoration
    c. confrontation
    d. forging a symbolic bond

23. Compared with women, grieving men __________ (p. 660)
    a. receive more social support.
    b. express distress less directly.
    c. express distress more directly.
    d. adjust to loss more easily.

24. Compared to those who lose loved ones to an unexpected event, bereaved people who lose their loved ones after a prolonged illness tend to feel __________ (p. 661)
    a. more emotionally overwhelmed by the death.
    b. a greater "numbing" sense of shock and disbelief.
    c. more persistent anxiety resulting from long-term stressors.
    d. a more profound feeling that the death was "senseless."

25. People who have lost a loved one to __________ typically have a prolonged grieving process, complicated by feelings of guilt, shame, and rejection. (p. 661)
    a. a random accident
    b. war
    c. suicide
    d. a debilitating illness

26. After a child's death, the parents __________ (p. 661)
    a. often divorce, even if their marriage was strong before the death.
    b. often blame one another for their grief.
    c. can begin a process leading to firmer family commitments and growth.
    d. typically distance themselves from their surviving children.

27. Which of the following is an example of disenfranchised grief? (p. 662)
    a. a child grieving for a father who died before she was born
    b. an elder exhibiting little or no grief after the death of a spouse
    c. a crowd publicly grieving the death of a celebrity
    d. a gay man barred from attending his partner's funeral

28. Although elders are at risk for __________ because they often experience many deaths in close succession, they are often better equipped to handle these losses than younger adults. (p. 663)
    a. anticipatory grieving
    b. disenfranchised grief
    c. bereavement overload
    d. prolonged mourning

29. Unlike other Christian groups, Quakers __________ in times of mourning. (p. 664)
    a. focus mainly on "salvation by character"
    b. emphasize hope of heaven and fear of hell
    c. worship and grieve loudly and freely
    d. gather with close friends and family

30. Compared to lecture-format death education programs, experiential programs __________ (p. 665)
    a. are less likely to heighten death anxiety and may sometimes reduce it.
    b. often leave students more uncomfortable about death than when they entered.
    c. often prevent people from confronting their own mortality.
    d. are more likely to heighten death anxiety through exposure to death's reality.

PRACTICE TEST #2

1. The large majority of people in industrialized nations who die suddenly are victims of __________ (p. 640)
   a. medical malpractice.
   b. household accidents.
   c. stroke.
   d. heart attacks.

2. In the days or hours preceding death, a dying person often experiences __________ (p. 640)
   a. increased energy and movement.
   b. rising body temperature and blood pressure.
   c. lack of interest in food, water, and surroundings.
   d. an urgent desire to connect with other humans.

3. Individuals in a persistent vegetative state __________ (p. 641)
   a. continue to maintain activity in the cerebral cortex.
   b. have an absence of activity in the cerebral cortex.
   c. are considered legally dead in most U.S. states.
   d. often regain consciousness after aggressive intervention.

4. Compared to previous generations, today's youth are __________ (p. 642)
   a. more comfortable talking about death and dying.
   b. less knowledgeable of the basic facts of death.
   c. more removed from death due to cultural denial.
   d. more likely to lose a loved one to suicide.

5. For children, the first and most easily grasped component of the death concept is __________, followed by __________. (p. 642)
   a. permanence; inevitability
   b. applicability; causation
   c. cessation; permanence
   d. causation; permanence

6. Teenagers __________ (p. 643)
   a. often struggle with the death concept of "cessation."
   b. are fully aware that death happens to everyone.
   c. are usually factual, rather than fanciful, about death.
   d. tend to dwell on the possibility of unlikely early death.

7. Among Westerners, __________ seems to be the most important influence on limiting death anxiety. (p. 645)
   a. spirituality
   b. religiousness
   c. knowledge of death
   d. sense of self-efficacy

8. Estela, who is nearing the end of her life, takes comfort in the belief that she will live on through her children and grandchildren. Estela's belief in her lasting influence on the world is known as __________ (p. 645)
   a. ego integrity.
   b. spirituality.
   c. thanatology.
   d. symbolic immortality.

9. Terminally ill children __________ (p. 646)
   a. have lower death anxiety than other children.
   b. are usually unaware of their own impending deaths.
   c. are at risk for high death anxiety.
   d. rarely understand the basic facts of death.

10. Kübler-Ross's five-stage theory is best viewed as __________ (p. 647)
    a. coping strategies used by anyone under threat.
    b. a road map used by caregivers to guide the dying person.
    c. the series of steps a normal dying person follows.
    d. a model for developing bereavement interventions.

11. When asked about a "good death," most patients mention __________ (p. 648)
    a. being cared for in a hospital.
    b. having access to some sort of afterlife.
    c. the importance of planning their own funeral.
    d. maintaining and enhancing relationships.

12. Professional caregivers of the terminally ill __________ (p. 649)
    a. often fail to provide empathetic care.
    b. report a lack of emotional attachment to patients.
    c. often have high death anxiety.
    d. often have low death anxiety.

13. What is an advantage of a home death? (p. 651)
    a. The quality of caregiving is usually higher in the home setting.
    b. The home offers a familiar, intimate, and loving setting for dying.
    c. Home deaths are less stressful on family members before and after the death.
    d. Homes are especially well-equipped to handle the patient's comfort and medical needs.

14. The central belief of the hospice approach is that __________ (p. 652)
    a. medical choices should be made by an objective third party in order to ease patients' psychological strain.
    b. quality of life is the most important issue surrounding a person's journey toward death.
    c. terminally ill patients should always be able to die in their own homes.
    d. contact with family members is secondary to monitoring the patient's condition.

15. Studies concur that __________ in nursing homes. (p. 653)
    a. feelings of sadness and depression are rare among dying patients
    b. most dying patients' spiritual and emotional needs are addressed
    c. dying patients suffer from high levels of untreated pain
    d. family members of dying patients tend to be well-informed on their treatment

16. Why is music particularly effective in easing the distress of dying patients? (p. 653)
    a. Music triggers the production of endorphins, which help to reduce pain.
    b. Music offers patients a "portal" in which to relive pleasant past experiences.
    c. Hearing typically functions longer than the other senses.
    d. Music encourages patients to express their emotional states.

17. Public acceptance of euthanasia is __________ (p. 654)
    a. low, even in passive euthanasia cases.
    b. low, unless the patient is in extreme pain.
    c. high, with the exception of active euthanasia cases.
    d. high, except when the patient's permission has not been obtained.

18. In North America, use of passive euthanasia for terminally ill patients and those in a persistent vegetative state is considered __________ (p. 655)
    a. immoral and unethical.
    b. a legal act that must be approved by the courts.
    c. permissible only for the most elderly patients.
    d. an ordinary part of normal medical practice.

19. Assisting a suicide is illegal in __________ (p. 657)
    a. Canada and most U.S. states.
    b. the United States, but not in Canada.
    c. all industrialized nations.
    d. all Western European nations.

20. In the Netherlands, doctors can legally provide active euthanasia under certain conditions. What does research on the Dutch experience reveal about this practice? (p. 658)
    a. Approximately 40 percent of all deaths in the Netherlands are due to voluntary active euthanasia.
    b. Dutch doctors routinely sidestep ethical guidelines and grant all euthanasia requests, including those of healthy patients.
    c. Because so few terminal patients request active euthanasia, actual deaths have been fairly easy to monitor.
    d. Euthanasia practices are difficult to monitor; some Dutch doctors report administering active euthanasia without following legal standards.

21. Mourning refers to the __________ (p. 659)
    a. experience of losing a loved one by death.
    b. acknowledgment that loss is inevitable and preparing emotionally for it.
    c. culturally specified expression of the bereaved person's thoughts and feelings.
    d. universal norms that guide our behavior when a loved one dies.

22. The grieving process is best viewed as a set of __________ (p. 660)
    a. fixed stages.
    b. responsibilities.
    c. emotions.
    d. tasks.

23. According to the dual-process model of coping with loss, effective coping requires people to __________ (p. 660)
    a. focus solely on their grief, without external distractions.
    b. move back and forth between grieving and attending to life changes.
    c. find comfort in religious or spiritual beliefs in the afterlife.
    d. become active in causes that honor the dead person's life or manner of dying.

24. People who lose a loved one after a period of prolonged dying have time to engage in __________ and may feel less overwhelmed immediately following the death. (p. 661)
    a. confrontation
    b. bereavement counseling
    c. restoration
    d. anticipatory grieving

25. Adjusting to death is easier when __________ (p. 661)
    a. the survivor understands the reasons for the death.
    b. the death is sudden and unanticipated.
    c. it takes place in a hospital rather than at home.
    d. a person experiences several deaths in close succession.

26. Compared to widowed elders, young and middle-aged widows and widowers __________ (p. 662)
    a. have a shorter, less intense grieving period.
    b. display more negative outcomes.
    c. display more positive outcomes.
    d. are more likely to reject bereavement interventions.

27. One of the best ways to help a grieving person is by __________ (p. 663)
    a. giving advice aimed at hastening recovery.
    b. discussing one's own experiences with death.
    c. listening sympathetically and "just being there."
    d. encouraging the person to spend some time alone.

28. In times of mourning, nearly all of the world's religions __________ (p. 664)
    a. encourage free, outspoken expressions of grief.
    b. value composure and calmness of the bereaved.
    c. offer consoling accounts of the aftermath of death.
    d. use music to trigger the release of deep emotion.

29. Most bereaved individuals __________ (p. 665)
    a. require medication to deal with their grief.
    b. refuse bereavement services, even when available.
    c. will not achieve restoration without counseling.
    d. seek out bereavement interventions of some kind.

30. What is an example of an experiential activity in a death education course? (p. 665)
    a. a lecture on medical and funeral services
    b. a discussion about the ethical issues surrounding death
    c. a confidential question-and-answer period
    d. a discussion with a terminally ill patient

CROSSWORD PUZZLE SOLUTIONS

PUZZLE 1.1

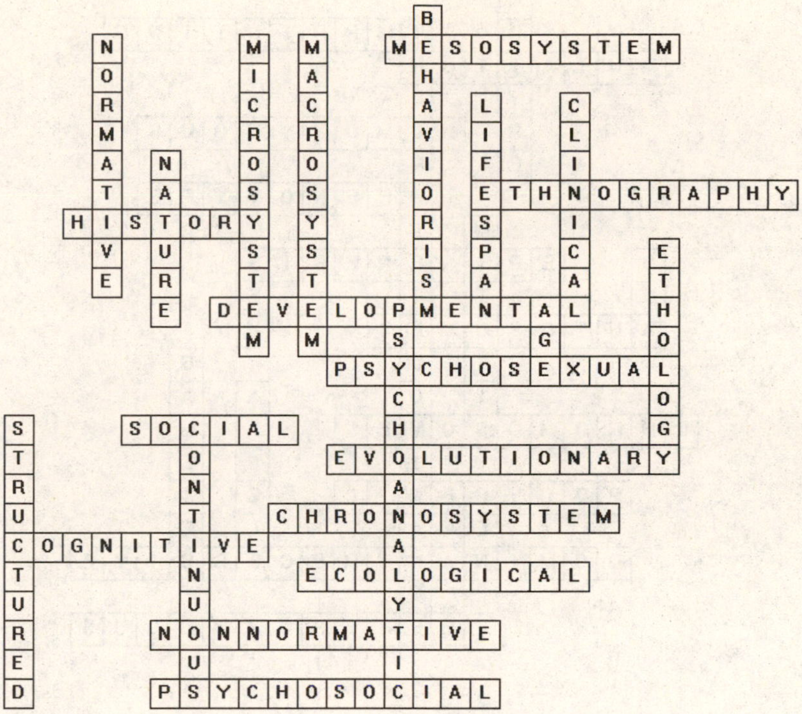

PUZZLE 1.2

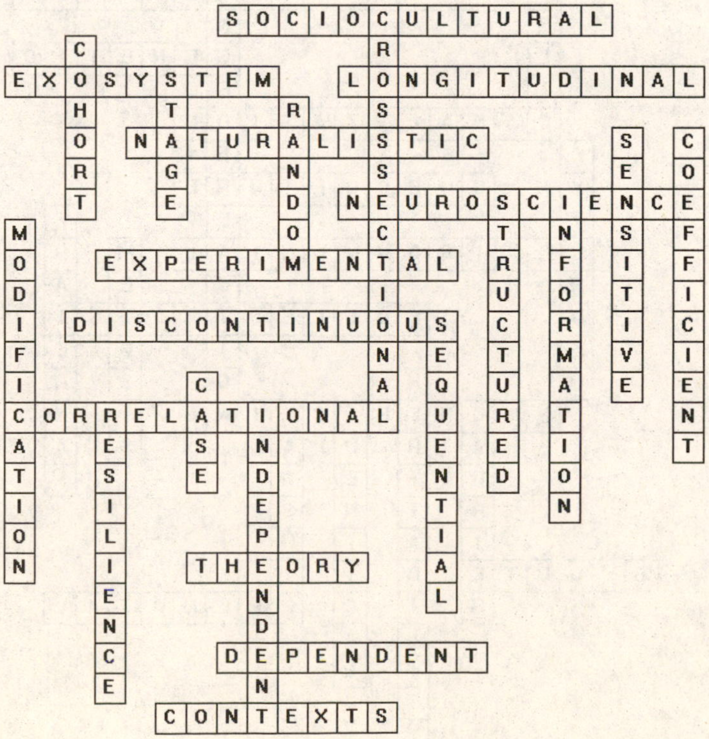

PUZZLE 2.1

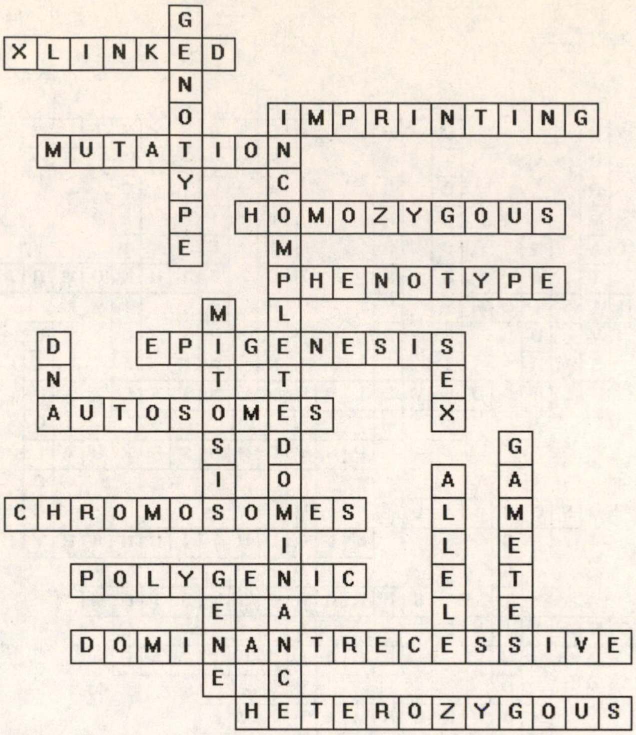

PUZZLE 2.2

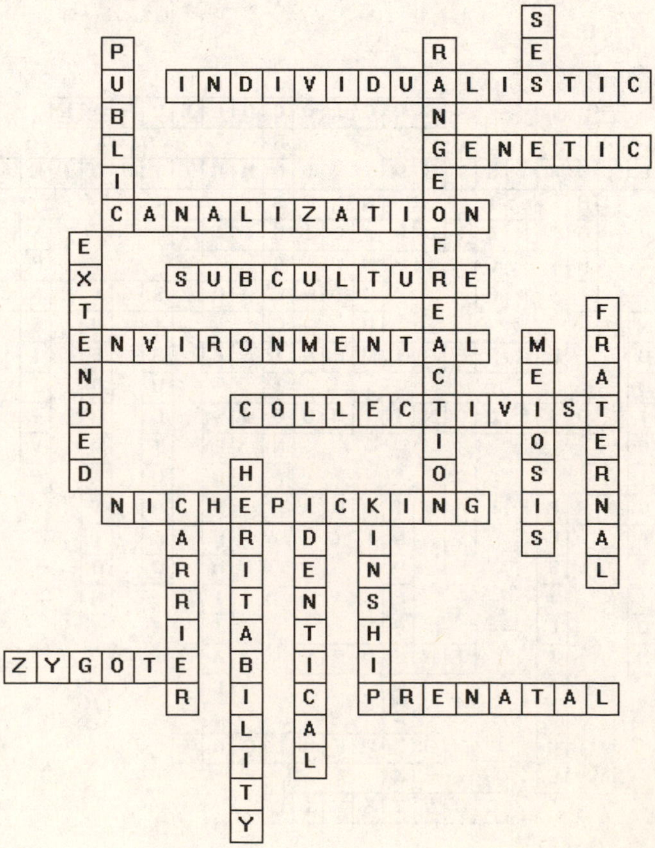

PUZZLE 3.1

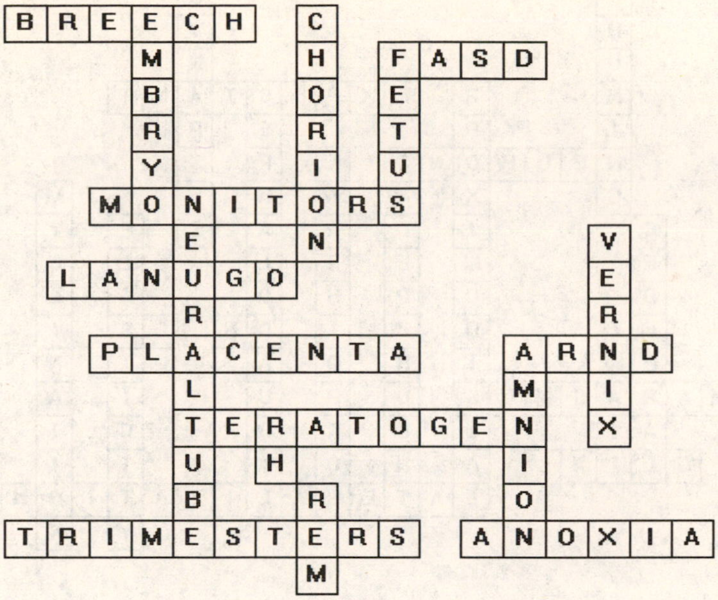

PUZZLE 3.2

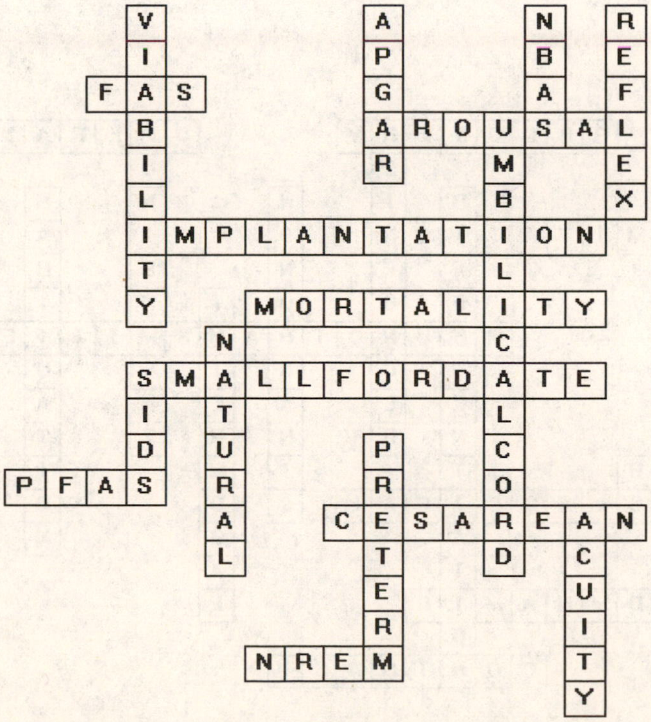

PUZZLE 4.1

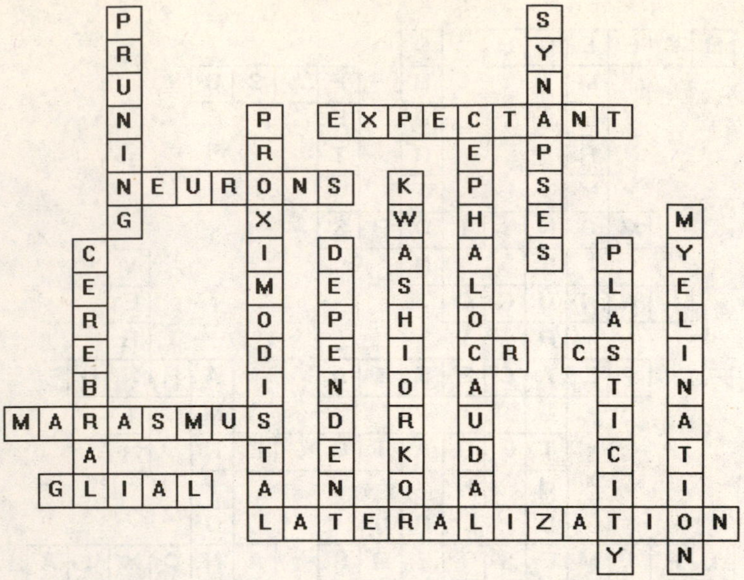

PUZZLE 4.2

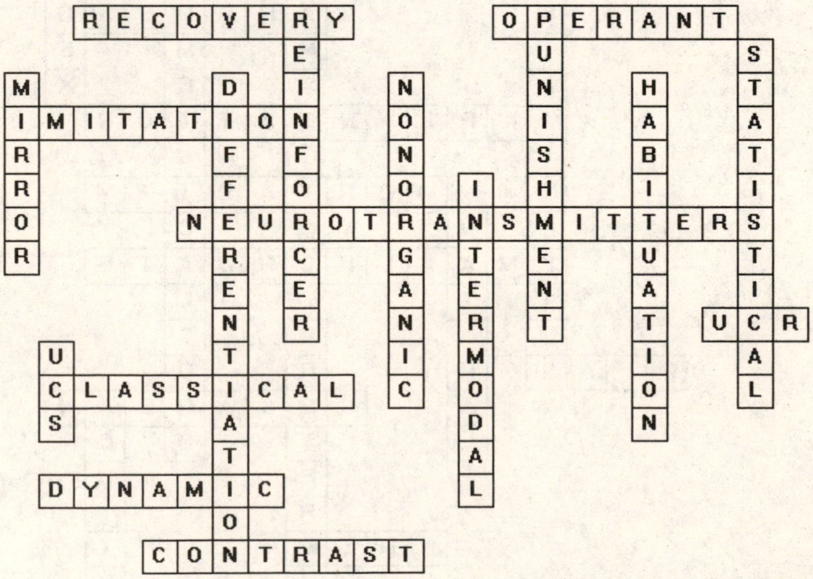

PUZZLE 5.1

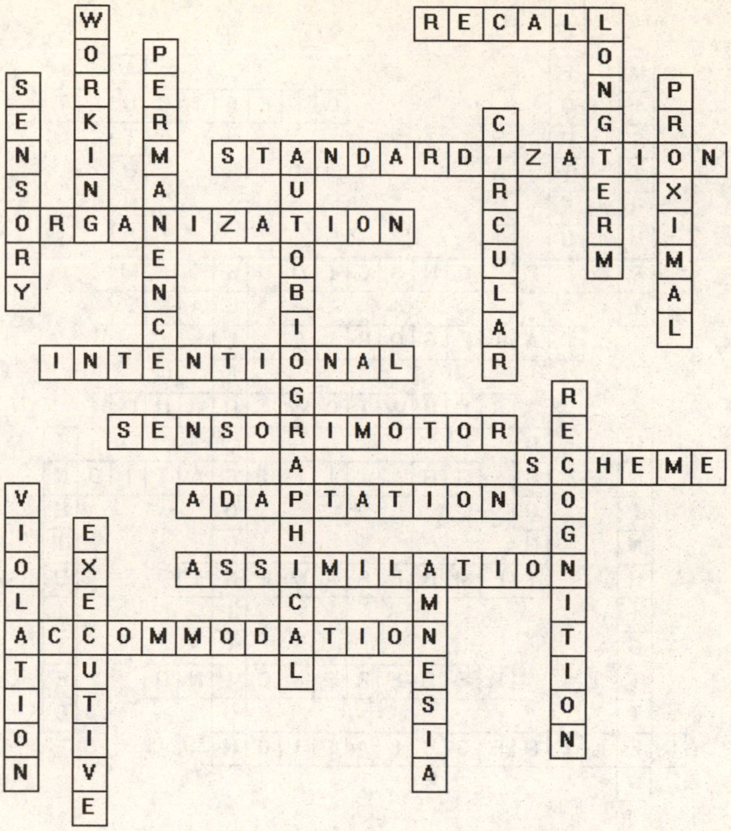

PUZZLE 5.2

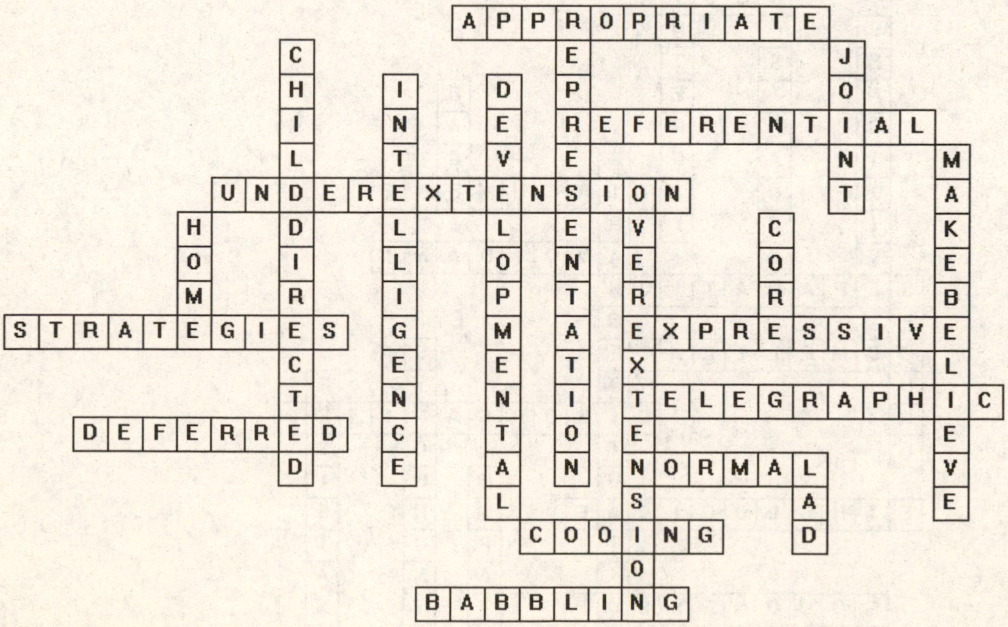

PUZZLE 6.1

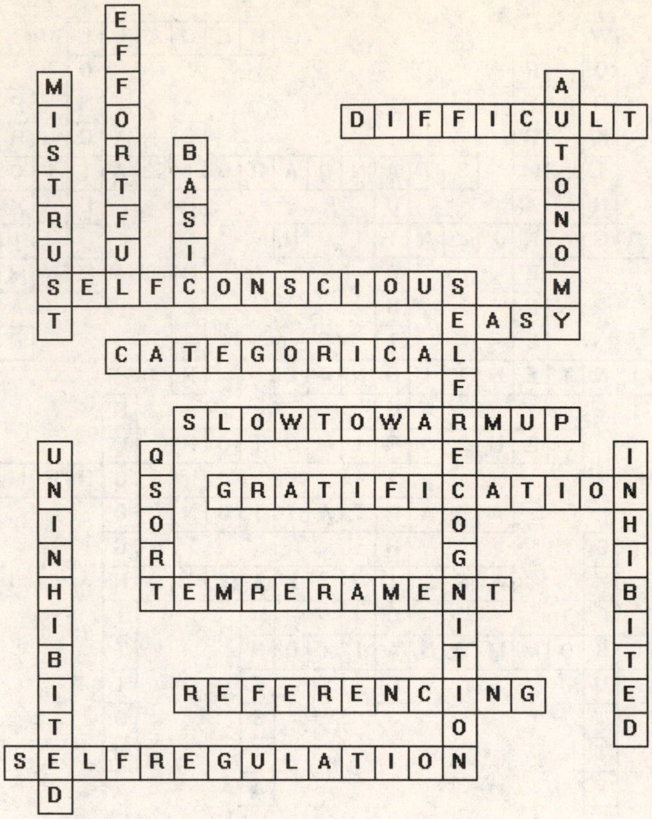

PUZZLE 6.2

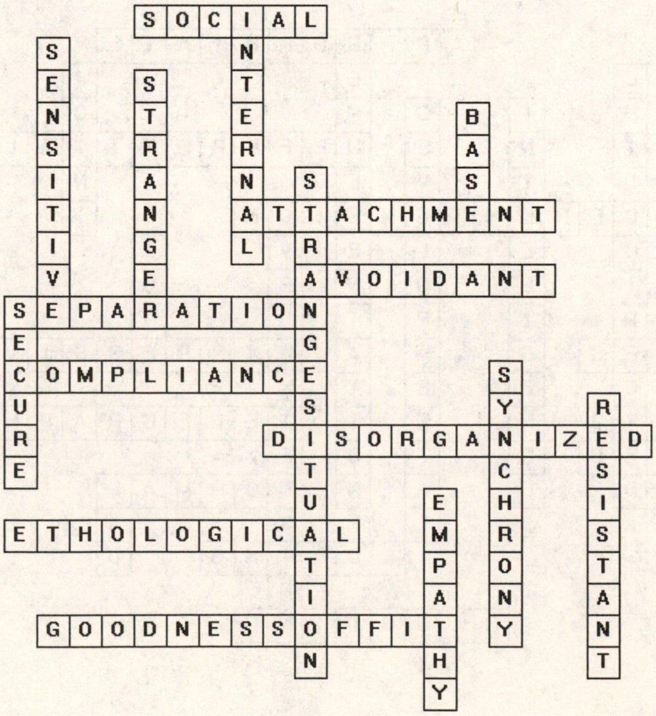

PUZZLE 7.1

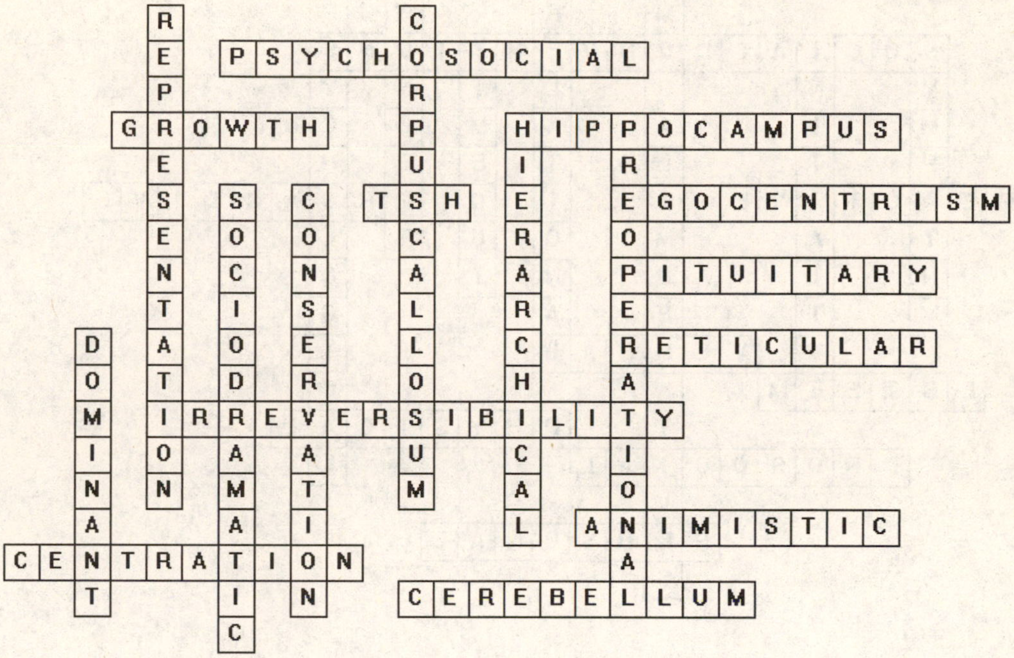

PUZZLE 7.2

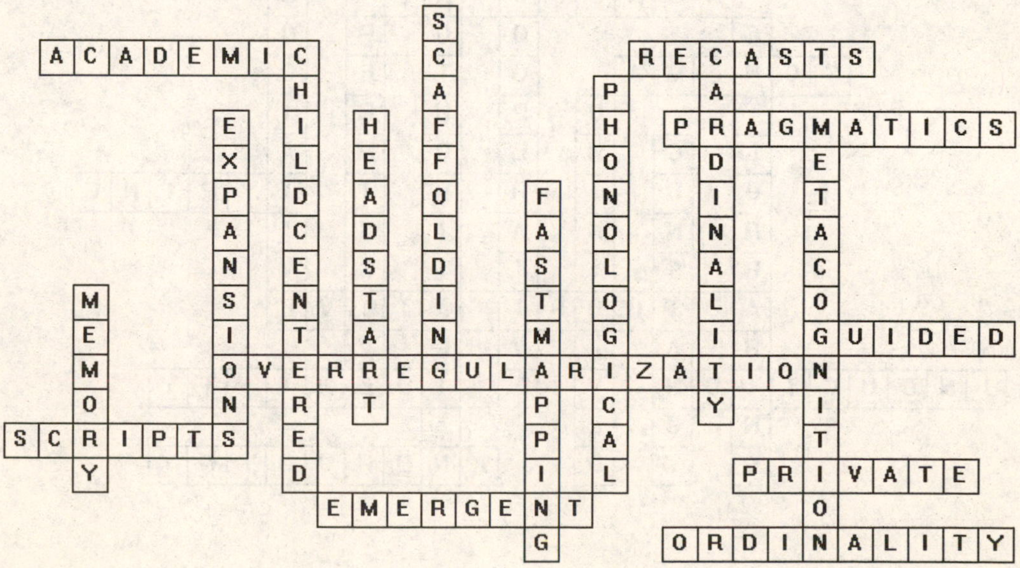

PUZZLE 8.1

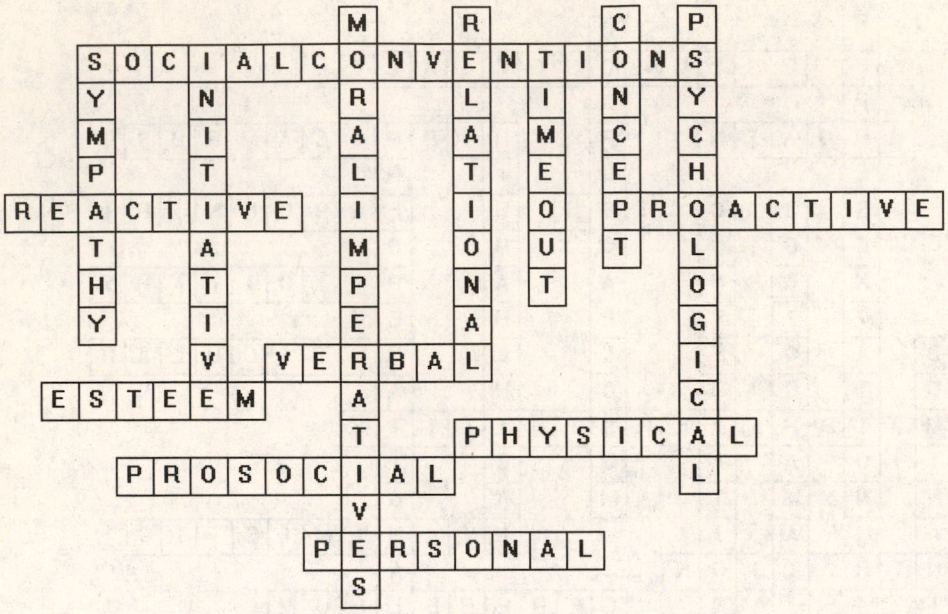

PUZZLE 8.2

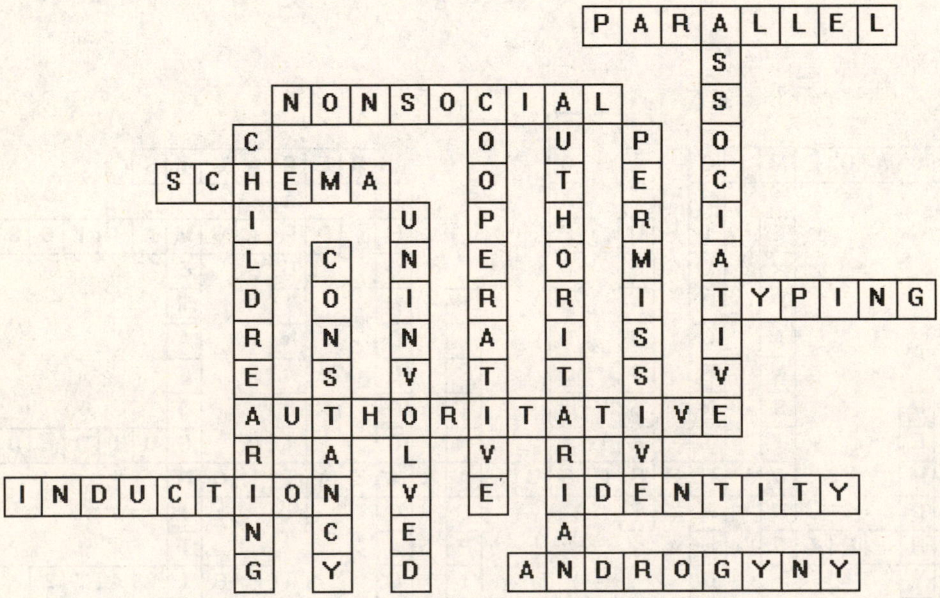

PUZZLE 9.1

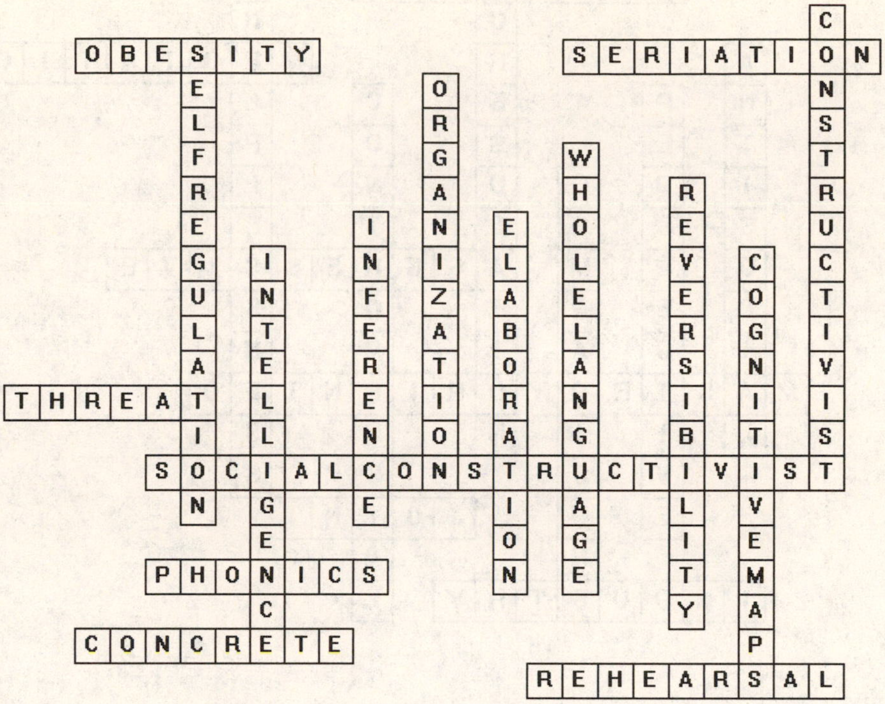

PUZZLE 9.2

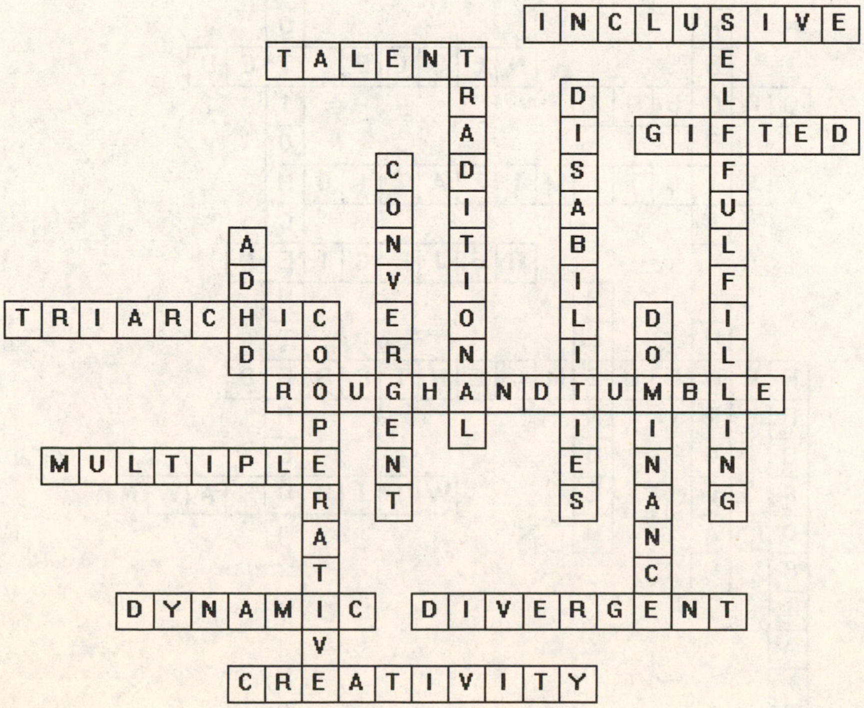

PUZZLE 10.1

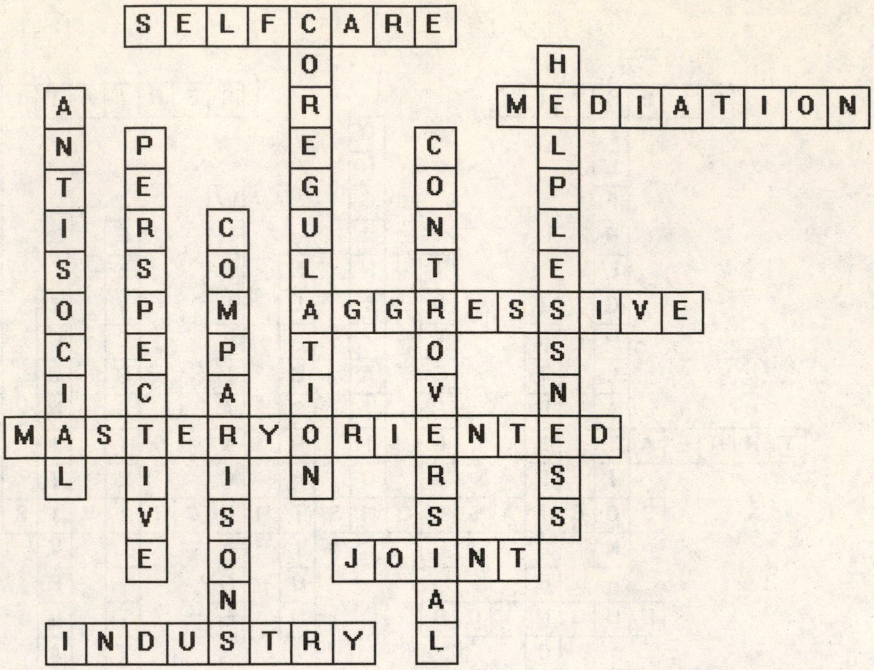

PUZZLE 10.2

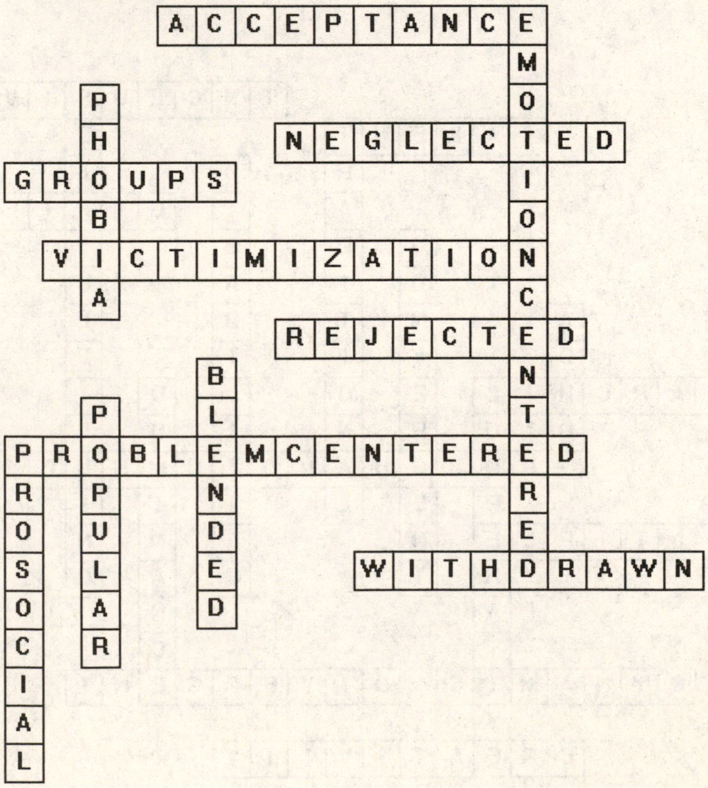

PUZZLE 11.1

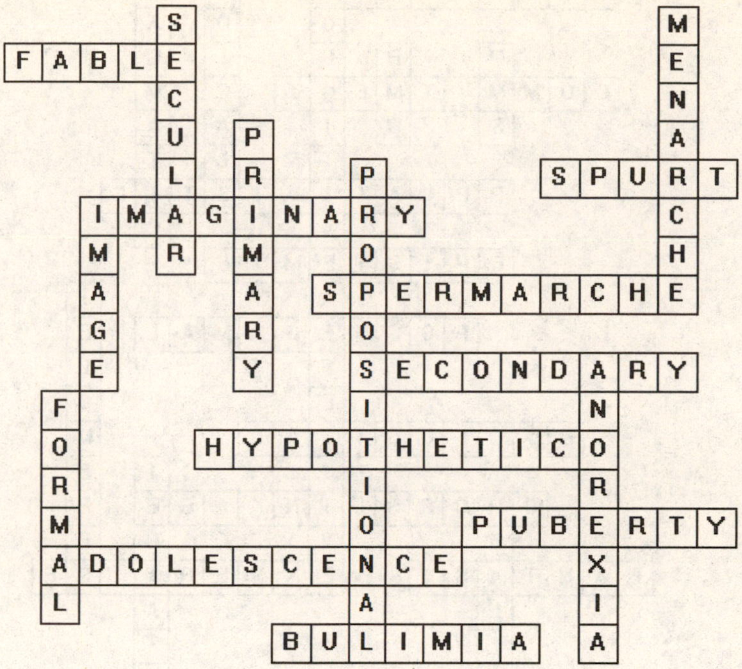

PUZZLE 12.1

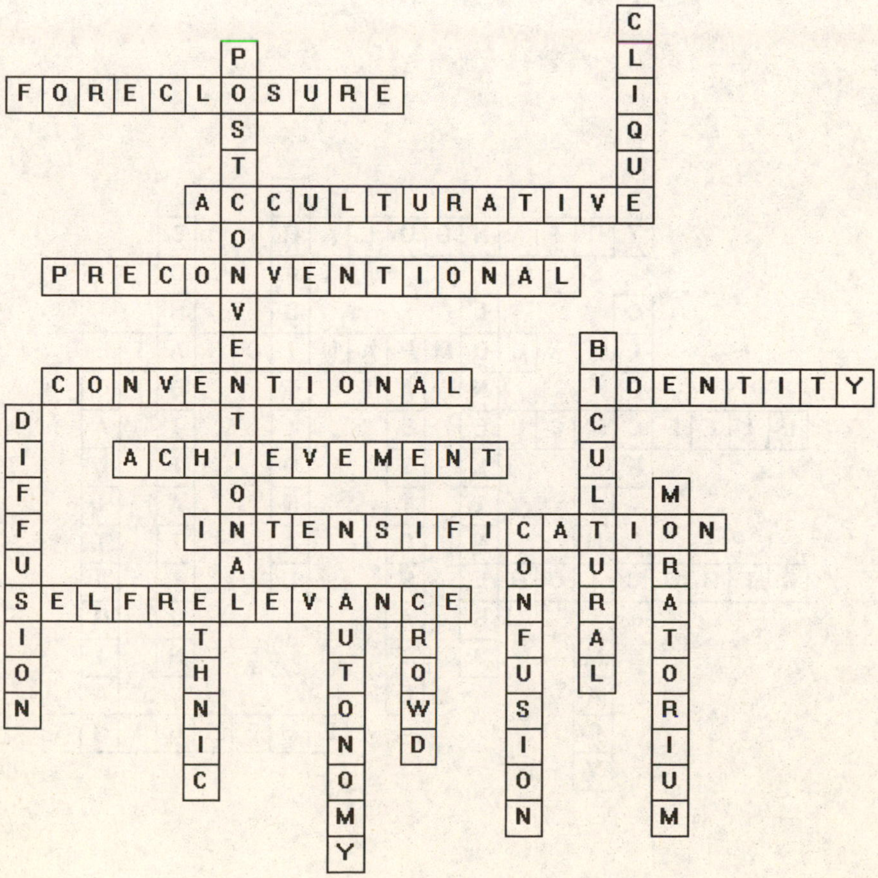

PUZZLE 13.1

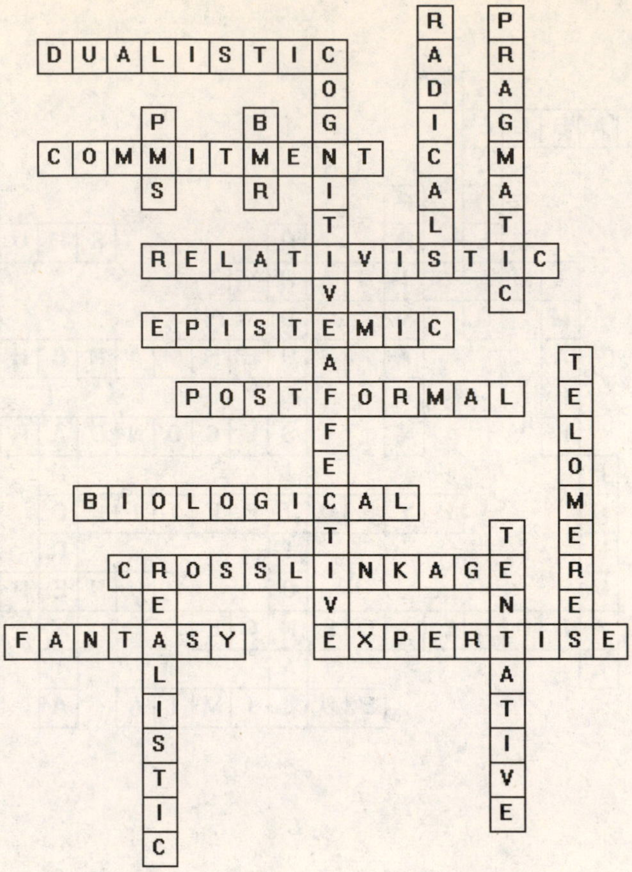

PUZZLE 14.1

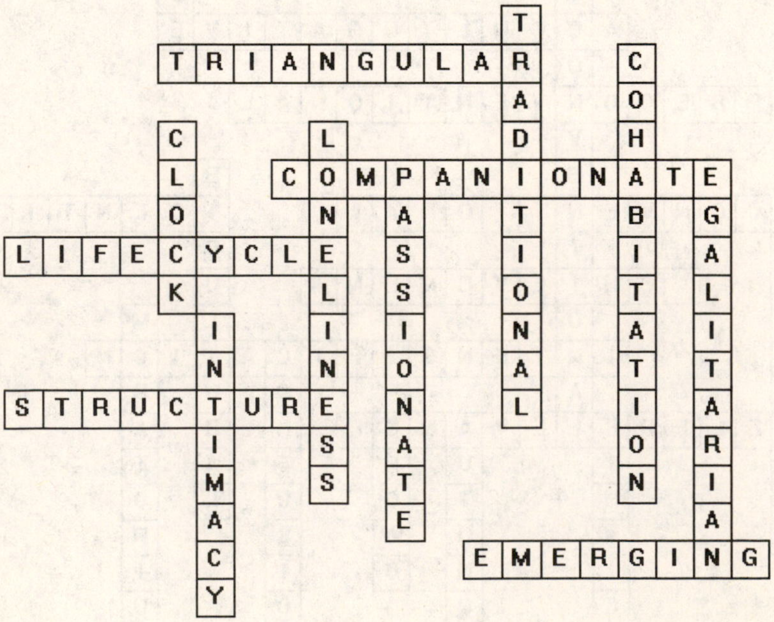

PUZZLE 15.1

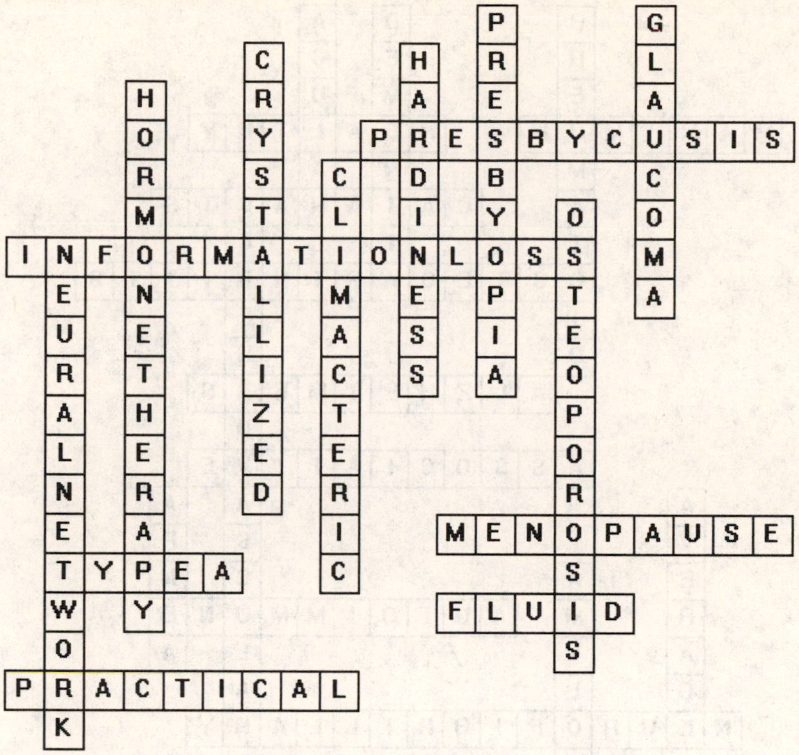

PUZZLE 16.1

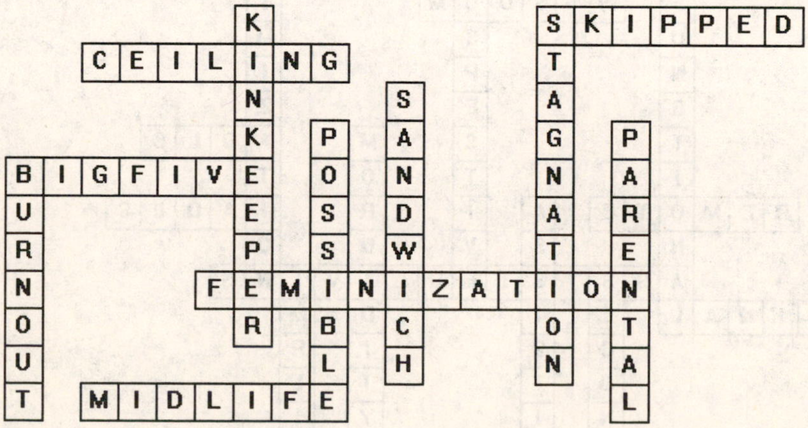

PUZZLE 17.1

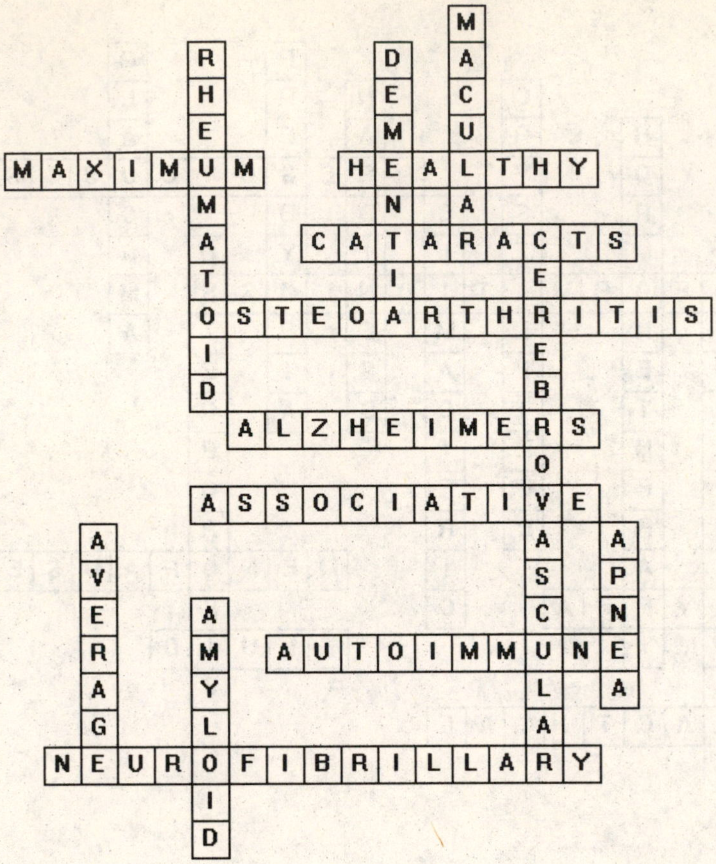

PUZZLE 17.2

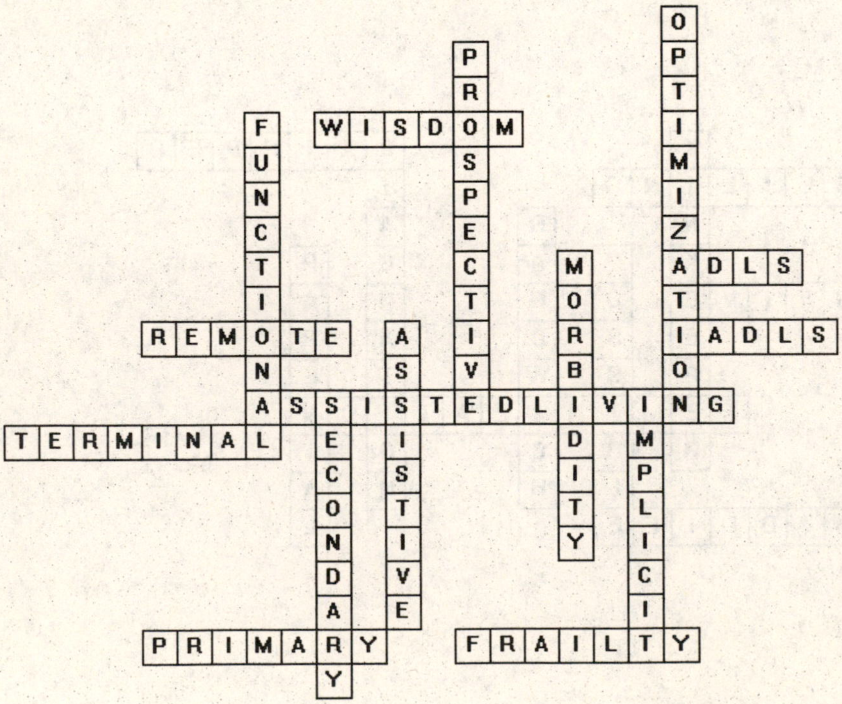

PUZZLE 18.1

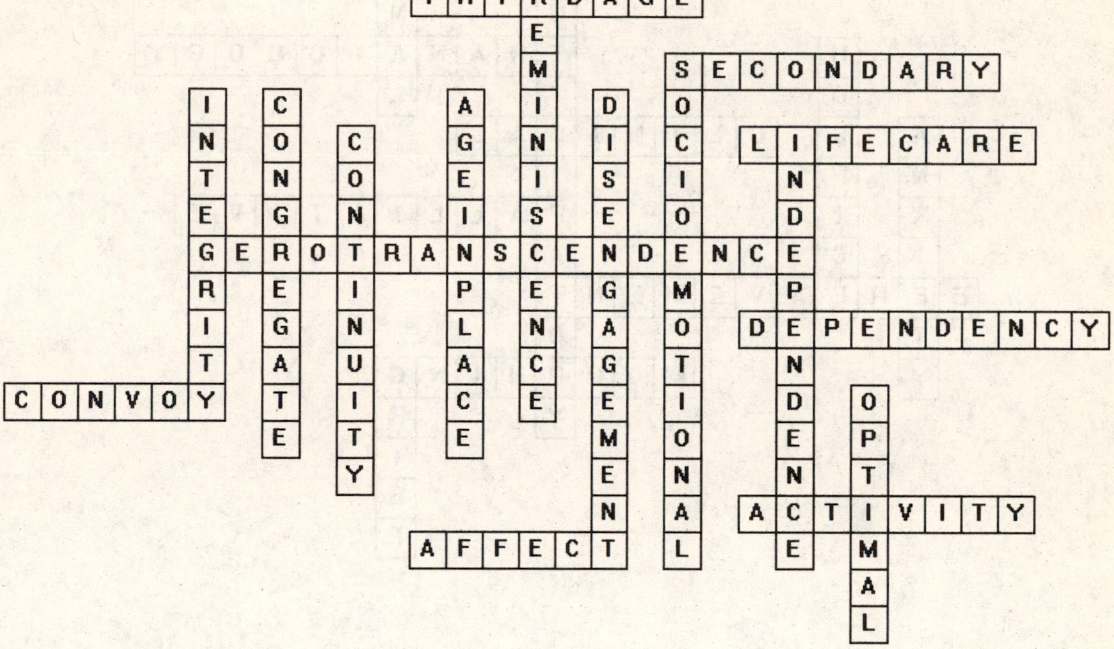

PUZZLE 19.1

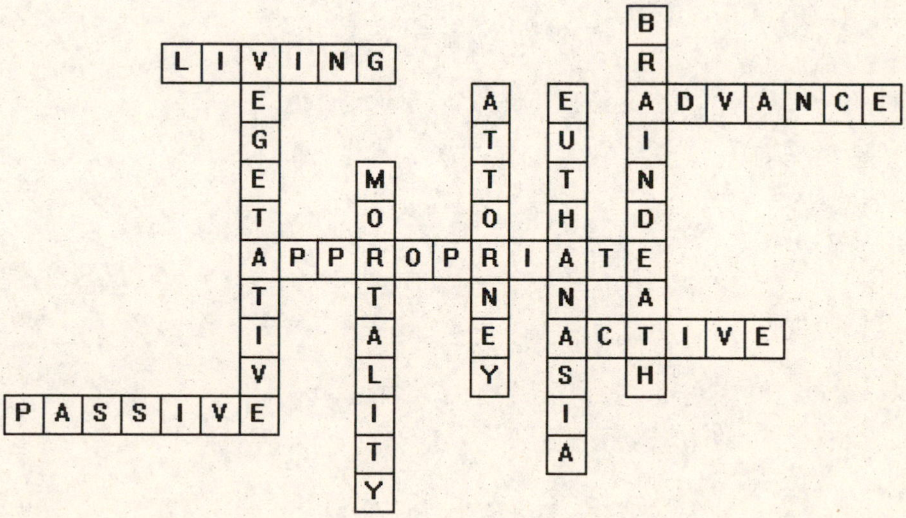

PUZZLE 19.2

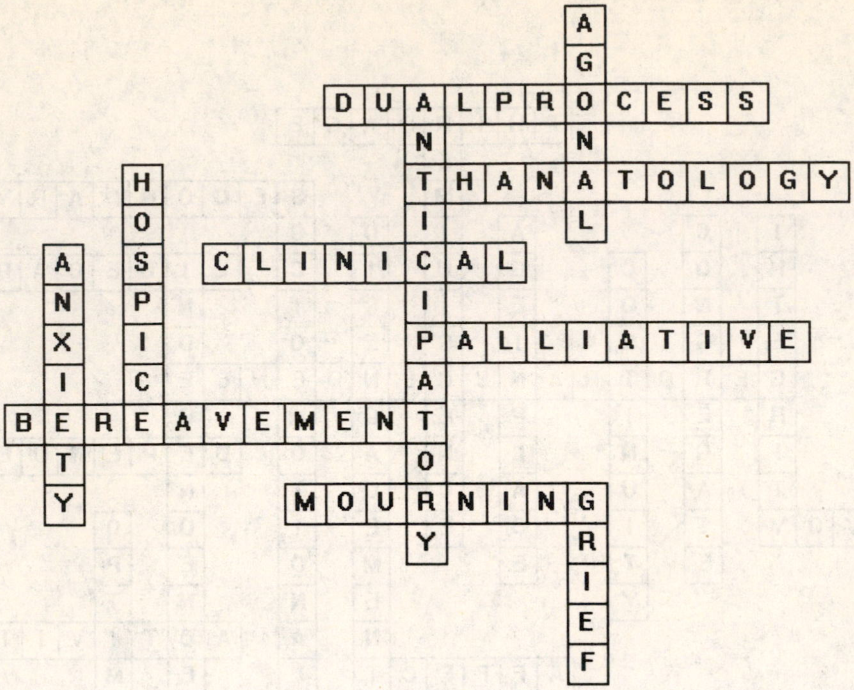
AGONAL
DUALPROCESS
ANTICIPATORY
THANATOLOGY
HOSPICE
ANXIETY
CLINICAL
PALLIATIVE
BEREAVEMENT
MOURNING
GRIEF

ANSWERS TO PRACTICE TESTS

CHAPTER 1

Practice Test #1

1. a	2. d	3. b	4. a	5. c
6. b	7. c	8. a	9. d	10. c
11. c	12. a	13. a	14. d	15. c
16. c	17. d	18. b	19. b	20. c
21. c	22. d	23. c	24. b	25. c
26. b	27. d	28. d	29. d	30. b

Practice Test #2

1. c	2. c	3. d	4. c	5. b
6. d	7. d	8. d	9. b	10. a
11. a	12. d	13. b	14. c	15. d
16. a	17. c	18. b	19. c	20. c
21. b	22. a	23. d	24. d.	25. b
26. a	27. c	28. a	29. d	30. c

CHAPTER 2

Practice Test #1

1. b	2. a	3. d	4. a	5. b
6. c	7. c	8. b	9. d	10. b
11. a	12. c	13. d	14. b	15. c
16. a	17. c	18. c	19. b	20. a
21. c	22. a	23. d	24. b	25. c
26. a	27. a	28. c	29. d	30. b

Practice Test #2

1. b	2. c	3. c	4. a	5. d
6. c	7. b	8. a	9. c	10. c
11. b	12. a	13. c	14. d	15. c
16. c	17. b	18. d	19. a	20. b
21. b	22. a	23. d	24. c	25. a
26. c	27. b	28. c	29. a	30. d

CHAPTER 3

Practice Test #1

1. c	2. b	3. c	4. d	5. a
6. b	7. c	8. d	9. b	10. a
11. b	12. a	13. b	14. d	15. a
16. c	17. d	18. c	19. d	20. c
21. a	22. d	23. a	24. d	25. b
26. a	27. c	28. b	29. d	30. a

Practice Test #2

1. b	2. b	3. a	4. b	5. c
6. c	7. b	8. b	9. c	10. d
11. a	12. a	13. d	14. c	15. a
16. d	17. a	18. b	19. c	20. b
21. c	22. b	23. a	24. c	25. b
26. d	27. a	28. c	29. b	30. c

CHAPTER 4

Practice Test #1

1. d	2. c	3. b	4. b	5. d
6. d	7. a	8. b	9. d	10. d
11. c	12. b	13. b	14. d	15. c
16. b	17. d	18. c	19. a	20. b
21. c	22. b	23. a	24. b	25. d
26. c	27. d	28. a	29. c	30. d

Practice Test #2

1. b	2. b	3. b	4. d	5. c
6. a	7. b	8. a	9. c	10. b
11. d	12. a	13. d	14. c	15. c
16. c	17. a	18. b	19. d	20. a
21. d	22. b	23. a	24. b	25. a
26. b	27. c	28. a	29. b	30. b

CHAPTER 5

Practice Test #1

1. d	2. c	3. d	4. c	5. a
6. a	7. a	8. a	9. d	10. a
11. b	12. a	13. d	14. b	15. d
16. a	17. c	18. b	19. c	20. a
21. c	22. b	23. b	24. c	25. c
26. d	27. a	28. a	29. b	30. d

Practice Test #2

1. d	2. b	3. a	4. a	5. d
6. b	7. c	8. d	9. b	10. c
11. c	12. c	13. b	14. c	15. c
16. a	17. d	18. d	19. c	20. d
21. a	22. d	23. b	24. c	25. a
26. c	27. d	28. b	29. b	30. d

CHAPTER 6

Practice Test #1

1. d	2. d	3. a	4. b	5. d
6. d	7. a	8. d	9. b	10. d
11. b	12. c	13. d	14. a	15. d
16. b	17. a	18. c	19. a	20. c
21. d	22. d	23. c	24. a	25. c
26. d	27. b	28. d	29. d	30. c

Practice Test #2

1. b	2. b	3. d	4. a	5. c
6. d	7. c	8. d	9. b	10. d
11. d	12. b	13. d	14. c	15. a
16. b	17. a	18. c	19. a	20. c
21. d	22. c	23. c	24. c	25. a
26. d	27. c	28. b	29. d	30. a

CHAPTER 7

Practice Test #1

1. d	2. a	3. c	4. b	5. a
6. d	7. a	8. b	9. d	10. a
11. d	12. c	13. c	14. d	15. b
16. d	17. c	18. c	19. a	20. b
21. c	22. d	23. c	24. b	25. d
26. b	27. c	28. b	29. c	30. b

Practice Test #2

1. c	2. d	3. a	4. c	5. a
6. b	7. c	8. d	9. b	10. c
11. d	12. a	13. b	14. d	15. c
16. a	17. d	18. c	19. b	20. a
21. b	22. d	23. c	24. a	25. d
26. b	27. a	28. c	29. b	30. d

CHAPTER 8

Practice Test #1

1. a	2. c	3. a	4. c	5. d
6. d	7. a	8. b	9. c	10. a
11. b	12. a	13. b	14. d	15. a
16. d	17. c	18. a	19. d	20. c
21. b	22. d	23. d	24. a	25. b
26. b	27. d	28. c	29. b	30. c

Practice Test #2

1. b	2. c	3. b	4. d	5. a
6. c	7. c	8. a	9. c	10. c
11. b	12. c	13. b	14. b	15. a
16. b	17. d	18. a	19. c	20. b
21. c	22. d	23. d	24. a	25. a
26. c	27. a	28. d	29. c	30. b

CHAPTER 9

Practice Test #1

1. a	2. d	3. c	4. b	5. a
6. b	7. b	8. d	9. b	10. a
11. a	12. c	13. a	14. d	15. b
16. d	17. c	18. b	19. c	20. c
21. a	22. c	23. d	24. b	25. d
26. a	27. d	28. c	29. c	30. b

Practice Test #2

1. b	2. c	3. b	4. a	5. d
6. b	7. c	8. a	9. c	10. c
11. d	12. a	13. c	14. b	15. a
16. c	17. b	18. b	19. d	20. b
21. a	22. b	23. d	24. d	25. b
26. a	27. c	28. d	29. a	30. d

CHAPTER 10

Practice Test #1

1. b	2. a	3. d	4. b	5. a
6. c	7. c	8. a	9. b	10. a
11. b	12. d	13. b	14. c	15. c
16. b	17. d	18. d	19. a	20. c
21. d	22. a	23. c	24. b	25. d
26. d	27. c	28. a	29. d	30. b

Practice Test #2

1. c	2. d	3. a	4. d	5. c
6. b	7. a	8. d	9. a	10. d
11. c	12. b	13. d	14. a	15. b
16. c	17. b	18. d	19. a	20. c
21. a	22. b	23. c	24. a	25. c
26. d	27. a	28. c	29. b	30. d

CHAPTER 11

Practice Test #1

1. c	2. d	3. a	4. b	5. d
6. c	7. b	8. a	9. b	10. d
11. c	12. d	13. d	14. b	15. c
16. a	17. d	18. a	19. c	20. b
21. b	22. b	23. b	24. a	25. d
26. a	27. c	28. d	29. b	30. c

Practice Test #2

1. d	2. b	3. c	4. a	5. c
6. c	7. a	8. c	9. b	10. d
11. b	12. a	13. b	14. d	15. b
16. c	17. a	18. b	19. a	20. d
21. c	22. b	23. a	24. c	25. b
26. d	27. a	28. a	29. b	30. a

CHAPTER 12

Practice Test #1

1. d	2. a	3. b	4. b	5. d
6. c	7. a	8. b	9. d	10. b
11. b	12. b	13. d	14. b	15. c
16. a	17. a	18. d	19. b	20. a
21. c	22. a	23. c	24. a	25. c
26. d	27. d	28. d	29. a	30. c

Practice Test #2

1. c	2. b	3. c	4. a	5. d
6. c	7. a	8. c	9. b	10. b
11. d	12. b	13. a	14. b	15. c
16. b	17. c	18. c	19. a	20. a
21. d	22. b	23. c	24. b	25. d
26. c	27. a	28. b	29. c	30. c

CHAPTER 13

Practice Test #1

1. b	2. b	3. b	4. a	5. c
6. c	7. d	8. a	9. b	10. b
11. b	12. d	13. c	14. b	15. d
16. a	17. b	18. d	19. b	20. d
21. c	22. c	23. a	24. d	25. b
26. d	27. c	28. a	29. d	30. c

Practice Test #2

1. a	2. a	3. b	4. c	5. c
6. d	7. c	8. a	9. d	10. a
11. d	12. b	13. c	14. b	15. d
16. c	17. b	18. b	19. a	20. d
21. c	22. d	23. b	24. c	25. c
26. b	27. a	28. d	29. d	30. c

CHAPTER 14

Practice Test #1

1. d	2. b	3. d	4. b	5. a
6. a	7. c	8. c	9. b	10. a
11. d	12. d	13. a	14. b	15. d
16. a	17. b	18. d	19. a	20. a
21. d	22. c	23. a	24. a	25. c
26. d	27. a	28. d	29. c	30. a

Practice Test #2

1. c	2. c	3. d	4. c	5. d
6. b	7. b	8. b	9. b	10. b
11. a	12. d	13. a	14. c	15. b
16. d	17. c	18. b	19. c	20. a
21. d	22. c	23. a	24. d	25. b
26. a	27. c	28. b	29. d	30. b

CHAPTER 15

Practice Test #1

1. d	2. a	3. d	4. b	5. d
6. c	7. d	8. b	9. c	10. a
11. b	12. c	13. d	14. b	15. c
16. c	17. a	18. b	19. a	20. a
21. b	22. c	23. d	24. a	25. c
26. d	27. d	28. b	29. b	30. a

Practice Test #2

1. b	2. c	3. a	4. a	5. c
6. d	7. a	8. a	9. c	10. d
11. b	12. b	13. a	14. d	15. c
16. a	17. b	18. b	19. c	20. a
21. d	22. d	23. c	24. b	25. d
26. b	27. b	28. c	29. c	30. a

CHAPTER 16

Practice Test #1

1. d	2. b	3. b	4. d	5. c
6. c	7. a	8. b	9. a	10. c
11. b	12. d	13. c	14. a	15. b
16. d	17. a	18. c	19. c	20. a
21. b	22. d	23. c	24. d	25. c
26. d	27. c	28. b	29. b	30. d

Practice Test #2

1. b	2. d	3. c	4. a	5. c
6. b	7. a	8. a	9. c	10. a
11. c	12. c	13. c	14. a	15. c
16. c	17. d	18. a	19. b	20. b
21. b	22. d	23. b	24. a	25. c
26. a	27. c	28. c	29. a	30. d

CHAPTER 17

Practice Test #1

1. c	2. d	3. b	4. a	5. d
6. d	7. c	8. c	9. a	10. d
11. c	12. a	13. c	14. b	15. d
16. d	17. c	18. a	19. c	20. b
21. c	22. b	23. d	24. a	25. c
26. b	27. c	28. c	29. c	30. a

Practice Test #2

1. c	2. a	3. d	4. b	5. d
6. b	7. a	8. c	9. d	10. b
11. a	12. d	13. b	14. a	15. d
16. b	17. c	18. a	19. d	20. c
21. b	22. d	23. c	24. a	25. d
26. b	27. a	28. d	29. c	30. b

CHAPTER 18

Practice Test #1

1. b	2. c	3. a	4. d	5. c
6. a	7. b	8. d	9. a	10. b
11. d	12. c	13. a	14. c	15. b
16. a	17. c	18. b	19. d	20. d
21. c	22. b	23. c	24. a	25. a
26. b	27. c	28. d	29. a	30. b

Practice Test #2

1. d	2. b	3. c	4. d	5. b
6. b	7. c	8. a	9. b	10. a
11. c	12. d	13. b	14. c	15. c
16. a	17. b	18. a	19. d	20. c
21. b	22. c	23. d	24. b	25. c
26. c	27. a	28. d	29. a	30. c

CHAPTER 19

Practice Test #1

1. c	2. c	3. a	4. b	5. d
6. c	7. a	8. b	9. d	10. d
11. c	12. b	13. d	14. a	15. b
16. c	17. d	18. c	19. a	20. d
21. a	22. c	23. b	24. c	25. c
26. c	27. d	28. c	29. a	30. a

Practice Test #2

1. d	2. c	3. b	4. c	5. a
6. b	7. a	8. d	9. c	10. a
11. d	12. d	13. b	14. b	15. c
16. c	17. d	18. d	19. a	20. d
21. c	22. d	23. b	24. d	25. a
26. b	27. c	28. c	29. b	30. d

NOTES

NOTES

NOTES

NOTES

NOTES

NOTES

NOTES

NOTES

NOTES

NOTES

NOTES